A
SHAKESPEARE MUSIC
CATALOGUE

The five volumes of *A Shakespeare Music Catalogue* constitute an invaluable reference tool: a comprehensive and detailed documentation of all music—published and unpublished, from Shakespeare's day to the present—in any way related to Shakespeare's life and work. No single work has ever before attempted to draw together such a mass of information, from many countries of the world, on this significant aspect of Shakespeare's dramatic art and cultural influence.

The music listed includes operas, ballets, overtures, tone-poems, songs, and various types of incidental music (for stage, radio, film, and television productions). The entry for each composition cited provides, whenever possible, information on its vocal and instrumental requirements, its publication history, and its first performance. The first three volumes deal with music and musical stage directions for the plays (arranged alphabetically) and with settings of the sonnets and narrative poems. The fourth volume contains indices of Shakespeare's titles and lines, the titles of musical works, and composers, arrangers, editors, librettists, etc. The final volume provides an entirely new research aid: a selected annotated bibliography of writings, in various languages, on the subject of Shakespeare and music.

Readers of the *Catalogue* will, for the first time, enjoy ready access to a broad range of Shakespeare-related compositions and to the diversity of critical verdicts pronounced upon them. Theatre directors will be able to select appropriate music for stage performance, and literary scholars, musicologists, and cultural historians, among others, will find a wealth of documentation, unavailable in other published sources, to assist them in their different fields of scholarly endeavour.

A
SHAKESPEARE
MUSIC
CATALOGUE

BRYAN N. S. GOOCH
DAVID THATCHER

ODEAN LONG
Associate Editor

*Incorporating material collected and
contributed by*
CHARLES HAYWOOD

IN FIVE VOLUMES

VOLUME IV

Indices

CLARENDON PRESS · OXFORD
1991

Oxford University Press, Walton Street, Oxford OX2 6DP
Oxford New York Toronto
Delhi Bombay Calcutta Madras Karachi
Petaling Jaya Singapore Hong Kong Tokyo
Nairobi Dar es Salaam Cape Town
Melbourne Auckland
and associated companies in
Berlin Ibadan

Oxford is a trade mark of Oxford University Press

Published in the United States
by Oxford University Press, New York

British Library Cataloguing in Publication Data
(data available)

Library of Congress Cataloging in Publication Data
Gooch, Bryan Niel Shirley, 1937–   .
A Shakespeare music catalogue.
1. Shakespeare, William, 1564–1616—Songs and
music—Bibliography.   2. Shakespeare, William, 1564–1616—
Musical settings—Bibliography.   I. Thatcher, David Sambourne, 1937–   .
II. Long, Margaret Odean, 1946–   .   III. Haywood, Charles, 1904–   .   IV. Title.
ML134.5.S52G6   1991   016.78'00822   89–9270
ISBN 0–19–812944–0

Text processed by Oxford Text System
Printed and bound in
Great Britain by Biddles Ltd,
Guildford and King's Lynn

CONTENTS

INDEX TO SHAKESPEARE'S TITLES AND LINES

A lively flourish of trumpets
5037
A Lover's Complaint
20584–20585
A lover's eyes will gaze an eagle blind
6338–6339
A Midsummer Night's Dream
9266–10989
A woman's face with Nature's own hand
painted
19476–19478
Absent thee from felicity a while
3694
Accuse me thus: that I have scanted all
20344–20348
Against my love shall be as I am now
19867
Against that time (if ever that time come)
19737–19742
Ah, wherefore with infection should he live
19927
Alack, what poverty my Muse brings forth
20228
Alas, 'tis true, I have gone here and there
20287–20290
All the world's a stage
964–976
All's Well That Ends Well
1–105
. . . . Although I joy in thee
13824
An old hare hoar
13825
And Crispin Crispian shall ne'er go by
4803
And I do love thee; therefore go with me
10294
And let me speak to th' yet unknowing world
3695
And let me the canakin clink, clink
12214–12234
And my ending is despair
15501
And will 'a not come again?
3696–3713
Angels and ministers of grace defend us!
3714
Antony and Cleopatra
106–385

Arise, fair sun, and kill the envious moon
13826
As a decrepit father takes delight
19675–19678
As an unperfect actor on the stage
19488–19490
As doth that orbed continent the fire
17425
As fast as thou shalt wane, so fast thou
grow'st
19281–19282
As in a theatre the eyes of men
12751
As Shafalus to Procrus, I to you
10295
As You Like It
386–2017
Be as thou wast wont to be
10296–10299
Be not afeard, the isle is full of noises
15502–15506
Be not too tame neither
3715
Be wise as thou art cruel, do not press
20467–20470
Before you can say "come" and "go"
15507–15510
Being your slave, what should I do but tend
19800–19809
Beshrew that heart that makes my heart to
groan
20436–20437
Betwixt mine eye and heart a league is took
19732–19734
Blow, blow, thou winter wind
977–1219
Blow, winds, and crack your cheeks! rage,
blow!
6019–6021
But be contented when that fell arrest
20030–20031
But do thy worst to steal thyself away
20125–20129
But look, the morn in russet mantle clad
3716–3717
But love, first learned in a lady's eyes
6340
But shall I go mourn for that, my dear?
18946–18950

But soft, what light through yonder window breaks?
13827

But wherefore do not you a mightier way
19317–19318

But wherefore do you droop? why look you sad?
5642

By Gis, and by Saint Charity
3718

By the pricking of my thumbs
7368

. . . by the roses of the spring
17426

By the simplicity of Venus' doves
10300

Canst thou, O cruel, say I love thee not
20525–20530

Come, civil night
13828

Come away, come away, death
17427–17676

Come, cousin, canst thou quake and change thy colour
13041

Come, gentle night, come, loving, black-brow'd night
13829–13830

Come ho, and wake Diana with a hymn
8420

. . . . Come let's away to prison
6022

. . . . Come, my queen, take hands with me
10301

Come, poor babe
18951

. . . . Come, seeling night
7369

Come, sisters, cheer we up his sprites
7370

Come, thou monarch of the vine
285–305

Come unto these yellow sands
15511–15594

Coriolanus
2265–2431

Could great men thunder
7811

. . . . Could I find out
2520

Cupid laid by his brand and fell asleep
20539–20542

Cymbeline
2432–2885

. . . daffadils,/That come before the swallow dares, and take
18952

Devouring Time, blunt thou the lion's paws
19462–19475

Did not the heavenly rhetoric of thine eye
6341

Do not call it sin in me
6342–6343

Do nothing but eat, and make good cheer
4637–4641

Do thou stand for my father and examine
4471

Done to death by slanderous tongues
11372–11374

Double, double, toil and trouble
7371–7372

Doubt thou the stars are fire
3719–3739

Dream on thy cousins smothered in the Tower
13042

Enter, solemnly tripping one after another, six personages
5038

Fair is foul, and foul is fair
7373

Fair love, you faint with wand'ring in the wood
10302

Farewell? a long farewell to all my greatness!
5039

Farewell, dear heart, since I must needs be gone
17677

Farewell! God knows when we shall meet again
13831

Farewell, thou art too dear for my possessing
20079–20099

Fathers that wear rags
6023–6024

Fear no more the heat o' th' sun
2521–2628

Fie on sinful fantasy!
9199–9208

First my fear, then my cur'sy, last my speech
4642

Flout 'em and scout 'em!
15595

Flower of this purple dye
10303

Fools had ne'er less grace in a year
6025–6027

For bonny sweet Robin is all my joy
3740–3742

For God's sake let us sit upon the ground
12752

For Night's swift dragons cut the clouds full fast
10304

For shame deny that thou bear'st love to any
19278–19280

For Time is like a fashionable host
16561

Freeze, freeze, thou bitter sky
1220
Friends, Romans, countrymen, lend me your
ears!
5484–5485
From fairest creatures we desire increase
19176–19187
From the east to western Inde
1221–1222
From you have I been absent in the spring
20177–20197
Full fadom five thy father lies
15596–15789
Full many a glorious morning have I seen
19645–19661
Gallop apace, you fiery-footed steeds
13832–13833
Gamouth I am, the ground of all accord
14649
Get you hence, for I must go
18953–18963
Give me some music. Now good morrow,
friends
17678
Give sorrow words. The grief that does not
speak
7374
. . . . Go with me
15790
. . . (God, if thy will be so)
13043–13044
. . . . God's goodness hath been great to thee
4919–4920
Good friends, sweet friends, let me not stir you
up
5486
Good morrow, masters, put your torches out
11375
Good night, good night! Parting is such sweet
sorrow
13834–13837
Good shepherd, tell this youth what 'tis to love
1223–1224
Good sister, wrong me not, nor wrong yourself
14650
Had I but died an hour before this chance
7375
Hamlet
2886–4291
Hand in hand, with fairy grace
10305–10309
Hark, hark, the lark at heaven's gate sings
2629–2809
Have at you then, affection's men-at-arms
6344
Have more than thou showest
6028
He is dead and gone, lady
3743–3745

He lives in fame that died in virtue's cause
16421
He that has and a little tiny wit
6029–6033
Health to my sovereign, and new happiness
4643
Heat not a furnace for your foe so hot
5040
Hence! home, you idle creatures, get you
home!
5487
1 Henry IV
4292–4520
2 Henry IV
4521–4689
1 Henry VI
4844–4884
2 Henry VI
4885–4928
3 Henry VI
4929–4965
Here will we sit, and let the sounds of
music
8421
Here's a knocking indeed! If a man were
7376
Hey, Robin, jolly Robin
17679–17686
. . . hinder not my course
18468
His beard was as white as snow
3746
"Hold thy peace, thou knave," knight?
17687–17691
Honour, riches, marriage-blessing
15791–15815
How all occasions do inform against me
3747
How all the other passions fleet to air
8422–8423
How can I then return in happy plight
19533–19539
How can my Muse want subject to invent
19679–19682
How careful was I, when I took my way
19735–19736
How far that little candle throws his beams!
8424
How heavy do I journey on the way
19743–19748
How like a winter hath my absence been
20150–20176
How many thousand of my poorest subjects
4644
How now, my love? why is your cheek so
pale?
10310
How oft when thou, my music, music play'st
20378–20405

How should I your true-love know
3748–3788
How silver-sweet sound lovers' tongues by
night
13838–13839
. . . . How sour sweet music is
12753
How sweet and lovely dost thou make the
shame
20140–20142
How sweet the moonlight sleeps upon this
bank!
8425–8481
I am gone, sir
17692–17713
I am informed throughly of the cause
8482
I am never merry when I hear sweet music
8483
I am your spaniel; and, Demetrius
10311
I dreamt there was an Emperor Antony
306–307
I grant thou wert not married to my Muse
20072
I have a faint cold fear thrills through my veins
13840
. . . I have/Immortal longings in me. Now no
more
308
I have serv'd Prince Florizel, and in my time
wore three-pile
18964
I know a bank where the wild thyme blows
10312–10349
I never saw that you did painting need
20073
I shall no more to sea, to sea
15816–15817
I, that please some, try all, both joy and
terror
18965
I'll follow you, I'll lead you about a round
10350
If I profane with my unworthiest hand
13841–13843
If it do come to pass
1225–1226
If love make me forsworn, how shall I swear to
love
6345–6348
If music be the food of love, play on
17714–17743
If my dear love were but the child of state
20369–20370
If she be made of white and red
6349–6356
If the dull substance of my flesh were thought
19724–19727

If there be nothing new, but that which is
19811–19814
If thou survive my well-contented day
19641–19644
If thy soul check thee that I come so near
20443–20445
If we shadows have offended
10351
If you have tears, prepare to shed them now
5488
Immortal gods, I crave no pelf
16375–16377
In Belmont is a lady richly left
8484
In faith, I do not love thee with mine eyes
20471–20473
In loving thee thou know'st I am forsworn
20537–20538
. . . . In such a night as this
8485
In sweet music is such art
5041
In the old age black was not counted fair
20374–20377
In youth when I did love, did love
3789–3806
Is it for fear to wet a widow's eye
19275–19277
Is it thy will thy image should keep open
19846–19861
Is this a dagger which I see before me
7377
It is my lady, O, it is my love!
13844–13845
It is not the fashion to see the lady the epilogue
1227
. . . it is not yet near day
13846
It was a lover and his lass
1228–1585
It will have blood, they say; blood will have
blood
7378
Jog on, jog on, the foot-path way
18966–18989
Julius Caesar
5245–5567
King Henry V
4690–4843
King Henry VIII
4966–5244
King John
5568–5653
King Lear
5654–6190
King Richard II
12612–12776
King Richard III
12777–13085

King Stephen was and-a worthy peer
12235–12243

. . . . Know that we have divided
6034

Lady, by yonder blessed moon I vow
13847–13848

Lawn as white as driven snow
18990–19027

Let me confess that we two must be twain
19671–19674

Let me not to the marriage of true minds
20305–20343

Let me play the fool
8486–8487

Let not my love be call'd idolatry
20246–20256

. . . . Let not virtue seek
16562

Let those who are in favour with their stars
19500–19508

Life's but a walking shadow, a poor player
7379–7380

Like as the waves make towards the pibbled shore
19815–19845

Like as to make our appetites more keen
20349

Lo as a careful huswife runs to catch
20476–20477

Lo in the orient when the gracious light
19219–19226

. . . . Look how the floor of heaven
8488–8489

Look in thy glass and tell the face thou viewest
19196–19200

Lord of my love, to whom in vassalage
19509–19513

Love is merely a madness, and I tell you
1586

Love is my sin, and thy dear virtue hate
20474–20475

Love is too young to know what conscience is
20535–20536

Love like a shadow flies when substance love pursues
9209–9210

Love looks not with the eyes but with the mind
10352

Love, love, nothing but love, still love
16563–16566

Love's Labour's Lost
6191–6691

Macbeth
6692–7586

Make me a willow cabin at your gate
17744–17748

Measure for Measure
7587–8046

. . . men are April when they woo, December
1587

Methinks I am a prophet new inspir'd
12754

Mine eye and heart are at a mortal war
19729–19731

Mine eye hath play'd the painter and hath stell'd
19492–19499

Much Ado About Nothing
10990–11652

. . . . Music do I hear?
12755–12756

Music to hear, why hear'st thou music sadly
19227–19274

My bounty is as boundless as the sea
13849–13850

My glass shall not persuade me I am old
19483–19487

My love is as a fever, longing still
20505–20518

My love is strength'ned, though more weak in seeming
20213–20227

My mistress' eyes are nothing like the sun
20417–20430

My mother had a maid call'd Barbary
12244

My tongue-tied Muse in manners holds her still
20077

Nay, take my life and all, pardon not that
8490

Night's candles are burnt out, and jocund day
13851

No exorciser harm thee
2810

No longer mourn for me when I am dead
19932–19975

No more be griev'd at that which thou hast done
19666–19670

No more dams I'll make for fish
15818–15823

No! Time, thou shalt not boast that I do change
20362–20368

Not from the stars do I my judgment pluck
19298–19302

Not marble nor the gilded monuments
19775–19789

Not mine own fears, nor the prophetic soul
20268–20274

Now all the youth of England are on fire
4804

Now I am alone
3807

Now is the winter of our discontent
13045

Now it is the time of night
10353
Now my charms are all o'erthrown
15824
.... Now, my fair'st friend
19028
Now the hungry lion roars
10354–10363
Now, until the break of day
10364
O, be some other name!
13852
O, call not me to justify the wrong
20462–20466
O England! model to thy inward
greatness
4805
O for a Muse of fire, that would ascend
4806–4807
O for my beads! I cross me for a sinner
2246
O, for my sake do you with Fortune chide
20291
O, from what pow'r hast thou this pow'rful
might
20531–20534
.... O gentle sleep!
4645–4647
O God of battles, steel my soldiers' hearts
4808
.... O God, thy arm was here
4809–4811
O happy fair!
10365–10376
O heart, heavy heart
16567–16569
O how I faint when I of you do write
20064
O how much more doth beauty beauteous
seem
19765–19774
O, how this spring of love resembleth
18469–18470
O, how thy worth with manners may I sing
19683–19686
O, lest the world should task you to recite
19976
O me! what eyes hath Love put in my head
20519–20524
O mighty Caesar! dost thou lie so low?
5489
O mistress mine, where are you roaming?
17749–18061
O, never say that I was false of heart
20276–20286
O, pardon me, thou bleeding piece of earth
5490
O serpent heart, hid with a flow'ring face!
13853

O, she doth teach the torches to burn bright!
13854
.... O sleep! O gentle sleep!
4648
O that this too too sallied flesh would melt
3808–3810
O that you were yourself! but, love, you are
19296–19297
O, the recorders!
3811
O then I see Queen Mab hath been with you
13855–13856
O thou, my lovely boy, who in thy power
20372–20373
O Thou whose captain I account myself
13046–13047
O truant Muse, what shall be thy amends
20212
O weary night, O long and tedious night
10377
O, what a rogue and peasant slave am I!
3812
On a day—alack the day!
6357–6371
On the ground
10378–10381
Open your ears; for which of you will stop
4649
Or I shall live your epitaph to make
20065–20071
Or if there were a sympathy in choice
10382
Or whether doth my mind being crown'd with
you
20301
Orpheus with his lute made trees
5042–5208
Othello
11653–12539
... our cause is ripe
5491
Our doubts are traitors
7812
Our remedies oft in ourselves do lie
83
Our revels now are ended. These our actors
15825–15828
Over hill, over dale
10383–10426
Pardon, goddess of the night
11376–11390
.... Parting is such sweet sorrow
13857
Pericles
12540–12611
Philomele, with melody
10427–10439
Poor naked wretches, wheresoe'er you are
6035–6036

Poor soul, the centre of my sinful earth
20487–20504

. . . remember this:/God and our good cause
fight upon our side
13048

Romeo and Juliet
13086–14215

Roses, their sharp spines being gone
19169–19172

Round about the cauldron go
7381

Say that thou didst forsake me for some fault
20103–20105

Shall I compare thee to a summer's day
19322–19461

She bids you on the wanton rushes lay you
down
4472

. . . she never told her love
18063–18076

Sigh no more, ladies, sigh no more
11391–11590

Sin of self-love possesseth all mine eye
19862–19866

Since brass, nor stone, nor earth, nor
boundless sea
19883–19904

Since I left you, mine eye is in my mind
20296–20300

Since my dear soul was mistress of her choice
3813

Since nought so stockish, hard, and full of
rage
8491

Since once I sat upon a promontory
10440

Sleep dwell upon thine eyes, peace in thy
breast!
13858–13859

". . . sleep" — the innocent sleep
7382

Sleepest or wakest thou, jolly shepherd?
6037–6038

So am I as the rich whose blessed key
19752

So are you to my thoughts as food to life
20032–20043

So is it not with me as with that Muse
19479–19482

. . . (so it came to pass)
10441

So now I have confess'd that he is thine
20438–20439

So oft have I invok'd thee for my Muse
20057–20060

So shall I live, supposing thou art true
20130–20132

So sweet a kiss the golden sun gives not
6372–6376

. . . . Soft stillness and the night
8492

Some glory in their birth, some in their skill
20115–20124

Some say that ever 'gainst that season comes
3814–3825

Some say thy fault is youth, some wantonness
20144–20149

Sometime we see a cloud that's dragonish
309

Speak of me as I am; nothing extenuate
12245

Spread thy close curtain, love-performing night
13860–13861

Sweet are the uses of adversity
1588

Sweet flower, with flowers thy bridal bed I
strew
13862

Sweet love, renew thy force, be it not said
19790–19799

Sweet lovers love the spring
1589

Sweet Moon, I thank thee for thy sunny beams
10442

Swithold footed thrice the 'old
6039

Take all my loves, my love, yea, take them all
19687–19702

Take but degree away, untune that string
16570

Take, O, take those lips away
7813–8024

Teach me, dear creature, how to think and
speak
2247

Tell me where is fancy bred
8493–8666

Th' expense of spirit in a waste of shame
20406–20416

That god forbid that made me first your
slave
19810

That I did love thee, Caesar, O, 'tis true
5492

That lord that counsell'd thee
6040

That sir which serves and seeks for gain
6041–6044

That strain again, it had a dying fall
18077–18079

That thou art blam'd shall not be thy defect
19930–19931

That thou hast her, it is not all my grief
19706–19707

That time of year thou mayst in me behold
19977–20029

That very time I saw (but thou couldst not)
10443

That you were once unkind befriends me now
20355–20357

The clock strook nine when I did send the nurse
13863

The cloud-capp'd tow'rs, the gorgeous palaces
15829–15841

The Comedy of Errors
2018–2264

The crow doth sing as sweetly as the lark
8667

The current that with gentle murmur glides
18471–18472

The forward violet thus did I chide
20198–20206

The fox, the ape, and the humble-bee
6377–6378

The god of love
11591

The honey-bags steal from the humble-bees
10444

. . . the isle is full of noises
15842–15843

The little Love-god, lying once asleep
20543–20550

The man that hath no music in himself
8668–8670

The master, the swabber, the boatswain, and I
15844–15858

The Merchant of Venice
8047–8797

The Merry Wives of Windsor
8798–9265

The moon shines bright. In such a night as this
8671–8672

The other two, slight air and purging fire
19728

The Passionate Pilgrim
20586–20752

The Phoenix and Turtle
20753–20768

The poor soul sat sighing by a sycamore tree
12246–12371

The quality of mercy is not strain'd
8673–8681

The Rape of Lucrece
20769–20783

. . . the readiness is all
3826

The Taming of the Shrew
14216–14690

The Tempest
14691–16298

The Two Gentlemen of Verona
18348–18666

The Two Noble Kinsmen
19158–19175

The weïrd sisters, hand in hand
7383–7384

The Winter's Tale
18667–19157

The woosel [ousel] cock so black of hue
10445–10453

The words of Mercury are harsh after the songs of Apollo
6379

Then hate me when thou wilt, if ever, now
20106–20114

Then is there mirth in heaven
1590–1594

Then let not winter's ragged hand deface
19215–19218

There is a tide in the affairs of men
5493

There is a willow grows askaunt the brook
3827

There is some soul of goodness in things evil
4812

There's not the smallest orb which thou behold'st
8682

There's rosemary, that's for remembrance
3828–3830

Therefore the moon (the governess of floods)
10454

. . . . These our actors
15859

They bore him barefac'd on the bier
3831–3843

They that have pow'r to hurt, and will do none
20133–20139

Thine eyes I love, and they as pitying me
20433–20435

Things base and vile, holding no quantity
10455

This above all: to thine own self be true
3844

This castle hath a pleasant seat, the air
7385

This day is call'd the feast of Crispian
4813–4814

. . . this ditty, after me
10456

This England never did, nor never shall
5643–5644

This fortress built by Nature for herself
12757

This is a sleepy tune. O murd'rous slumber!
5494

This is the state of man: to-day he puts forth
5209

This royal throne of kings, this sceptred isle
12758–12766

This was the noblest Roman of them all
5495

Those hours that with gentle work did frame
19205–19214

Those lines that I before have writ do lie
20302–20304
Those lips that Love's own hand did make
20484–20486
Those parts of thee that the world's eye doth
view
19929
Those pretty wrongs that liberty commits
19703–19705
Thou art as tyrannous, so as thou art
20431–20432
Thou art so fat-witted with drinking of old sack
4473
Thou blind fool, Love, what dost thou to mine
eyes
20446–20451
. . . thou owest God a death
4474
Thou speakest aright
10457
Thou trumpet, there's my purse
16571
Thrice the brinded cat hath mew'd
7386–7390
Through the forest have I gone
10458
Through the house give glimmering light
10459–10466
Thus can my love excuse the slow offense
19749–19751
Thus is his cheek the map of days outworn
19928
Thus sometimes hath the brightest day a cloud
4921
Thy bosom is endeared with all hearts
19632–19640
Thy gift, thy tables, are within my brain
20361
Thy glass will show thee how thy beauties
wear
20055–20056
Till thou applaud the deed. Come, seeling night
7391
Timon of Athens
16299–16388
Tir'd with all these, for restful death I cry
19905–19926
'Tis better to be vile than vile esteemed
20358–20360
'Tis now the very witching time of night
3845
'Tis ten to one this play can never please
5210
Titus Andronicus
16389–16431
To be, or not to be, that is the question
3846–3862
To me, fair friend, you never can be old
20229–20245

To sleep, perchance to dream — ay, there's the
rub
3877
. . . to thine own self be true
3878
To-morrow, and to-morrow, and to-morrow
7392–7398
To-morrow is Saint Valentine's day
3863–3876
Troilus and Cressida
16432–16584
Twelfth Night
16585–18347
Two loves I have of comfort and despair
20478–20483
Under the greenwood tree
1595–1818
Unthrifty loveliness, why dost thou spend
19201–19204
Up and down, up and down
10467–10469
Venus and Adonis
20784–20821
Vows are but breath, and breath a vapour is
6380
Was it the proud full sail of his great verse
20078
"Was this fair face the cause," quoth she
84–85
We are not the first
6045
. . . . We are such stuff
15860–15861
Weary with toil, I haste me to my bed
19514–19532
Weaving spiders, come not here
10470
Wedding is great Juno's crown
1819–1831
Were't aught to me I bore the canopy
20371
. . . . What a piece of work is a man
3879
What angel wakes me from my flow'ry bed?
10471
What harmony is this? My good friends, hark!
15862
What is your substance, whereof are you made
19753–19764
. . . . What music is this?
16572–16573
What potions have I drunk of Siren tears
20350–20354
What shall he have that kill'd the deer?
1832–1865
What thou seest when thou dost wake
10472
What's in the brain that ink may character
20275

When daffadils begin to peer
19029–19067
When daisies pied, and violets blue
6381–6491
When forty winters shall besiege thy brow
19188–19195
When griping griefs the heart doth wound
13864–13869
When he shall hear she died upon his words
11592
When I consider every thing that grows
19303–19316
When I do count the clock that tells the time
19283–19295
When I have seen by Time's fell hand defaced
19868–19882
... when I shall die
13870
When icicles hang by the wall
6492–6644
When in disgrace with Fortune and men's eyes
19540–19587
When in the chronicle of wasted time
20257–20267
When most I wink, then do mine eyes best see
19708–19723
When my love swears that she is made of truth
20452–20461
When shall we three meet again?
7399–7407
When shepherds pipe on oaten straws
6645
When that I was and a little tiny boy
18080–18200
When thou shalt be dispos'd to set me light
20100–20102
When to the sessions of sweet silent thought
19588–19631
When you shall these unlucky deeds relate
12372
Where art thou, Muse, that thou forget'st so
long
20207–20211
Where hast thou been, sister?
7408
Where is the number of our English dead?
4815
Where should this music be? I' th' air, or th'
earth?
15863–15866
Where the bee sucks, there suck I
15867–15964
Where the place?
7409
Wherein I spoke of most disastrous chances
12373

While you here do snoring lie
15965–15983
Whilst I alone did call upon thy aid
20061–20063
White his shroud as the mountain snow
3880–3883
Whither should I fly?
7410
Who doth ambition shun
1866
Who is it that says most, which can say more
20074–20076
Who is Silvia? what is she
18473–18637
Who will believe my verse in time to come
19319–19321
Whoever hath her wish, thou hast thy *Will*
20440–20442
Whose golden touch could soften steel and
stones
18640
Why didst thou promise such a beauteous day
19662–19665
Why is my verse so barren of new pride
20044–20054
Why, let the strooken deer go weep
3884
... why should proud summer
6646
Will you buy any tape
19068–19092
Wilt thou be gone? it is not yet near day
13871–13878
Wilt thou have music? Hark, Apollo plays
14651
Would I were sleep and peace, so sweet to
rest!
13879
Ye elves of hills, brooks, standing lakes, and
groves
15984–15985
You are three men of sin, whom Destiny
15986
You do look, my son, in a mov'd sort
15987
You heavens, give me that patience, patience I
need!
6046
You spotted snakes with double tongue
10473–10574
You sunburn'd sicklemen, of August weary
15988
You that choose not by the view
8683–8684
Your love and pity doth th' impression fill
20292–20295

INDEX TO TITLES OF MUSICAL WORKS

Titles beginning with Arabic or Roman numerals can be found under the initial letter of the first work, e.g., '1 Henry IV' appears under 'H' and 'XII English & Italian Songs' appears under 'E'. Less specific titles, e.g., 'III' and 'Nine Songs', are not indexed.

A Bank of Violets 18286
A Bergomask Dance 10641
A Birthday Greeting 87, 6117
A Book of Shakespeare's Songs 21318
A Calendar Set 4491
A Cantata and Four English Songs 5097
[A Case of Human Flesh] 8737
A Catalogue of Incidents in Romeo & Juliet 13908, 21129
A Cento, Consisting of Ballads, Rounds, Glees, & a Roundelay, Cavatinas, Canzonettas, Duettinos, Terzettos, and a Quartettino 4643
A Chamber Symphony 1891, 12769, 14658
A Choral Calendar (Winter) 6632
A Choral Miscellany 15721, 17685
A Clown's Song 18109
A Collection of Ayres, Compos'd For the Theatre, and upon other Occasions 10180
A Collection of Songs of various kinds, and for Different Voices 6475
A Collection of the Vocal Music in Shakespear's Plays . . . 21310, 21311
A Comedy of Errors 2148, 2201
A Compleat Score of the Solemn Dirge in Romeo and Juliet as perform'd at the Theatre Royal in Covent Garden 13102
A Concise, and Easy Treatise on Singing . . . 2869
A Consolation 19568
A Country Dance. Much ado about nothing 11648
A Cry From The Wilderness 4831
[A Cry of Players] 20881
A Dance of Clowns 9826
A Dialogue in the Opera, call'd the Fairy Queen 10180
"A Dirge" 15679
A Dirge. in Cymbeline of Shakespear's 2445
A Dirge of Love 17490
A Divided Duty 3477, 5948, 10041, 11974, 13506, 15309
[A Douăsprezecea noapte = Twelfth Night] 16642
A Double Life 12462
A Double Madrigal 20647

A Dream Tryst 19337
A Fairy Blessing 10360
A Fairy Lullaby 10520
A Fairy Pastoral 10346
A Fairy Song 10924
A Farewell 16561
A Favorite Duett Sung by Mrs. Crouch and Mr. Kelly with universal applause in the Tempest 15078
A Favorite Song Sung by Mrs. Crouch with universal applause in the Tempest 15078
A favourite Air 18675
A favourite Air composed by Dr. Arne 14764
A favourite Glee for Three Voices 1844
A Favourite Song in Coriolanus 2396
A Favourite Song, sung by Mrs. Abington in Twelfth-Night 16610
A few lines from Shakespear's Merchant of Venice 8461
A First Set of Pieces from Shakespeare's Plays 21354
A Forest Rondo[:] Shakespearean Fantasy 10400, 10431, 10470, 10507, 15539
A Garland of Fairy Music 10582
A Garland of Shakespearian and other Old Fashioned Songs 1487, 6368, 15724
A Garland of Sonnets 19326, 19591, 20309, 20893
A Girdle Round the Earth (Six Shakespeare Songs) 1005, 1276, 1620, 10388, 10481, 15630
A Glee 6475
A Goodly Heritage 1694, 6560
[A Heaven Blessed Maiden] 8757
A Hollywood Midsummer Night's Dream 10161
A Jig called Macbeth 7013
[A King In New York] 4089
A Life on the Ocean Wave 9005
A Little Act Upon the Blood 12439
[A Little Scene to Monarchize] 4401, 4583, 4753, 4946, 5010, 5880, 12702, 12940
A Little Shakespeare Suite 17762
A Little Tiny Boy 17007
A Lonely Romeo 14095
A Love Song 17808

A Lover and His Lass 1248, 1282, 1300, 1489, 1577, 2005
[A Lover's Complaint] 20584
A Lover's Eyes can gaze an Eagle blind[,] A Cantata, Sung by Mr. Braham . . . in The Merry Wives of Windsor 3733, 6673, 8876
A lover's eyes will gaze an eagle blind 6338
A Lover's Plea 21222
A Lyric Ode on the Fairies, Aerial Beings, and Witches of Shakespeare 21055
A Mad Song 7525
A Mad Song[:] Beneath The Poplar's Shadow 7526
A Madrigal 21252
[A makrancos hölgy = The Taming of the Shrew] 14306, 14524
A Masque (Shakespeare's "Tempest") 15295
[A Megera Domada = The Taming of the Shrew] 14274
A Menagerie 6391
A Merry Heart 18969, 18973 18983
A Merry Note 6607
A Midsummer Dream 9759
A Midsummer Eve 10629
A Midsummer Night Screame 20955
A Midsummer Nightmare, or The Fairies in Bottom's Garden! 10789
A Midsummer Night's Dream 9266, 9278, 9280, 9295, 9296, 9309, 9318, 9323, 9328, 9329, 9342, 9351, 9355, 9360, 9367, 9374, 9375, 9378, 9382, 9384, 9385, 9397, 9398, 9401, 9402, 9411, 9412, 9422, 9424, 9425, 9426, 9428, 9439, 9441, 9450, 9482, 9486, 9490, 9491, 9543, 9547, 9555, 9556, 9572, 9576, 9579, 9583, 9588, 9678, 9876, 9880, 9887, 9915, 9934, 9941, 9945, 9952, 9955, 9961, 9989, 9995, 9998, 10014, 10025, 10031, 10032, 10033, 10034, 10039, 10040, 10042, 10079, 10102, 10103, 10121, 10127, 10135, 10141, 10146, 10170, 10171, 10174, 10280, 10284, 10743, 10974, 14103
[A Midsummer Night's Dream] 9267, 9268, 9269, 9272, 9274, 9285, 9288, 9290, 9291, 9292, 9294, 9297, 9302, 9311, 9312, 9317, 9319, 9322, 9325, 9334, 9346, 9349, 9350, 9352, 9353, 9354, 9356, 9357, 9361, 9362, 9368, 9369, 9376, 9377, 9386, 9389, 9391, 9392, 9394, 9409, 9414, 9415, 9421, 9423, 9433, 9434, 9440, 9446, 9456, 9458, 9459, 9460, 9464, 9474, 9476, 9483, 9484, 9495, 9499, 9502, 9504, 9506, 9512, 9514, 9516, 9519, 9521, 9529, 9531, 9557, 9562, 9563, 9565, 9570, 9573, 9577, 9582, 9586, 9587, 9591, 9598, 9599, 9608, 9609, 9610, 9612, 9614, 9615, 9631, 9645, 9709, 9726,

9741, 9762, 9797, 9862, 9865, 9866, 9867, 9868, 9869, 9870, 9873, 9879, 9881, 9893, 9897, 9901, 9902, 9913, 9914, 9920, 9921, 9922, 9923, 9926, 9930, 9931, 9932, 9935, 9939, 9949, 9951, 9953, 9954, 9962, 9968, 9972, 9982, 9993, 9997, 10001, 10003, 10004, 10005, 10006, 10015, 10017, 10019, 10026, 10038, 10045, 10046, 10048, 10056, 10057, 10058, 10073, 10077, 10080, 10081, 10082, 10084, 10088, 10090, 10091, 10093, 10095, 10097, 10099, 10101, 10108, 10109, 10110, 10213, 10236
A Midsummer Night's Dream[:] Fantasia on the music composed for Shakespeare's Fairy Play 9680
'A Midsummer Night's Dream.' Music by Felix Mendelssohn-Bartholdy 9735
A Midsummer Night's Dream[:] Overture 9855
[A Midsummer Night's Dream Selection] 9721
A Midsummer Night's Dream-Suite 9355
A Midsummer Nights [sic] Dream 10721
A Miscellany of Love Songs 19363
A Modern Ecstasy 7563
[A Modern Hamlet] 4092
A Muse of Love[:] Five Elizabethan Love Lyrics 7862
A Musical Appendix 8122
A musical evening with Shakespeare 21325
A Musical Homage 5090
A Musical Merchant of Venice 8417
A New Duett introduced in the Merchant of Venice at the Theatre Royal, Drury Lane. . . . 8324
A New Edition of Shakespear's Poor Barbara 12244
A New Scotch Song 14679
A New Song in the Tempest, Sung by Mis [sic] Cross to her Lover, who is supposed Dead 15218
A New Willow Song 12284
A Nice Derangement of Epitaphs 3700, 15632
A Night in Elfland 10975
A Night in Fairyland 10632, 10781, 10783, 20932
A Pageant of Characters from William Shakespeare (on the 400th anniversary of his birth) 1594, 6045, 8490, 10442, 12372, 21083
A Pageant of Empire 20923
[A Part Song] 21091
A Poor Soul Sat Sighing 12267, 12279, 12336
A Portrait of Feste 18209
A Portrait of Imogen 2815
A Portrait of Shylock 8711
A Prayer for Peace 13044
A Prelude to Battle 13046

A Princess of Kensington 10778
"A Question Answered" 8666
A Renaissance Garland 20265
A Roaming Romeo 14137
A Round 18064
A Roundel 10726
A Roundelay in Canon 2003
A Rustic Lay 1296
A Sad Tale's Best for Winter 18763
A Sailor 15632
A Scene from Shakespeare 7572
A Sea Dirge 15649, 15660, 15669, 15671, 15674, 15683, 15687, 15709, 15723, 15724, 15731, 15739, 15770, 16152
A Sea Dirge (Full fathom five) 15745
A Sea Song 15715
A Second Set of Pieces from Shakespeare's Plays 21359
A Secular Requiem (The Phoenix and the Turtle) 20763
A Selection from Pyramus and Thysbe 10976
A Selection of English Songs 14779, 14780
a Selection of Famous Mendelssohn Melodies 9841
A Selection of Rodgers & Hart Songs 2210
A Selection of Rodgers and Hart Songs 2214
A Serenade 19702
A Series of Shakespeare's most Beautiful Songs 2868, 8589, 14161, 15701, 18295
A Set Of Songs 9210
A Shakespeare Fantasia 21158
A Shakespeare Garland 1188, 1544, 1795, 5188, 6481, 6622, 11560, 17646, 18027
A Shakespeare Lullaby 10537
A Shakespeare Overture 21128
A Shakespeare Prelude 21179
A Shakespeare Sequence 1336, 1662, 5085, 7887, 15664, 17728, 17878, 18508
A Shakespeare Set 1606, 6596, 8427, 11500, 15617, 15725, 18063
A Shakespeare Song Book 21353, 21356
A Shakespeare Song Cycle 1138, 1204, 1570, 1810, 3856, 5495, 6021, 6371, 8656, 8677, 19446, 19585, 19625, 19903, 20114, 20122, 20724
A Shakespeare Sonnet 19694
A Shakespeare Sonnet (No. 138) 20457
A Shakespeare Suite 1414, 8484, 8600, 10436, 19253, 19569, 19738, 20090
A Shakespeare Suite "Richard III" 13015
A Shakespeare Symphony[:] Symphony No. 3 4474, 6340, 12752, 15859, 15985
A Shakespeare Triad 7879, 11440, 19040
A Shakespearean Cantata 20984
A Shakespearean Duo 972, 19568
A Shakespearean Prologue 252, 2364, 3538, 4449, 4618, 4791, 4875, 4914, 4956, 5033, 5468, 5638, 5974, 7225, 12003, 12741, 13023, 13543, 16366, 16418

A Shakespearean scherzo: Titania and Her Elvish Court 10689
A Shakespearian Cycle[:] The Twelve Months musically illustrated 318, 6659, 10665, 11602, 12771, 16071, 18234, 19113, 20174
A Shakespearian Madrigal (Sigh no more, Ladies) 11562
A Shaksperian Fantasia 14703, 14761, 15116, 15576, 21102
A solemn Dirge in Romeo and Juliet 14122
A Solemn Music 19973
A Solo Requiem 19935
A Song 7866
A Song for Each Season 1064
"A Song for William" 19411
A Song from Shakespear's Cymbeline 2845
A song in Love Betray'd . . . sung by Mr. Davis 18267
A Song in the Comedy of Love makes the Man 4285
A Song in the Tempest 15926
A Song (in Timon of Athens) Sung by the Boy 16338
A Song of Orpheus 5013, 5014, 5221
A Song of Spring 1413
A Song of Thanksgiving 4809
A Song of Willow 12275
A Song set by Mr. Henry Purcell 18296, 18311
A Song Set by Mr. John Eccles, Sung by Mr. Knapp in the Tragedy of Hamlet, Prince of Denmark 3047
A Song Set by Mr. John Welldon[,] the words by Shakspear 8009
A Song Sung by Mr. Mason in Magbeth [sic] 7100
A Song sung by the Girl in the Tempest 15218
A Song to Portia 8777
A Song To The Queen 8741
A Song with a Symphony in Troilus and Cressida 16469
A Sonnet 19974, 20448, 20463
A Sonnet Voyage 19541, 19590, 19816, 19979
A Spring Garland 1545
A Spring Song 1487, 1517
A Stratford Suite 21284
A Suite of Music (In the Olden Style) Incidental to Shakespeare's Henry VIII 4976
A Suite of Music Incidental to Shakespeare's Merchant of Venice 8300
A Suite of 5 Songs from Palgrave's Golden Treasury 7886, 17520
A Summer Day 7002
A Summer's Day 19343, 19454
[A Tempestade] 15138
A Time for Us (Love Theme from Romeo & Juliet) 13419
"A Timely Thought" 5228

A Triad of Songs 19950
A Twelfth Night Song Cycle 17471, 17697, 17802, 18095
A Twelfth Night Suite 16715
A Two-Part Song in the Play called Henry the Fifth[,] Set by Mr. H. Purcell 4840
A Veteran 3700
A Village Romeo and Juliet 14077, 14083
[A Village Romeo and Juliet] 14079
A Williamsburg Songbook 2911
[A Windsori víg nők = The Merry Wives of Windsor] 8919
A Winter's Song 6623
A Winter's Tale 18810, 18931, 18951
A woman's love 18472
A Wood Nymph 10768
A Wood-Song 1708
A 12-a Noapte 16850
[A 12-a noapte = Twelfth Night] 16593
Absence 20167, 20180
Absent in the Spring 20183
Ach Seele, Centrum meiner sünd'gen Erde 20489
Acht Shakespeare-Lieder 1084, 2680, 7913, 15690, 15910, 17560, 18151, 19081
Act 2d. Chorus 15115
Adagio 19495
Adagio de Roméo et Juliette 13573
Adieu 17710
Adieu, Good Man Devil 16965
Aetherblau 2755
Aforisme engleze 4812
Afsked 14172
After Reading Shakespeare 4828, 6091, 8708, 10703, 12428, 16109, 19273, 19630, 19844
Against that time, if ever that time come 19739
Against the time 19738
Age and Youth 20660, 20683
Ages 971
Agincourt 4798, 4799, 4842
Ah! Robin! Jolly Robin! 18347
Ah! Sì per voi 12155
Ah sì per voi giàdsento 12143
Ah, sirrah! quoth-a we shall 4530
"Ah spiegar potessi a lei" in the opera of Romeo e Giulietta 13762
Ah vieni nel tuo sangue 12127
[Ahogy tetszik = As You Like It] 529, 564, 756
A-hunting we will go 21293
Air de Juliette dans Roméo et Juliette 13814
Air de "l'Anneau Perdu et Retrouvé" 9246
Air De Montano 11624
Air. De Montano et Stéphanie 11618, 11619, 11627
Air de Roméo et Juliette 13813
Air D'Othello 12117

Air From Otello 12046
Air from 'The Fairy Queen' 10230
Air, "Full Fathom Five" 15480
Air (on G String) 10245
Airs Choisis de Montano et Stéphanie 11623
Airs de l'opéra 'Falstaff' d'Ad. Adam 8994
Airs detachés D'Hylas Et Silvie 16200
Airs in the Pageant 21121
Āksta dziesma 20888
Alarums and Excursions 21165
Alas, Poor Ghost 3885
Alas Sweet Lady 4252, 21084
Alas 'tis true 20290
"Alas, 'tis true, I have gone here and there" 20288
Album de 30 Transcriptions sur les œuvres de Tschaikowsky 3471
Album of Nine English Songs 10352, 11473, 17737
Album of Six Old English Airs 444, 12258
Alexander Balus 350, 8036
Alfernes Sang af Shakespeares "En Skjærsommernats Dröm" 10539
All Hearts 19632
[All Night Long] 12450
All of greane willowe 12246
All Seasons shall be Sweet 6636, 10348
All that Glitters 8785
All that glitters is not Gold 8730, 8782, 8784, 8786, 8791, 8876
All That Glitters Isn't Gold 8780, 8797
All The World's A Stage 692, 964, 969, 973, 975, 976, 1965, 1973, 1974, 1985, 1986, 1991
All The World's A Stage . . . If Music Be The Food Of Love 965, 17725
All Will Be Well 10380
Allegro 15900
Allegro maestoso 19780
[Alles durcheinander] 89
All's Well Dances 3
All's Well That Ends Well 3, 4, 5, 11, 12, 13, 14, 16, 32, 42, 60, 61, 67, 68, 70, 72, 73, 82, 86, 98, 100, 21121
[All's Well That Ends Well] 1, 2, 7, 8, 10, 17, 22, 26, 38, 39, 40, 43, 44, 45, 46, 49, 50, 56, 66, 69, 71
All's Well that Ends Well (A 1980's RKO Musical) 94, 11632
'All's Well That Ends Well'. Music for Shakespeare's play 25
[All's Well That Ends Well: or Love's Labour Won] 79, 6676, 10791, 12475, 13071, 14101, 18281, 18652, 19686, 20751
Alonso's Grief 15498, 16150
Alpha et Omega 278
[Als Büblein klein an der Mutter Brust. Trinklied des Falstaff] 9146
[Als Büblein klein an der Mutterbrust] 9074

Always true to you in my fashion 14600
Ambleto 4264, 4268, 4276, 4288
Americles 12605
Amiens 1926
Amien's [sic] Song 1058
Amiens Sings 1212
Amiens' Song ("Blow, Blow, Thou Winter Wind") 1155
[Amleth] 4104
Amleth und Fengo 4277
Amleto 2991, 3575, 3579, 3692, 3693, 3893, 3909, 4010, 4138, 4146, 4149, 4157, 4166, 4168, 4181, 4182, 4280
[Amleto] 2993, 2999, 3070, 3130, 3343, 4150
Amleto di Buzzolla 4147
Amleto[.] Gran Marcia Danese 3576
Amleto[.] Marcia Funebre 3577
Amleto, Principe di Danimarca 4154
Amor possente nome 12144
Amor Titus Schwadronikus oder die Pfahlbauern 16430
[Amor vincit omnia] 6257
Amours de Cassandre 21239
Amphitrite's Song: "Halcyon days, now wars are over" 14711
[An Age of Kings] 21193
An Album of Short Pieces illustrating Portraits of Shakespearian Characters 316, 1897, 3959, 5218, 5507, 6657, 7447, 8695, 9221, 10641, 12402, 13915, 16050, 19110
An die Musik II 17715
An Early English Eclogue: Five Pastoral Pieces for String Quartet 475
An eine schöne Frau 4198, 14130
An Elizabethan Song Book 1444
An English Requiem (They shall rise again) 2625
An Epithalamium (Wedding Song) 10260
An Evening with Shakespeare 21043
[An Evening With Will Shakespeare] 20840
An Inconsequent Ballad 20734
An Introduction to 'A Midsummer Night's Dream' 9457
An Invitation 20719
An Ode for Music 5123
An Ode on the Spirits of Shakespeare 21055
An Ode Upon dedicating a Building to Shakespeare which was Erected by the subscription of the Noblemen & Gentlemen in the Neighbourhood of Stratford upon Avon 20902
[An old hare hoar] 13825
An Olivia 17622
An Overture to Shakespeare's Macbeth 7077
An Overture to William Shakespeare's 'Twelfth Night' 18206
An Sylvia 18560
Ancient Suite 13204

And A' Babbled of Green Fields 4822
And how should I your true love know 3758
And Let Me A Canakin Clink 12228
And let me the Canakin 12219
And let me the canakin clink 11696, 12215, 12222, 12224
And let me the canakin clink. Iago's drinking song from "Othello" 12226
And let me the canakin clink (Iago's Song) 12225
And Let Me the Canikin Clink 295
And Let Me The Canniken Clink 11884
And Let The Canakin Clink (Iago's Song) 12225
And When He Dies . . . 13870
And will 'a not come again? 2981, 3706
And will he not come again? 3697, 3699, 3702, 3703, 3705, 3709, 3710, 4021, 4058
And will he not come again (Shakespear's Ophelia) 3712
Andante Cantabile 17245
Andante sostenuto 18965
Andronico 16431
[Ang Negosyante ng Venecia = The Merchant of Venice] 8195
Angels and ministers of grace 3714
[Anjuman = Banquet] 13406
Ann Hathaway 20945, 21039
Anna und Williams 21137
Anne Boleyn 5232
Anne Hathaway 21004
Anne Hatheawaye 21024
Années de Pèlerinage, deuxième année, Italie 12114
Another Op'nin', Another Show from Kiss Me, Kate 14604
Ant visu medeliu 20573
Antemusic 17715
Anthem and Deviant Variations 14267
Anthem for our time 20760
Anthony & Cleopatra. On the Water 316
Anthony and Cleopatra 187, 363, 383
[Anthony and Cleopatra] 111, 206
Antimusic 17715
Antoine et Cléopâtre 226, 264, 333, 368, 372, 377
[Antoine et Cléopâtre] 119, 121, 123, 134, 135, 138, 171, 197, 218
Antonii i Kleopatra 284
[Antonii i Kleopatra] 148, 177, 178, 180, 183, 195, 208, 214, 230, 273
Antonio e Cleopatra 126, 276
[Antonio e Cleopatra] 154
[Antonius a Kleopatra] 149, 168, 240, 257
Antonius en Cleopatra 270, 282
[Antonius és Cleopatra] 136
[Antonius és Kleopatra] 212
Antonius och Cleopatra 112, 117
Antonius och Kleopatra 202, 224

Antonius und Cleopatra 157, 159, 185, 259, 348
[Antonius und Cleopatra] 124, 145, 150, 162, 191, 219, 220, 233, 239, 242, 243
Antonius und Kleopatra 251, 271, 283
[Antonius und Kleopatra] 141, 170, 211, 255
[Antoniusz i Kleopatra] 153, 181, 184, 223
Antony 5484, 5486, 5488, 5489, 5490, 5492
Antony & Cleopatra 200, 204
Antony and Cleopatra 108, 109, 110, 137, 142, 147, 152, 169, 193, 222, 228, 234, 235, 236, 237, 248, 256, 261, 262, 268, 269, 323
[Antony and Cleopatra] 107, 113, 114, 115, 116, 120, 130, 131, 132, 133, 140, 143, 144, 146, 151, 155, 156, 158, 160, 161, 163, 164, 165, 167, 172, 173, 174, 175, 176, 179, 186, 189, 190, 192, 196, 198, 200, 201, 203, 205, 207, 209, 210, 215, 216, 221, 227, 231, 245, 247, 249, 258, 310, 317, 325, 327
Antony and Cleopatra[.] Music for the Stratford Production 166
Anything Goes 20582
[Ào Sài Luó = Othello] 12212
[Ào Shì Luó = Othello] 11763, 11814
Apemantus's Grace 16376
Apemantus's Song 16375
Apementus's [sic] Grace 16377
Apocalyptica 6090
Apotheos 21006
Apparition of Eight Kings 6773
Après la Tempête 16283
April 318, 20191
Aprilisi rege (Shakespeare nyomán irta Auguste Dorchain) 17341
Aprílová komedie 17379
Archer's Glee 1992
Arden 947
[Arden de Feversham] 20833
Arden muss Sterben 20937
[Arden of Faversham] 20853, 20857
Are You Lonesome To-night? 1979
Aria, The Virgin Queen's Dramatic Monologue 21033
Arie des Macbeth: Was sonst wohl das Alter verkläret 7330
Ariel 14849, 15418, 15439, 15449, 15504, 15526, 15581, 15635, 15760, 15943, 15948, 15984, 15992, 15993, 15998, 15999, 16009, 16010, 16014, 16017, 16023, 16029, 16030, 16033, 16036, 16044, 16045, 16048, 16050, 16051, 16053, 16062, 16068, 16073, 16082, 16083, 16087, 16088, 16089, 16092, 16100, 16103, 16114, 16115, 16117, 16118, 16120, 16121, 16122, 16123, 16126, 16133, 16134, 16135, 16136, 16142, 16145, 16146, 16157, 16170,

16220, 16235, 16243, 16248, 16254, 16259, 16264, 16266, 16276, 16277, 16279, 16281, 16290, 16293
[Ariel] 16186
Ariel in Flight 16056
Ariel in the cloven pine 16209
Ariel, mélodie 16102
Ariel Schottische 16147
Ariel Settings 16284
"Ariel" Song 16260
Ariel Songs 15558, 15594, 15716, 15788, 15964
Ariel. Symphony No. 2 16247
Ariel Valse 16144, 16187
Ariel Valse de Salon 16047
Ariel Waltz 16054
Ariel Waltz on Melodies by W. Meyer Lutz 16187
Ariel's Adieu to Prospero 16226
Ariel's Fairy Song 15960
Ariel's Five Little Songs 15510, 15557, 15713, 15920, 15978
Ariel's Flight 16028
Ariels Gesang nach Shakespeare's 'Sturm' 16005
Ariels Lied 15690
Ariel's Magic Music 15212
Ariel's Mockery 15627
Ariel's Music 15566
Ariels Sang 16228, 21067
Ariels Sång Nr. 1 15560
Ariels Sång Nr. 2 15923
Ariel's Sea Dirge 15783
Ariels [sic] Song 10904, 16245
Ariel's Song 14728, 14808, 14848, 15113, 15525, 15580, 15588, 15654, 15672, 15675, 15696, 15759, 15873, 15888, 15914, 15937, 16015, 16163, 16171
Ariel's Song (a) 15556
Ariel's Song (b) 15711
Ariel's Song (Caprice) 16072
Ariel's Song, "Come unto these Yellow Sands" 15191
Ariel's Song, 'Full Fathom Five' 15212, 15743
Ariel's Song II aus 'The Tempest' 15263
Ariel's Song in the Tempest 14757, 14778
Ariel's Song (Where the bee sucks) 14807, 14808, 14845, 15215
Ariel's Song, "While You Here Do Snoring Lie" 14924
Ariel's Songs 15540, 15547, 15549, 15587, 15665, 15689, 15697, 15775, 15894, 15909, 15913, 15954, 15973, 15975, 16161, 16172
Ariel's Songs from The Tempest of William Shakespeare 15585, 15768, 15951
Arietta aus dem Singspiel "Der Othello in Wien". Arie der "Wäscherin" 12464
Ariette de "l'Anneau Perdu et Retrouvé" 9246

Ariette, valse de Roméo et Juliette 13668

'Ariia Dzhul'etty: K tragedii Shekspira "Romeo i Dzhul'etta"' [Juliet's Aria: To Shakespeare's Tragedy Romeo and Juliet] 13829

Arioso 3819

Arise! 2643

Arise, ye subterranean winds 14725, 14732, 14736

Arise, ye subterranean winds from "The Tempest" 14750

Arise, Ye Subterranean Winds . . . From the music to "The Tempest" 14752

[Arlequin Cruello, Parodie D'Othello] 12444

Arm Seelchen 12320, 12338

Arne Selected Songs 453, 14843

Arrig Trold: Bryllupsmarsch [and] Taffelmusik 14455

Arrive, arrive o mort 17582

Art Thou Weary, Heavy Laden? (Nocturne from "Midsummer Night's Dream") 9682

[As alegres Comadres de Windsor = The Merry Wives of Windsor] 8840

As In A Theatre 12751

As it fell upon a day 20593, 20608, 20609, 20611, 20612, 20631, 20645, 20653, 20657, 20676, 20682, 20727, 20728, 20729, 20732, 20739

As You Like It 387, 389, 392, 464, 467, 479, 480, 484, 485, 491, 492, 505, 508, 524, 530, 531, 548, 551, 552, 562, 566, 568, 580, 583, 584, 592, 607, 616, 628, 631, 694, 721, 754, 758, 776, 797, 798, 801, 820, 827, 842, 860, 861, 862, 863, 864, 869, 876, 878, 879, 904, 910, 924, 928, 929, 931, 932, 933, 945, 956, 959, 961, 963, 1873, 1883, 1884, 1888, 1901, 1912, 1925, 1931, 1934, 1945, 1946, 1947, 1984, 1999, 19226, 20368, 20523, 20741, 20806, 21121

[As You Like It] 393, 396, 459, 461, 462, 463, 471, 474, 476, 477, 486, 490, 500, 501, 506, 507, 509, 511, 512, 514, 517, 518, 519, 520, 523, 525, 528, 533, 537, 539, 540, 544, 547, 553, 565, 569, 571, 572, 573, 578, 579, 581, 585, 587, 588, 590, 597, 598, 601, 603, 610, 614, 615, 617, 618, 619, 625, 627, 629, 632, 639, 640, 641, 643, 644, 645, 647, 660, 662, 663, 664, 666, 668, 678, 682, 685, 686, 688, 691, 695, 697, 701, 705, 706, 711, 713, 718, 719, 720, 722, 724, 732, 734, 735, 737, 738, 741, 752, 755, 757, 764, 765, 766, 769, 770, 771, 780, 781, 782, 786, 794, 795, 804, 809, 814, 818, 821, 829, 832, 835, 836, 839, 841, 843, 844, 849, 851, 857, 865, 866, 867, 874, 875, 877, 881, 882, 885, 886, 887, 889, 892, 899, 908, 919, 920, 921, 923, 926, 930, 934, 1933

As You Like It (A Shakespearean Idyll) 1919

'As you like it' eller Livet i skoven 611

'As you like it'. Forspill og scene 388

'As you like it' Overture 1944

As you like it (Shakespeare transmogrified) 951

Ashmansworth 7385

Assisa a piè d'un salice 12055, 12082, 12140, 12145

Assisa a piè d'un Salice[,] Romance D'Otello 12130

Assisa A Piè D'Un Salice[,] Romance from Rossini's Opera Otello 12158

'Assisa a piè d'un salice', Romance, in the Opera of Otello 12074

Assisa a piè d'un salice, The favorite Romance, in Rossini's Opera, Otello, with variations 12097

Assisa à [sic] piè d'un Salice 12124, 12163

At Oberon's Court 10151

At the Boar's Head 4463, 4629, 19294

At the Drop of Another Hat 14182

At the Sign of the Angel or A Little Touch of Harry in the Night 4500, 4671

[Athéni Timon] 16317, 16325

[Atomic Shakespeare] 14677

Aubade 2454, 2788, 2801, 19129

Auf bluhenden Pfaden 14084

Auf morgen ist Sankt-Valentinstag 3873

August 16071

Aus A. Lindner's Bearbeitung von Shakespeare's "Timon von Athen" 16386

Aus dem Sommernachtstraum 10934

Aus den lustigen Weibern v. Nicolai 9113

Aus der Musik zu Shakespeares 'Der Sturm'[:] Erste Suite 15274

Aus der Musik zu Shakespeares 'Der Sturm'[:] Zweite Suite 15274

Aus der Musik zu Shakespeare's Kaufmann von Venedig 8260

Aus der Musik zu Shakespeare's Richard III. 12918

Aus der Musik zu Viel Lärmen um Nichts[:] Drei Stücke für Klavier 11161

Aus der Musik zu Viel Lärmen um Nichts[:] Vier Stücke für Violine und Klavier 11161

Aus 'Der verliebte Pilger' 20668

Aus Oberons Zauberreich 10621

[Aus Romeo und Juliet auf dem Dorfe: "Tritt in mein Haus"] 14084

Aus Shakespeare's Othello 12016

"LIV" aus Shakespeare's Sonette 19768

Aus Shakespeare's "Twelfth night"[:] Süßer Tod . . . 17621

Aus Shakespeares Welt 1936, 4043, 9235, 12436, 18255, 18648

Aus Shakspeare's: "Wie es euch gefällt" 1153, 21075

Aus Shakspears 'Was ihr wollt' 17517, 17690, 17875, 18129

Aus "Was ihr wollt" 18165
Aus "Was ihr wollt" von Shakespear 17565
Ausgewählte Lieder 2749
Autolycus 19036, 19115
Autolycus' Song 18974, 19001, 19007,
    19008, 19082
Autolycus's Song 19049
Autolycus'-Song 18884
Autolycus—Songs 18923
Automne shakespearien 20011
Av musikken til Shakespeares Romeo og Julie
    13277
av scenemusikken til Julius Caesar på
    Nationaltheatret 1947 5332
Ave Maria 12201
Avon 8754
Awakening Music 10011
Ayres for the Theatre 10189
Az vagy nékem 20020
Az Vagy Nékem . . . (Shakespeare: Sonnet
    LXXV) 20035

B

Babes in the Wood 10125
Bacchanale dans l'Opéra Macbeth 7334
Bacchanalian Humoresque 16627
Bacchanalian Song 303
[Back Street Romeo] 14047
Background Music to Julius Caesar 5333
44me. Bagatelle sur Otello, Opéra de G. Rossini
    12110
Balcony Music 13500
Baletní hudba z opery 'Hamlet, náš současník'
    3688
Balfe's Celebrated Operas, 'Joan of Arc,' and
    'Falstaff' 9002
Ballad composed for the Princess Signatelli
    Ruffo 7407
Ballad of King Lear 6149
Ballad, Willow; Willow 12314
[Ballade et Valse d'Ophélie, transcriptions
    variées sur Hamlet] 3658
Ballads from Over the Sea 18058
Ballata di Falstaff 4485, 4660, 9227
[Ballet d'Hamlet] 3660
Ballet Music from Shakespeare's Play The
    Tempest 15457
Ballet Music from Shakespeare's Play The
    Winter's Tale 18940
Ballet Of Reapers And Water-Nymphs 15989
Balletten Mackbeth 7289
Balletten Romeo og Juliette af Hr. Galeotti
    13807
[Balthasar's Song] 11014
Balthasar's Song from Much Ado About
    Nothing 11397

'Balthasar's Song' (Shakespeare) 11273
Balthazar's Song 11516
Ban Ban, Caliban 16012, 21112
Banquet Scene and Minuet 11025
Banquet-Scene, from Verdi's Opera, Macbeth
    7356
Banquo's Buried 7496
Banquo's Ghost 7457
Baō Fēng Yǔ [The Tempest] 15051
Barcarolle 8082
Barcarolle d'Oberon 10857, 10867
Barcarolle with Words 8082
Barocco. Suite Nr. 5 18682
Be My Love 20629
Be not afeard 15505
Be Not Afear'd[,] A Second Song for Caliban
    from Shakespeare's "Tempest" 15503
Be not afeared, the isle is full of noises 15502
Beach Girl 16197
Beatrice 11607, 11608, 11652
Beatrice & Benedict 11350, 11351
Beatrice and Benedick 11603
Beatrice and Benedict 11352, 11593
Béatrice et Bénédict 11343, 11347, 11349,
    12469
[Béatrice et Bénédict] 11344
Béatrice et Bénédict[,] Ouverture de Hector
    Berlioz 11354
Béatrice et Bénédict[:] Sicilienne 11348
Beatrice Theme 11009
Beatrice und Benedict 11353, 11355
Beatrice und Benedict—Ouvertüre 11346
Beaucoup de Bruit pour rien 11107, 11120,
    11367
[Beaucoup de bruit pour rien] 11011, 11061,
    11241
Beauties of Shakespere 21039
Beautiful Beatrice 11651
Beautiful Dreams 14054
Beauty and Truth 11716, 19774
"Beauty is but a vain" 20619
Beauty's Valuation 20739
Beauty's Vanity 20722
Behold your faithful Ariel 14757
Bei Lunas Schimmer 13848
Being Your Slave 19802, 19803, 19804,
    19807, 19826
Being your slave, what should I do 19800
Being your slave, what should I do but tend
    19805
[Beliebte Klavierstücke] 2753
Bells are Ringing 14115
Belmont 8484
Belwin string orchestra folio 9780
[Benátský kupec = The Merchant of Venice]
    8277, 8282, 8318
Benedick's Wedding 21121
[Benisu no Shônin = The Merchant of Venice]
    8321

Berceuse 9381
Bergomask Dance 9370
"Better than All" 19367
Bettlerlied aus dem Wintermärchen 18746
Betwixt mine eye and heart a league is took 19732
Beyond Compare 19442
Beyond the desart mountains 14679
Beyond The Fringe 21273
Bianca 14689
Bid Me Discourse 16667, 16669, 16674, 16675, 16678, 16679, 16682, 20797
Biorn 7550
Bird Song 10449
1935 Birthday Festival 20876
Birthday Festival Ov[erture] 1933 20874
Birthday Festival, 1934 20875
Birthday Festival 1936 20877
Bishop's Popular Duet 'As It Fell Upon A Day' 2046
Blæs, blæs, du vintervind 1078
Blase, blase Winterwind 1123
Blaubart und Othello oder Die Folgen der Eifersucht 12474
Bless This House 9862
Blind Cupid 10352
Bližženci 17421
Bliznetsy [The Twins] 17408
Blow 1103
Blow, blow 987, 996, 1067, 1079, 1085, 1089
Blow, blow thou winter wind 402, 409, 412, 415, 417, 418, 419, 421, 423, 427, 434, 436, 446, 450, 453, 455, 493, 526, 546, 580, 672, 856, 979, 981, 982, 985, 986, 988, 989, 990, 991, 992, 993, 994, 995, 997, 998, 999, 1002, 1004, 1005, 1006, 1008, 1009, 1010, 1012, 1013, 1014, 1015, 1016, 1018, 1019, 1020, 1022, 1024, 1025, 1026, 1027, 1028, 1029, 1030, 1031, 1035, 1037, 1038, 1039, 1044, 1045, 1046, 1051, 1053, 1054, 1056, 1057, 1058, 1061, 1062, 1063, 1065, 1069, 1070, 1071, 1073, 1074, 1075, 1077, 1078, 1079, 1080, 1081, 1082, 1083, 1087, 1090, 1091, 1093, 1094, 1095, 1097, 1098, 1099, 1100, 1101, 1102, 1105, 1106, 1107, 1108, 1109, 1111, 1112, 1114, 1116, 1117, 1119, 1120, 1121, 1122, 1124, 1125, 1126, 1127, 1128, 1130, 1131, 1132, 1133, 1136, 1137, 1138, 1139, 1141, 1142, 1143, 1144, 1145, 1146, 1147, 1149, 1150, 1151, 1152, 1154, 1157, 1158, 1160, 1161, 1164, 1166, 1168, 1169, 1170, 1171, 1173, 1175, 1176, 1177, 1178, 1179, 1180, 1181, 1182, 1187, 1188, 1190, 1191, 1192, 1193, 1195, 1198, 1199, 1200, 1201, 1202, 1203, 1204, 1205, 1207, 1208, 1209,
1210, 1213, 1214, 1216, 1217, 1218, 1219, 1923
[Blow, blow, thou winter wind] 1001, 1017, 1034, 1036, 1040, 1076, 1096, 1135, 1140, 1159, 1186, 1189
Blow, Blow Thou Winter Wind (from: As You Like It) 980
Blow blow thou winters [sic] wind 408, 1959, 8876
Blow, blow, thou Winter's Wind 435, 449, 1215
Blow, Blow thou winter-wind 425
Blow, Blow, Thou Wintry Wind 428, 1050, 1072, 1148, 1954
Blow, Blow, Winter Wind 1052
Blow The Wind 16065
Blow Thou Winter Wind 984, 1007, 1066, 1156, 1183
Blow Winds 6021
Blue Lagoon 16210
Blumenlese aus der Oper: Der Widerspänstigen Zähmung 14577
Blumenlied 20199
'Bog Kupidon dremal v tishi lesnoi (153-i sonet)' ['Cupid laid by his brand and fell asleep' (153rd Sonnet)] 20540
Bogojavljenska noć 16975
[Bogojavljenska noć = Twelfth Night] 17195
Bolingbroke March 12742
Bonjour l'Amour 24
Bonnie Sweet Robin 3740
[Book for the Recording of Titus Andronicus] 16397
Bottom the Weaver 10676
Bottom's Dream 9767, 10157, 10639, 16202
Bottom's Dream from "A Midsummer Night's Dream" 10135
Bottom's Song 10446
Bouře 14981, 14982, 14983, 15207, 15414, 15459, 15460
[Bouře = The Tempest] 14880, 15043, 15232, 15280, 15301, 15456
Bourée and Gigue from the Music to Much Ado About Nothing 11101, 11102
Bourrée 11216
Bourrée from the Music to the Masque in Shakespeare's 'Merchant of Venice' 8348
Boy's Own McBeth 7533
Boy's Song 254
[Bräker] 20844
Bridal Song as sung in Twelfth Night at Her Majesty's Theatre 17184, 19174
Bright Celia's Charms 20988
Bright in the Dark Directed 19723
Brilliant Rondo, for the Piano Forte, on Henry R. Bishop's Air 'When In Disgrace' 18368
Brindisi[:] Si colma il calice. From Verdi's Opera Macbeth 7355
British Songs 19000, 19074

Britisk Rapsodi 7743
[Broken Lance] 6122
Bröllops-Marsch ur Lustspelet 'Så tuktas en
    argbigga' 14500
Brush Up Your Shakespeare 14600, 14625
Brutus 5516, 5537
Bühnenmusik 596, 731, 2056, 2092, 2973,
    3119, 6870, 8315, 14874, 18756, 18889
Bühnenmusik Romeo und Julia 13489
Bühnenmusik zu 'Der Sturm' 15028
Bühnenmusik zu 'Der Widerspenstigen
    Zähmung' 14305, 14358
Bühnenmusik zu 'Die Lustigen Weiber von
    Windsor' 8922
Bühnenmusik zu 'Ein Sommernachtstraum'
    9299, 9566, 9928
Bühnenmusik zu 'Gewonnene Liebesmüh"
    14409
Bühnenmusik zu 'Hamlet' 3061, 3282
[Bühnenmusik zu 'Hamlet'] 2938
Bühnenmusik zu 'Hamlet, Prinz von
    Dänemark' 3488
Bühnenmusik zu '2 Herren aus Verona' 18383
Bühnen-Musik zu Julius Cäsar 5329
Bühnenmusik zu König Heinrich der Vierte
    4437
Bühnenmusik zu König Lear 5789
Bühnenmusik zu Macbeth 6950
Bühnenmusik zu 'Mass für Mass' 7673
Bühnenmusik zu 'Richard II' 12665
Bühnenmusik zu 'Romeo und Julia' 13489,
    13541
Bühnenmusik zu Shakespeare's Coriolan
    2351
Bühnenmusik zu Shakespeares 'Der Sturm'
    15042
Bühnenmusik zu Shakespeares Ein
    Wintermärchen 18789
Bühnenmusik zu Shakespeare's 'Wie es euch
    gefällt' 828
Bühnenmusik zu 'Was ihr wollt' 16795,
    16997, 17154, 18179
Bühnenmusik zu 'Wie es euch gefällt' 650,
    687, 927
Bühnenmusik zur 'Komödie der Irrungen'
    2136
Bühnenmusik–Troilus & Cressida 16536
Buria 16132
[Buria = The Tempest] 15435
Buria: Muzyka k drame V. Shekspira [The
    Tempest: Music to W. Shakespeare's Drama]
    14756
Buria [The Tempest] 15380, 16127, 16282
Burza 15143, 15189, 15282
[Burza = The Tempest] 14692, 14884, 14890,
    15031, 15159, 15172, 15214, 15216,
    15325, 15326, 15342, 15361
[Buscon sucht einen Othello] 12446
But not for love 1988

But shall I go moan [sic] for that my dear
    18946
But shall I go mourn 18702
But, Soft! 13827
Butler's Lives of the Saints 21197
By Gis, and by Saint Charity 3718
By the roses of spring 17426
By The Simplicity of Venus['] doves 10132,
    10134
By the simplicity of Venus's doves 10128
Bygone Days 4005

C

[Cacodémon roi] 12903
Cade 4923, 4924
Caesar, oh Caesar 5546
Café Crown 6136
Caio Martio Coriolano 2430
Caio Marzio Coriolano 2407
Cajo Mario 2401, 2404, 2405, 2410, 2412,
    2413, 2415, 2420, 2423, 2428, 2429
Cajo Marzio Coriolano 2411, 2418, 2425
Caliban 2397, 14856, 15395, 15818, 15820,
    15822, 16007, 16031, 16038, 16045,
    16081, 16099, 16109, 16119, 16167
[Caliban] 16192
Caliban & Ariel 16106
Caliban, A Rhapsody 16218
caliban and ariel 16061, 16069
Caliban II 16173
Caliban Impromptu 16074
Caliban in apartment 112 16258
Caliban[:] The Shakespeare Tercentenary
    Masque 1964, 9248, 15412, 20924
Caliban upon Setebos 16233, 16237
Caliban's Isle 16101
Caliban's Jigg 21121
Caliban's Masque 16008
Caliban's Song 15487, 15819
Caliban's speech 16160
Calypso style songs 2137
Can life be a blessing 16473
Can you not hit it my good man? 6206
Canakin clink 12218
Canço del marxant 21248
Canikin Song 12221
Cannibal-Caliban 16238
Canniken Clink 12220
Canon 4256
Canon: Lady Macbeth, with Witches' Chorus
    7373, 7383, 7388
Canonic Prelude No. 5 for Piano, 'Love's
    Labor's Lost' 6665
Canst thou, O cruel, say I love thee not 20528
Cantata Concertante: 'when dreams do show
    thee me' 19330, 19708

Cantata for a Summer's Day 19135
Cantata I 10750
Cantata II 4471
Cantata in Praise of Love 21227
Cantata: Lady Macbeth 7581
Cantata Piccola 7843, 20602
cantata prima (no longer mourn for me) 19968
cantata seconda (devouring time) 19471
Cantata #1 'Wedding' 15790
3 Canti di Shakespeare 21216
Canto di Romeo sulla Tomba di Giulietta 14133
Canzona Seria[:] A Hamlet Monologue 3965
Canzone 12114
Canzonet VII 7904
Cappriccio On The Seven Ages Of Man 1909
Capriccio Fantastico sull'Opera Otello di G. Verdi 12181
Capriccio, for the Piano Forte, In which is Introduced A Favorite Air, from Rossini's Opera of Othello 12141
Capriccio for the Piano Forte In which is Introduced Bishop's Favorite Air 'Bid Me Discourse' 16673
Caprice after Puck 10603
Caprice[,] 'As You Like It' 1882
Caprice élégante 20967
Cardinal Wolsey and Henry VIII 5218
Cardinal Wolsey's Soliloquy from Shakespear's Henry VIII 5039
Cariñi to Mio 4233
Carnevals-Scene, nach Motiven aus Richard Wagner's Opera Das Liebesverbot 7807
Carnival Song 7806
Carol of the holly 1211
Carol, Sonnet, and Song 19618
Carpe Diem 17830, 17925, 17957, 18053
[Carry on Cleo] 345, 5542
[Carry on Teacher] 14055
Cäsar 5515
Cäsario, oder die Verwechslung 17412
Castle Theme 7118
Catch 6377, 17008
Catch My Soul 12211
Catch[:] Stephano, Trinculo, And Caliban 15595
Catch that Catch can, or A Choice Collection of Catches, Rounds, & Canons 1845
Catch that Catch can: or The Musical Companion 1845
C. E. Horn's Celebrated Duet I Know A Bank 8887
Celebrated Overture to the Opera Otello composed by Rossini 12109
Célèbre valse de Roméo et Juliette 13733
Celestial Music 8478
Celý svět je scéna 974
Ceres' Song In the Tempest 14936, 14937

Cerises d'Amour 21204
César 5515
Cesare e Cleopatra 373
Cesario 17412, 17417
Četeri scene iz Šekspira 275, 6000, 8409, 10664
[Chabm Leil Kayitz = A Midsummer Night's Dream] 9596
Chacksfield plays Rodgers and Hart 2209
Chaconne from The Fairy Queen (Dance for a Chinese Man and Woman) 10252
Chaconne: Rosalind 954
Chairs 3877, 13041, 13045
Chanson 7969
Chanson d'amour 7849
Chanson d'Ariel 15694
Chanson de clown 17477
Chanson, de l'Anneau perdu et retrouvé 9243
Chanson de Printemps 6485
Chanson de Stéphano 13690
Chanson d'Hiver 6630
Chanson d'Ophélie 3743
Chanson du Saule 12332
Chanson funèbre 11378
Chansons de Shakespeare 1194, 1556, 1801, 1862, 2801, 3743, 6485, 6630, 7849, 8476, 8648, 17477
Chansons Galantes 20398
Chansons Pour Hamlet 3012
Chansons pour La Nuit des Rois 16995
Chanson-Zyklus auf Texte von Shakespeare 21217
Chant d'Amour aus der dramatischen Sinfonie 'Roméo et Juliette' 13579
Chant d'Amours 19853, 20101, 20436, 20444, 20526
Chant with Garlands 3932
Chant-funèbre 11379
2 Chants D'Ariel 15035
Charade For The Bard 20995
Charcoal Burner's Song 18289
Chariots 21285
Charm me asleep 20167
Chasse d'hylas et Silvie 16200
"Che accenti! ahimè!" Aria, Introduced by Signor Ivanoff, in the Opera of Otello 12484
Cheerfull Ayres Or Ballads 15068, 19025
Cheerfulness 8487
Chetyre fragmenta iz baleta 'Otello' [Four Fragments from the Ballet Othello] 12030
Chetyre romansa: Iz sonetov V. Shekspira [Four Romances: From the Sonnets of W. Shakespeare] 19791, 20155, 20177, 20474
Chetyre skazki [Four Tales] 6085
Chetyre soneta Shekspira [Four Sonnets by Shakespeare] 19515, 19646, 19735, 20487
Child of Earth with the golden Hair 10788
[Children in the Wood, or Harlequin Queen Mab, and the World of Dreams] 14054

[Chimes at Midnight] 4372, 4564
Chœur des chasseurs 1862
Choix D'Airs de l'Opéra, Otello de J. Rossini 12104
Choix d'airs tirés de l'opéra Macbeth 7251
Choix des plus heureuses pensées musicales de Rossini 12056
[Chor der Elfen] 9038
Chor zu Romeo und Julia[,] nach Shakespeare von Göthe 13361
Chor zu Romeo und Julie 13531
Choric Song 8719
Chorus 14712
Chorus & Dance of Nymphs & Reapers from Taubert's Music to Shakespeare's "Tempest" 15305
Chorus for the Pageant 21021
[Chorus of Fairies] 9704
Chorus of Peasants 12196
Chorus with Ballet, From Chelard's Opera of Macbeth 7255
Choruses of Caliban. A Shakespeare Masque 1964, 9248, 15412, 20924
Christmas Cradle-Song 2972
Christmastide 3821
Christopher Sly 14557, 14568
Chronicles of Love 19737, 19983, 20107, 20154
Cicha śmierci zejdź 17388
[Cimbelino] 2519
Cinco Poemas de Bécquer 3829
Cinq grimaces pour 'Le [sic] songe d'une nuit d'été' 9976
Cinq grimaces pour 'Un songe d'une nuit d'été' 9975
cinq interludes d'un Roméo et Juliette 13938
Cinq Refrains 7390
Cinque pezzi strumentali e due canzoni per 'Il mercante di Venezia' di W. Shakespeare 8369
Circle of fourths 21124
City Song 13901
Clarinet Concerto No. 2 4488
Clarinet Solo From The Trojans[:] The Capture of Troy (Act 1, Scene 6) 8750
Classic Gems 13891
Cleo 238
Cleopatra 277, 279, 281, 311, 315, 319, 329, 334, 356, 358, 359, 360, 362, 364, 366, 369, 376, 379, 381, 382, 385
[Cleopatra] 340
Cleopatra–A Dramatic Aria 308
Cleopatra's Dream 307
Cléopâtre 361, 367, 375, 14126
Cleopatre[:] Lady Wartons Faerwell [sic] 337
Cloten's Morgenlied 2803
Clouds 309
Clouds and Eclipses 332, 4487, 19670, 21178
Clowns [sic] Song From 'Twelfth night' 17256

Clown's Song 17696, 18023, 18083, 18113, 18120, 18137, 18141, 18142, 18172, 18191, 21207
Clown's Song (From King Lear) 6030, 18111
Clown's Song in Twelfth Night 17496
Clown's Songs 16637, 17447, 17775
Clownsong 18159
Co nepomine 19281, 19290, 19311, 19317
Cobweb, Moth and Mustardseed 10715
Coeurs à prendre 4193
[Cokoli chcete = What You Will] 17141
[Cokoli chcete aneb Večer tříkrálový = What You Will, or Twelfth Night] 16803, 17137
Cole 14610
Columbine 6656
Columbines 4240
Come & Go 15510
Come all ye songsters 10223, 10264
Come All Ye Songsters of the Sky 10201
Come and be my Juliet 14147
Come Away 17240, 17361, 17569, 17599, 17619, 18325, 18326, 18333, 18334, 18335, 18337, 18338, 18346
Come Away, Come Away 17522, 17623, 18327, 18332, 18341, 18345
Come away, come away, death 17430, 17437, 17442, 17463, 17465, 17471, 17476, 17478, 17479, 17488, 17495, 17497, 17512, 17513, 17540, 17543, 17550, 17554, 17555, 17558, 17567, 17579, 17594, 17601, 17602, 17618, 17620, 17646, 17649, 17657, 17675
[Come away, come away, death] 17457, 17509, 17531, 17533, 17534, 17551, 17584
"Come away, come away, death"[:] The Clown's Song from Shakespeare's "Twelfth Night" 17541
Come Away Death 8271, 16618, 16620, 16621, 16622, 16623, 16627, 16636, 16637, 16640, 16697, 16708, 16738, 16745, 16815, 16965, 16992, 17008, 17012, 17036, 17076, 17090, 17103, 17163, 17246, 17355, 17427, 17428, 17429, 17434, 17438, 17439, 17440, 17441, 17444, 17445, 17446, 17447, 17448, 17451, 17452, 17454, 17455, 17460, 17462, 17464, 17466, 17467, 17468, 17469, 17470, 17472, 17474, 17481, 17484, 17485, 17487, 17489, 17490, 17493, 17494, 17498, 17499, 17500, 17501, 17503, 17504, 17506, 17507, 17510, 17518, 17521, 17523, 17524, 17526, 17528, 17529, 17530, 17535, 17536, 17537, 17538, 17542, 17544, 17546, 17547, 17548, 17559, 17562, 17568, 17570, 17571, 17573, 17574, 17576, 17577, 17580, 17586, 17587, 17590, 17592, 17595, 17600, 17603, 17605, 17607, 17608, 17609,

17611, 17613, 17615, 17624, 17625,
17629, 17633, 17635, 17636, 17639,
17641, 17642, 17643, 17644, 17647,
17648, 17650, 17651, 17652, 17653,
17654, 17658, 17659, 17660, 17661,
17662, 17663, 17664, 17667, 17668,
17669, 17671, 17673, 17676, 18270,
18274, 21089
[Come Away Death] 16619, 16704, 16900,
17135, 17228, 17318, 17338, 17432,
17640
Come away death[,] Clowns [sic] song in
"Twelfth Night" 17502
Come away death (Dirge) 17475
Come Away Death[,] Feste's Song in
Shakespeare's Twelfth Night 17502
"Come Away, Death" (from "12th. Night")
17173
Come away, Hecate! 6927
Come away—come away 18336
Come, Black-Browed Night 13830
Come Buy 18995
Come buy! Come buy! 19000, 19074
Come Buy of Me 18999
Come Come My Good Shepherds 18678
Come Follow, Follow Me[.] Song of the Fairie
Queen 10914
Come Follow Me 10915, 10918, 10935
Come Follow Me (Queen Mab's Song) 10909
Come, gentle night 14189, 14194, 14197,
14204, 14205
Come, high or low 7544
Come live with me 20678
Come Live With Me, And Be My Love 20720,
20739
.... Come, my queen, take hands with me
10301
Come, my Queen, take my hands 9334
Come, O sea, and bring me sleep 12609
Come o'er the bourn 6145
Come o'er the bourn, Bessy, to me 5695
.... Come, seeling night 7369
Come Sisters! 7370
Come thou Monarch 285, 294
Come, thou monarch of the vine 125, 173,
289, 292, 298, 299, 336
[Come Thou Monarch of the Vine] 182, 304
Come to Dust! 2543
Come Unto These Golden Sands 15587
Come unto these yellow Sands 14704, 14705,
14706, 14709, 14712, 14713, 14715,
14719, 14720, 14723, 14724, 14729,
14734, 14735, 14737, 14738, 14739,
14740, 14742, 14744, 14746, 14747,
14751, 14757, 14848, 14850, 14905,
14916, 14950, 14957, 14961, 15168,
15289, 15317, 15373, 15511, 15514,
15517, 15518, 15519, 15521, 15522,
15524, 15528, 15529, 15532, 15533,

15534, 15536, 15537, 15540, 15541,
15542, 15543, 15545, 15546, 15548,
15549, 15550, 15551, 15553, 15554,
15557, 15558, 15559, 15561, 15562,
15563, 15565, 15567, 15572, 15574,
15575, 15576, 15577, 15578, 15582,
15585, 15586, 15589, 15591, 15593,
15594, 16184
[Come unto these yellow sands] 15520, 15527,
15552
Come Unto These Yellow Sands & Full Fathom
Five[,] Chorus of Nymphs from Taubert's
Music to Shakespeare's "Tempest" 15306
Come unto these yellow sands. Ariel's Song in
Shakespeare's Tempest 14717
Come vi piace 696, 714, 772
[Come vi piace] 595
[Comedia de Equivocaciones] 2018
Comedia erorilor 2127
[Comedia Shel Tauyat = The Comedy of
Errors] 2167
Comedy and Errors 2261
Comedy of Errors 2031, 2183, 2199, 2235
Comedy Tremolo 14290
[Comic Medley Overture] 11711
Command Performance–an entertainment in
divers scenes for tape recorder with songs
and mirth 1949, 2387, 2550, 4065, 4492,
4663, 5077, 5227, 5535, 6112, 8720,
10747, 13064, 14027, 16164, 16578,
19130
Comme il vous plaira 513, 952, 1907
[Comme il vous plaira] 535, 577, 684, 689,
817, 893
Comme il vous plaira, ("Die Namenlose"),
mazurka 1930
"Como la brisa que sangre orea . . ." 3829
[Como Quisieres = As You Like It] 838
Complete Incidental Music and Songs 859
Comus 10227, 14727
Comus[:] Suite from the Ballet 10227
Concert Overture for Brass Band "Henry V"
4823
Concert overture on Shakespeare's 'Merchant
of Venice' 8693
Concert overture on Shakespeare's 'Twelfth
Night' 18220
Concert pour clavecin et petit orchestre 16079
Concertante 19118
Concerto for piano and mixed chorus 20640
Concerto pour violon et orchestre 16078
Concerto (The 'Tempest') 16111
Concert-Ouvertüre (Romeo und Julia) 13924
Concert-ouvertüre zu König Lear 6087
Concert-Ouvertüre zu Romeo und Julie 13942
Concinamus[:] A Song Book for Schools 1466,
14830
Consequences of the Deed 6773
Consolation (When in disgrace) 19553

(Containing An Introduction & Air from Otello) 12060

Conte d'Avril 17341

Conte d'Avril[:] Marche Nuptiale 17342

Conte d'Avril[:] Romance 17343

Conte d'Avril, 1ère suite 17344

Conte d'Avril, 2ème suite 17345

[Conte d'hiver] 18828, 18857

Cordelia 5989, 6067, 6074, 6100, 6110, 6163, 6165, 6182, 6183, 6185, 6186, 6187

Cordélia 6015, 6146, 6188

Cordelia aus 'König Lear' 6056

Cordelia, or the British Heroine: On Occasion of the menac'd Invasion from France. (Address'd to the Ladies) 6190

[Cordelia Victorious] 6123

Cordelia: "We are not the first" 6045

Cordelia's Song 6115

2 cori di Shakespeare 21205

Coriolan 2273, 2279, 2280, 2305, 2313, 2351, 2373, 2374, 2391, 2417

[Coriolan] 2271, 2276, 2285, 2286, 2292, 2297, 2300, 2302, 2308, 2309, 2310, 2314, 2320, 2330, 2331, 2337, 2345, 2356, 2358, 2366, 2370, 2388, 2389, 2390, 2392, 2394, 2395

[Coriolan, ein Heldenleben] 2293

Coriolano 2277, 2377, 2409, 2414, 2416

[Coriolano] 2319

Coriolano, o l'Assedio di Roma 2421

Coriolanus 2267, 2270, 2274, 2282, 2290, 2295, 2301, 2307, 2315, 2318, 2322, 2332, 2333, 2346, 2347, 2348, 2349, 2350, 2352, 2353, 2361, 2365, 2367, 2368, 2371, 2372, 2379, 2383

[Coriolanus] 2265, 2266, 2272, 2284, 2287, 2288, 2289, 2294, 2296, 2298, 2306, 2311, 2316, 2317, 2321, 2323, 2324, 2326, 2327, 2328, 2334, 2335, 2338, 2340, 2343, 2344, 2354, 2362, 2363, 2369, 2378, 2386

Coriolanus Music 2278

Coro di Donne nel Sogno di una notte d'estate di Mendelssohn 9685

[Coronation Anthem] 12777

Coronation March 4977, 4978

Coronation March and Hymn 4984

Coronation March and Hymn (Based on two Themes from the music to Henry VIII) 4977, 4984

Coronation March (From The Music To Shakespeare's 'Henry VIII') 4991

Coronation March (Prelude to Act IV) From the Music to Henry VIII 4983

Coronation Marches 4978

Corydon 20736

Costard 6657

Counsel to Girls 21306

Country Dance 10597, 11309, 14019, 14483

Country Fellow's Song 4641

[Country Life] 4499

Country Song 1383

Cowslips 10634

Cowslip's Bell 16104

Crabbed Age & Youth 20622, 20655, 20722

Crabbed age and youth 8876, 8881, 20591, 20594, 20595, 20597, 20606, 20610, 20623, 20624, 20626, 20630, 20632, 20639, 20650 20656, 20657, 20661, 20662, 20665, 20667, 20674, 20678, 20679, 20680, 20708, 20709, 20710, 20711, 20717, 20724, 20733, 20745

[Crabbed age and youth] 20721

Crabbéd Aged And Youth 20607

Crabbed Age and Youth cannot live together 20600

[Crabbed age and youth cannot live together] 20601

Cravin' for the Avon 21269

Credo des Jago 12194

Cressida 16559, 16577, 16583

Criseyde 16576

Crispin's Day 4813

Cruel Tears 12481

Crystal Drops 16385

Csak addig Gyászolj . . . (Shakespeare: Sonnet LXXI) 19949

Čtyři profily podle Shakespeara 331, 4924, 5224, 19128

Cuckoo 6391, 6400, 6453

Cuckoo Song 6263, 6679

Cuckoo-Buds 6656

Cum vă place 602

[Cum vă place = As You Like It] 386, 710, 748, 816

Cupid's Doomsday 8034, 11613

Cymbelin 2439, 2513, 19141

[Cymbelin] 2442, 2470, 2495, 2497, 2500, 2510, 2517

Cymbeline 2432, 2433, 2454, 2461, 2485, 2490, 2494, 2503, 2504, 2506, 2507, 2511, 2515, 2682, 2816, 2819, 2828, 2832

[Cymbeline] 2440, 2443, 2448, 2449, 2450, 2451, 2458, 2459, 2460, 2462, 2465, 2466, 2467, 2468, 2469, 2474, 2476, 2477, 2478, 2480, 2481, 2482, 2484, 2487, 2489, 2491, 2505

Cymbeline March 2831

Cymbeline Mazurka 2822, 2829

Cymbeline[:] Musique de scène pour la tragédie de Shakespeare 2437

Cymbeline Polka 2823

Cymbeline. Skuespil af Shakespeare . . . 2485

Cymbeline Valse 2814

Cymbeline Waltzes 2818

Cypress 18225

Cztery eseje 4884, 4928, 4965

D

'"Dacă oamenii . . ."' ['Would men . . .']
    4812
Daffodils 19108
Daffodils that come before the swallow dares
    18952
Daisies 6688, 21068
Daisy 3952
Dance 8074, 10189
Dance and Slumber Song 14956
Dance in Cymbeline 2444
Dance Music 9574
Dance of Jolly Conspirators 16719
Dance of Masquers 13517
Dance of Nymphs and Reapers 15215
Dance of Puck 10740
Dance of the Clowns from 'A Midsummer
    Night's Dream' 9758
Dance of the Haymakers 10251
Dance of the Shapes & Dance of the Island. 2
    dances from the Tempest 15007
Dance of the Twelve Satyrs 18880
Dance of Witches from 'Macbeth' 6725
Dance—for Shakespeare's Tempest 15389
Dances from Shakespeare's 'Tempest' 15372
Dances from Shakespeare's Time 21282
Dances of Shapes 15215
[Danish Anthem] 2946
Danse—'Perdita' 18782
Dansons Belle Suzon! 24
[Dark Lady] 20826, 20836
Dark Night, Gentle Night 7840
Darn that dream 10287
Das arme Kind 11993
[Das Leben des Timon von Athen] 16327
[Das Leben Koenig Heinrich des Fuenften]
    4716
[Das Liebesverbot] 7810
Das Liebesverbot oder Die Novize von Palermo
    7805
[Das Trauerspiel von Julius Caesar] 5258
Das Wintermärchen 18776, 18831, 18927
[Das Wintermärchen] 18667, 18674, 18693,
    18739, 18750, 18752, 18765, 18771,
    18779, 18791, 18799, 18808, 18813,
    18819, 18823, 18833, 18835, 18837,
    18845, 18852, 18860, 18862, 18863,
    18865, 18867, 18890, 18893, 18897,
    18898, 18899, 18903, 18913, 18922
Daughters of Lear 6002
David Garrick 21275
Dawn 13851
Day and Night 14108
De koopman van Venetië 8121
[De koopman van Venetië] 8116
De Leeuwerk zingt . . . 2639
De Montano et Stéphanie 11620
[De muntre koner i Windsor = The Merry
    Wives of Windsor] 8812
De Musica 21221
De Profundis 13239
[De storm] 15024, 15355
De vrolijke vrouwtjes van Windsor 9220
[De Vrolijke Vrouwtjes van Windsor = The
    Merry Wives of Windsor] 8841, 8890
Dear pretty youth 15221
[Dear Pretty Youth] 15219
Death Music 13239
Death of Ophelia 4081
Decameron 12129
December 12771
Declamations ("Full of Tongues") 16423
Defend Me Still 21219
Defilir Marsch nach Motiven des Singspiels:
    Othellerl der Mohr von Wien 12456
Deh calma, o ciel, nel sonno 12164
'Deh calma, oh ciel . . .' aus der Oper Othello
    von Rossini 12107
Deh! calma oh Ciel nel seno 12125
Den genfundne Ophelia 4174
Den Jomfru sad med Sorgen. (Af "Othello")
    12302
[Den lille prinsen af Danmark] 4101
"Dengang jeg var kun saa stor som saa . . ."
    16782
Dengang jeg var kun saa stor som saa. (Af
    "Helligtrekongersaften") 18143
Dengang jeg var ung og elskovsfuld. (Af
    "Hamlet") 3793
[Dente por dente = Measure for Measure]
    7631
Deo Gracias (God Be Thanked) 4833
[Der bestrafte Brudermord oder Prinz Hamlet
    aus Dännemark] 4086
Der blinde Sänger 19516
[Der Dritte Richard] 12966
Der durch den Fall des grossen Pompejus
    erhöhte Julius Caesar 5560
Der ewige Kreis 19895
Der Frühling 6418, 6443, 6463
Der Frühling. (Spring.) 6480
Der Herr ist mein Licht 8682
Der Kaufmann von Venedig 8154, 8164,
    8214, 8257, 8258, 8261, 8370, 8405
[Der Kaufmann von Venedig] 8065, 8096,
    8130, 8135, 8137, 8145, 8155, 8157,
    8158, 8162, 8179, 8181, 8190, 8200,
    8201, 8203, 8207, 8209, 8228, 8232,
    8243, 8251, 8255, 8262, 8273, 8274,
    8283, 8284, 8286, 8295, 8305, 8308,
    8327, 8338, 8339, 8341, 8353, 8362,
    8371, 8389
[Der Kleine Prinz von Dänemark] 4128
[Der Komödie der Irrungen] 2121
[Der Krieg der Rosen] 4856, 4898, 4941
[Der Liebe Leid und Lust] 6238

Der Londoner Verlorene Sohn 20856
[Der Londoner verlorene Sohn] 20895
Der Mohr von Venedig 12020
Der Morgen 2802
[Der nackte Hamlet] 4118
Der Narr 18255
3. Der Narr beschließt 18129
Der Nordische Liedergruss 7997
Der Opern-Konzertist 9058
Der Orkan 15475
[Der Rest ist Schweigen] 4093
Der Schiffbruch 15428
Der Schlummer wohn' 21245
Der Schwan von Pesaro 12157
Der Sommernachtstraum 9618
Der Spiegel des Hamlet 3601
Der Sturm 14875, 14900, 14904, 14993,
    15140, 15259, 15283, 15304, 15313,
    15331, 15390, 15411, 15416, 15451,
    15455, 15463, 15468, 15472, 15496,
    15497, 16098, 16261
[Der Sturm] 14853, 14902, 14903, 14914,
    14929, 14946, 14960, 14963, 14964,
    14967, 14972, 14975, 14976, 14984,
    14992, 14996, 14999, 15001, 15029,
    15044, 15087, 15089, 15094, 15095,
    15101, 15132, 15133, 15136, 15151,
    15152, 15195, 15202, 15226, 15237,
    15244, 15251, 15256, 15262, 15303,
    15310, 15314, 15315, 15316, 15322,
    15327, 15337, 15339, 15343, 15344,
    15350, 15351, 15357, 15360, 15366
Der Sturm, oder Die bezauberte Insel 15469,
    15471
Der Sturm oder die verzauberte Insel 15471
Der Tod der Kleopatra 265
Der Tod des Antonius 370
Der Totengräber—The Gravedigger 3791
Der var en Svend med sin Pigelil. (Af "Som
    man behager") 1356
Der Widerspänstigen Zähmung 14571
[Der Widerspänstigen Zähmung] 14580
Der Widerspenstigen Zähmung 14232, 14310,
    14317, 14348, 14384, 14388, 14487,
    14488, 14506, 14545
[Der Widerspenstigen Zähmung] 14224,
    14225, 14233, 14247, 14249, 14253,
    14258, 14260, 14293, 14296, 14300,
    14318, 14322, 14329, 14331, 14333,
    14339, 14340, 14342, 14343, 14345,
    14346, 14351, 14352, 14357, 14365,
    14367, 14372, 14373, 14374, 14375,
    14377, 14379, 14387, 14395, 14396,
    14397, 14398, 14404, 14415, 14416,
    14424, 14435, 14439, 14445, 14447,
    14450, 14460, 14469, 14470, 14471,
    14474, 14489, 14491, 14496, 14498,
    14514, 14518, 14525, 14533, 14534,
    14547, 14554

Der Winter 6599, 6620
Des Narren Lied, aus Shakespeare's "Was ihr
    wollt" 17491
Des Pförtners Morgenlied aus Shacespear's
    Macbeth 7571
Descent into Epilogue 7539
Desdemona 12175, 12382, 12397, 12429,
    12501, 12539
Desdemona i Otello, Venetsianskii mavr
    [Desdemona and Othello, Venetian Moor]
    12135
Desdemona singt 12436
Desdemona Walzer 12380
"Desdemona, Won't You Feed Me, Please"
    12538
'Desdemonan laulu' [Desdemona's Song]
    12315
Desdemona's Song 11824, 12291, 12331,
    12342, 12366
Desdemona's Willow Song 12248
Desdémone 12111, 12493
Desdémone Endormie 12412, 12413, 12414,
    12415, 12416
Desdémone Valse 12381
Desdemonia 12537
Desiat' sonetov Shekspira [Ten Sonnets of
    Shakespeare] 19247, 19296, 19524, 19609,
    19953, 20048, 20069, 20111, 20223,
    20540
Det Guddommelige Tivoli 14108
Deuteromelia: or The Second part of Musicks
    melodie, or melodius Musick. Or Pleasant
    Roundelaies . . . 17691
Deutsche Lieder 17525
Deux Chansons de 'Comme il vous plaira' de
    Shakespeare 1023, 1307
Deux Fantaisies sur des thèmes de l'Opéra:
    Macbeth de G. Verdi 7322
Deux Marches solennelles du 'Roi Lear' 6057
Deux Mélodies 978, 11394
Deux poèmes de Shakespeare 7969, 19717
Deux Sonates Pour Le Piano Forte 2001,
    14688, 16234
Deux Sonnets de Shakespeare 20575
Devouring Time 19467, 19473
Devouring time. Sonnet 19 19466
[Dì Shí Er Yì = Twelfth Night] 17365, 17407
Diafonia 19537
'Dialog Gamleta s sovest'iu' [Hamlet's Dialogue
    with His Conscience] 4246
Dialog o hudbě 20402
Dialog o lidské důstojnosti 20138
Dialog s vnitřním hlasem 19923
Dialogue between Coridon and Mopsa from
    "The Fairy Queen" 10207
Dialogue in praise of the owl and the cuckoo
    6417, 6541
Dialogue: Kate and Bianca 14650
Diaphony 19537, 19624, 19722

Dichterworte 12770
Did not the heavenly rhetoric of thine eye 6341
Dido and Aeneas 8046
Die Aeolsharfe 16201
[Die beiden Gastmahle oder Der Verschwender] 7522
[Die beiden Veroneser] 18386, 18426, 18437, 18441, 18456
Die bezähmte Widerspenstige 14558
[Die bezähmte Widerspenstige] 14330
Die bezauberte Insel 15428
Die Ermordung Cäsars 5480
Die Feenkönigin 10258
[Die Feier des Bundes der Liebe] 16201
Die Geisterinsel 15404, 15415, 15419, 15426, 15454, 15465, 15500
[Die Geschichte Koenig Heinrichs des Vierten] 4341, 4546
[Die Geschichte von König Heinrich dem Vierten] 4428, 4601
[Die gezähmte Megäre] 14433
Die Hamletmaschine 4175
Die Hamlet-Saga 3580
Die Insel des Prospero 15468
Die Irrtümer der Zauberei 10292
[Die jämmerliche Tragödie von Titus Andronicus] 16416
Die Komödie der Irrungen 2143, 2144, 2178
[Die Komödie der Irrungen] 2021, 2049, 2066, 2067, 2070, 2091, 2095, 2096, 2098, 2111, 2113, 2114, 2119, 2123, 2131, 2140, 2145, 2146, 2150, 2151, 2157, 2169, 2179, 2182, 2185, 2190, 2197
[Die Kunst der Zähmung] 14406
Die Liebenden von Verona 13810
Die lustige Witwe 9265
Die lüstigen Weiber 9156
[Die lustigen Weiber] 9142
Die lustigen Weiber von Windsor 9006, 9015, 9016, 9018, 9023, 9040, 9045, 9058, 9063, 9064, 9071, 9072, 9077, 9081, 9083, 9117, 9126, 9130, 9141, 9143, 9154
[Die Lustigen Weiber von Windsor] 8803, 8809, 8824, 8830, 8846, 8849, 8854, 8874, 8900, 8908, 8909, 8916, 8925, 8932, 8942, 8943, 8947, 8948, 8964, 8981, 9020, 9033, 9042, 9049, 9053, 9054, 9055, 9059, 9061, 9067, 9073, 9078, 9080, 9086, 9089, 9090, 9092, 9095, 9097, 9104, 9105, 9108, 9109, 9110, 9122, 9125, 9128, 9133, 9137, 9138, 9140, 9144, 9145, 9147, 9149, 9150
Die lustigen Weiber von Windsor — Lied des Falstaff 9106
Die lustigen Weiber von Windsor — Ouvertüre 9139
Die Maske 14152
Die Nacht 10221

Die Novize von Palermo 7805
Die Rundköpfe und die Spitzköpfe 8032
Die Shakespeare-Feier 796
[Die Shakespeare-Feier] 20884
[Die Tragödie von König Richard II] 12730
[Die Tragödie von Macbeth] 6931
[Die Tragödie von Richard dem Dritten] 12927
Die Traum-Fee (La Reine Mab) 13575
[Die unzertrennlich eins ich mit dir bin. . . .] 2063
[Die Weiber in Wien] 9241
Die widerspänstige Katharina 14586
Die Winzerbraut 14107
Die Wunderinsel 15430, 15477
Die Zähmung der Widerspänstigen 14492
[Die Zähmung der Widerspenstigen] 14289, 14299, 14302, 14332, 14349, 14378, 14419, 14477, 14495, 14532
Die Zauberinsel 15492
Die Zauberirrungen 10292
[Die zwei edlen Herren aus Verona] 18413
[Die zwei Herren aus Verona] 18457
Die Zwillinge 17421
[Die zwölfte Nacht oder Was ihr wollt] 17285
Diktaren och Tiden. Fri omtolkning av fyra Shakespeare-sonetter 19622, 19840, 19878, 19902
Dinah 2516
Dine Læber lad mig fly[,] Sang af Shakespeare's Lige for Lige 7743
Ding Dong Bell 8562
Dirge 2571, 2577, 2588, 2626, 11390, 13862, 14123, 17433, 17511, 17588
Dirge; Fear no more the heat o' the sun 2540
Dirge for Fidele 2552, 2605, 2618, 2619
Dirge for Imogen 2589
Dirge, for Romeo and Juliet 13155
Dirge from Cymbeline 2536, 2575
Dirge from Cymbeline ("Fear No More The Heat Of The Sun") 2607
'Dirge' from Music to 'Hamlet' 3327
Dirge from Shakespeare's "Cymbeline" 2581
Dirge in Cymbelin [sic] 2846
Dirge in Cymbeline 2596, 2850, 2855, 2871
[Dirge: Pardon Goddess Of The Night] 11133
Dirge — Romeo & Juliet 13103
Divertimento before Shakespeare's The Merry Wives of Windsor 8821, 9212
Divertimento, for the Piano Forte, with Flute Accompaniment (ad Lib.)[,] The Subject of the Rondo, The Celebrated Glee 'The Loadstars,' by William Shield 10376
Divertisement for the Piano forte, with an Accompaniment (ad libitum) for the Flute consisting of an Introduction & Andante, with Dr. Cooke's Glee, 'Hark! the lark at Heaven's gate sings,' As a Finale 2659
Divertissement für Bläserquintett und Cembalo 14662

[Dmitri Shostakovich: Music to Plays] 3419, 3422

[Dmitri Shostakovich: Popular Pieces] 3411

Do Much About Nothings: 13 Paradoxical Pithy Paraphrases for Punaccompanied Pchoir 11641

Do not call it sin in me 6342, 6682

Do nothing but eat 4640

Dobrou noc 13835

Doch sei getrost, wenn jene Haft mich trifft 20030

Dogberry (& Verges) 11597

Dogberry March 11121

[Doi tineri din Verona = The Two Gentlemen of Verona] 18356

Doll Tearsheet's Rant 21121

Dorian Gray 14099, 19764, 20343

Dorian Gray Suite 14099, 19764

Dorian Waltz 13207

Dorinda lamenting the loss of her Amintas 15424

Double-Trouble 7586

Doubt that the Stars are fire 3720, 3721, 3732, 3739

Doubt thou. . . . 3725

Doubt Thou The Stars 3731

Doubt thou the stars are fire 3726, 3736, 3737, 3738

[Doubt thou the stars are fire] 3719

Down by the Avon's Flowing Stream 21038

Dramatic Banquet: Shakespearean Men 3586, 5479, 12603, 12749, 16370

Dramatic Overture (After seeing Ernesto Rossi perform 'Hamlet') 4029

Dramatic Overture for Richard III 12822

9 Dramatic Poems after Robert Browning 16233

Dramatic Reading 4060

Dramaticheskie stseny[:] Tret'ia siuita iz baleta 'Otello' [Dramatic Scenes: Third Suite from the Ballet Othello] 12410

Dream city 10271

Dream Pictures 10607

Dreams 15453

Dreamstuff; The Musical Tempest 15450

Drei Chansons aus Shakespeares Romeo und Julia 13628

Drei Gedichte von W. Shakespeare 2600, 8612, 18551, 21072

Drei Klavierstücke 10655

Drei Lieder der Ophelia (Aus 'Hamlet') 3781, 3843, 3876

Drei Lieder der Ophelia aus Shakespeares 'Hamlet' 3775, 3842, 3873

Drei Lieder des Narren aus Shakespeare's "Was ihr wollt" 17665

Drei Lieder (Three Songs) von Shakespeare 1574, 17663, 18044

Drei Narrenlieder aus Shakespeares 'Was ihr wollt' 16607

Drei Sätze aus 'Romeo und Julie' Symphonie von Hector Berlioz 13576

[Drei Shakespeare Lieder] 21209

Drei Shakespeare-Lieder 4921, 5493, 20136

Drei [sic] Herren aus Verona 18463

Drei Sonette von William Shakespeare 19716, 19899, 20447

Drie Sonnetten van Shakespeare 19721, 19727, 19734

[Driekoningenavond = Twelfth Night] 16987, 17182

Drinking Song 4637, 4639, 21218

Drinking Song . . . As Sung In "The Taming of the Shrew" produced at the Adelphi Theatre 4668, 14359

[Droom van een Midzomernacht] 10065

Dry those Eyes 14950, 15196, 15197, 16229

Du rummer alt, der er mig dyrebart. Sonnet af Shakespeare 19635

Duel Music 13229

Duell 20515

Duet In Timon Of Athens 16341

Duet of Sonnets 19489, 19494

Duet—"As It Fell Upon A Day" 2034

3 duets from 'As You Like It' 841

Duett 21021

Duett zwischen Reich und Spärlich 9036

Duetto, for [Two Cats] 12044

Duetto nell'Opera Romeo e Giulia 13808

Duetto—Rosalind & Celia 20741

Dumaine's Sonnet 6210

Duncan March 6840

Dunsinane Blues 7497

Duo Brillant Sur Oberon 10815

Duo de Montano et Stéphanie 11625

Duo d'Otello, chanté par Dupres et Barroilhet, Rossini 12065

Duo d'Otello[,] Op: de G. Rossini 12160

Duo pour Piano et Violon Sur des motifs d'Oberon de Weber 10882

Duologue: Romeo and Juliet 13766

Dva fragmenta (Kolybel'naia i Pantomima) iz muzyki k tragedii V. Shekspira 'Gamlet' [Two Fragments (Lullaby and Pantomime) from Music to W. Shakespeare's Tragedy Hamlet] 3414

Dva otryvka[:] Iz opery 'Ukroshchenie stroptivoi' [Two Fragments: From the Opera The Taming of the Shrew] 14643

[Dva Pechal'nykh Marsha = Two Mournful Marches] 2382

Dva šlechtici veronští 18399

Dva soneta Shekspira [Two Sonnets of Shakespeare] 19506, 19524, 19609, 19662, 19961, 20220

Dva tantsa[:] Iz baleta 'Romeo i Dzhul'etta' [Two Dances: From the Ballet Romeo and Juliet] 13791

'Dva tantsa' [Two Dances] 16961

[Dva vernoští páni = The Two Gentlemen of Verona] 18407

[Dva verontsa = The Two Gentlemen of Verona] 18395, 18396, 18400, 18403, 18410

[Dvamata verontsi = The Two Gentlemen of Verona] 18408, 18446

[Dvanaiseta nosht = Twelfth Night] 17045, 17420

[Dvanaiseta nosht: komedia ot Shekspir = Twelfth Night: Comedy by Shakespeare] 16761

[Dvanajsta noč = Twelfth Night] 17241

Dve p'esy[:] Iz muzyki k tragedii V. Shekspira 'Gamlet' [Two Pieces: From the Music to W. Shakespeare's Tragedy Hamlet] 3474

Dvě písně na slova Williama Shakespeara 974, 19281, 19290, 19311, 19317

Dve serenady iz komedii Shekspira 'Dvenadtsataia noch'' [Two Serenades from the Shakespeare Comedy Twelfth Night] 16964

Dve skazki [Two Tales] 3997

[Dvenadtsataia noch' = Twelfth Night] 16589, 16615, 16624, 16628, 16649, 16688, 16721, 16723, 16774, 16847, 16934, 16938, 16946, 16961, 16964, 16972, 16980, 16984, 17042, 17071, 17099, 17112, 17138, 17140, 17151, 17152, 17157, 17216, 17221, 17270, 17297, 17304, 17366, 17369, 17370, 17424

[Dvenadtsataia noch' ili Kak vam ugodno = Twelfth Night, or What You Will] 17156

Dvenadtsataia noch' [Twelfth Night] 17293, 17408, 17419

[Dwaj panicze z werony = The Two Gentlemen of Verona] 18397

[Dwaj panowie z werony = The Two Gentlemen of Verona] 18401, 18423, 18454

[Dwaj szlachcice z werony = The Two Gentlemen of Verona] 18381

'Dzhul'etta' [Juliet] 13883

E

Early English Lute Songs and Folk Songs 18308

Early Georgian Songs 5099

East Cheap Minuet 21121

Easy for Both 10767

Easy to play selections with lyrics from West Side Story 13623

Eaux-Fortes 3960, 16053

Eccho Song, 'twixt Ferdinand and Ariel 14859

Echo Song 14860

Écossaise[:] Duo des Pages 1556

Edgar and Fool 5977

[Edgar's Song] 5819

[Edmund Ironside] 20831

[Edwin Booth] 14042

E'en As The Sun 20806

[Een midzomernachtsdroom] 10086

Een Midzomernachtsdroom 9383

[Een Midzomernachtsdroom] 9568, 9950

Een Winteravondsprookje 18729

[Een Winters Verhaal] 18769

E'er you can say come and go 14757

Egipetskie nochi [Egyptian Nights] 341, 342, 357

Egy kislány meg egy legény 1549

Eia, wohl mir 21231

Eight Ancient English[,] Spanish and Scotch Ballads, with two Glees for four Voices 3739

Eight Scenes from the Tragedy of Macbeth 7248

Eight Shakspere Songs 1408, 1716, 2691, 7929, 8598, 10530, 11483, 17950

Ein Bursch und Mägdlein flink und schön 1259

Ein Bursche mit der Liebsten 1386

[Ein Charleston für Lady Macbeth] 7521

Ein Cyklus lyrisch-dramatischer Gesänge nach Shakespeares Sonetten 19502, 19777, 19937, 20030, 20032, 20310, 20383, 20419, 20489, 20506

Ein Liebster und sein Mädel 1509

Ein Liebster und sein Mädel fein. Lied der Pagen aus "Wie es euch gefällt" von Shakespeare 1542

Ein Liebster und sein Mädel schön 1531, 1557

[Ein Liebster und sein Mädel schön] 1254, 1344

[Ein Mittsommernachtstraum] 9332, 9487, 9877, 10036

Ein neuer Sommernachtstraum 10156

Ein Sommernachtstraum 9462, 9463, 9465, 9497, 9590, 9617, 9620, 9729, 9732, 9875, 9904, 9905, 9906, 9909, 9910, 9911, 10020, 10115, 10148, 10210, 10288, 10610, 10631, 10737, 10988

[Ein Sommernachtstraum] 9270, 9279, 9301, 9303, 9308, 9310, 9313, 9316, 9327, 9333, 9344, 9372, 9387, 9388, 9393, 9399, 9404, 9405, 9419, 9427, 9429, 9430, 9431, 9437, 9442, 9445, 9453, 9454, 9455, 9461, 9475, 9478, 9481, 9492, 9493, 9494, 9496, 9500, 9509, 9513, 9515, 9522, 9523, 9525, 9528, 9532, 9533, 9534, 9540, 9542, 9545, 9546, 9549, 9551, 9560, 9569, 9578, 9581, 9601, 9602, 9604, 9606, 9616, 9641, 9676, 9863, 9864, 9874, 9878, 9883, 9884, 9885, 9889, 9890, 9892, 9894, 9895, 9896, 9908, 9912, 9916, 9917, 9927, 9947, 9957, 9959, 9960, 9964, 9969, 9979, 9980, 9981, 9983, 9985, 9986, 9987, 9990, 9994, 10027,

[Ein Sommernachtstraum] (*cont.*)
  10037, 10069, 10074, 10085, 10107,
  10111, 10112, 10117, 10185, 10820
Ein Sommernachtstraum von Shakespeare 9619
[Ein Sturm] 15086
Ein unbekannter Kanon (fünfstimmig) auf den
  Geiger Ignaz Schuppanzigh 4501, 4674,
  9258
Ein Wintermährchen [*sic*] 18859
Ein Wintermärchen 18746, 18802, 18805,
  18879, 18934, 18945, 19154
[Ein Wintermärchen] 18715, 18744, 18745,
  18796, 18798, 18800, 18842, 19111
Eine Musik zu Schakespeare's 'Viel Lärmen
  [u]m Nichts' 11161
Eine Schottische Tragödie 7267
Einige Hexenscenen aus Schackespear's
  Macbeth 7110
Einlage zum Kaufmann von Venedig 8231
Einleitung zu Hamlet 4059
Einst, der Tag ist einerlei 20668
[El Mercader de Venecia] 8217
[El Rey Lear] 5704
El sueño de una noche de verano 9249, 10777,
  20929
Electronic Incidental Music for Macbeth 7171
Elegia e Canto 8436
Elegie 16782
Elegie aus: Cymbeline 2600
Elegy 2534, 2556, 2560, 3751
Elegy from Shakespear's Cymbeline 2593
Elegy I 6365
Elegy, I. M. Noel Newson 2583
Elegy on the supposed Death of Fidele 2844
[Elegy on the supposed Death of Fidele] 2865
Elegy—"Done to death" 11372
'Elfenlied' aus 'ein Sommernachtstraum' von
  William Shakespeare[:] 'über Tal, über
  Höh'n' 10064
Elfenlied (Fairy Song) aus Shakespeare's
  Sommernachtstraum 10571
Elfenmarsch aus dem "Sommernachtstraum"
  9706
Elfin Dance 9826
Elftes Quartett für zwey Violinen, Bratsche und
  Violoncelle ['Serioso'] 12534
'El'fy. Iz komedii V. Shekspira "Son v Ivanovu
  noch"'' [Elves. From W. Shakespeare's
  Comedy A Midsummer Night's Dream]
  10917
Elizabeth, Princess of England 5212
Elizabethan & Shakespearean Musicke for the
  Recorder 21292
Elizabethan Love and Bird Songs 17511
3 Elizabethan Partsongs 20091
Elizabethan Songs 17853, 20852
[Elmonda di Valenza] 6133
Elseneur 4161, 7542
Elsinore 3578

Elskovsvise 16782
En Blanc et Noir 13670
En gutt gikk ut på elskovssti 9470
En Jægersmand drogiud 807
En Marge de Shakespeare 3898, 8687, 13893,
  19460
En midsommarnattsdröm 9275, 9524, 10098,
  10291
[En midsommarnattsdröm] 9271, 9315, 9406,
  10078
[En skærsommernattsdrøm] 9538
En sommarnattsdröm 9242, 10772, 20912
[En Sommernattsdrøm] 9435, 9473, 10235
En vintersaga 18909
[En vintersaga] 19137
[En vintersaga = The Winter's Tale] 18682
Enchiridion 10744
Encounter 20014
Ende gut, alles gut 41, 81
[Ende gut, alles gut] 6, 18, 27, 31, 34, 36, 48,
  52, 55, 57, 58, 59, 62, 65
Ende gut, alles gut! 33
Ende gut, alles gut. All's well that ends well
  102
Ende gut—alles gut 91
Engender'd in the Eyes 8594
England 5644, 12761, 12762
England's Minstrel King 21059
England's Pleasant Land 4805, 5643, 12757
Englisch Horn 1049, 6374, 6420, 15849
XII English & Italian Songs 15799
English Ayres. 1598-1612 12262
English Lyrics 1127, 1744, 6593, 7949,
  12337, 17979, 19960, 20282, 20665,
  21305
English Songs 19553, 19603, 19822, 20085,
  20391
58 English Songs by Composers chiefly of the
  Seventeenth and Eighteenth Century 10132,
  11007, 14724, 14793, 18533, 19011
XII English Songs in Score[,] Collected from
  Several Masques and other Entertainments
  15926
[Enrico IV] 4392, 4576
Ensembles for 17 12245
Enter Ariel 16227
Enter Three Witches 7449
Entracte 13935
[Entr'actes zu Heinrich IV] 4293, 4522
Entracts & Air for 'Measure' 7765
Entrance of Baptista 14431
Entrance of Katharina 14290
Entrance of the Clowns 9826
Entreactes zur Tragoedie: 'Hamlet' 3505
Entry Dance 10251
Éphéméride 19833
Epicedium! in Anthony & Cleopatra 122
Epicedium In Shakspear's Play of Antony and
  Cleopatra 122

Epilogue 2534, 7393, 15827, 19534
Epilogue from the Tempest 15824
Epilogue[:] "full fathom five" 15618
Epilogue Song 17317
Epilogue to Twelfth Night 17307
Epilogue—Clown's Song 16808
Episode aus einem Künsterleben 6178
Épisode de la vie d'un artiste 6167
Épisode de la vie d'un Artiste[:] Grande
   Symphonie Fantastique 6173
Épisode de la vie d'un Artiste[:] Simphonie [sic]
   Fantastique 6166
Epitaph on Quin 21277
Epitaph on Shakspear[']s Tomb 21027
Epithalame, Danse et Ariette de 'Roméo et
   Juliette' 13681
Epithalamium 15795
Epithalamium: "Thrice happy lovers" 10197
Er ist tot 3744
Ere you can say 15122
Ere you can say come, and go 15115
"Erinnerung"[:] Sonette LXXXIV 20074
Ernest Austin's Songs. Second Volume 11400
Ero 11366
errors 2241
Erstes Lied des Amiens 1802
Erstes Lied des Ariel 15772
Erzählung Imogens und Klage 2872
Erzählungen 12433
Es war ein Schäfer und Shäferin 1523
"Escena Lírica" del Acto V de Romeo y Julieta
   14038
Esquisse d'une fanfare[:] ouverture pour le Vᵉ
   acte de 'Roméo et Juliette' 13399
Esquisses 12065
Esquisses Vénitiennes 12412, 12413, 12414
Être Ou Ne Pas Être[,] Monologue d'Hamlet
   4041
Étude symphonique No. 2 3978
Études Mélodiques pour Piano d'après Schubert
   2758
Euphrosine ou Le Tyran corrigé 12479
Euryanthe 2885
Even as the sun with Purple colour'd face
   8876, 20807
Evening in the Forest 784
Evening Rondeau 10220
Ever 'Gainst That Season 3817
Every one that flatters thee 20590
Exerzitien 10744
Exit March—'Twelfth Night' 17294
Extra Song 90

F

Fain would I change that Note 21296
Fair Fidele 2849

Fair Friend, You Never Can Be Old 20237
Fair Fugitives 10949
Fair Is My Love 20659, 20718
Fair, Kind, And True 18764, 20246, 20251,
   20253, 20255
Fair Love 9918
Fair Olivia (Who is Sylvia?) 17340, 18611
Fair Titania (Old English Dance) 10732
Faire Citherea sitting by a Brooke[:] Second
   part 20737
Fairies 10487
Fairies' Lullaby 10501
Fairies' Song 10484, 10525
[Fairies' Song] 8865, 9420
Fair-weather Friend 6044
Fairy Chimes 8597
Fairy Duets . . . Selected from Mendelssohn's
   Music to the Midsummer Night's Dream
   9652
Fairy Glee 10986
Fairy Glee from the Midsummer Night's Dream
   10464
Fairy King Attend And Mark 9362
Fairy Land 10497
Fairy lead them up and down, Song in
   Shakspere's Midsummer Night's Dream 9362
Fairy Life 15916
Fairy Lullaby 10428, 10514
Fairy Music from Weber's 'Oberon' 10836
Fairy Scenes from Shakespeare 7486, 10726,
   16134
Fairy Song 9574, 9918, 10415, 10939
[Fairy Song] 9347
Fairy Songs (from M.N.D.) 9485
Fairy Sports 10845
Falling in love with love 2209, 2210, 2211,
   2213, 2214, 2216, 2219, 2220, 2221,
   2223, 2224, 2225, 2226, 2227, 2231, 2232
Falsa-staff 9190
"False Concolinel" 6226
False Cressid! 16580
Falstaf [sic] 8992, 8993
Falstaff 4468, 4469, 4473, 4476, 4477, 4478,
   4479, 4483, 4545, 4634, 4635, 4651,
   4652, 4653, 4654, 4658, 4817, 4818,
   8989, 8998, 9000, 9002, 9158, 9162,
   9177, 9178, 9179, 9180, 9196, 9218,
   9219, 9226, 9255
[Falstaff] 4367, 4385, 4494, 4495, 4537,
   4570, 4597, 4667, 4669, 4741, 8917,
   8973, 9237
[Falstaff a Princ Jindra = Falstaff and Prince
   Hal] 4303, 4525
Falstaff at the Boar's Head 4484, 4659
Falstaff Atto I Parte II 9183
Falstaff. Atto III. Parte II 9191
Falstaff (Caprice) 4475, 4650, 9213
Falstaff di G. Verdi 9186
'Falstaff' Fantaisie 9193

Falstaff In and Out of Love 9155
Falstaff osia Le tre Burle 9158
Falstaff, Polka brillante 8991
Falstaff Quadrille 9031
Falstaff. Quick Step. from O. Nicolai [sic] Opera
    9065
Falstaff Scherzo 9187, 9188
Falstaff . . . Menuet Du 3me Acte 9182
Falstaffs Lied: Einstens als Page 9185
Falstaff's Minuet 21121
Falstaff's Ragamuffins 4506
Falstaff's Serenade 9260
Falstaff's Song 4502
Falstaff's Song. "Give me a cup of sack, boy"
    4504
Family Music 21230
Fancie 8515
Fancies 8626
Fancies I 1079, 8578, 17924, 18526
Fancies II 1378, 2577, 2677, 6562
Fancy 8499, 8512, 8527, 8536, 8543, 8547,
    8553, 8559, 8578, 8584, 8617, 8661
Fancy (from the Merchant of Venice) 8550
Fancy's Knell 8574, 8713, 8725
Fanfare, Flourish, Sennet 13049
Fanfare for a Great Occasion 3516
Fanfare for Julius Caesar 5403
Fanfare for Will 21105
Fanfare[:] Homage to Shakespeare 21107
Fanfare—Postlude 4832
Fanfare—Prelude 4832
Fanfarer och marcher till Hamlet 3440
Fanfares 7632, 12657
Fanfares and Nocturnes for Romeo and Juliet
    13918, 21143
Fanfares, Flourishes, and Entr'acte Music for
    'Macbeth' 7233
Fanfares for Macbeth 6745
Fanfares for Shakespearean (Historical) Plays
    1943 21182
'Fanfary' [Fanfares] 3384
Fanfáry k Richardu III. 12976
Fantaisia on Otto Nicolai's Opera The Merry
    Wives of Windsor 9091
Fantaisie brillante sur la Marche et la Romance
    de l'Opéra Othello de Rossini 12094
Fantaisie brillante sur la Marche et la Romance
    d'Otello de Rossini 12090, 12170
Fantaisie Brillante Sur la Romance d'Otello de
    Rossini 12076
Fantaisie brillante sur La tempesta di F. Halévy
    15423
Fantaisie Brillante sur Roméo et Juliette 13703,
    13709, 13737
Fantaisie Brillante . . . Sur des motifs de l'Opéra
    Oberon 10860
Fantaisie de chase . . . introducing Sir Henry R.
    Bishop's Favorite Chorus Hark! each Spartan
    hound 10130

Fantaisie de Concert . . . sur des Motifs d'Otello
    de Rossini 12132
[Fantaisie d'Hamlet, Opéra d'Ambroise
    Thomas] 3671
Fantaisie Dramatique Sur La tempête drame de
    W Shakespeare 16213
Fantaisie Élégante sur des Motifs de l'Opéra
    Roméo et Juliette de Chs. Gounod 13724
Fantaisie Élégante sur Roméo et Juliette
    13665
Fantaisie et Variations Pour le Piano Sur la
    Marche d'Otello de Rossini 12093
Fantaisie Facile Pour Flûte & Piano sur la
    Romance favorite d'Otello, de Rossini 12074
Fantaisie sur des motifs de 'Falstaff', musique
    d'Ad. Adam 8996
Fantaisie sur des motifs de l'Otello de Rossini
    12048
Fantaisie sur des Motifs D'Oberon[,] Euryanthe
    et de Preciosa 10858
Fantaisie, Sur des Motifs et Sur la Barcarolle,
    De Oberon, de Weber 10823
Fantaisie sur la Merry Wives of Windsor 9047
Fanta[i]sie Sur la Romance D'Othello 12131
Fantaisie sur 'Le Songe d'une nuit d'été'
    20970, 20978
Fantaisie sur "Les joyeuses Commères de
    Windsor" 9124
Fantaisie sur l'opéra 'Falstaff' d'A. Adam 8995
Fantaisie sur Macbeth (Op: de Verdi) 7328
Fantaisie sur Oberon[,] Op: de C. M. Weber
    10888
Fantaisie sur Otello[,] Op. de Rossini 12080
Fantaisie sur Roméo et Juliette 13685, 13698,
    13707, 13708, 13747, 13750
Fantaisie variée sur la Romance d'Otello[:]
    'Assisa à pié [sic]' 12064
Fantaisie . . . on the Mermaid's Song, from
    Weber's Opera of Oberon 10842
Fantaisie-Pot Pourri sur Roméo et Juliette 13715
2 fantaisies brillantes . . . sur l'Opéra de
    Ambroise Thomas[:] Le Songe d'une Nuit
    d'été 20974
Fantaisies Concertantes (Pots-Pourris) 3650
Fantaisie . . . Sur des Motifs favoris de l'Opéra
    D'Oberon 10868
Fantaisie . . . Sur les Airs de Montano et
    Stéphanie 11626
Fantaisie . . . Sur une Barcarolle célèbre de
    l'Opéra Oberon de M. Weber 10843
Fantasia for the Harp, on Henry R. Bishop's
    favorite air 'Bid Me Discourse' 16668
Fantasia, for the Piano Forte, On favorite
    Subjects from Balfe's Opera, Falstaff 9003
Fantasia from Weber's Oberon 10863
Fantasia From Weber's Op: Oberon 10848
Fantasia "Full Fadom Five" 15776
Fantasia on Favorite Melodies from Bennett
    Gilbert's A Night in Fairyland 10784

Fantasia on Greensleeves 9165, 9166, 9167, 9168, 9169, 9170, 9171, 9176
Fantasia on Nicolai's Opera The Merry Wives of Windsor 9051, 9111
Fantasia on Oberon 10811
Fantasia on Otto Nicolai's opera, The Merry Wives of Windsor 9017
Fantasia on Songs of Shakespeare's time 21281
Fantasia on the Opera Macbeth 7317
Fantasia on Themes from Nicolai's Opera, Merry Wives of Windsor (Falstaff) 9135
Fantasia, On Themes From Verdi's Opera Macbeth 7357
Fantasia on Verdi's Macbeth 7335
Fantasia on Verdi's Otello 12198
Fantasia sulla Romanza nell'Otello 12118
Fantasia sull'opera Macbeth di Verdi 7329
Fantasia—'Falstaff' 9189
Fantasia—'Recollections of Mendelssohn' 9697
Fantasie über Mendelssohns Sommernachtstraum 9808
Fantasie und Variationen über den Marsch aus Othello 12093
21 Fantasies for a Lover and his Lass 1467, 21175
Fantasina über Motive aus Oberon von C. M. v. Weber 10827
Fantasy Overture Romeo and Juliet 13992
Fantasy-Overture 'Romeo & Juliet' 13985
Faradt vagyot 19924
Farewell 13831, 20084, 20085, 20088, 20090
Farewell! (Addio!) 20083
Farewell, dear heart 16697
Farewell, Dear Love 17677
Farewell, Earth's Bliss 2537
Farewell, master; farewell, farewell! 14906
Farewell! Thou Art too Dear 20094
Farewell! Thou Art Too Dear For My Possessing 20091, 20092, 20095, 20169
Faust und Yorick 4286
Favorite Airs from Otto Nicolai's Opera, The Merry Wives of Windsor (Die lustigen Weiber von Windsor) 9102
Favorite Airs Sung In Shakespeare's Play Of The Tempest, Composed By Purcell, Arne, and Linley 14705, 14768, 15117, 15481
Favorite Overture & March to Romeo and Juliet 13812
Favorite Songs from Shakespeare 21324
Fear no more 2452, 2457, 2521, 2529, 2530, 2539, 2548, 2549, 2551, 2554, 2564, 2566, 2569, 2572, 2573, 2576, 2587, 2606, 2621, 2817, 2883, 2884
Fear no more the heat o' th' sun 2523, 2525, 2586, 2830
[Fear no more the heat o' th' sun] 2526, 2544, 2574, 2599, 2608
Fear no more the heat o' the sun 2446, 2499, 2522, 2527, 2531, 2535, 2537, 2542,
2545, 2547, 2550, 2553, 2555, 2561, 2562, 2563, 2567, 2568, 2579, 2580, 2582, 2583, 2584, 2595, 2597, 2602, 2603, 2613, 2615, 2617, 2620, 2623, 2628
Fear no more the heat o' the sun (Dirge from Cymbeline) 2622
Fear no more the heat of the sun 2533, 2541, 2592, 2594, 2612, 2616, 2624, 2834, 21087
Feare no more the heate o' th' Sun 2528
February 11602
Feengesang 10416
Fem sånger (posthuma) 853, 5172
Femeia îndărătnică 14494
[Femeia îndărătnică = The Taming of the Shrew] 14241, 14252, 14452
Ferdinand und Miranda 15046
Fest Musik til Schackespeares Apotheos 21172
Feste 17489, 17679, 17688, 17700, 17828, 18106, 18230, 18242
Feste's Dance 18211
Feste's Songs 16715
Festival March 21116
Festival of Spring[:] Ballet Divertissement from the Opera 'Hamlet' 3686
'Fialke rannei brosil ia uprek (Sonet 99)' ['The forward violet thus did I chide' (Sonnet 99)] 20203
Fidele 2561, 2565, 2598, 2611
Fie on Fantasy 8852
Fie on sinful fantasy 8820, 8836, 8979, 9199, 9200, 9207, 9248
[Fie on Sinful Fantasy] 8872
Fie On This Quiet Life 9198
Field Song 1525
Fifth Fantasie[,] on the Favorite Air Come live with me and be my love 2045
Fifty Shakspere Songs 1038, 11439, 21319
Final del 2° Acto del Macbeth, convite con brindiz 7351
Final March of Triumph 6834
Finale 3421
Finale[:] Bid Me Discourse 16671
Finale Dance 2193
Finale.—Homage to Shakespeare 21043
Fire Angel 8167
Fire engelske sange 11550
Fire Engelske Sonetter til Tekster af Keats og Shakespeare 19243, 20261, 20393
First Recreations 10616
First Selection from the Ballet in 'Hamlet' 3629
First Set of Pieces (from The Fairie Queen) 10183
First sketch for the music of 'The First Part of King Henry the Fourth' 4318
First sketch for the music of 'The Second Part of King Henry the Fourth' 4534
Fisherman's Chorus from Dr. Bennett Gilbert's Operetta, A Night in Fairyland 10782

Five Centuries of Spring 20187
Five Christmas Madrigals 977
Five Elizabethan Lyrics 2565
Five Elizabethan Songs 1671, 5100, 15629, 15878
Five English Songs 1504
Five Improvisations 6473
Five Love Songs 6421
Five Miniatures 10345
Five Musical Moments 10717
Five Poets—Seven Songs 2554, 12288, 18112
Five Preludes after The Tempest 15997
Five Shakespeare Songs 1154, 1190, 6341, 6384, 6624, 7994, 8432, 8500, 10350, 10475, 10501, 11396, 11406, 11616, 15528, 15636, 15654, 17375, 17429, 17448, 17476, 17623, 17649, 17712, 17744, 17754, 17813, 18007, 18080, 18120, 18974, 19443, 21237
Five Shakespeare Songs. Second Set 2602, 7960, 18171
Five Shakespeare Sonnets 19504, 19829, 19954, 20238, 20321
Five Shakespearean Madrigals 1089, 3764, 4639, 7917, 17935
Five Shakespearean Songs 305, 1085, 1324, 1651, 5206, 6441, 8020, 8440, 10409, 11383, 11585, 12292, 15803, 17671, 18471
Five Shakespearean Sonnets 19229, 20213, 20257, 20379, 20471
Five Shakespearian Dances 21160
Five Shaksperian Songs 1052, 1668, 8559, 11449, 17522
Five Short Poems 6505
Five Songs from Shakespeare 4647, 7397, 8469, 11525, 12229
Five Songs from The Winter's Tale 18757, 18959, 18978, 19003, 19044, 19078
Five Songs of Ophelia (Ophelia's Lieder) 2970
Five Songs of Sorrow And Reconciliation 19190, 19286, 19994, 20350, 20356
Five Songs of Youth 8554
Five Songs, Prelude and Tango, for Lady Macbeth 7582
Five Sonnets 19213, 19627, 19843, 19879, 20272, 20281
Five Sonnets by William Shakespeare, Set to Musick 19232, 19339, 19493, 19595, 19906
Five Sonnets of Shakespeare 19293, 19299, 19450, 19629, 20141, 20147
Five Sonnet-Settings 19433, 19528, 19536, 19720, 20243
Five Standard Songs 14841
Five Theatrical Sketches (Divertimento No. 3) 2400, 16236
Five Tone Sketches 10739
Five Winter Songs 6583

Fleurs Italiennes 12045
Flexi Scores 20756
Flip Up In De Scidimadinck Jube Up In De Jubin Jube 7579, 12513, 13078, 14180
Flores de mi primavera 15696
Florizel 19104
[Florizel and Perdita, or The Winter's Tale] 18775
Flourish & Exeunt, Severally 21165
Flourish, Enter Chorus 4804
Flout 'em and scout 'em 14906, 15595
Flow on Silver Avon 21052
Flower Speech 19134
Flower-de-luce 19109
Flowers From My Garden 11649
Folie et Mort d'Ophélie 4061, 4068, 4069, 4071, 4074, 4084
"Follow me" 14705
Following Falstaff's Footsteps 9008
Fool talk 6111
Fool's Fanfare 536, 3016, 5721, 9379
Fools had ne'er less grace 6026
Fools had ne'er less grace in a year 5695
Fool's Song 17777
[Fool's Song] 5696
Fool's Song (from: King Lear) 6041
Fool's Songs 5976
Foot It Featly 16057
For a Field a Cloth of Gold 5226
For a Leavetaking 6379
For A Wedding 20311
For as the sun is daily old and new [sic] 20052
For bonny sweet Robin is all my joy 2981
For O, for O, the Hobbyhorse is Forgot 3895
For Ophelia 4066
For Shame Deny that Thou Bear'st Love to Any 19278
For the Rain 17008
For the Rain it Raineth 18146
For the Rain it Raineth Every Day 16965, 18098
For Thee Hath Beauty Deck'd Her Bow'r 10865
for Your delight 6392
Foraaret 6429
Foråret 6435
Forbear Sweet Wanton 21280
Forbidden Planet 16177
Foreboding 19741
Forest One 9293
Forest Songs 1200, 1806, 1863
Fortress of Tragedy 7539
Fortune and men's eyes 19566, 19569, 19570
Four Ballads. Three from Shakespear and one by Harwood 6521, 7846, 8525
Four Dances from 'Love's Labour's Lost' 6649
Four English Songs 18172
Four little Character-Sketches 10627
Four Madrigals[:] Settings of Four Poems of Wm. Shakespeare 2566, 6547, 11450, 17887

Four Marches composed by F. Mendelssohn Bartholdy 9833, 9834

Four Movements from West Side Story 13612, 13613

Four Musical Monologues 534

Four Musical Sonnets 19364

Four Nature Songs 15789

Four Old English Lyrics 1310

Four Old English Songs 1631, 5075, 19638

Four Pieces by Henry Purcell 10239

Four Pieces from the music to 'Macbeth' (1955) 6944

Four Poems on Springtime 6470

Four Rounds to Shakespeare Texts 1045, 1663, 17701, 17729

Four Seasons Songs 6570

Four Shakespeare Dances 7467, 13941, 14663, 18240, 21176

Four Shakespeare Pieces 3954, 10636, 13912

Four Shakespeare Songs 1019, 1078, 1144, 1215, 1230, 1360, 1619, 1634, 1696, 1731, 1816, 2521, 2525, 2628, 2793, 2796, 3696, 3709, 3776, 5161, 5171, 6427, 6435, 6454, 6517, 6561, 6588, 6589, 6644, 7399, 7817, 7860, 7931, 7939, 7983, 8441, 8517, 8536, 8603, 8605, 8684, 10387, 10473, 10502, 11393, 11512, 12219, 12238, 12291, 13866, 15658, 15712, 15714, 15758, 15888, 15919, 17442, 17543, 17580, 17587, 17771, 17961, 18084, 18123, 18161, 18475, 18546, 18620, 20410, 21045

Four Shakespeare Songs[:] 3rd Set 3774, 11506, 19058

Four Shakespeare Sonnets 19231, 19267, 19351, 19776, 19885, 19969, 19987, 20150, 20158, 20179, 20372, 20394, 20459, 20484, 20528, 20550

Four Shakespearean Songs 1838, 6396, 8539, 17831

Four Shakesperian Part-Songs 1704, 6574, 8587, 10336

Four Short Shakespeare Songs 3770, 7934, 15556, 15711

Four Sketches for As You Like It 1880

four songs and two dances for the 'midsummer night's dream' 10066

Four Songs for Love's Labour's Lost 6210

Four Songs from Shakespeare 1133, 5151, 19223, 19256

Four Songs from 'Twelfth Night' 17526, 17530, 17702, 17703, 17890, 17897, 18133, 18138

Four songs in praise of spring 1290, 18952, 19037

Four Songs of Celebration 18003

Four Songs of Schubert 18614

Four Songs of Solitude 1195

Four Songs to poems by Shakspeare 672, 11824

Four Sonnets by Shakespeare 19406, 19574, 19614, 20093

Four Texts in Music 15860

Four Trifles 10640

Four XVIIth Century Poems 5067

Fourteen Comic, Convivial, and Sentimental Songs 1987

Fourteen Pieces for the violin 10200

Fragment No. IV: Sonnet LXXIII 19990

Fragmente aus der Schauspielmusik 'Macbeth' 6944

Fragmente aus Lear 6009

Fragmenten van Shakespeare 8668, 13865

Fragments from the Music in Macbeth, composed by Matthew Locke 6982

Fragmenty iz baleta 'Otello' [Fragments from the Ballet Othello] 12030, 12032

'Fragmenty iz baleta "Romeo i Dzhul'etta"' [Fragments from the Ballet Romeo and Juliet] 13798

Fragmenty iz muzyki k tragedii V. Shekspira 'Gamlet' [Fragments from the Music to W. Shakespeare's Tragedy Hamlet] 3418

4 Frames for Improvisers 4060

Frankincense 19358, 19600, 19756, 20234, 20247

Franklin Square Song Collection 8881

Franz Nava's Operatic Favorites 7347

Franz Schubert: Ausgewählte Lieder 2776

Frauenbilder aus Shakespeare's Dramen 4214, 12501, 14157, 16219

Freeze, freeze, thou bitter sky 1220

Frescoes 6094

Friendly Duet 14182

Friends of Mine 8415

Friends Romans Countrymen 5484

Friendship 6044

"Frolics of the Laborers" From Shakespeare's A Midsummer-Night's Dream 9786

[From 'A Midsummer Night's Dream'] 9826

From a Sonnet by Shakespeare 20559

From an Antique Land 10903

From An Unknown Past 20679

From fairest creatures 19178, 19181

From Hamlet 4063, 4064

From Much Ado 11610

From Oberon in Fairyland 10952

From Romeo to Juliet and back again 13920

From Schakespeare to You 970, 3715, 4807, 7379, 15861, 17735

From Shakespeare 19270, 20098, 20267, 20731

From Shakespeare in Antony & Cleopatra 291

From Shakespeare in Cymbeline 2649

From Shakespeare's Garden 4240, 6688, 10928

From Shakespear's Cymbeline 2593

From The Fairy Hills 10705
From the Fantasy Overture: Romeo and Juliet
    13988
From the Five Winds 10585
From The Tempest 15793
From The Winter's Tale 19055
From this moment on 14608, 14635, 14637
"From You Have I Been Absent" 20187
From you have I been absent in the Spring
    20184, 20186
From you I have been absent in the spring
    20178, 20193
Frühling 6460
Frühlingslied 6446
Frühlingslied—When Daisies Pied 6415
Frühling—Winter 6420, 6543
Fulfilment 16838
Full Fadom five 15691, 15721, 15756, 15778,
    15789
Full Fadom Five[:] Five Shakespearean Songs
    15655, 15656, 15889, 17512, 18999
Full fadom five thy father lies 15655, 15656,
    15763
[Full fadom five thy father lies] 15609, 15614,
    15615, 15695, 15726, 15786
Full fathom 15622
Full Fathom Five 8493, 14712, 14714, 14715,
    14724, 14729, 14731, 14745, 14850,
    14905, 14916, 14950, 14957, 15004,
    15054, 15055, 15056, 15057, 15060,
    15063, 15066, 15068, 15168, 15180,
    15289, 15292, 15317, 15373, 15596,
    15597 15598, 15600, 15602, 15604,
    15605, 15606, 15608, 15610, 15611,
    15612, 15613, 15616, 15617, 15619,
    15620, 15621, 15623, 15625, 15626,
    15628, 15629, 15630, 15631, 15633,
    15634, 15636, 15638, 15639, 15641,
    15642, 15643, 15644, 15646, 15648,
    15650, 15652, 15653, 15657, 15658,
    15661 15663, 15664, 15665, 15667,
    15668, 15670, 15672, 15673, 15676,
    15680, 15681, 15682, 15684, 15685,
    15688, 15693, 15697, 15699, 15700,
    15702, 15703, 15704, 15705, 15707,
    15710, 15712, 15713, 15714, 15716,
    15717, 15718, 15719, 15720, 15722,
    15725, 15727, 15728, 15729, 15730,
    15733, 15734, 15735, 15736, 15737,
    15738, 15740, 15741, 15742, 15746,
    15747, 15748, 15749, 15752, 15754,
    15761, 15765, 15766, 15767, 15768,
    15769, 15771, 15773, 15774, 15775,
    15777, 15779, 15780, 15782, 15785,
    15788, 15802, 15827, 15850, 15866,
    15897, 16034, 16156, 16184, 17714
"Full fathom five thy father lies" 14703,
    14705, 14706, 14746, 15485, 15637,
    15645, 15677, 15692, 15758

Full fathom five thy father lies. Ariel's Song in
    Shakespeare's Tempest 14717
Full fathoms [sic] five 15698
Full many a glorious morning 19653, 19654,
    19655, 19658
Full many a glorious morning have I seen
    19656
. . . full of sound and fury . . . 7481
Funérailles d'Imogène 2864
[Funeral March] 2918
[Funeral March for the Last Scene of Hamlet]
    4190
Funeral March from "Hamlet" 3514
Funeral Song 11381, 11383
Fünf Lieder nach Shakespeare 1110, 1725,
    7936, 11487, 17585
Fünf Ophelia-Lieder 2970
Fünf Shakespeare Sonette 19182, 19308,
    19565, 20119, 20208
Fünf Shakespeare-Lieder 850, 1165, 1531,
    1787, 1860, 17239, 17634
Fünf Shakespeare-Sonette erklingen 19177,
    19283, 19349, 19479, 19503
Fünf Shakespeare-Sonetten 20561
Fünfzehn Shakespeare-Sonette 19187, 19925,
    19972, 20024, 20099, 20274, 20336,
    20403, 20435, 20439, 20460, 20483,
    20504, 20530, 20542
für William 21007
Furies Dance 6705
Furlana per Forte-Piano nel Ballo Otello
    12210
Fürs Haus 3744
Furtuna 14901, 15010
[Furtuna = The Tempest] 15328
Fúvósötös, vagy amit akartok . . . or, What You
    Will (Shakespeare) 18322
Fye on Sinful Fantasy 8953, 9204, 9205, 9206
Fyra vinjetter till Shakespeares en vintersaga
    18806
Fyra visor ur Som ni behagar 559

G

G. Verdi. Otello[.] Dramma lirico. Atto Primo[.]
    Scena I. Urgano 12183
Galliard for Katherine & Petruchio 14655
Gallimaufry 4490, 4662, 9263, 19146
Galop from The Merry Wives of Windsor.
    Founded on Otto Nicolai's Opera 9028
[Gamlet = Hamlet] 2920, 2985, 3000, 3014,
    3090, 3091, 3106, 3115, 3193, 3194,
    3196, 3197, 3227, 3229, 3284, 3362,
    3364, 3384, 3406, 3421, 3423, 3494,
    3592, 3603
Gamlet [Hamlet] 3359, 3409, 3410, 3475,
    3569, 3983, 4038

Gamlet, Prints' Dans'kyi [Hamlet, Prince of
  Denmark] 3268
[Gamlet. Prints Datskii = Hamlet, Prince of
  Denmark] 3502
Gamlet, prints datskii [Hamlet, Prince of
  Denmark] 3581
Garrick's Monody on Shakspeare 21048
Garrick's Monody on The Death of Shakespeare
  21048
Gaudia mundana 5080
'Gavot (No. 4) iz stseny "Myshelovka"'
  [Gavotte (No. 4) from the 'Mousetrap' Scene]
  3359
Gavotte. De La Cour Du Roi Henri IV 4514,
  4682
Gavotte, Romeo e Giulietta 14017
Gay Dances for trio from Shakespeare 20852
'Gde, krasotka, ty guliaesh'? (Pesnia shuta)' ['O
  mistress mine, where are you roaming?'
  (Song of the Fool)] 16961
Gedicht von Shakespeare aus dem Lustspiel
  "Wie es euch gefällt" 1561
4 Gedichten van M. Nijhoff 19143
Geisterinsel 15427
Geistermarsch aus Macbeth 7044
"Gelehnt an die Cypress" aus "Othello" 12052
3 gem. Chor nach Gedichten von William
  Shakespeare 20049, 20669
Gems from Shakespeare[:] Five Beautiful Songs
  1166, 5170, 6478, 7982, 18016
Gentle Ophelia 4255
Genug 17734
Georget et Georgette 16195
Gesænge aus Shakespeare's Schauspielen 1700,
  2682, 3707, 3794, 8581, 17561
Gesaenge aus Shakspeare's Was ihr wollt.
  Kaufmann von Venedig. Wie es euch
  gefällt[.] Sommernachtstraum. Der Liebe
  Müh' umsonst 1543, 6480, 6620, 8640,
  10565, 17645, 18026
Gesang 18560, 18562
Gesang an Sylvia 18549
Gesang (An Sylvia) aus Shakespeare's "Die
  beiden Edelleute von Verona" 18560
Gesang der Desdemona im Othello 12361
Gesang der Isabella 7805
Gesang im Walde 21223
6 Gesänge aus Herders Sammlung der
  Volkslieder 7911
4 Gesänge aus 'Stimmen der Völker' von J. G.
  Herder 12311
Gesänge des Autolycus 19132
Gesänge im Klavierauszuge aus der Geisterinsel
  15465
Get You Hence 18683, 18700, 18702, 18958,
  18962, 18963
Get you hence for I must go 18675, 18718,
  18757, 18953, 18959
"Get You Hence" from The Winter's Tale 18768

Ghost of Hamlet's Father 3586
Ghost Sung [sic] 13042
Gillette de Narbonne 103
Girls of the future 12492
Gitarre Duos aus Shakespeares Zeit 21291
Giulietta e Romeo 13168, 13643, 13775,
  13785, 13790, 14030, 14118, 14121,
  14212, 14213, 14215
[Giulietta e Romeo] 13555, 13782, 13805
Giulietta e Romeo fra 14199
Giulietta e Romeo Intermezzo 14120
Giulio Cesare 5277, 5278, 5477, 5481, 5559,
  5562
[Giulio Cesare] 5271, 5286, 5378, 5428
Give Me Back My Heart 21301
Give sorrow words 7374, 7378, 7391
Give Us This Night 14050
Gjensyn 14172
Glee 7985, 8580
Glee & Chorus 19226, 20806
Glee for Five Voices 20712
Glee for four Voices (In answer to Sigh no more
  Ladies) 11643
Glee[.] Perform'd at Shakespear's Jubilee 20998
Glee V 2861
Glee VI 2873
Gli equivoci 2238
Gli sposi in contrasto 14593
Glorianna 21271
Glossolalie 61 7291
Gloucester 13054
"Glück" 10382
Gneo Marzio Coriolano 2408
Go Lovely Rose 14290
God, and our good cause 13048
. . . . God's goodness hath been great to thee
  4919, 4920, 21011
Golden Thoughts 10166
Goldene Blumenkrone . . . 3666, 9113, 13727
Goldene Töne 7330, 9185, 12194
Gondellied aus dem Schauspiel "Der Kaufmann
  von Venedig" von W. Shakespeare 8775
Gone with the Wind 18285
Goneril 6162
Goneril's Lullaby 6155, 6157, 6161
Good Company 1682, 6555
Good Friends Sweet Friends 5486
Good King Hal 4458, 4625, 4797
Good Night 20742
Good night, good rest 5269, 20658, 20672,
  20743
Good Night! Parting is Such Sweet Sorrow!
  13834
Good Time Johnny 9009
Goodbye, Little Dream, Goodbye 14059
Good-night 13859
Goodnight With a Lullaby 10523
Grab Me a Gondola 21269
Grabgesang 2559, 2590

Grablied eines Landmannes (aus Shakespeare's Cymbelin) 2601

Grablied—Fear No More 2557

Grace (from the music to "Henry VIII.") 4977

Grace In All Simplicity 20767

Graceful Dance ('Malvolio') 17185

Graceful Dance. No. III from the Incidental Music to Shakespeare's Henry VIII 5022

Graceful Dance (No. III) from the Incidental Music to Shakespeare's Henry VIIIth 5020

Græd ikke meer, du lille Mø! (Af "Stort Besvær for Ingenting") 11456

Græd ikke mer 11530

[Gran capriccio di Concerto . . . sull'Op. Guglielmo Shakespeare di T. Benvenuti] 20911

Grand duo de concert . . . sur des motifs d'Oberon de Weber 10851

Grand Duo, Sur la Barcarolle D'Oberon 10824

[Grand March] 852

Grand March from 'Henry VIII' 5024

Grand March (From the Music to Shakspere's Play of 'King John') 5649

Grand Potpourri From the Opera of 'Otello' 12190

Grand Quatuor en Partition pour deux Violons, Alto, et Violoncelle 4265, 9264

Grand Selection from G. Verdi's Opera: 'Falstaff' 9195

Grand Selection from Gounod's Opera Romeo and Juliet 13756

Grand Selection from Gounod's Opera 'Roméo é [sic] Giulietta' 13687

Grand Selection from Macbeth 6994

Grand Selection 'Macbeth' No. 1 7299

Grand Selection (No. 1)[:] 'Il Mercante di Venezia' 8414

Grand Selection 'Romeo And Juliet' 13694

Grand Trio Pour Harpe, Piano-forte et Violin, sur Les motifs favoris de Macbeth[,] Opéra de Verdi 7326

Grand Triumphal March in the Tragedy of Coriolanus 2283

Grande Fantaisie dramatique sur La Tempête, drame de Shakespeare 16213

Grande fantaisie pour le piano à 4 mains sur 'Otello' de Rossini 12149

Grande fantaisie pour le piano sur des motifs d'Otello, de Rossini 12115

Grande Fantaisie Symphonique 3559

Grande Fête des Capulets 13572

Grande Mosaïque sur Roméo et Juliette 13686

Grande Ouverture du Roi Lear 6058, 6062

Grande Sonate pour le Pianoforte ['Pastoral'] 19148

Grave Digger[']s Song 3789

[Gravedigger's Song] 3358

Graverens Vise 3802

Greasy Joan 6618

Great Caesar 5549

Great Moments with Tchaikovsky[:] Third Selection of His Most Famous Melodies 13968

[Great Shakespear's Image from its hallow'd Base] 21054

Green Ways 18225

Green Willow 12285

Greensleeves 9172, 9173, 9174, 9175

Gregorian Chant 13229

Gróf Romeo 14116

Grosse characteristische Ouvertüre zu Shakespeare's Macbeth 7077

Grosse Fantasie aus Verdi's 'Othello' 12208

Grosse Simphonie zu Shakespeare's 'Richard der Dritte' 13053

Großes Potpourri aus dem Musical West Side Story 13598

Grußworte 15805

Guglielmo Shakespeare 20909, 20910

Guido et Ginevra, ou La peste de Florence 14201

Guten Morgen, 's ist Sankt Valentinstag 3876

Gwen 6686

H

H. Hugo Pierson Album 7955

[Ha layla hashvem assar = Twelfth Night] 16639, 17218, 17290

Ha Orpheusz lantja szólt . . . 5124

Hai Ho 1476

Hǎi Lí Dé Hūn Yīn . . . [The Marriage of Helena. . . .] 35

Hail, All Hail To The Queen 8748

Hail! Caesar, Hail! 5534

Hail, Shakespeare, Hail 20950

Hair 4164

Hal 4460

Halcyon Days 14712, 14718

Half the fun 314

Hållilå, uti storm och i regn 17222, 17223

Hallowed And Gracious Is The Time 3825

[Halom Leil Kaiz = A Midsummer Night's Dream] 10002

[Halts Maul du Schuft!] 17199

[Ham Hamlet] 3161

[Hamelesch Lear = King Lear] 5673

Hamlet 2894, 2897, 2900, 2912, 2914, 2915, 2916, 2927, 2933, 2935, 2937, 2943, 2952, 2958, 2964, 2966, 2968, 2969, 2975, 2976, 2989, 2994, 2995, 3001, 3011, 3017, 3022, 3023, 3024, 3032, 3034, 3035, 3037, 3039, 3040, 3042, 3044, 3053, 3059, 3065, 3066, 3072, 3078, 3082, 3083, 3084, 3085, 3086, 3087, 3096, 3118, 3121, 3122, 3123, 3134, 3142, 3150, 3154, 3162, 3180,

3183, 3213, 3215, 3233, 3234, 3235,
3237, 3246, 3253, 3254, 3257, 3262,
3265, 3280, 3286, 3287, 3289, 3292,
3314, 3320, 3332, 3366, 3369, 3371,
3374, 3398, 3399, 3431, 3435, 3438,
3441, 3447, 3454, 3456, 3457, 3466,
3467, 3468, 3469, 3470, 3472, 3473,
3476, 3478, 3486, 3492, 3498, 3512,
3513, 3535, 3539, 3540, 3543, 3549,
3555, 3556, 3566, 3572, 3584, 3587,
3588, 3589, 3598, 3602, 3605, 3615,
3616, 3619, 3621, 3623, 3624, 3625,
3626, 3633, 3634, 3635, 3636, 3637,
3638, 3639, 3641, 3644, 3645, 3646,
3649, 3650, 3653, 3654, 3655, 3656,
3659, 3661, 3662, 3663, 3665, 3667,
3668, 3670, 3674, 3675, 3676, 3678,
3679, 3680, 3681, 3682, 3685, 3707,
3747, 3794, 3807, 3808, 3848, 3859,
3892, 3897, 3899, 3929, 3931, 3935,
3936, 3937, 3938, 3939, 3940, 3941,
3944, 3958, 3959, 3964, 3980, 3981,
3982, 3984, 3985, 3986, 4013, 4045,
4047, 4048, 4052, 4054, 4107, 4181,
4206, 4211, 4254
[Hamlet] 2886, 2887, 2888, 2889, 2892,
2893, 2895, 2896, 2898, 2899, 2901,
2902, 2907, 2908, 2909, 2913, 2917,
2922, 2923, 2924, 2925, 2926, 2928,
2929, 2930, 2931, 2932, 2936, 2939,
2940, 2941, 2942, 2944, 2945, 2947,
2948, 2949, 2950, 2951, 2953, 2954,
2957, 2959, 2960, 2961, 2962, 2967,
2978, 2979, 2981, 2982, 2983, 2984,
2986, 2987, 2990, 2996, 2997, 3002,
3003, 3005, 3006, 3007, 3009, 3010,
3013, 3015, 3021, 3026, 3028, 3029,
3030, 3033, 3036, 3038, 3043, 3045,
3046, 3048, 3049, 3051, 3052, 3054,
3055, 3056, 3057, 3058, 3062, 3063,
3064, 3067, 3068, 3071, 3073, 3074,
3075, 3076, 3077, 3079, 3080, 3081,
3088, 3089, 3092, 3094, 3097, 3099,
3100, 3102, 3103, 3104, 3105, 3108,
3109, 3110, 3112, 3114, 3116, 3117,
3120, 3124, 3125, 3126, 3132, 3135,
3141, 3143, 3146, 3147, 3148, 3149,
3152, 3153, 3155, 3156, 3157, 3160,
3164, 3165, 3166, 3167, 3168, 3169,
3170, 3171, 3172, 3173, 3174, 3175,
3176, 3179, 3181, 3182, 3184, 3185,
3186, 3188, 3191, 3192, 3195, 3198,
3199, 3200, 3201, 3202, 3204, 3205,
3207, 3208, 3209, 3210, 3211, 3212,
3214, 3218, 3219, 3220, 3221, 3222,
3223, 3225, 3226, 3228, 3230, 3231,
3232, 3236, 3238, 3240, 3241, 3242,
3248, 3249, 3251, 3252, 3255, 3258,
3261, 3263, 3264, 3266, 3267, 3269,

3270, 3273, 3276, 3277, 3278, 3279,
3283, 3285, 3287, 3288, 3290, 3293,
3294, 3295, 3296, 3299, 3303, 3304,
3307, 3308, 3309, 3310, 3311, 3312,
3313, 3315, 3316, 3317, 3319, 3323,
3324, 3325, 3326, 3328, 3329, 3331,
3333, 3334, 3335, 3336, 3338, 3339,
3340, 3341, 3344, 3345, 3347, 3348,
3349, 3350, 3351, 3352, 3353, 3354,
3355, 3357, 3363, 3365, 3368, 3372,
3373, 3375, 3376, 3377, 3379, 3380,
3381, 3382, 3383, 3385, 3386, 3387,
3388, 3389, 3390, 3391, 3393, 3394,
3395, 3396, 3400, 3401, 3402, 3403,
3404, 3407, 3408, 3426, 3427, 3428,
3429, 3432, 3434, 3436, 3442, 3443,
3445, 3446, 3448, 3450, 3451, 3452,
3455, 3459, 3460, 3462, 3463, 3464,
3465, 3479, 3480, 3482, 3483, 3491,
3493, 3495, 3496, 3497, 3499, 3500,
3501, 3506, 3507, 3509, 3510, 3511,
3517, 3518, 3520, 3522, 3523, 3524,
3525, 3526, 3528, 3529, 3531, 3533,
3534, 3536, 3537, 3541, 3544, 3546,
3547, 3550, 3552, 3553, 3570, 3664,
3966, 4004
Hamlet & Elsie Norr 4031
Hamlet a Ofelie 4046
Hamlet and Ophelia 3515, 4216
Hamlet and the Colleen Bawn 4139
Hamlet der Travesti[e]rte 4130
Hamlet. Elsinore Version 3288
[Hamlet ESP] 4094
Hamlet[:] Fantaisie sur l'opéra de Ambroise
Thomas 3640
'Hamlet' Fantasia 3862
Hamlet: Five Preludes to Shakespeare's
Tragedy 3891
Hamlet Galop! Homage to Edwin Booth 3920
[Hamlet in Unterschlamdorf] 4133
[Hamlet in Wittenberg] 4135
Hamlet, Mazurka 4016
Hamlet Music 3272, 3337
Hamlet. Musikaliska vignetter 3367
Hamlet[,] musique sur le drame de Shakespeare
3018
Hamlet, náš současník 3688
Hamlet[.] Ofelias sånger 2903
Hamlet on Ice 4087
Hamlet, opéra d'Ambroise Thomas 3672
Hamlet[,] Opéra de Ambroise Thomas 3673
Hamlet[.] Ophelia 3991
Hamlet or 'Naked Hamlet' 4163
Hamlet, or Why Did September Mourn? 4137
Hamlet ou Le Noble Fou 3571
Hamlet ou les suites de la piété filiale 4114
Hamlet, Prince de Danemark 3687
[Hamlet, Prince de Danemark] 3217
Hamlet[,] Prince of Denmark 4185

Hamlet, Prince of Denmark, Or The Sport, The
  Spook, and The Spinster 4140
Hamlet[,] Prins af Danmark 3900
Hamlet, Prinz von Dänemark 3159
[Hamlet Prinz von Dänemark] 3259, 3260,
  3356
[Hamlet, Prinz von Tandelmarkt] 4107, 4126
Hamlet, scène et air d'Ophélie 3647
Hamlet. Seelenstudie.—A Psychic Sketch 4008
Hamlet Speaks to Ophelia 4081
Hamlet Suita 4028
Hamlet Suite 3420, 3619
Hamlet, the Black Prince of Denmark 4213
[Hamlet: The First Quarto] 3430
Hamlet, the Musical 3607
Hamlet, the Prince 3591
Hamlet und Ophelia 3991
Hamlet[:] Valse d'Ophélie 3627
Hamlet von Thomas 3666
Hamlet, Waltz 4017
Hamlet Was A Melancholy Dane 4243
Hamlet Ye Dane. A Ghost Story 4205
[Hamlet 1603] 3177, 3274
Hamlet, 2ème Quadrille 3630
Hamlet[.] 5th Act 2956
Hamlet . . . Doute de la Lumière 3651
Hamleti laulud [Songs of Hamlet] 4079
Hamletiana 4032
Hamlet . . . La Fête du Printemps 3652
Hamlet . . . La fête du printemps & Airs de
  ballet 3683
Hamlet-ouverture 3968
Hamletovska Improvisace 3967, 21150
Hamlet-rapsodi 3367
Hamlets 3599
Hamlets ånd 4212
Hamlets erster Monolog 3809
Hamlets erster und zweiter Monolog 3809,
  3858
Hamlet's Father's Ghost's Music, Ltd 4208
Hamlet's Letter to Ophelia 3728, 3735
Hamlets Monolog 3857
Hamlet's Soliloquy. "To be, or not to be" 3847
Hamlet's theme 3437
Hamlets zweiter Monolog 3858
Hamlet-Sinfonie 3615
Hamlet-soliloquy 4098
Hamlet-Suite[:] drei Orchesterstücke aus der
  Musik zu Shakespeares 'Hamlet' 3483
Hamlet-symphony 3979
Hamlet-Tagträume 3216
Hamletto, or Prosciuttino 4177
Hammlet 3589
[Hanashim Haalizot Mevindzor = The Merry
  Wives of Windsor] 8988
Hand in hand 10305, 10308
Hand in hand with fairy grace 10306, 10307,
  10309, 10606
Harebells 2821

Hark! 2629
Hark, hark 2677, 7544, 16204
Hark! Hark! Each Spartan hound 10131,
  10133
Hark! Hark! The Ecch'ing [sic] Air 10254
Hark! Hark! the lark 2446, 2449, 2457, 2473,
  2483, 2493, 2631, 2632, 2633, 2634,
  2636, 2641, 2642, 2645, 2663, 2665,
  2669, 2670, 2671, 2673, 2675, 2676,
  2677, 2686, 2687, 2691, 2692, 2694,
  2697, 2700, 2701, 2704, 2706, 2713,
  2714, 2716, 2718, 2719, 2721, 2722,
  2723, 2726, 2727, 2729, 2730, 2732,
  2734, 2735, 2736, 2739, 2740, 2741,
  2743, 2750, 2751, 2752, 2754, 2756,
  2757, 2760, 2761, 2767, 2770, 2771,
  2772, 2773, 2774, 2775, 2780, 2781,
  2782, 2786, 2787, 2789, 2792, 2793,
  2796, 2797, 2800, 2806, 2826
[Hark! Hark! The Lark] 2472
Hark, hark, the lark at heaven's gate sings
  2698, 2762, 2798, 2808
[Hark, hark, the lark at heaven's gate sings]
  2661
Hark! Hark! the Lark at Heav'ns [sic] Gate
  Sings 2799
Hark! Hark! The Lark From 'Cymbeline' by
  Shakespeare 2769
[Hark, hark the lark (Horch, horch die Lerch)]
  2748
Hark! Hark! The Lark. Morning Serenade
  2712
Hark! Hark! the Lark! Serenade from
  "Cymbeline" 2784
[Hark! Hark the Lark (Ständchen)] 2717
Hark! Hark! the Lark!—Serenade—(From
  "Cymbeline" by William Shakespeare) 2778
Hark! hark! the watch dogs &c. 14729
"Hark! hark, the watchdogs bark" 14705
Hark! how all things 10265
Hark, How All Things in One Sound Rejoice
  10202
"Hark! how all things with one sound rejoice"
  10197
Hark, how the Songsters 16339, 16350
Hark! how the songsters of the grove 16347
Hark the ech'ing air! 10190, 10223, 10266
Hark! the Echoing Air 10233, 10234, 10253
Hark! the echoing air a triumph sings 10247
Hark! The Echoing Air (From "The Fairy
  Queen") 10192
Hark! the echoing air[,] From the Opera "The
  Fairy Queen" 10217
Hark! The Echoing Air[,] Song From The Opera
  "The Fairy Queen" 10238
Hark the Lark 2650, 2653, 2656, 2668, 2672,
  2693, 2696, 2724, 2725, 2766, 2795,
  2807, 2809
[Hark the Lark] 2689

Hark! the Lark at Heaven's Gate Sings 2651, 2652, 2655, 2657, 2702

[Hark, the Lark at Heaven's gate sings] 2492

Hark! The Lark at Heav'n's Gate Sings 2658, 2660

Hark! the Lark at Heavn's [sic] Gate Sings 2654, 2679, 2703

Hark 'Tis the Lark 2881

[Harlequin Puck, or The Elfin Changeling and the Enchanted Statue] 10762

Harmonious Young Men 2529

Három mondat a Rómeó és Júliából 13926

Három Shakespeare Szonett 19949, 19997, 20035

Harp & Other Pedals 21194

Hart's Thirteenth Set of Quadrilles, Selected from Mathew Locke's Original Music in Macbeth . . . 6983

[Hasocher Mivenezia = The Merchant of Venice] 8071, 8072, 8289, 8323

Hate 20110

Hawthorn 6078

Haydn's Celebrated Canzonets 18069

[He 'Lies Like Truth'] 7541

[He Striggla Pou Egine Arnaki = The Taming of the Shrew] 14390

He that has a little tiny wit 5695

He that has and a little tiny wit 6032

He that is thy friend 20642

He that is thy friend indeed 20707

Heart-Broken Ellen 10901

Hearts and Hands 93

Heavily! 11377

Hebdomade 1337

Hecuba; or, Hamlet's Father's Deceased Wife's Sister 4144

Heigh Ho, The Holly 977, 1088

Heigh-Ho! For A Husband 11635

Height of Summer 6428

[Heinrich der Sechste] 4865

[Heinrich der Vierte] 4347, 4369, 4549, 4561

[Heinrich der Vierte, Erster Theil] 4443

Heinrich der Vierte 1. Teil 4429

Heinrich der Vierte 2. Teil 4602

Heinrich IV. 4380, 4517, 4519, 4568, 4686, 4688

[Heinrich IV.] 4350, 4354, 4365, 4368, 4370, 4416, 4417, 4419, 4444, 4551, 4552, 4559, 4560, 4562, 4591, 4592, 4594, 4613

[Heinrich IV., Erster Teil] 4321

Heinrich IV, I 4433

Heinrich IV, II 4605

[Heinrich IV., Zweiter Teil] 4536, 4582

Heinrich V 4733, 4767

[Heinrich V.] 4692, 4749, 4760, 4766, 4772

[Heinrich VI.] 4874, 4913, 4955

[Heinrich VI, Erster Teil] 4863, 4904

Heinrich VIII. u. seine Frauen 5004

[Held Henry] 4764

[Hellig tre Kongers Aften eller Hvad I selv vil kalde det = Twelfth Night or What You Yourself Will Name It] 16590

Hellig Trekongers Aften 17638

Helligtrekongers aften 16890

Helligtrekongers Aften, eller Hvad man vil 17165

[Helligtrekongers Aften eller Hvad man vil = Twelfth Night, or What You Will] 17187

Helligtrekongersaften 16829, 17031

[Helligtrekongersaften] 17210

Helligtrekongersaften eller Hvad man vil 16830

Hence With Your Trifling Deity 16343, 16345

Hendrich den Fierdes Jagt 4508, 4677

[Henri IV] 4306, 4411, 4527, 4589

[Henri IV, 1re partie] 4374

"Henri VIII" 5240

[Henric al IV-lea = Henry IV] 4442, 4611

Henrik den 4de 4349, 4550

[Henrik IV] 4300, 4524

[Henry Harevyi = Henry the Fourth] 4420, 4595

Henry, Him of Eight 5233

Henry IV 4311, 4324, 4334, 4396, 4516, 4531, 4543, 4580, 4685

[Henry IV] 4319, 4330, 4381, 4542, 4569

Henry IV Part I 4309, 4316, 4323

Henry IV Part II 4530

Henry IV, Part One 4343

Henry IV, Part 1 4295, 4328, 4338, 4356, 4375

Henry IV, Part 2 4523

1 Henry IV 4292, 4294, 4297, 4298, 4301, 4302, 4304, 4305, 4307, 4313, 4317, 4320, 4322, 4327, 4329, 4331, 4332, 4333, 4335, 4336, 4339, 4340, 4344, 4345, 4346, 4351, 4358, 4360, 4363, 4366, 4377, 4382, 4383, 4384, 4386, 4387, 4388, 4389, 4395, 4398, 4402, 4405, 4406, 4407, 4409, 4413, 4423, 4426, 4427, 4430, 4432, 4434, 4435, 4436, 4438, 4441, 4446, 4447, 4450, 4452, 4453, 4454, 4455, 4456

2 Henry IV 4521, 4526, 4533, 4535, 4538, 4540, 4541, 4544, 4548, 4566, 4571, 4572, 4573, 4574, 4587, 4598, 4603, 4606, 4607, 4608, 4616, 4620, 4621, 4622, 4623, 4624

Henry Purcell 14749

Henry Purcell[:] Music from "The Dramatic Works" 10261

Henry Purcell[:] Orpheus Britannicus[,] Seven Songs 18314

Henry Purcell[:] Orpheus Britannicus[,] Six Songs 18304

Henry Purcell[:] Ten Duets 16347

Henry R. Bishop's Admired Duet 'As It Fell Upon A Day' 2047

Henry R. Bishop's Celebrated Air Bid Me
  Discourse 16681
Henry the Eighth 5242
Henry the Fifth 4830
Henry the 8th 4993, 4997
Henry V 4690, 4702, 4706, 4721, 4744,
  4747, 4785, 4802
[Henry V] 4717, 4774
Henry V. Birthday night Fanfare 20873
Henry V Choruses 4775
Henry VI 4847, 4850, 4861, 4889, 4892,
  4903, 4932, 4935, 4945
Henry VIII 4998, 5011, 5243, 5244
Henry VIII[:] A Suite of Music (In the Old
  English Style) 4976
1 Henry VI 4857, 4858, 4860, 4867, 4868,
  4870, 4876, 4879
2 Henry VI 4886, 4899, 4900, 4902, 4907,
  4908, 4915, 4918
3 Henry VI 4942, 4944, 4949, 4950, 4957,
  4960
[Henryk V] 4748
[Henryk VIII czyli Wszystko to prawda =
  Henry VIII or All Is True] 5032
Herb-grace 3953
Here A Dance Of Clowns 10650
Here sleeps Titania 10660
Here's Lawn as white as driven Snow 18992
Hermia 10590
Hermione 18928, 18929, 19110
Hermione Waltz 19099
Herne le Chasseur 9254
Heroic Elegy 4821
Herrin mein 17987
Herstory III: Jehanne de Lorraine 4880
Herzelied 4241
Heures de Loisir 1930
Hexenchöre zu 'Macbeth' 7498
Hexenscenen aus Macbeth 7149
Hexenskat oder Der Streik der Hexen 7274
Hey ho! the Wind and the Rain 17309, 18122,
  18125, 18131, 18171, 18175, 18190,
  18200
Hey, ho, the Wind and the Rain (Feste's Song
  from Twelfth Night) 17310
Hey, Lo [sic], the wind and the rain 18085
Hey, Nonny 11573
Hey, Robin! 16965, 17682, 17683, 17685
Hey, Robin, jolly Robin 16697, 17217, 17679
Heyday 21014
Heyday—reprise 21014
High With Crowned Immortals Dwelling
  21046
Highlights from Kiss me, Kate 14639
Highlights from 'West Side Story' 13604
Hin Torden-Bolig 3973
. . . hinder not my course 18468
Hip-hip Horatio 4278
Hither, Come Hither 1734

[Ho, Ho, Julia] 14065, 20886
Hobgoblin 10593
Hochzeitmarsch [sic] 9716
Hochzeitmarsch [sic] und Elfenreigen aus der
  Musik zu Shakespeare's
  Sommernachtstraum von Felix Mendelssohn
  Bartholdy 9750
Hochzeit-Marsch [sic] zu Shakespeare's
  Sommernachts Traum von Felix
  Mendelssohn Bartholdy 9830
Hochzeitsmarsch 9627, 9730, 9740, 9752
[Hochzeitsmarsch] 9811
Hochzeitsmarsch aus dem
  Sommernachtstraum 9666, 9837
Hochzeitsmarsch aus 'Ein
  Sommernachtstraum' 9787, 9813
[Hochzeitsmarsch aus Shakespeare's
  Sommernachtstraum] 9809
Hold thy peace 16697, 17688, 18292
[Hollywood Revue of 1929] 14052
Holmes's First Trio[:] Sir H. R. Bishop's Favorite
  Aria 'Bid Me Discourse' 16672
Holmes's Second Trio[:] Sir H. R. Bishop's
  Popular Subject As It Fell Upon A Day 2039
Holmes's Third Trio[:] Sir H. R. Bishop's
  Favorite Aria Should He Upbraid 18365
Holofernes 6691
Homage to Shakespeare 1889, 13910, 18218
Home Made 21208
Honeysuckle 10635, 11649
Honour, riches 15804
Honour, riches, marriage blessings [sic] 14941
Honour, riches, marriage-blessing 14961,
  15798, 15800, 15808, 15810, 15815
[Honour, riches, marriage-blessing] 15796,
  15809, 15811
Horatios Monolog 3695
Horch, horch 2667, 2684, 2685
Horch, horch, die Lerch 2648, 2755, 2794
[Horch, horch, die Lerch am Himmelsthor
  singt] 2805
Horn's Celebrated Duett, of I Know A Bank
  Whereon The Wild Thyme Blows 8877
Hörspielmusik 11872
Hörspiel-Musiken 7776
[Hotspur] 4422
[House of Strangers] 6118
How all occasions do inform against me 3747
How All The Other Passions 8422
How all the other passions fleet to air 8423
How can I then return 19533
How Imperfect is Expression 16610
How like a Winter 1953, 19508, 20152,
  20153, 20160, 20165, 20175
How like a winter hath my absence been
  20156, 20162, 20164, 20172
[How like a winter hath my absence been]
  20150
How oft, my music 20385

How oft, when thou, my muse, music play'st 20394

How oft, when thou, my music 20391, 20392, 20400

"How oft when thou, my music, music play'st" 20381

How Oft When Thou My Music Playest 20390

How oft, when you, my music 20397

[How shall I my true love know] 3767

How Shall I Your True Love Know 3754

How shall my muse want subject to invent 19681

How Shall We Honour Him? 21093

How shou'd I your true love know 2919

How Should I Know 3777

How should I your true love know 2981, 3244, 3949, 4058, 4200, 21142

How should I your true love know[:] Sketches of unbalanced Ophelia 3955

How Should I Your True Love Know (Sung by Ophelia in Shakespeare's "Hamlet") 3780

How should I your true-love know 3749, 3751, 3752, 3755, 3757, 3761, 3762, 3764, 3769, 3772, 3774, 3776, 3782, 3785, 3786, 3787

[How should I your true-love know] 3756, 3779

How sweet, How silver sweet 13839

How sweet the Moon light 8452

How Sweet The Moonlight 8426, 8427, 8440, 8441, 8448, 8461, 8466, 8472, 8475, 8480, 8710

How Sweet the Moonlight Sleeps 8430, 8432, 8434, 8437, 8438, 8439, 8446, 8450, 8451, 8454, 8462, 8463, 8467, 8468, 8471, 8473, 8479, 8481, 8760

How Sweet The Moonlight Sleeps On Yonder Bank 8696

How sweet the moonlight sleeps upon this bank! 8431, 8443, 8445, 8449, 8453, 8469

[How sweet the moonlight sleeps upon this bank!] 8428, 8444, 8455, 8458, 8460

Huit Scènes de Faust 4141, 14072

Humor im Laubenlied 17545

Humoresque 14356

Humours of Eastcheap 21121

Hunt Music 6652

[Hunting Song] 793

Huntsmen and Horsewomen 6664

Hvad ni vill 16654

Hvis du vil ligge her 1696

Hvis du vil ligge her under de grønne Træer. (Af "Som man behager") 1679

[Hylas et Silvie] 16200

Hymen: "Then is there [mirth] in heaven" 1594

Hymen's Song 1826

Hymen's Song, Then is there Mirth in Heaven 1590

Hymn for Shakespeare's Birthday 21005

Hymn of Victory (Finale) from Macbeth 7358

Hymn to Cynthia 8363

Hymns at heaven's gate 19523, 19559, 19564, 20161

Hymnus mysticus 10654

I

I am Gone 17698, 17705

I am gone, sir 17692, 17693, 17695, 17697, 17699, 17700, 17702, 17703, 17704, 17709, 17711, 17712, 17713

I am gone, sir, and anon, sir 16640, 16697

I Am Prospero (Reflections on 'The Tempest') 16039

I Capuleti e i Montecchi 14191

I Capuleti ed i Montecchi 14191

I do counsel that your playtime 21267

I dreamt there was an Emperor Antony 306

I due gentiluomini di Verona 18375

I Feel Pretty 13603

I Feel Pretty from "West Side Story" 13615

I Have Served Prince Florizel 18964

'I ia fialke tak s ukorom govoril' ['The forward violet thus did I chide'] 20200

I Know A Bank 8882, 8884, 8886, 9961, 10312, 10314, 10316, 10319, 10320, 10321, 10322, 10323, 10324, 10325, 10326, 10327, 10330, 10331, 10336, 10338, 10340, 10341, 10343, 10344, 10345, 10349

I Know A Bank[,] C. Horn's celebrated Duet 8887

I know a bank (Idyll) 10666

[I know a bank where the wild thyme blows] 10315, 10328, 10347

I Know A Bank Whereon The Wild Thyme Blows 8878, 8883, 8885, 10318

"I Know A Bank Whereon The Wild Thyme Grows" (Midsummer Night[']s Dream) 8880

I know a Bank whereon the wilde thyme grows 10329

I Know I Love in Vain 97

I know the [sic] bank whereon the wild thyme blows 8876, 10757

I Mercenari 16232

1 I moan 20654

2 I moans 19539, 20405

3 I moans 19531

I Shall Never Forget Him 20883

I shall no more to sea, to sea 14906

"I Want A Lonely Romeo" 14095

I Want to Play Hamlet 4196

'Ia daleko, moi drug, vesnoi byl ot tebia' ['From you have I been absent in the spring'] 20182

'Ia krasavitsei gordoi ubit . . . (Pesnia shuta)' [I
am slain by a fair, cruel maid . . . (Song of
the Fool)] 16961
'Ia vinovat. Iz kinofil'ma "Adam zhenitsia na
Eve"' [I'm To Blame. From the Film Adam
Marries Eve] 20344
Iago, a study 12440
Iago and Othello 12428
Iago's Trinklied, mit Chor 12232
Iced Arshole of Shakespeare 6023
Ich bin fort, Herr, und aufs Wort Herr 17706
Ich sag euch ab, O Sterne 14151
[Ich wollte, meine Tochter läge tot zu meinen
Füssen und hätte Juwelen in den Ohren]
8735
Icicles 6605
Idyll[:] Under the greenwood tree 2013
If I Profane[:] Sonnet from "Romeo and Juliet"
13843
If I profane with my unworthy hand 13841
If it do come to pass 1225
If love had lent you twenty thousand tongues
20796
If Love Make Me Forsworn 6345, 6347, 20749
[If love make me forsworn, how shall I swear
to love] 6346
If Love's A Sweet Passion 10254
"If Love's A Sweet Passion," from The Fairy
Queen 10198
If Love's A Sweet Passion[,] Song and Chorus
from "The Fairy Queen" 10248
If Music & Sweet Poetry Agree 20722
If music and sweet poetry 20669
"If Music Be. . . ." 17726
If Music be the food of Love 17714, 17716,
17717, 17718, 17721, 17723, 17724,
17729, 17730, 17732, 17736, 17737,
17740, 17742, 17743, 18290, 18298,
18299, 18300, 18301, 18303, 18304,
18305, 18308, 18309, 18310, 18313,
18314, 18315, 18316
If music be the food of love, play on 17721,
17722, 17728, 17738
If Music Be The Food Of Love (Stop The Band)
18287
If she be made of white and red 6350, 6351,
6353, 6354
[If she be made of white and red] 6355
"If there be nothing new" 19812
If thou be mine 21249
If thou survive my well-contented day 19641,
19643
If You Have Tears 5488
"Ihn wieder zu seh'n, meinen Romeo" aus
"Romeo und Julie" 13561
[Ikalabindalawang Gabi = Twelfth Night]
16940
Il Capriccio corretto 14690
Il Cigno pesarese 12162

Il Coriolano 2406, 2426, 2427
Il gioco dei potenti 4845, 4846, 4887, 4888,
4930, 4931
Il Mercante di Venezia 8117, 8151, 8220,
8394, 8412, 8413, 20256
[Il mercante di Venezia] 8048, 8149, 8250
[Il peccato di Anna] 12448
[Il racconto d'inverno] 18801
Il Rodrigo 6135
Il Sogno di Titania 10175
Il Sogno d'una notte d'estate 10270
I'll Marry You Sunday 14584
I'll sail upon the dog-star 21297
Illuminations (d'après Arthur Rimbaud) 4260
Illustrations Musicales pour les Contes de
Perrault et autres histoires merveilleuses
2454, 5723, 9381, 14951
Illustrations of Shakespear 3729, 6338, 13847
Illustrations of Shakespeare 10712, 11607,
13960, 16118, 16119, 18251
Illyrian Dances 10741, 14020, 18260
Illyrisches Abenteuer 17380
[Iluf Hasoreret = The Taming of the Shrew]
14238
Ilustracja muzyczna do 'Hamleta' W.
Shakespeare'a 3330
Ilustracja muzyczna do 'Króla Henryka VI'
Shakespeare'a 4862
Im Frühling 1492
Im Garten 14153
I'm no stingy Romeo 14175
Im Sommer 1725
Im Sommer (Symphony No. 9 in E minor)
10943
Im Winter 1110
Images of Love 20979
Imaginings of William Shakespeare 20843
Imelda de' Lamartazzi 14192
Imod vandmanden 3827
Imogen 2518, 2851
Imogena 2498
[Imogena (Tsimbelin) = Imogen (Cymbeline)]
2434
Imogène ou la Gageure Indiscrète 2837
Impatience 13863
Impressions at Wellesley 10695
Improved Edition of Haigh's Duets, from
Macbeth 6990
'Improvisata'. ('Af samma stoff som drömmar')
16096
Improvisation 15828
Improvisation sur des Airs favoris de l'opéra
Les joyeuses Commères de Windsor 9075
Improvisation Sur des motifs de l'Opéra Falstaff,
(Merry Wives of Windsor) 9084
In a Fairy Wood 10606
In A Stratford Garden 21138
In Another Part of the Forest 1224
In, "As you like it" 1784

In Belmont lives a lady 8728
In ConGruitEES 6134
In der Früh' 2804
In different light 4834
In Fairyland 10413, 10658
In Florizel and Perdita or the Winter's Tale. Sung by Miss Brent and Mr. Mattocks 18680
In Green Ways 1690
In Hayti 14112
In Lovers' Eyes 19781
In May 1523
In Memoriam. "To Fair Fidele's Grassy Tomb" 2875
In Midsummer Night['] s Dream 9286
In Portia's Park 8260
In Praise of Dance 20852
In Praise of Mercy 8681
In Praise of Music 5061, 8429
In Ringtime 1327
In Sad Cypress 17578, 18229
In Shakespeare's Days 20931
In Spring 1287
In Springtime 1479, 5065
In such a night 8672
In Sweet Music 5013, 5222
In sweet music is such art 5138
In the Forest 10624
In the Merry Month of May 20730
In the pretty Spring time 1978
In The Spring Time 1398
In the Springtime 1297, 1373, 1388, 1564
In Windsor Forest 9163, 9164
In Youth When I Did Love 3801
In youth, when I did love, did love 2981
Incantation as Sung by Miss Leak, Master Welsh, Mrs. Bland, in the Favorite Interlude of the Fairy Festival 10770
Incedental [sic] music from Hamlet 3519
Incidental Music 700, 3484, 3485, 4310, 4787, 5321, 5697, 7757, 8223, 8224, 9448, 9603, 9992, 10021, 10049, 11182, 11915, 12807, 13476, 13512, 14515, 15345, 16703, 16969, 17226, 18704
Incidental Music: A Comedy of Errors 2175
Incidental Music And Dances To Shakespeare's 'The Winter's Tale' 18790
Incidental Music and Song for Antony and Cleopatra 244
Incidental music and songs 15157, 17115, 17288
Incidental Music and Songs for 'A Midsummer Night's Dream' 10076
Incidental music and songs for 'The Winter's Tale' 18895
Incidental music and songs for Twelfth Night 16665, 16748
Incidental Music And Songs To Shakespeare's 'Tempest' 15088

Incidental music composed for William Shakespeare's The Tempest 15199
incidental music for A Midsummer Night's Dream 9305, 9306, 9358
[Incidental music for 'A Midsummer Night's Dream'] 9339
incidental music for a National Shakespeare Co. production 13129, 14235, 18684
[Incidental music for All's Well That Ends Well] 47
incidental music for Antony and Cleopatra 118
incidental music for As You Like It 472, 489, 661, 870
Incidental Music for Coriolanus 2341
incidental music for Cymbeline 2441
Incidental music for guitar from The Old Vic 1980 Production The Merchant of Venice 8215
Incidental music for Hamlet 3093, 3163, 3178, 3291
Incidental music for Henry IV, Part I 4348
Incidental music for Henry IV, Part 1 4394
[Incidental music for Henry IV, Part 2] 4579
Incidental Music for Henry V 4718, 4771
incidental music for Julius Caesar 5262, 5437
Incidental music for King Lear 5765, 5863, 5945, 5950, 5954
[Incidental Music for King Lear] 5927
Incidental music for 'Love's Labour's Lost' 6319
[Incidental music for Love's Labour's Lost] 6271
incidental music for Macbeth 6741, 6748, 6911, 6937, 7184
Incidental Music for 'Measure for Measure' 7697, 7713, 7753, 7773, 7777
Incidental Music for 'Merchant of Venice' 8051
Incidental Music for 'Merry Wives' 8968
Incidental music for 'Midsummer night's dream' 9956
incidental music for Much Ado about Nothing 11027, 11142
Incidental Music for Othello 11714, 11733, 11941
incidental music for Richard II 12622, 12696, 12735
Incidental Music for Richard III 13003, 13011, 13029
Incidental Music for Romeo & Juliet 13122
Incidental Music for Romeo and Juliet 13109, 13139, 13178, 13373
[Incidental Music for Romeo and Juliet] 13343
Incidental Music for Shakespeare's A Midsummer Night's Dream 9452
Incidental Music for Shakespeare's 'Hamlet' 3041
Incidental Music for Shakespeare's 'Julius Caesar' 5361

Incidental Music for Shakespeare's King Lear 5751

Incidental Music for Shakespeare's 'The Merchant of Venice' 8176

Incidental Music for Shakespeare's Twelfth Night 16811

Incidental Music for Shakespear's 'The Tempest' 15347

incidental music for The Comedy of Errors 2030

[Incidental music for The Comedy of Errors] 2154

Incidental Music for 'The Merchant of Venice' 8328

Incidental Music for the National Theatre of Great Britain's Shakespeare Quatercentenary production of Othello 11786

Incidental Music For The Play Julius Caesar 5300

incidental music for The Taming of the Shrew 14239, 14240, 14361, 14430

Incidental music for The Tempest 14970, 14995, 15003, 15075, 15081, 15239, 15277, 15278

Incidental music for: The Tragedy of Othello 11944

[Incidental music for The Winter's Tale] 18840

Incidental Music for Troilus and Cressida 16452

[Incidental music for Troilus and Cressida] 16509

incidental music for Twelfth Night 16653, 16730, 16904

incidental music for Two Gentlemen of Verona 18355

Incidental Music for William Shakespeare's A Midsummer Night's Dream 9416

Incidental Music for William Shakespeare's The Merchant of Venice 8138

Incidental Music for William Shakespeare's Twelfth Night 16798

Incidental Music from 'Othello' 11998

Incidental Music From Shakespeare's Play A Midsummer Night's Dream 9888

Incidental music from 'The Tempest' 15190

Incidental Music 'Hamlet' 3095

Incidental Music [Othello:] Stratford-on-Avon 11697

Incidental Music[:] Shakespeare's 'A Midsummer Night's Dream' 9418

Incidental Music specially composed for 'The Tempest' 15235

[Incidental Music: 'The Taming of the Shrew'] 14480

Incidental music: 'The Tempest' 15445

Incidental music to A Midsummer Night's Dream 9304, 9400, 9948, 9966

Incidental Music to A Midsummer-Night's Dream 9664

Incidental Music to 'All's Well That Ends Well' 15

Incidental music to 'Antony and Cleopatra' 127

Incidental Music to 'Coriolanus' 2291

Incidental Music to Cymbeline 2471

Incidental music to 'Hamlet' 2974, 3203

Incidental Music to 'Hamlet' (in Afrikaans) 2998

Incidental Music to Henry IV 4352, 4507, 4676

Incidental Music to 'King John' 5592

Incidental Music to King Lear 5868

Incidental Music to 'Love's Labour's Lost' 6226

Incidental Music to Macbeth 7121, 7195, 7202

Incidental Music to Merchant of Venice 8090

Incidental Music To Much Ado About Nothing 11033, 11196, 11253

Incidental Music to 'Othello' Film 11781

Incidental Music to Richard II 12728

Incidental Music to Richard III 13024

Incidental Music to Shakespeare's Henry VIII 5020

Incidental music to Shakespeare's Macbeth 6764, 6847

Incidental Music to Shakespeare's Merchant of Venice 8304

Incidental Music to Shakespeare's play, Henry VIII 5020

Incidental music to Shakespeare's play, Twelfth night 17183

Incidental Music to Shakespeare's 'The merchant of Venice' 2731, 8136

Incidental Music to Shakespeare's The Winter's Tale 18896

Incidental Music to Shakespeare's Twelfth Night 16772, 17175

Incidental Music to The Comedy of Errors 2112

Incidental music to The Merchant of Venice 8084, 8301, 8302, 8364

Incidental music to The Merry Wives of Windsor 8935, 8982

[Incidental Music to 'The Merry Wives of Windsor'] 8972

Incidental Music to the Play 'Julius Caesar' 5379

Incidental Music to the Story of Juliet 13169

Incidental Music to 'The Taming of the Shrew' 14273, 14376, 14451, 14665

Incidental Music to 'The Tempest' 14856, 14857, 14879, 15022, 15247, 15288

Incidental music to The Winter's Tale 18726

Incidental music to Twelfth Night 16652, 16866, 16944, 16979

Incidental Music to Two Gentlemen of Verona 18384

Incidental Music[:] Twelfth Night 16697

Incidental music with songs for 'Twelfth Night' 16767

Incidental Music written for the 'Little Theatre' production of King Lear 5830

Incidental music—Antony and Cleopatra 213

Incidental song 9574

Inconstancy 11419

Ingratitude 1129

Intemperancias (1962) 3828

Interlude 14483

4 intermèdes musicaux 17582, 17708, 17958, 18163

Intermezzi per il Macbeth di Shakespeare 7494

Intermezzi per la 'Tempesta' 15217

Intermezzo 7475, 14431

'Intermezzo' [and] 'Nocturno' from F. Mendelssohn's: 'Midsummer Night's Dream' 9737

Intermezzo from Macbeth 6924

Intermezzo from 'The Merchant of Venice' 8303

Intermezzo from the music to Henry VIII 4977

Intermezzo Funèbre 12847

Intermezzo och Epilog ur 'En Vintersaga' 18807

Intermezzo (Prelude to Act 2 'Henry VIII') 4986

Intermezzo[:] The Walk to the Paradise Garden 14081

Intrada 7743

Introduction 15179, 19537

Introduction à La Tempête de Schakespeare 16064

Introduction à la Tempête de Shakespeare 16064

Introduction and Allegro 2877

Introduction and Allegro for Strings 2876

Introduction and Postlude to 'Othello', Act I, Scene III 12398, 21131

Introduction de 'Roméo et Juliette' 13682

Introduction, The Three Witches on the Heath, The Witches Greet Macbeth, Prophecy 7448

Introduction to Act I 18695

Introduction to Act 2d. Royal Gaelic March 6941

Introduction to Ye Tempest 15179

Invitation to Madrigals 1433

Invocation 8420

Invocation of the Night 13833

Invocation to Bacchus 293

Irrungen 2202

Is It Thy Will? 19855

"Is it thy will thy image should keep open" 19854

Isn't it a crime 14115

. . . It is not yet near day 13846

It Was A Golfer And His Lass 1971

It Was A Lass 2012

It was a Lording's Daughter 20664, 20677

It was a lording's daughter, the fairest one of three 20686

It was a Lordling's Daughter 8876, 20596, 20636, 20649, 20688, 20716, 20745

It Was A Love And His Lass 1575

It was a Lover 1230, 1235, 1237, 1257, 1261, 1267, 1301, 1306, 1319, 1329, 1390, 1403, 1411, 1450, 1457, 1498, 1507, 1512, 1555, 1583

[It was a lover] 1522

It was a Lover & his Lass 1954

It was a lover and his lass 493, 580, 726, 758, 856, 925, 1228, 1231, 1233, 1234, 1236, 1238, 1239, 1240, 1241, 1242, 1243, 1245, 1246, 1249, 1251, 1252, 1253, 1255, 1256, 1258, 1262, 1263, 1264, 1265, 1266, 1269, 1270, 1273, 1274, 1275, 1276, 1277, 1278, 1279, 1280, 1281, 1284, 1285, 1286, 1290, 1291, 1292, 1293, 1294, 1298, 1299, 1302, 1303, 1304, 1305, 1308, 1310, 1311, 1312, 1313, 1314, 1315, 1316, 1317, 1318, 1323, 1324, 1325, 1326, 1328, 1331, 1333, 1335, 1336, 1337, 1338, 1342, 1343, 1345, 1346, 1348, 1349, 1350, 1351, 1352, 1353, 1355, 1358, 1359, 1360, 1362, 1363, 1364, 1365, 1366, 1367, 1369, 1370, 1371, 1372, 1374, 1375, 1379, 1381, 1382, 1383, 1385, 1387, 1389, 1391, 1393, 1396, 1397, 1399, 1400, 1404, 1407, 1408, 1409, 1410, 1412, 1414, 1415, 1417, 1418, 1419, 1421, 1422, 1423, 1424, 1425, 1427, 1428, 1429, 1430, 1431, 1432, 1433, 1434, 1435, 1436, 1437, 1438, 1439, 1440, 1441, 1442, 1443, 1445, 1446, 1447, 1449, 1451, 1452, 1453, 1454, 1455, 1458, 1459, 1460, 1461, 1462, 1463, 1464, 1466, 1469, 1471, 1472, 1474, 1475, 1477, 1478, 1481, 1482, 1484, 1486, 1488, 1490, 1491, 1493, 1496, 1497, 1499, 1500, 1501, 1502, 1503, 1504, 1505, 1506, 1508, 1510, 1511, 1513, 1515, 1516, 1518, 1524, 1527, 1528, 1529, 1530, 1532, 1534, 1535, 1536, 1537, 1538, 1539, 1541, 1544, 1545, 1548, 1550, 1551, 1553, 1554, 1559, 1560, 1562, 1563, 1565, 1569, 1570, 1572, 1574, 1576, 1579, 1582, 1584, 1585, 1960, 8271, 21029, 21090

[It was a lover and his lass] 1229, 1247, 1250, 1309, 1347, 1380, 1401, 1405, 1406, 1416, 1494, 1514, 1540, 1547, 1552, 1578

"It was a lover and his lass" from "As You Like It" 1473

It Was A Lover And His Lass (from Shakespeare's "As You Like It") 1468

"It was a Lover and His Lass" the song in the Comedy "As you like it" 1456

It was a lover and his lasse 1444, 1448

It was the Nightingale 6666, 14035
Italia 13312
Italialainen sarja musiikista näytelmään
    Venetsian kauppias 8707
Italian café music 11931
Italian song: "Amatemi ben mio" 13546
[Iulii Tsezar' = Julius Caesar] 5255, 5349,
    5381, 5449, 5451
Iuliu Cezar 5440
I've Come To Wive It Wealthily In Padua
    14632
Iz angliiskoi poezii [From English Poetry]
    19767
[Iz muzyki k spektakliu 'Mnogo shuma iz
    nichego' = From the Music to the Play
    Much Ado About Nothing] 11053
'Izbrannye p'esy iz baleta "Romeo i
    Dzhul'etta"' [Selected Pieces from the Ballet
    Romeo and Juliet] 13797

J

Ja, wir sind Widerhall 8682
[Jack and the Beanstalk; or Harlequin and the
    Midwinter Night's Dream] 20887
Jack Manning's Modern-dress production of
    Macbeth in Africa 7026
Jacques [sic] 1881, 7583
Jago 12470
Jak se vám líbí 606, 670, 775
[Jak se vám líbí = As You Like It] 499, 510,
    574, 674, 704, 743, 767, 774, 840, 890
Jak wam się podoba 830
[Jak wam się podoba = As You Like It] 457,
    498, 532, 542, 620, 621, 623, 624, 649,
    656, 659, 677, 725, 733, 800, 868, 888,
    901, 902
[Jak wam się podoba. Ćiczenie = As You Like
    It. Workshop] 707
[Jak zkrotit saň = The Taming of the Shrew]
    14438
January 6632, 6659, 6685
Jaro v Shakespeara 21200
Jazz-suite af musiken til Shakespeares Trold
    kan tæmmes . . . 14448
Je pars Monsieur 17708
Je te vois en rêve 19717
Jed z Elsinoru 3590
Jeleneti zene Shakespearea 'Macbethjéhez'
    6917
Jeleneti zene (William) Shakespeare 'Sok
    hühó semmiért' 11145
Jerusalem 14088
Jessica 8397, 8695, 8701
Jessica Valse 8700
Jessica—A Portrait 8792
Jessika 8399

Jeunesse d'Anne Boleyn 5236
Jig 3421
[Jig] 3422
Jigg 10240
Jill 19459
[Jindřich IV] 4393, 4424, 4578, 4599
[Jindřich V.] 4755
[Joe Macbeth] 7514
Jog on 18702, 18757, 18968, 18977, 18978,
    18988
Jog On, Jog On 18795, 18975, 18976, 18984,
    21142
Jog on, jog on, the Foot-path Way 18869,
    18987
[Jog on, jog on, the foot-path way] 18966,
    18981, 18982
Jog on the Footpath Way 18970, 18980,
    19120
[Johan uten land = John without Land]
    5601
[John de la lune Falstaff] 4497, 4670, 9240
John Falstaff 4465, 4631, 9014
John Hooton 12173
Jolly Robin 17681
Joy 11638
[Jubal] 12459
Jubilee Minuet 21121
[Jubilee Ode in Memory of Shakespeare]
    21074
Jubilee Song 21021
Jugend-Lieder 2683, 12319
Jules César 5368, 5387, 5392, 5513, 5557,
    5563, 5565
[Jules César] 5290, 5293, 5303, 5325, 5452
Jules César (R. Schumann) Ouverture 5523
Julia 14157
[Julia Caesar] 5539
Julia i Romeo 13784
Julia und Romeo 13637
Julie 13861
Juli[e]'s Leichenbegängnis aus 'Romeo u.
    Julie' 13567
Juliet 13894, 13897, 13916, 13943, 14160,
    14184, 14207
Juliet, a study 14025
Juliet and Romeo 14102
Juliet Mazurka 14203
Juliet Minuet 13338
Juliet to Romeo 14124
Juliet Valses 13898
Juliet Waltz 13909
Julieta y Romeo 14198
Juliet's Dump 13941
Juliet's Farewell 13876
Juliet's Song 14209
Juliet's Song. "A Sweet Good Night!" 14029
Juliet's Terror 13517
Julietta 14011
Juliette 13893, 13959

Juliette et Roméo 13627, 14111, 14164
[Juliette et Roméo] 13761, 14053
Julije Cezar 5320
[Julije Cezar] 5313
Julio César 5478
[Julio César] 5302, 5395
Julius Caesar 5230, 5247, 5249, 5252, 5257,
  5265, 5281, 5287, 5289, 5291, 5296, 5299,
  5301, 5304, 5309, 5316, 5317, 5322, 5330,
  5332, 5340, 5346, 5350, 5364, 5371, 5384,
  5388, 5398, 5412, 5415, 5422, 5423, 5429,
  5436, 5443, 5444, 5446, 5457, 5471, 5472,
  5473, 5482, 5483, 5497, 5499, 5505, 5506,
  5512, 5514, 5518, 5531, 5552, 5561,
  19532
[Julius Caesar] 5246, 5250, 5253, 5254, 5261,
  5263, 5268, 5269, 5272, 5275, 5276, 5280,
  5282, 5284, 5285, 5295, 5298, 5306, 5308,
  5311, 5312, 5314, 5319, 5323, 5324, 5328,
  5334, 5335, 5337, 5342, 5345, 5347, 5348,
  5352, 5353, 5354, 5355, 5357, 5359, 5360,
  5362, 5363, 5365, 5372, 5373, 5374, 5376,
  5377, 5382, 5383, 5385, 5389, 5390, 5391,
  5393, 5396, 5397, 5399, 5404, 5406, 5408,
  5410, 5411, 5414, 5417, 5418, 5419, 5421,
  5424, 5425, 5427, 5433, 5435, 5438, 5439,
  5442, 5445, 5450, 5454, 5456, 5458, 5459,
  5460, 5461, 5462, 5463, 5465, 5467,
  20743
Julius Caesar[:] Grand March 5401
Julius Caesar Jones 5566
Julius Caesar Overture 5511
Julius Caesar Overture (Prod. 'Julius Caesar')
  5424
[Julius Caesar—Overture] 5453
Julius Cäsar 5274, 5305, 5327, 5343, 5366,
  5464, 5475, 5476, 5524, 5525, 5526
[Julius Cäsar] 5248, 5260, 5267, 5288, 5294,
  5297, 5307, 5315, 5318, 5326, 5336, 5338,
  5341, 5358, 5369, 5375, 5394, 5405, 5407,
  5413, 5416, 5430, 5431, 5432, 5434, 5448,
  5455, 5474, 5500, 5501
[Julius See-sawcer, or a Storm in a Tea-Cup]
  5541
Juliusz Cezar 5256, 5380, 5402
[Juliusz Cezar] 5266, 5386
July 19113
June 18234
Juno and Ceres, from The Tempest 15814
Junos och Ceres Sång 15806
Juno's Song, In The
  Tempest 14936, 14938
Just Keep on Lovin' Till I
  Tell You to Stop. The Story
  of a Dusky Romeo 14134
Just my Luck 16186
[Jyuuni Ya = Twelfth Night]
  16867, 17070, 17109,
  17364

K

'K chemu tvoi ston?' [To what are you
  moaning?] 21234
[Kabuki Othello] 12447
'Kak chasto videl ia v lugakh . . .' ['Full many a
  glorious morning have I seen'] 19651
[' "Kak dvizhetsia k zemle morskoi priboi . . ." '
  = 'Like as the waves make towards the
  pibbled shore'] 19821
'Kak ia sravno tebia s roskoshnym letnim
  dnem' ['Shall I compare thee to a summer's
  day?'] 19384
'Kak ni zhelalab ty ukryt'sia ot menia' ['But do
  thy worst to steal thyself away'] 20125
'Kak solovei o roze' [As the Nightingale Sings
  of the Rose] 11157
Kak solovei o roze (Pesnia iz muzyki k komedii
  V. Shekspira 'Mnogo shuma iz nichego') [As
  the Nightingale Sings of the Rose (Song from
  the Music to W. Shakespeare's Comedy
  Much Ado About Nothing)] 11158
'Kak ty mogla skazat', chto mnoiu ne liubima'
  ['Canst thou, O cruel, say I love thee not']
  20527
[Kak vam eto ponravitsia = As You Like It]
  773
Kak vam eto ponravitsia [As You Like It] 652
Kako vam drago 515, 673
[Kako vam drago = As You Like It] 819, 898
[Kakor vam drago = As You Like It] 671
[Kakto vi kharesva = As You Like It] 543, 712
'Kantsona' [Canzona] 16901
[Kar hočete = What You Will] 16629, 16794,
  16916, 16994, 17001, 17271, 17321
[Karasawagi = Much Ado About Nothing]
  11144
'Karnaval'nyi marsh iz muzyki k tragedii
  Shekspira "Romeo i Dzhul'etta" ' [Carnival
  March from Music to Shakespeare's Romeo
  and Juliet] 13314
Karnevalslied 7805
Kassation für neun Instrumente 18441
Kateřina a Petrucio 14672
Katerina Izmailova 7551
Katharina and Petruchio (Burlesque) 14675
Katharina (Shakespearian Portraits) 14659
Katharina's Tarantella 14663
Katharine 4828
Katherine 14670
Katherine & Petruchio 14458
Katherine and Petruchio 14298
[Katherine and Petruchio] 14336
[Katov Beeinechem = As You Like It] 653,
  762
Kaufmann von Venedig 8380, 8581
[Kaufmann von Venedig] 8337
Kaufmann von Venedig V. Akt 8211

Kaupmaður í Feneyjum 8326
[Kean] 12472
Kein gülden Fürstenbild, kein Marmelstein 19777
Kein Sonnenglanz . . . 20422
Kenilworth, A Masque of the days of Queen Elizabeth 8760
[Kesäyön unelma = A Midsummer Night's Dream] 9403, 9466, 9489
Ki, zene vagy 19268
Kiedy narcyzy wyjrzą w świat 19041
[Kildar] 7554
"Kind fortune smiles" 14705, 14724, 14950
Kind Fortune Smiles (Ariel's Song) 14717
"Kind Fortune Smiles", The Celebrated Duet, Sung by Miss Coveney and Mr. Horn 15037
King Duncan's March from Macbeth 7352
King Henry the Eighth 4969
King Henry V 4697, 4699, 4736, 4738, 4757, 4768, 4778, 4793, 4794, 4795
[King Henry V] 4694, 4695, 4696, 4698, 4700, 4701, 4703, 4705, 4707, 4709, 4713, 4714, 4715, 4719, 4720, 4722, 4723, 4724, 4726, 4727, 4728, 4730, 4731, 4732, 4735, 4739, 4740, 4742, 4743, 4745, 4746, 4750, 4751, 4752, 4756, 4761, 4762, 4769, 4770, 4773, 4777, 4790, 4792, 4796, 4825
King Henry VIII 4966, 4968, 4973, 4974, 5006, 5016, 5026, 5027, 5035, 5213
[King Henry VIII] 4967, 4972, 4975, 4977, 4981, 4994, 4995, 4996, 4999, 5002, 5003, 5005, 5012, 5017, 5018, 5030, 5031, 5211, 5216
King Henry's Soliloquy 4644
King Henry's Song "Youth Will Needs Have Dalliance" 5020
King John 5570, 5572, 5585, 5593, 5600, 5620, 5627, 5630, 5632, 5636, 5641, 5647
[King John] 5568, 5569, 5576, 5577, 5578, 5579, 5581, 5583, 5584, 5586, 5587, 5591, 5595, 5597, 5598, 5608, 5611, 5613, 5614, 5616, 5618, 5624, 5626, 5628, 5631, 5634, 5639
King Lear 5657, 5674, 5680, 5682, 5688, 5689, 5694, 5699, 5703, 5705, 5707, 5714, 5717, 5719, 5720, 5728, 5738, 5750, 5757, 5758, 5766, 5781, 5786, 5787, 5820, 5828, 5829, 5834, 5864, 5896, 5914, 5915, 5916, 5930, 5940, 5941, 5942, 5952, 5972, 5979, 5980, 5998, 6004, 6016, 6017, 6060, 6061, 6088, 6092, 6109, 6156
[King Lear] 5664, 5666, 5681, 5683, 5684, 5699, 5706, 5709, 5710, 5711, 5712, 5713, 5715, 5716, 5722, 5732, 5734, 5735, 5754, 5756, 5761, 5767, 5769, 5771, 5772, 5777, 5778, 5779, 5782, 5785, 5788, 5798, 5800, 5807, 5808, 5814, 5816, 5825, 5826, 5839, 5841, 5842, 5847, 5852, 5853, 5857, 5858, 5862, 5870, 5874, 5878, 5879, 5881, 5897, 5901, 5902, 5905, 5917, 5919, 5920, 5926, 5928, 5931, 5932, 5933, 5937, 5939, 5949, 5953, 5956, 5957, 5958, 5969, 5971, 5973, 5977, 6012, 6014
King Lear and Cordelia 6089
King Lear And His Daughters Queer 6154
[King Lear Ballet] 6136
King Lear Fragments 6020, 6036, 6046
King Lear Is In 6097
King Lear March 6076
King Lear Overture 6077
King Lear Suite 6069, 6073
King Lear Variations 6048
King Lear's Blues 6165
[King Lear's Wife] 6125
King Richard II 12614, 12618, 12619, 12631, 12637, 12639, 12643, 12644, 12653, 12660, 12685, 12703, 12714, 12726, 12727, 12731, 12744, 12745, 12746
[King Richard II] 12613, 12617, 12623, 12624, 12629, 12635, 12640, 12641, 12642, 12658, 12659, 12666, 12667, 12668, 12670, 12687, 12688, 12691, 12695, 12697, 12700, 12701, 12704, 12712, 12715, 12719, 12721, 12732, 12739, 12740, 12742, 12743, 12767
King Richard III 12792, 12803, 12818, 12843, 12844, 12847, 12865, 12882, 12897, 12909, 12923, 12977, 12978, 12990, 12991, 12992, 12993, 12994, 13007, 13014, 13027, 13028, 13050
[King Richard III] 12778, 12779, 12790, 12791, 12794, 12795, 12801, 12812, 12817, 12824, 12826, 12828, 12832, 12834, 12836, 12845, 12852, 12855, 12857, 12862, 12866, 12868, 12869, 12875, 12880, 12881, 12887, 12889, 12890, 12891, 12893, 12894, 12896, 12907, 12912, 12913, 12917, 12918, 12919, 12922, 12924, 12925, 12928, 12931, 12935, 12936, 12939, 12941, 12946, 12948, 12953, 12967, 12968, 12969, 12970, 12971, 12974, 12979, 12987, 12995, 13005, 13018, 13020
King Richard The Second[,] Act IV Song: Retired From Any Mortal's Sight 12708
King Stephen 12237
King Stephen song 12236
King Stephen was a worthy peer 11696, 12238, 12241, 12452
[King Stephen was and-a worthy peer] 12240
Kirei wa kitanai, kitanai wa kirei 7386, 7402, 7408
Kísérőzene 8199

[Kísérőzene Shakespeare Macbethjéhez = Incidental Music to Shakespeare's Macbeth] 7185
Kiss Me, Kate 14597, 14603, 14615
[Kiss Me, Kate] 14598
"Kiss Me Kate" Choral Selection 14634
Kiss Me Kate Medley 14607
Kiss Me, Kate[:] Selection 14597
Kisses Sue'd [sic] For 7957
[Kjøbmanden i Venedig] 8244
Kjöbmannen i Venedig 8173, 8174
[Kjøbmannen i Venedig] 8076, 8356
Klagt nicht mehr 11553
Klänge der Liebe 9837
Klavier-Kompositionen zu eurythmischen Formzeichnungen von Rudolf Steiner 10064, 15330
Kleine Blumen, kleine Blätter 10893
Kleine Theater-Suite (Aus der Musik zu Shakespeares 'Zwei Herren aus Verona') 18406
Kleiner Opernfreund 9083
Kleines Dekameron 18244
Kleopatra 272, 366, 371, 384, 14127
[Kleopatra] 339
Kleopatra (po tragedii U. Shekspira 'Antonii i Kleopatra') [Cleopatra (after W. Shakespeare's Tragedy Antony and Cleopatra)] 267
Klubko 10451
Knocking Piece 15687
. . . . Know that we have divided 6034
[Koenig Richard II] 12647
[' "Kogda na sud bezmolvnykh tainykh dum . . ." ' = 'When to the sessions of sweet silent thought'] 19602
'Kogda na sud bezmolvnykh, tainykh dum (30-i sonet)' ['When to the sessions of sweet silent thought' (30th Sonnet)] 19609
'Kogda sred' khartii ia vremen' davno minuvshikh' ['When in the chronicle of wasted time'] 20262
'Kogda umru, menia oplakibai ne dole . . .' ['No longer mourn for me when I am dead'] 19951
Kolybel'naia iz muzyki k tragedii V. Shekspira 'Gamlet' [Lullaby from the Music to W. Shakespeare's Tragedy Hamlet] 3416
Kom alhier, Tood!... 17450
Kom nader, dood 16820
Kom nu hit, död! 17222
Kom nu kun, kom nu kun, Død! (Af "Helligtrekongersaften") 17539
[Komedia omylek = The Comedy of Errors] 2103, 2170, 2188
[Komedie Masopustu (Dvanáctá noc) = Carnival Comedy (Twelfth Night)] 17230
[Komedie omylů = The Comedy of Errors] 2141

Komedie plná omylů 2075
[Komedie plná omylů = The Comedy of Errors] 2074, 2160, 2166, 2186
[Komediia oshibok = The Comedy of Errors] 2020, 2109, 2110, 2138, 2153, 2164, 2174, 2184
Komm herbei . . . 17552, 17581, 17637
Komm herbei, komm herbei, Tod 17563, 17674
"Komm herbei, komm herbei, Tod!" Lied des Narren aus "Was ihr wollt" von Shakespeare 17575
Komm herbei, Tod 17239, 17453, 17560, 17585, 17634, 18255
[Komm herbei, Tod!] 17486
Komm herbei Tod aus "Was ihr wollt" 17606
Komm herbei, Todt! 17557
Komm herbei . . . Aus Shakespears: Was ihr wollt 17525
Komm, o Tod 17566
Komödie der Irrungen 2027, 2028, 2056, 2176, 2196, 2242, 2250
[Komödie der Irrungen] 2052, 2062, 2069, 2073, 2083, 2100, 2115, 2124, 2155, 2161, 2173, 2181
Komödie der Irrungen[,] Eine Shakespeare-Ouvertüre 2253
Komplette Bühnenmusik 17205
Kompletterande scenmusik till 'En midsommarnattsdröm' 9417
Komposition für Hornpipes 17200
[Komposition für Jazz-Ensemble/Beat-Gruppe] 9984
[Komposition für Orchestra und Pop-Gruppe] 17201
Konec vše napraví 20, 21
[Konec vše napraví = All's Well That Ends Well] 19, 64
[Konets—delu venets = All's Well That Ends Well] 51
Kong Lear 5760, 5774, 5802, 5833
[Kong Lear] 5791, 5906
Kong Lear for Fjernsynsteatret 1984 5866
Kong Richard III 12884
[König Cymbelin] 2447, 2508
[König Cymbeline] 2496
[König Heinrich der Fünfte] 4758
[König Heinrich der Sechste, Erster Theil] 4864
[König Heinrich der Sechste, Zweiter Theil] 4947
[König Heinrich der Vierte] 4308, 4379, 4415, 4425, 4529, 4567, 4600
[König Heinrich der Vierte, Zweiter Teil] 4577
König Heinrich IV 4439, 4609
[König Heinrich IV.] 4312, 4355, 4361, 4362, 4378, 4399, 4418, 4440, 4532, 4553, 4556, 4557, 4593, 4610
[König Heinrich V.] 4763
[König Heinrich VI.] 4871, 4910, 4952

[König Heinrich VIII.] 5009
[König Henry IV.] 4448, 4617
[König Henry V.] 4789
König Johann 5573, 5610
[König Johann] 5589, 5596, 5602, 5606,
    5607, 5612, 5615, 5617, 5622, 5623,
    5625, 5635, 5637
König Johann oder Der Ausstieg 5646
König Lear 5658, 5659, 5773, 5822, 5823,
    5837, 5851, 5855, 5947, 5983, 5995,
    5999, 6049, 6059, 6079, 6102, 6107, 6108
[König Lear] 5679, 5698, 5739, 5740, 5741,
    5745, 5746, 5747, 5748, 5749, 5752,
    5759, 5770, 5775, 5783, 5793, 5794,
    5796, 5810, 5815, 5817, 5831, 5838,
    5850, 5856, 5869, 5875, 5887, 5889,
    5898, 5904, 5907, 5908, 5910, 5911,
    5912, 5913, 5929, 5944, 5955, 5960,
    5962, 5965, 5966, 5967, 5968, 6086
König Lear–eine keltische Passion 5995
König Richard der Dritte 12854
[König Richard der Dritte] 12839, 12840,
    12861, 12900, 12950, 12951, 12972,
    12996
[König Richard der Zweite] 12648, 12674,
    12681, 12683, 12711, 12716
König Richard II. 12621, 12655
[König Richard II] 12645, 12661, 12698,
    12710, 12718, 12733, 12734
König Richard III 12998
[König Richard III] 12783, 12827, 12831,
    12838, 12858, 12864, 12888, 12892,
    12929, 12932, 12933, 12934, 12937,
    12945, 12959, 12963, 12964, 12997,
    12999, 13002, 13021
[Koning Lear] 5899
2. Konzert für Klavier und Orchester 20416
Köpmannen i Venedig 8066, 8140, 8171,
    8268, 8299, 8383, 8384
[Köpmannen i Venedig] 8172, 8334
Kordeliia ('Mest'') [Cordelia ('Revenge')] 6189
Koriolan 2336, 2376
[Koriolan] 2268, 2269, 2299, 2304, 2325,
    2339, 2359, 2375
[Koriolanus] 2342
[Koriulanus] 2275
[Korol' Genrikh VIII = King Henry VIII] 5019
[Korol' Lir = King Lear] 5667, 5730, 5803,
    5804, 5809, 5840, 5843, 5854, 5867,
    5871, 5884, 5891, 5892, 5900, 5903,
    5921, 5922, 5923, 5924, 5925, 5943,
    5946, 5963, 6006
Korol' Lir [King Lear] 6005
Korol' Lir[:] Siuïta z muzyky do tragediï V.
    Shekspira [King Lear: Suite from the Music
    to W. Shakespeare's Tragedy] 5843
[Korol' Richard III] 4961, 12788, 12873,
    12878, 12910, 13031
[Král Jindřich IV] 4404, 4585

Král Lear 6103, 6104
[Král Lear] 5662, 5685, 5686, 5687, 5737,
    5753, 5883, 5885, 5886
[Kral Lir = King Lear] 5733, 5792
[Kralj Henrik V.] 4776
Kralj Lear 5692, 5693, 5813, 5985, 20581
[Kralj Lear] 5909
Krämerlied 19081
[Król Henryk IV] 4299, 4353, 4364, 4391,
    4558, 4575
[Król Jan] 5604
Król Lear 5918
[Król Lear] 5661, 6075
[Król Lir] 5872, 5876, 5894
[Król Ryszard II] 12626, 12690, 12747
[Król Ryszard III] 12789, 12914, 12956
Kronborg: 1582 3595
Krönungs-Marsch 12918
'Kto osuzhdaet tvoi bespechnyi nrav (Sonet
    96)' ['Some say thy fault is youth, some
    wantonness' (Sonnet 96)] 20144
Kuckuck als Spottvogel (Spring). From Love's
    labour [sic] lost 6467
Kuckuckslied aus "Verlorene Liebesmüh" von
    Shakespeare 6491
[Kuinka äkäpussi kesytetään = The Taming of
    the Shrew] 14219, 14353
[Kumonosu-Djo] 7529
Kung John 5640
Kung Lear 5678, 5895
[Kung Lear] 5824
[Kung Richard III] 12833
Kuningas lähtee Ranskan [The King Goes
    Forth to France] 4843
Kuningas Lear 5811, 6080
[Kuningas Lear] 5821
Kuningas Staffan 11747
Kupec Benátský 8281
[Kupec benátský = The Merchant of Venice]
    8056, 8194, 8196, 8202, 8230, 8317
Kupiec wenecki 8306
[Kupiec wenecki = The Merchant of Venice]
    8086, 8204, 8206, 8248, 8254
Kvartet No. 4. (Po motivam proizvedenii
    Shekspira) [Quartet No. 4 (after Motifs from
    Shakespeare's Works)] 21164
Kyrie . . . d'après Félix Mendelssohn-Bartholdy
    9805

L

L['] Amleto 4151
La bisbetica domata 14268, 14595
[La bisbetica domata] 14405, 14421, 14563
La Capricciosa corretta 14593
La Capricciosa corretta 14593
La Capriciosa Coretta 14593

La célestine 6139
La Chanson Du Saule 11836
La Cleopatra 365
[La comedia degli errori] 2076
[La comédie des erreurs] 2058
La commedia deglia equivoci 2149
La Damnation de Faust: Légende Dramatique 4141, 14072
La danse de Puck 10601, 10602
La dodicesima notte 16710, 16711
[La dodicesima notte] 16609, 16906, 16985, 17179, 17252
[La dodicesima notte o quel che volete] 17386
[La farce des joyeuses commères] 8918
[La Fierecilla Domada] 14218
La Finale 12374
La folie de Lady Macbeth 7276
La Forêt de Sénart, ou la Partie de Chasse de Henri IV 4510, 4679
La fôret magique 8742
La forza del destino 20982
La furia domata 14641
La giornata degli sbagli 2120
La Gioventù di Enrico Quinto (La Jeunesse d'Henry V) 4512, 4681
La Gioventù di Enrico V 4466, 4632
[La Gioventù di Enrico V] 4801
La Gioventù di Enrico V. del Maestro Mercadante 4467, 4633
La gioventù di Shakespeare ossia il sogno d'una estiva 9252
La gioventù di Shakespeare ossia il sogno d'una notte estiva 10792, 20944
La Giulietta 14196
[La légende de Macbeth] 7519
La Marjolaine 2838, 2840, 2841, 2842, 2843
La mégère apprivoisée 14256, 14589, 14590, 14645
[La mégère apprivoisée] 14265, 14362, 14380, 14381
[La mégère domptée] 14227
La moglie corretta 14593
La Mort de Cléopâtre 274
La Mort d'Ophélie 3987, 4186, 4239
La mort du roi Lear 6070
La morte di Cesare 5556, 5564, 5567
La morte di Cleopatra 374, 378, 380
La morte di Giulio Cesare 5555
La notte di lady 7245
La nuit des rois 16695, 16744, 17358
[La nuit des rois] 16616, 16751, 16752, 16754, 16999, 17020, 17032, 17126, 17139, 17194
[La nuit des rois, ou Ce que vous voudrez] 16659
[La planète Shakespeare, Le Conte d'hiver] 19138
La pluie des fleurs 12163
La Poule 8685
La Prière d'Otello 12167, 12168
La Prise De Troie 8746
La prosperità infelice di Giulio Cesare dittatore 5558
La rappresentazione per Enrico V 4737
La Romance d'Ariel 16217
La Romance Du Saule 12283
La scuola dei maritati 14593
La Sérénade de Schakspeare 2758
La tempesta 14920, 14921, 15111, 15398, 15421, 15441, 16021, 16211, 16250, 16261, 16275, 16278, 16296
[La tempesta] 14919, 15165, 15279, 15388, 15403
La Tempesta ossia Da un Disordine ne nasce un ordine 16253
[La Tempestat] 15166
La Tempête 14851, 14926, 14951, 15071, 15192, 15290, 15407, 15408, 15493, 16128, 16129, 16130, 16131, 16242, 16244
[La tempête] 14869, 14897, 14910, 14930, 14945, 14954, 15017, 15026, 15049, 15148, 15178, 15224, 15249, 15255, 15268, 16132
La Tempête[:] Ballet de l'opéra (Quadrille Brillant) 15494
La Tempête, ou l'île des bossus 15476
La Tempête, ou l'île des génies 15476
La Titania 10659
[La tragédie au Vaudeville] 12449
[La tragédie de Macbeth] 7027
[La tragédie d'Hamlet, Prince de Danemark] 3548
[La tragédie du roi Richard II] 12632, 12664, 12680
[La tragique histoire d'Hamlet, Prince de Danemark] 2977, 3239, 3346
La Trenise 7411
La Veronese Waltz 13312
[La vie de Timon d'Athènes] 16306
[La vie et la mort du roi Jean] 5580, 5590, 5603, 5609
Lady, by yonder blessed moon I vow 13847
Lady in the Dark 20375, 20380, 20407, 20418, 20505, 20531, 20537
Lady Mac 7431
Lady Macbeth 7273, 7295, 7502, 7539, 7558
Lady Macbeth Theme 6840
Lady M'bira Macbeth MacDrum 7555
Længsel 14172
[L'amant loup-garou, ou M. Rodomont] 9239
Lament for Fidele 2578
Lament: Hamlet's Song 4224
Lamentations of a Moor 11754
Lamento. Shakespeare. Horatio 3694
L'Amour d'Ophélia 3989
Land Of Our Birth 4811
Langs waar komt het lustbegin? 8504

L'Anneau Perdu et Retrouvé 9246
[L'Anneau Perdu et Retrouvé] 9243
L'après-midi d'un Puck 10744
Larghetto 12122
[Las Alegres Comadres de Windsor] 8974
Las bravías 14565
Las danzas de 'La Reina de las Hadas' 10216
Láska (Othello) 12387
Lásky hra osudná 6690
[Lásky lichá lest = Love's Labour's Lost] 6229
Lass, die geboren unter günst'gem Stern 19502
Last Chorus 21021
Latin Chant 11247
Lawn as White 19002
Lawn As White As Drifted Snow 19016
Lawn as white as driven snow 18702, 18718,
    18732, 18757, 18991, 19003, 19004,
    19005, 19011, 19012, 19013, 19014,
    19018, 19020, 19026, 19027
[Lawn as White as Driven Snow] 18714,
    19019
Lawn as white as driv'n snow 19010
Lay Thou Thy Hand In Mine 21062
[Le allegre comari de Windsor] 8970
Le Carillon d'Amour (Chanson de Portia) 8648
Le conte d'hiver 18712, 18824
Le Juif de Venise[,] d'après Schakspeare 8763
Le lagrime d'une vedova 14196
Le Lutin 10675
Le marchand de Venise 8070, 8109, 8392,
    8396, 8402, 8789
[Le marchand de Venise] 8064, 8079, 8081,
    8092, 8118, 8124, 8126, 8188, 8275, 8368
Le Maure de Venise 12178
Le More de Venise, ou Othello 12021
Le Nègre d'Alcantara 12207
Le petit Falstaff 9253
Le Retour à la Vie 3557, 14073, 15392,
    20913
Le Rêve d'Ariel 16094
Le Rêve d'Ophélie 4011, 4234
[Le rideau rouge (Ce soir, on joue Macbeth)]
    7518
[Le roi Cymbeline] 2486
[Le roi Jean] 5574, 5575
Le roi Lear 5672, 5723, 5845, 5890, 5997,
    6008, 6064, 6066, 6114, 6143, 6144,
    6147, 6151, 6152, 6153, 6158
[Le roi Lear] 5655, 5676, 5690, 5691, 5700,
    5708, 5736, 5743, 5818, 5859, 5860, 5861
Le Roi Lear (d'après Shakespeare et Holinshed)
    5999
(Le Roi Lear, prélude) 5724
Le Saphir 74, 75, 77
Le Singe [sic] d'une Nuit d'Été 10984
Le Sommeil de Juliette de l'Opéra Roméo et
    Juliette de Gounod 13653
Le Sommeil Du Roi Lear De Claude Debussy
    5725

Le Songe d'une Nuit d'Été 9256, 9381, 9754,
    9788, 10149, 10804, 10913, 20958,
    20962, 20963, 20967, 20968, 20972,
    20975, 20976
[Le songe d'une nuit d'été] 9284, 9348, 9380,
    9443, 9511, 9517, 9558, 9559, 9900,
    9919, 9929, 9946, 10052
Le Songe d'une nuit d'été d'A. Thomas
    20964
Le Songe D'Une Nuit D'Été (de Mendelssohn)
    Réminiscences 9636
Le Songe d'une nuit d'été, Ouverture 20961,
    20971
Le Songe d'une nuit d'été von Shakespeare
    9719
Le Songe d'une nuit d'été[:] 1er. Bouquet de
    Mélodies 20959
Le Songe d'une nuit d'été[:] 2e. Bouquet de
    Mélodies 20960
[Le tricaballac ou Juliette et Roméo] 14105
Le vieux coquet 9153
Le Vieux Coquet ou les deux Amies 9153
Le vieux garçon 9153
Lear 5805, 5988, 6009, 6091
[Lear] 6121, 6128, 6129
Lear: A Study 6068
Lear And His Daughters 6160
Lear Awake 5976
Lear Drums 5976
[Lear király = King Lear] 5806, 5938
Lear: "We two alone" 6045
Lear's Storm Soliloquy 6019
[Leben und Sterben König Johanns] 5571
Leben und Tod des Königs Makbeth (Makbeth
    der Hexenkönig) 6719
[Leben und Tod Richard des Dritten] 12797
Ledi Makbet Mtsenskogo uezda 7551
L'Édit Royal 6681
[Leer om Leer = Measure for Measure] 7605
Leichte Stücke aus Shakespeares Zeit 21290
Leivonlaulua 2681
Leken i skogen 609
L'Élève Advancé, Rondeau Instructif pour le
    Piano Forte, sur la Thême favori de Le Songe
    d'une Nuit d'Été 20973
Lelio oder die Rückkehr ins Leben 3561
Lélio ou Le Retour à la Vie 3557, 14073,
    15392, 20913
L'Enterrement d'Ophélie 3901, 3902
Leonatus and Imogen 2813, 19096
Leonce und Lena 21265
Leontes 18941, 19101, 19126, 19128
Les Adieux. Rêverie sur un motif de l'opéra de
    Ch. Gounod[,] Roméo et Juliette 13712
Les agréments d'Hylas et Silvie 16200
Les Amants de Vérone 13638, 13639, 13646
[Les amants de Vérone] 14051
Les amants de Vérone. Fantaisie Mosaïque pour
    piano 13641

Les Amants de Vérone . . . Cavatine de Roméo 13640
Les Amours d'Antoine et de Cléopâtre 375
Les Caprices de Beatrix 11312
Les cœurs fermés 8476
Les deux amies 9153
Les Deux Amies, ou Le Vieux Coquet 9153
Les Deux Amies ou le Vieux Garçon 9153
[Les deux gentilshommes de Vérone] 18394
[Les deux Macbeth, ou l'Apothéose de Ducis] 7264
Les Femmes de Shakespeare 4194, 4882, 5236, 6146, 7558, 12493
Les fleurs d'Ophélie 4228
Les Joyeuses Commères de Windsor 8815, 8816, 8829
[Les joyeuses commères de Windsor] 8805, 8835, 8838, 8842, 8843, 8844
[Les joyeuses épouses de Windsor] 8912
Les Lutins 10800
Les Méprises Par Ressemblance 2258, 2259, 2260
Les Noces d'or d'Oberon et Titania 10124
Les oiseaux artificiels 15145
Les Sérénades De Paris ou Les Petits Concerts De Société 9247
Les sorcières 7570
Les Soupirs de Roméo 13937
Les Troyens 8740
Let Me Confess 19673
Let Me Confess that We Two Must Be Twain 19671
Let me not to the marriage of true minds 20309, 20313, 20321, 20328, 20334
Let Me The Canakin Clink 12227, 12239
Let No Such Man Be Trusted 8669, 8752
"Let not my love be call'd idolatry" 20248, 20250
Let Not To The Marriage Of True Minds Admit Impediments 20315
Let Sind 1533
Let the Fifes and the Clarions 10268
Let those who are in favour 19504
Let Us Garlands Bring[:] Five Shakespeare Songs 1325, 2555, 17513, 17863, 18507
L'Été 5496
Let's be Merry (from Oberon) 10832
"Let's be merry," from Weber's "Oberon" 10835
Let's Sing and Play 995, 1609, 13851, 15522, 15621, 17787, 18969
Leylines 5701
L'Homme Armé 6770
[Lǐ ěr wáng Xì Jū Pèi Yuè = Recorded Background Music for the Drama King Lear] 5762
'Lǐ Er Wáng' Zhǔ Ti Yīn Yuè [King Lear Theme Music] 5795

Libro di Madrigali per 'Romeo e Giulietta' 13096
L'Idée fixe. Andante amoroso pour le piano d'après une mélodie de H. Berlioz 6174
Lieb und Leid 7955
Liebe im Mai 1283
[Liebe leidet mit Lust] 6224
[Liebes Leid und Lust] 6227, 6235, 6252
Liebesglocken 8260
[Liebesglück und Leid] 6258
[Liebesleid und Lust] 6273
Liebeslied 7913
Liebes-Lied des Narren 18033
Liebeslied–O Mistress Mine 17866
Lied 1519
[Lied] 7683
Lied aus dem "Sturm" 15912
Lied aus Heinrich VIII 5125
Lied aus Heinrich VIII von Shakespeare 5187
Lied aus Makbet 7566
Lied aus "Mass für Mass" von Shakespeare 7997
Lied aus Shakespeares "Heilige-Drei-Königs-Abend" 17596
Lied aus Shakespeare's "So wie es euch gefällt" 1480
Lied aus "Viola" von Shakespeare 17486
Lied aus "Was ihr wollt" 18154
Lied der Desdemona 11958, 12269, 12319, 12363
Lied der Desdemona. (Aus "Les Consolations des Misères de ma Vie," par Rousseau.) 12311
Lied der Desdemona, aus "Othello" von Shakespeare 12327
Lied der Desdemona aus Shakespeare's Othello 12367
Lied der Elfen 10569
Lied der Pagen 1334
Lied des Amiens (Edelmann des verbannten Herzogs) aus Shakespeare's "Wie es euch gefällt" 1206
'Lied des Ariel' aus 'Der Sturm' von William Shakespeare/'Wie die Bien' . . .' 15330
Lied des Autolycus 19009
Lied des Balthasar 11477
Lied des Balthasar, mit Chor 11574
Lied des Hausirers 19023
Lied des Lucius zu Shakespeares "Julius Caesar" 5436
Lied des Narren 18157
Lied des Narren aus Shakespeare's "Was ihr wollt" 17656
Lied des Narren aus "Was ihr wollt" 17556
Lied des Pagen 11161
Lied des Todtengräbers 3805
Lied des Todtengräbers aus Hamlet 3804
Lied des Totengräbers 3797
Lied des Totengräbers (aus "Hamlet") 3800

Lied des transferierten Zettel 10453
Lied vom Weidenbaum—Willow, Willow 12293
Lied von der Weide (aus Othello) 12340
Lied von Shakespeare 17458, 17459, 17486
Lied von Shakespeare. Aus: "Was ihr wollt."
  "Komm herbei, Tod!" 17486
Lied von Weide aus "Othello" 12321
Lied zum Kaufmann von Venedig 8375
Liedchen der Desdemona aus "Othello" 12316
7 Lieder aus Klaus Groth's Quickborn 17552
Lieder aus Shakespeare's dramatischen Werken
  nach der Übersetzung von A. W. Schlegel
  12321, 15912, 18154
Lieder aus Shakespeares Dramen 21232
Lieder des Narren 18136
Lieder des Narren aus Shakespeare 'Was ihr
  wollt' 17921, 18149
Lieder des Narren aus Shakespeares 'Was ihr
  wollt' 16861
4 Lieder des Narren aus Shakespeares 'Was ihr
  wollt' 17563, 17706, 17932, 18152
Lieder im Volkston 1522
Lieder nach Shakespeare 21244
Lieder von Fr. Schubert 2758
Lieder von Heidenreich, Baron v.
  Schlippenbach und Schakespear in Musick
  gesetzt 1519
14 Lieder zum Tages- und Jahreslauf 7576
Lie-low, Viola! 18279
Life and Death of King John 5588
[Lige for Lige = Measure for Measure] 7588,
  7743
Lightly tread, 'tis hallowed ground 10983
[Lika för Lika = Measure for Measure] 7587,
  7709
Like An Autumn Sky 1216
Like As The Waves 19817, 19822, 19836
Like as the waves make toward the pebbled
  shore 19820
Like as the waves make towards 19829
"Like as the waves make towards the pebbled
  shore" 19823
Like for like 7589
Lilac-Time 2723
Lines from the Bard 11927, 17197, 20684
Lions (A Dream) 101
'Liricheskaia stsena'. [Lyrical Scene] 16961
Listening to the Time 19287
Little Stars 9365
'Liubliu. Iz muzyki k telefil'mu "Adam zhenitsia
  na Eve"' [I Love You. From the Music to the
  Tele-Film Adam Marries Eve] 20214
'Liubliu, no rezhe govoriu ob etom (102-i
  sonet)' ['My love is strength'ned, though
  more weak in seeming' (102nd Sonnet)]
  20223
'Liubov' i muzyka' [Love and Music] 20569
Liubov'iu za liubov' [Love for Love] 11364
'Liubov'—moi grekh' ['Love is my sin'] 20474

'Liudskaia neblagodarnost'' [People's
  Ingratitude] 1185
Live with me 20638, 20647
Live with me and be my love 20615, 20637,
  20686
Livet i skoven 397, 807
LIVme Sonate 16234
Ljubezni trud zaman 6202
Llamadas 1145, 1764, 5162, 6465, 6603,
  10465, 10545, 19918
Lo! Hear [sic] the Gentle Lark 2042
Lo! Here, Beneath This Hallowed Shade 10938
Lo! Here the Gentle Lark 2035, 2036, 2040,
  2041, 2048, 20792, 20800, 20803
Lo, In the Orient 19223
Locke's Macbeth Music 6992
Lock's, Celebrated Music from Macbeth 6997
L'ombra di Banquo 7285
[L'onesto Jago] 12443
Longaville's Sonnet (Galliard) 6210
. . . . Look how the floor of heaven 8488, 8489
Look in thy glass 19197
Looking Westward 16193
[Loppiaisaatto = Twelfth Night] 16769, 17284
L'Orage 16297
Lord, how mine eyes 20669
Lord of my love 19509
Lorenzo 8695
Lorenzo and Jessica (Nocturne) 8718
Lorenzo to Jessica 8425, 8764
Los amantes de Verona 13636
[Los amantes de Verona] 13097
[Los tarantos] 14060
Lovbud og Lovbrud 6204
Love 8563
Love and Death: Four Elizabethan Lyrics 19984
Love and Let Love 17389
Love and Madness! 19168
Love and May 20748
Love and Music 20748
Love and Shapes High Fantastical 8433,
  10317, 17720, 19234
Love and Time 19594, 19985, 20109, 20216,
  20312
Love and Understanding Theme 14307
[Love Betray'd; or, The Agreeable
  Disappointment] 18267
Love in Idleness[,] Song in Shakspere's
  Midsummer Night's Dream 9362
Love is Labour Lost 6686
Love is merely a madness 1586
Love is not love 20324
Love laid his sleepless head 8960
"Love Like A Shadow Flies" 9210
Love like a shadow flies (Romance) 9225
Love, love 16548, 16555
Love, love, nothing but love 16451, 16460,
  16566
[Love, love, nothing but love, still love] 16565

"Love Me Just Like Romeo Loved Miss Juliet" 14112

Love Scene from Shakespeare's Romeo and Juliet 14023

Love Sonnets 19198, 19310, 19405, 19497, 19573, 19747, 19759, 19782, 20297, 20426, 20481, 20496

Love Theme 11088

Love Theme from Romeo and Juliet 13420, 13421, 13423, 13424, 13425, 13426, 13427, 13428

"Love-in-idleness" 10471, 10635

Lover and His Lass 911

Lovers and Madmen 911, 3527, 4614, 7790, 8979, 10087, 11326, 15356, 16545

Lovers in Illyria 17378

Lovers Love the Spring 1330, 1378, 1402, 1546

Love's Answer 20647

Love's Constancy 20329

Love's Despair 8001, 17562

Love's Enchantment 16808

Love's investments lost 6332

Love's labor [sic] lost 6663

Love's Labor's Lost 6336

Love's Labour Lost 6687

Love's Labour's Lost 452, 6195, 6203, 6211, 6215, 6218, 6223, 6231, 6232, 6233, 6245, 6251, 6253, 6267, 6277, 6288, 6294, 6295, 6296, 6299, 6300, 6301, 6307, 6314, 6315, 6316, 6318, 6320, 6328, 6329, 6330, 6335, 6655, 20430

[Love's Labour's Lost] 6191, 6192, 6194, 6197, 6198, 6199, 6207, 6209, 6212, 6216, 6219, 6221, 6222, 6228, 6239, 6243, 6244, 6246, 6247, 6250, 6254, 6259, 6261, 6262, 6264, 6265, 6266, 6269, 6270, 6272, 6274, 6279, 6280, 6281, 6282, 6284, 6285, 6287, 6289, 6290, 6298, 6304, 6306, 6308, 6310, 6313, 19458

Love's Labour's Lost (after Shakespeare) 6650

Love's perjuries 6368

Love's Philosophy 20421

Love's Recompense 19550

Loves [sic] ingratitude 8016

Love's Voices 17523, 17730, 17886, 18131, 18261

LSD 9520

[Lucius' Song] 19532

Lucky 6023

Lucretia-Suite 20778

Lucrezia 20769

Lullaby 4619, 9318, 9471, 9520, 9862, 10432, 10434, 10436, 10473, 10494, 10505, 10531, 10568, 21206

Lullaby for Titania 10427, 10564

Lullaby from A Midsummer Night's Dream 10433

Lullaby I 21225

Lullaby II 21225

Lullaby To The Fairy Queen Titania 10538

Lullabye for Titania 10522

[Luó Mî Ou Yù Zhū Lī Yè = Romeo and Juliet] 13549

Lustige Weiber, Polka comique über Motive aus Nicolai's 'Lustige Weiber' 9123

Lustspiel-Entreact No. 3 11308

Lustspiel-Suite 'Der Widerspenstigen Zähmung' 14674

Lute Music of Shakespeare's Time 21287

Lyric Recitation of the Garden Scene in Romeo & Juliet 14037

Lyric Suite 7440

4 Lyrics 17968

Lyrische Stücke 7441

Lystige viser 6537

M

[Maat voor Maat = Measure for Measure] 7761

Macbet 7258

Macbet ossia [Due] spettri al convito 7257

Macbeth 6694, 6697, 6708, 6710, 6714, 6727, 6728, 6729, 6733, 6737, 6742, 6750, 6751, 6752, 6768, 6769, 6771, 6772, 6775, 6781, 6788, 6792, 6793, 6795, 6801, 6802, 6806, 6807, 6811, 6819, 6820, 6821, 6825, 6830, 6835, 6845, 6846, 6848, 6849, 6850, 6857, 6867, 6873, 6875, 6880, 6885, 6893, 6901, 6902, 6909, 6910, 6914, 6942, 6945, 6949, 6951, 6953, 6964, 6965, 6968, 6969, 7000, 7010, 7020, 7035, 7039, 7040, 7044, 7047, 7049, 7060, 7067, 7069, 7074, 7075, 7081, 7086, 7087, 7098, 7104, 7109, 7126, 7130, 7146, 7147, 7150, 7156, 7157, 7160, 7162, 7165, 7178, 7179, 7187, 7201, 7206, 7210, 7211, 7217, 7226, 7229, 7230, 7231, 7232, 7239, 7242, 7243, 7250, 7259, 7260, 7266, 7268, 7270, 7271, 7275, 7278, 7280, 7283, 7284, 7286, 7288, 7289, 7293, 7296, 7298, 7305, 7313, 7336, 7339, 7342, 7347, 7350, 7359, 7361, 7364, 7366, 7377, 7412, 7419, 7423, 7426, 7427, 7428, 7429, 7432, 7436, 7447, 7450, 7458, 7466, 7483, 7484, 7488, 7492, 7493, 7550, 7562, 7573

[Macbeth] 6693, 6695, 6696, 6698, 6701, 6703, 6704, 6718, 6721, 6722, 6726, 6731, 6732, 6734, 6738, 6740, 6743, 6744, 6753, 6754, 6757, 6758, 6760, 6761, 6762, 6763, 6766, 6767, 6774,

[Macbeth] (cont.)
6776, 6777, 6779, 6780, 6782, 6784,
6785, 6786, 6787, 6789, 6790, 6791,
6794, 6797, 6798, 6799, 6800, 6803,
6804, 6805, 6808, 6809, 6810, 6815,
6816, 6817, 6818, 6822, 6823, 6826,
6828, 6829, 6831, 6832, 6836, 6837,
6838, 6841, 6842, 6843, 6844, 6852,
6853, 6856, 6858, 6859, 6860, 6861,
6863, 6868, 6869, 6872, 6876, 6877,
6884, 6886, 6887, 6889, 6890, 6891,
6892, 6895, 6896, 6898, 6899, 6900,
6903, 6904, 6905, 6907, 6912, 6913,
6915, 6916, 6918, 6919, 6920, 6921,
6923, 6924, 6928, 6929, 6932, 6933,
6934, 6935, 6938, 6939, 6947, 6948,
6954, 6955, 6956, 6957, 6958, 6959,
6961, 6962, 6963, 6966, 6967, 6973,
6989, 7001, 7007, 7008, 7009, 7011,
7016, 7017, 7021, 7022, 7024, 7028,
7029, 7030, 7031, 7033, 7034, 7036,
7038, 7041, 7042, 7043, 7046, 7048,
7050, 7053, 7054, 7055, 7056, 7057,
7059, 7062, 7063, 7064, 7068, 7070,
7072, 7078, 7079, 7080, 7082, 7083,
7084, 7085, 7088, 7089, 7090, 7091,
7092, 7093, 7094, 7095, 7096, 7097,
7099, 7102, 7103, 7106, 7107, 7108,
7111, 7112, 7113, 7114, 7115, 7116,
7122, 7123, 7124, 7125, 7128, 7129,
7131, 7132, 7136, 7141, 7143, 7144,
7145, 7148, 7151, 7153, 7158, 7159,
7161, 7164, 7168, 7170, 7172, 7173,
7174, 7175, 7177, 7180, 7181, 7186,
7188, 7189, 7190, 7191, 7199, 7200,
7204, 7205, 7207, 7209, 7215, 7216,
7218, 7219, 7220, 7221, 7222, 7223,
7224, 7234, 7235, 7236, 7416, 7487,
7490, 7524
Macbeth a čarodějnice 7478
[Macbeth a čarodějnice = Macbeth and the
Witches] 7479
Macbeth a Jigg 7013
Macbeth Be-witched! 7580
[Macbeth. Brindisi] 7301, 7302
Macbeth by Verdi 7365
Macbeth, Convito con Brindisi de L'Opéra de
Verdi 7310
Macbeth de Verdi 7333
Macbeth[:] Deux interludes symphoniques
7242
Macbeth, Fantaisie Brillante, sur l'Opéra de
Verdi 7338
Macbeth[:] Fantaisie de Salon 7348
Macbeth. Fantaisie, Motifs de l'Opéra de Verdi
7311
'Macbeth' (For Folon) 6946
Macbeth. (from Verdi's Opera.) Quadrille 7319
Macbeth Galop 7324

Macbeth[:] Grand Selection from G. Verdi's
Opera 7360
Macbeth: Impressions from Shakespeare 7487
Macbeth[:] In Three Throes and a Tragedy
7559
Macbeth Incidental Music 6725
Macbeth. Introduction du 2d acte 7290
Macbeth[:] Lied des Pförtners 7576
Macbeth Mixture 7495
[Macbeth nach Shakespeare] 7508
Macbeth Ominous 6905
Macbeth[,] Opéra de G. Verdi 7337, 7344
Macbeth. Opéra de Verdi 7304, 7306, 7316,
7321, 7327
Macbeth[,] Opéra de Verdi[:] Brindisi 7323
[Macbeth, ou Les Sorcières De La Forêt]
7282
Macbeth ou les trois Sorcières 7455
Macbeth Overture 7175, 7176, 7465
Macbeth Quadrilles, Selected from the Music by
Matthew Locke 6993
Macbeth Quadrilles, The Melodies Selected from
Matthew Locke's Tragedy of Macbeth 6978
Macbeth, Skizza k scenĕ Shakespearových
Macbeth a čarodějnice 7477
Macbeth: sleepwalking music 7277
Macbeth the Knife 7548
Macbeth (Verdi) Fantaisie 7314
Macbeth. (Verdi's) Valse 7320
Macbeth (von Shakespeare) 7469, 7470
Macbeth. 3 Fantaisies Élégantes, sur des motifs
de Giuseppe Verdi 7303
Macbeth-Discord's [sic] (Under the Stage) 6706
Macbeth = March 6706
Macbeth . . . Marche 7139
Macbeth's Theme 6894
Macbeth. . . . Shakespeare útán 7489
Macbeth—Sound 6709
'Macbeth'—Theatre Music 7120
[Macbett] 7240, 7516, 7517, 7528
Macbetto 7292
[Macbetto] 7547
MacBird 7513
[MacBird] 7520
Macduffs = March [sic] 6706
Machbeth 7032
Macht der Töne 5192
Mackbeth 7013, 7286
Mactreth 7538
Mad Hamlet 3613
Mad Lady Macbeth 7446
Mad Madrigals 20562
Mad Ophelia 4075
Mad Scene 4081
Mad Scene from the opera "Hamlet" 3657
[Mademoiselle Cleopatra] 338
Madness in great ones 3928
Mad-regals from Shakespeare, or Bye-Bye,
Bardie 21028

Madrigal 7835, 7852, 7952, 8551, 8613, 8623, 13258, 20671, 20794
Madrigal à la Musique (Henry VIII de Shakespeare) 5063
Madrigal and Minstrelsy 19577
Madrigal (I) 7973, 20614
Madrigal (II) 8629, 20614
Madrigal III 20462
Madrigal IV 20525
Madrigal V 20614
Madrigal VI 19851, 20614
Madrigal VII 20618
Madrigálok 19268, 19924, 20020, 20347
Madrigals from Shakespeare 988, 2636, 8499
Madrigals Three 1312
Mae Bywyd Mor Llawen (This Life Is Most Jolly) 1115
Magbet 6908
Magic Banquet 15212
Magic Time 6680
[Mài Kè Bái Si = Macbeth] 6922
Maids and the Men[,] Dialogue from Purcell's Fairy Queen 10212
Maienzeit 1357, 1573
Mailied 896
Mai-Lied von Shakespeare 1321
Main Theme from Hamlet Overture 3946
Makbet 6720, 6952, 7269, 7279, 7453
[Makbet] 6711, 6717, 6746, 6749, 6765, 6851, 6864, 6930, 6936, 6943, 6944, 7023, 7037, 7066, 7076, 7169
Makbetas [Macbeth] 6724
Makbeth 6735, 6824, 7167, 7396
[Makbeth] 6702, 7154, 7155
Make me a willow cabin 17012, 17744, 17745, 17748
Make me a willow cabin at your gate 17746
Malcolm 7414, 7415
Malcolm's March 7467
Maléfice 7390
Maljat Yhteen Taas 11747
Malvina 78
Malvolio 17383, 17393, 18226, 18251
Malvolio and the letter 18261
Malvolio[.] Graceful Dance 17186
Malvolio March 16719
Malvolio's Aria ("Tis But Fortune") 17375
[Manatsu no Yo no Yume = A Midsummer Night's Dream] 9996
Manjula's Song: Dil Dharke (Heartbeat) 344, 12460
Männer 20067
Männerschwüre oder Verlorene Liebesmüh' 6324
Maquillage 7265
March 3128, 5470, 18763, 19113
[March] 4710, 5924, 6854
March: Bassanio 8049
March Burlesque 14307

March for Hamlet 3129
March from the Suite Poétique[,] Introduced as the Pageant March in Mr. Beerbohm Tree's production of 'Richard II' at His Majesty's Theatre 12714
March 'Hamlet' 3127
March in Richard the Third 12785
March of the Tribunes 5507
March Praetorian 129
March: Prince of Arragon 8101, 8290
March to the Scaffold 6169
March to the Scaffold From 'Symphonie Fantastique' by Berlioz 6172
March to the Scaffold from the Fantastic Symphony 6175
Marche au Supplice 6177
[Marche des Chasseurs d''Hamlet'] 3642
Marche des Noces du Songe d'une Nuit d'été 9692
Marche des Noces du Songe d'une Nuit d'été de F. Mendelssohn-Bartholdy 9849
[Marche d'Hamlet] 3643
Marche d'Ophélie 3977
Marche d'Otello 12096
Marche du Songe de [sic] nuit d'été 9691
Marche du Songe d'une Nuit d'Été 9663
Marche du Supplice 6176
Marche Funèbre de 'Hamlet' 4192
Marche Funèbre d'Hamlet 4192
Marche funèbre d'Ophélia '1' 3977
Marche funèbre pour la dernière scène d'Hamlet 4187, 4188, 4191
Marche nuptiale 9642, 17346
Marche Nuptiale du Songe D'Une Nuit D'Été 9662, 9703, 9831
Marche nuptiale du Songe d'une nuit d'été de Mendelssohn 9695, 9743
Marche Nuptiale (Hochzeits-Marsch aus der Musik zu Shakespeare's Sommernachtstraum) 9654, 9783
Marche Sarcastique from 'Hamlet' 3412, 3413
Marche solennelle de Hamlet 3632
Marche sur Otello (de Rossini) 12159
Marche triomphale d'Hamlet 3019
Marche Troyenne from the Opera 'The Taking of Troy' 8745
Marcia degli Elfi 9651
Marcia di nozze 9653, 9756, 9839
Marcia Eroica, from Rossini's Opera, Otello 12121
Marcia Funèbre voor het slot van Shakespeare's 'Coriolanus' 2385
Marcia Nuziale 9661
Marcus Antonius 330, 331
Marguerite d'Anjou 4882
Maria 13603
Maria from 'West Side Story' 13593, 13611, 13616, 13621
Mariana 8025, 8027

Mariana's Song 7934, 7989
Marigold 2820
Marina's Song 12545
[Márna lásky snaha = Love's Labour's Lost]
6225, 6291
[Marowitz's Hamlet] 4131
Marriage of true minds 20327
Marriage Song 15204, 15803
[Marsch der Könige] 7138
Marsch über Themas aus der Oper Die Lustigen
Weiber von Windsor 9056
[Marsch und Chor der Elfen] 9861
Marsch ur Konung Richard den Tredje 12980
Marsch zu Romeo und Julia 13361
3 Marscher til Shakespeares sørgespil Richard
den 3die 12981
Marsch-Vorspiel zum zweiten Acte von
Shakespeare's 'Sturm' 16110
'Marsh Fortinbrasa' [Fortinbras' March] 3384
'Marsh' [March] 16961
Marsz do IV aktu trag. Hamlet 3302
Marzio Cajo Coriolano 2431
Marzio Coriolano 2419, 2422, 2424
Mascarade du Marchand de Venise 8345
Mascarade (Overture to 'The Merchant of
Venice') 8296
Maskernes Dans fra Musikken til 'Stor Ståhej
for Ingenting' 11272
Maski[:] Iz baleta 'Romeo i Dzhul'etta' [Masks:
From the Ballet Romeo and Juliet] 13803
Masks 13945
Masque 16370
Masque by Herne's Oak 9214
Masque in the Tempest 14757, 14894
Masque of Peleus & Thetis 8751
Masque (Three Dances from 'As You Like It')
593
Masquerade 4461, 4627
Mass für Mass 7600, 7601, 7618, 7634, 7693,
7705, 7719, 7755, 7767, 7803
[Mass für Mass] 7593, 7596, 7607, 7610,
7617, 7620, 7621, 7646, 7649, 7651,
7653, 7656, 7658, 7661, 7662, 7667,
7669, 7670, 7675, 7678, 7680, 7682,
7684, 7686, 7687, 7688, 7690, 7694,
7698, 7702, 7703, 7704, 7720, 7724,
7728, 7734, 7740, 7745, 7747, 7758,
7766, 7768, 7769, 7772, 7774, 7778,
7789, 7792, 7800, 7802
Master Melodies from the Classics 2715
Măsură pentru măsură 7636
[Măsură pentru măsură = Measure for
Measure] 7801
Matin shakespearien 19575
'Matrosskaia pesnia: "Nash shkiper,
botsman . . .": Iz komedii Shekspira "Buria"'
[Sailor's Song: 'Our master, boatswain . . .':
From Shakespeare's Comedy The Tempest]
15855

Matthew Locke[:] Three Songs 6988
Mavritanskiĭ tanets[:] Iz baleta 'Otello' [Moorish
Dance: From the Ballet Othello] 12033,
12036
May 4491, 6659
May the God of Wit 10267
[May the God of Wit inspire] 10196
Mazurka Des Fleurs 14069
Measure for Measure 3811, 5494, 7590, 7595,
7599, 7604, 7611, 7613, 7619, 7644,
7645, 7647, 7648, 7659, 7689, 7699,
7700, 7722, 7723, 7726, 7739, 7750,
7762, 7763, 7764, 7786, 7796, 7798,
7799, 7804, 7869, 8042, 8044, 8045,
8483, 8670, 10456, 15862, 17727, 21121
[Measure for Measure] 7591, 7594, 7598,
7602, 7606, 7609, 7614, 7616, 7622,
7624, 7625, 7627, 7630, 7633, 7638,
7639, 7641, 7642, 7643, 7652, 7655,
7657, 7663, 7664, 7665, 7676, 7677,
7695, 7710, 7711, 7712, 7715, 7716,
7717, 7718, 7730, 7731, 7732, 7733,
7737, 7738, 7746, 7749, 7751, 7756,
7759, 7775, 7781, 7784, 7787, 7791, 7793
Measure for Pleasure 8037
Measures and Minuets 16058
3 Meditations on Sonnets by Shakespeare
19432, 19838, 19965
Meet Cole Porter At The Piano 14620
Meet Richard Rodgers At The Piano 2220
[Mehuma Raba Al Lo Davar = Much Ado
About Nothing] 11018
Meilė ir mirtis Veronoje [Love and Death in
Verona] 14070
Mein Auge war ein Maler 19503
Mein Leben ist wie Fieber, stets begehrend
20506
Mein Mädchen hat nicht Augen wie zwei
Sonnen 20419
Mein Schicksal 19647
Mélange Pour Le Piano, Sur les plus jolis Motifs
D'Otello De Rossini 12040
Mélange sur Othello de Rossini 12086
Melodier af Adam Oehlenschläger til Digte af
forskjellige Forfattere 10539, 17596
Melodies by Schubert 2761
Melodiia.-Vstrecha.-Serenada [Melody.-
Encounter.-Serenade] 13088
Melodrama (Macbeth) 7127
Melodramatische Musik zu Macbeth 7058
Melodramatische Traummusik zu Richard III
12920
Mélodrame[:] Le Sommeil de Desdémone
12417
Melody From The Fantasy-Overture "Romeo
and Juliet" 13979
Melody-Harmony[:] A Re-Study of the
Shakespeare Play-Songs 1456, 17765
Memories of Schubert 2786, 18586

Memory 19620
[Men Are Not Gods] 12454
Mendelssohn[:] Excerpts from His Greatest Works 9624
Mendelssohnana 9801
Mendelssohn's Wedding March 9622, 9701, 9766, 9790, 9794, 9795, 9827
[Mendelssohn's Wedding March, First Movement] 9822
Mendelssohn's Wedding March, From A Midsummer Night's Dream 9842
[Mendelssohn's 'Wedding March' from 'A Midsummer Night's Dream'] 9773
Mendelssohn's Wedding March, in the Midsummer Night's Dream 9699
Mendiant du ciel bleu 2393
Menuet ze Shakespearovy hry 'Lásky lichá lest' 6229
Menuetti näytelmään Paljon melua tyhjästä 11600
Mera Za Meru 7666
[Mera za meru = Measure for Measure] 7707, 7782
Mera za meru [Measure for Measure] 7679
Mercante de Venezia 8796
Merchant of Venice 8054, 8131, 8352, 8359, 8360, 8361
Mercutio 13855
Mercutio, a study 14024
Mercy 8677
Mercy Cycle 8675
Mermaid's Song (Gesang der Meermädchen) from Oberon 10874
Mermaid's Song (Oberon—Weber) 10879
Merrily 15881
Merry Heart 18948
[Merry Wives] 8804
Merry Wives 8971
Merry Wives of Windsor 8827, 8907, 8984, 9041, 9114, 9229, 21121
[Merry Wives of Windsor] 9050, 9116
Merry Wives of Windsor Galop 9021
Merry Wives of Windsor Overture 9052, 9087, 9098
[Merry Wives of Windsor Overture] 9057, 9060, 9082, 9085, 9096
[Mesure pour mesure] 7626, 7628, 7681, 7691, 7742, 7779
Metamorphoses 15706
Metoikos 19908
Miarka za miarkę 7597, 7760
[Miarka za miarkę = Measure for Measure] 7612, 7706, 7714, 7785
Mice and Rats 5977
Mid Summer Night [sic] Dream. Selection from A. Thomas 20966
Midnight Revels at Hernes' Oak 9232
Midsommardrömmen 10973
Mid-summer 10155

Midsummer Mishigass 9769
Midsummer Night 10348
Midsummer Night Revels 10786
Midsummer Night's Dream 9273, 9413, 9571, 9589, 9715, 9745, 9800, 9882, 9899, 9978, 10009, 10050, 10096, 10120, 10139, 10661, 10667, 10670, 10906
Midsummer Night's Dream (Mendelssohn.) 9812
Midsummer Night's Dream (Nocturne) 9801
[Midsummer Night's Dream: Wedding March] 9632, 9725
Midsummer Nocturne 10954
Midsummer Song 10460
Midsummernight's Dream 9330, 9816, 9817, 10282
Midsummernight's Dream II 9331
'Midsummernight's Dream' Overture 9832
[Midzomernacht 77] 10763
[Midzomernachtsdroom] 10028
Mignon 10805
Military March 11200
[Milo za drago = Measure for Measure] 7729, 7783
[Minden jó, ha jó a vége = All's Well That Ends Well] 23, 54
Mine Eye Awake 19847
Mine eye hath play'd the painter 19499
Mine Eye Hath Played the Painter and Hath Stell'd 19493
Mingle, Mingle 7544
Miniaturen zu dem Lustspiel 'Zwei Herren aus Verona' von Shakespeare 18351
Miniatyrsvit ur kompletterande scenmusik till 'En midsommarnattsdröm' 9417
Minstrel's Song 21062
. . . mint testnek a kenyér . . . 20037
Minuet 8376, 11216, 14356
Minuet[:] No. 2. from the Incidental Music to Romeo and Juliet 13136
Mirage 15832
Miranda 15448, 15991, 16000, 16004, 16011, 16016, 16035, 16042, 16058, 16085, 16089, 16108, 16133, 16141, 16142, 16149, 16166, 16219, 16239, 16249, 16267, 16271, 16272, 16280, 16286, 16294, 16298
Miranda dalla 'Tempesta' di G. Shakespeare 15397
Miranda ('Der Sturm' von Shakespeare) 16153
Miranda or "True Love has found its Way" 16295
Miranda (Posledniaia bor'ba) [Miranda (The Last Struggle)] 15436
Miranda-Miranda 16285
Miranda's Song 14856, 16212
Mirrors 19205, 19645
Miss Leake's [sic] Favorite Song in Vortigern 20865

Mistah Shakespeah 14131, 21012
Mister Othello 12497
Mistress Mine 17795, 17844
'Mistress Mine' Waltz 17916
Mistress Page and Mistress Ford 9230
[Misura per misura] 7650
Mit Shakespeares XXX. Sonett 19631
[Miten haluatte = As You Like It] 665, 669
[Mitta mitasta = Measure for Measure] 7672
[Mletački trgovac = The Merchant of Venice]
  8372
'Mne pokazalos', chto byla zima' ['How like a
  winter hath my absence been'] 20155
'Mne pokazalos', chto byla zima (Sonet 97)'
  ['How like a winter hath my absence been'
  (Sonnet 97)] 20168
[Mnogo hrupa za nič = Much Ado About
  Nothing] 11285
[Mnogo shuma iz nichego = Much Ado About
  Nothing] 11013, 11024, 11053, 11059,
  11098, 11153, 11157, 11211, 11236,
  11237, 11279, 11288, 11336
[Mnogo shuma iz-za . . . serdets = Much Ado
  from the Heart] 11363
Mnoho povyku pro nic 11023
[Mnoho povyku pro nic = Much Ado About
  Nothing] 11089, 11228, 11230, 11238,
  11239, 11286, 11293
mobile for shakespeare 19757, 19769
Mockery 6447, 6488
Modern Music 13824
'Moi genii, moi angel, moi drug . . .' [My
  Inspirer, My Angel, My Friend . . .] 4251
Molodost' moia [My Youth] 20569
Molto rumore per nulla 11366
[Molto rumore per nulla] 11103, 11251
Mon bon Ami 9247
Mondaufgang aus 'Die lustigen Weiber von
  Windsor' 9119
[Mondaufgang und Elfenchor] 9103
[Mondchor] 9039, 9132
Mondi celesti e infernali 13773
Monolog Horatios 3695
Montagues and Capulets (from 'Romeo and
  Juliet' Ballet) 13801
Montano et Stéphanie 11617, 11628
Monument Scene 11247
Moon Canticle 10454
Moon Magic 8465
Moonlight 8459, 8709
Moonlight Sketches 8709
Moorish March 8238
Mopsa 19147, 19149, 19152, 19155, 19157
"Mor bêr y lloergan gwsg." 8438
More fun 20472
Morgen Ständchen 2710
Morgengesang 2674, 2683, 2707
Morgengruss 2662
Morgenlied 7560

Morgenständchen 2666, 2695
Morning 3716
Morris Dance From The Music To Henry VIII
  4988
Mortality 8039
Mosaïc[:] Summer Night Dream 9644
Moth 6648
[Moth's Song] 20430
Motive aus "Oberon" von Weber 10893
Motto 17678
Mourning 13922
2nd Movement of the Intermezzo from the
  music to 'Midsummer Night's Dream' 9643
Mr. Charke's Medley Overture 11711
Mr. Corbet's Musick in the Comedy call'd Henr.
  the 4th Play'd all the time of the Publick Act
  in Oxford 4326
Mr. Corbetts Musick in the Comedy call'd the
  agreeable Disappointment 18267
Mr. Hamlet of Broadway 4159
Mr. Hamlet of Broadway Selection 4160
Mr. Paisible's T[unes] in Timon of Athens 16332
Mr. Peasable's [sic] Ayres in the Comedy call'd
  the Humors of Sr [J]ohn Falsstaf 4496
Mr. Purcell's in Timon of Athens 16332
Mr. Shakespeare's Timetrek 20918
Mr. W.S. 20916
Mrs. Jordan's Favorite Song in Vortigern
  20865
Mrs. Quickly 21121
Much Ado About Nothing 11001, 11002,
  11003, 11019, 11020, 11039, 11040,
  11042, 11051, 11064, 11066, 11070,
  11077, 11078, 11081, 11091, 11092,
  11093, 11094, 11100, 11101, 11106,
  11135, 11152, 11197, 11253, 11256,
  11260, 11275, 11290, 11297, 11298,
  11299, 11300, 11304, 11306, 11318,
  11328, 11332, 11333, 11369, 11540,
  11595, 11639, 19702, 20746, 21121
[Much Ado About Nothing] 10990, 10991,
  10993, 11000, 11004, 11015, 11016,
  11028, 11029, 11034, 11037, 11038,
  11048, 11050, 11052, 11056, 11057,
  11063, 11065, 11069, 11072, 11076,
  11079, 11080, 11083, 11084, 11085,
  11087, 11090, 11095, 11099, 11109,
  11110, 11117, 11134, 11139, 11146,
  11147, 11148, 11154, 11155, 11156,
  11171, 11172, 11177, 11178, 11180,
  11184, 11187, 11188, 11189, 11193,
  11195, 11198, 11202, 11206, 11207,
  11210, 11218, 11220, 11223, 11227,
  11231, 11232, 11233, 11234, 11240,
  11245, 11248, 11250, 11252, 11253,
  11254, 11255, 11257, 11261, 11263,
  11274, 11280, 11281, 11284, 11289,
  11310, 11313, 11319, 11320, 11331,
  11334, 11338, 11594

Much ado about nothing; or, she loves me? 11345

Much ado about Nothing Waltz 11016

[Mudasawagi = Much Ado About Nothing] 11277

[Muhumah raba al lo davar = Much Ado About Nothing] 11199

Multimedia-Spiel 15261

Muntra fruarna i Windsor 8915, 8987

Murdering Macbeth 7246

Music 5093, 5140

Music & Sound for 'Measure for Measure' by Wm. Shakespear 7637

Music & Sound for Shakespeare's 'Cymbeline' 2457

Music and Poetry 20747

Music and Songs for Shakespeare's Twelfth Night 17229

Music and songs for the play 'Hamlet' 3532

. . . . Music do I hear? 12756

Music for 'A Midsummer Night's Dream' . . . 9337, 9451, 9918

[Music for A Midsummer Night's Dream] 9477

Music for 'A Midsummernight's Dream' 9276, 9277

Music for a production of As You Like It at Allington Castle[,] Kent 1971 504

Music for Antony and Cleopatra 217

Music for 'As You Like It' 394, 563, 715

[Music for As You Like It] 613

Music for 'Hamlet' 2904, 2905, 2906, 3004, 3008, 3113, 3140, 3545, 3933, 4019

Music for 'Henry IV, Part 1' 4359

Music for 'Henry IV, Part 2' 4555

Music for 'Julius Caesar' 5251, 5259

Music for 'King Henry the Fourth, Part 1' 4296

Music for King Henry VIII Act IV Scene II 5225

Music for 'King Lear' 5660, 5718, 5763, 5863

[Music for 'King Lear'] 5797

Music for 'Lady Macbeth' 7507

Music for Love's Labour's Lost 6226, 6297, 6351, 6399, 6529, 6652

Music for 'Macbeth' 6700, 6778, 6866, 6879, 6998, 7061, 7071, 7137

[Music for Macbeth] 6755

Music for 'Measure for Measure' 7592, 7608

Music for Midsummer Night's Dream 10043

Music for 'Much ado about Nothing' 10995, 10996

[Music for Much Ado About Nothing] 11126

Music for 'Othello' 11661, 11691, 11952

Music for 'Prospero's Story' 15579, 15757, 15946

Music for 'Richard III' 12782, 12915

[Music for Richard III] 13032

[Music for Romeo and Juliet] 13353

Music for Shakespeare 20834

Music for Shakespeare '70 20890

Music for Shakespeare's 'As You Like It' 651

Music for Shakespeare's 'Hamlet' 3481

Music for Shakespeare's King John 5629

Music for Shakespeare's Measure for Measure 7771

Music for Shakespeare's Othello 11976

[Music for Shakespeare's play 'As You Like It'] 699

Music for Shakespeare's Romeo and Juliet 13188, 13902

Music for Shakespeare's 'Tempest' 14868

[Music for Shakespeare's Tempest] 15241

Music for Shakespeare's 'The Merchant of Venice' 90, 8161, 8355

Music for Shakespeare's 'The Tempest' 15370

[Music for Shakespeare's The Tempest] 14957

Music for Shakespeare's The Twelfth Night; or, What you will 17092

Music for Shakespeare's Twelfth Night 8725, 16737, 17116

Music for 'Taming of the Shrew' 14510

Music for the Classical Tragedy 3054, 5299, 6822, 13197

Music for 'The Comedy of Errors' 2191

Music for The Fool in 'King Lear' 5654

Music for 'The Merchant of Venice' 8055, 8382

Music for 'The Merry Wives of Windsor' 8802

Music for the Opening of Macbeth 6839

Music for the Spheres 10440

Music for 'The Taming of the Shrew' 14223, 14368

Music for 'The Tempest' 14698, 14699, 15004, 15005, 15006, 15073, 15348, 15364, 15376

[Music for the Tempest] 15016

Music for 'The Tempest' by William Shakespeare 14944

Music for the Wedding 9673

Music for 'The Winter's Tale' 18673, 18735, 18826

Music for Theatre No. 17 9611

Music for Theatre No. 6 12908

Music for 'Troilus and Cressida' 347, 16435, 16468, 16528

Music for 'Twelfth Night' 16604, 16605, 16606, 16707, 16714, 17051, 17176

[Music for Twelfth Night] 16865

Music for Winds, Percussion, and Prepared Piano 4261

Music from Shakespeare's Day 21288

Music from Shakespeare's plays 21354, 21359

[Music from the Columbia Picture's Release 'Taming of the Shrew'] 14456

Music From The Royal Shakespeare Company Production 1974 2501

Music in 'The Play Measure for Measure' 7640

Music in the Tempest 14757, 15115

Music Introduced In Macbeth 6985

Music Is 5041 17373

Music of Shakespeare's Time 21286
Music That Brings Sweet Sleep 5176
Music to Accompany Shakespeare's 'A
    Midsummer Night's Dream' 9300
Music to Antony & Cleopatra 139
Music to 'Antony and Cleopatra' 241
Music to commit burglaries by 20470
Music to Hear 1159, 11521, 19245, 19253,
    19255, 19256, 19257, 19259, 19260,
    19261, 19262, 19264, 19267, 19271
[Music to Hear] 19261
Music To Hear, Why Hear'st Thou Music
    Sadly? 19232, 19233, 19242
[Music to hear, why hear'st thou music sadly?]
    19231
Music to Henry VIII 4997
Music to Lear 6013
Music to Love's Labours Lost 6255
Music to Macbeth 6940
[Music to Macbeth] 6813
Music to Selected Sonnets of William
    Shakespeare 19252, 19831, 20494, 21058
Music to Shakespeare's 'As You Like It' 557
Music to Shakespeare's 'Miching Mallecho', it
    means 'Mischief' 3622, 19809, 19866
Music to Shakespeare's Plays . . . A
    Midsummer Night's Dream 21321, 21345
Music to Shakespeare's Plays . . . As You Like
    It 21349
Music to Shakespeare's Plays . . . The Tempest
    21322
Music to Shakespeare's Plays . . . Twelfth Night
    21346
Music to Shakespeare's Tempest 14710
Music to Shakespeare's 'The Tempest', from the
    Second Suite for orchestra 15275
Music to "The Fairy Prince" 10767
Music to the Masque in Shakespeare's
    'Merchant of Venice' 8345, 8348
Music to the 'Merchant of Venice' 8097, 19685
[Music to the play 'Hamlet'] 2934
[Music to the play 'Macbeth'] 6730
[Music to the play the 'Tempest'] 14864
Music to 'The Taming of the Shrew' 14383
Music to The Tempest 14987
Music to Twelfth Night for Stratford 17000
Music Written For A Midsummer Night's
    Dream 9410
Musica di Camera 18064
Música para la Comedia El Mercader de
    Venecia 8225
Música para la Comedia Noche de Reyes 17018
Musical Highlights From Cleopatra 340
Musical Illustrations of Bishop Percy's 'Reliques
    of Ancient English Poetry' 12309
Musical Illustrations of Shakspere 3729, 6338,
    12314, 13847
Musical Illustrations of the Beauties of
    Shakespeare 3729, 6338, 12314, 13847

Musiche di scena per il 'Macbeth' di
    Shakespeare 7203
Musiche di scena per il 'Sogno di una notte di
    mezza estate' di Shakespeare 10068
Musiche di Scena per 'La Dodicesima Notte' di
    Shakespeare 17319
Musiche di scena per La tempesta 14980
Musiche di scena per 'Le Allegre Commare di
    Windsor' di Shakespeare 8975
Musiche per Amleto di Shakespeare 3504
Musiche per 'Giulietta e Romeo' di Shakespeare
    13524
Musiche per 'Kean' 4132, 12466
Musiche per La Tempesta 15335
Musiche per l'Amleto 3503
Musick in Timon of Athens 16338
Musick to heare 19265
Music's Praise 5117
Musiikkia näytelmään Antonius ja Cleopatra
    194
Musiikkia näytelmään Julius Caesar 5245
Musiikkia Näytelmään Kuningas Lear 5656
Musiikkia näytelmään Kuten haluatte 555
Musiikkia näytelmään Macbeth 6692
Musiikkia näytelmään Miten äkäpussi
    kesytetään 14216
Musiikkia näytelmään Venetsian kauppias
    8047
Musiikkia William Shakespearen näytelmään
    Kuningas Lear 5865
[Musik for the dances and songs in 'As You
    Like It'] 749
Musik fra Shakespearetiden bearbejdet og
    instrumenteret til Brug for Det. kgl. Teaters
    Opførelse af Hamlet 2890
Musik fra Shakespeare-Tiden bearbejdet og
    instrumenteret til Brug for Det kongelige
    Teaters Opførelse af Hamlet ny Udgave 2891
Musik für 'Der Widerspenstigen Zähmung'
    14468
Musik für Hamlet 3098
Musik für Klavier und Mezzosopran nach
    Worten von Shakespeare, Dostojewski,
    Whitman und Goethe 19891
Musik für Klavier und Sopran nach Worten
    von Shakespeare und dem Ev. Johannis, Kap.
    XII, 24 15900, 18965, 19495, 19780
Musik für Zwei 18231
Musik mit ihrem Silberklang 13864
Musik til Dürrenmatts skuespil Kong John[,]
    Det kgl. Teater 1969 5605
Musik til Hamlet 3066
Musik til Helligtrekonger Hørespil 17204
Musik til hørespillet Romeo og Julie 13455
Musik til Kantate-Forspillet ved Shakespeare-
    mindefesten 16228, 21067
Musik til Romeo og Julie 13297
Musik til Shakespeares Helligtrekongersaften
    eller Hvad I vil 16782

Musik til Shakespear's Købmanden i Venedig 8292

Musik til Shakespears 'Trold kan tæmmes' i funktionalistisk Bearbejdelse af Henry Hellssen 14448

Musik til Stadsteaterns föreställning av Shakespeares Othello 11785

Musik til W. Shakespeares The Tempest i Marianne Rolfs Oppsetning . . . 15312

Musik til William Shakespeare 20860

Musik till Hamlet 3190

Musik till Henrik IV 4410, 4588

Musik till Julius Caesar 5356

Musik till Kung Lear 5936

Musik till 'Så tuktas en argbigga' 14309

Musik till Shakespeares 'En Vintersaga' 18806

Musik till Stormen 14876

Musik till Trettondagsafton 16814

Musik till William Shakespeares Henry IV 4408, 4586

Musik um Shakespeare[:] Altenglische Virginalmusik 18323, 21289

[Musik zu Cymbelin] 2479

Musik zu 'Cymbeline' 2509

Musik zu dem Trauerspiele Macbeth 7217

[Musik zu Der Kaufmann von Venedig] 8293

Musik zu 'Der Sturm' 15025

Musik zu 'Der Sturm' von W. Shakespeare 15091

Musik zu 'Ein Sommernachtstraum' von William Shakespeare 10083

[Musik zu Ein Wintermärchen] 18855

Musik zu einem Märchenspiel 10020

Musik zu Fernsehspiel 5466

Musik zu Hamlet 3138, 3206

[Musik zu Hamlet] 3453

Musik zu Hamlet, Langsamer Satz 3542

Musik zu Hexenküche in Macbeth 7140

[Musik zu Julius Cäsar] 5420

Musik zu 'König Lear' von William Shakespeare 5836

[Musik zu Macbeth] 7117

Musik zu 'Maß für Maß' 7754

Musik zu Pantomime in Hamlet 3375

[Musik zu Richard III] 12853

Musik zu Shakespeare's Cymbelin 2456

[Musik zu Shakespeare's Cymbelin] 2455

Musik zu Shakespeares 'Cymbeline' 2509

Musik zu Shakespeares 'Der Sturm' 15274, 15352

[Musik zu Shakespeare's 'Ein Sommernachtstraum'] 10114

[Musik zu Shakespeares 'König Johann'] 5621

Musik zu Shakespeare's König Richard der Dritte 13000

Musik zu Shakespeare's Königsdramen nach der Dingelstedt'schen Bearbeitung 4433, 4605, 4767, 12725

Musik zu Shakespeare's Macbeth 7192, 7193

[Musik zu Shakespeare's 'Macbeth'] 6723, 6874, 7237

Musik zu Shakespeare's Othello 11658, 12001

Musik zu Shakespeare's Richard III 13009

[Musik zu Shakespeares 'Richard III'] 12961

[Musik zu Shakespeares 'Romeo und Julie'] 13445

[Musik zu Shakespeares Sonett Nr. 116] 8191, 20339

Musik zu Shakespeare's 'Sturm' 15331, 15332, 16070

Musik zu Shakespeares Tragödie Julius Caesar 5447

Musik zu Shakespeares Viel Lärm um Nichts 11123

Musik zu Shakespeare's 'Was ihr wollt' 16828, 16905, 17276

Musik zu Shakespeares 'Wie es Euch gefällt' 913

Musik zu Shakespeares 'Wie es Euch gefällt' . . . Suite (fünf Sätze) für Orchester 913

Musik zu Shakespeares 'Wintermärchen' 18878

[Musik zu Shakespeares 'Wintermärchen'] 18692

Musik zu 'Sommernachtstraum' 10257

Musik zu 'Timon' von Shakespeare 16362

Musik zu Viel Lärm um Nichts 11308

Musik zu W. Shakespeares Der Kaufmann von Venedig 8182

Musik zu W. Shakespeares Der Sturm 15045

Musik zu W. Shakespeare's Tragödie 'König Lear' 5668

Musik zu W. Shakespeares Wintermärchen 18776

Musik zu 'Was ihr wollt' 16696, 16963, 16966

Musik zu 'Was ihr wollt' von W. Shakespeare 16905

Musik zu 'Was ihr Wollt' von William Shakespeare 17029

Musik zu 'Wie es euch gefällt' 938, 941

[Musik zu 'Wie es euch gefällt'] 796

Musik zu 'Zwei Herren aus Verona' von William Shakespeare 18406

Musik zum Eurythmischen Cyklus aus 'Ein Sommernachtstraum' 10030

[Musik zum König Lear] 5659

Musik zum Macbeth 6699

[Musik zum 'Sturm'] 15266

Musik zum 'Wintermärchen' 18883

Musik zum Wintermärchen von Shakespeare 18924

Musik zur König Lear 5981

Musik zur Musica buffa 'Komödie der Irrungen' von Shakespeare 91

Musikalisches Vorspiel zu Der Widerspenstigen Zähmung 14446

Musikantenlied 2688

Musiken till Trettondagsafton (Shakspeare) 17232

Musikk til A. Brinckmanns Oppsetning av 'King Lear' på det Norske Teatret 5951

Musikk til Pål Løkkebergs Oppsetning . . . av Shakespear's tragoedie Romeo and Juliet 13509

Musikk til W Shakespeares Troll kan temmes i Marianne Rolfs oppsetning 14512

Musikvinjetter till Shakespeares Troilus och Kressida 16487

Musique de la Reine des Fées[:] Ouverture 10182

[Musique de scène pour 'Coriolan' de W. Shakespeare] 2329

Musique de scène pour Hamlet 3025, 3243, 3489

Musique de scène pour la Mégère apprivoisée 14286

Musique de scène pour Le Marchand de Venise 8062

Musique de scène pour: 'Le Songe d'une Nuit d'Été' 9324

Musique de scène pour Percussions 6906

Musique de scène pour Richard II de W. Shakespeare 12625

Musique de Scène . . . de Roméo et Juliette 13342

Musique pour Hamlet 3916

Musique pour La Mégère Apprivoisée 14386, 14412

Musique pour la Tragédie du Roi Lear 5727

Musique pour 'Le Conte d'Hiver' de Shakespeare 18877

Musiques pour le Roi Lear 5724

[Muziek bij 'de Vrolijke Vrouwtjes van Windsor' = Music in The Merry Wives of Windsor] 8904

Muziek bÿ Macbeth van W. Shakespeare 7198

Muziek bÿ Midzomernachtsdroom van W. Shakespeare 10063

Muzik zu Shakespeare: Ein Sommernachtstraum 9906

Muzik zur Musica buffa 'Komödie der Irrungen' von Shakespeare 2195

Mūzika F. Bruknera lugai 'Elizabete, Anglijas karaliene' 19799

Muzika kum tragediiata 'Khamlet' [Music for the Tragedy Hamlet] 2963

Mūzika un dziesmas V. Šekspīra lugai 'Liela brēka, maza vilna' 11149, 19798

Mūzika V. Šekspīra lugai 'Divpadsmitā nakts' 17158

[Muzyka do Hamleta = Music to Hamlet] 3302

[Muzyka do 'Króla Henryka IV' = Music to King Henry IV] 4412, 4590

Muzyka do przedstawienia 'Sceny z Szekspira' 20848

Muzyka do 'Sen nocy letniej' 9447

Muzyka do Shakespeare'a 'Król Henryk IV.' 4397, 4581

Muzyka do sztuki 'Burza' 15000

Muzyka do sztuki 'Hamlet' 3101

Muzyka do sztuki 'Król Ryszard II' 12651

Muzyka do sztuki 'Romeo i Julia' 13235

Muzyka do sztuki 'Wieczór trzech króli' 16843

Muzyka k tragedii Shekspira 'Gamlet' [Music to Shakespeare's Tragedy Hamlet] 3359

Muzyka k tragedii V. Shekspira 'Korol' Lir' [Music to W. Shakespeare's Tragedy King Lear] 5668

Muzyka k 'Zimnei skazke' Shekspira [Music to Shakespeare's The Winter's Tale] 18877

'Muzykal'nyi antrakt' [Musical Entr'acte] 16961

My Bounty, my love 3734, 13849, 13850

[My Darling Clementine] 4115

My flockes feed not 20725

My Flocks Feed Not 20586, 20675

My glass shall not persuade me I am old 19486

My Juliet[:] A Shakespearean Coon Song ("Oh! ain't you comin' out My Juliet?") 14156

My Love Is As A Fever 20507, 20509

My Love is as a Fever Longing Still 20508

My love is strengthen'd, though more weak in seeming 20217, 20218

My love is strengthened 20225

My Mistress' Eyes 20423, 20425, 20427

My mistress' eyes are nothing like the sun 20420, 20424

My Roguish Julie 14135

Mycket väsen för ingenting 11073, 11264, 11330

Myrsky 15187

Mystery's Song: "I am come to lock all fast" 10197

N

['Na smert' Koriolana v tragedii Shekspira' = On the Death of Coriolanus in Shakespeare's Tragedy] 2382

Na tri kralja ili kak hočete 16832

Naar Enden er god saa er alting godt 80

Naar til Lyren Orpheus sang. (Af "Henrik den Ottende") 5108

Nachklänge aus der Oper: Der Widerspänstigen Zähmung 14578

Nächtliche Vision 10655

Nah' mir mit dem Lippen nicht 7892

Nähe des Geliebten 21214

[Naked Hamlet] 4110

Nancy's The Name 21025

[Napraznite usilia na liubovta = Love's Labour's Lost] 6220

Når Enden er god 29

Narodnyi tanets[:] Iz baleta 'Romeo i Dzhul'etta' [Folk Dance: From the Ballet Romeo and Juliet] 13799

Narrenlied aus "Was ihr wollt" 17545

[Narrenlieder] 16749, 17166

Narren-Lieder und Bühnenmusik aus 'Was ihr wollt' 17041

Narrenlied—Fool's Song 6031

Narrens sista visa 17232

'Nas razluchil aprel" ['From you have I been absent in the spring'] 20177

Naslouchání času 19287

'Ne govori, moi drug', chto serdtse izmenilo' ['O, never say that I was false of heart'] 20279

'Ne izmeniaisia, bud' sami soboi (13-i sonet)' ['O that you were yourself! but, love, you are' (13th Sonnet)] 19296

'Ne plach', krasavitsa' [Don't Weep, My Beauty] 11428

'Neath the Greenwood Tree[:] Pastoral 1941

Neguțătorul din Veneția 8069

Nell'Otello 12120

Nemesis 16421

[Nenagradjeni ljubavni trud = Love's Labour's Lost] 6303

[Neshei Windsor Haalizot = The Merry Wives of Windsor] 8950

Never Doubt I Love 3724, 3729, 3730

Never Say Fail 7565

Nevestele vesele din Windsor 8839, 8850, 8997

[Nevestele vesele din windsor = The Merry Wives of Windsor] 8831, 8855

[Nevihta = The Tempest] 15285

New Canzonet 7946

New Dance: S & Titus Dance 16398

New Readings, from Shakespeare 20993

New Tunes to Choice Words 10924

Next, winter comes slowly 10222

Nézd: Életem oly évszak . . . (Shakespeare: Sonnet LXXIII) 19997

Nicht jene Muse hab ich mir erwählt 19479

Nicht länger trauere um mich 19937

[Nichts ist so stockisch. . . .] 8491

Nichts kann den Bund zwei treuer Herzen hindern 20310

12th Night at the Crossroads 18282

Night Images 17425

12th Night Music 16955, 18654

Night of the Moonspell 10272

Night Songs 8480

Nightshriek 7367

Nimble Cymbeline 2882, 4159

"Nimbly Nimbly Dance" (Macbeth) 6979

Nimm, o nimm—Take, O Take 7880

Nine Shakespeare Songs by Thomas Augustine Arne 455, 2850, 6501, 14848, 16620

Nine Songs from Shakespeare 1236, 1598, 2632, 5046, 6381, 6494, 15600, 17434, 18476

Nine Traditional Songs 3762

[No Bed for Bacon] 20938, 20986

No longer mourn 19939, 19952, 19966, 19969

No Longer Mourn for Me 19941, 19946, 19955, 19958, 19960

No longer mourn for me when I am dead 19938, 19940, 19943, 19954, 19970

No more be grieved at that which thou hadst done 19667

No more dams 15484, 15823

No more dams I'll make for fish 14906, 14950, 14957, 15481

'No Non Temer.' From Rossini's Otello 12146

"No, Time, thou shalt not boast" 20364

No Women Mr. Shakespeare 20957

Noaptea regilor 16760

'Noch' listvoiu chut' kolyshet' [Night is Scarcely Stirring with Leaves] 11157

Noch'[:] Stsena iz baleta 'Otello' [Night: Scene from the Ballet Othello] 12030

Nochecita de San Juan 10163

Nocturne 3845, 8238, 9826, 13828, 19711

Nocturne[:] A Midsummer Night's Dream 9859

Nocturne de Gabriel Fauré 8767

Nocturne de Shylock 8769

Nocturne du Songe d'une Nuit d'Été de Mendelssohn 9857

4e Nocturne en mi bémol majeur 10707

Nocturne from A Midsummer Night's Dream 9796, 9823

[Nocturne from A Midsummer Night's Dream] 9660

Nocturne. From 'A Midsummer Nights [sic] Dream' 9814

Nocturne; from Midsummer night's dream 9760

Nocturne From The 'Midsummer Night's Dream' 9656, 9770

Nocturne. (How Sweet The Moonlight Sleeps) 8456

Nocturne [in G minor] 4269

Nocturne: Midsummer Night's Dream 9843

Nocturno 9860

Nocturno from 'Midsummernight's Dream' 9702

Noh Hamlet 3608

[Noite de Reis = Twelfth Night] 16750

'Noktiurn[:] Iz muzyki k fil'mu "Otello"' [Nocturne: From the Music to the Film Othello] 11813

'Noktiurn (iz muzyki k komedii V. Shekspira "Dvanadtsataia noch'")' [Nocturne (from the Music to W. Shakespeare's Comedy Twelfth Night] 16962

Non m'inganno il mio rivale 12153

Nostr'omo, il mozzo, il fabbro ed il padrone 15846
Not from the stars do I my judgment pluck 19299
Not Marble, nor the Gilded Monuments 19779
[Not marble, nor the gilded monuments] 19776
Not marble . . . (nor gilded monuments) 19789
"Not Wisely, But Too Well" 12495, 12512
. . . notes of Music 19246, 19385, 19477, 19511, 19672, 19729, 19793, 20068, 20320, 20480, 20648
Notturno 9628, 21210
[Notturno] 13932
Notturno aus dem Sommernachtstraum von Mendelssohn-Bartholdy 9761
Notturno aus "Ein Sommernachtstraum" 9807
Notturno (dall Opera 'La Bisbetica Domata') 14595
Notturno from 'A Midsummer Night's Dream' 9637
Notturno. (Midsummer Night's Dream) 9714
Novelletten 7475, 10631
November 10665
Now and Then 4143, 20915
Now I am alone 3807
"Now the hungry lion roars . . ." 9926, 10355, 10356, 10361, 10363
Now the hungry Lions roar 10754
Now The Hungry Lyon Rores 10357
"Now, until the break of day" 9926, 10364
Now winter comes slowly 10241
Nu dricker jag dig till 13840
[Nuit des rois] 16720
Nuptial hymn 14906
Nuptial March 16013

O

O, be some other name! 13852
"O bid your faithful Ariel fly" 15115, 15117, 15118, 15120, 15123, 15124, 15125, 15126, 15127
O Bid Your Faithful Ariel Fly. Song, in "The Tempest" 15121
O, by rivers, by whose falls 16676
O by rivers, from Shakespeare's The Merry Wives of Windsor 16670
O England! model to thy inward greatness 4805, 5643, 12757
O For A Muse of Fire 4806
O from what Power hast Thou this Powerful Might 20532
O Gentle Sleep 4646, 4684
"O God of Battles" 4808
O happy fair! 10366, 10369, 10371, 10372, 10374

O Happy Fair, or The Load-Stars 10370, 10373
O happy, happy fair 10369
O Heart Heavy Heart 16548, 16569
O Heart, O heart, O heavy heart! 16568
"O heavy heart" 16567
O! how much more doth beauty 19766
O how should I your true love know? 3783
O lásce 20317
O Let Me Play The Fool 8486
O ma maîtresse 17958
O Me! What Eyes Hath Love Put in My Head 20520
O meisje mijn 16820
O meisjes, zucht niet . . . 11410
O Mistress Mine 16627, 16637, 16697, 16745, 16746, 16815, 16965, 17007, 17008, 17062, 17102, 17117, 17245, 17246, 17749, 17750, 17751, 17752, 17753, 17754, 17756, 17758, 17759, 17760, 17762, 17763, 17764, 17765, 17767, 17768, 17769, 17770, 17772, 17773, 17774, 17775, 17776, 17780, 17781, 17782, 17786, 17787, 17788, 17790, 17791, 17793, 17796, 17797, 17798, 17799, 17800, 17802, 17804, 17805, 17806, 17807, 17808, 17809, 17810, 17811, 17812, 17813, 17814, 17817, 17818, 17820, 17821, 17822, 17823, 17824, 17825, 17827, 17828, 17829, 17830, 17831, 17833, 17834, 17835, 17836, 17837, 17838, 17840, 17841, 17846, 17847, 17848, 17850, 17851, 17852, 17853, 17855, 17857, 17860, 17861, 17863, 17865, 17869, 17870, 17873, 17876, 17877, 17878, 17881, 17882, 17883, 17884, 17885, 17886, 17887, 17888, 17889, 17890, 17891, 17892, 17893, 17894, 17895, 17896, 17897, 17899, 17900, 17901, 17902, 17904, 17906, 17907, 17909, 17911, 17912, 17913, 17915, 17918, 17919, 17922, 17923, 17924, 17926, 17927, 17929, 17930, 17931, 17934, 17935, 17937, 17939, 17940, 17941, 17943, 17944, 17945, 17948, 17949, 17950, 17951, 17952, 17953, 17954, 17955, 17956, 17959, 17961, 17963, 17964, 17965, 17966, 17967, 17970, 17971, 17972, 17973, 17974, 17975, 17978, 17979, 17983, 17984, 17985, 17986, 17988, 17989, 17991, 17992, 17993, 17994, 17997, 17998, 17999, 18000, 18001, 18002, 18004, 18005, 18006, 18007, 18008 18010, 18012, 18013, 18014, 18015, 18016, 18017, 18020, 18021, 18022, 18024, 18025, 18027, 18028, 18029, 18030, 18031, 18032, 18034, 18035, 18036, 18037, 18038, 18039, 18040, 18042, 18043, 18044,

18046, 18048, 18049, 18050, 18052,
18054, 18055, 18058, 18059, 18060,
18062, 18246, 18269, 18283, 21142
["O Mistress Mine"] 17908
O Mistress Mine (Clown's Song) 17981
O Mistress Mine (from Twelfth Night) 17864
O Mistress Mine[.] Jester's Song from
Shakespeare's "Twel[f]th Night" 17761
O Mistress Mine (NOT a song of good life)
17784
O mistress mine, where are you roaming?
17771, 17839, 17843, 17845, 17856,
17969, 17976, 17995, 18018
[O mistress mine, where are you roaming?]
17778, 17779, 17789, 17794, 17801,
17826, 17849, 17859, 17862, 17868,
17903, 17920, 17928, 17946, 17947,
17960, 17977, 17996, 18057
O Mistresse myne 17758
O Mistris Myne 17758
O My America 16205
O never say that I was false of heart 20277,
20281, 20282, 20285
O Note So Dear 6414
O O O O That Shakespeherian Rag 6159, 6450,
6585, 10531, 15976
O! Orlando 950
O Pardon Me 5490
"'O, prikhodi, moia smert'. . ." (Pesnia shuta)'
['O, come, my death . . .' (Song of the Fool)]
16961
O Proserpina 19028
O Schatz, auf welchen Wegen 17932
O sleep, O gentle sleep 4647
O smrti 19824
O take those lips away 7931
O, the twelfth day of December 16697
O 'Tis A Glorious Sight To See, An Admired
Scena, from Weber's Opera Of Oberon 10870
O Wall 10651
O Weary Night 9918
O, Willow, Willow 12264
Oberon 10589, 10638, 10742, 10807, 10809,
10812, 10816, 10819, 10829, 10837,
10841, 10847, 10850, 10853, 10854,
10869, 10871, 10873, 10877, 10878,
10881, 10891, 10892, 10940
Obéron 10826, 10885, 10967
Oberon & Titania 10658
Oberon de Ch. M. de Weber 10861
Oberon (de Weber) 10887
Oberon Duet 10849
Oberon[,] Fantaisie on Admired Airs 10894
Oberon, Fantaisie sur l'Opéra de C. M. von
Weber 10810
Oberon flowersqueezing [sic] song 10472
Oberon, grand duo sur l'opéra de Weber
10825

Oberon[:] Grande Fantasia Brillante
(Containing The Most Favorite Airs)
10897
Oberon[,] König der Elfen 10864, 10899
[Oberon, König der Elfen] 10803
Oberon[:] Les Nymphes de la Mer 10872
Oberon[,] Opéra de Weber 10830
Oberon, or the Elf king's oath 10807
Oberon Overture 10828, 10889
Oberon Polkas 10794
Oberon Quadrille 10896
Oberon, Quadrille Brillant, sur l'Opéra de C. M.
von Weber 10852
Oberon[,] Roi des Elfes 10803
Oberon, The Enchanter 10982
Oberon—Ouvertüre 10840
Oberon's Court. or Songs of the Fairies 10787
Oberon's Festival 10969
Oberon's Song 10339, 10461, 10463
Obertura para el Rey Lear 6101
October 20174
Ode to Music 8464
Ode to Rosalind 1875
Ode to Shakespeare 19314, 19449, 19473,
20829, 21082
[Ode to Shakespeare] 21010
Ode to the Memory of Shakespeare 21010
'Odinochestvo Gamleta' [Hamlet's Solitude]
3384
O'er Hill and Dale 1911
Of Love and Time (Ren-ai To Toki Ni Tsuite)
19269, 19313, 19448, 19626
Of Love: Songs from Shakespeare 7968, 15741,
18004
Of Three Shakespeare Sonnets 19306, 19517,
19849
Ofelia 4217
Ofelia's [sic] Songs from 'Hamlet' 3133
Ofelias vise 4220
"Oh! Bid your faithful Ariel fly" 15116
Oh, Brother! 2239
[Oh, Death, his face my shroud hath hid]
21273
Oh! for my beads 2246
Oh Happy Bride 2836, 10773
Oh, happy fair 10367
Oh! How Much More Doth Beauty Beauteous
Seem 19765
"Oh How Much More Doth Beauty Beauteous
Seeme" 19770
Oh, how the Spring of Love 18470
Oh, It Is Pleasant To Float, The Celebrated
Barcarolle, from Weber's Oberon 10831
Oh Mighty Caesar 5489
Oh Mistress Mine 17854, 17914, 17968,
17980, 18019, 18047, 18051
Oh! Mistress Mine[:] The Clown's Song 17936
Oh Mistress Mine Where Are You Roaming?
17755

Oh! Never Say That I Was False of Heart
    20276, 20280, 20286
"Oh! Pluck not yet those spring flowers rare."
    Ophelia's Song 3628
Oh, Sir John 9009
Oh That This Too, Too Solid Flesh Would Melt
    3808
Oh The Green Willow! 12306
Oh Thou my lovely boy 20372
Oh! willow, willow, willow! 12252
Oko za oko 7654
[Oko za oko = Measure for Measure] 7615, 7752
Old English Composers 10243
Old English Songs 1454, 11542
Old English Songs, amorous, festive & divine
    8019
Old English Tunes 3949
Old Folks At Home 4273
Old Song 17473
Old Tunes for Young Fiddlers 1464
Olivia 18208, 18215, 18227, 18236, 18237,
    18243, 18250, 18343
Olivia Theme 17277
['Olivia' Theme] 16817
Olivia's Song 18331
Oluja 15491
[Oluja = The Tempest] 15250, 15341
Ombre d'Hamlet 4193
Omkring Hamlet 3604
On a day 6360, 6363, 6367, 6668, 20685,
    20742
On A Day, Alack The Day 20672, 20681,
    20686, 20713
On a day—alack the day! 6357, 6358, 6362,
    6366, 6368, 6370, 6371
On Cloe Sleeping, taken from Shakespear 20781
On Music 12755
On the Ground 9289, 10094, 10378
On Time—On Age 19288, 19309
Once upon a crime 7543
One Hand, One Heart from "West Side Story"
    13617, 13618
One hundred lyrics and lyrical passages from
    the plays and poems of William Shakespeare
    21362
One Hundred Songs of England 17759
One More Gaudy Night 266
One world; or, A midsummer night's dream
    10167
Opéra de Verdi[:] Macbeth 7331, 7332
Ophelia 1998, 3567, 3574, 3600, 3753, 3886,
    3905, 3906, 3911, 3925, 3927, 3945,
    3957, 3963, 3999, 4000, 4005, 4006,
    4007, 4014, 4033, 4057, 4083, 4184,
    4197, 4214, 4235, 4248, 4253, 4267, 4290
[Ophelia] 4095, 4109
Ophélia 3894, 3914, 3919, 3923, 3924, 3943,
    3948, 3972, 3975, 4020, 4024, 4039,
    4209, 4210, 4223, 4258, 4279, 4291

Ophelia Dances 3970
Ophelia. In Hamlet 5. Aufzug, 6. Auftritt 3551
Ophelia March 3300
Ophelia Polka 3903
Ophelia. Reverie 3947
Ophelia (Shakespearian Portraits) 3988
Ophelia Sings 3749, 3832, 3864
Ophelia singt 4043
Ophelia (Songs for Soprano and Orchestra after
    Arthur Rimbaud) 4197
Ophelia Valse 4055
Ophelia (Vision Triste) 4049
Ophelia Waltzes 4056
Ophelia Will Fool You 4282
Ophelia-Fragmente 4226
Ophelia-Lieder 3708
Ophelia-no-Uta [Ophelia Songs] 4078
Ophelia's Air 4266
Ophelia's Airs in Hamlet 4080
Ophelia's Airs in Shakspeare's Play of Hamlet
    3322
Ophelia's Dream I 4067
Ophelia's Dream II 4067
Ophelia's funeral march 3425
Ophelia's Lament 4082
Ophelia's Lieder 2970
Ophelia's mad scene 4077
Ophelia['s] Mad Scene 3527
Ophelia's Mad Song 3759, 4062
Ophelia's madness 3689
Ophelia's Prayer 4009
Ophelia's Song 3696, 3763, 3768, 3770,
    3778, 3784, 3993, 4199
Ophelia's song on the death of her father 3841
Ophelia's Songs 3174, 3706, 3761, 3835,
    3868, 3998
Ophelia's Songs from Hamlet 3998
Ophelia's Songs sung by Mrs. Jordan in Hamlet
    2919
Ophelia's Waltz 4018
Ophélie 3898, 3922, 3960, 3974, 4051, 4194,
    4202, 4260, 4275
[Ophélie] 4103, 4244
[Ophélie. Valse, composée sur les motifs
    d'Hamlet d'Ambroise Thomas] 3631
[Opowieść zimowa = The Winter's Tale]
    18856, 18900, 18901, 18908
Opposites 20683
Orchestersuite zu 'Der Sturm' 16049
Orchester-Vorspiel zu Shakespeare's 'Macbeth'
    7471
Orchester-Vorspiel zu Shakespeare's 'Othello'
    12421
Orchester-Vorspiel zu Shak[e]speare's 'Romeo
    und Julia' 13952
Orchester-Vorspiel zu Shakespeare's 'Sturm'
    16095
Orchestra Studies for Bassoon; From the Works
    of Peter I. Tchaikovsky 13998

[Orchestral Scenes for 'The Tempest'] 16019
Ordo modalis 20784, 20842
"Orfeus med sin lutas klang" ur "Henrick VIII" 5172
Original Music of Desdemona's Song in Othello 12270
Original music to 'Dream Fantasy'—a reworking of 'Midsummer Nights [sic] Dream' 9971
Orpheus 5048, 5061, 5070, 5071, 5072, 5084, 5100, 5105, 5127, 5128, 5130, 5142, 5205, 5217
Orpheus and his lute 5043
Orpheus Britannicus . . . 10180, 10190
Orpheus Britannicus . . . The Second Book . . . 7525, 10180, 16338
Orpheus en sy luit 5120
Orpheus' Laute 5122
Orpheus (Lucius' Song) 5230
Orpheus Music 5113
Orpheus sang. Aus Shakespeares Heinrich VIII 5158
Orpheus sjöng vid lutans toner 5132
Orpheus with his lute 4971, 4972, 4973, 4977, 4985, 4993, 5000, 5005, 5007, 5013, 5015, 5034, 5042, 5044, 5046, 5047, 5049, 5050, 5051, 5052, 5053, 5054, 5055, 5057, 5059, 5064, 5067, 5074, 5075, 5076, 5077, 5079, 5081, 5083, 5085, 5086, 5090, 5091, 5092, 5094, 5095, 5096, 5098, 5099, 5101, 5103, 5104, 5105, 5107, 5109, 5110, 5111, 5112, 5114, 5115, 5116, 5117, 5118, 5119, 5120, 5121, 5126, 5129, 5131, 5133, 5134, 5136, 5137, 5139, 5144, 5145, 5146, 5147, 5148, 5149, 5150, 5151, 5152, 5153, 5154, 5155, 5157, 5159, 5160, 5161, 5163, 5164, 5165, 5166, 5169, 5170, 5171, 5173, 5174, 5175, 5176, 5177, 5178, 5179, 5180, 5181, 5182, 5183, 5184, 5185, 5186, 5188, 5189, 5191, 5193, 5194, 5195, 5196, 5197, 5198, 5199, 5200, 5203, 5204, 5206, 5207, 5208
[Orpheus with his Lute] 4970
Orpheus With His Lute[.] From the music to "Henry VIII" 4979
Orpheus with his lute made trees 5058, 5162, 5190, 5235
[Orpheus with his lute made trees] 5068, 5082, 5141
Ostragobolus 18930
O.T. 12482
Otello 11668, 11705, 11706, 11875, 11885, 11914, 12017, 12022, 12030, 12038, 12056, 12057, 12077, 12081, 12083, 12088, 12116, 12138, 12142, 12152, 12162, 12180, 12184, 12185, 12377, 12385, 12393, 12408, 12409

[Otello] 11654, 11662, 11667, 11673, 11690, 11693, 11700, 11710, 11723, 11726, 11729, 11735, 11744, 11745, 11751, 11764, 11767, 11771, 11772, 11774, 11777, 11803, 11805, 11809, 11810, 11811, 11817, 11818, 11820, 11823, 11825, 11826, 11837, 11839, 11843, 11849, 11850, 11857, 11863, 11874, 11897, 11900, 11903, 11905, 11925, 11934, 11935, 11936, 11945, 11948, 11949, 11960, 11966, 11968, 11972, 11981, 11982, 11983, 11985, 11988, 11991, 12009, 12079, 12099, 12100, 12101, 12195
Otello: A Favourite Overture by Rossini 12123
Otello. 'Ah! Si Per Voi' 12078
Otello. (Ave Maria.) 12197
Otello De Rossini 12067, 12113, 12129
Otello di G. Verdi 12182, 12186, 12187
Otello di Rossini 12073
Otello, Elisabetta et Barbier 12105
Otello et autres Pièces 12106
Otello. Grand Selection 12192
Otello i Desdemona [Othello and Desdemona] 12029
[Otello, il moro di Venezia] 11920
Otello: Il Morodi di Valenzia 12471
Otello[:] Muzyka k fil'mu po tragedii Shekspira [Othello: Music to the Film after the Tragedy of Shakespeare] 11811
Otello (Opéra De Rossini) 12050, 12051, 12102, 12154
Otello; ossia, L'Africano in Venezia 12038
Otello ou Le More de Venise 12038
Otello. Tragicheskaia poema po V. Shekspiru [Othello. Tragic Poem after W. Shakespeare] 12028
Otello y Desdemona 12483
Otello. . . . Catiello l'Africano 12174
Otello-Tamburo 12478
Otelo 11783
[Otelo] 11888, 11990, 12015
Othellerl. Der Mohr von Wien 12456
Othello 11663, 11664, 11677, 11679, 11680, 11681, 11683, 11694, 11695, 11703, 11709, 11713, 11716, 11718, 11721, 11732, 11734, 11741, 11748, 11761, 11762, 11766, 11768, 11789, 11838, 11842, 11848, 11852, 11861, 11867, 11869, 11873, 11901, 11909, 11912, 11929, 11961, 11962, 11963, 11964, 11965, 11973, 11975, 12008, 12013, 12023, 12025, 12166, 12188, 12189, 12379, 12383, 12394, 12395, 12396, 12400, 12406, 12424, 12425, 12426, 12427, 12431, 12434, 12490, 12492, 12498, 12503, 12504, 12510, 19774
[Othello] 11653, 11655, 11656, 11659, 11660, 11665, 11666, 11669, 11670,

[Othello] (*cont.*)
 11671, 11672, 11675, 11676, 11678,
 11684, 11685, 11686, 11687, 11688,
 11689, 11692, 11696, 11698, 11699,
 11702, 11707, 11708, 11712, 11715,
 11722, 11724, 11725, 11727, 11728,
 11731, 11736, 11737, 11739, 11740,
 11742, 11743, 11746, 11749, 11750,
 11752, 11753, 11755, 11756, 11757,
 11758, 11759, 11760, 11770, 11773,
 11775, 11776, 11782, 11784, 11787,
 11788, 11790, 11791, 11792, 11793,
 11795, 11796, 11797, 11799, 11800,
 11801, 11802, 11804, 11806, 11808,
 11819, 11821, 11822, 11827, 11829,
 11830, 11831, 11833, 11834, 11840,
 11841, 11844, 11845, 11846, 11847,
 11851, 11853, 11854, 11855, 11856,
 11858, 11859, 11860, 11865, 11866,
 11868, 11870, 11871, 11876, 11877,
 11878, 11879, 11880, 11881, 11882,
 11883, 11886, 11887, 11889, 11890,
 11891, 11892, 11893, 11894, 11895,
 11898, 11899, 11902, 11904, 11906,
 11907, 11908, 11911, 11913, 11916,
 11918, 11919, 11921, 11922, 11923,
 11924, 11926, 11928, 11930, 11932,
 11933, 11937, 11939, 11940, 11942,
 11947, 11950, 11951, 11954, 11955,
 11956, 11957, 11959, 11967, 11969,
 11970, 11977, 11978, 11979, 11980,
 11984, 11987, 11989, 11992, 11993,
 11994, 11995, 11996, 11997, 11999,
 12000, 12002, 12005, 12007, 12010,
 12011, 12179, 12384, 12392, 12407,
 12411, 12418
Othello & Desdémone 12500
Othello (A Symphonic Portrait in Five Scenes
 after Shakespeare) 12422
Othello[:] A Tragedy in Three Spasms and a
 Final Kick 12494
Othello and Desdemona 12027
Othello Ballet Suite 12172
Othello (de Rossini.) 12041, 12045, 12062
[Othello, der Mohr in Wien] 12464, 12465
Othello der Mohr von Venedig 11862
Othello. Entreacte No. 3 11993
'Othello' Fantaisie 12202
Othello[:] Fantasia on Rossini's Opera 12161
Othello[:] Incidental Music to Glen Byam
 Shaw's 1956 Production 11794
Othello Mesél 12176
Othello, Mohr von Venedig[,] Oper von Rossini
 12070
Othello, Moren i Venedig 11917
'Othello' oder 'Der Mord war nicht nötig'
 12453, 12477
Othello og narren 12451
Othello[,] Opéra de Rossini 12112

[Othello ou le More de Venise] 12210
Othello, Ouverture 12075, 12139
Othello Overture 12401
"Othello" Prière 12047
'Othello' Showcase 12199
Othello Story 12211
'Othello' Suite 11720
Othello. The Moor 12402
Othello und Desdemona 12027
Othello[.] 1er acte[.] Pas de Deux 12043
Othello-Fantasie 12128
Othello—Romanze der Desdemona 12063
Othello-Suite 11747
Othelo 11682
Otto Nicolai's Falstaff or The Merry Wives of
 Windsor Quadrille 9024
Otto Nicolai's Falstaff or The Merry Wives of
 Windsor Valse 9025
Où butine l'abeille je butine aussi 15035
Our Beauties Are Not Ours 19055
Our Love was New 20227
Our Love was young 20227
Our Minutes Hasten To Their End 19844
Our revels 15825
Our Revels Now Are Ended 15826, 16204
Out, Damned Spot 7499
Out of Town 9759
Ouverture à grand Orchestre de la Tragédie:
 Macbeth 7165
Ouverture à grand orchestre de l'opéra: Die
 Geister-Insel 15415
Ouverture à grand Orchestre sur le sujet
 d'Othello 12438
Ouverture à la tragédie de Shakespeare 'Roméo
 et Juliette' 13974
Ouverture aus dem Schauspiele William
 Shakespeare 20860
[Ouvertüre aus Shakespeares
 'Sommernachtstraum'] 9742
Ouverture 'Cymbeline' 2811
Ouverture d'Antoine et Cléopâtre d'Après la
 Tragédie de Shakespeare 313
Ouverture de Coriolan 2403
Ouverture de la tragédie 'Antonius et
 Cléopâtre' [*sic*] de Shakespeare 324
Ouverture de la Tragédie: Macbeth 7165
Ouverture de l'Opéra: Montano et Stéphanie de
 H. Berton 11622
Ouverture de L'opéra Oberon de C. M. de
 Weber 10862
Ouverture de l'Opéra Titania 10152
Ouverture de Montano et Stéphanie (Op: de
 Berton) 11621
Ouverture de Othello 12403
Ouverture del dramma Un Sogno d'una notte
 d'estate 9765
Ouverture des Joyeuses Commères de Windsor
 9216

Ouverture D'Hamlet[,] Tragédie de Shakespeare 3994

Ouvertüre[:] Die lustigen Weiber von Windsor 9068

Ouverture d'Oberon 10886

Ouverture D'Oberon de Weber 10828

Ouverture D'Othello. (Rossini) 12095

Ouverture, Driekoningenavond 18256

Ouverture du Roi Lear 6063

[Ouverture du 'Roi Lear'] 6095

[Ouvertüre: Ein Sommernachtstraum] 9727

Ouverture et Douze favorites et brillantes Pièces de l'Opéra 'Macbeth' 7256

Ouverture för stor orkester till W. Shakespeares Antonius och Cleopatra 321

Ouverture for Trumpets (aus "The Fairy Queen") [sic] 10186

Ouvertüre für Orchester zu W. Shakespeare's Tragödie 'König Lear' 5668

Ouverture héroïque et Marche des Impériaux de la Tragédie 'Jules César' de Shakspeare 5452

Ouvertüre in C-dur zu Shakespeares 'Komödie der Irrungen' 2252

Ouvertüre Julius Cäsar 5527

Ouverture, King John 5650

Ouverture, les Joyeuses Commères de Windsor 9216

Ouvertüre: Midsummer Night's Dream 9844

Ouvertüre Nr. 5 für Orchester, zum Trauerspiel 'Julius Caesar' von Shakespeare 5508

[Ouvertüre Othello] 12136, 12137

Ouverture per 'Il racconto d'inverno' ('The Winter's Tale') 19102

Ouverture per la commedia 'Pene d'amor perdute' di Shakespeare 6661

Ouverture Portia 8691

Ouverture pour la comédie 'Beaucoup de bruit pour rien' de Shakespeare 11145

Ouverture pour la Tempête 16003

Ouverture pour la tragédie 'Macbeth' de Shakespeare 6917

[Ouverture pour la Tragédie: Roméo et Juliette] 13919

Ouverture til et romantisk lystspill av Shakespeare 21149

Ouverture til Shakespeare's Othello 12430

Ouverture til the Tempest 16158

Ouverture till Shakespeare's 'Antonius och Cleopatra' 320

Ouvertüre und sämtliche Muzik zu 'Hamlet' von Shakespeare 3144

Ouvertüre und Zwischenakts-Musik zu Shakespeare's 'Romeo und Julia' 13218

Ouverture voor Driekoningenavond 18252

Ouverture voor Shakespeare's Blijspel: 'De getemde Feeks' 14673

Ouvertüre zu dem Schauspiel 'Richard III' 13000

Ouvertüre zu den Lustigen Weibern von Windsor 9233

Ouvertüre zu der Oper Romeo und Julie 13822

Ouvertüre zu Die lustigen Weiber von Windsor 9076

[Ouvertüre zu Die Zähmung der Widerspenstigen] 14425

Ouvertüre zu einem Lustspiel von Shakespeare 21170

Ouvertüre zu einem Trauerspiel 13884

Ouvertüre zu Hamlet 3896, 3961, 4035

[Ouvertüre zu Hamlet] 4025

[Ouvertüre zu Hamlet von Joseph Joachim] 3962

Ouvertüre zu König Lear 5999, 6065, 6105

Ouvertüre zu Macbeth 6888, 7418, 7476

[Ouvertüre zu Macbeth] 6812, 7463

Ouvertüre zu Macbeth nebst der ersten Szene der drey Hexen 6739

Ouvertüre zu Shakespeares 'Der Sturm' 15352

Ouvertüre zu Shakespeare's Die beiden Veroneser 18647

Ouvertüre zu Shakespeares Hamlet 4053

Ouvertüre zu Shakespeares Heinrich IV 4480, 4655

Ouvertüre zu Shakespeare's Heinrich IV von Joseph Joachim 4481, 4656

Ouvertüre zu Shakespeare's König Johann 5648

Ouvertüre zu Shakespeares 'König Lear' 6106

Ouvertüre zu Shakespeares Lustspiel Die lustigen Weiber von Windsor 9233, 9234

Ouvertüre zu Shakespeares Macbeth 7491

Ouvertüre zu Shakespeare's Othello 12435

[Ouvertüre zu Shakespeares 'Othello'] 12419

Ouvertüre zu Shakespeares Richard III 13059, 13061, 13062

Ouvertüre zu Shakespeare's Romeo und Julia 13958

Ouvertüre zu Shakespeares Schauspiel Der Kaufmann von Venedig 8358

Ouvertüre zu Shakespeare's Sommernachtstraum 9618, 9712, 9720, 9810, 9854

[Ouvertüre zu Shakespeares Sommernachtstraum] 9629, 9771

Ouvertüre zu Shakespeare's Sturm 16107, 16139

Ouvertüre zu Shakespeare's 'Timon von Athen' 16378, 16380

Ouvertüre zu Shakespeares 'Wie es Euch gefällt' 913

[Ouvertüre zu Shakespeares 'Wie es Euch gefällt'] 916

Ouvertüre zu Shakespeare's 'Wintermärchen' 19112

[Ouvertüre zu Shakespeares 'Wintermärchen'] 19105

Ouvertüre zu Shakespeare's 'Zähmung der
    Widerspänstigen' 14666
Ouvertüre zu Shakspeare's Julius Cäsar 5520,
    5521, 5522
Ouvertüre zu Shakspeare's 'Zähmung der
    Widerspänstigen' 14666
Ouvertüre zu Sommernachtstraum 9647
Ouvertüre zu 'Was ihr wollt' 18214
Ouvertüre zum Sommernachtstraum 9710
Ouvertüre zum Trauerspiel Hamlet 4027
Ouvertüre zum Trauerspiel 'Othello' 12423
Ouvertüre zur komischen Oper: 'Der
    Widerspänstigen Zähmung' 14579
Ouvertüre zur Oper: Die lustigen Weiber von
    Windsor 9069, 9115
Ouvertüre zur Oper: Macbeth 7254
[Ouvertüre zur Oper: 'Was ihr wollt'] 18223
Ouvertüre-Macbeth 7263
Ouvertures per il Teatro di Shakespeare[:] N. 3-
    'Il Mercante di Venezia' 8690
Ouvertures per il Teatro di Shakespeare[:] N. 4
    'Giulio Cesare' 5498
Ouvertures per il Teatro di Shakespeare[:] N. 5
    'Il Racconto d'Inverno' 19102
Ouvertures per il Teatro di Shakespeare[:] No.
    2-'La Dodicesima Notte' 18210
Ouvertures per il teatro di Shakespeare[:] N.1.
    'La Bisbetica Domata' 14654
Over hill, Over dale 1006, 1277, 6518, 9363,
    9364, 9365, 9371, 9471, 9862, 9926,
    9961, 9999, 10384, 10386, 10387, 10388,
    10389 10390, 10393, 10394, 10396,
    10397, 10398, 10399, 10404, 10405,
    10407, 10408, 10409, 10410, 10414,
    10417, 10422, 10423, 10424, 10425,
    10426, 10482, 10588, 10643, 10799,
    10951, 15631, 17469
[Over hill, over dale] 9359
Over Hill, Over Dale, A Fairy Glee 10391
Over Hill, Over Dale[.] Fairy Song 10412
Over hill, over dale, Song in Shakspere's
    Midsummer Night's Dream 9362
Overtura Alla Tragedia Giulio Cesare di
    Shakespeare 5504
Overture 2400, 7228, 8227, 8309, 8313,
    10243, 10992, 14290, 14307, 16236,
    17084, 18695, 18763, 21121
[Overture] 9774
Overture & Entr'acts to Macbeth 6882
Overture & Operatic Marches in the Grand
    Burlesque The Magic Horn 10856
[Overture, A Winter's Tale] 19095
Overture after Shakespeare's 'Much Ado About
    Nothing' 11604
Overture and Incidental Music 7183
Overture and Incidental Music to Cymbeline
    2463
[Overture and Incidental Music to Shakspere's
    Henry IV] 4414

Overture and Incidental Music to The Tempest
    15205
Overture and Music Cues to King Lear 5799
Overture and Music Cues to Twelfth Night
    16931
Overture and Music Incidental to Shakspere's
    Play of King Henry the Eighth as performed
    at The Royal Princesses Theatre 4993
[Overture and Music to Katherine & Petruccio]
    14263
Overture and Songs[:] Shakespeare's 'The
    Tempest' 14985
Overture[:] Antony & Cleopatra 337
Overture[:] Beatrice and Benedict 11357
Overture for 'A Midsummer Night's Dream'
    10592
Overture from the Music to Henry VIII 4977
Overture 'Hamlet' 3327
Overture in D major 10195
Overture in Mr. P. Opera 15218
Overture in The Moor of Venice 11835
Overture 'King Henry V' 4693, 4826
Overture 'Macbeth' 7413, 7454, 7473
Overture. 'Merry Wives of Windsor' 9112
Overture 'Midsummer Night's Dream' 9694
Overture (Much Ado about Nothing) 11598
[Overture No. 2: 'Cymbeline'] 2812
Overture 'Oberon' 10875
Overture. Otello 12089
Overture. Othello 12134
[Overture, 'Othello'] 12391
Overture, Richard III 12850
Overture 'Romeo and Juliet' 13510
Overture[,] selected chiefly from the airs in
    Shakspeare's Plays 1954, 4085, 7510,
    16179, 18266, 19136
Overture: Strike Up The Bard 21169
Overture[:] Taming Of The Shrew 14582
[Overture 'The Comedy of Errors'] 2139
Overture, 'The Globe Playhouse' from the Suite
    From Henry V 4783
Overture (The Tempest) 14749
Overture[:] Titus Andronicus 16425
Overture to A Midsummer Night's Dream
    9684, 9733, 9753
[Overture to A Midsummer Night's Dream]
    9708
Overture To A Shakespeare Comedy 14473
Overture to a Shakespearean Drama 21110
Overture [to Act IV] 8074
Overture to Ambroise Thomas's Le Songe d'une
    nuit d'Été (Midsummer Night's Dream)
    20965
Overture to 'Anthony and Cleopatra' 312
Overture to 'As you like it' 550, 1868, 1879,
    1899
[Overture to 'As You Like It'] 1920
Overture to 'Hamlet' 3002, 3069
Overture to King John 5599, 5645

Overture to King Lear 6063
Overture to Macbeth 7434
Overture to Mendelssohn's Midsummer Night's Dream 9677
Overture To Merry Wives Of Windsor 9088
[Overture to 'Miranda'] 15996
Overture to 'Much Ado About Nothing' 11596
Overture to Nicolai's Merry Wives of Windsor 9046
Overture to 'Othello' 12103
Overture to 'Richard III' 12848
Overture to Romeo and Juliet 13934
Overture to Shakespeare's 'As You Like It' 1917
Overture to Shakespeare's Comedy, As You Like It 1904
Overture to Shakespeare's Comedy Twelfth Night 18235
[Overture to Shakespeare's Julius Caesar] 5532
[Overture to Shakespeare's 'King Lear'] 6051
Overture to Shakespeare's 'Macbeth' 6796, 7437, 7465
Overture to Shakespeare's Macbeth[,] composed as an introduction to the celebrated Witch Music attached to that tragedy 7077
Overture to Shakespeare's Midsummernight's dream 9618
Overture to Shakespeare's play The Tempest 16001
Overture to Shakespeare's Richard III 12847
Overture to Shakespeare's 'The Taming of the Shrew' 14234
Overture to Shakespeare's 'The Tempest' 16093
Overture to Shakespeare's Tragedy, Macbeth 7459
Overture to Shakespeare's Tragedy Richard III 12849
Overture to Shakespeare's Twelfth Night 18213
Overture to Shakespear's Play 'Antony & Cleopatra' 322
Overture to Shakespear's Play Cymbeline 2824
Overture to Shakspeare's Merchant of Venice 8698
Overture to Shakspeare's Romeo & Juliet 13934
Overture to 'Taming of the Shrew' 14320
Overture to The Tempest 14957, 16027, 16090
Overture to 'The Tragedy of Coriolanus' 2380
Overture to 'Twelfth Night' 17356
Overture to Weber's Celebrated Opera Oberon 10838
Overture to 'West Side Story' 13605
Overture 'Twelfth Night' 18220
Overture: Yorick 3908
Overtüre zu Shakespeares 'Cymbeline' 2827

Overtüre zum Sommernachtstraum 9778
Overture—'As You Like It' 811
[Overture—'As You Like It'] 494
Overture—Hamlet 3992
Overture—'Macbeth' 6883, 7459
Overture—'Othello' 12004
Overture—Prologue From the Opera 'Romeo and Juliet' 13736
Owls, Pussycats, Cabbages, and Kings: Musical Growth Through Modern Songs and Serial Piano Pieces 1300, 1633, 6645, 10446
Oxford Blues 21148
Oxlips & Crown Imperial 19108
Oxlips and Violets 10333

P

[Paano Man ang Ibig = As You Like It] 657
Pagenlied 1520, 1521, 1936
Pagenlied aus der Musik zu Shakespeare's 'Wie es Euch gefällt' 913, 914
Pagernes Sang af "As you like it" 1533
[Paljon melua tyhjästä = Much Ado About Nothing] 11335
[Palju kära ei millestki = Much Ado About Nothing] 11150
Pandarus Sings 16564
Pandarus Sings (higher) 16564
Pandarus' Song 16545
[Pangarap sa Isang Gabi ng Gitnang Tag-Araw = A Midsummer Night's Dream] 9526
[Panic Button] 14046
Pan's Anniversary, or the Shepherd's Holyday 20981
Pansies 3952, 4240
Pantalon 3887
Pantomime 3996
[Pantomime zu Hamlet] 3151
Par les bois 21196
Pardon, Goddess 11385
Pardon, goddess of the night 11042, 11097, 11104, 11128, 11135, 11214, 11224, 11287, 11384, 11387, 11388, 11389
[Pardon, Goddess of the night] 11219, 11386
Pardon Goddess of the Night[,] Dirge from Shakspeare's "Much ado about nothing" 11071
Parting 13837
. . . . Parting is such sweet sorrow 13857
Partitura del Hamlet 2988
Partituret til William Shakpear 20860
Passacaglia[:] 'Death of Falstaff' 4780
Passamezzo and Saltarello: Richard II 12749
Passionate Pilgrim. VIII 20723
Pastoral 1639
Pastoral Symphony 9262
Pastorale 20134

Pateticheskaia uvertiura 'Iulii Tsezar''
[Pathetic Overture 'Julius Caesar'] 5529
Patterns for Close-Harmony 3730
Pavane from Romeo and Juliet 13228
Pavane-Fantasia 19244
Pavanne: Anne Bullen 5036
Peace Lives Again 13043
Peasblossom 10635
Péchés de vieillesse 14176
Pedlar's Song 19075, 19076, 21061
Peg-a-Ramsay 16697
Peines d'Amour Perdues 6322, 6675
[Peines d'amour perdues] 6196, 6208, 6230,
6278, 6305
['Pejlingar' = 'Bearings'] 20866
Pelissier's Columbian Melodies 15196
Pene d'amore perdute 6201
[Pene d'amore perdute] 6275
Pensées 3855
2 Pensées caractéristiques 3945, 16042
People Are Saying 21009
Per la recuperata salute di Ophelia 4283
Perchance to Dream 4171
Perdita 18938, 18942, 19100, 19103, 19114,
19116, 19121
Perdita oder ein Wintermärchen 18926
[Perdita or The Royal Milkmaid] 19140
Perdita's Song[,] "The nest of the Dove is
rifled" 19145
Perfection 21026
[Pericle] 12560
[Pericle, Principe de Tiro] 12581
[Pericle principe di Tiro] 12541
Pericle re di Tiro 12601
Pericles 12544, 12550, 12551, 12555, 12556,
12562, 12563, 12564, 12567, 12576,
12585, 12595, 12598, 12599, 12600,
12603, 12604, 12606, 12608, 12611
[Pericles] 12540, 12542, 12543, 12548,
12549, 12552, 12553, 12554, 12557,
12558, 12565, 12568, 12569, 12574,
12575, 12578, 12579, 12580, 12582,
12583, 12584, 12586, 12587, 12593,
12594
[Périclès, Prince de Tyr] 12547
Pericles Prince of Tyre 12596, 12602
[Perikles] 12546, 12590, 12591, 12597
[Perikles, Fürst von Tyrus] 12570, 12589
[Perikles von Tyrus] 12571, 12592
Perles Enfantines 20975
Perles Mélodiques 20976
Perles musicales 9653
5 pesen na sl. R. Bernsa i U. Shekspira [5 Songs
to the Words of R. Burns and W.
Shakespeare] 17990, 21234
'Pesenka Dzhul'etty: Iz muzyki k spektakliu
"Romeo i Dzhul'etta"' [Juliet's Song: From
the Music to the Play Romeo and Juliet]
13389

'Pesenka o korole Stefane' [Little Song of King
Stephen] 12242
'Pesn' Iago. K tragedii Shekspira "Otello"'
[Iago's Song. From Shakespeare's Tragedy
Othello] 11949
'Pesn' Oberona' [Oberon's Song] 10303
'Pesn' Ofelii' [Ophelia's Song] 3502
'Pesn' shuta iz komedii V. Shekspira
"Dvenadtsataia noch'"' [Song of the Fool
from Shakespeare's Comedy Twelfth Night]
18118
Pesni iz muzyki k komedii V. Shekspira
'Dvenadtsataia noch' ili Kak vam ugodno'
[Songs from the Music to W. Shakespeare's
Comedy Twelfth Night, or What You Will]
16961
Pesni iz muzyki k spektakliu 'Vindzorskie
nasmeshnitsy' [Songs from the Music to the
Production The Merry Wives of Windsor]
8897
Pesni shuta i Ballada Kordelii iz spektaklia
'Korol' Lir' [Songs of the Fool and Cordelia's
Ballad from the Play King Lear] 5924
'Pesni shuta iz muzyki k spektakliu "Korol'
Lir"' [Songs of the Fool from Music to the
Play King Lear] 5924
'Pesnia Avtolika iz muzyki k "Zimnei skazke"
V. Shekspira' [Autolycus' Song from the
Music to W. Shakespeare's The Winter's
Tale] 18888
['Pesnia Desdemony' = Desdemona's Song]
12318, 12326
'Pesnia Desdemony' [Desdemona's Song]
12353
'Pesnia Desdemony ob ive iz muzyki k tragedii
"Otello"' [Desdemona's Willow Song from
the Music to the Tragedy Othello] 12357
'Pesnia lesa' [Forest Song] 8897
'Pesnia mogil'shchika iz tragedii "Gamlet"'
[Song of the Grave-digger from the Tragedy
Hamlet] 3803
['Pesnia mogil'shchikov' = Grave-digger's
Song] 3502
'Pesnia Mshcheniia' [Song of Vengeance] 8897
'Pesnia Ofelii' [Ophelia's Song] 3997, 4245
'Pesnia (ot "Tsimbelina")' [Song (from
Cymbeline)] 2705
'Pesnia p'ianykh' [Drinking Song] 11157
'Pesnia Robina' [Robin's Song] 8897
'Pesnia shuta iz komedii "Dvenadtsataia
noch'"' [Fool's Song from the Comedy
Twelfth Night] 18187
'Pesnia shuta' [Song of the Fool] 17990
P'esy iz baleta 'Otello' [Pieces from the Ballet
Othello] 12030, 12035
P'esy iz baleta 'Romeo i Dzhul'etta' [Pieces
from the Ballet Romeo and Juliet] 13796
Pět fantasií ma symfonické básně Zdeňka
Fibicha 12395, 14982

Peter Quince at the Clavier 10903
Petit Concert 8644
Petite Fantaisie mignonne sur Oberon de Weber 10855
Petite Fantaisie pour le piano sur le choeur des gardes-chasse du Songe d'une nuit d'été 20969
Petite Fantaisie sur Roméo et Juliette 13706
Petite Fantasie On Airs From 'The Tempest' 14738, 14822, 15125
12 Petites Fantaisies en forme d'Amusemens [sic] instructifs sur des thêmes favoris des Opéras italiens 7342
Petitions and Interludes 21215
Petruccio 14680
Petruchio 14585, 14653, 14661
[Petruchio Waltz] 14287
[Petruchio's Song] 14269
Phallstaff's Phollies 1963
Phantasie 10916
Phantasien über Motive aus Opern, Oratorien und Cantaten 9064
Philomel 10429, 10435, 10515, 10547, 10574
"Philomel, with melody" 10607
Philomele, with melody 10430, 10439
Piano Quintet 14856, 15994
Piano selection from 'Othello' 12206
Piat' pesen iz muzyki k komedii V. Shekspira 'Mnogo shuma iz nichego' [Five Songs from the Music to W. Shakespeare's Comedy Much Ado About Nothing] 11157
5 Pieces after The Tempest 15997
Pièces Intimes 1907
Pilgramage [sic] To Thee 19319
Pinch Theme 2193
Pioneer American Composers[:] A Collection of Early American Songs 12281, 15197
Piosnka obłąkanej Ofelii 3302
Piosnka Pazia 7882
Pirame et Thisbé 10977
Pirame et Tisbé 10953
Piramo e Thisbe 10978
Piramo e Tisbe 10150, 10944, 10947, 10963, 10971, 10976, 10980, 10981
Piramus und Tisbe 10985
Píseň na Shakespeara 17553
Píseň o koni 19751
Píseň Šaška 16810
[Play Macbeth] 7509, 7523, 7530
Play without Players 21140
Pleasant Pastimes 16120
Plump Jack 4462, 4628, 4800
Plumpy Bacchus 229
Plus de soupirs, ô Belles 11430
Pochod k slavnosti Shakespearově 21171
Poème I 8706
Poème symphonique d'après Shakespeare 5513
Poèmes d'Automne 4209

5 Poèmes für Violine und Klavier nach Texten von Shakespeare, Petrarca, Majakowskij, Heine und Verlaine 8706
Poetry Set in Jazz 11527
'Pogodi! . . .' [Wait! . . .] 14185
Pohádka zimního večera 19123, 19124
'Pokhodnaia pesnia Benedikta' [Marching Song of Benedict] 11053
Polacca—"Sweet Charming Hope" 10129
Polka-Mazurke sur Roméo et Juliette 13749
'Polno vam', krasavitsy, polno vsdykhat" ['Sigh no more, ladies'] 11394
Pomp and Circumstance (Land of Hope and Glory) 12518
Pomp and Circumstance March No. 1 12524
[Pomp and Circumstance Marches] 12514
Pomp and Circumstance Military March No. 4 12523
Pomp and Circumstance (No. 1) 12516, 12522, 12525, 12528
Pomp and Circumstance (No. 1 and No. 2) 12519
Pomp and Circumstance (No. 3) 12526
Pomp and Circumstance (No. 4) 12527, 12529, 12530
Pomp and Circumstance (No. 5) 12517, 12521, 12532
Pomp and Circumstance Nr. 1 12531
Pomp And Circumstance[:] Themes from Marches Nos. 1 and 4 12520
Poor Barbara 12299
Poor Corydon 630, 20744
Poor soul, the centre of my sinful earth 20495
Poore soule 20492
Pop 6134
Pops 6134
Popular English Melodies 16675
Popular Recitations with Musical Accompaniment 692, 8219
Portia 5550, 8687, 8689, 8699, 8705, 8708
'Portia.' A Graceful Measure 8686
Portia und Nerissa 8260
Portia's Bede 8390
Portraits: Five Songs about Musicians 5070
Portrety[:] Pervaia siuita iz baleta 'Otello' [Portraits: First Suite from the Ballet Othello] 12408
Porzia 8418
Poskromienie złośnicy 14407
[Poskromienie złośnicy = The Taming of the Shrew] 14285, 14341, 14401, 14402, 14434, 14490, 14501, 14539, 14555, 14556
'Posledniaia pesnia shuta' [Last Song of the Fool] 16961
Postavy ze Shakespeara 3859, 7396, 10451, 13861, 18176
[Post-Hamlet] 4088
Postlude 14039

Pot-pourri per Pianoforte sopra temi di Rossini 12142

Potpourri[:] The Taming of the Shrew 14574

Potpourri über Themas aus der Oper: Macbeth, von A. H. Chélard 7252

Potpourri . . . d'après des thèmes favoris de l'Opéra: Guillaume Shakspeare 20861

Potpourri . . . Sur des Motifs de l'Opéra Macbeth de G. Verdi 7341

Pound Sterling 10764

[Poveste de iarnă = The Winter's Tale] 18686

'Pozdno noch'iu (Pesnia shuta)' [At Night (Song of the Fool)] 16961

Pozdvižení v Efesu 2200

Praise God On High 7005

Präludium 10655

Prayer Response 15501

Preciosa 11615

Předehra k Shakespeareovské komedii 21147

Preghiera 12151

Prelude 2254, 11112, 13229, 14039

Prélude à Roméo et Juliette 14013

Prelude Act II 11088

Prelude Act III 11294

Prelude Act V 11246

Prelude and Fanfares for 'Hamlet' 3361

Prelude and Postlude: The Shipwreck 15093

Prélude et Divertissement[:] La Tempête—Ariel et les Esprits 16080

Prelude: 'Ferdinand and Miranda's Love Motive' 15215

Prelude for 'The Tempest' 14955

Prelude 'Pericles' 12577

Prélude pour 'La Tempête' de W. Shakespeare 15035

Prélude pour le drame Henry VIII de Shakespeare 5215

Prelude: 'Prospero's Hour's Now Come' 15215

Prelude "Richard III" 13016, 13017

Prelude: 'The Distraction of the Shipwrecked Lords' 15212

Prelude to Act IV. of 'Othello' 12404

Prelude to [Act IV] Scene I[:] Antonio 8074

Prelude to [Act IV] Scene I[:] Bassanio 8049

Prelude to [Act IV] Scene I[:] Portia 8309

Prelude to [Act IV] Scene I[:] Prince of Morocco 8165

Prelude to [Act IV] Scene I[:] Shylock 8313

Prelude to Hamlet 3187, 4022

Prelude to Scene I 8074

Prelude to Shakespeare's Play, Romeo and Juliet 13214

Préludes 10601

Preludio ad una commedia de W. Shakespeare (Twelfth Night) 18239

Preludio e morte di Macbeth 7501

Preludio per 'Riccardo III' di Shakespeare 13051

Preludio sinfonico alla tragedia Amleto 3890

Premier Potpourri tiré de l'opéra Oberon 10844

Pretty Ring Time 1272, 1566

[Pretty Ring Time] 1568

Prière d'Otello de Rossini 12171

Primavera 10364, 10533

Primrose 19108

Prince Hal 4486, 4661, 4839

Prince Hamlet 3611

[Prince Hamyul] 4106

[Prince of Players] 4099, 6124, 13068, 14048, 18271

Princes 13069

Prinz Methusalem 14114

Příroda. Život a Láska 12387

Prison Scene 12649

Přízrak otce Hamleta 4044

Processional: Julius Caesar 5479

Processional March 12847

Processional March. No. 1 from the Incidental Music to Shakespeare's Henry VIII 5021

Prolog 7380

Prolog für Troilus und Cressida 16582

Prolog til et Drama af Shakespeare 20850

Prologue 2534, 8429, 20018, 20731

Prologue, Episode and Interlude 9163

Prologue from 'West Side Story' 13592

Proportions 8422, 8667, 8673

'Prosnis' liubov'!' [Awaken, Love!] 19791

Prospero 15987, 16017, 16018, 16168

[Prospero] 15206

Prosperos Abschied von den Elementärgeistern 15416

Prosperos Beschwörungen[:] Fünf symphonische Stücke (nach Shakespeares 'Der Sturm') 16148

Prospero's Island 16020

Prospero's Magic Island 15490

Prospero's Spell 16041

Puck 10143, 10164, 10579, 10580, 10581, 10591, 10595, 10596, 10598, 10612, 10613, 10617, 10618, 10619, 10622, 10623, 10627, 10640, 10642, 10652, 10657, 10672, 10673, 10676, 10684, 10685, 10691, 10695, 10697, 10706, 10709, 10712, 10715, 10717, 10718, 10724, 10726, 10727, 10729, 10730, 10733, 10745, 10759, 10800, 10961

Puck & Titania 10679

Puck[:] A Comedy Overture 10722

Puck and the Fairies[:] Suite for Piano[,] From Fairy Scene in Shakespeare's 'Midsummer Night's Dream' 10594

[Puck and the Magic Flower] 10802

Puck and Titania 10711

Puck Fair 10970

Puck In The Belfry 10945

Puck is King 10966

Puck Pictures 10637

Puck Polka 10692
Puck (The Mischief Maker) 10704
Puck's Birthday 10648
Puck's Dance 10609
Pucks Liebeslied 10979
Puck's Minuet 10645
Puck's Pieces 10942
Puck's Song 10350, 10351, 10395, 10413,
10749, 10902
Puck—The Minstrel 10585
Purcell[:] Selected Songs 14746
Purcell[:] Ten Selected Songs 10247
Purcell[:] 40 Songs 10223, 14726,
18298
Purgatorio 19914
Pwy yw Sylvia? (Who is Sylvia?) 18505
Pyrame e Thisbé 10987
Pyrame et Thisbé 10955
Pyramus and Thisbe 10138, 10140, 10158
Pyramus und Thisbe 10289, 10776, 10898,
10900, 10948, 10959
Pyramus und Tisbe 10289

Q

1er Quadrille des bals de la cour 3677
Quadrille from The Merry Wives of Windsor.
Founded on Otto Nicolai's Opera 9029
Quadrille. Le Saphir 76
[Quadrille nach Motiven der Oper Hamlet von
A. Thomas] 3669
Quadrilles from M. W. Balfe's Grand Opera of
Falstaff as Performed at The Promenade
Concerts à la Musard 9004
Quand j'étais tout 18163
Quartet No. 6 10919, 16221
Quattro liriche per i versi di Leopardi,
Shakespeare, Goethe e Mallarmé
20389
Quatuor pour Deux Violons, Viola et
Violoncelle ['Harp'] 14190
Queen Elizabeth's Minuet 21121
Queen Mab 13856, 13888
Queen Mab. Fairy Dance 14214
Queen Mab Interlude 13500
Queen Mab or the Fairies Jubilee, A Cantata
compos'd for the Jubilee at Stratford upon
Avon Which was held in Honour of the
Immortal Shakespeare[,] September the 6th
and 7th 1769 21020
Queen Mab[:] Shakespeare Poem No. 7
14033
Queen Mab Sleeps 13961
Queen Mab's Waltzes 13889
Queen of the Nile 130
Quiet Pilgrimage 2627

R

R. and J. Cues 4-8 13227
R Loves J 14090
Racconto d'inverno 18706, 19153
Rage and Sorrow 13853
Raindrops 18102
Raise The Cup, Raise The Bowl 21062
Raitalaulu 11747
[Ran] 6131
'Ranenyi olen'. Iz muzyki k p'ese Shekspira
"Kak vam eto ponravitsia"' [The Wounded
Deer. From the Music to Shakespeare's Play
As You Like It] 1906
Raub der Schönheit 19895
Rauschende Engel 4183
Re Enrico IV 4314, 4315
[Re Enrico IV—Parte II] 4547
[Re Giovanni] 5594
Re Lear 5702, 5832, 5987, 5992, 5996, 6053,
6054, 6055, 6099
Recital-Collage-Shakespeare 83, 967, 1587,
2520, 4642, 4648, 4649, 5040, 5210,
5485, 6646, 7376, 7812, 10455, 16562
Récitatif et Cavatine de Roméo et Juliette
13813
Recitativ des Fluth und Falstaff 9036
Recitative and Aria from "Romeo and Juliet"
13860
Recitatives: "Great Neptune" [and] "Aeolus
You Must Appear" 14712
Recollections of Mendelssohn's Midsummer
Night's Dream 9718, 9846
Recollections of Shakespeare 1902, 6658,
6976, 7456, 14705, 16067
Recollections of Shakspeare 428, 8883, 21161
Récréations Lyriques des jeunes Pianistes . . .
3685
Recueil D'Airs à 4 Parties Tirez des Opéra [sic]
Tragédies & Comédies de Monsr. Henry
Purcell 10182
Recviem pentru o fată 20714, 20776
Red Rose 20801
Reflections 15879
Regarding Faustus 20360
Regele Lear 5742, 5846
[Regele Lear] 5959
[Regele Richard III] 12975
Regenlied 18151
[Reiten lassen: "Hopp, mein Kindchen"] 9062
Reiters Leid und Freud 19749
Remember not! 19950
Remembrance 19599, 19603, 19613, 19625
Remembrance of Things Past 19597, 19630
Remembrances 1994
Réminiscences D'Oberon 10821
Reminiscences from 'The Taming Of The
Shrew' 14359

Reminiscences of Mendelssohn's 'Midsummer Night's Dream' 9847
Reminiscences of Shakespeare 1888, 3944, 7436, 16037
Reminiscenze dell'Opera Otello di G. Verdi 12200
Reminiscenze des Macbeth di Verdi 7308
Renaissance Sweet: Music for 'As You Like It' 810
Rendimi lieto appieno[:] Scena e duetto 4150
Retir'd From Any Mortal's Sight From King Richard The Second 12707
Retraite (1er Chant d'Amiens) 1801
[Return from the Hunt] 5924
Return Revolting Rebels 16344
[Return revolting rebels] 16342
Revue 16199
Rhapsodie 10655
Rhum et eau en juillet 13675
Rhythm on the River 21259
Ričard II 12671
[Ričard II] 12654
Ricardus Impius, Angliæ Rex, ab Henrico Richmondæ Comite vita simul et regno exitus 13082
Riccardo Duca di Yorck 13084
Riccardo II 12630, 12679
[Riccardo II] 12650
Riccardo III 12810, 12811, 13038, 13081, 13083
[Riccardo III] 12784
[Richard al III-lea = King Richard III] 12809, 12819, 12872
Richard de Gloucester 12944
[Richard de Tweede = Richard II] 12673
Richard den Anden 12713
Richard den Tredje 12980
"Richard der Dritte" 13080
Richard II 12615, 12616, 12627, 12634, 12652, 12678, 12689, 12725, 12737
[Richard II.] 12633, 12638, 12662, 12663, 12672, 12675, 12677, 12682, 12693, 12694, 12699, 12705, 12709, 12717, 12720, 12724
Richard II Quarante 12776
[II. Richárd] 12729
Richard III 12787, 12793, 12796, 12798, 12802, 12804, 12805, 12816, 12835, 12837, 12842, 12947, 12952, 13001, 13008, 13012, 13022, 13033, 13034, 13035, 13039, 13055, 13056, 13060, 13063, 13076
[Richard III] 12800, 12806, 12815, 12820, 12829, 12841, 12856, 12860, 12863, 12867, 12874, 12883, 12885, 12886, 12898, 12901, 12902, 12904, 12916, 12921, 12926, 12938, 12954, 12955, 12957, 12960, 12965, 12983, 12988, 13037, 13040
Richard III: Ouverture pour la tragédie de Shakespeare 13052
Richard III Overture 12851
[Richard III, Part Two] 13067
[III. Richárd] 12989
Richard III's Liv og Død 12870
Richard the III 12786
Richard The Third 12973, 13076
[Richard the Third] 12986
Richard The Third Quadrille 13057
Richard 2nd 12656
Richmond's Prayer From "Richard III" 13047
Rickard III 12808
[Rickard III] 13010
Riddle of the World 3879, 7506, 7811, 12373
Riddle Song 6226
Rigaudon by Rameau 1354
Right Up Your Alley 14076
[Rihard II] 12612
[Rikhard III] 12823
Ritter Hans von Dampf 9013
Roamin' Romeo 14200
Robbing Around 19140
Robert Johnson[:] Ayres, Songs and Dialogues 2631, 6927, 15066, 18962
Robert Schumann's Ouvertüren 5526
Robin Goodfellow Quadrilles 10795
Rock, brass, stone, earth and love 19892
Rock musical score for Shakespeare's As you like it 950
Rockabye Hamlet 3595
Rockbeth 7537
Rodgers & Hart Notebook 2216
Rodrigo di Valenza 6135, 6140
'Romanc Mirandy iz opery "Buria" (po Shekspiru)' [Miranda's Romance from the Opera The Tempest (after Shakespeare)] 15380
Romance 14431, 14499
Romance aus Macbeth 7569
Romance de Desdemona de l'opéra Othello (Rossini) 12042
Romance de Roméo et Juliette 13634
Romance de Rossini 12097
Romance de Shakespear, chantée par Desdemona dans Othello 12346
Romance de Shakespear[,] Chantée par Desdémone dans Othello 12346
Romance du Saule 11778, 11779, 12358
Romance du Saule de Rossini 12133
Romaneska 11112
[Romanoff and Juliet] 14049, 14058, 14063
'Romans Bal'tazara' [Balthasar's Romance] 11053
'Romans Benvolio: Iz muzyki k spektakliu Romeo i Dzhul'etta' [Benvolio's Romance: From the Music to the Production Romeo and Juliet] 13279

'Romans "Kogda na sud bezmolvnykh tainykh dum"' [Romance 'When to the sessions of sweet silent thought'] 19596

'Romans Violy' [Romance of Viola] 16961

Romansy na slova U. Raleia, R. Bernsa i V. Shekspira [Romances on the Words of W. Raleigh, R. Burns, and W. Shakespeare] 19920

Romansy na slova V. Shekspira [Romances to the Words of W. Shakespeare] 19709, 19848, 20065, 20108

Romantisk Svit (ur musiken till 'Köpmannen i Venedig') 8383

Romanza 20852

Romanza del salice 12165

Romanza di Caterina 14595

Romanze aus: Der Kaufmann von Venedig 8612

Romanze aus Othello 12389

Romanze der Desdemona 12072

Romanze des Fenton 9035

Romea 14210

Romeo 13123, 13892, 13895, 14068, 14140, 14143, 14145, 14146, 14176

Romeo & Juliet 13309, 13310, 13340, 13429, 13990, 19705, 20123

[Romeo & Juliet] 13275, 13680

Romeo & Juliet[:] Ballet Suite No. 2 13947

Romeo & Juliet Fantasia 13903

Romeo & Juliet: New Wave 13629

Romeo & Juliet[.] Selection from the Opera 13729

Romeo & Juliette Polka 13931

[Romeo + Julija] 14062

[Romeo a Julia] 13210

Romeo a Julie 13151, 13245, 13246, 13247, 13293, 13396, 13398, 13410, 13905, 13930, 14012

[Romeo a Julie] 13167, 13209, 13251, 13264, 13267, 13272, 13393, 13458, 13469, 13485, 13532, 13535, 13550, 13925

Romeo and Giulietta 13261

Romeo and Juliet 13098, 13099, 13100, 13124, 13144, 13156, 13157, 13164, 13177, 13180, 13186, 13187, 13189, 13192, 13197, 13199, 13203, 13219, 13220, 13221, 13228, 13230, 13232, 13234, 13238, 13263, 13287, 13328, 13368, 13370, 13378, 13405, 13413, 13439, 13460, 13461, 13483, 13492, 13493, 13494, 13495, 13496, 13504, 13505, 13513, 13514, 13521, 13524, 13545, 13548, 13556, 13557, 13559, 13632, 13719, 13767, 13770, 13783, 13788, 13809, 13818, 13874, 13896, 13900, 13910, 13911, 13913, 13917, 13939, 13957, 13960, 13968, 13975, 13984, 13994, 13999, 14008, 14022, 14032, 14075, 14080, 14109, 14128, 14138, 14142, 14144, 14149, 14159, 14168, 14169, 14178, 14183

[Romeo and Juliet] 13091, 13092, 13093, 13101, 13107, 13108, 13111, 13115, 13117, 13119, 13120, 13127, 13132, 13135, 13136, 13138, 13150, 13152, 13158, 13161, 13174, 13175, 13176, 13181, 13190, 13195, 13198, 13205, 13206, 13208, 13211, 13216, 13217, 13223, 13233, 13256, 13257, 13259, 13268, 13274, 13276, 13307, 13312, 13315, 13316, 13324, 13325, 13327, 13338, 13339, 13348, 13349, 13350, 13351, 13354, 13355, 13356, 13357, 13358, 13359, 13367, 13371, 13372, 13376, 13379, 13386, 13388, 13392, 13395, 13397, 13408, 13409, 13415, 13416, 13418, 13431, 13432, 13433, 13435, 13437, 13440, 13442, 13443, 13447, 13452, 13454, 13457, 13465, 13466, 13468, 13473, 13474, 13479, 13486, 13491, 13511, 13518, 13519, 13520, 13529, 13530, 13534, 13538, 13539, 13540, 13542, 13725, 13887, 13899

Romeo and Juliet (from the Musical Comedy Breaking into Society) 14089

Romeo and Juliet (Incidental Music) 13463

Romeo and Juliet[:] Introduction and Finale 13993

Romeo and Juliet (Limited) 14129

Romeo and Juliet Love Theme 13980

Romeo And Juliet Overture 14004

Romeo and Juliet (Pavane) 14026

Romeo and Juliet Selection 13687

Romeo and Juliet Suite 13945, 13948

Romeo and Juliet (The Balcony Scene) 13824, 13915

Romeo and Juliet (Theme from the Overture) 13970

Romeo and Juliet (Tschaikowsky) 13977

Romeo and Juliet Waltz 13677, 13844

Romeo and Juliet Waltz Song 13652

Romeo and Juliet Waltz . . . On the Celebrated Valse Song & Other Airs 13660

Romeo and Juliet were Punks 13629

Romeo and Juliet—Mignonette 13751

Romeo and Juliette 13998

[Romeo and Juliette] 13137

[Romeo at Julieta] 13285

Romeo, Dzhul'etta i t'ma [Romeo, Juliet and Darkness] 14071, 14104

Romeo e Giulia 13808

Romeo e Giulietta 13762, 13774, 13776, 13777, 13778, 13779, 13780, 13781, 13785, 14206

[Romeo e Giulietta] 13166, 13303, 13417

[Romeo és Julia] 13201, 13278, 13412, 13497

Roméo et Juliette 13308, 13335, 13347,
13360, 13562, 13563, 13574, 13577,
13633, 13647, 13648, 13649, 13650,
13654, 13655, 13657, 13658, 13661,
13662, 13666, 13667, 13671, 13672,
13673, 13676, 13678, 13679, 13683,
13684, 13695, 13696, 13697, 13699,
13701, 13704, 13705, 13710, 13713,
13714, 13716, 13717, 13718, 13720,
13721, 13722, 13726, 13728, 13731,
13732, 13734, 13738, 13739, 13742,
13743, 13746, 13748, 13752, 13753,
13754, 13755, 13760, 13811, 13821,
13875, 13914, 13933, 13967, 13989,
13991, 14001, 14002, 14009, 14155,
14208
[Roméo et Juliette] 13141, 13145, 13162,
13184, 13185, 13270, 13330, 13344,
13401, 13464, 13508, 13516, 14003
Roméo et Juliette[:] Ballet 13741
Roméo et Juliette[:] Choeur. 'l'heure s'envole'
13691
Roméo et Juliette Fantaisie 13723, 13744,
13745
Roméo et Juliette[:] Invocation 13564
Roméo et Juliette[:] La Reine Mab ou la Fée des
Songes 13570
Roméo et Juliette[:] Les adieux de Roméo 13692
Roméo et Juliette (Op. de Berlioz) Scène du Bal
13571
Roméo et Juliette, Opéra de C. Gounod 13757
Roméo et Juliette[,] Opéra de Ch. Gounod
13664
Roméo et Juliette[,] Opéra de Gounod 13669
[Roméo et Juliette, ou, Catastrophes d'Amour]
14043
Roméo et Juliette[:] Valse ariette 13693
Roméo et Juliette[:] Valse Brillante sur l'Opéra
de Ch. Gounod 13735
Romeo Gavotte 13956
[Romeo i Dzhul'etta = Romeo and Juliet]
13088, 13110, 13118, 13133, 13142,
13194, 13196, 13200, 13226, 13279,
13282, 13288, 13289, 13290, 13295,
13298, 13313, 13337, 13369, 13389,
13400, 13434, 13438, 13467, 13484,
13527, 13551, 13795, 13973
Romeo i Dzhul'etta[:] desiat' p'es dlia fortepiano
[Romeo and Juliet: Ten Pieces for Piano]
13949
Romeo i Dzhul'etta[:] Muzykal'nye zarisovki k
tragedii V. Shekspira [Romeo and Juliet:
Musical Sketches to the Tragedy by W.
Shakespeare] 13923
Romeo i Dzhul'etta[:] Pervaia siuita [Romeo
and Juliet: First Suite] 13944
Romeo i Dzhul'etta [Romeo and Juliet] 13105,
13106, 13299, 13300, 13791, 13793,
13996

Romeo i Dzhul'etta[:] Siuita z muzyky do tragedii
Shekspira [Romeo and Juliet: Suite from the
Music to Shakespeare's Tragedy] 13313
Romeo i Dzhul'etta[:] Tret'ia siuita [Romeo and
Juliet: Third Suite] 13951
Romeo i Dzhul'etta: Uvertiura-fantaziia [Romeo
and Juliet: Overture-Fantasy] 14000
Romeo i Dzhul'etta[:] Vtoraia siuita [Romeo
and Juliet: Second Suite] 13946
[Romeo i Giulietta] 13215
Romeo i Julia 13112, 13173, 13302, 13331
[Romeo i Julia] 13113, 13179, 13225, 13255,
13271, 13283, 13284, 13286, 13345,
13381, 13382, 13453, 13552
Romeo i Julia—walc z opery 13759
Romeo i Julija 13645
[Romeo i Zhulieta = Romeo and Juliet] 13191,
13336
Romeo in Georgia 14179
[Romeo in Julija] 13086, 13104, 13114,
13526, 13553, 13554
Romeo, Julie a Tma 14093
[Romeo, Julie a tma = Romeo, Juliet and
Darkness] 14067
Romeo, My Only Romeo 14181
Romeo och Julia 13134, 13480, 13547
[Romeo och Julia] 13095, 13148, 13202,
13265, 13311, 13470
[Romeo och Juliet] 13090
Romeo og Giulietta 13807
Romeo og Julie 13094, 13147, 13224, 13273,
14172
[Romeo og Julie] 13277
Romeo og Julie suite 13273, 13921
Romeo Polka 13955
[Romeo şi Julieta] 13140, 13213
Romeo to Juliet 14132
Romeo u. Julie 14018
Romeo und Julia 13125, 13126, 13149,
13163, 13222, 13241, 13243, 13306,
13326, 13471, 13533, 13628, 13630,
13635, 13771, 13787, 13804, 13815,
13819, 13823, 13965, 13966, 13972,
14057, 14167
[Romeo und Julia] 13121, 13128, 13131,
13143, 13154, 13160, 13165, 13172,
13193, 13212, 13231, 13237, 13240,
13242, 13244, 13249, 13250, 13252,
13253, 13254, 13260, 13262, 13269,
13291, 13292, 13294, 13296, 13301,
13317, 13318, 13319, 13321, 13322,
13323, 13341, 13352, 13362, 13364,
13365, 13366, 13383, 13384, 13387,
13402, 13403, 13411, 13414, 13430,
13441, 13446, 13449, 13450, 13451,
13459, 13475, 13478, 13482, 13487,
13488, 13490, 13499, 13501, 13502,
13503, 13507, 13515, 13522, 13528,
13536, 13537, 13987

Romeo und Julia auf dem Dorfe 14077, 14100
Romeo und Julia und die Finsternis 14094
Romeo und Julia[:] Visionen für Orchester 13886
Romeo und Julie 13560, 13565, 13566, 14107, 14113
[Romeo und Julie] 14064
Romeo und Julie von Gounod 13727
[Romeo Ve Yulia = Romeo and Juliet] 13333, 13334, 13385
Romeo Waltz 13954
Romeo! (What did Ro-me-owe?) 14186
Romeo y Julieta 13320
[Romeo y Julieta] 13182, 13374, 13523, 14045
Romeo-moï sosed [Romeo, My Neighbour] 14097
Romeo's farewell to Juliet[:] Shakespearian Sketch No. 1 13885
Romeo's Good Night 13838
Romeo's Ladder 14165, 14170, 14173
Romeo's Lament 13907
Romeo's Serenade 13891
Romeu e Julieta 13983
[Romeu e Julieta] 13170, 13346
[Romey and Julie] 14041
[Romio to Juliet = Romeo and Juliet] 13462
Ronde nocturne dans le jardin de Juliette 13935
Rondeau 10211, 10239, 10240
Rondeau Allemand sur des Motifs d'Oberon de Ch. M. de Weber 10884
Rondeau: Ophelia 3585
Rondeau[:] Second movement from 'The Fairy Queen' 10229
Rondino über 'Die lustigen Weiber von Windsor' 9034
Rosalind 604, 961, 1222, 1869, 1876, 1881, 1889, 1894, 1897, 1898, 1905, 1913, 1921, 1928, 1929, 1932, 1935, 1939, 1976, 2002, 2006, 2007, 2014, 2015, 6689
Rosalind and Orlando 1918
Rosalind (Gavotte) 1890
[Rosalind in Arden] 1958
['Rosalind' ou 'Comme il vous plaira'] 779
Rosalinda 960
[Rosalinde ou Comme il vous plaira] 458
Rosalind's Madrigal 2009, 2016
Rosalind's Minuet 21121
[Rosalynde in Arden] 1956
Rose of May: A Threnody for Ophelia 4073
Rosemary 3830, 3952, 4231, 4240
Rosen für Julia 14154
Rosencrantz and Guildenstern 4122
[Rosencrantz and Guildenstern are Dead] 4134
[Rosenkriege] 4866, 4906, 4948
Roses their sharp spines being gone 9334, 19173

[Rosornas krig = Wars of the Roses] 4445, 4615, 4788, 4872, 4873, 4911, 4912, 4953, 4954, 12738, 13013, 13019
Rossini: Othello 12119
Rossini Waltzer 12071
Rossini's Celebrated Overture to Othello 12053
Rossinis [sic] Admired Opera of Otello 12068
roulette of moments 7375, 12753
Round 7821, 8622
Roundel 9203, 10498
Royal Gaelic March. (Introduction to the Banquet Scene.) From the music to 'Macbeth' 6940
Royal Winter Music[:] First Sonata on Shakespearean Characters 1896, 3957, 10638, 13054, 13913, 16048
Royal Winter Music[:] Second Sonata on Shakespearean Characters 7446, 10639, 13079, 18222
'Rozumna bud" ['Be wise'] 20467
Rue 3952
Rugged Romeo 14195
Rumba-Fortinbras 3913
Rundtanz der "Lustigen Weiber von Windsor" 9235
[Rüpelkomödie] 9444
[Ruusujen sota = Wars of the Roses] 4852, 4894, 4937
[Ryszard III] 12879, 12930, 13004

S

Så tuktas en argbigga 14257, 14309
[Så tuktas en argbigga = The Taming of the Shrew] 14552, 14553
Så tuktas en argbigga[:] Bröllops-Marsch 14500
Sad and Solemn music 5220
Sad Cypress 17631
[Saga för Vintern] 18838
Sailor Song 15850
Saint Withold footed thrice the wold 6119
Salad Days 351, 352
Saltarelle intercalée dans le ballet de Roméo et Juliette 13663
Salute to Summer 1660, 2669
Sam Crowell's Quadrilles on airs from popular comic songs 14150
Sammlung der beliebsten Opern in Form von Potpourris 9016
San ivanjske noći 9548, 9977
San letnje noći 9508
[San letnje noći = A Midsummer Night's Dream] 9942, 10071
[San ljetne noći = A Midsummer Night's Dream] 9943
Sang af "Cymbeline" 2485

Sang af "Kjøbmanden i Venedig" 8569
Sang af Shakespeare af "Som man behager" 1060
Sange af Shakspeare 1356, 1679, 3793, 5108, 11456, 12302, 17539, 18143
Sange til Shakespeare's 'Helligtrekongersaften' 16782
Sankt Amor—oder: Die Verteidigung der Liebe 6344, 21079
Sarabande[:] No. 1. from the Incidental Music to Romeo and Juliet 13136
Šašek 18176
Satyres Masque 19139
Satyrtanz 18777
Saudades 8006
Say tho' you strive to steal yourself away 20128
Say thou wilt roam with me 10796
Scarlett 18285
Scen musik till Julius Caesar efter Ravels La valse 5426
Scène dans la Caverne des Sorcières (IVme Acte, Scène 1re) de la tragédie 'Macbeth' 7421
Scéna z Macbetha 7477
Scene and Mercutio from Romeo and Juliet (Ballet) 13950
Scène d'Amour aus 'Roméo et Juliette' 13568
Scène dans la Caverne des Sorcières . . . de la tragédie 'Macbeth' 7422
Scène de Somnambulisme de Macbeth 7287
Scène Finale[:] Macbeth[,] Les Sorcières—Le Festin—L'Apparition—Les Fanfares du Couronnement 7460
Scène Finale[:] Macbeth—Les Sorcières—Le Festin—L'Apparition—Couronnement du Roi Malcolm 7460
[Scene from Act Three] 5924
Scene from 'Hamlet' 3934
Scene from Macbeth 7387
Scene From The Tempest 14707
Scene Hecate 7263
Scène Muziek bij Shakespeare's 'Merchant of Venice' 8332
Scene Tunes for the Tragedy of Macbeth 7073
Scenemusik til Julius Caesar af William Shakespeare 5344
Scene-musik til W. Shakespear's 'Et Vintereventyr' 18670
Scènes dramatiques 7460, 7461, 12417, 13935, 16080
Scenes from 'As You Like It' 473
Scenes from Hamlet 3224
Scenes from Macbeth 7448, 7499
8 Scenes from Shakespeare (with a Prologue) 1952, 4925, 7503, 8721, 10752, 12442, 14034, 16174, 18263
Scenes from Shakespeare's 'The Tempest' 16124

Scenes from The Fairy Queen 10208
Scénická hudba ke hře W. Shakespeara Co dobře skončí 88
Scénická hudba ke hře W. Shakespeara Jak se vám líbí 708
Scénická hudba ke hře W. Shakespeara Komodie omylů 2126
Scénická hudba ke hře W. Shakespeara Mnoho povyku pro nic 11191
Scénická hudba ke hře W. Shakespeara Sen svatojánské noci 9594
Scénická hudba ke hře W. Shakespeara Večer tříkrálový 17043
Scénická hudba ke hře W. Shakespeara Zkrocení zlé ženy 14403
Scenmusik till Hamlet 2921
Scenmusik till Kärt besvär förgäfves 6240
Scen-och Entr'actsmusik till Kung Lear 5776
2 Schakespeare-Suites 8904
Schauspielmusik 805, 806, 3271, 3521, 5633, 7133, 7134, 7748, 9963, 11262, 13448, 17038, 17213, 18428
[Schauspielmusik] 7527
Schauspielmusik: Suite d-Moll 13329
Schauspielmusik zu Shakespeares 'Was ihr wollt' 16837
Schauspielmusik zum 'Sommernachtstraum' 9480
Schauspiel-Ouvertüre 16270, 19151
Scherzetto 10738
Scherzetto (Mab) aus 'Roméo et Juliette' 13569
Scherzo 9826
Scherzo & Cortege on themes from 'Julius Caesar' 5351
Scherzo aus dem Sommernachtstraum 9806
Scherzo aus der Musik zu Shakespeares 'Ein Sommernachtstraum' 9687
Scherzo aus der Musik zu Shakespeare's Sommernachtstraum 9693
Scherzo du Songe d'une Nuit d'Été 9739, 9747
Scherzo du Songe d'une Nuit d'Été de Mendelssohn 9792, 9804
Scherzo d'Un Songe d'une Nuit d'été de Mendelssohn 9659
Scherzo from 'A Midsummer Night's Dream' 9638, 9700, 9749, 9782
Scherzo, from 'A Midsummer Night's Dream,' by Felix Mendelssohn-Bartholdy. 9724
[Scherzo, from Incidental Music to 'A Midsummer Night's Dream'] 9777
Scherzo from 'Midsummer Night's Dream' 9639
[Scherzo from Midsummer Night's Dream] 9825
Scherzo From Midsummer Nights [sic] Dream 9841
Scherzo From The 'Midsummer Night's Dream' 9655

Scherzo (Midsummer Night's Dream) 9690, 9845
Scherzo (Midsummer-Night's Dream) 9705
Scherzo, notturno e marcia nuziale dal 'Sogno di una notte di mezza estate' 9818
Scherzo. (Puck and Titania) 10711
Scherzo—'Midsummer Night's Dream' 9820
Schlusslied des Narren 18193
Schlusslied des Narren aus "Was ihr wollt" 18178
Schlusslied des Narren zu Shakespear's "Was ihr wollt" 18164
Schnittertanz 15046
Schön Röslein rot 20668
Schöne Opern-Melodien 9106
Schubert Album 18594
Schubert Fragments 2752
Schubert in Blue 301, 2728, 18574
Schubertana 2773
Schubertiana. Fantasia on Melodies by Franz Schubert 2733
Schubertiana. Fantasia on Melodies by Franz Schubert (2d Selection) 2785
Schubert's Celebrated Song Hark The Lark! At Heav'n's Gate Sings 2759
Schubert's 'Hark, Hark the lark' 2747
Schubert's Six Popular Songs 2756, 18587
Schubert's Songs 2738
[Score for 'The Haunted House Hamlet'] 4090
Score for The Tempest 15141
Score for 'Twelfth Night' 16716, 17035
Scots Duets 16218
[Scrambled Hamlet] 4117
Sea Change 15662, 16176
Sea Dirge 15603, 15732
Sea Lullaby 15661
Sea Murmurs 2644
Sea Nymphs &c. 14729
Sea Pictures 16251
Seachange 15613, 15842, 16055
Seals of Love 7848, 7872, 8014
Sea-magic 16134
"Sea-Nymphs hourly ring his knell" 14705
Searching 20009
Seasonal Songs 1134
Seasons Such as These 6035
Sechs Instrumental-Sonette 19453
Second Book of Diverse Songs, Sounds and Thoughts 1087
Second Choral Fantasia on National Airs 1472
Second Grand Selection 'Macbeth' 7300
Second Set of Pieces (from The Faerie Queen) 10184
Second Sett of Dr. Haydn's VI Original Canzonettas 18068
Second Year Schubert 18589
Seconde Étude Symphonique 3978
Secrecy's Song uit "The Fairy Queen" 10206
See The Heavens Smile 14712, 14733

[See! the Heavens smile] 14708
Seemannslied 15849
Sein oder Nichtsein 4230, 4247
Šekspir u Muzici 17418
Šekspīra mūzika [Shakespeare's Music] 19208, 19220, 19510, 19633, 19649, 19683, 19688, 20219, 20545
Select Airs, from Rossini's celebrated Opera of Othello 12054
Select Pieces, From Rossini's favorite Opera of Otello, as performed at the King's Theatre 12126
Selection from Ch. Gounod's Grand Opera Romeo and Juliet 13688
Selection from C. M. v. Weber's Opera: 'Oberon' 10889
Selection from Kiss Me, Kate 14613
Selection from O. Nicolai's Opera Falstaff 9066
Selection from Romeo and Juliet 13386
Selection from the Incidental Music composed for Mr. Richard Mansfield's Revival of Shakespeare's Richard III 12847
Selection from the Suite Othello 11719
Selection from Verdi's Opera Macbeth 7309
Selection From Weber's Opera Oberon 10866
Selection from West Side Story 13626
Selection Of Famous Melodies From Works By Tschaikowsky 13981
Selection of Themes from the Music to Much Ado About Nothing 11101
Selection of Themes from the Music to Shakespeare's Romeo and Juliet 13228
Selection 'Romeo e Giulietta' 13700
Selection—A Souvenir of Shakespeare 1923, 4021, 8029, 18246, 18646, 19120
Selections from 'A Midsummer Night's Dream' 9735
[Selections from O. Nicolai's Opera Merry Wives of Windsor] 9148
Selections From The Music In Macbeth 6814
Selections from 'West Side Story' 13582, 13583, 13585, 13586, 13600, 13601, 13609, 13614, 13624
Sem' pesen dlia golosa i fortepiano iz Shekspira [Seven Songs for Voice and Piano from Shakespeare] 1185, 3803, 6619, 12231, 12242, 12357, 18187
Sem' stikhotvorenii A. Bloka [Seven Poems by A. Blok] 4245
[Sen kresne noči = A Midsummer Night's Dream] 9535
Sen noci svatojánské 9326, 9468, 10060, 10123, 10144, 10281, 10285
[Sen noci svatojánské = A Midsummer Night's Dream] 9407, 9467, 9498, 9510, 9564, 9592, 9967, 10022, 10023, 10024, 10053, 10054, 10055, 10072
Sen nocy letniej 9550, 9593, 9772

[Sen nocy letniej = A Midsummer Night's Dream] 9287, 9338, 9396, 9518, 9527, 9536, 9539, 9738, 9898, 9936, 9938, 9973, 9974, 10029, 10035, 10059, 10105, 10116
Sen nocy letniej—Marsz weselny z uwertury do . . . 9779, 9858
[Sen svatojánské noci = A Midsummer Night's Dream] 10010
[Sen Wieszcza = A Midsummer Night's Dream] 9872
Sensations 13763
September 16071
[Ser Dzhon Fal'staf = Sir John Falstaff] 4421, 4596, 8949
Seraphic Songs for the Serene Psyche (for Shakespeare's Comedy: As You Like It) 541
Serenada 16901
'Serenada Benedikta (iz muzyki k komedii V. Shekspira "Mnogo shuma iz nichego")' [Benedick's Serenade (From the Music to Shakespeare's Much Ado About Nothing)] 11059
'Serenada Borakhio' [Borachio's Serenade] 11157
'Serenada Fentona' [Fenton's Serenade] 8897
'Serenada iz muzyki k spektakliu V. Shekspira "Ukroshchenie stroptivoi"' [Serenade from the Music to Shakespeare's Play The Taming of the Shrew] 14312
'Serenada (iz muzyki k tragedii Shekspira "Romeo i Dzhul'etta")' [Serenade (From the Music to Shakespeare's Tragedy Romeo and Juliet)] 13088, 13089
'Serenada Klavdio' [Claudio's Serenade] 11157
'Serenada' [Serenade] 16961
'Serenada Slendera' [Slender's Serenade] 8897
Serenade 21021
Sérénade de Shakespeare 2720
Sérénade du Page de Roméo et Juliette 13758
Serenade from Cymbeline 2763, 2764, 2765
Serenade (Hark, hark, the Lark) 2742
Serenade. (Hark! Hark! the Lark.) Ständchen 2737
Serenade in a Gondola 19685
Serenade: On Five English Poems 20412
Serenade (Ständchen) 2768
Serenade to Music 8474
Serious Glee 15829
Serious Glee (the Words from Beaumont & Fletcher's t. Two Noble Kinsmen) 19172
Set by Mr. Lampe 18950, 18979
Settings 5487, 10311, 10379
Settings to Four English Lyrics 18104
Seven ages 968
Seven Sea Poems 15676
Seven Shakespeare Sketches 2254, 3990, 4824, 6660, 6664, 8711, 9225, 9232, 10666, 14010, 14669, 16072

Seven Shakespeare Songs 1067, 1686, 2573, 6431, 17911, 18147, 18520
Seven Shakspere Songs 1097, 2586, 5136, 6448, 6581, 17579, 18539
Seven Songs by Elizabethan Composers 15057
Seven Songs from Shakespeare 1035, 17510, 19464, 19554, 19992, 20044, 20302
Seven Sonnets by William Shakespeare 19812, 19823, 19854, 20236, 20248, 20260, 20288
Seven Sonnets of Shakespeare 19742, 19859, 20041, 20105, 20113, 20245, 20502
[Seven Sonnets/Sieben Sonette] 19212, 19839, 19967, 20304, 20333, 20354, 20450
Seventeen Songs By Purcell 18310
Shadows 21060
Shaekespeare's fool 21253
Shake On A Barre 21156
Shakespear 20896
Shakespear Sonnet 19369
Shakespear svit för Kammerorkester ur musiken 'En midsommarnattsdröm' 9524
Shakespeare 20997, 21017, 21019, 21064, 21126, 21134, 21261
Shakespeare & All That Jazz 99, 355, 1975, 2264, 2398, 2551, 2860, 4204, 4503, 4675, 4836, 4883, 4927, 4964, 5237, 5553, 5652, 6150, 6526, 6684, 7371, 7497, 7564, 8041, 8765, 9261, 10294, 10908, 11637, 12496, 12610, 12775, 13072, 14141, 14684, 16216, 16384, 16429, 16581, 16745, 17724, 18291, 18653, 19142, 19357, 19489, 20583, 20585, 20752, 20768, 20782, 20810
Shakespeare Album 1066, 1685, 5114, 6364, 17910, 18518
Shakespeare and Elizabeth Unmasked 20846
Shakespeare and Ragtime 21271
Shakespeare and the Indians 20926
Shakespeare Blues 21050
Shakespeare Cantata 943, 20901
Shakespeare Character Dances 329, 10729, 12434, 14670
Shakespeare Characters 1921, 4014, 8705, 9230, 10691, 13943, 16088, 18242, 18243
[Shakespeare: Cotillon. Danza finale] 20934
Shakespeare Dance 10700, 16105
3 Shakespeare Duets 8718, 14026, 14675
Shakespeare et pire encore 21030
Shakespeare Festival[,] Stratford-on-Avon[,] August 1919 8826
Shakespeare Fragments 10500, 15651, 17508
[Shakespeare in America] 20851
Shakespeare Lieder 1165, 17634
15 Shakespeare Lieder 2938
Shakespeare March 21168
Shakespeare missed the boat 20943
Shakespeare Music 21119

Shakespeare Music[:] A Collection of Uncommon and Rare Pieces of Shakespeare Music 21312

Shakespeare Music (Music of the Period) 21323

Shakespeare never repeats 21049

Shakespeare Ode 21055

Shakespeare og Kronborg 4105, 20855

Shakespeare Overture 6662, 21152

Shakespeare Party 20941

Shakespeare Portraits 8701, 16083

Shakespeare Quadrilles 3887, 5496, 7411, 8685, 12374

Shakespeare Recitation 14006

Shakespeare Rock 21278

Shakespeare said 21063

Shakespeare Series 19813, 20221

Shakespeare, Shakespeare 21073

"Shakespeare Snapshotted" 21057

Shakespeare Song 1962, 20896

Shakespeare Songs 85, 991, 996, 1061, 1105, 1251, 1257, 1261, 1359, 1412, 1532, 1610, 1723, 1773, 1819, 1837, 2527, 2543, 2588, 2643, 3705, 3753, 3790, 4637, 5055, 5058, 5110, 6394, 6510, 6601, 7898, 7991, 8503, 8571, 8641, 9203, 10544, 10547, 11377, 11381, 11389, 11408, 11485, 11529, 11563, 12216, 12282, 12303, 15526, 15622, 15635, 15710, 15795, 15808, 15816, 15820, 15873, 15881, 16013, 16376, 16569, 17454, 17705, 17783, 18016, 18089, 18948, 18956, 18996, 19013, 19036, 19178, 19183, 19189, 19197, 19578, 19718, 19876, 19919, 20039, 20126, 20131, 20428, 20476, 20498, 20517, 20661, 20678, 20685

2 Shakespeare Songs 10320, 10490, 21243

3 Shakespeare songs 1107, 1108, 1417, 1724, 2589, 5140, 6602, 15934, 17999, 21228

4 Shakespeare Songs 15502, 15534, 15646, 15863, 21241

Shakespeare Songs and incidental music for 'Twelfth Night' and 'Midsummer Night's Dream' 9574, 17008

3 Shakespeare Songs from 'Winged Cupid' 1286, 8524, 11417

Shakespeare Sonnet 20556

Shakespeare Sonnet XVIII 19451

Shakespeare, Sonnet LX 19837

Shakespeare, Sonnet No. XLII 19707

Shakespeare sonnet: no. 116 20337

Shakespeare Sonnets 19233, 19255, 19346, 19519, 19545, 19597, 19632, 19641, 19667, 19687, 19732, 19754, 19800, 19820, 19871, 19887, 19938, 19986, 20084, 20110, 20135, 20156, 20178, 20217, 20232, 20246, 20258, 20277, 20293, 20313, 20388, 20397, 20409, 20425, 20446, 20490, 20544, 20547, 20568

2 Shake-Speare Sonnets 19521, 20364

Shakespeare Sonnets, Set 2 19201, 19207, 19215

Shakespeare: Soul of an Age 20859

Shakespeare Theme 21144

"Shakespeare." ("Waggish Will of Avon") 21071

[Shakespeare Wallah] 344, 12460

Shakespeare 2000 21042

Shakespearean Bidford Morris Dances 21127

Shakespearean Characters 315, 1895, 10633, 16045

Shakespearean Concerto 21099

3 Shakespearean Dances 1932, 16133

Shakespearean Madrigals 1240, 6502, 7823, 8497, 9200, 11402, 17692, 17768, 18478

[Shakespearean Melodies] 5270

Shakespearean Moods 21177

Shakespearean Overture 11701, 21097

Shakespearean Rhapsody[:] Prospero and Miranda 16046

Shakespearean Selection 11769

Shakespearean Sequence 958, 7281, 10177

Shakespearean Serenade 4804, 5037, 5038

Shakespearean Songs 986, 1241, 1600, 7824, 7825, 8498, 12266, 15604, 15844

4 Shakespearean Songs in Swing 1217, 1585, 11588, 18060

Shakespearean sonnet cycle 19257, 19410, 19653, 20264, 20328

Shakespearean Suite 4832, 10738, 14019, 18258, 19129

Shakespearean Women 954, 3585, 5036, 7373, 7383, 7388, 14650

Shakespeareana 20951

Shakespeare-fragments 1586, 7410, 8423

Shakespeare-Gesänge 2699, 2872, 18549

Shakespeare-Lieder 6460, 7958, 10416, 13873, 17987, 18553, 19749, 19778, 20199, 20671, 21214

3 Shakespeare-Liederen 16820

Shakespeare-March 21151

Shakespeare-monológok 7377, 13855, 15987

4 Shakespeare-Ouverturen 7471, 12421, 13952, 16095

Shakespeare's a bore 21051

Shakespeare's Battle Prayer 4808

Shakespeare's Birth Day 20999

Shakespeare's Cabaret 20948

Shakespeare's Carol 442

Shakespeare's Christmas Carol 3818

Shakespeare's Dramatic Songs 7004, 14729

Shakespeare's Epitaph 21044

Shakespeare's Epitaph as Inscribed upon the Pedestal on an Urn, under the Shade of a Mulberrytree in a Garden near Prescot 21040

[Shakespeares Falstaff] 4371, 4563, 4729, 8902

Shakespeare's Festival Quadrille 1910, 2251, 4003, 7464, 16084, 21159

Shakespeare's First One Hundred Thousand 1961, 2257, 2835, 8733, 10761, 12461, 16191, 18275, 20885

Shakespeare's Flowers[:] A Second Garland 2821, 3953, 6078, 6656, 10635, 19109

Shakespeare's Flowers [first set] 2820, 3952, 4922, 10634, 19108, 20801

Shakespeare's Grand March in 'Lear' 6050

Shakespeare's Henry VIII 5020

Shakespeares Jubilee Voluntary 21101

Shakespeare's Kingdom 20923

Shakespeare's Lieder 1196, 1802, 2803, 3805, 10569, 11574, 12232, 12363, 15772, 15953, 18033, 19023

Shakespeare's Lovers in a Garden[:] A Flower Masque 17464, 20952

Shakespeare's Love's Lost[,] An Elegy. Sung at the Tomb of a young Virgin 20687

Shakespeares Macbeth 7263

Shakespeare's Merrie Meeting 4170, 4835, 7544, 8758, 10799, 14681, 16204, 20950

Shakespeare's Minuet 21121

Shakespeare's Not For Us 21066

Shakespeare's Revived Play of the 'Merry Wives of Windsor' 1959, 8730, 8876, 10757, 20176, 20745, 20807

Shakespeare's Romeo and Juliet 14021

Shakespeare's Serenade 20628

[Shakespeare's Serenade] 2746

Shakespeare's Seven Ages 1972

Shakespeare's Seven Ages, Illustrated by Music & Poetry 1981

Shakespeare's Songs 21358

Shake-speares Sonnets 19560, 19608

Shakespeare's The Tempest 15440, 15461

Shakespeare's Voice to Rome 5651, 20992

Shakespeare's Willow 12280

Shakespeare's Winteravond Sprookje 19143

[Shakespeare's Women] 20824

Shakespeare-Sinfonie 335, 4664, 5536, 12774, 13065, 14031, 16579

Shakespeare-Sonette 19236, 19642, 19827

4 Shakespeare-sonetter 19255 20293, 20397, 20425, 20446, 20547

Shakespeare-Songs 1041, 2557, 3791, 6031, 6415, 7393, 7880, 12293, 17514

3 Shakespeare-Songs 7818, 17430, 17755

Shakespearesque 21211

Shakespeare-Suite 488, 9871, 18350, 21224

Shakespeare-Suite I 8182, 15045, 18776

Shakespeare-Suite II 15045, 16905, 18776

2 Shakespeare-szonett 20298, 20352

Shakespearian Air 21153

Shakespearian Airs 21113

Shakespearian blues 20991

Shakespearian Grand March 21167

Shakespearian love 21130

Shakespearian Studies 3999, 10676

Shakespearian Suite 3913, 5499, 7424, 13896, 18211, 21062

Shakespearian Tercentenary March 21104

Shakespeariana, Set I 20572

[Shakespeariment] 14061

Shakespearistan East of Suez 21258

Shakespearovské fresky 4046, 6104, 14012, 14672

Shakespearovské variace 330, 4044, 4923, 5223, 5530, 6103, 19126

Shakespear's Celebrated Poor Barbara 12244

Shakespear's description of Winter from Love's labour [sic] lost 6595

[Shakespear's Duel] 4127, 20688

Shakespear's Duel and Loadstars 4127, 10369, 20688

Shakespear's Garland or the Warwickshire Jubilee[,] Being a Collection of Ballads &c. as Perform'd in the Great Booth at Stratford upon Avon 21021

Shakespear's Head 21255

Shakespear's Loadstars 10369

Shakespears [sic] Shrew 14686

Shakespears [sic] Tomb 20896

Shakesperian Songs 1210, 1582, 1814

Shakesperian Songs For Schools 1181, 1538, 1791, 2795, 7986, 10344, 10422, 10562, 11552, 15944, 18019, 18622

Shakesperina: Five Scenes From Shakespeare 21189

Shakspeare! 21274

Shakspeare Commemoration Fantasia 413, 6979, 8880, 21125

Shakspeare Gavotte 21122

Shakspeare ovvero Il sogno d'una notte d'estate 9245, 9251, 10775, 10785, 20919, 20933

Shakspeare's Dramatic Songs 84, 298, 423, 1397, 1823, 1857, 1866, 2594, 2657, 3838, 4640, 5133, 5220, 6026, 7923, 8592, 10308, 10361, 10555, 11385, 11478, 12224, 12325, 14802, 15122, 15484, 15804, 17312, 17573, 17941, 18535, 18675, 19010, 21309

[Shakspeare's Early Days] 20825, 20889

Shakspeare's Seven Ages of Man 1915

Shaksperian Fantasia 413, 6979, 8880, 21125

Shaksperian Overture 9819, 14743, 14826, 15065, 21173

Shaksperian Quadrilles 21120

Shaksperian Sketches 3885, 8025, 15989

[Shaku Niwa Shaku = Measure for Measure] 7671

Shall I Compare Thee 19331, 19333, 19334, 19337, 19338, 19344, 19350, 19357, 19370, 19373, 19375, 19376, 19382,

19389, 19400, 19404, 19407, 19408, 19410, 19423, 19425, 19427, 19437, 19441, 19443, 19446, 19449, 19458, 19468
Shall I compare thee to a summer day? 19346
Shall I compare thee to a summer's day 19326, 19329, 19332, 19335, 19336, 19339, 19340, 19343, 19345, 19347, 19353, 19354, 19355, 19362, 19363, 19364, 19377, 19378, 19379, 19380, 19381, 19383, 19386, 19387, 19392, 19393, 19394, 19398, 19399, 19401, 19402, 19412, 19413, 19415, 19416, 19419, 19421, 19429, 19434, 19435, 19436, 19438, 19439, 19444, 19445, 20190
Shall I compare you? 19461
'Shame' and 'Shakespeare'[,] Introducing 'When Mr. Shakespeare Comes To Town' and 'Ain't Dat A Shame' 21077
'Shater frantsuzskoi korolevy. Iz muzyki k tragedii V. Shekspira "Korol' Lir"' [The Tent of the French King. From Music to W. Shakespeare's Tragedy King Lear] 5844
She Bids You Upon The Wanton Rushes Lay You Down 4472
She Lov'd Not Wisely But Too Well 12491
She loved not wisely, but too well 12506
. . . she never told her love 18063, 18066, 18068, 18069, 18070, 18071, 18072, 18074, 18075, 18076, 18288
[. . . she never told her love] 18073
She Never Told Her Love and My Mother Bids Me Bind My Hair 18071
Shepherd's Dance 18725, 18811, 19110
Shepherds' Dance from "Henry VIII" 4977, 4980
Shepherd's Dance from Henry VIII Dances 4992
Shepherds' Dance From The Music To Henry VIII 4989
Shepherd's Song 18694
Shest' p'es: Iz baleta 'Otello' [Six Pieces: From the Ballet Othello] 12035
Shest' sonetov Shekspira [Six Sonnets of Shakespeare] 20578
Shest' stikhotvorenii Mariny Tsvetaevoi [Six Poems of Marina Tsvetaeva] 4246
"Should he upbraid" 14676, 14687, 18362, 18363, 18364, 18366, 18367, 18369, 18370
Should love make me forsworn 6312
Shrew 14363, 14559
Shylock 8167, 8390, 8397, 8398, 8404, 8406, 8407, 8408, 8410, 8411, 8416, 8697, 8714, 8717, 8727, 8766, 8768, 8770, 8771, 8772, 8778, 8790
Shylock[:] Duo uit het 2ᵉ Bedrÿf (Portia en Bassanio) 8390
Shylock: "Nay, take my life and all" 8490

Shylock, or Old 60 Per Cent 8762
Shylock; or, The Venus of Venice 8739
Siciliana 11036
Sie trugen ihn auf der Bahre bloß 3842, 3843
Sieben Ophelia Lieder aus Hamlet 3708, 3741, 3746, 3765, 3836, 3869, 3882
Sieben Schauspiellieder nach Shakespeare 2688, 3797, 6446, 6577, 11477, 18157, 19009
Siegel der Liebe 7958
Sigh I must Henry 11646
Sigh No More 11135, 11326, 11391, 11392, 11393, 11398, 11412, 11442, 11449, 11450, 11465, 11478, 11504, 11572, 11573, 11636, 11645, 11647
[Sigh no more] 11521
Sigh no more Ladies 11006, 11008, 11042, 11046, 11054, 11055, 11090, 11091, 11224, 11287, 11395, 11400, 11401, 11402, 11403, 11406, 11407, 11408, 11411, 11414, 11415, 11417, 11418, 11422, 11423, 11425, 11426, 11427, 11429, 11431, 11436, 11437, 11439, 11440, 11441, 11443, 11445, 11448, 11451, 11452, 11453, 11454, 11457, 11460, 11461, 11462, 11464, 11466, 11467, 11471, 11472, 11473, 11474, 11475, 11476, 11479, 11480, 11481, 11483, 11484, 11485, 11486, 11488, 11490, 11492, 11494, 11495, 11497, 11498, 11499, 11500, 11502, 11503, 11505, 11506, 11507, 11508, 11509, 11510, 11511, 11512, 11513, 11514, 11515, 11517, 11518, 11519, 11520, 11523, 11525, 11527, 11528, 11529, 11531, 11532, 11533, 11534, 11535, 11536, 11537, 11539, 11540, 11541, 11542, 11543, 11544, 11545, 11546, 11548, 11549, 11550, 11551, 11552, 11554, 11555, 11556, 11558, 11559, 11560, 11561, 11563, 11564, 11565, 11566, 11567, 11568, 11569, 11570, 11575, 11576, 11577, 11578, 11579, 11580, 11581, 11582, 11584, 11585, 11586, 11588, 11589, 11590, 11611, 11614
[Sigh no more, ladies] 11141, 11201, 11219, 11404, 11455
Sigh No More Ladies & Blow, Blow Thou Winter Wind 1218, 11589
Sigh no more, Ladies. Balthasar's song from "Much Ado About Nothing" 11459
Sigh No More Ladies. Balthazar's Song, in Shakespere's Play "Much Ado About Nothing" 11547
Sigh no more ladies from Much Ado 11007
Sigh No More Ladies from Much Ado About Nothing 11526

Sigh No More Ladies[,] From Shakespeare's
  Much Ado About Nothing 11203
Sigh no more, ladies, sigh no more 11396,
  11433, 11463, 11557, 11633
[Sigh no more, ladies, sigh no more] 11424,
  11438, 11482, 11489, 11501
Signaler og Scenemusik til Kong Lear 5768
Silhouettes[:] Neuf Portraits musicales 4024
Silks and Satins 7549
Silversweet Sound 14108
Silvia 18491, 18499, 18536, 18537, 18555,
  18557, 18659, 18664
Silvia from Shakespear 18532
Simfoniia No. 5 'Sonety Shekspira' [Symphony
  No. 5 'Shakespeare's Sonnets'] 4225, 19915,
  20005
Sin of self-love 19865
Since Brass 19901
Since Brass, nor Stone 19903
Since Brass, Nor Stone, Nor Earth 19897
Since Brass, nor Stone, nor Earth, nor
  Boundless Sea 19886, 19887
[Since brass, nor stone, nor earth, nor
  boundless sea] 19885
Since I left you, mine eye is in my mind 20299
Sinfonia 4026
Sinfonia dell'Otello del Signor Mº Rossini
  12039
Sinfonia dell'Otello di Rossini 12085
Sinfonia nell'opera 'Rodrigo di Valenza' 6141
Sinfonia Nr. 4 (Shakespeariana) 21162
Sinfonia per il Hamlet 4026
Sinfonia 6 19870
[Sinfonie Nr. VI. 'König Lear'] 6096
Sinfonie Nr. 3 5510
Sinfonie zur Tragoedie Hamlet 3505
Sinfonische Einleitung zu Shakespeare's
  'Macbeth' 7452
Sing and Dance (Pastoral) 10666
Sing, Heigh-ho! 1055
Sing immer Sing 2810, 8664, 12369, 17672,
  20738
Sing In Harmony 1171, 15053
Sing, the Muse 982, 1597, 11398, 20994
Sing Willow 11884, 12445
Sing Willow, Willow, Willow 12313
Sing Willow-Willow-Willow 12349
Sing with Tschaikowsky 13970
Singout 12256
Sir Andrew Aguecheek 18222
Sir Andrew's Galliard 18240
Sir Henry R. Bishop's Celebrated Song Bid Me
  Discourse 16680
Sir H. R. Bishop's Admired Melodies, Selected
  From His Popular Operas 2034, 10129
Sir Jack! 4459, 4626
Sir John Falstaff 4482, 4657, 9222
Sir John in Love 9163
[Sir Thomas More] 20828

Sir Toby 18205
Sir Toby's and Sir Andrew's Entrance 16862
Siuita iz baleta 'Gamlet' [Suite from the Ballet
  Hamlet] 3569, 3582
Siuita iz muzyka k komedii V. Shekspira
  'Dvenadtsataia noch' ili Kak vam ugodno'
  [Suite from the Music to W. Shakespeare's
  Comedy Twelfth Night, or What You Will]
  16961
Siuita iz muzyka k tragedii V. Shekspira 'Korol'
  Lir' [Suite from the Music to W.
  Shakespeare's Tragedy King Lear] 5843
[Siuita iz muzyki k kinofil'mu 'Gamlet' = Suite
  from Music to the Film Hamlet] 3424
Siuita iz muzyki k komedii Shekspira 'Mnogo
  shuma iz nichego' [Suite from the Music to
  Shakespeare's Comedy Much Ado About
  Nothing] 11157
Siuita iz muzyki k spektakliu 'Antonii i
  Kleopatra' [Suite from the Music to the Play
  Antony and Cleopatra] 230
Siuita iz muzyki k tragedii V. Shekspira 'Romeo
  i Dzhul'etta' [Suite from the Music to W.
  Shakespeare's Tragedy Romeo and Juliet]
  13118, 13882
Siuita Venetsianskii kupets [Suite: The
  Merchant of Venice] 8365
Sivu 940 6022
Six Characters from Shakespeare 1887, 4479,
  4654, 6074, 9219, 10623, 11597, 16035
Six Country Scenes 16104
Six Declamatory Songs 2663, 3714, 3850
Six Elizabethan Lyrics 1706
Six Elizabethan Songs 6493, 9318, 17433, 18694
Six Fantaisies Brillantes 3656
Six Favorite Airs from Verdi's Opera Macbeth
  7349
Six Humorous Part-Songs 14144
Six Love Songs 3736
Six morceaux choisis, transcriptions des vieux
  maîtres 14804
Six Musical Episodes from Shakespeare with
  Original Setting for Children 949, 2514,
  3573, 9007, 10145, 15410, 18932
Six on TV 2338, 5917, 13465
Six Recreations, From the Classical Works of
  Mendelssohn, Hummel, Cramer & Spohr
  9714
Six Renaissance Lyrics 20096
[Six Romances on Verses by English Poets]
  19920
Six Shakespeare Songs 833, 1011, 1289,
  1449, 1624, 1626, 5072, 5109, 6283,
  6425, 6554, 7845, 7848, 8523, 8527,
  9999, 10487, 11418, 11457, 12268,
  12279, 15517, 15608, 15872, 17217,
  17311, 17444, 17473, 17772, 17809,
  18096, 18098, 18490, 18491, 20641,
  21142

six Shakespearean Songs 1818, 8024, 10574
Six Shakespearian Sketches 4822, 8696, 10650, 16057, 18229, 20767
Six Songs for two voices, from Shakespeare 1624, 7845, 8523, 12279, 18096, 18490
Six Songs from Shakespeare 2247, 2834, 6375, 6671, 7951, 10339, 10415, 16184, 17981, 18269
Six Songs in Harlequin's Invasion, Cymbeline, and Midsummer Night's Dream, &c. 2438, 9286, 20830
Six Songs of Love 6449
Six Songs, The Poetry selected from the Works of Shakspere 6666, 14035, 17995, 19421, 19654, 20095, 20169, 20190, 20796
Six Sonnets of Shakespeare 19299, 19394, 19691, 19955, 20184, 20250
Six Sonnets of William Shakespeare 19611, 19637, 19758, 19805, 20092, 20164
Six Tudor Songs 12259
Six Variations Pour le Piano Forte, Sur l'Entrée d'Ariel dans l'Opéra de l'Isle des Esprits 15465
Sixteen Favorite Airs Selected from Rossini's celebrated Opera of Otello 12108
Sixteen Sonnets of William Shakespeare 19196, 19228, 19304, 19323, 19462, 19540, 19589, 19743, 19775, 19869, 19884, 19977, 20106, 20229, 20306, 20417
Sixteen Standard Songs of Shakespeare 21350
Skærsommernatsdrøm 9432
Sketches from Twelfth Night 17247
Skizz till Amiens sång "Blås, blås, du vintervind" ur "Som Ni behagar" 853
Skizza ke scéně: "Makbeth a čarodějnice" ze Shakespearea 7477
Skizzer till en 'Macbeth'-musik för Radion 7105
Slain by love 17666
Slavnostní průvod ku Shakespearově slavnosti v roku 1864 v Praze 21171
Sleep 4645, 7382
"Sleep dwell upon thine eyes" 13858
Sleep No More 7536
Sleep of Miranda and Ariel Theme 15212
Sleepest or wakest 5977
"Sleep'st or Wak'st thou, Jolly Shepherd" 6037
Slings and Arrows 3910
Slotlied 16820
Sluha Oktaviánův nad zavražděným Caesarem 5530
[Slutet gott, allting gott] 9
Sly ovvero La Leggenda del Dormiente Risvegliato 14648
Smallwood's Dance Album for Little Folks 18237
Småtrold 10961
'Smezhaia veki' ['When most I wink'] 19709
Smíření Bruta s Casiem 5530

So are you to my thoughts 20036
"So are you to my Thoughts as Food to Life" 20033
So Hallow'd Is the Time 3823
So In Love 14616, 14618, 14622, 14623, 14624, 14629, 14631, 14633
So life goes on: Henry IV, Part I, Welsh song 4505
So Oft I Invoked Thee 20059
"So runs the World away" 3884
So Sweet A Kiss 6375, 6376
So sweet a kiss the golden sun gives not 6373
So wie es euch gefällt 1700
Soft in the East 9238
Sogno di una notte d'estate 10168, 10179
Sogno di una notte di mezza estate 9321
[Sogno di una notte di mezza estate] 9607, 9886, 9965
Sogno d'una notte d'Estate 9828
Sogno d'una notte di mezza estate 9345
[Sok hűhó semmiért = Much Ado About Nothing] 11062
Solarium 3717, 11375
Solche Macht ward süßen Tönen 5201, 8492, 13869, 18640
'Soldatskii tost' [Soldier's Toast] 12231
Solemn Music 5720
Solemn Overture Romeo and Juliet 13940
Soliloquy 3405, 3926
Soliloquy from Hamlet 3855
Soliloquy Music From King Lear 5826, 6081
Soliloquy V: From Hamlet 3846
Soll ich dich einem Sommertag vergleichen 19324, 19349
Som man behager 481, 637, 777, 789, 790, 791, 792
[Som man behager = As You Like It] 658, 744
Som man behager eller Livet i skoven 586
Som Ni behagar 456, 478, 853
[Som ni behagar = As You Like It] 482, 831, 845, 854
Som ni vill ha det 872
[Som ni vill ha det = As You Like It] 642
Some glory in their birth 20122
Some Glory In Their Birth, Some In Their Skill 20117
Some say 20148
Some Say That Ever 'gainst the Season 3824
Some say thy fault is youth 20145
Some Select Songs As they are Sung in the Fairy Queen 10180
Some Shakespeare Fairy Characters 10715, 13961, 19122
Some Wine Ho! 12229
Something is rotten 3564
Something Rich and Strange 15543, 15677, 15903
Something's Rockin' in Denmark 3595
Sometime 309

Somewhere 13603
Somewhere from 'West Side Story' 13596, 13597, 13622
Sommerlied 15910
Sommernachtstraum 9472, 9648, 9711, 9746, 9840, 10147, 10626
[Sommernachtstraum] 9561, 9626
Sommernachtsträume Walzer 10630
Sommernachtstraum-Musik 10075
Sommernattsdrømmen 9470
[Son v letniuiu noch' = A Midsummer Night's Dream] 9552, 9940, 10007, 10016, 10067
Sonata quasi una Fantasia per il Clavicembalo o Piano-Forte 8781
Sonata quasi una Fantasia per il Clavicembalo o Piano-Forte ['Moonlight'] 6180
5 Sonatas on Shakespeare Themes 20561
LIVme Sonate ['Appassionata'] 7585
Sonate pour le Piano Forte 5239
LIme Sonate pour le Pianoforte 11650
2 soneta [2 Sonnets] 20565
3 Soneta V. Shekspira [3 Sonnets of W. Shakespeare] 20570
Sonetele nr. 73, 75, 97 de Shakespeare 20019, 20042, 20171
[Sonets] 20552
Sonett 6374, 19842
Sonett von Shakespeare 20189
[Sonette] 20551
3 Sonette von William Shakespeare 19771, 19785, 19795
4 Sonety Miłosne—Four Love Sonnets 19488, 19790, 20116, 20151
Sonety (Na slova V. Shekspira i drugikh poetov) [Sonnets (To Words by Shakespeare and Other Poets)] 19365, 19602, 19634, 19821, 20066
Sonety na texty renesančních básníků 19824, 20317
Sonety Shekspira [Sonnets of Shakespeare] 19284, 19522, 19555, 19745, 20539
Sonety V. Shekspira [Sonnets of W. Shakespeare] 19384, 19651, 19951, 19999, 20125, 20182, 20200, 20262, 20279, 20527
Song 1752, 5231, 5279, 8773
[Song] 20472
Song and Dance (Act V, Sc. i) 9998, 19175
Song at Dawn 13878
Song: Celia 20368
Song: Come Away, Death 17480
Song Cycle No. 1 19988
Song Cycle[:] To Poetry 19428
Song[:] 'Fancy' 8344
Song for Massed Choir: Sonnet No. 106 20263
Song for Today 5491
Song from Cymbeline 2614
Song from "Henry the Eighth" 5102
Song From Incidental Music To "Twelfth Night" 16953
Song from Measure for Measure[:] Take, O take those lips away 7998
Song from Much Ado about Nothing—Done to Death by slanderous tongues 11373
Song from Shakespeare's Much Ado About Nothing 11232
Song from "The Tempest" 15974
Song from The Winter's Tale 18960
Song in The Comedy call'd Love betraid, Sung by Mrs. Bracegirdle 18268
Song in the Tempest 15464
Song in the Two Gentlemen of Verona 18444
Song No. IV[:] "Fox-Trot"[,] To Be or Not to Be 4233
Song of Hiems 6226
Song of Oberon 10296
Song of Spring (When Daisies Pied) 6448
Song of the Fairies 10383
Song of the Fairy 10385
Song of the Fairy Queen 10932
Song of the Huntsmen 493
Song of the Lady-in-Waiting 18763
Song of the Little Fairies 9184
Song of the Owl and the Cuckoo 6210
Song of the Peddlar [sic] 19091
Song of the Pedlar 18990, 19086
Song of the Pedlar (The Song of Autolycus) 19092
Song of the Shepherds 18809
Song of the Spirits 15530
Song of Ver 6226
Song of Winter 6563, 6582
Song of Winter. (When Icicles Hang By The Wall) 6581
Song Pearls 6604
Song: Rosalind 20523, 20806
[Song: Sigh No More Ladies] 11133
Song: Silvius 20806
Song (Sonnet) 19240
Song: Touchstone 20741
Song Tune 10240
Song Tune: Blow, Blow, Thou Winter Wind 411
Song Tune: When Daisies Pied 411
Song: Who Is Sylvia? 18481
Song—"By The Simplicity of Venus" 10129
Songe d'une nuit d'été 9438, 10160, 10656, 10714, 10950
[Songe d'une nuit d'été] 9320, 9958, 10092
Song . . . in Robin Good-fellow 10758
Song—"It Was A Lover And His Lass" 2034
Song—'Lo! here the gentle lark' 2037
Song—"Low! Here The Gentle Lark" 2034
Songs & Underscore For 'The Tempest' 15170
Songs and Choruses from Incidental Music to Clemence Dane's Play Will Shakespeare 20899

Songs and Dances for Master Will of Stratford (A Midwinter Night's Dream) 10756, 20847

Songs and Incidental Music for As You Like It 495, 727

Songs and incidental music for Shakespeare's Tempest 15173

Songs and Incidental Music for The Merry Wives of Windsor 8823

Songs and Incidental Music for 'The Taming of the Shrew' 14261

Songs and incidental music for 'The Winter's Tale' 18882

Songs and Music from 'The Tempest' 15346

Songs and Spells 21238

Songs by Franz Schubert 2713

Songs by George Friderick Handel 17844

Songs Composed And In Part Written By The Late Rev. John Park 5146, 6457

Songs Composed by St. Vincent Jervis 17554, 19952

Songs for a Winter Night 10398

Songs for Ariel 15317, 15582, 16207

Songs for Dov 15583, 16207

Songs for 'Hamlet' 3244

Songs for the Fool 5755

Songs for The Winter's Tale 18958, 18977, 19002, 19043, 19077

[Songs for 'Will'] 20832

Songs from a Midsummer Night's Dream 9471

Songs from 'As You Like It' 693, 763, 1496, 1753

Songs from Love's Labours [sic] Lost 6333

Songs from Shakespeare 580, 1104, 1411, 1722, 2587, 2693, 6586, 7910, 8579, 10523, 11091, 12313, 15700, 15914, 16815, 17484, 17555, 17929, 18103, 18544, 20686

Songs from Shakespeare[:] The Earliest Known Settings 21317

Songs from Shakespeare's Plays 299, 1152, 1225, 1518, 1593, 1770, 1828, 1853, 3718, 3777, 3801, 3875, 7970, 8627, 10452, 10546, 11388, 11514, 12228, 12241, 12349, 15567, 15742, 15823, 15856, 15936, 15979, 16566, 17620, 17711, 18006, 18177, 18559, 18963, 18964, 18984, 19016, 19060, 19087

Songs from Shakespeare's Plays and Popular Songs of Shakespeare's Time 21355

Songs from Shakespeare's Tempest 15584, 15764, 15817, 15857, 15981

Songs from Shakespeare's Tragedies 21357

Songs from the plays by Shakespeare 1079, 1378, 1697, 2577, 2677, 6562, 8578, 17924, 18526

Songs from the Plays of William Shakespeare With Dances 21320

Songs from the text of Shakspeare 97, 2263, 2851, 7557, 10901, 12491, 14125, 16580, 18288

Songs from the Text of Shakspeare, The Vocal Album of Her Most Gracious Majesty, Queen Victoria, 1843 12491, 18288, 21120, 21276

Songs from 'Twelfth Night' 17472, 17497, 17536, 17595, 17681, 17698, 17709, 17807, 17843, 17899, 17970, 18097, 18114, 18141

3 Songs from Twelfth Night 16748

Songs in a Farmhouse[:] A Cycle of Traditional Songs 1424

Songs in Arden 1333, 1658, 1843

Songs in the Opera of Hamlet as they are Perform'd at ye Queens Theatre 4276

Songs in Winter 19562

Songs nach Texten von William Shakespeare 1041, 2557, 3791, 6031, 6415, 6539, 7393, 7880, 12293, 17514, 17678, 17866

Songs of a Wayfarer 19046

Songs of Ariel from Shakespeare's Tempest 15509, 15555, 15708, 15918, 15986

Songs of Come and Gone 6564, 19049

Songs of Juliet 13831, 13853, 13863, 13878

Songs of Love and Irony 1402, 6447, 18537

Songs of Love and Parting 19376

Songs of Ophelia 2971

Songs of Praise 20499

Songs of Shakespeare 294, 1053, 10511, 11451, 12222, 12237, 15667, 15895, 17524, 18511

Songs of Springtime 1729, 11490

Songs of the British Isles 1473, 3786, 12264

Songs of the clown from Shakespeare's 'Twelfth night' 16965

Songs of the Fairies 10414, 10437, 21303

Songs of the Fairies, or Oberon's Court 10787

Songs of the Fool 17546, 17906, 18145

Songs of the Nativity 3820

Songs of the Poets 10366

Songs of Youth 7989

Songs of Youth and Springtide 20595

3 songs to Shakespeare Sonnets 19932, 20080, 20130

Songs to the Plays of Shakespeare 21351, 21352

Songs To 'The Winter's Tale' 18790

[Sonho de uma Noite de Verão] 9544

Sonnet 11642, 19254, 19426, 19428, 19452, 19562, 19605, 19618, 19638, 19659, 19668, 19710, 19873, 19889, 20000, 20029, 20265, 20307, 20557, 20563, 20571, 20651, 21133

Sonnet à Ophélie 4281

Sonnet Cycle 19832

Sonnet, De Shakespeare 20398

[Sonnet de Shakespeare 147] 20511

Sonnet for Caesar 5502

Sonnet for Piano 19271

Sonnet for Sister Kate 14656

Sonnet for Woodwind Quintet & Tenor 19360
Sonnet from Romeo and Juliet 13842
Sonnet from The Passionate Pilgrim 20735
Sonnet in search of a Moor 12390
Sonnet Lines 19249, 19298, 19893
Sonnet of Shakespeare 19832, 20050
Sonnet Sequence 20558, 21003
Sonnet. ("Shall I compare thee to a Summer's day?") 19414
Sonnet to Hank Cinq 4819
Sonnet: When I have seen by Time's fell hand defaced 19872
Sonnetina #5 19396
Sonnets 19303, 19588, 19846, 19852, 20086, 20305, 20355, 20406, 20440, 20478
4 Sonnets d'Ariel 15520, 15615, 15875, 15969
Sonnets de Shakespeare 20567
Sonnets: for [. . . .] 19193, 19681, 20334
Sonnets for Orchestra 19299
Sonnets from Shakespeare 19238, 19465, 19650, 19789, 19807, 19926, 19947, 20025, 20148, 20365
Sonnets of Shakespeare, Selected from a complete Setting and Miscellaneous Songs 6472, 15570, 18183, 19211, 19217, 19224, 19527, 19810, 19814, 19867, 19964, 20016, 20071, 20146, 20289, 20290, 20700, 20775
Sonnets of Summer and Sorrow 19395, 19561, 20003, 20514
Sonnets of Time 19612, 19875, 20008
Sonnets to sundry notes of music 20715
2 sonnets 19981, 20382
Sonnett [sic] 19327, 19835, 20330
5 Sonnette von William Shakespeare 19481, 20043, 20053, 20139, 20723
Sosedi [Neighbours] 14097
Souffle, souffle, vent du nord 1023
Soul and Death 20490
Soul of the age, Shakespeare, rise! 21053
Soul of the Age th' applause delight and wonder of our Stage my Shakspere rise 21081
Sound the tucket sonance and the note to mount 4816
Sounds and Sweet Ayres: A Garland for William Shakespeare 1214, 10573, 15593, 21096
Sounds of Desolation and Joy 7374, 7378, 7391
Soundtrack for Macbeth 6897
Sous bois (2d Chant d'Amiens) 1194
Souvenir de Macbeth de G. Verdi 7325
Souvenir de Rossini. Fantaisie de Salon, sur l'Opéra Otello 12169
Souvenir de Shakespeare 21108
Souvenir de Verona (The Ball of The Capulets) 13881

Souvenir D'Otello 12086
[Souvenir d'Otello] 12150
Souvenir d'Otello et de Bianca et Faliero 12150
Souvenirs de Marjolaine 2839
Souvenirs de Verdi 7325
Souvenirs d'Otello 12087
Souvenirs of the Opera 3639
Spiegelfuge 3826
Spiegelszene 12770
Spiel und Lied für Imogen 2699
Spielmusik zum 'Sommernachtstraum' 10214
Spirit all limitless, Ode to Shakespeare 21015
Spirit Puck 10620
Spiv' Ofeliy do tragediy 'Gamlet' Shekspyra [Songs of Ophelia to the Tragedy Hamlet by Shakespeare] 3268
Spohr's Overture to the Tragedy of 'Macbeth' 7166
Spotted Snakes 10543
Spring 6200, 6322, 6383, 6398, 6412, 6419, 6421, 6423, 6425, 6432, 6435, 6439, 6441, 6449, 6450, 6455, 6462, 6474, 6476, 6481, 6486, 6489, 6679
Spring and Winter 6393, 6397, 6408, 6520, 6527, 6533
['Spring' and 'Winter'] 6236
Spring Carol 1937
Spring from 'Love's labour [sic] lost' 6293
Spring Song 1271, 1571, 6392, 20181
Spring song, Winter song 6440, 6569
Spring Things 1589
Spring (When Daisies Pied And Violets Blue) 6433
[Spring 1600] 18273
Springtime 1289
"Springtime is Ring-time" 1983
['"Sravniu li s letnim dnem tvoi cherty . . ."' = 'Shall I compare thee to a summer's day'] 19365
St. Crispin's Day (March) 4824
St. Valentine's Blues 3874
Stability 3813
Staffordshire Jubilee 21121
Stages 556, 20845
Stammbuch-Blätter 1118, 21231
Standard English Songs 447, 14744, 14828, 15127
Ständchen 2664, 2680, 2709, 2715, 2728, 2738, 2749, 2776, 2783
Ständchen aus: Die beiden Veroneser 18551
Ständchen aus Shakespeare's Cymbeline 2638
Ständchen für Silvia 18648
'Ständchen,' (Hark! The Lark At Heaven's Gate Sings) 2745
[Ständchen (Horch', horch', die Lerch')] 2753
Ständchen von Shakespeare 2758
Standup Shakespeare 20942
Star-cross'd 13644
'Statue Music' for 'WT' 18768

Stephano's Song 15847, 15858
Still Music 16548
Still Telling What is Told 20054
10 stjerne melodier 4227, 14166
'Stomyvshysia, vzhe smerti ia blagaiu' ['Tir'd with all these, for restful death I cry'] 19907
Stor ståhei for ingenting 11292
Stor ståhej for ingenting 11030, 11272
10 Storiettes 10604
"Storm" 15196, 16230
Storm Scene 16862
Stormen 14696, 14886, 15014, 15183, 15274, 15284, 15385, 16273
[Stormen] 14755, 14928, 14971, 15338
Stormen av Shakspere 14854
[Stracone zachody miłości = Love's Labour's Lost] 6248, 6249, 6268, 6276, 6292
[Strange Brew] 4096
Stratford 18276, 20896
Stratford Adventure 20823
Stratford Minuet 21121
Stratford Music 10597, 13901, 21117
Stratford Revels 20940
Stratford Sonata 21123
Stratford Suite[:] Four Shakespearean Scenes 1875, 5212, 9214, 13049
Streich leise Saiten, Musikant 17734
[Streichquartett] 14187
Streichtrio 3996
String Quartet in D, after Shakespeare's 'Measure for Measure'[:] 'Escalus, — my Lord' 8028
String Quartet No. 1 in A major 1995
Strophe 3995
1-aia stsena IV-go deistviia iz tragedii 'Makbet'' [1st Scene of the IVth Act of the Tragedy Macbeth] 7421
'Stsena iz baleta "Romeo i Dzhul'etta"' [Scene from the Ballet Romeo and Juliet] 13794
'Stsena v peshchere ved'm (iz "Makbeta")' [Scene in Witches' Cave (from Macbeth)] 7421
Stseny po V. Shekspiru [Scenes According to W. Shakespeare] 7279
Stsenyi i tantsy iz baleta 'Romeo i Dzhul'etta' [Scenes and Dances from the Ballet Romeo and Juliet] 13791
Study & Pleasure 8478
Sturm 14866, 15302
[Sturm] 15181, 15231
Stürm, du Winterwind 1049
Stürm, stürm du Winterwind 1113, 1118, 1165
Sturmlied 1084
Sturmlied — Blow, Thou Winterwind 1041
Sturm-Suite zu Shakespeares 'Der Sturm' 15352
Succès Mélodiques . . . Sur Les Opéras De Verdi 7336

Such Sweet Thunder 314, 3928, 4819, 5502, 7431, 10608, 12390 13906, 14656, 21124
Suita z baletu Macbeth 7297
Suita Ze Shakespeara 7433, 14657, 18216, 19107
Suitable for either Lady or Gentleman, Romeo & Juliet, Serio Comic Medley 14028
Suite: 'A [sic] Winter's Tale' 18687
Suite aus der Musik zu Shakespeares 'Wie es euch gefällt' 915
Suite aus Hamlet 3566
Suite Danoise 2922
Suite dramatique (Coriolanus) 2384
Suite Élisabéthaine 9511
Suite (Fantasy — Air — Finale) for String Orchestra (on a Shakespearian Tune) 3950
Suite for Orchestra 18221
Suite for Recorders 8026
Suite for the J. Arthur Rank motion picture 'Romeo and Juliet' 13524
Suite for Violin and Pianoforte from the music to Shakespeare's Hamlet 4042
Suite fra Kjøbmannen i Venedig 8174
Suite from 'As You Like It' 783
Suite from Hamlet 2893
Suite from Henry V 4781, 4782, 4784
Suite from 'Henry VIII' 4998
Suite from Incidental Music to the Film 'Hamlet' 3423
Suite from King Lear 5839
Suite from Orpheus Britannicus 16340, 18315
Suite from 'The Fairy Queen' 10193, 10209, 10256
Suite From the Masque Music The Merchant of Venice 8347
Suite From The Music To Shakespeare's Hamlet 3137, 3956
Suite from the Music to Shakespeare's Henry VIII 4977
Suite from The Music to Shakespeare's Romeo and Juliet 13228
Suite from 'The Tempest' 15021, 15032
Suite from the Tempest (Divertimento) 15400
Suite from Twelfth Night in Elizabethan Style 16748
Suite für kleines Orchester zu Shakespeares Sommernachtstraum 9567
Suite In Five Movements 16351
Suite: Music from King Richard II 12646
Suite nach der Bühnenmusik zu König Lear von Joseph Haydn 5663
Suite pour 'Beaucoup de bruit pour rien' 11116
Suite Pour Sextuor avec Piano sur le Songe d'une Nuit d'Été 10731
Suite ur musiken till Shakespeares Stormen 14854
Suite — 'Mascarade' 8346
Sullivan's Incidental Music to Henry VIII 5023

Summer Gardens 16112
Summer is Gone 21308
Summer-Dances 9277
Summernight's Dream 9273
Sun 19655
Sundered Majesty 5994
Sung by Master Vernon 10755
Sung by Miss Radley 21021
Sung by Miss Young, As one of the Muses to the Statue of Shakespear in Harlequin's Invasion 20829
Sung by Mr. Andrews at Sadlers [sic] Wells in the Entertainment of The Tempest 14753
Sung by Mr. Beard, in (Much ado about nothing) 11005
Sung by Mr. Denman, & Mr. Street 14950
Sung by Mr. Dodd in Harlequin's Invation [sic] 20830
Sung by Mr. Lowe in as you like it 398
Sung by Mr. Lowe in the Merchant of Venice 8059
Sung by Mr. Lowe in Twelfth Night 16617
Sung by Mrs. Baddley [sic] in As you like it 399
Sung by Mrs. Chambers in the Character of Jessica in the Merchant of Venice 8723
Sung by Mrs. Clive 14953
Sung by Mrs. Clive in as you like it 398, 6667
Sung by Mrs. Clive in the Comedy call'd the Universal Passion 11612
Sung by Mrs. Clive in Twelfth Night 8722, 16617
Sung by Mrs. Hodgson in the Play call'd Timon of Athens 16313
Sung by Mrs. Mozeen 14953
Sung by Mrs. Scot and Mr. Vernon in Midsummer Night[']s Dream 9286
Sung by Mrs. Vincent in Cymbeline 2438
Sung in the Machines by Ariels [sic] Spirits 15431
Sunlight Sketches 12772
Sunny Airs And Sober 8666, 11590, 17676
Sunrise 20795
Sunset 12772
Sunset Songs 7392
Süss' Liebe liebt den Mai 1526
Süsser Tod 17443, 17610
[Süßer Tod, süßer Tod, komm] 17655
Svadebnyi marsh: Iz muzyki k komedii V. Shekspira 'Son v letniuiu noch'' [Wedding March: From the Music to Shakespeare's Comedy A Midsummer Night's Dream] 9672
[Svatebni pochod = Wedding March] 9736
Svit nr. 1 ur Musik till Köpmannen i Venedig 8140
Svit nr. 2 ur musiken till Köpmannen i Venedig 8140
Svit nr. 2 ur Stormen. Efter skisser från 1917, 1921, 1946 14854
Svit nr 7 112

Svit ur musiken till En vintersaga 18909
Swan Song 4158, 5234, 6137, 20028
Sweet and Twenty 17783, 17785, 17803, 17872, 17942, 17982, 18003
Sweet Anne Page 9231
Sweet Cytherae [sic] 20616
Sweet Cytherea, sitting by a brook 20617
Sweet Harmony 8421, 18077
Sweet Love Renew Thy Force 19797
Sweet Lovers 1589
Sweet lovers love the spring 1232, 1377, 1495
Sweet Music 5156, 8219
Sweet o' the Year 19067
Sweet rose 20604, 20670
Sweet Rose, Fair Flower 20722
Sweet Uses of Adversity 1588
Sweet Will 20949
Sweet William 20917
Sweet Willy 21021
Sweet-and-Twenty 17815, 17816, 18041
Sweetest Bard 20989
Sweetest Bard that ever Sung 20908
Sweetness 14136
Sweets to the Sweet 4198, 14130
Swingin' the Dream 10287
Swithold Footed 5977
Sylvia 18488, 18499, 18526, 18540, 18627, 18643, 18645, 18656, 18657, 18658, 18660, 18661, 18662, 18663, 18665, 18666
'Sylvia' by William Shakespeare 18453
Sylvia ("Who is Sylvia?") 18588
IV. Symfonie. Dialogy s vnitřním hlasem 7380, 19923, 20138, 20402
XII. Symfonie pro housle violu a orchestr 'shakespearovská' 4045, 5531, 14671, 19127
Symphonic Dances from 'West Side Story' 13581
Symphonic Impressions of the Glendower scene in Henry IV, Part I 4489
Symphonic Poem 'King Lear' 6113
Symphonic Poem 'Macbeth' 7500
Symphonic Poem: Shakespeare's Tempest 16086
Symphonic Prelude "The Magic Island" 15990
Symphonic Sketches 10593
Symphonie Fantastique 6171
Symphonie Fantastique[:] Episode in the Life of an Artist (Movements No. II and No. IV) 6170
Symphonie pour Grand Orchestre 16077
Symphonie pour Othello 12386
Symphonische Dichtung nach Shakespeares Sturm 16086
Symphonischer Prolog zu Shakespeare's Othello 12405
Symphony, from The fairy queen. Act IV 10224

Symphony in C 18099
Symphony in E Minor 16137
Symphony in One Movement 19541
Symphony No. 1 17591, 20007, 20070, 20411
Symphony No. 2 (Even To the Edge of Doom) 20338
Symphony No. 2: Monumentum 19788
Symphony No. 3 3969
Symphony (no. 3) in C 6647
[Szeget szeggel = Measure for Measure] 7674, 7692, 7780
Szentivánéji álom 9944
[Szentivánéji álom = A Midsummer Night's Dream] 9530, 9937

T

Ta-Dah! 11360
Taglied 13873
"Take All My Love", A Ballad, Sung by Mr. Horn 15037, 19701
"Take All My Loves" 11260, 19689, 19702
Take all my loves, my love 19691
Take all my loves, my love, yea, take them all 19687
Take Back The Golden Gifts of Love 2263
Take it slow 8756
Take, O Take 7823, 7824, 7825, 7840, 7898, 7909, 7912, 7917, 7938, 7962, 8000, 8022
Take O' Take These Lips Away 7970
Take, o take those lips away 7613, 7623, 7629, 7632, 7696, 7725, 7816, 7817, 7822, 7826, 7827, 7830, 7831, 7841, 7842, 7845, 7847, 7851, 7855, 7856, 7857, 7860, 7862, 7865, 7867, 7868, 7870, 7873, 7876, 7878, 7881, 7884, 7885, 7887, 7888, 7890, 7891, 7895, 7896, 7897, 7899, 7901, 7902, 7907, 7910, 7914, 7915, 7916, 7919, 7920, 7924, 7925, 7929, 7939, 7944, 7947, 7948, 7949, 7950, 7953, 7954, 7956, 7960, 7965, 7966, 7967, 7968, 7974, 7975, 7981, 7982, 7983, 7984, 7987, 7991, 7993, 7994, 7995, 8002, 8004, 8006, 8007, 8011, 8012, 8016, 8017, 8019, 8020, 8024, 8029
[Take, O, take those lips away] 7819, 7829, 7854, 7875, 7928, 7937, 8023
"Take, O Take Those Lips Away" from M for M 7660
Take, O Take Those Lips Away (Seals of Love) 7861
Take Oh Take 7828, 7864, 7932, 7992, 8013
Take, Oh Take[.] Page's Song from Measure for Measure 7930
Take, oh! take those lips 7923

Take, Oh, Take Those Lips Away 7795, 7797, 7815, 7818, 7820, 7832, 7836, 7837, 7846, 7858, 7859, 7871, 7877, 7879, 7889, 7893, 7894, 7900, 7903, 7905, 7906, 7908, 7918, 7921, 7926, 7927, 7933, 7940, 7941, 7942, 7945, 7951, 7959, 7961, 7963, 7972, 7986, 7988, 8010, 8018, 8031
Take, Oh Take Those Lips Away[:] A Dancing Song 8043
"Take, Oh take those lips away" from Shakespeare's "Measure for Measure" 8005
Take, Oh! Take Those Lips Away, (The Passionate Pilgrim.) introduced in Measure for Measure 7935, 21065
Take Thine Auld Cloak 11884
Take Those Lips Away 7790, 7814, 7863, 7922, 7999
Taková ztráta krve 19751
[Tal Como as Guste] 17206
Talvi 6598
Taming of the Shrew 14220, 14303, 14457, 14458, 14505, 14516, 14517, 14591, 14594, 14682
[Taming of the Shrew] 14660
Taming of the Shrew. Opera by H. Goetz 14575, 14576, 14581
Taming of the Shrew Quadrille on H. Goetz's Opera 14572
Taming of the Shrew Waltz on Goetz's Opera 14573
Taming of the Shrew[:] Wedding Procession 14267
'Tanets antil'skikh devushek iz baleta "Romeo i Dzhul'etta"' [Dance of the Maids from the Antilles from the Ballet Romeo and Juliet] 13794
'Tanets' [Dance] 16961
Tanets iz muzyki k tragedii Shekspira 'Gamlet' [Dance from the Music to Shakespeare's Tragedy Hamlet] 3415
Tanglin' hearts 1968
Tango 18957
Tantsuiushchii Kipr[:] Vtoraia siuita iz baleta 'Otello' [Dancing Cyprus: Second Suite from the Ballet Othello] 12409
Tanz der Luft- und Meergeister 15046
Tarantella nel Gran Ballo Macbeth 7366
Tarry Here With Me And Love[,] Sung by Mrs. Kennedy in the Comedy of Errors 2065
Tatíček Willi 20987
Te Deum 5013
Teach Me, Dear Creature 2247
Teatersvit nr. 2 ur musiken till 'Stormen' 15183
Teatersvit nr. 4 (Köpmannen i Venedig) 8268
["'Tebe l' menia pridetsia khoronit'..."' = 'Or I shall live your epitaph to make'] 20066

'Tebe l' menia pridetsia khoronit'' ['Or I shall live your epitaph to make'] 20065
'Tebe l' menia pridetsia khoronit' (81-i sonet)' ['Or I shall live your epitaph to make' (81st Sonnet)] 20069
[Téli Rege = The Winter's Tale] 18741, 18875
Tell Me Where 8497, 8604
Tell me where is Fancy 8507
Tell me where is fancy bred 8083, 8087, 8091, 8098, 8099, 8107, 8150, 8178, 8186, 8218, 8221, 8264, 8271, 8279, 8297, 8298, 8300, 8355, 8381, 8493, 8494, 8496, 8498, 8500, 8501, 8502, 8503, 8508, 8509, 8510, 8511, 8513, 8516, 8517, 8519, 8520, 8521, 8522, 8523, 8524, 8525, 8529, 8531, 8534, 8535, 8537, 8538, 8539, 8540, 8541, 8542, 8544, 8545, 8546, 8549, 8552, 8554, 8555, 8557, 8558, 8560, 8561, 8564, 8565, 8566, 8567, 8570, 8571, 8572, 8573, 8575, 8577, 8579, 8583, 8585, 8587, 8593, 8595, 8596, 8598, 8599, 8600, 8601, 8603, 8605, 8606, 8607, 8609, 8610, 8611, 8615, 8616, 8618, 8619, 8620, 8621, 8626, 8627, 8628, 8630, 8631, 8634, 8635, 8636, 8638, 8639, 8641, 8642, 8643, 8645, 8646, 8647, 8650, 8651, 8652, 8653, 8656, 8660, 8662, 8663, 8665, 8724, 8758, 16620, 21018
[Tell me where is Fancy bred] 8153, 8229, 8288, 8322, 8506, 8528, 8548, 8590, 8602, 8625, 8655
"Tell me where is fancy bred" from Shakespeare's "Merchant of Venice" 8649
Tell me where is Fancy bred, From Shakespear's Measure for Measure 8525
Tell Me, Where Is Fancy Bred (from "The Merchant of Venice") 8586
Tell me where is fancy &c. 8592
Telmah 4142, 7534, 13070
Tempest 14697, 14881, 15209, 15321, 15358, 16063
[Tempest] 16194, 16288
Tempest in a teapot 16203
Tempest Now 15437
[Tempest, or, The Enchanted Island] 15196
Tempest, reminiscences of Shakespeare 16113
Tempest Songs 15003
Tempête 16025
Tempête, Ariel 16026
Ten Shakespeare Sonnets 19352, 19547, 19755, 19801, 20055, 20159, 20259, 20278, 20287, 20314
Ten Songs And Dances Of The Playhouse By Henry Purcell (1659-1695) 10255
Ten Songs from John Wilson's Cheerful Ayres or Ballads (1659) 15060, 19026

Tenth Set of Admired Quadrilles, Selected from Henry R. Bishop's Favorite Operas 16682
Terzetto 18067
Tévedések vígjátéka 2203
[Tévedések vígjátéka = The Comedy of Errors] 2064
Th' Expense of Spirit 20410, 20412
Th' expense of spirit in a waste of shame 20409
Thanksgiving for Victory 4809
Thanksgiving Hymn 4977
Thanksgiving Hymn (Prelude to Act 5, 'Henry VIII') 4987
That Hallowed Season 3820
That I am Foresworn for Thee 6364
That I Did Love Thee 5492
That Shakespearian Rag 21080
That strain again 18078, 18079
That Strain Again: It Had A Dying Fall 2868, 14161, 18295
That Time of Year 19978, 19984, 19988, 19994, 20009, 20010, 20025, 20026
That Time of Year Thou Mayst in Me Behold 19980, 19993, 19995, 20001, 20015
That You Were Once Unkind, Befriend Me Now 20356
The Acrobats 21272
[The Airs and Chorusses, in the Monody, on the Death of Mr. Garrick] 21054
The Alps and Andes of the Living World 4145
The Amateur Conjuror 16186
The Answer to "Sigh no more Ladies" 11640
The Ariel Galop 16262
The Ariel Polka 16076, 16256, 16257
The Ariel Sylph 16287
The Ariel Valse 16091
The Ariel Waltzes 16097, 16143, 16289
The Ariels [sic] Songs in the Play call'd the Tempest 14859, 15387, 15424, 15431
The Arrival of the Bride 9768
The Arrow in the Heart 17451, 17786, 18484
The Avon Quadrille 1939, 1998, 4057, 6689, 10735, 16142
The Awakening of the Statue 18880
The Backward Boy 16186
The Balaclava Charge 4837
The Ballad of Romeo and Juliet 13765
The Ballad Opera Robin Goodfellow 10793
The Banks Of the Avon 429, 2043, 20907
The Banquet Dance, from the Music to the Tempest 15293
The Banquet Dance. (Shakespeare's "Tempest") 15295
The Bard of Avon[:] A Shakespearean Suite 1047, 1339, 1665, 5087, 10401, 10508, 15830, 15864, 16572, 17879, 18293, 20633, 21035
The Bard of Avon Quadrille 21157
The Bard of Avon Quadrilles 21115

The Bargain 14499

The Beauties of Purcell 10196, 14707, 14708, 14712, 15219, 16341, 16342, 16343, 16344

The Beauty of Bath 1965

The Best Hour 9838

[The Big Show] 6127

The Bird of Dawning Singeth all Night Long 3918

The Birthday of Oberon 10226

The Birth-Place, The Grave and the Home of the Bard 21070

The Bloody Crown 7238

The Boys from Syracuse 2206, 2217

The Bridge of Khazad Dûm 7584

The 'Bronze' Album. Seven Pieces, by Arne, Lawes, Mazzella, G. Dyson, etc. 10766

[The Caesar Conspiracy] 5469

The Caledonian Pocket Companion . . . 7073

The Candle 8424

The Capulets' Ball 14010

The Cares of Lovers 16340

The Castle of the Spider's Web 7529

The Cauldron 7381

The Celebrated Brindisi in the Opera of Macbeth by Verdi 7363

The Celebrated March in Henry 4th 4520, 4689

The Celebrated Music in Macbeth 6999

The Celebrated Music, in Shakespeare's Tragedy, Macbeth, attributed to Matthew Locke, A.D. 1672 6991

The Celebrated Music introduced in the tragedy of Macbeth 6996

The Changing Year 19417

The Children's Tschaikowsky 13979

The Child's First Grief 21295

The Cloud capt Towers 15835

The cloud capt tow'rs 15833

The Cloud-capp'd Towers 15839, 15840, 15841

The cloud-capt Towers 15834, 15836, 15837, 15838

The Clown 18099

The Clown in the Churchyard 3790

The Clown Song from "Twelfth Night" 18195

The Clown's Song 18142

The Clown's Song from Shakespeare's "Twelfth Night" 17541, 18107

The Clown's Songs from Shakespeare's Twelfth Night or What You Will 17540, 17682, 17704, 17902, 18144

The Clown's Songs from Shakespere's Comedy Twelfth Night 17635, 18015, 18185

The Clown's Songs in Shakespeare's 'Twelfth Night' 17495, 17836, 18110

The Cobblers' Song from "Locrine" 21056

The Cole Porter Song Book 14621

The Comedy of Errors 2026, 2050, 2054, 2055, 2068, 2072, 2079, 2080, 2081, 2093, 2105, 2152, 2177, 2187, 2194, 2198, 2204, 2205, 2236, 2243

[The Comedy of Errors] 2019, 2022, 2024, 2025, 2029, 2053, 2057, 2059, 2060, 2061, 2071, 2078, 2086, 2087, 2088, 2089, 2090, 2094, 2097, 2101, 2102, 2104, 2106, 2107, 2108, 2118, 2122, 2125, 2128, 2129, 2130, 2132, 2133, 2134, 2135, 2142, 2147, 2156, 2158, 2159, 2162, 2163, 2165, 2168, 2171, 2172, 2180, 2189, 2192, 2248, 2249, 2255

The Comick Masque of Pyramus and Thisbe 10162

The Commemoration Ode written for the 300th Anniversary of the birth of Shakespeare 21037

The Community Sing-Song Book 427, 1459, 11546, 14809

The Complaint 7813

The Compleat Works 99, 355, 1975, 2264, 2398, 2860, 4204, 4503, 4675, 4836, 4883, 4927, 4964, 5237, 5553, 5652, 6150, 6684, 7564, 8041, 8765, 9261, 10908, 11637, 12496, 12610, 12775, 13072, 14141, 14684, 16216, 16384, 16429, 16581, 18291, 18653, 19142, 20583, 20585, 20752, 20768, 20782, 20810

The Cordelia Valse 6184

The Coronation in Shakspeare's Play Henry = Fourth (2nd Part) 4528

The Coster Othello 12502

The course of true love 10310

The Course of True Love Never Did Run Smooth 10901

The Crow Doth Sing as Sweetly 8667

The Cuckoo 6402, 6413, 6490, 21095

The Cuckoo and the Owl 6394, 6522

The Cuckoo Song 455, 6205, 6409

The Cuckoo. Sung by Mrs. Jordan in the Comedy of As You Like It 400

The Cuckow 6445, 6575

The current that with gentle murmur glides 18471

The Dairymaids 8038

The Dance in the Play of Macbeth 7013

The Dances from The Faery Queen 10249

The Dances From The Fairy Queen 10250

The Dark Lady Within 20375

The Darling Buds of May 19455

The Dawn of Peace 5238

The Day is Done 14039

The Dead Bride 14125

The Death of Hamlet (Elegy) 3990

[The Death of King Lear] 6000

The Death of Yukio Mishima 20414

The deaths of Pyramus and Thisbe: a masque 10442

The Deceived 7941

The Deer Song 8969
The Defeat of Macbeth 6940
[The Derby] 6138
The Dirge from Shakespeare's Cymbeline 2604
The Dirge in Cymbaline [sic] 2854, 2856
The Dirge in Cymbeline 2859
The Dirge in Cymbeline, Sung by Mr. Lowe 2436
The Dirge of Fidele 2570
[The Dream] 10259, 10664
The Duke of Milan 15393
The Dumb Show[:] Hamlet, Act III, Scene II Mime Music 3174
The Echoing Green 1391
The Education of H*Y*M*A*N K*A*P*L*A*N 5547, 7545
The Eighteenth Sonnet 19361
The Electric Tempest 15396
The Elfin Glade 10605
The Elizabethan Age 1962, 18276, 20896
The enchanted island 15386, 15401, 15995
The Enchanted Isle 14856, 16162
The Enchanted Isle[:] Scenes from Shakespeare's 'Tempest' 10790, 15433, 20750
The Enchanted Wood 10769, 16196
The English Opera; or The Vocal Musick in Psyche, with the Instrumental Therein Intermix'd. To which is Adjoyned The Instrumental Musick in the Tempest 15444
The English Songs 20755
[The Escapade of Launcelot Gobbo] 8409
The Essential Cole Porter 14605
[The Expectation of Cleopatra] 275
The Eye of Anguish 6004
The Fair Inconstant 7996
The Faires [sic] 10751
The Fairies 5235, 6682, 10276, 11633, 16206
The Fairies' Dance 10833
"The fairies fugitives" [sic] 10949
The Fairies' Lullaby 10485
The Fairie's [sic] Lullaby 10437, 10438
The Fairies' Song 10484, 10502, 10521, 10923
The Fairy Blessing 10305
The Fairy Bridal 10153
[The Fairy Favour] 10771
[The Fairy Festival] 10770
The Fairy Glee 10933
The Fairy Prince 10765
The Fairy Queen 10180, 10191, 10194, 10228, 10237, 10241, 10905, 10926, 10930, 10931
The Fairy Ring 10577, 10912
The Fairy Song 10499, 10929
The Falstaff Polka 9093
The Family of Man 1951
The favorite Act Symphonies to Macbeth 7212
The Favorite Airs, Assisa A Piè and Aurora Ah Sorgerai 12061
The Favorite Airs from Nicolai's Opera The Merry Wives of Windsor 9107
The Favorite Airs, in Shakespeare's King Henry V 4725
The favorite Airs In the Opera of Otello 12049
The Favorite Airs, in W. M. Balfe's Opera, of Falstaff 8999
The Favorite Cavatina[,] Sweet Rose, fair flower 20739
The Favorite Madrigal, "It was a Lordlings [sic] Daughter" 20613
The Favorite March from Macbeth 7343
The Favorite March in Richard the Third 12785
The Favorite Quartetto of Where the Bee Sucks 14950
The favorite Romance of the Captive of Spilberg 12536
The Favorite Song Sung by Master Welsh in the Fairy Festival 10770
The Favorite Song Sung by Miss Leak, in the Fairy Festival 10770
The Favorite Song Sung by Miss Wentworth in the Fairy Festival 10770
The Favorite Trio, Sung by Mrs. Bland, Master Welsh & Miss Wheatley, in the Fairy Festival 10770
The Favourite Airs She Wore A Wreath And Even As The Sun 8879
The Favourite New Overture to The Tempest 14950
The Favourite new Songs & Duet in the Fairy Tale. . . . Perform'd at the Theatre Royal in Drury Lane 9282
The Favourite Scotch Airs . . . As they are Perform'd in the Tragedy of Macbeth at the Theatre Royal In the Haymarket 6713
The favourite Song of "Where the bee sucks" 14950
The Feast of Crispian 4814
The Feast of Spring[:] Ballet from the Opera 'Hamlet' 3648
The Festival of Spring! 7006
The First Book of Apollo's Banquet . . . 10180
The First Booke of Ayres. Or Little Short Songs . . . 1423
The Fisherwoman's Song 16186
The Five Kings 4325, 4539, 4711, 12636
The five Songs in As You Like It 856
The Food of Love 17731, 18203, 18280
The Fool Speaks 17701
The Fool (6 short songs from 'King Lear') 6024, 6025, 6028, 6029, 6040, 6042
The Fools and The Fairies 10000
The Fool[']s Music in King Lear 5654
The Fool's Song 6033, 18123
The Footpath Way 18986

The Forest of Arden 1886
The Forester's Song 1833
The forsaken Maid. A New Song in the Tragedy call'd Double Falsehood by Shakespear 20849
The forward violet 20201
The Four Chorus's in the Tragedy of Julius Caesar 5540
The Four Seasons 6614
The four songs of the Clown from Shakespeare's 'Twelfth Night' 17305
The fox, the ape, and the humble-bee 6378
The French Air in Twelfth Night. Sung by Mrs. Abington 16610
The Friendly Wish 15799
The frolicks of Queen Mab 14174
The Fruit of Love 1602, 5056, 6386, 10476, 11409, 15845, 19032
The Gamut Duet 19845
The Garden Scene from Shakespeares Romeo and Juliet 14171
The Garden Scene from Shakespear's Romeo and Juliet 14171
The Gardens of Adonis 20786
The Gay Venetians 8395
[The Genuine Music Hall Version of The Merry Wives of Windsor] 9008
The Gertrude Waltz 4274
[The Ginger-bread Man] 12307
The Gipsy Queen Quadrilles 16671
The Globe 21109
The god of love 11043, 11591, 11631
The Grace of Todd 10774
The Gracious Time 3816, 3822, 4167
The Gravedigger's Song 3244, 3796, 3799
The Green Willow 12348
The Greenwood Tree 1745
The Guests 14074
The Hallowed Season 3815
[The Hamlet of Stepney Green] 4121
The Hamlet Rondo 4050
The Happy Juliet 13407
The Harmonist or Eight New Glees and Madrigals from the Classic Poets 20652
The Harpsichord 20388
The Heights 16198
[The History, Murders, Life, and Death of Macbeth] 7244
[The History of King Lear] 5790
The Home of Titania 10937
The Honeybags 9918
The Hood of the Woods Meets the Dark Lady of the Sonata: In Memoriam Steven A. Olick III 21198
The Horn 1837, 1841
The Hotspur Song 4513
[The House of York] 4855, 4897, 4940, 12895
The Hunting Song in Love in a Forrest 1955
The Huntsman's Roundelay 1855

The Huntsmans [sic] Song in Love in a Forest 1955
The Instrumental Musick used in the Tempest 15444
The Introduction and Air, Come unto these Yellow Sands From the Tempest 14722
The Introduction and Air, Let's have a Dance upon the Heath, from Macbeth. Composed by Locke 6980
The Introductory Symphony, Airs, Recitatives, Dance, and Choruses, in the Tragedy of Macbeth 6972
The Inviolable Voice 4803, 4815
The Invitation 20625
The Island Revisited 16020
The Isle 15843
The Isle Is Full of Noyses 15842
[The Jewish King Lear] 6126
The Jubilee 21021
The Juliet Valses 13964
[The Karl Marx Play] 18283
The Kid from Stratford 20954
The King 4643
The King's Grief 6047
The King's Song 6322
The King's Sonnet 6210
The Knot Garden 95, 16207
The Lad of Stratford 20980
The Lark 20788
The Lark at Break of Day 19571
The Lay of the Willow 12491
[The Life and Death of Sir John Falstaff] 4373, 4565, 8906
[The Light Grief] 21220
"The Lion's Song" 10159
The little Love-god 20459, 20547
"The little love-god lying once asleep" 20543, 20544
The Load-Stars 10369
The Loneliness and Gloom of Leontes 18763
The Lonely Shepherd 19122
The Lord is my Shepherd 9696
The Lordling's Daughter 20652
The lover and his lass 1420
The Lowly Lover 20082
The Lusty Horn 1851
The Lyrics and Incidental Music from Twelfth Night 16857
The Macbeth Quadrilles, Selected from Mathew Locke's Celebrated Music . . . 6995
[The Magic Christian] 4129
The Man I Marry 21261
The Mantle of Night 15610
The Marriage of True Minds 20318
The Marriage Song Sung by Mrs. Hudson in the agreeable Disapointment [sic] 18277
The Masque in Timon of Athens 16338
The Masque of Juno & Ceres 16180
The Master, The Swabber 15856

The master, the swabber, the boatswain and I
  14906, 15844
[The master, the swabber, the boatswain, and
  I] 15851, 15852
The May Song 189
The May! the May! 1361
The Melodies of Tchaikowsky 13979
The Merchant 8738
The Merchant of Venice 8073, 8083, 8105,
  8111, 8112, 8113, 8128, 8129, 8139,
  8146, 8147, 8148, 8152, 8156, 8186,
  8210, 8216, 8222, 8265, 8280, 8312,
  8320, 8330, 8349, 8350, 8373, 8385,
  8386, 8387, 8391, 8393, 8400, 8419,
  8704, 8774, 11614
[The Merchant of Venice] 8050, 8052, 8053,
  8058, 8067, 8068, 8075, 8077, 8078,
  8080, 8085, 8088, 8089, 8093, 8100,
  8102, 8104, 8106, 8108, 8110, 8114,
  8115, 8119, 8120, 8123, 8127, 8132,
  8133, 8134, 8141, 8142, 8143, 8144,
  8159, 8160, 8163, 8166, 8167, 8169,
  8170, 8175, 8177, 8178, 8180, 8184,
  8185, 8187, 8192, 8197, 8198, 8208,
  8212, 8213, 8226, 8233, 8234, 8235,
  8236, 8237, 8239, 8240, 8241, 8242,
  8245, 8246, 8247, 8252, 8253, 8256,
  8259, 8263, 8266, 8269, 8270, 8271,
  8272, 8276, 8278, 8291, 8294, 8296,
  8307, 8310, 8311, 8314, 8316, 8319,
  8325, 8333, 8335, 8340, 8342, 8343,
  8354, 8357, 8366, 8367, 8374, 8377,
  8378, 8379, 8731
The Mermaid's Song, From Weber's Oberon
  10846, 10890
The Mermaid's Song from Weber's Opera
  Oberon 10895
The Mermaid's Song[,] 'Oh! 'Tis Pleasant To
  Float On The Sea.' from Weber's Celebrated
  Opera 10880
The Mermaid's Vesper Song 10910
The Merry Adventures of Falstaff 9198
'The Merry Bachelor'[:] Five Elizabethan Lyrics
  11468
The Merry Elves 21303, 21304
The Merry Month of May 189
The Merry Wives of Windsor 8808, 8810,
  8820, 8834, 8837, 8848, 8853, 8862,
  8863, 8867, 8875, 8927, 8960, 8961,
  8962, 8967, 8983, 8985, 8986, 9037,
  9129, 9211, 9215, 9221
[The Merry Wives of Windsor] 8798, 8799,
  8801, 8806, 8807, 8813, 8814, 8822,
  8825, 8828, 8832, 8833, 8845, 8847,
  8851, 8860, 8861, 8864, 8866, 8868,
  8870, 8873, 8888, 8889, 8891, 8893,
  8896, 8898, 8903, 8913, 8914, 8920,
  8928, 8930, 8931, 8936, 8940, 8941,

8944, 8946, 8952, 8963, 8965, 8966,
  8980, 9043, 9044, 9118
[The Merry Wives of Windsor: Grand Selection]
  9079
[The Merry Wives of Windsor: Operatic
  Selection] 9048
"The Merry Wives of Windsor" Overture 9120,
  9131
The Merry Wives of Windsor[,] Overture from
  O. Nicolai's Opera 9151
The Merry Wives of Windsor, Polka 9100
The Merry Wives of Windsor Quadrille 9027,
  9101
The Merry Wives of Windsor Quadrilles 9031
The Merry Wives of Windsor Valse 9094
The Merry Wives of Windsor within the
  Compass of the Flute 9257
The Merry Wives of Windsor . . . (Otto Nicolai)
  9134
The Midsummer Marriage 10806
The Midsummer Night's Dream 10688
The Midsummer Night's Dream Waltz 10736
The Mikado; or, The Town of Titipu 12486
The Mines of Sulphur 12468
The 'Miranda' Valse 16075
The Miranda Waltzes 16269
The Mirror 19754
[The MND Show] 10273
The Moaning Song 11339
The Modern Caliban 16218
The Monkey Opera or The Making of a
  Soliloquy 4179
The Montagues and the Capulets 13948
The Moon 10263
The Moon shines bright 8671
The Moor of Venice 12375
[The Moor of Venice] 11835
The Morning 2863
The Morning Chase 16424
The much admir'd Act Symphonies to
  Coriolanus 2360
The much Admir'd Overture to Coriolanus
  2360
The much admir'd Overture to Cymbeline
  2502
The much admir'd Overture to Macbeth 7212
The Mulberry Tree 21021, 21121
The Muse 19679, 20034, 20045, 20058
The Music for animating the Statue, in
  Shakespeare's play of the Winter's Tale
  18699
The Music for Hamlet 3306
The Music for Twelfth Night 17077
The Music Hall Shakespeare 21032
The Music in Macbeth 6813, 7003, 7004,
  7213
The Music in Macbeth, Composed by Matthew
  Locke 6975
The Music in Shakespeare's 'Tempest' 15115

The Music in Shakespeare's Tragedy of Macbeth 6976

The Music in Shakespeare's Twelfth Night 4666, 5229, 6120, 9236, 16180, 16666, 18650, 19661, 19700, 19773, 20740, 20804

The Music in The Tempest 14818

The Music in the Tempest as alter'd by Dryden & Davenant 15179

The Music Played At The Banquet in "The Fairy Prince" 10766

The Music to Shakespeare's Hamlet 3136

The Music to Shakespeare's Julius Caesar 5423

The Music To Shakespeare's Play The Tempest 15293

The Music to Shakespeare's Tempest 15293

The Musical Golconda, or, Beauties of Melody 435, 7906

The Musick in Harlequin Ranger 21255

The Musick in the Comedy of the Tempest 14702, 15179, 15218

The Musick in the Comedy of Twelfth Night 16621

The Musick in the Play call'd Sawney the Scot or ye Tameing ye Shrew 14679

[The Musick of Mac-beth] 6971

The Mystery of Hamlet[,] King of Denmark or What We Will 4111, 20868

The Naked Hamlet 4097

[The Net] 12172

The New Air in the Tempest. Sung by Mrs. Farrell, In the Character of Ariel 14757

The New National Song Book 21009

The new Sheep-Shearing Song in the Winter's Tale 18678

The New Songs in the Pantomime of the Witches[,] The Celebrated Epilogue in the Comedy of Twelfth Night[,] A Song in the Two Gentlemen of Verona . . . to which are added . . . a favourite French Air Sung in the Comedy of Twelfth Night by Mrs. Abington 17307, 18444

The New-Born King 3819

[The Newfoundland Tempest] 16181

The Night I Played Richard the Third 13074

The Noble Heart[:] A Tribute to Shakespeare 1950, 3834, 8556, 10748, 11447, 13854, 15848, 19285, 21034

The Old King's Lament 6084

The Ophelia Polka 3942

The Order of the Coronation 5037

The Original Music in Macbeth as Composed by Matthew Locke 6986

The original Music in the Witches scene in Middleton's comedy of the Witch, from a MS. of that age in the Editor's possession 6925

The Original Music, introduced in the Tragedy of Macbeth, Composed by Matthew Locke . . . 6977

The Original Music to Middleton's Tragi-Comedy of "The Witch." Temp. James I 6926

The Original Musick in the Tempest 14950, 15115

The Original Songs Airs & Chorusses which were introduced in the Tragedy of Macbeth in Score[,] Composed by Matthew Locke 6705, 6971

The Original Songs, Dances, &c. in Romeo and Juliet Up to Larks 14044

The Ousel Cock 9334, 10445, 10452

The Ouselcock 10447

The Ouzel Cock 10450

The Overture & Music in Shakespeare's Comedy of Errors 336, 1954, 2032, 4085, 6119, 6496, 6669, 7510, 8031, 8724, 12445, 16179, 18266, 18649, 19136, 20739, 20803

The Overture and Music to Shakspere's Tempest 15009

The Overture[,] Entr. & Actes & Music to Henry 5th 4725

The Overture, Songs, Airs, & Chorusses, in the Jubilee or Shakspear's Garland as Performed at Stratford upon Avon, and the Theatre Royal Drury Lane. To which is added a Cantata called Queen Mab or the Fairies Jubilee 21021, 21121

The Overture, Songs, Chorusses &c. in the Battle of Hexham or Days of Old 4881, 4926, 4962

The Overture, Songs, Duetts, Glees, & Chorusses In Shakespeare's Play of the Two Gentlemen of Verona 1953, 6668, 10754, 14676, 18361, 19508, 19587, 19882, 20026, 20128, 20175, 20286, 20742, 20805

The Owl 6495, 6501, 6536, 6642

"The owl is abroad" 14705, 14950, 15486

The Owl Song 6205, 6645

The Padua Town Band Awaits the Arrival of the Wedding Party 14669

The Passing Seasons. Summer 1892

The Passionate Pilgrim 20627, 20673, 20722

The Pedlar 18869, 18989, 18996

The Pedlar and The Cow 18989

The Pedlar[:] "Will you buy any tape" 19069

The Pedlar's Song 18998, 19021, 19133

The Pedlar's Song From Shakespeare's "The Winter's Tale" 19072

The Perdita Waltzes 19140

The Phoenix and the Turtle 20758, 20759, 20761, 20765, 20766, 21086

[The Phoenix and the Turtle] 20753

The Phoenix and Turtle 20754

The Plaint: "Oh! let me for ever weep" 10197

The Plaint uit The Fairy Queen 10206

(The Play of Love) 4400

"The Play's The Thing" 4238

'The play's the thing' from Shakespeare's drama 'Hamlet' 3812

The Pleasures of Youth 1508, 20680

The Poet 21203

The Poet's Corner 21168

The Polite Pilot 16186

The Polonius Platitudes 4070

The Poor Soul 12288

The Poor Soul Sat Sighing 12255, 12268, 12270, 12292, 12301, 12312, 12325

[The poor soul sat sighing by a sycamore tree] 12290, 12300, 12310, 12329, 12330, 12343, 12351, 12368

The Popular Melody, Known As Bid Me Discourse 16677

'The Popular Shakespeare'[:] Songs from the Plays of Shakespeare 1073, 1372, 1692, 6433, 6557, 7901, 11463, 17550, 17918, 18148, 18523, 19005, 19045, 19080

The Potion Scene 13377

The Power of Music 5065

The Prince of Denmark's March 4270

The Prince of Morocco's Fanfare & March 8087

The Quality of Mercy 8482, 8673, 8675, 8678, 8679, 8680

[The quality of mercy] 8676

The quality of mercy is not strain'd 8674

The Queen's Obsession 7539

The Rain, it raineth 18128, 18138

The rain it raineth every day 18185

The Rape of Lucrece 20772, 21041

The Rape of Lucretia 20779

The Reign of King Edward III 20841

The Rejected Lover 17604

The Rival Othellos 12507

The Road to Siberia from "Lady Macbeth of Mtsensk" 7553

The Rodgers and Hart Song Book 2221

The Rodgers and Hart Songbook 2208

The Romance of Numbers 6094

The Royal Jubilee Sonata. for the Piano Forte[,] Chiefly Selected from Kozeluch & Dussek[,] With Shakespeare's Jubilee Voluntary And Other Appropriate Airs 21101

The Rubicon 5545

The Russian Masqueraders 6664

The Sailor Drinks 15816

The Satyrs' Dance 19139

The Scythe of Time 19825

[The Sea and the Mirror] 16183

The Seagull 14036

The Seasons 6629

The Second Volume of Lyric Harmony Consisting of Eighteen entire new Songs and Ballads[,] The Words collected from the best Poets, ancient and modern . . . 2845, 20781

The Select Airs, in Rossini's Admired Opera Otello 12069

The Sequel to The Play of Love 4400

The Serenade Sung by Mr. Lowe in the Merchant of Venice 8059

The Servants of the Serpent 346

The Seven Ages 966, 1878

The Seven Ages of Man 534, 638, 953, 955, 972, 1870, 1874, 1908, 1982

The Seven Ages—Bottled 1957

The Sexton's Song 2910, 2911

The Shades of Night 20914

The Shakespeare Hymn Tune Book 1989, 2399, 2874, 4237, 6164, 7574, 10927, 11644, 12509, 14177, 16231, 18320, 19144, 20497

The Shakespeare Jazz 21270

[The Shakespeare Murders] 21263

The Shakespeare Musical Wreath 21166

The Shakespeare Quadrille 21111

The Shakespeare Quadrilles 1881, 1993, 7425, 7583, 16017, 21120

The Shakespeare Shake; or, The Funky Funk, or, The Shimmy Shake 21085

The Shakespeare Song Book 1091, 1396, 2584, 2687, 5131, 6576, 10527, 11476, 15915, 17940, 18534, 19008

The Shakespearian Song Book 1054, 1669, 3866, 5094, 6032, 6548, 7891, 10327, 10405, 11452, 15541, 15896, 17888, 18976, 19042, 20235, 20637

The Shakspeare Album, or Warwickshire Garland, Consisting of Ancient, Modern, & Traditional Songs &c. Illustrative of Shakspeare 21314

The Shakspeare Polkas 1894, 18219

The Shakspeare Vocal Album 21315

The Shaksperean Overture 480, 7511, 14246, 21106

[The Sheep-Shearing; or, Florizel and Perdita] 18679

The Shepherds' Dance 18809

The Shepherd's Invitation 20587, 20588

The Shepherds' March 18809

The Shepherds Masque 19139

"The Shepherd's Song" for The Winter's Tale 18768

The Ship goes up, up, up 16186

The Shipwreck 20791

The Shoemaker 4167

[The Shrew] 14277

The Siege of Time 19890

The Singing Parts in Shakespeare's Plays (Complete) 21360

The Sleep-Walking Scene[,] Macbeth 7261

The Smiths "Shakespeare's Sister" [sic] 21279

The Soldier Drinks 12216

The Solemn Dirge in Romeo and Juliet 13380

The Soliloquy 3849

The Song from Love's Labours Lost ("When daisys pied") 6267

The Song (Love's Labour's Lost) 6321
The Song Master[:] Ten Songs from Schubert
    2757
The Song of Agincourt 4702
The Song of Autolycus 19022
The Song of Lucius 5400, 20777
The songs & incidental music arranged &
    composed . . . for Granville Barker's
    production of A midsummer night's dream
    at the Savoy Theatre in January, 1914
    9998, 19175
The Songs and Duetts In the Blind Beggar of
    Bethnal Green; As perform'd by Mr. Lowe,
    and Mrs. Clive, at the Theatre-Royal, in
    Drury-Lane. With the Favourite Songs, Sung
    by Mr. Lowe, In The Merchant of Venice, At
    the said Theatre 6495, 8059
The Songs and Symphony's in the Masque of
    Venus and Adonis as they are Perform'd at
    the Theatre Royal . . . 20820
The songs from As you like it 1948
The Songs from Shakespeare's Plays, Part I
    21347
The Songs from Shakespeare's Plays, Part II
    21348
The Songs in Queen Mab As they are perform'd
    at the Theatre Royal in Drury Lane 10755
The Songs in the Comedies called As You Like
    It, and Twelfth Night 398, 6667, 8722,
    16617
The Songs in the Tempest or the Enchanted
    Isleland [sic] As they were perform'd at the
    Theatre Royal in Drury Lane by Mrs. Clive
    and Mrs. Mozeen 14953
The Songs of Autolycus from 'Winter's Tale'
    18834
The Sonnets of William Shakespeare 19227,
    19322, 19500, 19666, 19753, 19868,
    19883, 19905, 20079, 20115, 20133,
    20268, 20374, 20378, 20479
The Sphinx. From the opera "Antony and
    Cleopatra" 222
The Spirit of Night 14039
The Spirit's Song 21299
[The Spirit's Song] 21016
The Spring (Intermezzo) 6660
The Springtime of love 18649
The Stage Play of Human Life 1987
The 'Star' Choral Singer 11544
The star-crossed lovers 13906
The Statue Scene from 'Winter's Tale' 18786
'The Stolen Flower Queen.' A Child's
    Midsummer Night's Dream 10960
The Storm 15456, 18887
The Story of Constance (King John—
    Shakespeare) 5582
The Stratford Series of Shakespeare Songs 125,
    493, 2446, 2981, 4309, 4530, 4702, 4971,
    5269, 5695, 6205, 6206, 6756, 7613,

8083, 8820, 9334, 11042, 11043, 11696,
    11697, 12545, 13157, 14905, 14906,
    16451, 16697, 18373, 18702, 19173, 20743
The sweet o' the year 19037, 19054
The Sweet Season 1280, 3752
The Symphony & Choruses, in Macbeth . . . To
    which is added An Additional Symphony
    6981
The Taming of the Shrew 93, 2836, 4091,
    6672, 8752, 9250, 10773, 10780, 12452,
    14098, 14243, 14255, 14259, 14270,
    14278, 14279, 14280, 14291, 14292,
    14294, 14304, 14315, 14316, 14321,
    14338, 14347, 14355, 14393, 14451,
    14484, 14493, 14502, 14503, 14504,
    14508, 14509, 14546, 14548, 14549,
    14551, 14566, 14567, 14570, 14647,
    14664, 14665, 14685, 18270, 18278,
    18286, 19665, 19808, 19845, 19861,
    20124, 20143, 20227, 20342, 20451,
    20524, 20534, 20536, 20747, 20748,
    20749, 20808, 20809, 21121
[The Taming of the Shrew] 14217, 14221,
    14226, 14230, 14242, 14244, 14248,
    14251, 14262, 14266, 14272, 14275,
    14276, 14281, 14282, 14283, 14284,
    14290, 14295, 14298, 14308, 14311,
    14313, 14324, 14325, 14328, 14337,
    14344, 14359, 14366, 14382, 14385,
    14391, 14394, 14408, 14411, 14418,
    14426, 14427, 14428, 14436, 14449,
    14451, 14453, 14454, 14459, 14461,
    14462, 14464, 14466, 14472, 14473,
    14476, 14485, 14497, 14507, 14513,
    14520, 14521, 14523, 14528, 14529,
    14536, 14537, 14538, 14540, 14541,
    14542, 14543, 14544, 14550, 14561
The Taming Of The Shrew (Der
    Widerspänstigen Zähmung) 14583
The Tavern Song 4614
[The Teatrolley, or a Midsummer Night's
    Scream] 10760
The telecasters 7431, 12390
The Tempest 14700, 14701, 14737, 14741,
    14821, 14850, 14858, 14863, 14872,
    14882, 14898, 14915, 14922, 14934,
    14942, 14943, 14955, 14977, 14978,
    14990, 14991, 15008, 15012, 15019,
    15020, 15021, 15034, 15038, 15040,
    15096, 15105, 15106, 15109, 15110,
    15124, 15168, 15174, 15175, 15184,
    15200, 15208, 15218, 15222, 15234,
    15238, 15243, 15246, 15260, 15265,
    15281, 15286, 15293, 15298, 15299,
    15300, 15308, 15311, 15317, 15320,
    15324, 15362, 15365, 15373, 15374,
    15384, 15400, 15409, 15417, 15420,
    15425, 15429, 15445, 15458, 15462,
    15478, 15479, 15488, 15498, 16002,

The Tempest (*cont.*)
  16022, 16037, 16040, 16059, 16060,
  16125, 16140, 16175, 16214, 16241,
  16246, 16263, 16268, 16274, 16282,
  16291, 20340
[The Tempest] 14691, 14693, 14694, 14695,
  14748, 14754, 14852, 14855, 14861,
  14867, 14870, 14871, 14877, 14883,
  14888, 14889, 14892, 14893, 14895,
  14899, 14908, 14909, 14911, 14912,
  14913, 14916, 14917, 14918, 14925,
  14927, 14931, 14932, 14933, 14935,
  14939, 14940, 14947, 14949, 14950,
  14958, 14959, 14962, 14966, 14968,
  14969, 14973, 14974, 14979, 14988,
  14989, 14998, 15002, 15011, 15015,
  15018, 15023, 15027, 15030, 15032,
  15033, 15039, 15048, 15050, 15059,
  15070, 15072, 15074, 15076, 15077,
  15082, 15083, 15084, 15090, 15092,
  15097, 15098, 15100, 15102, 15104,
  15107, 15108, 15130, 15131, 15135,
  15137, 15142, 15144, 15146, 15147,
  15150, 15153, 15154, 15155, 15158,
  15160, 15161, 15162, 15163, 15164,
  15167, 15169, 15171, 15176, 15182,
  15185, 15186, 15188, 15193, 15194,
  15198, 15203, 15210, 15211, 15212,
  15213, 15215, 15223, 15225, 15228,
  15229, 15230, 15233, 15236, 15240,
  15242, 15245, 15248, 15252, 15253,
  15254, 15257, 15258, 15264, 15267,
  15269, 15270, 15271, 15272, 15273,
  15276, 15287, 15291, 15318, 15319,
  15323, 15329, 15333, 15349, 15359,
  15363, 15367, 15368, 15369, 15371,
  15372, 15377, 15379, 15383
The Tempest. Brilliant Fantasia on the
  incidental Music in Shakespeare's Play
  14739, 14823, 15487
The Tempest[:] Full Incidental Music 15334
The Tempest Galop 15297
'The Tempest' Music 15447
The Tempest[:] Music to the Comedy by
  William Shakespeare 14923
The Tempest, or the Enchanted Island 14859,
  15387, 15405, 15424, 15431, 15444,
  15464
The Tempest-March 16154
The Third Secret 16240
The Three Caskets or Venice Re-served 8753
The Three Romeos 14202
The Three Songs For The Player Queen From
  Hamlet 4072
The Three Witches 7400
The Tinker's Song 18949
The Titania Mazurka 10678
The Titania Polka 10583, 10702
The Titania Schottische 10690

The Tolling Bell 3861
The Tomb of Shakespear 21013
[The Tragedy of Julius Caesar] 5441
The Tragedy of Macbeth 7556
[The Tragedy of Marcus Brutus] 5538
The Triumph of Death 19942, 19948
The Trojans 8747
The Trojans at Carthage 8743
The Trojans In Carthage 8749
The Trumpets of Summer 21002
The Tunes in the 1st Act of Timon of Athens
  16332
The Turning Worlds 6094
The twelve points of the modified Mercalli
  earthquake scale 21247
The Two Gentlemen of Verona 18354, 18360,
  18372, 18382, 18387, 18431, 18435,
  18438, 18439, 18460, 18461, 18466,
  18467
[The Two Gentlemen of Verona] 18348,
  18352, 18353, 18358, 18374, 18376,
  18388, 18389, 18391, 18392, 18393,
  18398, 18402, 18409, 18416, 18418,
  18419, 18420, 18425, 18429, 18433,
  18436, 18442, 18447, 18451, 18458
[The Two Noble Kinsmen] 19158, 19159,
  19160, 19161, 19162, 19163, 19164,
  19166, 19167
The Unchangeable 20283
The Undiscover'd Country 2556
The Unveiling of the Statue 18843
The Valley Wind 6474
The Verdi Opera Album 12209
The Vicar of Wakefield 1967
The Vision 5038
The Vision of Ariel 16292
The Vision of Cleopatra 354
The Vocal Music to Shakespeare Plays[:]
  'Macbeth' 21340
The Vocal Music to Shakespeare's Plays[:] A
  Midsummer Night's Dream 21313
The Vocal Music to Shakespeare's Plays[:]
  Antony and Cleopatra 21333
The Vocal Music to Shakespeare's Plays[:] 'As
  You Like It' 21334
The Vocal Music to Shakespeare's Plays[:]
  'Cymbeline' 21335
The Vocal Music to Shakespeare's Plays[:]
  'Hamlet' 21326
The Vocal Music to Shakespeare's Plays[:]
  Henry IV Part II 21336
The Vocal Music to Shakespeare's Plays[:]
  'Henry The Eighth' 21337
The Vocal Music to Shakespeare's Plays[:]
  'King Lear' 21338
The Vocal Music to Shakespeare's Plays[:]
  'Love's Labour's Lost' 21339
The Vocal Music to Shakespeare's Plays[:]
  Measure for Measure 21341

The Vocal Music to Shakespeare's Plays.
Midsummer Night's Dream 21313
The Vocal Music to Shakespeare's Plays[:]
'Much Ado About Nothing' 21330
The Vocal Music to Shakespeare's Plays[:]
'Othello' 21331
The Vocal Music to Shakespeare's Plays[:]
'Romeo & Juliet' 21342
The Vocal Music to Shakespeare's Plays[:] The
'Merchant of Venice' 21327
The Vocal Music to Shakespeare's Plays[:] The
Merry Wives of Windsor 21329
The Vocal Music to Shakespeare's Plays[:] 'The
Tempest' 21332
The Vocal Music to Shakespeare's Plays[:] 'The
Winter's Tale' 21344
The Vocal Music to Shakespeare's Plays[:]
'Twelfth Night' 21328
The Vocal Music to Shakespeare's Plays[:] Two
Gentlemen of Verona 21343
The Vocal Musick in the Tempest 15431
The Walk to the Paradise Garden. Intermezzo
from 'A Village Romeo and Juliet' 14078,
14086
[The Wars of the Roses] 4859, 4877, 4878,
4901, 4916, 4917, 4943, 4958, 4959,
12905, 13025, 13026
The Warwickshire Lad 21021, 21023
The Warwickshire Lads 21022
The Wedding March 9635, 9646, 9649, 9667,
9713, 9789, 9791, 9850
The Wedding March from A Midsummer
Night's Dream 9848
The Wedding Masque from The Tempest
15175
The Wedding of Gloriana 6679, 11631
The Weird Sisters 7384
[The Weird Sisters: or, the Thane and the
Throne] 7532
The Wellington Quadrilles 15575
[The White Rose and the Red] 4712, 4851,
4893, 4936, 12825
The Whole of the Music in As You Like It . . .
To which are added The 3 songs composed
for the above Play by Dr. Arne 480, 19226,
20741, 20806
The Willow 12282, 12305, 12339
The Willow Cabin 18278
The Willow Song 11697, 11716, 12247,
12251, 12256, 12259, 12261, 12271,
12274, 12277, 12278, 12294, 12307,
12328, 12333, 12344, 12345, 12347,
12356, 12359, 12360, 12533, 12535
The Willow Song[:] 'A Poor Soul Sat Sighing'
12399
The Willow Song (Desdemona's Song in
Shakespeare's "Othello") 12260
The Willow Song (from 'Othello') 11717,
12263

The Wind and the Rain 17246, 18080, 18082,
18097, 18103, 18115, 18117, 18139,
18170, 18192, 18198, 18199, 18202
The Wind and the Rain (Twelfth
Night—Epilogue) 16815
The Winter Wind 1184
The Winter's Tale 18672, 18677, 18687,
18694, 18701, 18709, 18710, 18730,
18749, 18755, 18758, 18760, 18762,
18770, 18834, 18839, 18841, 18864,
18866, 18873, 18881, 18885, 18886,
18892, 18911, 18912, 18916, 18917,
18918, 18933, 18937, 19093, 19095
[The Winter's Tale] 18671, 18681, 18688,
18689, 18690, 18691, 18696, 18697,
18698, 18702, 18703, 18707, 18708,
18713, 18716, 18717, 18720, 18721,
18722, 18727, 18728, 18731, 18734,
18737, 18738, 18740, 18742, 18748,
18751, 18754, 18761, 18763, 18766,
18767, 18768, 18773, 18774, 18781,
18783, 18785, 18787, 18803, 18811,
18815, 18816, 18818, 18820, 18821,
18822, 18825, 18827, 18829, 18830,
18832, 18836, 18847, 18849, 18850,
18851, 18853, 18858, 18861, 18868,
18870, 18871, 18872, 18876, 18891,
18894, 18902, 18904, 18905, 18906,
18907, 18910, 18914, 18915, 18919,
18920, 18921, 18943, 19098
The Witches 1993, 7404, 7425
The Witches, and Fairies[:] An Ode in
Commemoration of Shakespear 21055
The Witches' Chant from 'MacBeth' 7445
The Witches Dance 7013
The Witches in Macbeth 7482
The Witches [sic] Song in the Tragedy of
Macbeth 6971
The Witches' Song 6988
the witness and revelation of the new tragedy
of King Lear 6013
The Wonderful Bell Song 8589, 15701
The Wonderful Year 6685
[The Wooden O] 20920
The Woosel-Cock 9471
The Words by Shakespear 5097
The Words by Shakespeare 20589
The words by Shakespeare in Antony &
Cleopatra 290
The words by Shakespeare in as you like it
1820
The words by Shakespeare in Cymbeline
2646
The words by Shakespeare in Henry the
Eight [sic] 5073
The words by Shakespeare in Love's labour
[sic] lost 6361
The words by Shakespeare in Measure for
Measure 7850, 7990

The words by Shakespeare in much ado about nothing 11380
The Words from Shakespeares Winters Tale 18997
The Works of Dove DoVale 4208
The Works of Henry Purcell 7526, 12708
The World A-Hunting Is 18023
The World and the Child 21246
The Youth of Shakespeare 21141
[Theater of Blood] 20864
Thème de l'opéra: Othello de Rossini 12098
Theme for Scottish March 7197
[Theme for the Country of Corba] 5310
Theme From Arden of Faversham 20853
Theme from Midsummer Night's Dream 9658
Theme from Military March No. 1 (Land of Hope and Glory) 12515
Theme from Military March No. 4 12515
Theme from Overture 'Romeo and Juliet' 13969
Theme from Romeo And Juliet 13971, 13982, 14005
Theme from "Romeo and Juliet" Overture 13981
Theme From the 'Romeo and Juliet' Overture 13997
Themes from Romeo and Juliet 13978, 13995
Themes from the Incidental Music to Mendelssohn's A Midsummer Night's Dream 9689
Then hate me when thou wilt 20114
Then is there mirth in heaven 1593
Then let me the Canakin clink 12214
Then let not Winter's ragged hand . . . 19215
Then they for sudden joy did weep 5695
"Then to Sea, Boys" 15853
Then to Silvia let us sing 18518
There dwelt a man in Babylon 16697
There Is A Willow Grows Aslant A Brook 3904
These Yellow Sands 15515
They bore him bare faced 3838
They bore him bare-fac'd 3244
They bore him barefac'd on his Bier 2919
[They bore him barefac'd on the bier] 3839
They bore him bare-faced . . . 3832
They bore him barefaced on the bier 2981, 3835
They That Have Power 20134
They that have power to hurt and will do none 20135
Thinkst thou to seduce me then 13159
Third Cantata 16169
Third Sonnet to Sundry Notes of Music 20605
Thirteen Standard Songs of Shakespeare 21316
Thirty-two lyrics from the plays of William Shakespeare 21362
This above all 3844
This Can't Be Love 2208, 2210, 2212, 2214, 2216, 2218, 2220, 2221, 2228, 2229, 2230, 2233

This Dear, Dear Land 12754
This England 12758, 12764
This Gap of Time 19117
This is the State of Man 5209
This Royal Throne 12765
This Royal Throne Of Kings 12760
This Royal Throne of Kings, This Sceptred Isle 5653, 12759
[This royal throne of kings, this sceptred isle] 12763
This Sceptred Isle 5653, 12759
[This Side Idolatry] 20879
This Sorry Scheme of Things 7398
This Was A Man 5495, 20872
Thorough bush, thorough brier 10403
Those hours . . . 19207
Those lips that love's own hand 20484
Those Pretty Wrongs that Liberty Commits 19703
"Thou art as tyrannous, so as thou art" 20431
Thou blind fool, Love 20446
Thou Know'st the Mask of Sealing Night 7557
Thou soft flowing Avon 20905, 20906, 20990, 20996
Thou soft-flowing Avon 20903, 20904, 20907, 20908
Thou, Trumpet 16571
Thought 19725
Thoughts of Melody 1752
Three Ariel Songs 15373
Three canzonets on love 7847
Three Choral Songs from 'As You Like It' 1069, 1365, 1687, 21047
Three Christmas Songs 1088
Three Couplets on the Charms of Women 21078
Three Dances from 'The Fairy Queen' by Henry Purcell 10219
Three Dances from the Incidental Music to King Richard II 12703
Three Dances from the Music to Henry VIII 4977, 4982
Three Dances From The Music To Shakespeare's Tempest 15294
Three Dances from 'The Palace of Puck' 10957
Three Diatonic Settings for 'Twelfth Night' 17501, 17850, 18116
Three Elizabethan airs; on the lines of Ophelia, in Hamlet, act 4, scene 5 4058
Three Elizabethan Partsongs 12360, 18031
Three Elizabethan Songs 6679, 11415, 11631, 12359, 18030
Three English Lyrics 21235
Three English Part-Songs 1373
Three English Songs 5156, 19271
Three English Sonnets 19909
Three Fancies 10660
Three Fragments from Lady Macbeth of Mtsensk 'Katerina Ismaila' [sic] 7552

Three from my den 21253
Three Kings 21294
Three Little Commentaries 12755
Three Little Elves 10684
Three Lyric Pieces 7439
Three Lyrics from the plays of Shakespeare 1209, 5204, 11582
Three Madrigals from Wm Shakespeare 7876, 8549, 9204
Three Madrigals On Song Texts From The Plays of William Shakespeare 2692, 7932, 17953
Three merry men 16697
Three New Old Songs 5169, 18012
Three Night Songs on Elizabethan Texts 10498
Three of Shakespeare's Sonnets 19400, 19567, 20201
Three Old English Songs 1428, 1430, 17854
Three Ophelia Songs 4222
Three Pastels 10648
Three Pastoral Songs 7915, 8582, 15911
Three Phrases from Romeo and Juliet 13827, 13852, 13879
Three Pieces for Organ 13014
Three Pieces from Arden Must Die 20937
Three Pieces from 'Romeo and Juliet' Ballet 13802
Three Pieces from 'The Fairy Queen' 10188, 10262
Three Pieces from the Incidental Music to The Merchant of Venice 8300
Three Pieces from the Opera A Midsummer Night's Dream 10284
Three Poems by Shakespeare 3740, 8563, 17896
Three Poems of the Sea 15113
Three Portraits from The England of Elizabeth 20897
Three Scenes from 'Hamlet', Ophelia's Story 4081
Three Seasonal Songs 1274
Three Sentences from the Romeo and Juliet for Strings 13926
Three Shakespeare Madrigals 1018, 1775, 7856, 7950, 8534, 8610, 11425, 15747, 17980, 18105, 19088, 20610
Three Shakespeare Settings 5173, 15572, 15754
Three Shakespeare Songs 289, 980, 987, 990, 1010, 1025, 1137, 1160, 1169, 1212, 1248, 1302, 1387, 1450, 1616, 1618, 1641, 1721, 1756, 1789, 1800, 2457, 2549, 2620, 2624, 2796, 3697, 4062, 4076, 5203, 6041, 6383, 6390, 6423, 6462, 6490, 6516, 6584, 6641, 6642, 7831, 7861, 7896, 7965, 7984, 8011, 8030, 8516, 8521, 8535, 8567, 8621, 8631, 8647, 9201, 10423, 10428, 10486, 10543, 10572, 11584, 12248, 12301, 15524, 15602, 15633, 15693, 15749, 15758, 15769, 15780, 15840, 15933, 15947, 16375, 17375, 17437, 17456, 17463, 17488, 17500, 17568, 17611, 17664, 17668, 17696, 17745, 17764, 17781, 17829, 17900, 17957, 17993, 18065, 18082, 18087, 18115, 18264, 19180, 19353, 21095
[Three Shakespeare Songs] 7987, 17643, 18022
Three Shakespeare Sonnets 19191, 19210, 19241, 19332, 19353, 19383, 19399, 19526, 19610, 19636, 19652, 19739, 19803, 19886, 19959, 19980, 20023, 20163, 20186, 20188, 20195, 20202, 20205, 20222, 20237, 20299, 20315, 20396, 20453
Three Shakespearean Madrigals 8497, 9200, 17692
Three Shakespearean Songs 1090, 1143, 1710, 3724, 6378, 15702, 15739, 15935, 18125
Three Shakespearean Sonnets 19447, 19586, 20022, 20424, 20455, 20495
Three Shakespeare-Songs 19486, 19499, 19970
Three Shakespearian Love Lyrics 1385, 11471, 17934
Three Shakespearian Love Songs 11579, 17661, 18042
Three Shakespearian Trios 8672, 13839, 20324
Three Songs by Schubert 18613
Three Songs for Ariel 15559, 15717, 15922
Three Songs for The Merchant of Venice 8103
Three Songs from 'As You Like It' 1011
Three Songs from Shakespeare 993, 1530, 1554, 1603, 2595, 3796, 5127, 5128, 5198, 6628, 7919, 7920, 7999, 8000, 11566, 17633, 17648, 17785, 17973, 18014, 18029, 18170, 18188, 18529
Three Songs From Shakespeare's 'As You Like It' 1122, 1484, 1738
Three Songs from Shakespeare's Twelfth Night 17493, 17594, 17833, 17969, 18109, 18169
Three Songs from 'The Fairy Queen' 10254
Three Songs from the Film 'Gone to Earth' 11611
Three Songs from 'The Tempest' 14850, 15519, 15571, 15612, 15753, 15874, 15941
Three Songs from 'Twelfth Night' 17253, 17466, 17796, 18093
Three Songs from William Shakespeare 6479, 15756, 19265
Three Songs of Longing 1128
Three Songs of Sadness 2533, 15625, 17462

Three Songs of Shakespeare 19855, 20659, 21061
Three Songs to Lyrics by Shakespeare 1383, 3763, 17562
Three Songs to Lyrics from Shakespeare 1383, 3763, 17562
Three Songs to Poems of Shakespeare 1409, 1718, 20660
Three Sonnets 19250, 19583, 20194, 20244, 20296, 20546
Three Sonnets by Shakespeare 19259, 19423, 20400
Three sonnets by William Shakespeare 19509, 19514, 19533
Three Sonnets from Shakespeare 19444, 19787, 20172, 20285, 20377, 20415, 21088
Three Sonnets from William Shakespeare 19434, 19761, 20193
Three Sonnets of Matthew Arnold 21017
Three Sonnets of Shakespeare 19289, 19418, 20013, 20117, 20218, 20520
Three Stratford Fanfares 20822
[Three Symphonic Portraits: Hamlet, Ophelia, Polonius] 4012
Three Theatre Portraits 16033, 18215
Three Tunes from Shakespeare's England 21283
Three very short songs 21201
Three Witches; from 'Macbeth' 7354
Three 17th Century Lyrics 8488
Threnody 18258
Threnos 20755, 20756, 20757
[Threnos: Beauty Truth and Rarity] 20764
[Þrettándakvöld (eða hvað sem þið viljið) = Twelfth Night (or What You Will)] 17283
Threw Away A Pearl 12420
Thrice happy Lovers 10223
Thrice the brindled cat hath mew'd 6756
Throne of Blood 7529
Through the forest have I gone 10458
Through the House 10466
Through the House from "A Midsummer Night's Dream" 9722
Through the house give glimmering light 9334, 10459, 10465
[Through the house give glimmering light] 10462
Through the Secret Gate 7389, 10358, 10519
Thus The Gloomy World 10205
Th'Wit to Woo 6413, 6536
thy black is fairest 20381, 20431, 20543
Thy bosom is endeared with all hearts 19636, 19637
"Thy Lips" 7943
Tide Life, Tide Death 9918
Tiden 19841
Tillyvally lady 16697
Time 19874

Time Changes 15692, 17567
Time Excursions 4342
Time Past IV 19604
Timon 16371
Timon af Athen 16358
[Timon Ateenalainen] 16335
Timon Atenski 16304
Timon Athénský 16326
[Timon athénský] 16359
Timon d'Athènes 16387
Timon d'Athènes: poème symphonique d'après Shakspeare 16381
[Timon din Atena] 16323
Timon i Athen 16299
Timon of Athens 16301, 16305, 16307, 16312, 16330, 16338, 16360, 16363, 16364, 16367, 16368, 16382
[Timon of Athens] 16300, 16302, 16308, 16310, 16314, 16315, 16328, 16329, 16331, 16336, 16352, 16354, 16373
Timon of Athens: A Symphonic Portrait after Shakespeare 16379
[Timon of Athens, The Man-Hater] 16338
Timon von Athen 16321
[Timon von Athen] 16303, 16309, 16318, 16324, 16353, 16356, 16357, 16361, 16365
Timone d'Atene 16311
[Timone d'Atene] 16337
Timone Misantropo 16388
Timons Abkehr 16374
[Timons Glück und Untergang] 16383
Tinker's Song (from A Winter's Tale) 19131
Tired of All These, for Restful Death I Cry 19906
Tired With All These 19909, 19926
Titania 9918, 10154, 10165, 10166, 10172, 10173, 10269, 10274, 10275, 10575, 10578, 10582, 10584, 10586, 10600, 10604, 10611, 10615, 10628, 10633, 10644, 10647, 10653, 10662, 10663, 10669, 10677, 10682, 10683, 10686, 10694, 10699, 10701, 10710, 10713, 10715, 10719, 10723, 10728, 10735, 10911, 10922, 10936, 10962, 10965, 10968, 10989
Titania and Donkey 10283
Titania and her Fairies 10641
Titania and Oberon 10703
Titania Dances in the Moonlight 10687
Titania Galop 10599
Titania Intermezzo 10649
Titania oder Liebe durch Zauberei 10152
Titania, ou Le Songe d'une Fée 10671
Titania Sleeps 10605, 10726
Titania[:] Three Fairy Sketches 10614
Titania Waltz 10646
Titania Walzer 10587
Titania's bower 10606

Titania's Court[:] Four Fairy Lyrics 10693
Titania's Cradle 10334, 10335
Titania's Dance 10680, 10696, 10739
Titania's Flight 10725
Titania's Lullaby 10503, 10504, 10551, 10916
Titania's Nocturne 10698
Titania's Rondel & Song 9436
Titania's Serenade 10975
Titania's Slumber Song 10616
Titania's Waltz 10624
Titania-Walzer nach Motiven der komischen Operette 'Die Afrikareise' 10988
[Tito Andronico] 16396
Titus 16419
Titus' Adagio 16405
Titus Andronicus 16390, 16391, 16401, 16405, 16407, 16417, 16420, 16425
[Titus Andronicus] 16389, 16393, 16394, 16395, 16398, 16400, 16402, 16403, 16404, 16406, 16408, 16409, 16410, 16411, 16412, 16413, 16414, 16427
[Titus, Titus!] 16428
Tjugondag Knut, eller, Vad Ni vill. En sångkomedi efter Shakespears lustspel Trettondagsafton 1969, 17413
To a Soldier Dying Young 19179
To Bacchus 305
To be 3610
'To be', odpověd' na hamletovskou otázku 3971
"To Be Or Not. . . ." 4207
To Be Or Not To Be 3848, 3850, 3853, 3854, 3856, 3860, 3921, 4015, 4162, 4195, 4203, 4215, 4218, 4219, 4227, 4229, 4232, 4236, 4249, 4250, 4257, 4263, 14166
[To Be or Not to Be] 4100, 4116, 8729, 8732
"To be or not to be" Blues 4201
To Be Or Not To Be. . . . What kind of a Question is that? 4176
To bee or not to bee [&c.] 3852
'To, chto tebia braniat, ne tvoi porok (Sonet 70)' ['That thou art blam'd shall not be thy defect' (Sonnet 70)] 19930
To Cordelia 6181
To Fair Fidele's Grassy Tomb 2847, 2848, 2857, 2858, 2862
[To fair Fidele's grassy tomb] 2870
To Fair Fidele's grassy tomb, Dirge in Cymbeline 2852
To Greet the Spring 9853
To keep my gentle Jessy 8060, 8061
To Lady Mac 7435, 21132
"To Live With Thee And Be Thy Love" 20592
To me, fair friend 20230, 20231, 20241
To me, fair friend, you never can be old 20232, 20233, 20236, 20238
To Me You Never Can Be Old 20235

To Miranda 16151
To Music 8472
To Prove My Love 19513, 20335, 20348
To sange af Livet i skoven 807
To Sange af Viola 17188
To See His Face 20805
To Shakespeare 20893
To shallow rivers 8820
To Sonetter af Shakespeare 19366, 19635
To Sylvia 18527, 18602, 18610
. . . to thine own self be true 3878
To Transfigure 20002
To Wet a Widow's Eye 15791, 19275, 19501, 19933, 20081
Tod, komm herbei—Death, Come Away 17514
Today 13073
Todtengräberlied 3806
Todtengräberlied aus "Hamlet" von Shakespeare 3798
Tomorrow and tomorrow 7397
To-morrow, and to-morrow, and to-morrow 7394, 7395, 7398, 7448
Tomorrow is Saint Valentine's day 2919, 3864, 3866, 3868, 3875
[To-morrow is Saint Valentine's day] 3871
Tomorrow is St. Valentine's Day 3244, 4058, 21142
Tomorrow 'tis St. Valentine's day 2981
Tone Poem—Henry V 4827
Toneelmuziek bÿ Macbeth van W. Shakespeare 7198
Tongs and Bones 10681
Tonight 13584, 13603
Tonight from: West Side Story 13590, 13591, 13594, 13595, 13610, 13619, 13620
Too soon the flowers of spring may fade 12669
Top of the Town 4098
Torch Dance From The Music To Henry VIII 4990
Totengräbers Lied 3795
[Touch and Go] 4155
Touchstone 1877, 1887, 1895, 1921
Touchstone, Audrey and William 1896
Touchstone[:] Portrait for Orchestra 1942
Touchstone's Frolick 21121
Tout est Bien qui Finit Bien 104, 105
[Tout est bien qui finit bien] 24, 28
Tout pour l'Amour, ou Juliette et Roméo 13633
Tout pour l'Amour, ou Roméo et Juliette 13633
towards anthony holborne 19230, 20880
[Tower of London] 12780, 12943
Traditions of Shakespeare 1457, 21155
[Tragédie du roi Lear] 5848
Tragedin om Konung Richard III 12781
Tragic Obsession 7539
[Tragicheskata istoriia na Khamlet prints Datski = The Tragedy of Hamlet, Prince of Denmark] 3027

Transcriptions élégantes 12042
2 Transcriptions Italiennes variées 12133
Trascrizioni dello Scherzo nel Sogno d'una
   notte d'estate di Mendelssohn 9829
Trauermarsch 3471
[Trauermarsch] 3275
Trauermarsch für die letzte Scene des Hamlet
   aus 'Tristia' 4189
Träum der Blinden 19516
Traurnyi marsh [Funeral March] 3502
Tre arie e quattro danze (con un'eco) per
   mezzosoprano e complesso da camera da
   'The Fairy Queen' di H. Purcell 10242
Tre av narrens visor ur Trettondagsafton
   17232
Tre Danser ur musiken till 'En
   midsommarnattsdröm' 10098
Tre engelske Sange med norsk Oversættelse
   7835
Tre marscher till Shakespeares Sorgespel
   Richard III 12980
Tre Pezzi nell'Opera Otello di G. Verdi 12191
Tre Sange af Schakespeare ved E. Lembcke
   3802, 11530, 17638
Tre Sånger ur musiken till 'Stormen' 15183,
   15560, 15806, 15923
Trebles All 1458
Trei Madrigale de William Shakespeare 7961,
   8620, 20674
Trei Sonete de Shakespeare 20386, 20408,
   20433
Trek de lippen vol venijn . . . 7833
Tres Cançons de Shakespeare 21240
Tres Sonets de Shakespeare 20576
Trettondagsafton 16650, 17177, 17214,
   17232
[Trettondagsafton = Twelfth Night] 16655,
   16781, 16993, 17222, 17326
Trettondagsafton, eller, Vad Ni vill 17347
[Trettondagsafton eller Vad ni vill = Twelfth
   Night, or What You Will] 17233
Tri pesni iz muzyki k komedii V. Shekspira
   'Mnogo shuma iz nichego' [Three Songs
   from the Music to W. Shakespeare's Comedy
   Much Ado About Nothing] 11157
Tri pisni z muzyky do komedii V. Shekspira
   'Dvanadtsiata nich' [Three Songs from the
   Music to W. Shakespeare's Comedy Twelfth
   Night] 16901
Tri Sonety zo Shakespeara 19714, 20392,
   20509
Tri stikhotvoreniia [Three Poems] 19982
Tri tantsa iz baleta 'Gamlet' [Three Dances
   from the Ballet Hamlet] 3581
Triade für Orchester 3995
Trincalo's [sic] Reel 21121
Trinity Church 9008
Trinklied 300, 11807
[Trinklied des Falstaff (Als Büblein klein)] 9121

Trinklied (Drinking Song) 301
Trinklied von Shakespeare 297
Trio: Celia, Rosalind, Touchstone 20741
Trio in B♭ 4259
Trio in the Winters [sic] Tale 18675
Trio: Juno, Ceres and Iris 14878
Trio—Get you hence 18763
Trip It In A Ring (From The Faerie Queen)
   10203
Trip No Further, Pretty Sweeting 17910
Trip, trip away 8876, 10757
Triptych 5152
[Troilo e Cressida] 16478
[Troilos och Kressida] 16500, 16522
Troilus 16575
Troilus & Cressida 16457, 16516, 16538
[Troilus a Kressida] 16459, 16474, 16505,
   16532
Troilus and Cressida 16438, 16453, 16461,
   16483, 16494, 16502, 16535, 16539,
   16551, 16552, 16554, 16558, 16559,
   16574, 16584
[Troilus and Cressida] 16432, 16433, 16434,
   16439, 16443, 16444, 16446, 16447,
   16451, 16455, 16456, 16467, 16481,
   16501, 16504, 16507, 16508, 16511,
   16513, 16515, 16519, 16521, 16523,
   16529, 16530, 16531, 16533, 16534,
   16541, 16546, 16547, 16556
Troilus e Cressida 16542
[Troilus en Cressida] 16463, 16540
Troilus et Cressida 16462, 16495
[Troilus et Cressida] 16442, 16498, 16543
[Troilus i Kressyda] 16518
Troilus i Kresyda 16512
[Troilus i Kresyda] 16437, 16477, 16510,
   16517, 16524
Troilus in Kresida 16450
[Troilus och Cressida] 16445
[Troilus og Cressida] 16490
Troilus und Cressida 16440, 16441, 16497,
   16537, 16560
[Troilus und Cressida] 16448, 16449, 16458,
   16464, 16466, 16470, 16471, 16475,
   16480, 16482, 16484, 16485, 16486,
   16488, 16489, 16491, 16492, 16493,
   16496, 16499, 16503, 16506, 16514,
   16520, 16525, 16526, 16527, 16549,
   16550, 16557
Trois Divertissements sur l'opéra de Macbeth de
   G. Verdi 7315
Trois Sonnets de William Shakespeare 19724,
   19996, 20491
Trois Transcriptions d'après Roméo et Juliette
   13578
Trois Transcriptions de Roméo et Juliette 13711
Troisième Grande Fantaisie . . . Sur des Thêmes
   de Rossini avec des Variations sur la
   Romance d'Othello 12092

Troisième Quatuor pour 2 Violons, Alte & Violoncelle des Quatuors 10946

Trojan March 8744

Trold kan tæmmes 14350

[Trold kan tæmmes = The Taming of the Shrew] 14222, 14399

Troll kan temmes 14245, 14334

Troll kan tœmmes 14335

tropes on the salve regina 4023

'Trudami iznuren, khochu usnut' (27-i sonet)' ['Weary with toil, I haste me to my bed' (27th Sonnet)] 19524

True & False Compare 20421

True Love 20342

Trumpet March 21121

Trumpet Sonata No. 2 16348

Trust not Man for he'll deceive you[,] Sung by Mrs. Abington in Twelfth Night 16610

Try romansa[:] Na slova V. Shekspira [Three Romances: On the Words of W. Shakespeare] 19907, 20467

Try romansa[:] Na slova V. Shekspira [Three Romances: To the Words of W. Shakespeare] 20560·

Trys Šekspyro sonetai 20554, 20566

Tschaikowsky Melodies 13988

Tschaikowsky Piano Arrangements For All To Play 13975

Tuba or not Tuba 3907

Turangalîla-Symphonie 14188

Turetskii marsh i narodnye stseny iz baleta 'Otello' [Turkish March and Folk Scenes from the Ballet Othello] 12034

Turn Then Thine Eyes 10204

Tush i tantseval'naia muzyka iz muzyki k tragedii V. Shekspira 'Gamlet' [Flourish and Dance Music from the Music to W. Shakespeare's Tragedy Hamlet] 3417

[Tutto è bene quel che finisce bene] 63

Tu-whit, To-who 6559, 6624

Två danser ur musiken till en vintersaga 18909

Två unga älskande det var[:] It was a lover and his lass 1426

[Tvillingarna = Twins, i.e., The Comedy of Errors] 2082

Tvillingerne 2084

[Tvillingerne = Twins, i.e., The Comedy of Errors] 2099

'Tvoia l' vina, chto milyï obraz tvoi (Sonet 61)' ['Is it thy will thy image should keep open' (Sonnet 61)] 19856

'Tvoia l' vina' [If Your Guilt] 19848

'Twas a lover and his lass 1911

Twee edellieden van Verona 18443

Twelfth Night 11616, 16595, 16613, 16623, 16641, 16647, 16657, 16693, 16699, 16709, 16712, 16717, 16724, 16734, 16736, 16745, 16747, 16755, 16770, 16788, 16791, 16799, 16812, 16815, 16816, 16818, 16819, 16833, 16873, 16874, 16942, 16996, 17002, 17003, 17009, 17052, 17063, 17068, 17106, 17147, 17153, 17171, 17207, 17211, 17231, 17247, 17259, 17260, 17261, 17262, 17263, 17264, 17265, 17266, 17267, 17268, 17278, 17279, 17289, 17291, 17292, 17315, 17317, 17328, 17335, 17337, 17350, 17353, 17357, 17359, 17368, 17375, 17381, 17392, 17416, 17422, 17423, 17750, 18204, 18212, 18245, 18249, 18262, 18339

[Twelfth Night] 16586, 16588, 16591, 16592, 16594, 16597, 16599, 16600, 16601, 16611, 16614, 16627, 16631, 16635, 16643, 16644, 16656, 16658, 16661, 16662, 16663, 16664, 16687, 16691, 16692, 16694, 16700, 16713, 16718, 16722, 16725, 16726, 16727, 16728, 16729, 16731, 16732, 16733, 16735, 16740, 16741, 16743, 16746, 16758, 16759, 16763, 16764, 16766, 16768, 16783, 16786, 16789, 16790, 16792, 16793, 16801, 16813, 16824, 16826, 16838, 16839, 16841, 16844, 16845, 16848, 16849, 16851, 16859, 16860, 16863, 16868, 16871, 16872, 16875, 16880, 16881, 16886, 16889, 16891, 16892, 16893, 16894, 16895, 16896, 16897, 16898, 16899, 16909, 16910, 16912, 16914, 16915, 16918, 16924, 16925, 16928, 16930, 16932, 16941, 16945, 16947, 16948, 16949, 16954, 16959, 16968, 16986, 16988, 16991, 17010, 17011, 17017, 17019, 17021, 17024, 17025, 17026, 17027, 17030, 17034, 17037, 17039, 17044, 17046, 17050, 17053, 17060, 17061, 17062, 17067, 17069, 17074, 17076, 17078, 17079, 17080, 17081, 17093, 17094, 17101, 17105, 17108, 17110, 17113, 17114, 17119, 17125, 17127, 17128, 17129, 17134, 17142, 17144, 17148, 17149, 17155, 17160, 17168, 17169, 17172, 17189, 17191, 17203, 17208, 17209, 17212, 17215, 17220, 17225, 17227, 17238, 17249, 17253, 17257, 17258, 17282, 17295, 17299, 17300, 17301, 17322, 17323, 17327, 17329, 17330, 17331, 17332, 17333, 17339, 17340, 17348, 17349, 17351, 17354, 17356, 17360, 17363, 18201, 18228, 19195

'Twelfth Night' (An Elizabethan Dance) 18324

Twelfth Night, An Entertainment 17470, 17677, 17695, 17800, 18094, 18290

Twelfth Night, or, what You will 21121

Twelfth Night Song 18344

Twelfth Night Songs 6377, 17445, 17693, 17773, 18085
Twelfth Night Suite 17055
Twelfth Night. Three Incidental Dances 18238
Twelfth Night—Incidental Music 17054
Twelve Celebrated Comic Songs 1982
Twelve English Songs 290, 1820, 2646, 5073, 6361, 7850, 11380
Twelve Magic Keys to Tuneland 18988
Twelve Old English Songs 1469
Twelve pieces of Music Selected from the favorite Drama of Venus and Adonis 20818
Twelve Songs from Herrick, Shakespeare, &c. 1269, 2641, 18489
Twenty Thousand Tongues 20808
Twenty-four lyrics from the plays of William Shakespeare 21362
Twilight 7420, 20021
Twilight of Love 20006
Two Arne Songs 443, 6498
Two Character Songs 14131, 21012
Two Choruses from "Antony and Cleopatra" 262
Two Dances from Ballet 'Romeo and Juliet' 13947
Two Dances from 'The Taming Of The Shrew' 14359, 14360
Two Elizabethan Songs 6471
Two English Cantatas and Four Songs 7866
Two Faces of Love 18024, 19438
Two Fairy Songs from A Midsummer Night's Dream 10323, 10397
Two Fragments from Shakespeare's 'As You Like It' 1551, 1798
Two Gentlemen from Verona 18450
Two Gentlemen of Verona 18349, 18357, 18378, 18404, 18415, 18432, 18448, 18464, 18465
Two Gents 18385
Two Heresies 18321
Two Interludes from Falstaff 4476, 4651, 4817
Two Little Songs 20672
Two Maids Wooing a Man 18956
Two Old English Songs 446
Two Ophelia Songs 3710, 3772
Two orchestral pieces to 'Roméo et Juliette' 13904
Two Picture-Pieces 7420
Two Pictures 7420
Two pieces for orchestra from Richard III 13039
Two Pieces for Strings from the film music Henry V 4778
Two Pieces from 'Henry V' 4778
Two Pieces from the Suite: The Fairy Ring 10578
Two Scenes from "Antony and Cleopatra" 262
Two Shakespeare Choruses 6568, 8451
Two Shakespeare Lyrics 6489, 6638

Two Shakespeare Madrigals 968, 1680, 6476, 6613
Two Shakespeare Pieces 1869, 16000
Two Shakespeare Sketches from 'The England of Elizabeth' 20898
Two Shakespeare Songs 1193, 1318, 1799, 5164, 6360, 8005, 8505, 8546, 8649, 10343, 11511, 11515, 15688, 15740, 15940, 17895, 18483, 19387, 19779, 20604
Two Shakespeare Songs for Schools 1812, 18194
Two Shakespeare Songs from 'As You Like It' 1331, 1655
Two Shakespeare Sonnets 19242, 19266, 19341, 19355, 19379, 19440, 19548, 19558, 19610, 19819, 19828, 20047
Two Shakespearean Settings 8475, 19445
Two Shakespearean Sketches 8271, 8703
Two Shakespearean Songs 6439, 6567, 7933, 8606, 12366, 15588, 15709, 15715, 17544, 19079
Two Shakespearean Sonnets 19320, 19378
Two Shakespearian Songs 18492
Two Shakespearian Songs for Baritone 1125, 17978
Two Shakespearian Songs for Contralto 1486, 12336
Two Shakespearian Songs for Mezzo-Soprano 5147, 10338
Two Shakespearian Songs for Tenor 2698, 17603
Two Songs and a Scene from 'Cymbeline' 2833
Two Songs for Feste 16640
Two Songs for Robin Goodfellow 10355, 10390
Two Songs from 'As You Like It' 758, 1157, 1774
Two Songs From Incidental Music To 'The Tempest' 15085
Two Songs from 'Love's Labour [sic] Lost' 6410, 6534
Two Songs from Shakespeare 1284, 2546, 6200, 6509, 8661, 15589, 15620, 17482, 17490, 17624, 17804, 17830, 18181
Two Songs from Shakespeare's 'A Midsummer Night's Dream' 10301, 10329
Two Songs from Shakespeare's The Tempest 15542, 15668
Two Songs from Shakespeare's "Twelfth Night" 17590, 17966
Two Songs from "The Passionate Pilgrim" 20595
Two Songs from The Tempest 15568, 15744
Two Songs from 'Twelfth Night' 17468, 17518, 17798, 17877
Two Songs of Amiens 1071, 1688
Two Songs of Ariel 15578, 15945

Two Songs of Autolycus 19020, 19090
Two Sonnets 19525, 19557, 19995, 20454
Two sonnets by William Shakespeare 20001, 20162
Two Sonnets from "Sonnets to sundry notes of music" 20641
Two Sonnets of Shakespeare 19550, 19794, 20351, 20615
Two Sonnets of Time 19825, 19890
Two Sonnets—Shakespeare 19258, 19783
Two Suites from The Fairy Queen 10246
Two Texts in Music 15860
Two Unison Songs from Twelfth Night 17713, 18198
'Ty pogrusti, kogda umret poet (71-i sonet)' ['No longer mourn for me when I am dead' (71st Sonnet)] 19953
'Ty vidish', ia dostig pory moi pozdneigoda' ['That time of year thou mayst in me behold'] 19999
Tyger: A Celebration of William Blake 20985
[Tymon Ateńczyk] 16355
'Ty-muzyka (8-i sonet)' ['Music to hear, why hear'st thou music sadly?' (8th Sonnet)] 19247
Tytus Andronikus 16415

U

Übergang von der Nacht zum Tage 11308
Udkast til Musik til Shakespeares Richard den Tredje[,] Det kgl. Teater 1951 12884
[Ukroćena goropadnica = The Taming of the Shrew] 14465
Ukročena trmoglavka 14254
[Ukročena trmoglavka = The Taming of the Shrew] 14531
[Ukroshchenie stroptivoi = The Taming of the Shrew] 14228, 14229, 14250, 14271, 14297, 14312, 14323, 14326, 14327, 14364, 14370, 14389, 14410, 14414, 14422, 14429, 14444, 14463, 14478, 14519, 14527, 14530, 14535
Ukroshchenie stroptivoi [The Taming of the Shrew] 14642
[Ukrotiavane na opurnichavata = The Taming of the Shrew] 14288, 14522
Ulrike 4153, 5544
Un Amant avec sa Belle 1307
Un Amour de Tchaikovsky 14003
[Un ballo nuovo] 4154
Un' Ora die Sollievo 4147
Un Othello 12476
Un Re in ascolto 15391
Un sogno di primavera 10798
Un Soir avec Shakespeare 20871
Un Songe de nuit d'été 10290

[Un vis din noaptea miezului de vară = A Midsummer Night's Dream] 9307
Und als ich ein winzig Büblein war 18152
Und der Regen der regnet jeglichen Tag 18224
Under det grønne Træ 807
Under the blossom 15907
Under the greenwood tree 402, 403, 405, 406, 407, 410, 416, 419, 420, 421, 423, 424, 426, 428, 431, 432, 434, 435, 437, 438, 440, 446, 447, 448, 455, 493, 527, 546, 572, 580, 672, 758, 856, 904, 905, 1595, 1596, 1597, 1598, 1600, 1601, 1603, 1604, 1605, 1606, 1607, 1609, 1610, 1612, 1614, 1615, 1616, 1618, 1619, 1620, 1621, 1622, 1623, 1624, 1625, 1626, 1627, 1628, 1630, 1631, 1632, 1633, 1634, 1636, 1637, 1638, 1641, 1642, 1643, 1644, 1648, 1651, 1652, 1653, 1654, 1655, 1656, 1658, 1660, 1661, 1662, 1663, 1667, 1668, 1669, 1670, 1671, 1672, 1673, 1674, 1675, 1676, 1677, 1680, 1681, 1682, 1683, 1684, 1685, 1686, 1687, 1688, 1689, 1690, 1691, 1692, 1693, 1694, 1695, 1696, 1697, 1698, 1699, 1702, 1703, 1704, 1705, 1706, 1707, 1709, 1710, 1711, 1712, 1713, 1716, 1717, 1718, 1719, 1720, 1721, 1722, 1723, 1724, 1729, 1730, 1731, 1732, 1733, 1736, 1737, 1738, 1739, 1740, 1743, 1744, 1747, 1748, 1749, 1750, 1751, 1753, 1755, 1756, 1759, 1760, 1761, 1764, 1767, 1768, 1769, 1770, 1771, 1772, 1773, 1774, 1775, 1776, 1777, 1785, 1786, 1788, 1789, 1790, 1791, 1792, 1793, 1794, 1795, 1796, 1797, 1798, 1799, 1800, 1804, 1805, 1806, 1807, 1809, 1810, 1811, 1812, 1813, 1814, 1815, 1816, 1817, 1818, 1872, 1903, 1914, 1923, 1924, 1927, 1940, 1954, 1964, 1980, 1997, 2000, 2004, 2008, 2010, 2011, 2017
[Under the greenwood tree] 1611, 1617, 1635, 1647, 1649, 1664, 1714, 1715, 1726, 1728, 1735, 1746
['Under the Greenwood Tree' and 'What shall He Have that killed the Deer'] 560
"Under The Greenwood Tree" (As you like it.) 413
Under The Greenwood Tree (Come Hither, Come Hither) 1990
Under the Greenwood Tree (Country Dance) 1892
"Under The Greenwood Tree" (from "As You Like It") 799, 1754
Under The Greenwood Tree. (Sicilienne.) 444
Under the greenwood tree who loves to sit with me 1640
Under the Holly Bough 4838

Under the Spreading Chestnut Tree 20580
Unsterblichkeit 19778
Unter des Laubdachs Hut 1763, 1787
[Unter des Laubdachs Hut] 1645
Unter dies Grünlaubdach nach Shakespeare
   1758
Unthrifty Loveliness 19201, 19202
Unto The Holly 1021, 1104
[Untune that String] 20867
Up And Down 9362, 9471, 10468, 10956,
   10964, 10972
Up and down, up and down (I will lead them
   up and down) 10608
Up on the Mountain, Live From That Good Old
   American Music Show, Nashville, Tennessee
   6142
Ur Musiken till Shakespeares Komedi 'Mycket
   väsen för ingenting' 11073
Ur musiken till Shakespeares
   'Trettondagsafton' 18254
'Use vzhe ia pro tebe rozpoviv' [I have told
   everything of your love] 20560
'Utrenniaia serenada: "Chu slysh', kak
   zhavoronok poet . . ."' [Morning Serenade:
   'Listen, how the lark sings . . .'] 2711, 2777,
   2779
Utrenniaia serenada[:] Iz baleta 'Romeo i
   Dzhul'etta' [Morning Serenade: From the
   Ballet Romeo and Juliet] 13800
Uvertira veseloj igri 21188
Uvertiura Iulii Tsezar' [Julius Caesar Overture]
   5529
[Uvertiura—Otello = Overture–Othello] 12378
'Uvy, moi stikh ne bleshchet noviznoi (76-i
   sonet)' ['Why is my verse so barren of new
   pride?' (76th Sonnet)] 20048
'Uzh esli ty razliubish'' ['Then hate me when
   thou wilt, if ever, now'] 20108
'Uzh esli ty razliubish' (90-i sonet)' ['Then hate
   me when thou wilt, if ever, now' (90th
   Sonnet)] 20111
Uzmi sve moje ljubavi 19185, 19472, 19538,
   19697, 19731, 19763, 20063, 20295

V

['V razdum'e bedniazhka' = A Poor Woman]
   12287, 12354
V sadu[:] Val's iz baleta 'Otello' [In the Garden:
   Waltz from the Ballet Othello] 12030
['"V tvoei grudi ia slychu vse serdtsa . . ."' =
   'Thy bosom is endeared with all hearts']
   19634
Vádolj assai 20347
Vægtersang 7438
Valse Ariette 13651
Valse Brillante sur Roméo et Juliette 13674

Valse de Juliette 13730
Valse from the Music to the Masque in
   Shakespeare's 'Merchant of Venice' 8348
Valse Ophelia 3976
Variationi per Chitarra sulla Cavatina favorita:
   De! calma oh ciel: O Gott hab' Mitleid:
   dell'Opera: Otello 12084
Variations Brillantes Quasi Fantasia sur la
   Marche d'Otello 12066
Variations Brillantes . . . Sur le Duo Favori de la
   parodie d'Othello, le Maure à Vienne 12457
Variations For Concert Flute on 'The Mermaid's
   Song' 10834
Variations for Orchestra (The Mask of Night)
   13832, 21103
Variations on a Theme of Robert Johnson
   15062, 21145
Variations on "Bonny Sweet Robin" (Ophelia's
   Song) 4034
(Variations on Last Rose of Summer) 20689
X Variations pour le Clavecin ou Piano-Forte
   Sur le Duo La Stessa, la Stessissima del'Opera
   Falstaff ossia le tre Burle 9159
VIII. Variations pour le forte piano sur l'air: Ich
   küsse dich o Schleier: aus der Geister Insel
   von Herrn Kapelmeister Reichard [sic] 15466
XII Variations pour le Piano-Forte sur L'Air
   d'Ariel de l'Opéra: Die Zauberinsel 15465
Variations pour le Piano-forte sur un motif
   favori de l'Opéra Oberon 10814
Variations 'Seven Ages of Man' 1900
Variazioni sopra la romanza e la preghiera
   dell'Op. Otello di Rossini 12156
Vasarvidžio nakties sapnas 10118
Veanus, and young Adonis sitting by hir[:]
   First part 20737
Večer tříkrálový 16802, 16810, 16858,
   16927, 17145, 17146, 17303, 17399
[Večer tříkrálový = Twelfth Night] 16630,
   16648, 16684, 16685, 16689, 16885,
   16936, 16967, 16981, 17065, 17131,
   17242
[Večer tříkrálový nebo cokoli chcete = Twelfth
   Night, or What You Will] 16971, 16978,
   17190
Večer v Belmontě 8692
Vedi nas, doroga . . . [Lead Us, Road . . .] 20553
[Veel drukte om niets = Much Ado About
   Nothing] 11058
[Veel Gemin, Geen Gewin = Love's Labour's
   Lost] 6256
[Veel Leven om niets = Much Ado About
   Nothing] 10994, 11049, 11295
Veglie d'un Solitario 7466
Vendor's Song 18694
[Veneetsia kaupmees = The Merchant of
   Venice] 8193
[Venetsian kauppias = The Merchant of
   Venice] 8189

[Venetsianskii kupets = The Merchant of Venice] 8329, 8336
Venetsianskii kupets [The Merchant of Venice] 8063, 8205
Venetsianskii mavr [Venetian Moor] 12030
Venetsiia. Noktiurn iz muzyki k (p'ese) V. Shekspira 'Otello' (iz muzyki k kino fl'mu) [Venice. Nocturne from the Music to W. Shakespeare's Othello (From the Music for the Film)] 11812, 11815
Venez jusqu'à ces sables d'or 15035
Venezia e Napoli 12114
Venus & Adonis 20821
Venus and Adonis 20646, 20785, 20802, 20811
venus and adonis suite 20785
Vénus et Adonis 20812, 20813, 20814, 20815, 20816, 20817
Venus und Adonis 20819
Verdi Album 12201
Verdi's Macbeth 7318
Verdi's Macbeth March 7312
Verdi's Macbeth Quadrille 7345
Vergänglichkeit 19818
Verlassen 7936
Verlorene Liebesmüh' 6234
[Verlorene Liebesmüh'] 6302, 6311, 6317
[Veronští šlechtici = The Two Gentlemen of Verona] 18459
Verschmähte Liebe (nach Shakespeare) 17583
Verschwunden ist die [finstre] Nacht 7560
Verwandlung zum Esel 9520
Veselé paničky Windsorské 8811, 8857
[Veselé paničky windsorské = The Merry Wives of Windsor] 8892, 8934
[Vesele Windsorčanke = The Merry Wives of Windsor] 8976
[Veselé windsorské paničky = The Merry Wives of Windsor] 8858, 8859, 8901, 8921, 8924, 8954, 8955, 8956, 8957, 8959
Veta za vetu 7603
[Veta za vetu = Measure for Measure] 7668, 7685, 7735
Victoria Waltz 787
[Viel Getu' um nichts] 11115
Viel Lärm um Nichts 11021, 11022, 11167, 11173, 11174, 11176, 11204, 11205, 11268, 11291, 11296, 11314, 11321, 11342, 11361, 11362, 11365, 11370, 11606, 19274
[Viel Lärm um Nichts] 10998, 10999, 11010, 11031, 11032, 11035, 11041, 11044, 11045, 11047, 11067, 11068, 11074, 11075, 11086, 11096, 11105, 11113, 11114, 11118, 11119, 11125, 11127, 11130, 11131, 11132, 11136, 11137, 11138, 11140, 11143, 11159, 11163, 11164, 11165, 11166, 11168, 11169, 11170, 11179, 11181, 11185, 11186,
11194, 11208, 11209, 11212, 11213, 11217, 11221, 11226, 11229, 11235, 11243, 11249, 11259, 11266, 11269, 11270, 11271, 11278, 11302, 11303, 11305, 11307, 11315, 11316, 11322, 11324, 11325, 11327, 11329, 11337
Viel Lärmen um Nichts 11162
[Viel Lärmen um Nichts] 11267, 11317, 11323
Vier Gedichte nach Heine, Shakespeare und Lord Byron 10453
Vier Sonette 20088, 20492
Vignettes[:] Five Miniature Songs 18983
Vihar 14896
[Vihar = The Tempest] 15336
Vijf Shakespeare-Liederen 2639, 7833, 8504, 11410, 17450
Vilhelm Stenhammars svit ur musiken till Romeo och Julie 13481
[Vindsorskie kumushki = The Merry Wives of Windsor] 8800
[Vindzorskie kumushki = The Merry Wives of Windsor] 8945
Vindzorskie kumushki [The Merry Wives of Windsor] 9022
[Vindzorskie nasmeshnitsy = The Merry Wives of Windsor] 8869, 8897, 8905, 8938, 8939, 8951, 8958
[Vindzorskie prokaznitsy = The Merry Wives of Windsor] 9152
Vinter 6537, 6556
Vinteren 6561
Viola 16882, 17376, 17377, 17388, 17397, 17398, 17401, 17402, 17410, 17421, 18207, 18217, 18218, 18219, 18247, 18248, 18330
[Viola] 17188
Viola und Sebastian 16773
Viola Valse 18253
Viola Waltz 18328
Viola Waltzes 18329
Violet 10634
Violinkonzert 16078
Virgo Gemma Nominatur 11135
Virtues and Vices 18462
Virtuous, Upright, Clever 21062
Visa Pour l'Amour 14164
Viser frå min gitar 4220
vision d'ariel 14910
Visitations 2393
[Visul unei nopți de vară = A Midsummer Night's Dream] 10061
Vivace 14356
Vive Henri IV 4515, 4683
Vive Henry Quatre 4511, 4518, 4680, 4687
[Vízkereszt = Twelfth Night] 16742, 16796, 16797, 16835
[Vízkereszt, vagy amit akartok = Twelfth Night, or What You Will] 17059

Vocal and incidental music to Shakespeare's A
    midsummer night's dream 9605
Vocal Duets (Secular) 17487
Vocal Magazine Consisting of Canzonets,
    Madrigals 12314
Vocal Melody 11005
Vocal Selection From 'Much Ado About
    Nothing' 11135
'Voi, v'iuga, voi sil'nyi' ['Blow, blow, thou
    winter wind'] 978
Voices 15506
Vokaliz Desdemony [/] Pesnia pro ivu iz muzyki
    k fil'mu 'Otello' po tragedii V. Shekspira
    [Desdemona's Vocalise and Song of the
    Willow from the Music to the Film Othello
    after W. Shakespeare's Tragedy 11811
Vokal'nyi tsikl 'Chetyre serenady na stikhi
    Shekspira' [Vocal Cycle: Four Serenades to
    Poetry by Shakespeare] 6442, 6571, 11470,
    19505, 20513
Vold mot Lucretia 20778
Volpino il Calderaio 14562
Volshebnaia noch' [An Enchanting Night]
    10119
[Voluptuous Slave Theme] 19809
Von schönstem Wesen wünschen wir
    Vermehrung 19177
'Vorrei Che Il Tuo.' From Rossini's Otello
    12147
Vorspiel zu 'Shakespeare' 21163
[Vortigern] 20865
Vows are but breath 6380
'Vstuplenie i pesn' torzhestvuiushchei liubvi'
    [Introduction and Song of Triumphant Love]
    16961

W

W krainie melodii 9858, 13759
W młodości — ach! — czemu wiek ten zgasł . . .
    3792
[W Weronie = In Verona] 13302
Wack ado 11629
Waldgesang 1659
Waldhymnus 1059, 1678, 8447
Wall 10122
Waltz from 'Romeo and Juliet' 13702
Waltz from The Merry Wives of Windsor.
    Founded on Otto Nicolai's Opera 9030
Walzer od[er] Was ihr wollt 18244
War [sic] of the Roses, parts I and II 4849,
    4891, 4934, 12814
Warning 15976
Warsong 4493, 4665, 13066
[Warui Yatsu Hodo Yoku Nemuru = The Bad
    Sleep Well] 4125
Warwickshire Lads 21121

Warwickshire Lasses 21121
Warwickshire Minuet 21121
Was es heisst: zu lieben 1223
Was ihr wollt 16645, 16800, 16919, 16922,
    16952, 16982, 16989, 16990, 17016,
    17064, 17120, 17234, 17235, 17239,
    17254, 17352, 17372, 17385, 17394,
    17403, 17404, 17406, 17561, 18340,
    18342
[Was ihr wollt] 16587, 16598, 16602, 16603,
    16608, 16625, 16626, 16632, 16633,
    16638, 16646, 16651, 16660, 16683,
    16686, 16698, 16701, 16706, 16756,
    16762, 16765, 16771, 16776, 16777,
    16780, 16784, 16785, 16787, 16804,
    16805, 16807, 16809, 16821, 16822,
    16823, 16825, 16827, 16834, 16852,
    16853, 16854, 16855, 16856, 16864,
    16869, 16870, 16876, 16878, 16879,
    16883, 16884, 16887, 16902, 16903,
    16907, 16913, 16917, 16920, 16921,
    16929, 16939, 16943, 16951, 16956,
    16957, 16960, 16970, 16973, 16974,
    16976, 16983, 16998, 17006, 17014,
    17015, 17022, 17028, 17049, 17056,
    17058, 17066, 17075, 17082, 17083,
    17086, 17087, 17088, 17089, 17095,
    17096, 17100, 17104, 17107, 17111,
    17118, 17121, 17122, 17123, 17124,
    17130, 17132, 17136, 17159, 17161,
    17162, 17167, 17170, 17174, 17178,
    17180, 17181, 17192, 17193, 17198,
    17243, 17244, 17248, 17250, 17251,
    17274, 17275, 17280, 17281, 17286,
    17298, 17302, 17306, 17320, 17324,
    17334, 17336, 17367, 18257
Was Ihr wollt 17057
Was ihr wollt oder Die Schiffbrüchigen von
    Illyrien 17387
[Was ihr wollt oder Die zwölfte Rauhnacht]
    16585
Was ist Sylvia? (Who is Sylvia?) 18574
Was kriegt der, der den Hirsch erlegt? 1860
Was Mrs. Macbeth Really Sleeping? (When She
    Took That Famous Walk) 7549
Was this fair face 84
"Was This Fair Face The Cause?" 85, 90, 8355
[Was werden wir beginnen] 9070
[Wat u maar wilt = What You Will] 16820
[Wat u wilt] 891
Watchman's Song 7442, 7443
Water-Scenes. Five Illustrations 4006
We are Spirits of another sort 9362
We cobblers lead a merry life 21092
We Happy Few 4814
We Loved Not Wisely, But Too Well 12505
We Two 19278, 19362, 19551, 19601,
    19671, 19703, 19940, 20508, 20532
Weary with toil 19514, 19530

"Weary With Toil" from Sonnet XXVII by
William Shakespeare 19529
Weary with toil, I haste me to my bed 19519,
19526
Weather Tis Nobler 987, 6383, 18082
Weber's Admired Opera Oberon 10817
Weber's Celebrated Overture To Oberon 10813
Weber's Oberon 10839
Weber's Overture to Oberon 10876
Wedding Carol . . . from the Incidental Music
to Romeo and Juliet 13136
Wedding Is Great Juno's Crown 763, 856, 884,
1819, 1823, 1828, 1831
[Wedding is great Juno's crown] 1824
Wedding March 4759, 9633, 9640, 9697,
9744, 9748, 9757, 9780, 9801, 9802,
9841, 9852
[Wedding March] 9621, 9634, 9650, 9657,
9669, 9670, 9679, 9683, 9707, 9728,
9751, 9776, 9781, 9851
Wedding March and Scherzo from Midsummer
Night's Dream 9784
Wedding March (From 'A Midsummer Night's
Dream') 9625, 9673, 9688, 9731, 9824
Wedding March from Mendelssohn's
Midsummer nights [sic] Dream 9623
Wedding march, from 'Midsummer Night's
Dream' 9674, 9833, 9834
Wedding March from 'Midsummer Night's
Dream' by Felix Mendelssohn 9755
Wedding March from Midsummer-Night's
Dream 9668
Wedding March, from Midsummernights [sic]
Dream 9793
[Wedding March from Music to Midsummer
Night's Dream] 9803
Wedding March From the incidental music to
'A Midsummer Night's Dream' 9665
Wedding March (from "The Midsummer
Night's Dream") 9770
Wedding March from the music to
Shakespeare's "Midsummer Night's Dream"
9856
Wedding March (Mendelssohn) 9671, 9763,
9815, 9836
Wedding March (Midsummer Night's Dream)
Composed by F. Mendelssohn Bartholdy
9835
Wedding March (Midsummer Night's Dream,
Op. 61) 9624
Wedding March—Mendelssohn 9698
Wedding Music 8168, 14082
Wedding Song 15802
Wedding Song for John Armstrong and Lori
Burns 1827
Wedding-Album 9856
[Wedding-March] 9775
Wedding-Song 15791
Weep you no more 21305

Weep you no more, sad fountains 21300
[Wéi Ní Sí Shàng Rén = The Merchant of
Venice] 8388
Weidenlied 11807
Welch [sic] Song 4451
[Wēn Shǎ Dē Fèng Liǔ Niǎng Mén = The
Merry Wives of Windsor] 8856
Wend', o wende diesen Blick 7853, 7911,
7964, 7971
[Wend', o wende diesen Blick] 8003
Wenn die Narcissel schau'n durch's Moos von
Shakespeare 19041
Wenn in der Leiden hartem Drang 13867
Wer ist Silvia? 18553
Were Thine That Special Face[:] Beguine
14609
[Wesołe kumoszki z Windsoru = The Merry
Wives of Windsor] 8911, 9099
Wesołe kumoszki z Windsoru uwertura 9026
[Wesołe windsorskie kobiety = The Merry
Wives of Windsor] 8894, 8899
West Side Story 13581, 13588, 13589
[West Side Story] 13603, 13606
West Side Story Selection 13587, 13608
West Side Story[:] Selection for Orchestra
13602
What A Piece Of Work Is Man 4164
What is a Youth. From The Paramount Picture
"Romeo and Juliet" 13422
What is love? 18285
What is thy substance 19762
What is your substance, whereof are you made
19758, 19761
"What Poor Fools We Mortals Be" 10921
What Potions Have I Drunk In Siren Fears
20350
What shall he have 1840
What shall he have that kill'd the deer? 833,
1832, 1838, 1839, 1843, 1848, 1849,
1850, 1856, 1857, 1858, 1859, 1861,
1863, 1865, 2033, 2038, 2044
What shall he have that killed the deer? 856,
922, 1923, 1954, 2043
What shall he have that kills the Deere 1845
What shall we have that killed the deer 1853
What Then Is Love? 8511
"What Thou See'st" 9362
What wakes this new Pain in my breast 18265
What win I if I gain 20774
What Would Shakespeare Have Said 21259
When April Came 1273
When Birds Do Sing 672, 1581
[When daffodils begin to peer] 19031, 19039,
19053, 19056
When Daffodils 19043, 19059
When Daffodils Begin to 'Pear 18733
When daffodils begin to peer 18675, 18702,
18757, 19030, 19035, 19038, 19040,
19042, 19044, 19045, 19046, 19047,

When daffodils begin to peer (*cont.*)
19048, 19051, 19057, 19058, 19060,
19063, 19064, 19065, 19066
When Daffodils Begin to Peer[,] "We must
disguise ourselves" 18751
When daffodils begin to peere 19061
When daisies pied 402, 414, 423, 429, 430,
434, 439, 441, 443, 445, 447, 452, 815,
6213, 6381, 6384, 6390, 6395, 6396,
6399, 6401, 6403, 6405, 6406, 6407,
6422, 6427, 6430, 6431, 6434, 6436,
6437, 6448, 6454, 6457, 6458, 6461,
6464, 6468, 6469, 6470, 6471, 6473,
6477, 6478, 6487, 6525, 6600, 6671, 6674
When [daisies] pied 6426, 6670
When Daisies pied and Violets blue 401, 422,
454, 6451, 6456, 6465
[When daisies pied, and violets blue] 6387,
6389, 6438, 6444, 6452, 6483
When Daisies Pied And Violets Blue. Cuckoo
Song in "Loves Labours [*sic*] Lost" 6404
When Daisies Pied and Violets Blue, The
Cuckoo Song 433
When daisies pied (Cuckoo Song) 6410
When Daisies pied[:] the Cuckoo Song 453
When daisies py'd, &c. 6482
When Dasies [*sic*] pied 6479
When fair Ophelia 4284
When forty winters 19189, 19193
When Forty Winters Shall Besiege Thy Brow
19190
When griping grief 13157, 13866
When grypinge griefes 14193
When hawthorn buds 10368
When Hawthorn Buds. (O Happy Fair.) 10375
When He Sat Writing 21031
When I Consider 19314
When I consider everything that grows 19305
When I Do Count The Clock That Tells The
Time 19286
When I Have Often Heard 10254
"When I have often heard young maids
complaining" 10197
When I have seen by Time's fell hand defaced
19871
When I have seen the hungry Ocean gain
19882
When icicles 6214
When Icicles Hang 1147, 6510, 6564, 6566,
6568, 6596, 6605
When Icicles Hang by the Wall 815, 6283,
6494, 6497, 6498, 6499, 6502, 6503,
6505, 6508, 6509, 6512, 6514, 6516,
6517, 6518, 6519, 6521, 6523, 6528,
6529, 6531, 6538, 6544, 6545, 6547,
6549, 6550, 6551, 6552, 6555, 6558,
6560, 6565, 6572, 6573, 6574, 6576,
6578, 6579, 6580, 6581, 6588, 6589,
6591, 6592, 6593, 6597, 6601, 6602,
6603, 6608, 6610, 6611, 6616, 6621,
6625, 6628, 6631, 6636, 6637, 6640,
6643, 6644, 6672, 6674
[When icicles hang by the wall] 6507, 6515,
6587, 6635
When icicles hang by the wall (Owl Song)
6534
When in disgrace 19544, 19549, 19567,
19572, 19581, 19584
When in disgrace: Sonnet XXIX 19563
When in disgrace with fortune 19542, 19552,
19587
When in disgrace with Fortune and men's eyes
19545, 19546, 19548, 19551, 19557,
19558, 19560
When in happier days we wandered 10797
When in the chronicle of wasted time 20258,
20260, 20264
When In The Sessions Of Sweet Silent Thought
19598
When Is the Proper Time to Drink 21062
When it is the time of Night 8730, 8876,
10757
When most I wink 19713, 19714
When Mr. Shakespeare comes to Town 21008
When Mr. Shakespeare Comes to Town or "I
Don't Like Them Minstrel Folks" 4242,
7575, 21076
When my love says that she is made of truth, I
do believe her 20455
When my love swears 20550
When My Love Swears That She Is Made Of
Truth 20453
When Portia Sings 8776
When Shakespeare's ladies sing 20930
When shall we three meet again? 6756, 7568,
7577
When Shall We Three Meet Again? The
Witches Glee 7405, 7406
When Sweet Sixteen 1966
When that I was 16627, 16745, 17312,
18089, 18101, 18112, 18133, 18147,
18158, 18168, 18177, 18272, 20863
When that I was a little tiny boy 16697,
17173, 17313, 17316, 18086, 18096,
18100, 18114, 18167, 18186
When that I was and a little tiny boy 17217,
17308, 17311, 17314, 18084, 18087,
18088, 18093, 18094, 18104, 18105,
18106, 18110, 18116, 18130, 18145,
18148, 18150, 18161, 18169, 18173,
18181, 18194, 18269
[When that I was and a little tiny boy] 17219,
18091, 18121, 18135, 18160, 18162,
18166, 18197
"When that I was and a tiny little boy" 18144,
18188, 18196
When that I was but a little tiny boy 17012
When the Cat's Away 9161

When Thou My Music, Music Playest 20399
When To The Sessions 19592, 19621
When to the sessions of sweet silent thought
19591, 19593, 19595, 19601, 19608,
19611, 19616
When we shall hear she died 11592
When you shall these unlucky deeds relate
12372
Where are you roaming, O Mistress mine?
18061
Where corals lie 16251
Where Is Fancy Bred? 8582, 8659
Where should this music be? 15863
Where the Bee 15897
Where the Bee Sucks 10279, 10920, 14758,
14760, 14761, 14762, 14763, 14765,
14766, 14767, 14768, 14769, 14770,
14771, 14772, 14773, 14774, 14775,
14776, 14779, 14780, 14781, 14782,
14783, 14784, 14785, 14786, 14787,
14788, 14790, 14791, 14792, 14793,
14794, 14796, 14797, 14799, 14800,
14802, 14803, 14804, 14805, 14806,
14809, 14810, 14812, 14813, 14815,
14816, 14819, 14820, 14821, 14822,
14823, 14824, 14825, 14827, 14828,
14829, 14830, 14831, 14832, 14834,
14835, 14836, 14837, 14838, 14839,
14841, 14842, 14843, 14844, 14846,
14847, 14850, 14905, 14957, 14987,
15053, 15057, 15060, 15061, 15063,
15064, 15066, 15067, 15068, 15168,
15227, 15317, 15356, 15373, 15432,
15867, 15870, 15871, 15872, 15874,
15876, 15878, 15879, 15880, 15882,
15883, 15884, 15887, 15889, 15894,
15895, 15896, 15899, 15901, 15902,
15905, 15911, 15913, 15915, 15919,
15920, 15921, 15924, 15925, 15927,
15928, 15929, 15931, 15932, 15933,
15934, 15935, 15936, 15940, 15942,
15944, 15945, 15949, 15952, 15954,
15957, 15958, 15964, 16112, 16222,
16224, 16225
Where the Bee sucks. Ariel's Song 14814
Where the Bee sucks from Shakespeare's Play
of The Tempest 14759
Where the bee sucks (from The Tempest) 15890
Where the bee sucks (Pastorale) 14817
"Where The Bee Sucks," Song and "Come
Unto These Yellow Sands," Chorus of
Nymphs from Taubert's Music to
Shakespeare's "Tempest" 15307
Where The Bee sucks[,] The Popular Melody
from Shakespeare's Tempest by Dr. Arne
14798
Where the bee sucks, there lurk I 16206
Where the bee sucks, there suck I 15903,
15922, 15947, 15951

[Where the bee sucks, there suck I] 15875,
15892, 15893, 15917, 15962
Where the nodding violet grows 10941
Where the place? 7409
Where The Rainbow Ends 8679
Where the wild thyme blows 10313, 10337
Wherefore Do You Droop. . . . 5642
While you here do snoring lie 14906, 14957,
15115, 15122, 15966, 15970, 15973,
15975, 15978, 15979, 15982, 15983
[While you here do snoring lie] 15968, 15969,
15977
While you here doth sleeping lie 15965
"Whilst I alone did call upon thy aid" 20061
White and Red 6356
[White and Red] 6241
White his Shroud 2919
White Rose 4922
Whither should I fly? 7410
Who doth ambition shun 1866
Who is Silvia? 18373, 18473, 18484, 18489,
18495, 18496, 18500, 18501, 18504,
18519, 18520, 18521, 18522, 18523,
18524, 18529, 18535, 18546, 18550,
18552, 18554, 18571, 18623, 18626,
18632, 18635
[Who is Silvia] 18417
[Who is Silvia? what is she] 18494, 18506,
18538, 18545, 18547, 18624
Who is Sylvia 17062, 18377, 18379, 18434,
18448, 18474, 18475, 18476, 18477,
18478, 18479, 18480, 18482, 18490,
18492, 18493, 18497, 18498, 18502,
18503, 18507, 18508, 18509, 18510,
18511, 18512, 18513, 18514, 18515,
18516, 18517, 18525, 18528, 18530,
18531, 18534, 18539, 18541, 18542,
18543, 18544, 18548, 18556, 18558,
18559, 18561, 18563, 18564, 18565,
18566, 18567, 18568, 18569, 18570,
18572, 18573, 18575, 18576, 18577,
18578, 18579, 18581, 18582, 18583,
18585, 18586, 18587, 18589, 18590,
18592, 18593, 18595, 18596, 18597,
18598, 18600, 18601, 18603, 18604,
18605, 18606, 18609, 18612, 18613,
18614, 18615, 18618, 18619, 18620,
18621, 18622, 18625, 18629, 18630,
18631, 18633, 18636, 18637, 18638,
18639, 18646, 18651, 18655
[Who is Sylvia?] 18405, 18430
Who is Sylvia? (An Silvia.) 18594
Who is Sylvia? from Shakespeare's Two
Gentlemen 18533
"Who Is Sylvia?" from The Two Gentlemen of
Verona 18392
"Who is Sylvia?" from Two Gentlemen of
Verona 18415, 18591, 18607
Who is Sylvia (Was ist Sylvia?) 18599

Who Seeketh Beauty 21307
Who Sees His True Love 20799
Who will believe my verse 19320
Who's your hatter 14150
Who's your hatter polka or the popular comic song 14150
Why can't you behave? 14602
Why Hear'st Thou Music Sadly? 19273
Why is my verse so barren 20049
Why is my verse so barren of new pride 20047
Why is Springtime Ringtime? 1977
Widmungen aus den Sonetten von William Shakespeare 19371, 19476, 19484, 20118
Wie Brot dem Leben bist du den Gedanken 20032
"Wie die Blume" aus Shakespeare's "Viel Lärm um Nichts" 11609
Wie erkenn' ich dein Treulieb vor den andern nun? 3775
Wie erkenn' ich mein Treulieb? 3781
Wie es euch gefällt 468, 469, 605, 648, 683, 736, 846, 847, 848, 850, 871, 896, 907, 940
[Wie es euch gefällt] 390, 391, 395, 465, 483, 497, 502, 503, 521, 522, 549, 554, 558, 567, 570, 575, 576, 582, 591, 594, 599, 600, 612, 622, 626, 633, 635, 654, 655, 675, 676, 679, 680, 702, 703, 716, 717, 723, 728, 729, 739, 742, 745, 746, 747, 750, 751, 760, 761, 768, 778, 785, 788, 803, 812, 813, 823, 825, 826, 837, 855, 858, 873, 880, 883, 894, 895, 900, 903, 906, 909, 912, 917, 918, 936, 937, 942
Wie es Euch gefällt 1996
Wie es euch gefällt. Vorspiel zu einer Komödie 1943, 10100
Wie Ihr wollt ('As you Like it') 1916
Wie oft, wann du, Musik mir musizierest 20383
[Wieczór trzech króli = Twelfth Night] 16690, 16753, 16775, 16831, 16877, 16937, 16950, 16958, 16977, 17005, 17033, 17072, 17073, 17085, 17098, 17143, 17196, 17202, 17269, 17272, 17273, 17296, 17325
[Wieczór trzech króli lub co chcecie = Twelfth Night, or What You Will] 16634, 16705, 17362
Wiele hałasu o nic 11265
[Wiele hałasu o nic = Much Ado About Nothing] 10997, 11012, 11017, 11082, 11151, 11160, 11190, 11192, 11222, 11242, 11301, 11311
Wild Thyme 10635
Will Shakespeare 20838
[Will Shakespeare] 20854, 20882, 20894, 20900
Will you buy any tape 18675, 18700, 18702, 18724, 18757, 19071, 19073, 19077, 19078, 19079, 19080, 19085, 19087, 19088, 19090, 19156
[Will you buy any tape] 19083, 19084
William Shakespeare Sonetts—Original and German Translations 19492, 19815, 20308
William Shakespeare[:] Two Songs From The Tempest Set By His Contemporary Robert Johnson . . . 15063
[William Shakespeares 'nackter' Hamlet] 4108
Willow! 12272
[Willow] 11864
Willow Cycle 12441
Willow Song 11943, 12254, 12266, 12303, 12304, 12341
Willow, tit-willow 12486
Willow, Willow 12250, 12253, 12257, 12262, 12281, 12308
Willow, Willow, Willow 12258, 12296, 12309, 12335, 12337
"Willow-song" from Shakespeare's Othello 12350
Will's Birthday Suite 2540, 6111, 21014
Wilt thou be gone love 13871, 13872
Wind Song 21114
Windsor Ladies 9008
Windsor Minuet 21121
[Windsorin Iloiset Rouvat = The Merry Wives of Windsor] 8910, 8923
Winter 1134, 6200, 6492, 6493, 6504, 6506, 6511, 6524, 6526, 6530, 6532, 6540, 6542, 6546, 6548, 6554, 6561, 6562, 6567, 6570, 6583, 6584, 6585, 6590, 6604, 6613, 6614, 6615, 6622, 6626, 6629, 6633, 6634, 6638, 6639, 19989
Winter in paradise 8035
Winter on Avon 1184, 1792, 3824, 6618, 20018, 20799
Winter (When Icicles Hang by the Wall) 6553, 6557
Winter Wind 1011, 1064
Winterlied 6577
Winterlied—When Icicles Hang 6539
Wintermärchen 18676, 18759, 18814, 18883
[Wintermärchen] 18747, 18854
Winter's Song 6586, 6627, 6641
Winter's Tale 18753, 18935, 19150
Wir sind Staub 8682
Witch Music 7372
Witches Dance 6705, 6783, 6871, 6982, 7424
Witches Fair And Foul 7371, 10294
Witches' Incantation//Overture to Macbeth 7434
Witches Scene 7486
Witch[e]s' Song 7399
With a Hey, and a ho! (It was a lover and his lass) 1288
With hey, ho, the wind and the rain 18095
With thee fair summer[']s joy appears 8876, 20176

[Woe is me] 4102
Wohlan! Begeht den Feiertag 1227
Wolsey 5223, 5224
Woman's Heart 12299
Woodbine 10928
Woodland dreams 10178
Woosel Cock Song 10087
words and music to The Tempest by Wm
  Shakespeare 15473
[Words are easy, like the wind] 20666
Words from Shakespeare 20209
Wordsongs 19689, 20507
Would I Were Sleep and Peace 13879
[Would You Win The World's Acclaim] 20839
W.S. Loves W.H. 20577
[Wszystko dobre, co kończy się dobrze = All's
  Well That Ends Well] 30, 37
[Wszystko dobre co się dobrze kończy = All's
  Well That Ends Well] 53
Wǔ Dao Yīn Yuè [Dance Music] 16369
[Wú Shì Shēng Fēi = Much Ado About
  Nothing] 11183
Wú Shì Shēng Fēi [Much Ado About Nothing]
  11359
Wunderbar 14601, 14602, 14612, 14617,
  14619, 14626, 14627, 14628, 14630,
  14636, 14638

Y

Y Dymhestle (The Tempest) 16265
Y Gwydd (The Weaver's Song) 4309
Ye Life and Deathe of Bad Macbethe 7567
Ye Songe of Macbethe 7567
Ye Songes of Will Skakspere Newe Sett in
  Musik 1308, 6373, 8541, 15884, 17839
Ye Spotted Snakes 9378, 9469, 9999, 10475,
  10486, 10490, 10492, 10499, 10506,
  10518, 10527, 10529, 10533, 10535,
  10552, 10553, 10554, 10555, 10556,
  10557, 10558, 10559, 10560, 10570
Yellow Leaves 19986
Yellow Sands 15227
Yeoman's Song 20852
Yet Still She Is The Moone 6651, 21118
Yorick 4165, 20946
[Yorick] 20837
You must sing a-down a-down 2981
You spotted snakes 9334, 9340, 9926, 10011,
  10012, 10013, 10277, 10278, 10474,
  10480, 10481, 10482, 10483, 10488,
  10489, 10491, 10495, 10497, 10510,
  10511, 10516, 10524, 10528, 10530,
  10536, 10541, 10544, 10546, 10561,
  10562, 10563, 10566, 10572
You Spotted Snakes: fairy chorus from "A
  Midsummer-Night's Dream" 10496

You Spotted Snakes from A Midsummer
  Night's Dream 9723
You spotted snakes with double tongue 10478,
  10526, 10532, 10545, 10567, 10573
[You spotted snakes with double tongue]
  10517, 10534
You sunburnt Sicklemen 15988
You that choose not by the view 8684
Your Awful Voice 14726
Your love and pity 20293
Your Own Thing 17395, 17405, 20939, 20947
Your sister's drown'd 3827
You're the top 20582
Youth 556, 20845
Youth and Age 18010, 20635
Yuè Jū Yin Bin Qǔ [Shaoxing Opera Verses]
  18944
Yule-Tide 3814

Z

Z Krále Leara 6116
Z Macbetha 7504
Zadarnicele jocuri de iubire 6260
Zähl ich die Glocke, die die Zeiten mißt 19283
[Zähmung der Widerspenstigen] 14231,
  14301, 14413, 14467, 14511
'Zastol'na' [Drinking Song] 16901
'Zastol'naia' [Drinking Song] 16961
Ze Shakespeara 7433, 14657, 18216, 19107
Ze Sonetů 20038
Zehn Variationen über das Thema: 'La stessa,
  la stessissima' aus der Oper: Falstaff von
  Salieri 9159
Zes Symphonische Epigrammen 4262
[Zhizn' i smert' korolia Richarda tret'ego =
  The Life and Death of King Richard the
  Third] 12871
Zhōng Xià Yiè Zhi Mèng [A Midsummer
  Night's Dream] 10113
'Zima' [Winter] 6619
[Zimna prikazka = The Winter's Tale] 18817
Zimní pohádka 18793, 18874, 19127
[Zimní pohádka = The Winter's Tale] 18711,
  18736, 18743, 18797, 18846, 18848,
  19125
[Zimniaia skazka = The Winter's Tale] 18784,
  18888
Zimniaia skazka [The Winter's Tale] 19106
Zimska bajka 18792
[Zimska pravljica = The Winter's Tale] 18668,
  18669
Zither Garland 3903, 10587, 12380
[Zkrocení zle panny = Taming of the Shrewish
  Maiden] 14592
Zkrocení zlé ženy 14236, 14237, 14264,
  14486, 14526, 14569, 14671

[Zkrocení zlé ženy = The Taming of the
Shrew] 14314, 14371, 14420, 14423,
14437, 14440, 14441, 14442, 14443,
14481, 14482, 14588

Zpěvy a hry na úryvky ze Shakespeara 6116,
7504, 20038

Zu Shakespeares Gedicht: Where the bee
sucks . . . 14994

Zu Shakespeare's Jubiläum, 23 April 1864
21094

Zu Shakespeare's Richard III. 13060

Zur Beherzigung 11487

Zur Maienzeit 21229

[Zwei aus Verona] 18449

[Zwei Edelleute aus Verona] 18445

Zwei Gesänge aus der Musik zur Shakespeare's
'Wie es euch gefällt' 896

Zwei Herren aus Verona 18350, 18351, 18411

[Zwei Herren aus Verona] 18380, 18390,
18412, 18414, 18424, 18427, 18440,
18455

Zwei Kapricen über Themas von Mendelssohn
9706

Zwei kleine Serenaden 2804

Zwei Leichte Sonaten nach Motiven aus den
Opern: 'Oberon' und 'Euryanthe' von C. M.
v. Weber 10891

Zwei Lieder aus Shakespeare's Was ihr wollt
17222

Zwei Shakespeare-Lieder 1283, 13864

Zwei Shakespeare-Sonette 20579

Zwei Sonette 19642, 20100

Zwei Sonetten 19420, 19962

Zweierlei Mass 7708

[Zweierlei Maß] 7721, 7736, 7741, 7744,
7770

Zweite Ballade 4037

Zweites Lied des Amiens 1196

Zweites Lied des Ariel 15953

Zwischenmusik zu Anthony and Cleopatra [sic]
188

[Zwölfte Nacht oder Was ihr wollt] 17133

INDEX TO COMPOSERS, ARRANGERS, AND EDITORS

Names are listed alphabetically. In cases in which 'van', 'von', 'de', 'de la', etc., are part of the name, the 'v' or 'd', etc., has been taken as the initial letter for indexing purposes, so that Hans von Bŭlow, for example, is listed as 'von Bŭlow, Hans'. However, in cases in which the composer or arranger is better known by surname alone, the indexing will follow suit, for example, 'Beethoven, Ludwig van'.

a Becket, Thomas
  Lear 5654
Aaltoila, Heikki Johannes 1905–
  Caesar 5245; Macbeth 6692; Merchant 8047; Shrew 14216
Abady, H. Temple 1903–1970
  Also known as Tim Abady
  1 Henry IV 4498; 2 Henry IV 4521; Othello 11653; Tempest 14691
Abbott, Alain André Yves 1938–
  Also writes under the pseudonym 'Allan MacNell'
  Hamlet 4061
Abbott, Ernest Hamlin
  Hamlet 4136
Abbott, G. W.
  Twelfth Night 16585
Abbott, Roy
  Dream 9266
Aberer, Rolf, arr.
  Shrew 14598
Abington, Leonard
  Settings of Commemorative Pieces . . . 20988
Abondance, Alfred Eugène Charles   –1971
  1 Henry IV 4292
Abrahams, Paul
  Twelfth Night 16586
Absil, Jean 1893–1974
  Lear 5655
Abt, Franz Wilhelm, arr. 1819–1885
  Cymbeline 2710; Dream 9620
Abut, [?]
  Much Ado 10990
Accolla, Francesco
  Merchant 8048; Othello 11654
Achter, Morton
  Tempest 15511, 15596
Adam, Adolphe Charles 1803–1856
  Merry Wives 8989
Adam, Fritz 1904–
  Twelfth Night 16587; Winter's Tale 18667
Adamič, Bojan
  Hamlet 2886; Richard II 12612; Romeo 13086; Winter's Tale 18668, 18669

Adams, Carrie B. Wilson
  As You Like It 1832
Adams, Christine
  Merchant 8049
Adams, Daniel Marshall
  Sonnet 104 20230
Adams, David Stephen 1909–
  As You Like It 1228
Adams, James Alan
  All's Well 1; L.L.L. 6191
Adams, Joseph H.   –1938
  Dream 10575
Adams, Julius C.
  Sonnet 18 19327
Adams, Leslie 1932–
  As You Like It 1595
Adams, Roger
  Hamlet 2887; Macbeth 6693
Adamus, Henryk 1880–
  Tempest 14692
Addinsell, Richard Stewart 1904–1977
  1 Henry IV 4499; Macbeth 6694; Shrew 14217
Addison, John [1766?]–1844
  Merry Wives 9199; Twelfth Night 17749
Addison, John, arr. [1766?]–1844
  Macbeth 6972
Addison, John 1920–
  Hamlet 2888, 2889; Dream 9267; Twelfth Night 16588
Addiss, Stephen
  Merchant 8050; Richard II 12613; Tempest 14693
Adkins, Don
  Tempest 14694
Adlam, Frank
  Hamlet 3885; Measure 8025; Tempest 15989
Adler, Ernest, arr.
  Hamlet 3626, 3627; Romeo 13649; Twelfth Night 17342, 17343
Adler, Richard 1921–
  Twelfth Night 17373

Adolphe, Bruce
　Merry Wives 8798
Adolphson, Olle 1934–
　Measure 7587
Adrian, Walter 1897–
　Much Ado 11391
Advis, Luis
　Errors 2018
Aedonitskii, Pavel Kuz'mich 1922–
　Twelfth Night 16589
Aerts, Egide
　Lear 6143
African, An
　[Pseudonym used by Ignatius Sancho
　(1728–1780)?]
　Measure 7813; Settings of Commemorative
　Pieces . . . 20989, 20990
Agate, William John, arr.
　Tempest 14758; Two Gentlemen 18362
Ager, Laurence Mitchell 1904–
　Dream 10427
Ager, Milton 1893–1979
　Settings of Commemorative Pieces . . . 20991
Agerbæk, Lars
　Measure 7588
Agersnap, Harald, in part arr. 1899–1980
　Hamlet 2890, 2891; Twelfth Night 16590;
　Winter's Tale 18670
Agostini, Lucio
　Othello 11655
Aguado, Harry
　Errors 2019; Twelfth Night 16591
Aguilar, Emanuel Abraham 1824–1904
　Hamlet 3886
Aiken, G.
　As You Like It 1229
Aikin, William Arthur 1857–1939
　Much Ado 11392; Sonnet 18 19328
Aitken, Brian
　Hamlet 2892
Aitken, Robert Morris 1939–
　Hamlet 2893
Aitkenhead, Lindsay
　Macbeth 7507
Akaltan, Mithat
　Twelfth Night 16592
Aked, Lindsay Alfred 1930–
　As You Like It 1230; Cymbeline 2521;
　Macbeth 7399; Merchant 8493; Much Ado
　11393; Tempest 15597; Twelfth Night
　17714
Akimento, Fedor Stepanovich 1876–1945
　Dream 10303
Akimov, Fedor
　Dream 10296
Akimov, K.
　Errors 2020
Akses, Necil Kâzim 1908–
　Caesar 5246

Akutagawa, Yasushi
　Macbeth 6695
Alard, Delphin, arr.
　Romeo 13650
Alassio, Serafino, arr.
　Othello 12181, 12182
Alaszewski, Marek, in part arr.
　Dream 10117, 10181
Albert, Karel 1901–
　Hamlet 2894; Caesar 5247
Albertazzi, Valckenaere
　Tempest 16209
Albino, H. Hurlbutt
　Winter's Tale 18990
Albrechtsberger, Johann Georg 1736–1809
　1 Henry IV 4293; 2 Henry IV 4522
Alcock, Gilbert A.
　Henry VIII 5042
Alcock, John, Jr. 1715–1806
　Measure 7814
Aldea, Dan
　Twelfth Night 16593
Aldenhoff, Bernd
　Romeo 13087
Alderson, Albion Percy
　As You Like It 1231
Alderson, T. Albion
　Othello 12533
Aldis, Maud E.
　Twelfth Night 17751
Aldridge, Arthur N.
　Tempest 15598, 15867; Twelfth Night
　17427; Two Gentlemen 18473
Aldridge, T. A.
　Henry VIII 5043
Aleksandravičius, Zigmas 1911–1965
　Dream 10118; Sonnet 155 20554
Aleksandrov, Anatolii Nikolaevich 1888–1982
　Romeo 13088, 13880
Alekseev, S., arr.
　Cymbeline 2711
Alexander, Craig Jon
　Dream 9268
Alexander, Eric
　Much Ado 10991
Alexander, Josef 1910–
　As You Like It 977
Alexander, Sylvia
　Merry Wives 8799; Twelfth Night 16594
Alexander, William P. 1927–
　Winter's Tale 19093
Alexandre, Charles-Guillaume 1735–[circa
　1787]
　Also known as Charles-Guillaume Alessandro
　Tempest 16195
Alfano, Franco 1875–1954
　Tempest 16239
Alferaki, Akhilles Nikolaevich 1846–1919
　As You Like It 978; Much Ado 11394

Algero, Augusto
Antony 106; Shrew 14218

Aliab'ev, Aleksandr Aleksandrovich 1787–1851
Merry Wives 8800; Dream 10119; Tempest 15380

Alifantis, Nicu
As You Like It 386; Merry Wives 8997

Alig, Hellmut
Errors 2021; Caesar 5248

Allan, Cameron 1955–
As You Like It 387; Twelfth Night 16595; Settings of Commemorative Pieces . . . 21194

Allan, H.
Twelfth Night 16596

Allan, Trevor 1952–
Merchant 8051

Allanbrook, Douglas Phillips 1921–
Winter's Tale 18671; Sonnet 71 19932; Sonnet 87 20080; Sonnet 93 20130

Allbright, Terence
Dream 9269

Allegro, Elena
Merry Wives 8801

Allen, Campbell
L.L.L. 6192

Allen, Frank J.
Measure 7815

Allen, George Benjamin 1822–1897
Hamlet 4184

Allen, Jameson
Coriolanus 2265; Tempest 14695

Allen, John Jones
Romeo 13844

Allen, K. B.
Winter's Tale 18966

Allen, Liz
Richard III 12777

Allen, Marcus 1946–
Born Marcus Allen Donicht
Twelfth Night 17752

Allen, Paul Hastings 1883–1952
Measure 7816

Allen, Ray
[Raymond Allen?]
Othello 11656

Allen, Raymond
Twelfth Night 16597

Allen, Vivian
Merchant 8052

Allen, W. R.
As You Like It 1232

Allihn, Jochen
Hamlet 2895

Allison, Horton Claridge 1846–
Much Ado 11395

Allitsen, Francis 1849–1912
Pseudonym used by Mary Francis Bumpus; also known as Frances Allitsen
Antony 334

Allmann, George Joseph Oliver
Hamlet 3887; Caesar 5496; Macbeth 7411; Merchant 8685; Othello 12374

Allnatt, M. M.
Two Gentlemen 18468

Allon, Henry Erskine 1864–1897
Two Gentlemen 18474

Allport, Ronald Eric Harrison
Merchant 8053; Twelfth Night 17428

Allridge, H.
Settings of Commemorative Pieces . . . 21097

Allum, Charles Edward, arr.
Dream 9621

Allworth, Robert
Dream 10746

Allwright, Graeme
Hamlet 3878; P. Pilgrim 20586

Alm, Anders
Romeo 13090

Almila, Atso Aksel 1953–
Lear 5656, 6047; Shrew 14219

Alofsin, Anna Sarah
Much Ado 10992

'Alotta Peeple'
Hamlet 4137

Alpaerts, Flor 1876–1954
Cymbeline 2432; Merchant 8390

Alsfelt, Palle 1908–
Timon 16299

Alsina, Carlos Roqué
Dream 9270

Alsing, Hans Jörgen 1952–
Dream 9271

Alsleben, Julius 1832–1894
Twelfth Night 18201

Altaï, Armande
Pseudonym used by Armande Jeanne Maggini
Othello 11657

Altès, Ernest Eugène, arr. 1830–1899
All's Well 75

Althaus, Basil, arr.
Dream 9622

Altheimer, Bessie Miriam
Cymbeline 2629

Alvars, Elie Parish, arr.
Dream 9623

Alvensleben, Agibhard 1810–1886
As You Like It 979

Alwyn, William 1905–1985
Othello 12375; Tempest 15990

Alwyn, William Crowther
Henry VIII 5044

Amani, Nikolai Nikolaevich 1872–1904
Romeo 13829

Ambroise, Victor, arr.
Dream 9624; Romeo 13968

Ambros, August Wilhelm 1816–1876
Othello 11658

Ambros, Janusz
Hamlet 2896
Ambrose, Paul 1868–1941
As You Like It 1233; Twelfth Night 17753
Amdahl, Bjarne 1903–1968
As You Like It 388
Amdahl, Magne 1942–
As You Like It 389; Hamlet 2897; Measure
7589; Tempest 14696
Amend, Erwin
As You Like It 390, 391; Hamlet 2898;
Twelfth Night 16598
Ames, Craig
Dream 9272
Ames, John Carlowitz 1860–1924
1 Henry IV 4294; Richard II 12614; Sonnet
60 19817
Ames, William
1 Henry IV 4507; 2 Henry IV 4676
Amfitheatrof, Daniele 1901–1983
Also known as Daniele Amfiteatrov
Lear 6118
Amiel, Jon
Troilus 16432
Ammons, Lila
Romeo 13845
Amram, David Werner, III 1930–
All's Well 2; Antony 107, 108; As You Like
It 392, 393, 980; Coriolanus 2266; Hamlet
2899, 2900, 2901, 3696; 1 Henry IV 4295;
2 Henry IV 4523; Henry V 4690; Caesar
5249, 5250; K. John 5568; Lear 5657,
6041, 6048; Macbeth 6696, 6697, 6698;
Measure 7590, 7591, 7817; Merchant 8054;
Dream 9273, 10473; Much Ado 10993,
11396, 11616; Othello 11659, 11660;
Richard II 12615; Richard III 12778; Romeo
13091, 13092, 13093; Shrew 14220,
14221; Tempest 14697; Titus 16389;
Troilus 16433; Twelfth Night 16599,
16600, 16601, 17375, 17429, 17744,
17754, 18080, 18202; Two Gentlemen
18348, 18475; Winter's Tale 18672;
Settings of Commemorative Pieces . . .
21099
Anbild, Karol
Hamlet 2902
Anders, Erich 1883–1955
Pseudonym used by Freiherr Wolff von
Gudenberg
Lear 5658
Anders, Hermann
Phoenix 20753
Andersen, Allan
Shrew 14222
Andersen, Johannes, [in part arr.] 1890–1980
Romeo 13094
Andersen, Walther
Richard III 12779

Anderson, [?]
Romeo 14021
Anderson, Barry 1935–
Henry V 4816
Anderson, Doug
Errors 2022
Anderson, E. N.
As You Like It 1234
Anderson, Hilding, arr.
Two Gentlemen 18561
Anderson, Inger Yde
Much Ado 11397
Anderson, Laurie 1947–
Tempest 16210
Anderson, Michael
Dream 9274
Anderson, Michael Anthony
Richard III 12780
Anderson, R. Graham
L.L.L. 6492
Anderson, Ruth Marie
Macbeth 7369; Sonnet 17 19319
Anderson, Sam
All's Well 71
Andersson, Kjell 1937–
Hamlet 2903; Dream 9275; Richard III
12781; Romeo 13095
Anderton, Howard Orsmond 1861–1934
Cymbeline 2522; Measure 7818; Merchant
8494; Dream 10474; Twelfth Night 17430,
17755
Anderton, T[homas] [1836–1903]
Measure 7819
Anderton, Thomas 1836–1903
Antony 285; As You Like It 943; Hamlet
3814; Settings of Commemorative Pieces . . .
20901
André, Carl
Merchant 8686
André, J. B.
Twelfth Night 16602
André, Johann 1741–1799
Lear 5659; Macbeth 6699
Andrée, B.
Twelfth Night 16603
Andreozzi, Gaetano 1755–1826
Hamlet 4138; Caesar 5555; Dream 10944
Andrews, David 1915–
Sonnet 18 19329
Andrews, Dwight, arr.
Much Ado 11111
Andrews, George F.
As You Like It 1235
Andrews, Herbert Kennedy 1904–1965
Troilus 16434
Andrews, Mark 1875–1939
Twelfth Night 17756; Winter's Tale 19147
Andriessen, Gijs
Much Ado 10994

Andriessen, Jurriaan 1925–
As You Like It 394; Cymbeline 2811; Hamlet
2904, 2905, 2906; 1 Henry IV 4296; Caesar
5251; Lear 5660; Macbeth 6700; Measure
7592; Merchant 8055; Merry Wives 8802;
Dream 9276, 9277, 9278, 10576; Much
Ado 10995, 10996; Othello 11661; Richard
III 12782; Romeo 13096; Shrew 14223;
Tempest 14698, 14699, 14700, 15791;
Troilus 16435; Twelfth Night 16604,
16605, 16606; Winter's Tale 18673; Sonnet
9 19275; Sonnet 25 19501; Sonnet 71
19933; Sonnet 87 20081; Sonnet 128
20381; Sonnet 131 20431; Sonnet 154
20543

Andrus, Donald George 1935–
Macbeth 6701

Andrzejewski, Marek
Much Ado 10997

Andrzejewski, Zenon
Hamlet 2907; Lear 5661

Anelli, Joseph, arr.
Dream 10788

Anfossi, Pasquale 1727–1797
Antony 358; Coriolanus 2401

Angel, Antonio Ramirez
Romeo 13097

Anger, Mořic Stanislav 1844–1905
Lear 5662; Macbeth 6702; Merchant 8056;
Twelfth Night 17376

Angerer, Paul 1927–
As You Like It 395; Macbeth 6703; Measure
7593; Merry Wives 8803; Much Ado 10998,
10999; Shrew 14224, 14225; Twelfth Night
16607, 16608, 17431, 17757, 18081;
Winter's Tale 18674

Ángyal, [?]
Tempest 15382

Anholt, Simon
Hamlet 2908

Aniol, Edward
Hamlet 2909; Dream 9279; Richard III
12783

Anker, Bernt
Macbeth 6704

Annecchino, Arturo
Othello 12443; Richard III 12784; Twelfth
Night 16609

Anniko, Tom
As You Like It 396

[Anon.]
Antony 260, 353; As You Like It 1590,
1867; Coriolanus 2396; Hamlet 3789; K.
John 5569; Lear 5663; Macbeth 6705,
6706, 6707; Measure 7820; Merchant 8737;
Dream 10445; Much Ado 11000, 11591;
Othello 11662, 12214; Romeo 14022;
Tempest 14701, 14702, 15383, 15599,
15965, 15991; Winter's Tale 18675, 18946,

18967, 18991, 19029, 19068; Sonnet 155
20555; P. Pilgrim 20587; Settings of
Commemorative Pieces . . . 21100

[Anon.], adapter
Tempest 15595

[Anon.], ed.
Anthologies 21312

[Anon., in part arr.]
Twelfth Night 16610

Anon.
Antony 286, 359; As You Like It 397;
Cymbeline 2630, 2844; Hamlet 2910;
1 Henry IV 4508; 2 Henry IV 4677; K. John
5651; Lear 6179; Merry Wives 9257; Dream
10120, 10753; Much Ado 11648; Othello
12246, 12249, 12444, 12489; Richard III
12785; Romeo 14122; Tempest 14753,
15829; Twelfth Night 17432, 17687,
17758, 18265; Winter's Tale 18676; Venus
20787; Settings of Commemorative
Pieces . . . 20992, 20993, 21255

Anon., adapter
Henry VIII 5045

Anon., arr.
As You Like It 399, 400; Hamlet 3628,
3629; Henry VIII 5137; Macbeth 7299,
7300; Merchant 8346; Merry Wives 9178;
Dream 10182; Much Ado 11006, 11555;
Othello 12183, 12184; Romeo 13812;
Tempest 14703, 14759, 14760, 14761,
15116, 15480, 15575, 15576; Twelfth
Night 16667; Settings of Commemorative
Pieces . . . 20903, 21101, 21102

Anon., ed.
Settings of Commemorative Pieces . . . 21276;
Anthologies 21314; 21315

Anschütz, Johann Andreas, arr. 1772–1856
Also known as Joseph Andreas Anschütz
Settings of Commemorative Pieces . . . 20959,
20960

Anson, Hugo Vernon 1894–1958
Dream 10945

Anstruther, P. N.
As You Like It 1596

Antanėlis, Kęstutis 1951–
Romeo 14070

Antcliffe, Herbert 1875–
As You Like It 981

Anthony, David
Twelfth Night 16611

Anthony, Peter 1951–
Pseudonym used by Peter Anthony Martinez
Tempest 15384

Anthony, Phil
Twelfth Night 18287

Antill, John 1904–
Tempest 14754

Antolin, J.
Hamlet 2912

Antonietti, David, arr.
Hamlet 4147
Antonietti, Felice
Othello 12377
Antoniou, Theodore 1935–
Dream 9280; Romeo 13098
Aperghis, Georges 1945–
Hamlet 2913
ApIvor, Denis 1916–
Cymbeline 2523
Applebaum, Edward 1937–
Sonnet 18 19330; Sonnet 43 19708
Applebaum, Louis 1918–
All's Well 3, 4; Antony 109, 110; Coriolanus
2267; Cymbeline 2433; Hamlet 2914, 2915,
2916, 2917; 1 Henry IV 4297; Henry V
4691; Henry VIII 4966; Caesar 5252, 5253;
K. John 5570; Lear 5664, 5665; Macbeth
6708, 6709, 6710; Measure 7594, 7595;
Merchant 8057; Merry Wives 8804; Much
Ado 11001, 11002, 11003, 11004; Othello
11663, 11664, 11665; Richard II 12616;
Richard III 12786, 12787; Romeo 13099,
13100, 13101; Shrew 14226; Timon 16300;
Troilus 16436; Twelfth Night 16613,
16614; Two Gentlemen 18349; Winter's
Tale 18677; Settings of Commemorative
Pieces . . . 20822, 20823
Appleby, Benjamin William, arr.
As You Like It 1171; Tempest 15053
Araci, Elvan
Tempest 14755
Aramian, F. A.
Coriolanus 2268
Arandia Navarro, Jorge 1929–
Hamlet 3828
Araratian, Vaag Georgievich 1902–
Twelfth Night 16615
Arban, Joseph Jean-Baptiste, arr. 1825–1889
Hamlet 3630
Archer, J. Stuart, arr.
As You Like It 784; Dream 9625
Archer, Violet 1913–
Née Balestreri
As You Like It 982, 1597; Much Ado 11398;
Settings of Commemorative Pieces . . . 20994
Ardin, Leon
Antony 261
Arditi, Luigi, arr. 1822–1903
Hamlet 3631
Ardley, Neil Richard 1937–
Sonnet 18 19331; Settings of
Commemorative Pieces . . . 20995
Arends, Andrei Genrikh Fedorovich
1855–1924
Cymbeline 2434; 3 Henry VI 4961; Macbeth
6711; Richard III 12788
Arenskii, Anton Stepanovich 1861–1906
Tempest 14756

Arenson, Adolf
Twelfth Night 17377
Argento, Dominick J. 1927–
L.L.L. 6493; Romeo 13832; Shrew 14557;
Twelfth Night 17433; Settings of
Commemorative Pieces . . . 21103
Arimont, Jean 1916–
Pseudonym used by Ernest Majo; also known
as Ernest Majowski
Lear 6049
Ariosti, Attilio Malachia 1666–[1729?]
Coriolanus 2402
Aristides, Mosxhos 1929–
Dream 9281
Arizaga, Rodolfo 1926–
Sonnet 71 19934
Arkwright, Godfrey Edward Pellew 1864–1944
As You Like It 1236, 1598; Cymbeline 2632;
Henry VIII 5046; L.L.L. 6381, 6494;
Tempest 15600; Twelfth Night 17434; Two
Gentlemen 18476
Armand, Georges
Twelfth Night 16616
Armbruster, Carl
Hamlet 2918
Arment, Hollace E.
Merchant 8058
Armer, Elinor Florence 1939–
Merchant 8422, 8667, 8673
Armstrong, David 1927–
Hamlet 4139
Armstrong, John 1952–
Twelfth Night 17715
Armstrong, William Dawson 1868–1936
Romeo 13881
Arnatt, Ronald Kent 1930–
Settings of Commemorative Pieces . . . 21201
Arne, Michael [1740?]–1786
Errors 2023; Dream 9282; Winter's Tale
18678
Arne, Thomas Augustine 1710–1778
As You Like It 398, 983, 1591, 1599;
Cymbeline 2435, 2436, 2524, 2845; L.L.L.
6193, 6382, 6495, 6667; Macbeth 6712;
Merchant 8059, 8495, 8722; Dream 10765;
Much Ado 11005, 11399; Romeo 13102;
Tempest 14757, 15507, 15512, 15792,
15868, 15967; Twelfth Night 16617,
16621, 17435, 17436; Winter's Tale 18679,
18680; P. Pilgrim 20588; Lucrece 20781;
Settings of Commemorative Pieces . . . 20902
Arnejšek, Milenko
Romeo 13104
Arnell, Richard Anthony Sayer 1917–
Tempest 16240; Twelfth Night 18203
Arnold, Charles
Sonnet 109 20276
Arnold, George Benjamin 1832–1902
Settings of Commemorative Pieces . . . 20996

Arnold, Jay, arr.
Two Gentlemen 18562
Arnold, Malcolm Henry 1921–
Antony 111; Caesar 5254; Tempest 14850, 15513, 15601, 15869
Arnold, Samuel 1740–1802
1 Henry VI 4881; 2 Henry VI 4926; 3 Henry VI 4962; Dream 9283, 10769; Tempest 16196; Kinsmen 19168; P. Pilgrim 20589
Arnold, Samuel, in part arr. 1740–1802
Macbeth 6713
Arnold, Samuel, arr. 1740–1802
Hamlet 2919, 3748, 3831, 3863, 3880
Arp, Klaus
Othello 11666
Arpaia, William H.
Settings of Commemorative Pieces . . . 20997
Arrhén von Kapfelman, Eric Jacob 1790–1851
Macbeth 6714
Arrieu, Claude 1903–
Pseudonym used by Louise Marie Simon
Cymbeline 2437, 2511; Merchant 8062; Richard II 12776; Tempest 14851
Artamanov, Aleksei Pavlovich 1906–
Othello 12378; Twelfth Night 16624
Artem'ev, Eduard Nikolaevich 1937–
Hamlet 2920
Arthuys, Philippe
Macbeth 6716
Artok, Leo, arr.
Dream 9626, 9627, 9628; Much Ado 11162; Romeo 13651
Arundell, Dennis Drew 1898–
Born Arundel
Dream 10121; Tempest 14852; Winter's Tale 18681; Complaint 20584
Arundell, Dennis Drew, arr. 1898–
Born Arundel
Henry VIII 5134
Arzumanov, Valerii Grantovich 1940–
Sonnet 112 20292
Asaf'ev, Boris Vladimirovich 1884–1949
Also known under the pseudonym 'Igor' Glebov'
Caesar 5255; Macbeth 6717; Merchant 8063; Othello 11667, 11668; Romeo 13105, 13106
Aschaffenburg, Walter 1927–
Sonnet 18 19332; Sonnet 65 19886; Sonnet 73 19980
Aschenbrenner, John, in part arr.
Lear 5666
Ascolese, Domenico, arr.
Hamlet 3576
Ascone, Vicente 1897–
Macbeth 6718
Asherman, Eddie
Merchant 8779
Ashford, Emma Louise 1850–1930
As You Like It 984

Ashton, Archie Thomas Lee
Much Ado 11649
Asioli, Bonifacio, arr.
Othello 12039
Asoha
[Pseudonym used by ?]
As You Like It 1999
Aspa, Edwin [1835?]–1883
Henry VIII 5047
Asplmayer, Franz 172[8]–1786
Surname known in a number of forms, e.g., Aspelmayr, Aspelmeier, Asplmeyr, Aschpellmayr, and Appelmeyer
Macbeth 6719; Tempest 14853
Asriel, Andre 1922–
Two Gentlemen 18350, 18641
Aßhauer, Hans-Georg
Twelfth Night 16625
Aston, Peter 1938–
Hamlet 3697; Tempest 15602; Twelfth Night 17437
Atanasiu, Dudu
Othello 11669
Atherling, Theodore
Twelfth Night 17438
Atherton, Percy Lee 1871–1944
Hamlet 4140
Atkins, Richard
Pericles 12540
Ator, James Donald 1938–
Sonnet 15 19303; Sonnet 30 19588; Sonnet 61 19846; Sonnet 116 20305; Sonnet 120 20355; Sonnet 129 20406; Sonnet 135 20440; Sonnet 144 20478
Atovm'ian, Levin Tadessovich, arr. 1901–
Hamlet 3411; Romeo 13792, 13793
Atterberg, Kurt Magnus 1887–1974
Antony 112; Hamlet 2921; Macbeth 7412; Tempest 14854, 15385; Winter's Tale 18682, 19094
Atterberg, Kurt Magnus, in part arr. 1887–1974
As You Like It 456
[Atterbury, Luffman] [–1796]
Measure 7821
Attree, Richard
Tempest 14855
Attwater, John Post 1862–1909
As You Like It 1237; Cymbeline 2633; Dream 10383; P. Pilgrim 20590
Attwood, Thomas 1765–1838
Henry VIII 4967; Dream 10770
Atzler, Rich[ard], arr.
Dream 9629
Aubin, Tony Louis Alexandre 1907–1981
Hamlet 2922, 3888; Much Ado 11344; Troilus 16583
Aubrey, Alfred
Tempest 15992

Audran, Edmond 1840–1901
  All's Well 103
Auemüller, Hans
  Twelfth Night 16626
Auerbach, James
  Romeo 13107
Auerbach, Rudolph
  Merchant 8738
Auger, Jean Pierre
  Merchant 8064
Augustine, Reggie
  As You Like It 944
Augustyn, Rafał
  As You Like It 457
Aulagnier, Antonin, arr.
  Othello 12040
Auric, Georges 1899–1983
  As You Like It 458; Merry Wives 8805;
  Dream 9284
Auscher, Abel
  Pseudonym used by [?]
  Timon 16387
Aust, Konrad
  Henry V 4692; K. John 5571; Merchant
  8065; Othello 11670
Aust, Konrad, in part arr.
  Measure 7596
Auster, Lidiia Martinovna 1912–
  Romeo 14071
Austin, Dorothea
  Sonnet 5 19205; Sonnet 33 19645
Austin, Ernest 1874–1947
  Cymbeline 2634; Much Ado 11400
Austin, Frederic 1872–1952
  As You Like It 1238; Henry VIII 5048;
  Dream 10577; Much Ado 11401; Richard II
  12767
Austin, Frederic, arr. 1872–1952
  As You Like It 1424
Austin, Mabel Mae
  Much Ado 11009
Austin, Richard
  Antony 113
Aven, Richard
  Dream 9285
Avery, Stanley R., arr.
  Two Gentlemen 18563, 18564
Avison, Charles 1709–1770
  Romeo 14123
Avitabile, S.
  Henry V 4693
Avril, Hanns
  Much Ado 11010
Awner, Deborah
  1 Henry IV 4298; L.L.L. 6194; Romeo
  13108
Aylward, Theodore 1730–1801
  Cymbeline 2438, 2635; Dream 9286; Much
  Ado 11372; Twelfth Night 17439; Two

Gentlemen 18477; Settings of
  Commemorative Pieces . . . 20998
Ayres, Frederic 1876–1926
  As You Like It 1239; Measure 7822;
  Merchant 8496; Tempest 15514, 15603,
  15870; Winter's Tale 19030

B

B., L.
  Tempest 16211
Baas, Alexius
  As You Like It 985
Babbitt, Milton Byron 1916–
  Sonnet 71 19935
Babcock, Richard
  Settings of Commemorative Pieces . . . 20824
Babel, Armand Adrien Fernand
  Othello 11671
Baber, Joseph Wilson 1937–
  As You Like It 986, 1240, 1241, 1600,
  1868; L.L.L. 6502; Measure 7823, 7824,
  7825; Merchant 8497, 8498; Merry Wives
  9200; Much Ado 11402; Othello 12266;
  Tempest 15604, 15844; Twelfth Night
  17692, 17768; Two Gentlemen 18478;
  Settings of Commemorative Pieces . . . 21202
Babić, Bogdan
  Othello 11672
Bacewicz, Grażyna 1913–1969
  Macbeth 6720; Troilus 16437
Bach, Carl Philipp Emanuel 1714–1788
  Also known as Emanuel Bach
  Hamlet 3889
Bach, Emanuel [flor. 1870]
  Hamlet 2923
Bach, Fritz 1881–1930
  Much Ado 11011
Bach, Jan Morris 1937–
  As You Like It 987; L.L.L. 6383; Romeo
  13109; Twelfth Night 18082
Bach, Johann Christian 1735–1782
  Dream 10771
Bach, Johann Christoph Friedrich 1732–1795
  Caesar 5537
Bach, P. D. Q. '(1807–1742)?'
  Pseudonym of Peter Johann Schickele (born
  1935)
  As You Like It 1242; Two Gentlemen 18479
Bacher, Elman
  Tempest 15993
Bäck, Sven-Erik
  Merchant 8066
Bacon, Ernst 1898–
  Coriolanus 2397; 2 Henry IV 4645; Tempest
  14856, 14857, 15515, 15818, 15871,
  15994, 15995, 16212

Badenes, Garcia, arr.   –1959
  Merchant 8767
Baekers, Stephan 1948–
  Sonnet 5 19206
Baeyens, August-Louis 1895–1966
  Coriolanus 2371
Baeyertz, Paul
  Merchant 8067
Bagdasarian, E.
  Romeo 13110
Bagot, Maurice Louis Joseph
  Shrew 14227
Baildon, Joseph [circa 1727]–1774
  Merchant 8723
Bailey, Gerald H.
  Tempest 15386
Bailey, Larry
  Antony 114; Romeo 13111
Bailey, Parker 1902–
  As You Like It 1833; Henry VIII 5049
Bailly, Jean Gabriel
  Hamlet 2924
Bailly, Jean-Guy 1925–
  Hamlet 2925; Sonnet 138 20452
Baines, Herbert
  As You Like It 1243; Henry VIII 5050; L.L.L.
  6503; Much Ado 11403; Othello 12215;
  Tempest 15605; Twelfth Night 17769,
  18083
Baini, Lorenzo
  Romeo 13555
Bainton, Edgar Leslie 1880–1956
  Dream 10579; Twelfth Night 16627
Baird, Tadeusz 1928–1981
  Cymbeline 2439; Hamlet 2926, 2927;
  1 Henry IV 4299; 1 Henry VI 4844, 4884;
  2 Henry VI 4885, 4928; 3 Henry VI 4929,
  4965; Caesar 5256; Measure 7597; Dream
  9287; Much Ado 11012; Richard III 12789;
  Romeo 13112; Sonnet 23 19488; Sonnet 56
  19790; Sonnet 91 20116; Sonnet 97 20151
Bairstow, Edward Cuthbert 1874–1946
  Henry VIII 5051
Bajerski, Tomasz
  Coriolanus 2269; Romeo 13113
Bakaleinikov, Nikolai Romanovich
  1881–1957
  Lear 5667; Much Ado 11013; Othello
  11673; Twelfth Night 16628
Baker, Howard
  Dream 9288
Baker, Larry A. 1948–
  Hamlet 3877; Richard III 13041, 13045
Baker, M. Appleton
  Lear 6050
Baker, Terry S.
  Much Ado 11014
Baker, Thomas
  As You Like It 459

Baker, Thomas, in part arr.
  Much Ado 11015
Baker, Thomas, arr.
  Merry Wives 8877
Baker, Ward
  Richard III 13069
Baksa, Robert Frank 1938–
  As You Like It 988, 1601; Cymbeline 2636;
  L.L.L. 6504; Merchant 8499; Tempest
  15606; Twelfth Night 17440, 17770;
  P. Pilgrim 20591
Balakirev, Milii Alekseevich 1837–1910
  Lear 5668
Balamos, John
  As You Like It 945
Balanchivadze, Andrei Melitonovich 1906–
  Lear 5670; Shrew 14228
Balatka, Anton
  Romeo 13114; Twelfth Night 16629
Balatka, Antonín
  Twelfth Night 16630
Balay, Guillaume, arr. 1871–1943
  Merchant 8768
Baldamus, Gustav 1862–
  Richard III 13080
Baldridge, Richard 1926–[1970?]
  Macbeth 6721
[Baldwin, Ralph Lyman, arr.]
  Two Gentlemen 18565
Baldwin, Frederick R.
  Tempest 15996; Settings of Commemorative
  Pieces . . . 21104
Baldwin, Ralph Lyman, arr.
  Cymbeline 2712
Balentine, James Scott
  Tempest 14858
Bales, Richard Henry Horner 1915–
  Twelfth Night 17441; Two Gentlemen
  18480
Balfe, Michael William 1808–1870
  Hamlet 3554; 1 Henry IV 4509; 2 Henry IV
  4678; Merry Wives 8998; Much Ado 11404
Baliani, Carlo [circa 1680]–1747
  Hamlet 4264
Ball, Andrew, in part arr.
  Henry V 4694
Ball, John Meredith [1838?]–1915
  Lear 5671; Merchant 8068; Othello 12267;
  Romeo 13115; Twelfth Night 16631
Ball, John Meredith, in part arr.
  [1838?]–1915
  Much Ado 11016; Richard III 12790
Ball, Michael 1946–
  Cymbeline 2525; Twelfth Night 17442,
  17771, 18084
Ball, W[illiam?], arr. [1784–1869]
  Othello 12306
Ball, William 1784–1869
  Romeo 14124

Balling, Michael 1866–1925
  Antony 115; Henry V 4695; Macbeth 6722;
  Dream 9289
Ballinger, Cathryn
  Romeo 13117
Balmer, Luc 1898–
  Macbeth 6723
Balsys, Eduardas Kosto 1919–
  Macbeth 6724
Balzer, Klaus
  Othello 11674
Banasik, Michał
  Much Ado 11017
Banck, Carl 1809–1889
  Twelfth Night 17443
Banco, Gerhard
  Twelfth Night 16632
Bandini, Uberto 1860–1919
  Hamlet 3890
Banger, Georg, arr.
  Merry Wives 9016; Dream 9630
Banister, Henry Charles 1831–1897
  Cymbeline 2812
Banister, John, the Elder [circa 1625]–1679
  Tempest 14859, 15387, 15516, 15607
Bannelier, Charles, arr.
  Lear 6167
[Bannister, John, adapter] [1760–1836]
  Hamlet 4185; Macbeth 7556; Othello 12490
Bannister, Charles, arr. [1741?]–1804
  Macbeth 6973
Bantock, Granville 1868–1946
  Lear 6051; Macbeth 6725, 7413; Measure
  7826; Merchant 8674; Othello 12268;
  Tempest 15517, 15608, 15872, 16233;
  Twelfth Night 17444, 17772
Bantock, Granville, arr. 1868–1946
  As You Like It 2000; Errors 2033; Cymbeline
  2713; Dream 9631; Othello 12250; Romeo
  13652, 13969, 13970; Tempest 14762,
  15054; Twelfth Night 17759; Settings of
  Commemorative Pieces . . . 21293
Bantzer, Claus
  Twelfth Night 16633
Banzer, Alexander
  Shrew 14558
Baramishvili, Ol'ga Ivanovna 1907–1956
  Romeo 13118, 13882; Shrew 14229
Baranović, Krešimir 1894–1975
  Hamlet 2928; 1 Henry IV 4300; 2 Henry IV
  4524
Barbe, Helmut 1927–
  Two Gentlemen 18351, 18642
Barber, Samuel 1910–1981
  Antony 262; As You Like It 460
Barberis, Alberto
  Othello 11675
Barberis, Mansi 1899–1986
  Merchant 8069

Barbie, Richard Alan
  1 Henry IV 4458; 2 Henry IV 4625; Henry V
  4797; Shrew 14559
Barbieri, Carlo Emanuele 1822–1867
  Also known as Carlo Emanuele de Barbieri
  and as Carlo Emanuele di Barbieri.
  Winter's Tale 18926
Barboteu, Georges-Yves 1924–
  Macbeth 7238
Barbour, James Murray 1897–1970
  As You Like It 461; Romeo 13119
Bard, Vivian
  Dream 10580
Bardi, Benno 1890–
  Pseudonym used by B. Poswiansky
  Hamlet 2929; Henry V 4696; Merry Wives
  8806; Othello 11676; Richard III 12791;
  Romeo 13120; Tempest 14861; Two
  Gentlemen 18352
Barfoed, Søren 1950–
  Sonnet 73 19981; Sonnet 128 20382
Barfuss, Franciszek
  Twelfth Night 16634
Bargiel, Woldemar 1828–1897
  Romeo 13884
Bargiel, Woldemar, arr. 1828–1897
  Caesar 5521, 5522
Barker, David
  Twelfth Night 16635
Barker, G.
  [George Arthur Barker?]
  Much Ado 11405
Barker, George Arthur
  Sonnet 54 19765; P. Pilgrim 20592
Barker, Nathan   –[before 1891]
  Tempest 16241
Barker, Paul Alan 1956–
  Dream 10122
Barkley, Glen
  Dream 9290; Two Gentlemen 18353
Barkworth, John Edmond 1858–1929
  As You Like It 1244; 2 Henry VI 4886;
  Romeo 13556
Barkworth, John Edmond, arr. 1858–1929
  As You Like It 1425
Barlow, David Frederick 1927–1975
  Tempest 15997; Sonnet 155 20556
Barlow, Jeremy
  Errors 2024
Barman, Herb
  1 Henry IV 4301
Barmettler, Magi
  Romeo 13121
Barnard, Dorothy, arr.
  Much Ado 11532
Barnard, Francis
  Richard II 12617
Barnard, J. M.
  Tempest 15998

Barnby, Ethel
Twelfth Night 18324
Barnby, Joseph 1838–1896
As You Like It 1245
Barndt, Timothy
L.L.L. 6377; Twelfth Night 17445, 17693, 17773, 18085
Barnes, Chris
Measure 7598; Tempest 14862
Barnes, Edward
Macbeth 6726
Barnes, Edward Shippen
Settings of Commemorative Pieces . . . 21294
Barnes, Edward Shippen, arr.
Dream 9632; Two Gentlemen 18566
Barnes, Howard
Merchant 8780
Barnes, Milton 1931–
Romeo 13122
Barnes, Richard
Dream 9291
Barnett, Carol Edith Anderson 1949–
Hamlet 3829
Barnett, David 1907–
Sonnet 30 19592; Sonnet 97 20152
Barnett, John 1802–1890
All's Well 97; Errors 2263; Cymbeline 2851; Macbeth 7557; Dream 10312, 10901; Othello 12491; Romeo 14125; Troilus 16580; Twelfth Night 18288; P. Pilgrim 20593; Settings of Commemorative Pieces . . . 20999, 21000
Barnett, John Francis 1837–1916
Winter's Tale 19095
Barnier, Théodore Émile, arr. –1919
Caesar 5523; Settings of Commemorative Pieces . . . 20961
Baron, Maurice 1889–1964
Romeo 13885
Baron, Maurice, arr. 1889–1964
Two Gentlemen 18567
Barraine, Elsa 1910–
Lear 5672
Barratt, Carol, arr. 1945–
Dream 9633; Romeo 13971
Barratt, R., arr.
Dream 9634
Barratt, William Augustus 1874–
As You Like It 1246; Henry VIII 5052; Measure 7827; Dream 10310, 10313; Twelfth Night 16636, 16637, 17446, 17447, 17774, 17775, 17776, 18086
Barratt, William Augustus, arr. 1874–
As You Like It 401; Cymbeline 2714; Dream 9363; Much Ado 11533, 11635; Othello 12247; Tempest 15055; Two Gentlemen 18568
Barrell, Bernard 1919–
L.L.L. 6384; Merchant 8500; Dream 10475; Much Ado 11406; Twelfth Night 17448

Barrett, Augustus, in part arr.
[William Augustus Barratt (1874–   )?]
Dream 9292
Barrett, Paul
As You Like It 462
Barrett, William Alexander, arr. 1836–1891
As You Like It 402; Tempest 14763; Settings of Commemorative Pieces . . . 20904
Barri, Odoardo 1844–1920
Pseudonym used by Edward Slater
Romeo 13834
Barri, Richard, arr.
Much Ado 11345
Barrie, Denys
Sonnet 87 20082
Barrie, Lucy
Errors 2025
Barrie, Stuart, arr.
Othello 12515
Barrington, Clarence
Tempest 16197
Barrish, Seth
Hamlet 2930; Merry Wives 8807
Barron, Bebe
Tempest 16177
Barron, Louis 1920–
Tempest 16178
Barrow, Benjamin, arr.
Dream 9635
Barrows, John 1913–1974
Hamlet 2931
Barrows, Margaret Hamilton
Sonnet 18 19333
Barry, Augustus
Measure 7828
Barry, Charles Ainslie, arr. 1830–1915
Much Ado 11346
Barry, Frederick 1876–1943
Twelfth Night 17777
Barry, Gerald
Sonnet 155 20557
Barry, H. C.
Merchant 8739
Barry, John
Hamlet 3719
Barry, Katharine E.
Winter's Tale 19031
Barshai, Rudol'f Borisovich, arr. 1924–
Romeo 13794
Barskov, Oleg 1935–
Sonnet 27 19515; Sonnet 33 19646; Sonnet 48 19735; Sonnet 146 20487
Barthel, Karl-Heinz
Twelfth Night 16638
Barthélemon, François-Hippolyte 1741–1808
Cymbeline 2440; L.L.L. 6357; Settings of Commemorative Pieces . . . 21001

Barthélemon, François-Hippolyte, in part arr. 1741–1808
Macbeth 7239
Barthelemy, Claude André Pierre 1956–
Merchant 8070; Dream 9293
Bartholin, Birger 1900–
Romeo 13557
Bartholomew, Ann Sheppard 1811–1891
Née Mounsey; also known as Mrs. William Bartholomew and as Mrs. Mounsey Bartholomew
As You Like It 989; Merchant 8501; Dream 10902; Tempest 15999; Sonnet 54 19766; P. Pilgrim 20594
Bartholomew, [Marshall Moore] [1885–1978]
As You Like It 1247
Bartholomew, Ruth
Romeo 13123
Bartini, Gari
Also known as Gary Bartini
Hamlet 2932; Lear 5673; Merchant 8071, 8072; Much Ado 11018; Twelfth Night 16639
Bartlett, Homer Newton 1846–1920
Merchant 8502
Bartlett, Ian James, adapter 1934–
Twelfth Night 16640, 17449, 17694
Barton, David
As You Like It 463
Barton, Gerrard 1861–
As You Like It 990, 1248; Twelfth Night 18087
Barton, Oliver
Dream 9294
Barton, Todd
All's Well 5; Errors 2026; Coriolanus 2270; Hamlet 2933; 1 Henry IV 4302; Henry VIII 4968; Caesar 5257; K. John 5572; Lear 5674; L.L.L. 6195; Macbeth 6727, 6728, 6729; Measure 7599; Merchant 8073; Merry Wives 8808; Dream 9295, 9296; Much Ado 11019; Othello 11677; Richard II 12618, 12619; Richard III 12792; Romeo 13124; Shrew 14230; Tempest 14863; Titus 16390; Troilus 16438, 16439; Winter's Tale 18683
Barton, Todd, in part arr.
As You Like It 464; Henry V 4697; Much Ado 11020; Twelfth Night 16641; Two Gentlemen 18354
Barton-Armstrong, John 1923–
Hamlet 3555
Basarabescu, Gabriel
Twelfth Night 16642
Bashmakov, Leonid 1927–
Hamlet 2934; Macbeth 6730; Tempest 14864
Basili, Basilio 1803–1895
Macbeth 6731

Baskett, Lawrence E.
Tempest 15793
Basman, Ken
Othello 12492
Bass, Claude L. 1935–
Winter's Tale 18968
Bass, Howard, in part arr.
Twelfth Night 16643
Bassett, Leslie Raymond 1923–
Lear 5675; Dream 10454; Richard II 12620; Tempest 14865
Bastard, William, arr.
Merchant 8769
Bate, Stanley 1913–1959
Troilus 16558; Twelfth Night 16644
Bateman, David
Kinsmen 19158
Bath, Hubert Charles 1883–1945
As You Like It 1869, 1971; Dream 10581, 10582; Tempest 16000
Bath, J[ohn?]
Measure 7829; Tempest 15609; Twelfth Night 17778
Batista, Andres
Romeo 14040
Batiste, Édouard, arr.
Hamlet 3632
Batstone, Philip Norman 1933–
Phoenix 20754
Batta, Jos
Lear 6144
Battaglino, John
Dream 9297
Batten, Joseph
Twelfth Night 17779
[Battishill, Jonathan] [1738–1801]
Dream 10297
Battishill, Jonathan 1738–1801
Dream 9298
Battista, Ned
1 Henry IV 4459; 2 Henry IV 4626
Battmann, Jacques Louis, arr. 1818–1886
Hamlet 3633; Dream 9636; Othello 12041
Baudo, Serge 1927–
Sonnet 1 19176; Sonnet 71 19936
Baudrier, Yves 1906–
Lear 5676
Bauer, André
As You Like It 465; Merry Wives 8809; Othello 11678
Bauer, Hermann
Caesar 5258; Shrew 14231
Bauer, Robert Paul 1950–
Hamlet 3845; Romeo 13828
Baughan, Clare
As You Like It 466
Bauld, Alison 1944–
As You Like It 467; Macbeth 7496; Richard III 12793

Baumann, F., arr.
Romeo 13972
Baumann, Herbert 1925–
As You Like It 468, 469; Errors 2027;
Hamlet 2935; K. John 5573; Macbeth 6732,
6733; Measure 7600, 7601; Dream 9299;
Much Ado 11021, 11022; Othello 11679,
11680; Richard II 12621; Romeo 13125,
13126; Shrew 14232; Troilus 16440,
16441; Twelfth Night 16645
Baumfelder, Friedrich, arr. 1836–1916
Othello 12042
Baumgarten, Christl 1910–
Errors 2028; Othello 12269
Baumgarten, Karl Friedrich 1740–1824
Romeo 13127
Baumgartner, Walter
Tempest 14866
Baur, Antonio 1820–1884
Tempest 15388
Baur, Jürg 1918–
Romeo 13886
Bavicchi, John Alexander 1922–
L.L.L. 6505
Bax, Arnold Edward Trevor 1883–1953
Occasionally wrote under the pseudonym
'Dermot O'Byrne'
As You Like It 1249; Hamlet 4259; Twelfth
Night 17780
Baxter, Francis
Pseudonym used by Albert Reubrecht
Lear 6052
Baxter, Tom
Macbeth 6734; Richard III 12794
Bayer, Friedrich, arr.
Tempest 16128
Bayer, Wolfgang
Hamlet 2936; Romeo 13128; Shrew 14233;
Twelfth Night 16646
Bayford, Dudley E., arr.
Antony 352
Bayford, Frank Raymond 1941–
Tempest 15610
Bayley, Harold
Henry VIII 5054
Bayley, T. Harold R.
Cymbeline 2637, Venus 20788
Baynham, Thomas
Dream 10583
Baynon, Arthur [1889?]–1954
Romeo 14189
Baynton-Power, Henry
Antony 310; Henry VIII 5211; Much Ado
11593; Romeo 13887
Bažant, Jiří
Shrew 14560
Bazelon, Irwin Allen 1922–
Merry Wives 8810; Shrew 14234,
14652

Bazzini, Antonio 1818–1897
Lear 6053
Beach, John Parsons 1877–1953
Measure 7830
Beach, Mrs. Henry Harris Aubrey 1867–1944
Née Amy Marcy Cheney
Measure 7831; Dream 10384, 10428,
10459; Tempest 15518; Twelfth Night
17781
Beadell, Robert Morton 1925–
Much Ado 11407; Tempest 15611
Beale, James 1924–
Sonnet 97 20153
Beardslee, Sheila
Tempest 14867
Beattie, Herbert
Richard III 12795
Beaty, Dan 1937–
Dream 9300; Tempest 14868
Beaucarne, Julos 1943–
L.L.L. 6196; Tempest 14869; Troilus 16442
Beaulieu, [Joseph] [1895–1965]
As You Like It 1250
Beaumont, Geoffrey
Errors 2029
Beaumont, Henry
Twelfth Night 17782
Beck, Curt 1910–
Lear 5983
Beck, Jeremy Joseph 1960–
Henry VIII 5232; Romeo 13129; Shrew
14235; Winter's Tale 18684
Beck, Sydney, arr. 1906–
Much Ado 11443; Tempest 15056
Beck-Slinn, Edgar [1879?]–1936
As You Like It 991, 1251; Henry VIII 5055;
Merchant 8503; Much Ado 11408; Tempest
15873; Twelfth Night 17783
Beckemeier, Gregor
Romeo 13130
Beckemeier, Rüdiger
Romeo 13131
Becker, Gottfried 1879–1952
Richard III 12796
Becker, John Joseph 1886–1961
Caesar 5259; Tempest 15389
Becker, Michael
Tempest 14870, 14871
Becker, Udo
Lear 5677
Beckerman, Michael
Measure 7602
Beckert, Dieter
Dream 9301
Beckett, John, arr.
Dream 10183, 10184; Twelfth Night 18303,
18312
Beckett, Wheeler 1898–
Sonnet 18 19334

Beckett, Wheeler, arr. 1898–
Two Gentlemen 18569
Beckler, Stanworth R. 1923–
As You Like It 1870; Hamlet 2937
Beckler, Stanworth R., in part arr. 1923–
Othello 11681
Beckwith, John 1927–
Settings of Commemorative Pieces . . . 21002
Beckwith, John Christmas 1750–1809
Also known as 'Dr. Beckwith of Norwich'
Othello 12270
Beckwith, John Christmas, arr. 1750–1809
Also known as 'Dr. Beckwith of Norwich'
Tempest 14764
Beckwith, Joseph
Tempest 14872; Twelfth Night 16647
Bédard, Jean-Baptiste, arr. [circa 1765–circa 1815]
Much Ado 11618
Beddall, Rod
Tempest 14873
Bedford, Herbert 1867–1945
Merchant 8425; Romeo 13888, 14023;
Twelfth Night 17716
Bedřich, Jan 1932–
Macbeth 6735; Measure 7603; Merry Wives 8811; Dream 10123; Much Ado 11023;
Othello 11682; Shrew 14236, 14237;
Twelfth Night 16648
Beecham, Adrian Welles 1904–1982
L.L.L. 6322, 6372, 6385, 6506; Merchant 8391; Othello 12271; Twelfth Night 17784;
Sonnet 146 20488
Beecham, Thomas, arr. 1879–1961
Romeo 14078
Beechey, Gwilym E., arr.
Twelfth Night 18313
Beer, Ernst Hans
Caesar 5260
Beer, Jeff 1952–
Tempest 14874
Beer, Leopold J., arr.
Cymbeline 2715
Beer-Walbrunn, Anton 1864–1929
Hamlet 2938; Tempest 14875, 15390;
Sonnet 25 19502; Sonnet 55 19777; Sonnet 71 19937; Sonnet 74 20030; Sonnet 75 20032; Sonnet 116 20310; Sonnet 128 20383; Sonnet 130 20419; Sonnet 146 20489; Sonnet 147 20506
Beerman, Burton
Antony 116
Beethoven, Ludwig van 1770–1827
As You Like It 2001; Coriolanus 2403;
Cymbeline 2878; Hamlet 4265; 1 Henry IV 4501; 2 Henry IV 4674; Henry VIII 5239;
Lear 6180; Macbeth 6736, 7240, 7585;
Merchant 8781; Merry Wives 9258, 9264;
Dream 10946; Much Ado 11650; Othello

12534; Romeo 13558, 14187, 14190;
Shrew 14688; Tempest 16234; Winter's Tale 19148
Beethoven, Ludwig van, arr. 1770–1827
Merry Wives 9159
Beghon, Jean 1888–
As You Like It 992
Behr, Heinz-Otto
Macbeth 7508
Behrend, John Arthur Henry, arr. 1853–1935
Merchant 8301
Behrens, Jack 1935–
Dream 9302
Behrens, Robert
Romeo 13132
Behrsing, Hartmut
All's Well 6
Beier, Vladimir Petrovich 1905–1957
Much Ado 11024; Romeo 13133; Twelfth Night 16649
Beischer, Josef
Dream 9303
Beisert, Wolfgang
Richard III 12797
Beissel, Heribert
Hamlet 2939
Bell, Allan 1953–
Richard III 12798
Bell, Brian Stanley 1933–
Sonnet 130 20420
Bell, Daniel 1928–
Antony 117; Lear 5678; Macbeth 6737;
Twelfth Night 16650
Bell, Daniel, in part arr. 1928–
Romeo 13134; Tempest 14876
Bell, Edith
Much Ado 11025
Bell, William Henry 1873–1946
Hamlet 3891; Romeo 13559; P. Pilgrim 20595
Bellairs, Ralph H., arr.
Othello 12516
Bellak, J., arr.
Macbeth 7301
Bellear, [?]
Richard III 12799
Bellerby, Edward Johnson 1858–
P. Pilgrim 20596
Bellini, Vincenzo 1801–1835
Romeo 14191
Bellmann, Dietmar
Macbeth 6738; Twelfth Night 16651
Bellmann, Dietmar, arr.
Dream 10185
Bělohlávek, Jiří
Much Ado 11026
Below, Robert 1934–
Dream 9304; Twelfth Night 16652; Two Gentlemen 18481

Belvo, Jerry
  Winter's Tale 18685
Belza, Igor' Fedorovich 1904–
  Also known as a writer under the names of
  Igor Boelza and Igor Belza
  Sonnet 73 19982
Bement, Gwynn S., arr.
  Much Ado 11556
Bement, Rosalind
  Merchant 8074
Ben-Zissi, Fordhaus
  Hamlet 2940; Shrew 14238
Benary, Barbara 1946–
  Tempest 14877
Benda, Georg Anton 1722–1795
  Also known as Jiří Antonín Benda
  Macbeth 6739; Romeo 13560
Benda, Herman Christian 1759–1805
  As You Like It 470
Bendall, Wilfred Ellington 1850–1920
  As You Like It 1252; Merchant 8426
Bendall, Wilfred Ellington, arr. 1850–1920
  Dream 10779; Settings of Commemorative
  Pieces . . . 21268
Bendel, François, arr.
  Romeo 13653
Bendix, Max
  Romeo 13135
Bendix, Theo, in part arr.
  As You Like It 471
Bendl, Carl 1838–1897
  Romeo 13889
Benedict, Julius 1804–1885
  Also known as Jules Benedict
  Macbeth 7414; Dream 10808; Romeo
  13136, 13890; Tempest 16001; Twelfth
  Night 18204
Benedict, Julius, arr. 1804–1885
  Also known as Jules Benedict
  Tempest 14765
Beneš, Juraj
  1 Henry IV 4303; 2 Henry IV 4525
Benfey-Schuppe, Anna
  Also known as Anna Benfey-Shuppe
  Romeo 13137
Benger, Richard 1945–
  Tempest 15519, 15612, 15874
Benjamin, Thomas Edward 1940–
  As You Like It 1602; Henry VIII 5056; L.L.L.
  6386; Dream 10476; Much Ado 11409;
  Tempest 15845; Winter's Tale 19032
Benkert, Georg Felix
  Cymbeline 2638; Lear 6056, 6057
Bennato, Eugenio
  Pericles 12541
Bennell, Raymond
  Cymbeline 2526; L.L.L. 6387, 6507
Bennett, Edith Edwidge
  Tempest 14878

Bennett, Frank
  Caesar 5261
Bennett, George John 1863–1930
  Cymbeline 2813; Winter's Tale 19096;
  Sonnet 104 20231; Settings of
  Commemorative Pieces . . . 21295
Bennett, George John, arr. 1863–1930
  Dream 9637
Bennett, James Robert Sterndale, arr.
  Dream 9638, 9639
Bennett, Richard Rodney 1936–
  Hamlet 2941; Othello 12468; Tempest
  15613, 15842; Timon 16301; Sonnet 155
  20558; Settings of Commemorative
  Pieces . . . 21003
Bennett, Robert Russell 1894–1981
  Hamlet 2942; Macbeth 6740; Romeo 13138
Bennett, Robert Russell, arr. 1894–1981
  Shrew 14599
Bennett, Thomas Case Sterndale   –1944
  Also known as Thomas Case Sterndale-
  Bennett
  Measure 7832
Bennett, Tom
  Othello 11683
Bennett, William Sterndale 1816–1875
  Merry Wives 9211; Tempest 16002
[Benoist, François], arr. [1794–1878]
  Othello 12043
Benoît, Camille, arr. 1851–1923
  Romeo 13563
Benoit, Peter 1834–1901
  Cymbeline 2639; Measure 7833; Merchant
  8504; Much Ado 11410; Twelfth Night 17450
Bensa, Giuseppe
  Antony 360
Benshoof, Kenneth W.
  Antony 118; As You Like It 472; Errors
  2030; Cymbeline 2441; Caesar 5262;
  Macbeth 6741; Dream 9305, 9306; Much
  Ado 11027; Richard II 12622; Romeo
  13139; Shrew 14239, 14240; Twelfth Night
  16653; Two Gentlemen 18355
Benson, George 1943–
  Henry VIII 5057; Twelfth Night 17717
Benson, John Allanson 1848–1931
  As You Like It 473
Benson, Lionel Solomon
  Two Gentlemen 18482
Benson, Patrick, in part arr.
  Timon 16302
Bentoiu, Pascal 1927–
  Hamlet 2943, 3556; Dream 9307; Romeo
  13140; Shrew 14241; Two Gentlemen
  18356; Winter's Tale 18686
Benton, Daniel Joseph 1945–
  Merchant 8505; Two Gentlemen 18483
Bentz, Cecil
  Merchant 8075

Bentzon, Niels Viggo 1919–
  Macbeth 6742; Merry Wives 8812
Benvenuti, Tommaso 1838–1906
  Othello 12017; Settings of Commemorative
  Pieces . . . 20909
Berekashvili, Mamiia Titovich, arr. 1928–
  Romeo 13795, 13973
Bérel, Ant., arr. 1849–1902
  Pseudonym used by Antony Choudens
  Romeo 13654, 13655
Berenclow, Bernard Martin
  Hamlet 4266
Berens, Johann Hermann 1826–1880
  Merry Wives 9242; Dream 10772; Twelfth
  Night 16654; Settings of Commemorative
  Pieces . . . 20912
Berény, Henri 1871–1932
  Winter's Tale 18927
Beresi, Carlos Alberto
  Macbeth 7509
Beretta, Mario
  Timon 16303
Berg, Albert W., arr.
  Macbeth 7302; Romeo 13891
Berg, Gottfrid, arr.
  As You Like It 1426
Berg, Gunnar Johnsen 1909–
  Tempest 15825
Berge, Håkon
  As You Like It 474
Bergé, Irénée 1867–1936
  As You Like It 1253
Berger, Emile, arr.
  Tempest 14766
Berger, Francesco 1834–1933
  Dream 10584
Berger, Günter, arr.
  Dream 10186
Berger, Jean 1909–
  Henry VIII 5209
Berger, Ludwig 1777–1839
  As You Like It 1254
Bergese, Hans, arr. 1910–
  Dream 9907
Berggreen, A. P., arr.
  Dream 10540; Twelfth Night 17597
Bergh, Arthur 1882–1962
  As You Like It 993, 1603; Twelfth Night
  17785
Bergh, Sverre
  Hamlet 2944; Merchant 8076; Othello
  11684
Berghmans, José 1921–
  Antony 119; Hamlet 2945; Othello 11685;
  Romeo 13141
Berghorn, Alfred Maria 1911–1978
  Caesar 5475
Berghout, Johann Cornelis 1869–1963
  Hamlet 3892

Bergman, Sten 1942–
  Richard III 12800; Twelfth Night 16655
Bergmann, Walter Georg 1923–1988
  Also wrote under the pseudonym 'T. S.
  Walker'
  Tempest 15968
Bergmann, Walter Georg, arr. 1923–1988
  Also wrote under the pseudonym 'T. S.
  Walker'
  As You Like It 403; Dream 10187; Timon
  16339; Twelfth Night 18297
Beringer, Robert
  Settings of Commemorative Pieces . . . 21004
Berinskiǐ, S.
  Romeo 13142
Berio, Luciano 1925–
  Tempest 15391
Berk, Adele L. 1927–
  Much Ado 11411
Berkeley, Lennox Randal Francis 1903–
  Tempest 14879; Winter's Tale 18687, 19097;
  Settings of Commemorative Pieces . . . 21005
Berkovec, Jiří 1922–
  Coriolanus 2271; Cymbeline 2442; Macbeth
  6743; Tempest 14880
Berky, Carl 1934–
  As You Like It 475, 1871; Dream 10585
Berlin, Ben, arr.
  Romeo 13947
Berlioz, Louis Hector 1803–1869
  Also wrote under the pseudonym 'Pierre
  Ducré'
  Antony 263, 361; Hamlet 3557, 3563,
  4141, 4186, 4187; Lear 6058, 6166;
  Merchant 8740; Dream 10124; Much Ado
  11343; Othello 12018, 12469; Romeo
  13562, 13580, 14072, 14073, 14126;
  Tempest 15392, 16213; Settings of
  Commemorative Pieces . . . 20913
Berman, Norman L.
  Hamlet 2946, 2947; L.L.L. 6197; Richard II
  12623
Berman, Steven D.
  Twelfth Night 17378
Bermann, Friedrich
  Lear 5679; Dream 9308; Romeo 13143
Bernard, Anthony 1891–1963
  All's Well 7; Antony 120; As You Like It
  476; Coriolanus 2272; Cymbeline 2443;
  Hamlet 2948; 1 Henry IV 4304; Henry V
  4698; Henry VIII 4969; Caesar 5263; Lear
  5680; L.L.L. 6198; Macbeth 6744; Merchant
  8077, 8506; Dream 9309; Much Ado
  11028, 11594; Othello 11686; Richard II
  12624; Richard III 12801; Shrew 14242;
  Tempest 14881, 14882, 15614; Troilus
  16443; Twelfth Night 16656, 18088; Two
  Gentlemen 18357, 18358; Winter's Tale
  18688, 19098

Bernard, Anthony, in part arr. 1891–1963
Errors 2031; Romeo 13144; Twelfth Night 16657

Bernard, Guy-Charles-Léon-Georges –1979
Romeo 13145

Bernard, James
Twelfth Night 16658

Bernard, Raymond
Sonnet 128 20384

Bernard, Robert Victor 1900–1971
Hamlet 4193; Tempest 16003

Bernat, Robert
1 Henry IV 4305; 2 Henry IV 4526; Tempest 14883; Troilus 16444

Bernert, Helmut
Dream 9310

Bernheim, Lucien 1897–1984
Tempest 15520, 15615, 15875, 15969

Bernstein, Franz
Lear 6067

Bernstein, Laurence
Merry Wives 8813

Bernstein, Leonard 1918–1990
Romeo 13581

Bernstein, Rudolph I.
Hamlet 3564

Bersa, Blagoje 1873–1934
Hamlet 3893

Berteau, Gabriel, fils, arr.
Much Ado 11619

Berthier, Pascal Marie Jean Char
Twelfth Night 16659

Berthold, G., adapter 1795–1856
Pseudonym used by Robert Lucas Pearsall; see also Pearsall, Robert Lucas
Othello 12044

Berton, Henri Montan 1767–1844
Much Ado 11617

Bertoni, Ferdinando Giuseppe 1725–1813
Coriolanus 2404

Bertoni, Phillip
Merchant 8078

Beruh, [?]
Coriolanus 2378

Berwald, Franz Adolf 1796–1868
Settings of Commemorative Pieces . . . 21006

Berwald, William Henry 1864–1948
As You Like It 994, 1255, 1604; L.L.L. 6508; Merchant 8507

Besançon, Georges, arr. –1933
Much Ado 11347

Besly, Edward Maurice 1888–1945
As You Like It 1256; Merchant 8508

Besoyan, Richard Vaugh 1924–1970
Dream 10125

Bessant, John
Winter's Tale 18689

Besse, Jacques
1 Henry IV 4306; 2 Henry IV 4527

Bessières, Louise Émile Marie
Antony 121; Hamlet 2949

Best, Martin 1942–
As You Like It 1605; Pericles 12542; Tempest 15521, 15616, 15876; Twelfth Night 17451, 17786; Two Gentlemen 18359, 18484; Sonnet 8 19227; Sonnet 18 19322; Sonnet 25 19500; Sonnet 35 19666; Sonnet 53 19753; Sonnet 64 19868; Sonnet 65 19883; Sonnet 66 19905; Sonnet 87 20079; Sonnet 91 20115; Sonnet 94 20133; Sonnet 107 20268; Sonnet 127 20374; Sonnet 128 20378; Sonnet 144 20479

Best, William Thomas, arr.
Dream 9640

Bestor, Charles 1924–
Measure 7604, 8026

Betsumiya, Sadao
Hamlet 2950

Bett, Andrew, in part arr.
Merry Wives 8814

Betts, Lorne Matheson 1918–1985
As You Like It 1257, 1606; Henry VIII 5058; Merchant 8427; Tempest 15617; Twelfth Night 18063

Beuret, Michel André
Merchant 8079; Romeo 13627

Beuschel, Wolfgang
Twelfth Night 16660

Beuthin, John Christopher
Lear 6145

Beveridge, Thomas Gattrell 1938–
Henry VIII 5059

Bevis, T. A.
As You Like It 1258

Bew, George, in part arr.
Twelfth Night 16661

Bex, Armand Hubert 1925–
Richard II 12625

Bexfield, William Richard 1824–1853
Twelfth Night 18064

Beydts, Louis-Antoine-Pierre-Hector 1895–1953
Also known under the names Louis Beydts, Louis Hector Antoine Beydts, and Louis Antoine Hector Désiré Beydts
K. John 5574; Othello 11687

Beyer, Ferdinand 1803–1863
Hamlet 3894

Beyer, Ferdinand, arr. 1803–1863
Macbeth 7303; Merry Wives 9017; Othello 12045, 12046

Beyer, Mary Ann
Romeo 13870

Beyschlag, Adolf, arr.
Othello 12047

Bial, Carl, arr.
Romeo 13974

Bianchi, C. N., arr.
  Othello 12048
Bianchi, Francesco [circa 1752]–1810
  Coriolanus 2405; Caesar 5556; Dream 10947
Bibby, Gillian Margaret 1945–
  Macbeth 6745
Bibl, Rudolf, arr. 1832–1902
  Hamlet 3471
Bicât, Nicholas
  All's Well 72; Lear 5681, 5682; Pericles
  12543; Shrew 14243; Titus 16391; Two
  Gentlemen 18360
Bidgood, Thomas
  Dream 10586
Bieber, C. F. Egon 1887–
  Also wrote under the pseudonym 'Geno von
  Cöln'
  As You Like It 1259
Biehler, Helmut
  Othello 11688
Bielawa, Herbert 1930–
  Sonnet 116 20311
Bierey, Gottlob Benedikt 1772–1840
  Macbeth 7416; Dream 10948
Biesemans, J. P.
  Measure 7605
Biever, Curtis
  Sonnet 3 19196; Sonnet 8 19228; Sonnet
  15 19304; Sonnet 18 19323; Sonnet 19
  19462; Sonnet 29 19540; Sonnet 30 19589;
  Sonnet 50 19743; Sonnet 55 19775; Sonnet
  64 19869; Sonnet 65 19884; Sonnet 73
  19977; Sonnet 90 20106; Sonnet 104 20229;
  Sonnet 116 20306; Sonnet 130 20417
Bieżan, Andrzej   –1983
  Macbeth 6746; Tempest 14884
B[iggs], E[dward] S[mith] [–circa 1820]
  Cymbeline 2852
Biggs, Allan
  Winter's Tale 18953
Biggs, Edward Smith [–circa 1820]
  As You Like It 1607; Othello 12272;
  Winter's Tale 18992, 19069
Biggs, Howard
  Shrew 14561
Biggs, Ronald
  Twelfth Night 16662
Bihr, Jeffrey
  As You Like It 477; Dream 9311, 9312;
  Shrew 14244; Twelfth Night 16663
Bilchick, Ruth Coleman 1904–
  P. Pilgrim 20597
Biliński, Marek
  Hamlet 2951
Billard, Pierre
  K. John 5575
Billema, Charles Louis, arr.   –1915
  Also known as Carlo Billema
  Macbeth 7304, 7305

Billema, Raphael, arr.   –1874
  Macbeth 7306, 7307
Billgren, Jean 1944–
  As You Like It 478; Hamlet 2952
Billich, Carl
  Othello 11689
Billingsley, William
  1 Henry IV 4307
Billington, Thomas, arr. 1754–1832
  Cymbeline 2846
Bilse, Benjamin, arr. 1816–1902
  Merry Wives 9018
Bilton, Manuel
  Shrew 14653
Binder, Franz
  Dream 9313
Binet, Jean 1893–1960
  Coriolanus 2273; Hamlet 2953; Merry Wives
  8815
Bingham, Judith 1952–
  Merchant 8509; Othello 12019, 12439,
  12440; Romeo 14024, 14025
Bingham, Seth Daniels 1882–1972
  Twelfth Night 17452
Birch, John
  Much Ado 11029
Birch, Tim
  Lear 5683
Bird, Hubert C. 1939–
  Hamlet 3815
Biriotti, León
  Hamlet 2954
Biriukov, Iurii Sergeevich 1908–1976
  Othello 11690
Birknes, Tønnes, in part arr. 1871–1956
  Shrew 14245
Birnbaum, Daniel
  Measure 7606; Merchant 8080; Twelfth
  Night 16664
Birsner, Gerd 1953–
  Settings of Commemorative Pieces . . . 21007
Birtchnell, Arthur J.
  Cymbeline 2814
Birtwistle, Harrison 1934–
  As You Like It 479; Coriolanus 2274;
  Hamlet 2955, 3895; Caesar 5264; Tempest
  15618; Settings of Commemorative
  Pieces . . . 21105
Bischoff, Edgar 1912–
  Merchant 8081; Merry Wives 8816
Bischoff, Hermann
  Twelfth Night 17453
Bischoff, Kaspar Jakob 1823–1893
  Also known as Kaspar Jacob Bischoff
  Hamlet 3896
Bishop, Christopher
  Two Gentlemen 18458
Bishop, David
  Twelfth Night 16665

Bishop, [Henry] [flor. 1785]
Winter's Tale 18690
Bishop, Henry Rowley 1786–1855
Antony 122, 287, 336; As You Like It 1260,
1608, 1834, 1953; Hamlet 2956, 4085; 2
Henry IV 4666; Henry VIII 5060, 5229; Lear
6039, 6119; L.L.L. 6199, 6668; Macbeth
7510, 7511; Measure 7834, 8031; Merry
Wives 8817; Dream 10300, 10354, 10754;
Othello 12273, 12445; Shrew 14676;
Troilus 16567; Twelfth Night 18266; Two
Gentlemen 18469, 18649; Winter's Tale
18691, 19136; Sonnet 7 19219, 19226;
Sonnet 25 19508; Sonnet 29 19587; Sonnet
33 19661; Sonnet 40 19700; Sonnet 54
19773; Sonnet 64 19882; Sonnet 73 20026;
Sonnet 92 20128; Sonnet 97 20175; Sonnet
109 20286; Sonnet 123 20362, 20368;
Sonnet 148 20519, 20523; P. Pilgrim
20598, 20739, 20740, 20741; Venus
20789, 20803, 20804, 20805, 20806;
Settings of Commemorative Pieces . . . 20825
Bishop, Henry Rowley, in part arr. 1786–1855
As You Like It 480, 1954; Errors 2032;
2 Henry IV 4528; Dream 9314, 10127;
Shrew 14246; Tempest 16179, 16180;
Twelfth Night 16666; Two Gentlemen
18361, 18486; P. Pilgrim 20742; Settings of
Commemorative Pieces . . . 21106
Bishop, Henry Rowley, arr. 1786–1855
As You Like It 404, 1172; Cymbeline 2444,
2650; Lear 6120; L.L.L. 6496, 6669;
Macbeth 6974, 7405; Merchant 8637,
8724; Merry Wives 9236; Dream 10306,
10370; Much Ado 11534; Romeo 13103;
Tempest 14885, 15794, 15836, 16222; Two
Gentlemen 18485, 18650
Bishop, John D.
Much Ado 11629
Bissell, Keith Warren 1912–
As You Like It 995, 1609; Hamlet 3816;
Henry VIII 5061; L.L.L. 6509; Romeo
13851; Tempest 15522, 15619, 15620,
15621; Twelfth Night 17787; Winter's Tale
18969; Sonnet 49 19737; Sonnet 73 19983;
Sonnet 90 20107; Sonnet 97 20154
Bittner, Julius 1874–1939
Winter's Tale 18692
Biusseret, A.
Romeo 13146
Bizet, Georges Alexandre César Léopold
1838–1875
Hamlet 3565; Macbeth 7241
Bizet, Georges Alexandre César Léopold, arr.
1838–1875
Hamlet 3634, 3635, 3636, 3637; Merry
Wives 9019; Romeo 13656
Bjärhall, Sven
Hamlet 2957

Bjelkerud, Tomas 1956–
Dream 9315
Bjerno, Erling D. 1929–
As You Like It 481; Hamlet 2958; Romeo
13147; Settings of Commemorative
Pieces . . . 20826
Bjerre, Jens 1903–
Much Ado 11030
Björlin, Ulf 1933–
As You Like It 482; Hamlet 2959; Romeo
13148; Tempest 14886; Troilus 16445
Bjørset, Karl
Measure 7835
Blacher, Boris 1903–1975
As You Like It 483; Hamlet 2960, 3566,
3897; 1 Henry IV 4308; 2 Henry IV 4529;
Measure 7607; Much Ado 11031; Othello
12020; Romeo 13149, 13628; Shrew
14247; Twelfth Night 16683; Winter's Tale
18693
Blacher, Boris, in part arr. 1903–1975
Dream 9316
Black, Andrea
Romeo 13150
Black, Arnold
Lear 5684; Dream 9317
Black, Eugene
Settings of Commemorative Pieces . . .
21008
Black, Frank, arr.
[Frank J. Black (1894–1968)?]
As You Like It 1497; Much Ado 11557;
Tempest 14767; Twelfth Night 17308,
17722
Black, William Electric 1952–
Pseudonym used by Ian James
Romeo 13629
Blackall, Allen Keet 1877–1963
Twelfth Night 17718; Winter's Tale 18970
Blackburn, Adam
Troilus 16446
Blackburn, David Alexander
Richard III 12802
Blacking, John
Shrew 14248; Twelfth Night 17788
Blair, Brent
Hamlet 2961
Blair, Dean Garber 1932–
L.L.L. 6200
Blair, Hugh, arr. 1864–1932
Cymbeline 2716
Blake, Charles Dupee 1847–1903
Romeo 13892
Blake, Howard David 1938–
As You Like It 484, 996, 1261, 1610, 1819;
Cymbeline 2527; Henry V 4699; L.L.L.
6510; Tempest 15622; Twelfth Night
17454, 18089; Settings of Commemorative
Pieces . . . 21009

Blakeley, William 1852–
As You Like It 1262
Blaker, Charles R.
Sonnet 107 20269
Blanchard, T.
Merchant 8428
Blanco, Juan Marcos
Othello 12446
Blane, Ralph, arr.
Errors 2207
Blangenois, J., arr.
Dream 9641
Blank, Allan 1925–
Merchant 8510
Blank, Allan, in part arr. 1925–
Measure 7608; Othello 11691
Blasser, G., arr.
Merry Wives 9020
Blatný, Pavel 1931–
Lear 5685, 5686, 5687; Othello 11692;
Romeo 13151; Twelfth Night 16684, 16685,
17379
Blech, Leo 1871–1958
Shrew 14249
Blecharovitch, Misha
Coriolanus 2275
Bleive, Iogannes Mikhailovich 1909–
Shrew 14250
Blémant, L., arr.
Merry Wives 9179
Blessner, G.
Much Ado 11595
Blewitt, Jonathan 1782–1853
Also wrote under the pseudonym 'Colonel
Bolsover'
Merry Wives 8818
Bley, Volker
Twelfth Night 16686
Blezard, William
Tempest 14887; Titus 16392
Blickhan, Charles Timothy 1945–
Macbeth 6747
Bliesener, Ada Elizabeth Michelman
1909–
Sonnet 155 20559
Bliffert, Fred
Measure 7609
Blinov, Iu., arr.
Shrew 14643
Bliss, Arthur Edward Drummond 1891–1975
Tempest 14888; Settings of Commemorative
Pieces . . . 21107
Bliss, Arthur Edward Drummond, arr.
1891–1975
As You Like It 485
Bliss, Philip Paul, Jr., arr. 1872–1933
Cymbeline 2717
Bliss, Tamara
Twelfth Night 17455

Blitzstein, Marc 1905–1964
Henry VIII 5062, 5230; Caesar 5265; Lear
5688, 5689, 6068; Dream 9318, 10477;
Romeo 14074; Twelfth Night 16687;
Winter's Tale 18694, 18993, 19033
Bloch, Augustyn
Hamlet 2962; Caesar 5266; Richard II
12626
Bloch, Ernest 1880–1959
Lear 5984; Macbeth 7242, 7417
Bloch, J.
Twelfth Night 18090
Bloch, Josef
Also known as Joseph Bloch
Richard II 12768
Block, Frederick, arr.
Hamlet 3412
Block, Leon, arr.
Romeo 13582
Block, Steven D.
Macbeth 7243
Blocker, Frank
Dream 9319
Blodek, Vilém 1834–1874
Settings of Commemorative Pieces . . .
20827
Blodek, W.
[Vilém Blodek (1834–1874)?]
Merry Wives 9259
Blow, John 1649–1708
Venus 20811
Blum, Alla
Shrew 14251
Blum, Elias
L.L.L. 6358
Blunck, Erick
Much Ado 11032
Blunt, Joseph
As You Like It 486; K. John 5576; Romeo
13152; Tempest 14889; Kinsmen 19159
Blyth, Benjamin, arr.
Tempest 14704
Blyton, Carey 1932–
Merchant 8511
Bobchevski, Venedict [Petrov] [1895–1957]
Hamlet 2963
Bobescu, Aurel
Shrew 14252
Bobin, Gérard
Antony 123
Boboc, Nicolae 1920–
Hamlet 2964
Bobokhidze, IAkov Varlamovich 1931–
Twelfth Night 16688
Bobrow, Sanchie
As You Like It 487; Henry V 4700; Romeo
13153
Bochsa, Robert Nicolas Charles 1789–1856
Tempest 16242

Bochsa, Robert Nicolas Charles, arr.
1789–1856
Much Ado 11620; Othello 12049; Twelfth
Night 16668; Settings of Commemorative
Pieces . . . 21108

Bock, Fred 1939–
As You Like It 1263

Bodine, Bertha
Winter's Tale 18695

Bodley, G.
Twelfth Night 17789

Bodley, Seóirse 1933–
Tempest 16161

Body, John Stanley 1944–
Macbeth 6748

Boehm, Th[eobald], arr. [1794–1881]
Macbeth 7251

Boëllmann, Léon, arr. 1862–1897
Merchant 8770; Dream 9642

Boese, Julius
Caesar 5267

Boeswillwald, Pierre 1934–
Lear 5690

Boettger, T. G., arr.
Merry Wives 9021

Böffgen, Hans-Peter
Hamlet 4086

Bogard, Travis
Troilus 16447

Bogartz, David
Hamlet 2965

Bogatyrev, Anatolii Vasil'evich 1913–
Sonnet 43 19709; Sonnet 56 19791; Sonnet
61 19848; Sonnet 81 20065; Sonnet 90
20108; Sonnet 97 20155; Sonnet 98 20177;
Sonnet 142 20474

Boghen, Felice, arr.
Dream 10169

Bogorad, Ia., arr.
Merry Wives 9022

Bohdanov, Fedir 1904–
Macbeth 6749

Böhlmann, Ernst
Measure 7610; Shrew 14253

Bohm, Carl [1844–1920]
Tempest 16004

Böhm, Rainer
Romeo 13154; Troilus 16448

Bohon, Roy
Much Ado 11033; Othello 12274

Bohrer, Henry, arr.
Romeo 13657

Bohuňovský, Oldřich
Twelfth Night 16689

Boissot, Nannie
Dream 9320

Bok, Józef
Othello 11693; Tempest 14890; Twelfth
Night 16690

Bolcom, William Elden 1938–
Two Gentlemen 18372

Bollinger, Samuel 1871–1941
Merchant 8512

Bolton, Cecil, arr.
Romeo 13975

Bonamici, Ferdinando 1827–1905
Antony 362

Bonavia, Ferruccio 1877–1950
Much Ado 11412

Bond, Grahame 1943–
Hamlet 4087; Macbeth 7533

Bond, Victoria 1950–
Dream 10903

Bondeville, Emmanuel Pierre Georges 1898–
Antony 264; Hamlet 4260

Bondo, Margaret Allison
Romeo 14041

Bonell, Carlos, arr.
Dream 10188

Bonheur, Theodore
One of the sixty-two pseudonyms used by
Charles Arthur Rawlings; see also Telma,
Maurice
Romeo 14128

Bonnet, Joseph 1884–1944
Tempest 16243

Bononcini, Giovanni 1670–1747
Also known as Giovanni Buononcini
Caesar 5538

Bonotto, Robert
Much Ado 11034

Bonsor, James Brian 1926–
Settings of Commemorative Pieces . . .
20914

Booth, Josiah 1852–1930
As You Like It 1264

Borch, Gaston 1871–1926
Measure 7836

Borchard, Adolphe 1882–1967
Hamlet 3898; Merchant 8687; Romeo
13893; Sonnet 18 19460

Borchert, Dieter
Errors 2049

Bordes, Charles H. 1863–1909
Henry VIII 5063

Bordèse, Luigi 1815–1886
Hamlet 4194; 1 Henry VI 4882; Henry VIII
5236; Caesar 5557; Lear 6146; Macbeth
7558; Merchant 8763; Othello 12493

Borelli, Calisto, arr.
Romeo 13658

Borg, Kim 1919–
Hamlet 3749, 3832, 3864; Merry Wives
9201; Twelfth Night 17456, 18065

Borg, Kim, arr. 1919–
Twelfth Night 17223

Borgstrøm, Hjalmar 1864–1925
Hamlet 3899

Borini, César
Lear 6147
Borishansky, Elliot David 1930–
Sonnet 73 19978
Borisovskii, Vadim Vasil'evich, arr.
1900–1972
Romeo 13796, 13797, 13798
Born, Erwin
Troilus 16449
Børresen, Axel Ejnar Hakon 1876–1954
Hamlet 3900
Borris, Siegfried 1906–
As You Like It 488
Borroff, Edith 1925–
Settings of Commemorative Pieces . . . 21203
Borsetto, Dante 1955–
L.L.L. 6201; Dream 9321
Bortkevich, Sergei Eduardovich 1877–1952
Othello 12379
Borton, Alice
Cymbeline 2528
Börtz, Daniel 1943–
Sonnet 64 19870
Borwick, Douglas Bruce 1952–
As You Like It 489
Bosman, Tine
Dream 9322
Bosseur, Jean-Yves
Titus 16393
Bossi, Rinaldo Renzo 1883–1965
Shrew 14562
Bothén, Christer
Tempest 14891
Bottagisio, Carlo Pietro 1873–1949
Shrew 14563
Böttcher, Lukas
Much Ado 11035
Bottesini, Giovanni, arr. 1821–1889
Romeo 13659
Bottje, Will Gay 1925–
Hamlet 2966; Merchant 8429; Dream 9323;
Twelfth Night 18205
Bottle, Carol
Twelfth Night 18091
Bouchel, Joseph Marie Marcellin, arr. –1927
Romeo 13639
Boughton, Rutland 1878–1960
Henry V 4798; Troilus 16574
Boulanger, Lili 1893–1918
Tempest 16244
Boullard, Victor Léon Adolphe, arr. –1876
Othello 12050
Boultbee, Elizabeth
Hamlet 2967
Bourdon, Rosario, arr.
Cymbeline 2718
Bourgault-Ducoudray, Louis-Albert
1840–1910
Hamlet 3901

Bourgeois, Derek David 1941–
Settings of Commemorative Pieces . . . 21109
Bourgeois, Émile –1934
Lear 5691
Bourland, Roger 1952–
Hamlet 3846
Bourtayre, Jean-Pierre-Henri-Eugène
Hamlet 4195
Boury, Robert W. 1946–
Settings of Commemorative Pieces . . . 21110
Boustead, Alan
As You Like It 1611; Twelfth Night 17457
Bousted, Donald 1957–
Pericles 12544
Bovet, Guy 1942–
Dream 9324
Bowden, Emma B.
Much Ado 11036
Bowen, Douglas Deri
Henry VIII 4970
Bowers, Jane Gardner Riley
Henry V 4813
Bowie, William C. 1925–1970
Cymbeline 2529
Bowler, Tony
Winter's Tale 18696
Bowles, Anthony
Much Ado 11037; Twelfth Night 16691;
Winter's Tale 18697, 18698; Settings of
Commemorative Pieces . . . 20828
Bowles, Paul Frederic 1910–
Romeo 14042; Tempest 14892; Twelfth
Night 16692
Bowman, Rob
Much Ado 11038
Boxer, Stephen
Henry V 4701; Richard III 13067; Tempest
14893
[Boyce, William] [1711–1779]
Winter's Tale 18954
Boyce, Ethel Mary 1863–1936
As You Like It 1872; Dream 10460
Boyce, William 1711–1779
Cymbeline 2445; Merchant 8751; Romeo
13155; Tempest 14894; Winter's Tale
18699; Settings of Commemorative
Pieces . . . 20829, 20830, 21010
Boyd, Charles N., arr.
Dream 9643
Boyd, Jeanne
L.L.L. 6511
Boyd, Robert A.
Twelfth Night 17790
Boyer, Constance
Winter's Tale 18700
Boyle, Ina –1967
As You Like It 997
Boyle, Malcolm
Tempest 14895

Boys, Henry
  As You Like It 490; Dream 9325
Boys, Henry, arr.
  Lucrece 20780
Božič, Darijan 1933–
  Hamlet 2968, 4142; Lear 5692, 5693,
  5985; L.L.L. 6202; Macbeth 7534; Othello
  12470; Richard III 13070; Shrew 14254;
  Tempest 14896; Timon 16304; Troilus
  16450; Sonnet 155 20581
Brabant, Georges-Philippe
  Tempest 14897
Brabbins, Martyn
  Settings of Commemorative Pieces . . .
  20831
Brabec, Jindřich 1933–
  Dream 9326
Braceful, Fred
  Dream 9327
Bracewell, John L.
  As You Like It 491; Much Ado 11039;
  Richard III 12803
Brachet, P. Louis
  Hamlet 3903; Dream 10587; Othello 12380
Bradfield, David
  Errors 2050; Hamlet 2969; Lear 5694; L.L.L.
  6203; Macbeth 6750; Measure 7611; Dream
  9328, 9329; Othello 11694; Romeo 13156;
  Tempest 14898; Winter's Tale 18701
Bradfield, David, in part arr.
  Much Ado 11040; Shrew 14255
Bradfield, David, arr.
  Twelfth Night 16693
Bradshaw, Merrill 1929–
  Dream 9330, 9331; Sonnet 73 19984
Braham, [?]
  As You Like It 492
Braham, John 1774–1856
  Born John Abraham
  L.L.L. 6359; Merry Wives 8819, 9209;
  Shrew 14564; Twelfth Night 18278; Sonnet
  116 20342; P. Pilgrim 20747
Braham, Philip
  Hamlet 4143; Settings of Commemorative
  Pieces . . . 20915
Brahms, Johannes 1833–1897
  Also wrote under the pseudonym 'G. W.
  Marks'
  Hamlet 2970, 3698, 3750, 3833, 3865,
  3881; Twelfth Night 17458
Brahms, Johannes, arr. 1833–1897
  Also wrote under the pseudonym 'G. W.
  Marks'
  Hamlet 3962; 1 Henry IV 4481; 2 Henry IV
  4656
Braithwaite, S. H., arr.
  Tempest 15854
Bramall, Anthony
  Much Ado 11041

Bramel, Tom
  Caesar 5268
Brancato, Paul
  Twelfth Night 16694
Brand, Michael
  Tempest 14899
Brand, Oscar 1920–
  Caesar 5543; Macbeth 7535
Brandel, Rose
  Sonnet 15 19305; Sonnet 18 19335; Sonnet
  29 19542; Sonnet 30 19593
Brandman, Margaret Susan 1951–
  As You Like It 1220
Brandmüller, Theo 1948–
  Hamlet 2973
Brandt, Michel 1934–
  Othello 11695; Richard III 12804; Shrew
  14256; Twelfth Night 16695
Brandt, William Edward 1920–
  Hamlet 2974; Lear 6069
Brandts-Buys, Jan Willem Frans
  1868–1933
  Dream 10940
Brash, James   –1961
  Henry VIII 5064
Bratt, L. G., arr.
  Antony 321
Bratt, Leif 1897–
  Macbeth 6751
Bratton, John W.
  Hamlet 4196
Brauel, Henning 1940–
  Hamlet 4197
Brauel, Henning, arr. 1940–
  Lear 6010
Braun, Adolf 1946–
  Hamlet 2975
Braun, Leo, arr.
  Cymbeline 2719
Braunfels, Walter 1882–1954
  Antony 265; Macbeth 6752; Tempest
  16005; Twelfth Night 16696
Brawn, Geoffrey
  1 Henry IV 4500; 2 Henry IV 4671
Bream, Julian Alexander, arr. 1933–
  Macbeth 7439
Brearley, Herman [1877?]–1940
  Tempest 15393; Settings of Commemorative
  Pieces . . . 21296
Breckenridge, Almyra Morton
  Merchant 8082
Bredal, Ivar Frederik 1800–1864
  L.L.L. 6204
Bredemeyer, Reiner 1929–
  Hamlet 2976; Dream 9332; Tempest 14900
Brediceanu, Mihai 1920–
  Tempest 14901
Bregman, Buddy, arr. 1940–
  Errors 2208

Breit, Bert
Antony 124
Breitenstein, Henri
Hamlet 2977; Macbeth 6753
Breitmann, Carl, arr.
Twelfth Night 17916
Breitner, Walter
Tempest 14902
Brennecke, Ernest, arr. 1896–1969
As You Like It 1846
Brenner, Konrad
Hamlet 2978; Macbeth 6754; Dream 9333
Brent-Smith, Alexander 1889–1950
Also known as Alexander Brent Smith
Cymbeline 2530
Brenton, H. E.
Macbeth 7559; Othello 12494; Romeo
14129
Brepsant, Engebert, arr.
Dream 9644
Bresgen, Cesar 1913–
Merchant 8682; Sonnet 27 19516
Bresticzker, Jerzy
Measure 7612
Bretonneau, Émile   –1930
Coriolanus 2276
Bretonnière, Victor, arr.
Othello 12051
Breuer, Franz Josef
Tempest 14903
Breuer, Paul
Hamlet 2979
Brewer, Alfred Herbert 1865–1928
As You Like It 1265; Henry VIII 5065;
Twelfth Night 17791
Brewer, Alfred Herbert, arr. 1865–1928
L.L.L. 6497
Brian, William Havergal 1876–1972
Antony 354; As You Like It 998, 1266,
1612; Cymbeline 2531; Hamlet 3699; L.L.L.
6512; Measure 7837; Merchant 8513;
Dream 10478; Othello 12275; Richard II
12748; Tempest 15394, 15623; Twelfth
Night 17460; Sonnet 18 19336
Briccialdi, Giulio, arr. 1818–1881
Macbeth 7308
Bridge, Frank 1879–1941
As You Like It 999; Hamlet 3904; Sonnet 43
19710
Bridge, John Frederick 1844–1924
2 Henry VI 4919; Richard III 13043, 13048;
Settings of Commemorative Pieces . . . 21011
Bridge, John Frederick, adapter 1844–1924
Henry V 4808
Bridge, John Frederick, arr. 1844–1924
As You Like It 1427; Hamlet 3853; Twelfth
Night 17760
Bridge, John Frederick, ed. 1844–1924
Anthologies 21317

Bridge, Joseph Cox 1853–1929
As You Like It 1267
Bridges, Denim
Macbeth 6755
Bridgewater, Leslie [1894?]–1975
Antony 125, 288; As You Like It 493, 1000,
1268, 1613, 1835; Cymbeline 2446, 2532,
2640; Hamlet 2980, 2981; 2 Henry IV
4530; Henry V 4702; Henry VIII 4971,
5066; Caesar 5269; K. John 5577; Lear
5695; L.L.L. 6205, 6206, 6388, 6513;
Macbeth 6756; Measure 7613, 7838;
Merchant 8083, 8514; Merry Wives 8820,
9202; Dream 9334, 10479; Much Ado
11042, 11043, 11376, 11413; Othello
11696; Pericles 12545; Richard II 12627;
Richard III 12805; Romeo 13157; Tempest
14905, 14906, 15523, 15624, 15877;
Troilus 16451, 16563; Twelfth Night
17461, 17792, 18092; Two Gentlemen
18373, 18487; Winter's Tale 18702, 18947,
18955, 18971, 18994, 19034, 19070;
Kinsmen 19169, 19173; P. Pilgrim 20599,
20743
Bridgewater, Leslie, in part arr. [1894?]–1975
1 Henry IV 4309; Othello 11697; Twelfth
Night 16697
Bridgewater, Leslie, arr. [1894?]–1975
Dream 9645, 10189; Othello 12276
Bridgman, William C., arr.
Two Gentlemen 18570
Brierley, Eric
Two Gentlemen 18488
Briffaux, J., arr.
Macbeth 7309
Briggs, John R.
As You Like It 1963
Brigham, John W.
Romeo 14075
Bright, Dora Estella 1863–1951
Also known as Dora Estella Knatchbull
As You Like It 1269; Cymbeline 2641; Two
Gentlemen 18489
Brimé, Josef 1899–
[Also known as Josef Briné]
Shrew 14257
Brimhall, John, arr.
Romeo 13419, 13420, 13421, 13422
Brisman, Heskel 1923–
Troilus 16452
Brissac, Jules, arr. 1824–1895
Pseudonym used by Mrs. John Macfarren;
née Emma Marie Bennet
Macbeth 7310, 7311; Dream 10809, 10810
Brissler, Friedrich Ferdinand, arr. 1818–1893
Hamlet 3936; Merry Wives 9023, 9180;
Othello 12185, 12186
Bristow, George Frederick 1825–1898
Winter's Tale 18703

Britain, Radie 1908–
  Sonnet 127 20375; Sonnet 128 20380;
  Sonnet 129 20407; Sonnet 130 20418;
  Sonnet 147 20505; Sonnet 150 20531;
  Sonnet 152 20537
Britten, Edward Benjamin 1913–1976
  Lear 5986; Measure 7839; Merchant 8515;
  Dream 10135; Tempest 14907; Timon
  16305; Sonnet 43 19711; Lucrece 20779
Britten, Edward Benjamin, arr. 1913–1976
  Dream 10190, 10191; Twelfth Night 18304,
  18314
Britton, Phillip
  Cymbeline 2533; Tempest 15625, 15626;
  Twelfth Night 17462, 17793
Brixey, Andrew 1956–
  1 Henry IV 4310; Winter's Tale 18704
Broad, Charles Robin
  Shrew 14258; Twelfth Night 16698
Brockington, John
  Tempest 14908
Brockless, George Frederick
  Twelfth Night 18289
Brode, Hermann
  As You Like It 494; Caesar 5270
Brohn, Bill, arr.
  Romeo 13764
Bromley, Deborah
  As You Like It 946
Bromley, Wendolyn
  As You Like It 947
Bronskill, Richard Eric 1951–
  Shrew 14259; Twelfth Night 16699, 16700
Bronwer, Dieter
  Richard III 12806
Brook, Harry 1893–
  Twelfth Night 18325
Brook, Peter Stephen Paul 1925–
  Tempest 14909; Titus 16394
Brooke, H. Sullivan
  Romeo 13158
Brooks, Gary
  Macbeth 7536
Brooks, Walter William 1861–
  L.L.L. 6514
Brosig, Gerhard
  Errors 2051; Shrew 14260; Twelfth Night
  16701
Broughton, James 1833–1887
  Dream 10904; Tempest 16245
Brounoff, Platon G. 1863–1924
  Dream 10385
Brouwer, Leo
  Caesar 5271
Brower, Jay D., arr.
  Settings of Commemorative Pieces . . . 20956
Brown, Alexander 1929–1975
  Known as Sandy Brown
  Sonnet 18 19338

Brown, Allanson Gordon Yeoman 1902–
  As You Like It 1270
Brown, Arthur Henry, arr.
  Dream 9646
Brown, Charles Louis Georges 1898–
  Tempest 14910, 16006; Timon 16306
Brown, Christopher Roland 1943–
  Cymbeline 2534; Hamlet 3751; Merchant
  8516; Merry Wives 8821, 9212; Tempest
  15524; Twelfth Night 17463
Brown, Dorothy Riley
  Twelfth Night 17464
Brown, Douglas
  Caesar 5272; Merry Wives 8822
Brown, F. K. Sargent
  Dream 10588
Brown, Francis Henry, in part arr. 1818–1891
  Settings of Commemorative Pieces . . . 21111
Brown, Frank Edwin, arr. [1908–   ]
  As You Like It 405, 406; Dream 10192;
  Othello 11717
Brown, G. Barton
  Hamlet 4144
Brown, Gillian
  Twelfth Night 16702
Brown, Hubert S.
  Sonnet 18 19337
Brown, James, arr.
  Dream 10193, 10766
Brown, K.
  Twelfth Night 17794
Brown, K. A.
  [Keneth Arundel Brown (1891–   )?]
  As You Like It 1001
Brown, Mark
  Hamlet 2982
Brown, Mary Helen
  Twelfth Night 17795
Brown, Mrs. Bailey LeF.
  Caesar 5273
Brown, Richard
  As You Like It 1002
Brown, Stephen 1945–
  As You Like It 495; Merry Wives 8823;
  Shrew 14261
Brown, T. Conway, arr.
  Lear 6168; Othello 12517
Browne, Davy
  Dream 9335
Browne, H. E.
  As You Like It 1873
Browne, Tom
  Othello 11698
Brownjohn, Michael
  Lear 5696
Brozen, Michael 1934–
  Measure 7840; Tempest 15395
Bruce, Frank Neely 1944–
  Dream 10138; Tempest 14911

Bruce, Margaret Campbell, arr.
Othello 12277
Bruch, Max Karl August 1838–1920
Winter's Tale 18928
Bruči, Rudolf 1917–
Sonnet 30 19594; Sonnet 73 19985; Sonnet
90 20109; Sonnet 102 20216; Sonnet 116
20312
Bruck, Wilhelm
Pericles 12546
Brüggemann, Kurt 1908–
Twelfth Night 17380
Bruguier, David, arr.
Twelfth Night 16669
Brüll, Ignaz 1846–1907
Hamlet 3905; Macbeth 7418; Shrew 14689
Brumagne, Fernand Maximilien Nap
1887–1939
Merchant 8392
Brumby, Colin James 1933–
As You Like It 496, 1614, 1874; Cymbeline
2535; Merchant 8084; Twelfth Night
17465; Phoenix 20755, 20756, 20766
Brün, Herbert 1918–
1 Henry IV 4311; 2 Henry IV 4531; Lear
5697; Richard III 12807; Timon 16307;
Twelfth Night 16703
Brunotte, Karl Gottfried 1958–
Lear 6023
Brush, Ruth
Sonnet 128 20385
Bryan, Gordon 1895–1957
Tempest 15627
Bryan, Robert
Merchant 8430
Bryanton, Rob
Measure 7614
Bryars, Gavin, in part arr.
Timon 16308
Brydson, John Callis 1900–
Also known as John Brydson-Jones
As You Like It 1615
Brydson, John Callis, arr. 1900–
Also known as John Brydson-Jones
As You Like It 1428
Bryning, Percy L.
As You Like It 1004
Bucalossi, Ernest
Merchant 8085; Shrew 14262
Bucalossi, Procida, in part arr.
Shrew 14263
Bucalossi, Procida, arr.
Romeo 13660
Bucchi, Jean Louis, arr.
Romeo 13976
Buch, E.
Macbeth 6757
Buchanan, Dorothy
Tempest 14912

Büchi, Karl
As You Like It 497
Büchi, Karlheinz
Hamlet 2983
Buchman, Andrew William 1956–
Sonnet 8 19232; Sonnet 18 19339; Sonnet
24 19493; Sonnet 30 19595; Sonnet 66
19906
Bucht, Gunnar 1927–
Richard III 12808
Buchtel, Forrest Lawrence 1899–
1 Henry IV 4475; 2 Henry IV 4650; Merry
Wives 9213
Buciu, Dan 1943–
Sonnet 128 20386; Sonnet 129 20408;
Sonnet 132 20433
Buck, Dudley 1839–1909
As You Like It 1271; Hamlet 3847; 1 Henry
IV 4502; Tempest 16246
Buck, Rudolf
Macbeth 7560
Buckland, John
Macbeth 6758; Troilus 16453
Buckman, Ronald, in part arr.
Dream 9336
Buckmaster, Paul
Macbeth 6759
Buckner, Thomas Watson 1941–
Dream 9337; Romeo 13159; Twelfth Night
16704
Budík, Jaroslav
Macbeth 6760; Othello 11699
Budnitskii, Boris Il'ich
Sonnet 30 19596
Buevskyi, Borys Mykolaiovych 1935–
Sonnet 66 19907; Sonnet 140 20467;
Sonnet 155 20560
Buffer, Thomas
Tempest 14913
Buketoff, Igor, arr. 1915–
Romeo 14079
Bukin, V., arr.
Sonnet 102 20215
Bukowski, Mirosław
Dream 9338
Bukowski, Ryszard 1916–
As You Like It 498; Othello 11700; Twelfth
Night 16705
Bulis, Jiří 1946–
As You Like It 499; Measure 7615; Shrew
14264
Bull, Georges, arr.
Cymbeline 2839; Hamlet 3638; Romeo
13661; Settings of Commemorative
Pieces . . . 20962, 20963
Bull, John
As You Like It 500
Bullard, Alan 1947–
As You Like It 1272

Bullard, Frederick Field, arr. 1864–1904
Two Gentlemen 18571
Buller, John 1927–
Sonnet 15 19306; Sonnet 27 19517; Sonnet 61 19849
Bullock, Ernest 1890–1979
Twelfth Night 17466, 17796, 18093
Bungart, Heinrich, arr.
Othello 12052
Bunge, Sas 1924–1980
Henry VIII 5067; Twelfth Night 18206
Bungert, August 1846–
Hamlet 4198; Romeo 14130
Bunin, Revol' Samuilovich 1924–1976
Sonnet 155 20553
Bunnett, Edward 1834–1923
Dream 10386
Buot, Victor Mathurin   –1883
Macbeth 7419; Othello 12381
Burchard, Carl, arr.
Dream 9647, 9648
Burchardt, Carl, arr.
Merry Wives 9024, 9025
Burg, Bradley
Measure 7616
Burger, Ludwig
Caesar 5274
Burgess, Anthony 1917–
Born John Anthony Burgess Wilson; also writes under the pseudonym 'Joseph Kell'
Antony 289; As You Like It 1616; L.L.L. 6647; Dream 9339; Timon 16375; Settings of Commemorative Pieces . . . 20832, 20916
Burgess, F. W.
P. Pilgrim 20600
Burghardt, Hans-Georg 1909–
Sonnet 33 19647; Sonnet 60 19818
Burghauser, Jarmil, arr. 1921–
Macbeth 7478
Burgmüller, François, arr.
Romeo 13662
Burgmüller, Johann August Franz 1776–1824
Also known as August Friedrich Burgmüller
Macbeth 6761
Burgon, Geoffrey 1941–
As You Like It 501; Hamlet 4267; L.L.L. 6207; Macbeth 6762; Troilus 16454
Burk, Don L.
Twelfth Night 17467
Burke, Brendan
Troilus 16455
Burke, Brian
Sonnet 18 19340
Burkhard, Paul 1911–1977
As You Like It 502; Errors 2052; Cymbeline 2447; 1 Henry IV 4312; 2 Henry IV 4532; Caesar 5275; Measure 7617, 7618; Merry Wives 8824; Much Ado 11044; Romeo

13160; Tempest 14914; Timon 16309; Twelfth Night 16706
Bürkholz, Thomas
As You Like It 503; Lear 5698
Burkingshaw, Sydney 1911–
Dream 9340, 10314; Tempest 15628, 16160, 16162
Burleigh, Cecil Edward 1885–1980
Dream 10429
Burmeister, Richard
As You Like It 1223
Burnand, Arthur Bransby 1859–1907
Also wrote under the pseudonyms 'Anton Strelezki' and 'Stepán Esipoff'
Hamlet 3906, 4199; Measure 7841
Burnard, A.
As You Like It 1617; Henry VIII 5068; L.L.L. 6389, 6515; Dream 10315; P. Pilgrim 20601
Burney, Charles 1726–1814
Dream 9341, 10298, 10755
Burrell, Howard John
Winter's Tale 18930
Burrowes, John Freckleton, the Elder
Richard II 12629
Burrowes, John Freckleton, the Elder, arr.
Macbeth 6975; Merry Wives 8999; Othello 12053, 12054
Burrows, Benjamin 1891–1966
Hamlet 4200; Macbeth 7420; Measure 7842; Sonnet 22 19483; Sonnet 27 19518; Sonnet 29 19543; Sonnet 33 19648; Sonnet 50 19744; Sonnet 61 19850; Sonnet 128 20387
Burrows, Donald
As You Like It 504
Bursa, Stanisław
Merchant 8086
Burtch, Mervyn Arthur 1929–
As You Like It 505, 1005, 1006, 1273, 1274, 1275, 1276, 1277, 1618, 1619, 1620; Cymbeline 2536; L.L.L. 6390, 6516, 6517, 6518; Merchant 8517; Dream 9342, 10387, 10388, 10389, 10480, 10481, 10482; Tempest 14915, 15629, 15630, 15631, 15878; Twelfth Night 17468, 17469, 17797, 17798
Burton, H. Sanford
Much Ado 11414
Burton, Laura
Macbeth 6763; Romeo 13161
Burton, Stephen Douglas 1943–
Tempest 16247
Burwell, Paul
Hamlet 2984
Bury, Edward, arr.
Merry Wives 9026
Bury, Winifred
As You Like It 1278, 1621; Dream 10316; Twelfth Night 17799

Busby, Jim
  As You Like It 506
Busby, Thomas 1755–1838
  Macbeth 7244; Dream 10949
Busch, Carl Reinholdt 1862–1943
  As You Like It 1622; Henry VIII 4972,
  5069; K. John 5578
Busch, Siegfried 1943–
  Hamlet 3907
Buschmann, Rainer Glen
  Much Ado 11045
Bush, Alan Dudley 1900–
  Hamlet 4145; Macbeth 6764; Sonnet 18
  19341; Sonnet 60 19819
Bush, Alan Dudley, arr. 1900–
  Dream 10194
Bush, Geoffrey 1920–
  As You Like It 1279, 1280; Cymbeline 2537;
  Hamlet 3700, 3752, 3908; Henry VIII 5070;
  L.L.L. 6323, 6391; Measure 7843; Merchant
  8087, 8518, 8688; Much Ado 11415;
  Tempest 15632; Twelfth Night 17470, 17677,
  17695, 17719, 17800, 18094, 18290;
  Winter's Tale 19035; P. Pilgrim 20602
Bush, Geoffrey, arr. 1920–
  Caesar 5351; Dream 10128
Bushby, Maud
  As You Like It 1281; Dream 10483
Busky-Benedetti, Albina, arr. [circa 1869]–
  Dream 10811
Bussell, F. W.
  Merchant 8088
Bussmeyer, Hugo, arr.
  Hamlet 3639
Butera, Robert
  Sonnet 18 19342
Butler, Artie, arr.
  Shrew 14600
Butler, Eugene [Sanders] [1935–]
  As You Like It 1007, 1282
Butler, Geoff
  Tempest 16181
Butler, Roger Andrew 1948–
  Tempest 15396
Butsko, Iurii Markovich 1938–
  Hamlet 2985
Butskoi, Anatolyi Konstantynovych
  1892–1965
  Macbeth 6765
Butt, James Henry Baseden 1929–
  Henry VIII 5071; L.L.L. 6392; Dream 10484;
  Tempest 15525, 15879; Twelfth Night
  16707, 17381; Sonnet 18 19343; Sonnet 94
  20134; Settings of Commemorative
  Pieces . . . 21297
Butter, Wolf
  Hamlet 2986
Butterworth, Arthur 1923–
  Tempest 16007

Butterworth, Arthur, arr. 1923–
  Tempest 15275
Butterworth, David Neil 1934–
  Measure 7619; Merchant 8519; Much Ado
  11046, 11416; Tempest 14916, 15633;
  Twelfth Night 16709, 17696, 17745
Button, Henry Elliot, arr. 1861–1925
  Henry VIII 4978
Butz, Josef, arr.
  As You Like It 1523
Buzzi-Peccia, Arturo 1856–1943
  As You Like It 1623; Dream 10485; Winter's
  Tale 18995
Buzzi-Peccia, Arturo, arr. 1856–1943
  Othello 12187
Buzzolla, Antonio 1815–1871
  Hamlet 4146
Byass, Gilbert
  Winter's Tale 19099
Byers, David 1947–
  Tempest 16008; Settings of Commemorative
  Pieces . . . 21204
Byers, Patrick
  Tempest 14917
Byng, F. D.
  Timon 16310
Byrne, Andrew
  Hamlet 2987; K. John 5579; Lear 5699;
  Macbeth 6766; Merchant 8089
Byrns, Harold, arr.
  L.L.L. 6331

C

C., I.
  Henry VIII 5039
Caber, C.
  Pseudonym used by E. Jordan
  Twelfth Night 17801
Cable, Howard Reid 1920–
  As You Like It 1875; Henry VIII 5212;
  Merry Wives 9214; Richard III 13049
Cacavas, John, arr.
  Romeo 13423
Cachot, Michel
  Sonnet 140 20468
Cadenas, José I.
  Hamlet 2988
Cadier, A.
  Winter's Tale 18705
Cadman, Charles Wakefield 1881–1946
  Romeo 14131; Settings of Commemorative
  Pieces . . . 21012
Cadou, André Pierre   –1973
  Lear 5700; L.L.L. 6208; Macbeth 6767;
  Romeo 13162; Shrew 14265; Settings of
  Commemorative Pieces . . . 20833

Cadou, André Pierre, in part arr.   −1973
  Hamlet 2989; K. John 5580
Cadow, Paul
  As You Like It 1283; Measure 7620; Much
  Ado 11047; Romeo 13864
Cage, John Milton, Jr. 1912–
  Hamlet 3567
Caggiano, Nestore 1888–1918
  Hamlet 3909
Cagiada, Giovanni Battista
  Macbeth 7245
Cagnoni, Antonio 1828–1896
  Lear 5987
Cahn, Richard
  Twelfth Night 17471, 17697, 17802, 18095
Cain, David 1941–
  As You Like It 507; 1 Henry IV 4313; 2
  Henry IV 4533; Henry V 4703; Much Ado
  11048; Tempest 14918; Titus 16395
Cain, Noble 1896–1977
  Also wrote under the pseudonym 'John Forest'
  As You Like It 1008; L.L.L. 6519
Cairanne, Marius Pierre, arr.   −1910
  Othello 12413
Calabrese, Anthony 1938–
  Macbeth 7246
Calabrese, Rosalie 1938–
  Macbeth 7247
Calabrini, Pietro 1897–
  Tempest 16009
Caldara, Antonio 1670–1736
  Coriolanus 2406
Callaway, A. H.
  K. John 5581; Othello 11701
Callcott, John George 1821–1895
  Merchant 8431, 8520
Callcott, John Wall 1766–1821
  Cymbeline 2538; Measure 7844; P. Pilgrim
  20603; Settings of Commemorative
  Pieces . . . 21013
Callcott, William Hutchins 1807–1882
  Caesar 5497; Romeo 14132
Callcott, William Hutchins, arr. 1807–1882
  As You Like It 1173, 1535, 1856; Errors
  2034; Macbeth 6976, 7312; Merchant
  8060; Dream 10129; Tempest 14705,
  14768, 14769, 15117, 15481, 15837;
  P. Pilgrim 20727
Callender, Donald Francis
  Sonnet 18 19344
Calusio, Ferruccio, arr.
  Romeo 14119
Calvi, Gérard 1922–
  Pseudonym used by Grégoire Krettly
  Pericles 12547
Campanella, Philip
  Hamlet 2990; Othello 11702; Shrew 14266
Campanini, Gino 1949–
  Hamlet 2991; Macbeth 6768

Campbell, Arthur 1922–
  Merchant 8090
Campbell, Arthur, arr. 1922–
  Dream 10195
Campbell, Francis
  Twelfth Night 17803
Campbell, James B., arr.
  Henry V 4779
Campbell, William Vance, Jr.
  As You Like It 1009
Candael, Karel
  Much Ado 11049
Candlyn, Thomas Frederick Handel 1892–1964
  As You Like It 1010; Merchant 8521; Dream
  10486
Canepa, Luigi 1849–1914
  Richard III 13081
Canick, Michael
  Errors 2053; Caesar 5276
Canino, Bruno 1935–
  Settings of Commemorative Pieces . . . 21205
Canonica, Pietro 1869–1959
  Tempest 15397
Cantarini, Aldo
  Tempest 14919
Caplet, André 1878–1925
  Dream 10950
Capoianu, Dumitru
  Richard III 12809
Caracciolo, Luigi 1847–1887
  Sonnet 87 20083
Carafa, Michele 1787–1872
  Romeo 14133
Carbutt, Ann
  Othello 11703, 12278
Carcani, Giuseppe 1703–1779
  Also known as Giuseppe Carcano
  Hamlet 4268
Card, Edward John, arr.
  Merry Wives 9027
Cardana, Enea, arr.
  Othello 12055
Cardew, Herbert W.
  As You Like It 1284; Cymbeline 2539;
  Twelfth Night 17804
Cardew, Mary
  Merchant 8522
Cardinale, Joseph S.
  1 Henry IV 4460
Carey, Henry [circa 1689]–1743
  Also wrote under the pseudonyms 'Benjamin
  Bounce' and 'Signor Carini'
  As You Like It 1836, 1955; Hamlet 2992
Carey, Richard Durant 1916–
  Hamlet 3910
Carignani, Carlo, arr. 1857–1919
  Merry Wives 9181
Carl, Eugene M., Jr. 1953–
  Lear 5701

Carl, M.
  Also wrote under the pseudonym 'Carlo'
  Caesar 5476
Carl, Rüdiger
  Dream 9343
Carls, Lawrence D. F. 1949–
  Romeo 13163, 13630
Carlson, [?]
  Merchant 8393
Carlson, Charles Frederick 1875–1939
  Hamlet 3747, 3807, 3808, 3848; Caesar
  5484, 5486, 5488, 5489, 5490, 5492
Carlson, Roberta
  Shrew 14267
Carlton, Cyril
  Antony 311; As You Like It 1876, 1877;
  Coriolanus 2379; Hamlet 3911; L.L.L. 6648;
  Measure 8027; Merchant 8689; Dream
  10589, 10590, 10591; Othello 12382;
  Pericles 12608; Richard III 13050; Romeo
  13894, 13895; Tempest 16010, 16011;
  Troilus 16575; Twelfth Night 18207,
  18208; Two Gentlemen 18643; Winter's
  Tale 19100, 19101
Carluccio Leante, Francesco
  Also known by the surname Leante
  Settings of Commemorative Pieces . . . 21206
Carlyle, Edward, arr.
  Twelfth Night 16670
Carmichael, Mary Grant 1851–1935
  As You Like It 1285, 1624; Measure 7845;
  Merchant 8523; Othello 12279; Twelfth
  Night 17805, 18096; Two Gentlemen
  18490; Sonnet 18 19345
Carmichael, Mary Grant, arr. 1851–1935
  As You Like It 1429
Carmines, Alvin A. 1938–
  Much Ado 11050
Carnaby, William 1772–1839
  Dream 10905
Carnahan, Shirley
  Two Gentlemen 18374
Carnell, William
  As You Like It 1286, 1948; L.L.L. 6393,
  6520; Merchant 8524; Much Ado 11417
Carnini, Giorgio
  Hamlet 2993; Titus 16396
Carnochan, David
  Lear 5988
Carpenter, Gary
  Dream 9344
Carpenter, John Alden 1876–1951
  As You Like It 1287, 1878
Carpi, Fiorenzo 1918–
  Antony 126; Coriolanus 2277; Hamlet
  4088; 1 Henry IV 4314, 4315; 1 Henry VI
  4845, 4846; 2 Henry VI 4887, 4888; 3
  Henry VI 4930, 4931; Caesar 5277, 5278;
  Lear 5702; Macbeth 6769; Dream 9345;

Othello 11705, 11706; Richard II 12630;
Richard III 12810, 12811; Shrew 14268;
Tempest 14920; Timon 16311; Twelfth
Night 16710, 16711; Two Gentlemen
18375; Winter's Tale 18706
Carpi, Fiorenzo, in part arr. 1918–
  Tempest 14921
[Carr, Benjamin, arr.] [(1768)–1831]
  Twelfth Night 17822
Carr, Benjamin [1768]–1831
  L.L.L. 6521; Measure 7846; Merchant 8525;
  Othello 12280
Carr, Benjamin, arr. [1768]–1831
  Macbeth 7512
Carr, Edwin James Nairn 1926–
  Hamlet 4062; L.L.L. 6360; P. Pilgrim 20604
Carr, Ian
  Cymbeline 2540; Lear 6111; Tempest
  16012; Settings of Commemorative
  Pieces . . . 21014, 21112
Carriere, Berthold
  As You Like It 508, 509; Hamlet 2994;
  1 Henry VI 4847; 2 Henry VI 4889; 3 Henry
  VI 4932; Henry VIII 5231; Caesar 5279,
  5280; Lear 5703; L.L.L. 6209; Merry Wives
  8825; Dream 9346; Richard II 12631;
  Romeo 13164; Tempest 14922; Twelfth
  Night 16712; Winter's Tale 18707
Carriere, Berthold, arr.
  Errors 2117
Carrizosa, Eduardo
  Lear 5704
Carroll, Frank M. 1928–
  Errors 2054
Carroll, Jeff
  Winter's Tale 18708
Carrott, Livesey
  Twelfth Night 17806
Carson, Irwin
  Romeo 14076
Carswell, Ian
  Twelfth Night 16713
Carte, R., arr.
  Merry Wives 9000
Carter, [?]
  Cymbeline 2853
Carter, Anthony, arr.
  Lear 6169
Carter, Elliott Cook, Jr. 1908–
  Merchant 8091, 8526; Much Ado
  11051
Carter, John Wallace 1929–
  Measure 7847
Carter, William, arr.
  Dream 9649
Cartwright, Root
  P. Pilgrim 20605
Carulli, G., arr.
  Othello 12056

Caruso, Francesco 1919–1978
As You Like It 1625; Cymbeline 2541, 2642,
2815; Tempest 15634, 15819, 15880,
15970; Twelfth Night 16714, 17472,
17698, 17807, 18097, 18209
Caruso, Luigi 1754–1822
Hamlet 4150; Tempest 15398
Carver, Michael 1950–
Coriolanus 2278; Macbeth 6770; Twelfth
Night 16715
Cary, Tristram Ogilvie 1925–
Hamlet 2995; 1 Henry IV 4316; Caesar
5281; Lear 5705; Macbeth 6771, 6772;
Timon 16312
Casadesus, Henri Gustave 1879–1947
Othello 11707
Case, George Tinkler, arr.
Dream 9650
Case, Thomas
Twelfth Night 17808
Casey, Alice Myers
Macbeth 6773
Casey, James W.
Merchant 8782
Casey, Warren
Twelfth Night 16716
Cashman, Edward
Dream 9347; Othello 11708; Shrew 14269;
Settings of Commemorative Pieces . . .
20917
Cassels-Brown, Alastair K. 1927–
Cymbeline 2542; Sonnet 29 19544
Casson, Reg[inald] H.
Hamlet 4201
Castellini, John
As You Like It 1288
Castelnuovo-Tedesco, Mario 1895–1968
All's Well 73; Antony 312; As You Like It
1011, 1289, 1626, 1837, 1879; Coriolanus
2380; Cymbeline 2543, 2643; Hamlet 3753,
3790; Henry VIII 5072; Caesar 5498;
K. John 5645; Lear 6024, 6025, 6028, 6029,
6040, 6042; L.L.L. 6394, 6522, 6649;
Measure 7848; Merchant 8394, 8527, 8690,
8718; Merry Wives 9203; Dream 10487,
10592; Much Ado 11377, 11418, 11596;
Othello 12216, 12282; Romeo 14026;
Shrew 14654, 14675; Tempest 15526,
15635, 15795, 15816, 15820, 15881,
16013; Timon 16376; Twelfth Night 17473,
17809, 18098, 18210; Two Gentlemen
18491; Winter's Tale 18948, 18956, 18996,
19036, 19102; Sonnet 8 19233; Sonnet 18
19346; Sonnet 27 19519; Sonnet 29 19545;
Sonnet 30 19597; Sonnet 31 19632; Sonnet
32 19641; Sonnet 35 19667; Sonnet 40
19687; Sonnet 47 19732; Sonnet 53 19754;
Sonnet 57 19800; Sonnet 60 19820; Sonnet
64 19871; Sonnet 65 19887; Sonnet 71

19938; Sonnet 73 19986; Sonnet 87 20084;
Sonnet 90 20110; Sonnet 94 20135; Sonnet
97 20156; Sonnet 98 20178; Sonnet 102
20217; Sonnet 104 20232; Sonnet 105
20246, 20256; Sonnet 106 20258; Sonnet
109 20277; Sonnet 116 20313; Sonnet 128
20388; Sonnet 129 20409; Sonnet 146
20490; Sonnet 154 20544
Castiglioni, Niccolò 1932–
Twelfth Night 18099
Castil-Blaze, François Henri Joseph, in part arr.
1784–1857
1 Henry IV 4510; 2 Henry IV 4679
Castoldi, Giovanni
Romeo 13165
Castro, Dino 1920–
Merchant 8092
Catalisano, Gennaro
Coriolanus 2407
Catherine, Georges Robert, arr.   –1958
Cymbeline 2720; Much Ado 11348; Romeo
13564
Cathie, Philip
Much Ado 11052
Catrice, Andre Charles 1963–
Macbeth 7248
Cattani, Lorenzo [circa 1650]–1713
Coriolanus 2408
Cattini, Umberto Andrea
Romeo 13166
Caulfield, J[ohn], arr.
[John Caulfield, the Younger (circa 1775–   )?]
As You Like It 1972
Caulfield, John, ed.
[John Caulfield, the Younger (circa 1775–   )]
Anthologies 21310; 21311
Cavalli, Pietro Francesco 1602–1676
Also known as Pier Francesco Cavalli; his
surname is also known as Caletti, Caletto,
Bruni, Caletti-Bruni, and Caletto Bruni
Coriolanus 2409; Caesar 5558
Cavanna, Bernard
Dream 9348
Cavell, Stanley
Lear 5706
Cayre, Jean Michel
Macbeth 6774
Cazabon, A[lbert]
Tempest 15527
Cazabon, Albert
Caesar 5282; Lear 5707; Winter's Tale
18709
Cazabon, Albert, in part arr.
Merry Wives 8826, 8827; Othello 11709;
Twelfth Night 16717
Cazabon, Albert, [in part] arr.
Winter's Tale 18710
Cazaneuve, Édouard, arr.
Romeo 13663

Cazden, Norman, in part arr. 1914–1980
  Merry Wives 8828
Cazden, Norman, arr. 1914–1980
  Tempest 14923; Settings of Commemorative
  Pieces . . . 20834
Cearlock, Gary
  Pericles 12548
Cébron, Francis Jules
  Hamlet 2996
Cecil, H. M.
  Caesar 5283
Čelanský, Ludvík Vítězslav
  As You Like It 510
Cellier, Alfred 1844–1891
  As You Like It 511; Dream 10951; Twelfth
  Night 16718
Center, Ronald 1913–1973
  As You Like It 1290; Winter's Tale 18952,
  19037
Ceremuga, Josef
  Romeo 13167
Cerito, Alwin, arr.
  Shrew 14572, 14573
Černý, Vladimír
  Winter's Tale 18711
Cerren, Dorothy Vesta
  Tempest 14924
Cerri, Michael
  Othello 12447
Cervone, Michael A.
  Twelfth Night 17474, 17810
Cesi, Beniamino, arr.
  Merry Wives 9182
Cesi, Sigismondo, arr.
  Dream 9651
Chabrier, Alexis Emmanuel 1841–1894
  Tempest 15399
Chacksfield, Frank, arr.
  Errors 2209
Chadwick, George Whitefield
  1854–1931
  As You Like It 1291; Dream 10593;
  Much Ado 11419
Chagrin, Francis 1905–1972
  Pseudonym used by Alexander Paucker
  As You Like It 1012, 1292; Cymbeline 2544;
  Twelfth Night 17475
Chaikovskii, M.
  Othello 11710
Chailley, Jacques 1910–
  Hamlet 4202
Chailly, Luciano 1920–
  Romeo 13168
Chaine, Eugène, arr. 1819–
  Macbeth 7313
Chaitkin, David 1938–
  Lear 6035
Chalcraft, Rory
  As You Like It 512

Chalk, Leonard W.
  1 Henry IV 4317
Challinor, Frederick Arthur 1866–
  As You Like It 1627; Twelfth Night 17811
Chalmers, Marjorie
  Twelfth Night 16719
Chamberlayne, E. A.
  Tempest 16014
Chambers, Clifford
  As You Like It 1293
Chambers, Herbert Arthur, arr.
  Henry VIII 4979, 4980
Chambers, Herbert Arthur, ed.
  Anthologies 21353
Chambers, Ian
  Merchant 8093
Chamoux, André Léon Louis 1932–
  As You Like It 513; Coriolanus 2279;
  Macbeth 6775; Merry Wives 8829; Winter's
  Tale 18712
Champ, John
  Tempest 14925
Chandler, Mary 1911–
  L.L.L. 6523
Chandler, Mary, arr. 1911–
  Timon 16340; Twelfth Night 18315
Chandler, Philip Terrell
  Sonnet 18 19347
Chanler, Theodore Ward 1902–1961
  Twelfth Night 17812
Chapí y Lorente, Ruperto 1851–1909
  Shrew 14565
Chapin, Harry
  Dream 10139
Chaplin, Alan D. 1925–
  Sonnet 18 19348
Chaplin, Charles Spencer 1889–1977
  Hamlet 4089
Chapman, Edward Thomas
  As You Like It 1294, 1628
Chapman, Ernest, arr.
  Merchant 8741
Chappell, Herbert
  Winter's Tale 18713
Chappell, William 1809–1888
  As You Like It 1295, 1629
Chapple, Brian 1945–
  Merchant 8432; Tempest 15528, 15636;
  Twelfth Night 17476, 17813
Chardiny, Louis Claude Armand 1755–1793
  Surname also known as Chardin and as
  Chardini
  Merry Wives 9243
Charke, Richard [circa 1709]–1737
  Othello 11711
Charnell-White, Michael John 1946–
  Dream 10355, 10390
Charpentier, Gabriel 1925–
  Errors 2055; Cymbeline 2448; Hamlet 2997;

1 Henry IV 4318; 2 Henry IV 4534; Henry V 4704; Caesar 5284; Merchant 8094; Pericles 12549, 12550; Richard II 12632; Shrew 14270; Titus 16397, 16398; Twelfth Night 16720

Charpentier, Raymond 1880–
Coriolanus 2280

Chase, David Allen
Hamlet 4063

Chase, Leonard
Othello 11712

Chase, William Henry
Cymbeline 2645

Chatburn, Tom
Merchant 8395

Chater, James Michael 1951–
As You Like It 1013

Chatman, Stephen George 1950–
Merchant 8433; Dream 10317; Twelfth Night 17720; Sonnet 8 19234

Chatterton, F., arr.
Settings of Commemorative Pieces . . . 21113

Chatterton, John Balsir, arr. [1802?]–1871
Dream 9652

Chau, Ai Kian
Dream 9349

Chausson, Ernest Amédée 1855–1899
Hamlet 3743; Macbeth 7249; Measure 7849; Much Ado 11378; Tempest 14926; Twelfth Night 17477

Chavers, Nicky
Winter's Tale 18714

Chawner, C. F. F.
Sonnet 104 20233

Chelard, André Hippolyte Jean Baptiste 1789–1861
Also known as Chélard and as Hippolyte-André-Jean-Baptiste Chelard
Macbeth 7250

Chemin-Petit, Hans 1902–1981
Errors 2056

Chén Jing Gēn 1944–
Much Ado 11359; Romeo 14114

Chén Jūn
Twelfth Night 17382

Chep, Jean-Jacques
Lear 5708

Cheremukhin, Mikhail Mikhailovich 1900–
Hamlet 3568

Cherepnin, Nikolai Nikolaevich 1873–1945
Macbeth 7421

Cherkezishvili, N., arr.
Othello 12031

Cherniavsky, Vladimir
Tempest 14927

Chernick, Maurice, in part arr.
Caesar 5285

Chernysheva, L.
Twelfth Night 16721

Cherry, Don
Tempest 14928

Cherry, Richard 1897–1982
Hamlet 2998; K. John 5582; Romeo 13169; Settings of Commemorative Pieces . . . 21182

Cherry, Robert W., III 1966–
As You Like It 1973

Chervinskii, Nikolai Pavlovich 1925–
Hamlet 3569

Cheshire, John 1839–
Tempest 16015

Cheslock, Louis 1898–1981
As You Like It 1014

Chessid, Herman
All's Well 8; Errors 2057; 1 Henry IV 4319; Henry V 4705; Troilus 16456; Twelfth Night 16722

Chesworth, David
Dream 9350

Cheyette, Irving, arr.
Cymbeline 2721

Chiaffitelli, [?]
Romeo 13170

Chiaramello, Giancarlo 1939–
Coriolanus 2281; Hamlet 2999; Caesar 5286; Macbeth 6776; Merchant 8095; Romeo 13171

Chic, Léon Prudencio, arr. –1916
Macbeth 7314; Much Ado 11621

Chicorel, Ralph
As You Like It 1974

Chiesa, Michele, arr.
Dream 9653

Chignell, Robert 1882–1939
Coriolanus 2282; 1 Henry IV 4320; 2 Henry IV 4535; Henry V 4706; Caesar 5287; Merchant 8528; Romeo 13631; Tempest 15796; Troilus 16457

Chignell, Robert, arr. 1882–1939
Settings of Commemorative Pieces . . . 20900

Chihara, Paul Seiko 1938–
Tempest 15400; Settings of Commemorative Pieces . . . 21114

Chilcot, Thomas [circa 1700]–1766
Antony 290; As You Like It 1820; Cymbeline 2646; Henry VIII 5073; L.L.L. 6361; Measure 7850; Much Ado 11380

Childe, C. S.
Dream 10952

Childs, Barney Sanford 1926–
Cymbeline 2545; Measure 7851; Merchant 8529; Tempest 15637

Chimakadze, Archil Ivanovich 1919–
Hamlet 3000

Chimeri, Filippo
Lear 6133

Chipp, Thomas Paul, arr. 1793–1870
Tempest 14770

Chishko, Oles' Aleksandr Semenovich
1895–1976
Much Ado 11053, 11420
[Chisholm, Erik], arr. [1904–1965]
Tempest 14706, 14771
Chisholm, Erik 1904–1965
P. Pilgrim 20606
Chitz, Arthur 1882–
1 Henry IV 4321; 2 Henry IV 4536; Caesar
5288; Macbeth 6777; Measure 7621;
Merchant 8096; Merry Wives 8830; Richard
II 12633; Romeo 13172; Tempest 14929;
Troilus 16458; Winter's Tale 18715
Chomel, Léonce Vincent, arr.   –1935
Hamlet 3902; Romeo 13664
Chopin, Frédéric François 1810–1849
Born Fryderyk Franciszek Chopin
Hamlet 4269
Chorbajian, John 1936–
Henry VIII 5074; Twelfth Night 17478
Chorgolashvili, A.
Shrew 14271; Twelfth Night 16723
Choron, Alexandre-Étienne 1771–1834
Othello 12283
Chosson, Ernest
Tempest 14930
Choudens, Antony 1849–[1901]
Cymbeline 2879
Chouquet, Louise
Macbeth 7423
Chouquet, Louise, arr.
Macbeth 7315
Choy, David
Winter's Tale 18716
Chrislip, Frederic 1946–
L.L.L. 6210
Christiansen, Larry A. 1941–
Also writes under the pseudonym 'Gordon
Johnstone'
Merchant 8719
Christol, L., arr.
Hamlet 3640
Christopher, J.
Pseudonym used by Jordan Zankoff
Twelfth Night 18100
Chrystal, William Adamson 1931–
Pericles 12551; Twelfth Night 16724
Chubb, [?], in part arr.
K. John 5583
Chubb, John Frederick 1885–1966
As You Like It 1296
Chubb, T. Youres
Dream 10391
Church, Joseph
As You Like It 514; Richard III 12812;
Shrew 14272; Tempest 14931; Winter's Tale
18717
Churchill, Stuart, arr.
Romeo 13977

Chwatal, Franz Xavier, arr. 1808–1879
Dream 9654, 10812; Othello 12057
Chydenius, Kaj
All's Well 9
Cicognini, Alessandro
Othello 12448
Ciechan, Zbigniew 1929–
Romeo 13173
Cikker, Ján 1911–
Coriolanus 2372
Cimarosa, Domenico 1749–1801
Coriolanus 2410
Cimino, James
Twelfth Night 17479, 17699, 17814, 18101
Cimr, Edmund Ondřej, arr. 1861–1920
Othello 12395; Tempest 14982
Ciortea, Mircea
Merry Wives 8831
Čipera, Bohumil
Troilus 16459
Cipra, Milo 1906–1985
As You Like It 515; Hamlet 3001
Claoué, Yves Paul Marie 1927–
Errors 2058
Clapisson, Antoine-Louis 1808–1866
Also known as Antonin Louis Clapisson
Othello 12383
Clapp, Philip Greeley 1888–1954
Shrew 14566
Clare, [Edward], in part arr. [–1869]
Settings of Commemorative Pieces . . . 21115
Clark, Bradford
Lear 5709; Twelfth Night 16725
Clark, Dan Olin 1944–
Dream 9351
Clark, Dan Olin, in part arr. 1944–
Othello 11713
Clark, Harold
Measure 7852
[Clarke, Jeremiah] [(circa 1674)–1707]
[Also known as Jeremiah Clark and as
Jeremiah Clerk]
Titus 16425
Clarke, George W.
Romeo 14134
Clarke, Helen A.
Othello 12284; Twelfth Night 17480
Clarke, Henry Leland 1907–
Hamlet 3849; Merchant 8675
Clarke, [James] H[amilton Siree], arr.
[1840–1912]
Settings of Commemorative Pieces . . . 21281
Clarke, James Hamilton Siree 1840–1912
Cymbeline 2449, 2647; Hamlet 3002, 3912;
Lear 5710; Merchant 8097; Sonnet 39 19685
Clarke, Jeremiah [circa 1674]–1707
Also known as Jeremiah Clark and as
Jeremiah Clerk
Antony 337; Hamlet 4270; Timon 16313

Clarke, John 1770–1836
  Later known as John Clarke-Whitfeld
  Othello 12285
Clarke, John, arr. 1770–1836
  Later known as John Clarke-Whitfeld
  As You Like It 407; Cymbeline 2651;
  Macbeth 6977; Measure 7905; Dream
  10196; Tempest 14707, 14708, 15219;
  Timon 16341, 16342
Clarke, Maurice
  Romeo 14135
Clarke, Rebecca Thacher, arr. 1886–1979
  Also known as Mrs. James Friskin; also
  wrote under the pseudonym 'Anthony Trent'
  As You Like It 1430
Clarke, Rosemary
  Dream 9352
Clarke, Samuel
  As You Like It 1297
Clarke, Symon 1957–
  Sonnet 66 19908
Clarke, Terence John Osborne 1935–
  Antony 127; Dream 9353, 10318; Shrew
  14273; Winter's Tale 18718
Claudius, Otto 1795–1877
  Measure 7853
Clausen, Alf H., in part arr. 1941–
  Shrew 14677
Claussen, Wilhelm 1843–1869
  Othello 12384
Clay, Frederic 1838–1889
  Twelfth Night 16726
Clay, William P.
  Hamlet 3003
Clayton, Kenny
  Settings of Commemorative Pieces . . .
  20918
Clemens, Theodor L.
  As You Like It 1015
Clementi, [?]
  Tempest 16248
Clements, Constance E.
  Dream 10594
Clements, John Harvey, arr. 1910–
  As You Like It 1567; Cymbeline 2722
Clendon, Hugh
  Cymbeline 2816
Clérambault, Louis-Nicolas 1676–1749
  Dream 10953
Clerico, Francesco 1755–[after 1838]
  Hamlet 4151; Macbeth 7257, 7258
Clifford, Hubert John 1904–1959
  As You Like It 1880
Clifford, William
  Dream 9354
Clifton, John 1935–
  Macbeth 6778; Dream 9355
Clifton, John Charles 1781–1841
  As You Like It 1630; Twelfth Night 17721

Clifton, John Charles, adapter 1781–1841
  Merchant 8764
Clifton, John Charles, arr. 1781–1841
  As You Like It 408
Clinton, John, arr.
  Othello 12058, 12059
Clokey, Joseph Waddell 1890–1961
  As You Like It 1016
Close, Claude
  Cymbeline 2450
Clothier, Michael John 1930–
  Hamlet 3913; Caesar 5499; Macbeth 7424;
  Romeo 13896; Twelfth Night 18211
Clough-Leighter, Henry 1874–1956
  Also wrote under the pseudonym 'Louis
  Koppitz'
  As You Like It 1298
Clough-Leighter, Henry, arr. 1874–1956
  Also wrote under the pseudonym 'Louis
  Koppitz'
  Tempest 14709
Clutsam, George Howard, arr. 1866–1951
  Cymbeline 2723
Coates, Eric 1886–1957
  As You Like It 1299, 1631; Henry VIII
  5075; Merchant 8098, 8530; Much Ado
  11054, 11421; Twelfth Night 17815; Two
  Gentlemen 18492
Coates, Gloria Kannenberg 1938–
  Hamlet 3004
Coates, John, arr. 1865–1941
  Twelfth Night 16618
Coates, Kate, in part arr.
  Merchant 8100; Merry Wives 8832; Tempest
  14932
Coates, Leon 1937–
  Henry V 4707; Othello 11714
Coates, Matthew Francis
  Measure 7854
Coates, Simon, in part arr.
  Twelfth Night 16727
Cobleigh, Donald Edwards, arr.
  As You Like It 1431
Cockburn Clive
  As You Like It 516
Cockshott, Gerald Wilfred 1915–1979
  Twelfth Night 17481
Cocoran, John
  As You Like It 517
Cody, Robert Oswald 1928–
  Sonnet 30 19598
Cœdès, Auguste [1835?]–1884
  Hamlet 3914
Coelho, Luis Fernando
  Shrew 14274
Coenen, Paul 1908–
  Sonnet 1 19177; Sonnet 12 19283; Sonnet
  18 19349; Sonnet 21 19479; Sonnet 25
  19503

Coffin, Myra
    Shrew 14275
Cohen, Edward 1940–
    Sonnet 97 20157; Sonnet 123 20363
Cohen, Gerard Bernard
    Othello 11715
Cohen, Joel Israel 1942–
    Twelfth Night 16728
Cohen, Richard
    Dream 9356
Cohen, Robert S.
    As You Like It 518; Dream 9357; Twelfth
    Night 16729
Cohen, Steve 1954–
    Hamlet 3005; Dream 9358; Twelfth Night
    16730
Cohn, Chester
    Romeo 14136
Cohn, Gregory P., arr.
    Romeo 13583
Cohn, Zena
    As You Like It 519; Dream 9359; Twelfth
    Night 16731; Sonnet 18 19456
Coke, Roger Sacheverell 1912–[before 1982]
    Sonnet 71 19939
Colbran, Isabella Angela 1785–1845
    Also known as Signora Rossini
    Antony 128
Colburn, George 1878–1921
    Antony 363
Colby, Ruth Hartwell
    Merchant 8101
Cole, Frederick G.
    Much Ado 11422
Cole, Rossetter Gleason 1866–1952
    Merchant 8531
Cole, Sidney R.
    Dream 10595
Coleman, E[llen?] [1893?–1973]
    As You Like It 1017
Coleman, James
    Two Gentlemen 18494
Coleridge-Taylor, Samuel 1875–1912
    Othello 11716, 12286; Twelfth Night
    17817; Sonnet 54 19774
Collette, Buddy
    Hamlet 3006
Collier, S.
    Settings of Commemorative Pieces . . . 21015
Colline, Victor, arr.
    Merry Wives 9028, 9029, 9030
Collingwood, Arthur
    As You Like It 1632; Dream 10319, 10488;
    Twelfth Night 17818; Two Gentlemen 18495
Collingwood, Lawrance Arthur 1887–1982
    Macbeth 7259
Collins, A[nthony Vincent Benedictus?]
    [1893–1963]
    Twelfth Night 16732

Collins, Charles
    Romeo 14137
Collins, George W.
    Henry VIII 5213; Tempest 16016; Settings of
    Commemorative Pieces . . . 21116
Collins, Joe
    As You Like It 520; Cymbeline 2451; Romeo
    13174; Two Gentlemen 18376
Collins, Mary Ellen 1941–
    Also known as Mitzie Collins
    Dream 9360
Collins, Peter L., arr.
    Romeo 14091
Collison, Michele
    Twelfth Night 18102
Colonna, Luigi 1891–
    Sonnet 128 20389
Colot, Hildur
    Richard III 12813
Colville, Thomas L., arr.
    Tempest 14710
Coma, Abelardo
    Othello 12471
Coman, Nicolae 1936–
    Sonnet 8 19235
Combi, Pietro [circa 1808]–1853
    Antony 364
Comboul, E., arr.
    Romeo 13665
Combs, Ronald
    K. John 5584
Commer, Franz 1813–1887
    Cymbeline 2648
Condell, Henry, in part arr.   –1824
    Tempest 15401
Cone, Edward Toner 1917–
    Cymbeline 2546; Twelfth Night 17482
Conen, Johannes
    As You Like It 521
Congdon, David 1953–
    Sonnet 99 20198
Conley, Boris
    Tempest 14933
Conley, Brian
    Hamlet 3007
Connell, Edward
    Errors 2059; 1 Henry IV 4322; Lear 5711
Connell, Richard Lee
    Sonnet 18 19350; Sonnet 29 19546
Connelly, Gary Alyn, in part arr.
    Shrew 14276
Connolly, Joseph F., Jr.
    All's Well 92; Much Ado 11630
Connolly, Richard
    Merchant 8102; Twelfth Night 16733
Connor, [?], arr.
    Settings of Commemorative Pieces . . . 21282
Conrad, Hy
    Much Ado 11360

Conrad, Max
  As You Like It 522
Consorti, Alfredo
  Caesar 5477
Constantine, N., arr.
  Tempest 14772
Constantinides, Dinos Demetrios 1929–
  Hamlet 3008, 3915; Twelfth Night 16734
Conti, Niccolò
  Coriolanus 2411
Converse, Frederick Shepherd 1871–1940
  Hamlet 4152
Convery, Robert 1954–
  L.L.L. 6524; Measure 7855; Dream 10140;
  Tempest 15529, 15638; P. Pilgrim 20607
Conway, Roma
  As You Like It 523
Conyngham, Barry 1944–
  Hamlet 3009; Measure 7622
Cook, [?]
  Merry Wives 8833
Cook, Charles Stiebler, arr.
  Cymbeline 2652
Cook, John Ernest 1918–1984
  As You Like It 524; Cymbeline 2547;
  1 Henry IV 4323, 4324; 2 Henry IV 4537;
  Henry V 4708; 1 Henry VI 4848; 2 Henry VI
  4890; 3 Henry VI 4933; K. John 5585; L.L.L.
  6211, 6212; Merchant 8103, 8104, 8532;
  Merry Wives 8834; Richard II 12634;
  Romeo 13175; Shrew 14277; Tempest
  14934; Twelfth Night 16735, 17483,
  17819; Winter's Tale 18719
Cook, Patrick, in part arr.
  Romeo 13176
Cook, Ray, arr.
  Merry Wives 9010
Cook, T.
  Macbeth 6779
Cooke, Arnold Atkinson 1906–
  Merchant 8105; Sonnet 18 19351; Sonnet
  73 19987; Sonnet 97 20158; Sonnet 98
  20179
Cooke, Benjamin 1734–1793
  Antony 291; Cymbeline 2649, 2858; Dream
  10305; Winter's Tale 18997, 19071
Cooke, Deryck Victor 1919–1976
  Sonnet 18 19352; Sonnet 29 19547; Sonnet
  53 19755; Sonnet 57 19801; Sonnet 77
  20055; Sonnet 97 20159; Sonnet 106
  20259; Sonnet 109 20278; Sonnet 110
  20287; Sonnet 116 20314
Cooke, John
  Tempest 14935
Cooke, John, in part arr.
  Dream 9361
Cooke, Thomas Simpson 1782–1848
  Also known as Tom Cooke
  All's Well 93; Coriolanus 2283, 2381;
Cymbeline 2836; 2 Henry IV 4538;
  Merchant 8752; Dream 10304, 10392,
  10443, 10467, 10773; Shrew 14567,
  14649, 14651; Tempest 14936, 15797;
  Timon 16314; Sonnet 60 19845; Sonnet
  102 20227; P. Pilgrim 20608, 20748;
  Settings of Commemorative Pieces . . .
  20835
Cooke, Thomas Simpson, in part arr.
  1782–1848
  Also known as Tom Cooke
  Henry V 4709; Dream 9362; Venus 20808
Coole, Orlando
  Pseudonym used by Livingstone Gearhart
  Much Ado 11423
Coolidge, Lucy Frances 1948–
  Merchant 8533, 8725; Twelfth Night
  16736, 16737, 17484, 18103
Coolidge, Richard Ard 1929–
  As You Like It 1300, 1633; L.L.L. 6645;
  Dream 10446; Sonnet 73 19988
Cools, Eugène 1877–1936
  Hamlet 3916
Coombes, Douglas 1935–
  Lear 5712; Dream 10489; Twelfth Night
  17723
Coombs, John, arr.
  Romeo 13978
Cooney, Myron
  Hamlet 3570
Cooper, Charles Paston
  Also known as Charles Paston-Cooper
  Othello 12535
Cooper, Elmore
  Twelfth Night 18104
Cooper, Gerald Melbourne, arr.
  Dream 10197, 10198; Richard II 12707;
  Tempest 14711
Cooper, Joseph Thomas
  Merry Wives 9215
Cooper, June
  Tempest 14939
Cooper, Rose Marie, arr.
  As You Like It 1432
Cooper, Stanley
  Antony 129; Henry V 4710
Cooper, Wilbye, arr.
  As You Like It 409
Coote, Charles, the Elder 1809–1880
  As You Like It 1881, 1993; Macbeth 7425,
  7583; Tempest 16017
Coote, Charles, the Elder, arr. 1809–1880
  Merry Wives 9031
Coote, Charles, the Younger
  Romeo 13897
Coote, Charles, the Younger, arr.
  Tempest 16187
Cope, David Howell 1941–
  Richard II 12635

Copeland, Paul 1947–
Sonnet 65 19888
Copeman, Andy
Dream 9366
Copland, Aaron 1900–1990
Born Aaron Kaplan
1 Henry IV 4325; 2 Henry IV 4539; Henry V
4711; Dream 10954; Richard II 12636;
P. Pilgrim 20609
Copley, Ian Alfred 1926–
Dream 10320, 10490
Coquelet, Onésime Louise, arr. –1910
Hamlet 4188; Othello 12188, 12189, 12414
Coquelin, Gaston Adrien Adolphe, arr. –1939
Shrew 14590
Coraggio, Peter 1940–
Dream 9367
Corban, Michael A.
Tempest 15639, 15882
Corbett, H. M.
[H. M. Brickdale Corbett?]
Sonnet 30 19599
Corbett, William [circa 1669]–1748
1 Henry IV 4326; Twelfth Night 18267
Corder, Frederick 1852–1932
Shrew 14655; Tempest 15402, 15530,
15640, 16018, 16019; Twelfth Night 17485
Corelli, Marie 1855–1924
Romeo 13838
Corfe, Joseph [1741]–1820
Cymbeline 2859; Tempest 15641
Corfe, Joseph, arr. [1741]–1820
Tempest 14712; Timon 16343, 16344
Corigliano, John Paul 1938–
1 Henry VI 4849; 2 Henry VI 4891; 3 Henry
VI 4934; Richard III 12814
Corina, John Hubert 1928–
Measure 7856; Merchant 8534; P. Pilgrim
20610
Cornelius, Carl August Peter 1824–1874
Twelfth Night 17486
Cornelius, Harold
Merchant 8783
Corness, Jeffrey Mark 1961–
Hamlet 4090
[Cornet, Alessandre]
Hamlet 4271
Cornett, Alice
Merchant 8784
Corp, Ronald
Much Ado 11056; Winter's Tale 18720
Correll, Stephen
All's Well 86
Corri, Charles
Kinsmen 19160
Corri, Philip Anthony, arr. 1784–1832
Also wrote under the pseudonym 'Arthur
Clifton'
Tempest 14773

Corri, William, Jr.
Antony 130; As You Like It 525
Corroyez, Georges, arr.
Macbeth 7461
Cortés, Ramiro, Jr. 1938–1984
Antony 131
Costa, Alessandro 1857–1953
Hamlet 3917; Richard III 13051
Costandinos, Alec R.
Romeo 13632
Cotter, James
Lear 5713; Macbeth 6780; Merchant 8106;
Tempest 14940; Winter's Tale 18721
Cotton, W. [J.]
Much Ado 11424
Cottrau, Giulio 1831–1916
Lear 5989; Pericles 12601
Coucill, Christopher, in part arr.
Much Ado 11057
Coughlin, Bruce
All's Well 10; Antony 132; Dream 9368;
Winter's Tale 18722
Coulthard, Jean 1908–
Hamlet 3918; Sonnet 18 19353; Sonnet 75
20033; Sonnet 91 20117; Sonnet 102
20218; Sonnet 116 20315; Sonnet 138
20453; Sonnet 148 20520
Courtauld, S.
Sonnet 73 19989
Courtioux, Jean Godefroy Charles
Merry Wives 8835
Courvoisier, C., arr.
Merry Wives 9032
Cousins, John
Dream 9369
Covell, Roger 1931–
Hamlet 3010
Cover, Claude E.
Measure 7857
Coward, James 1824–1880
Measure 7858; P. Pilgrim 20611
Coward, James Munro
Winter's Tale 18723
Coward, Noël Pierce 1899–1973
Much Ado 11636
Cowdell, Ellen
As You Like It 1301
Cowell, Henry Dixon 1897–1965
Hamlet 3011, 3701; Lear 5714, 6043; L.L.L.
6349; Merchant 8683; Dream 9370, 10430;
Tempest 16163; Settings of Commemorative
Pieces . . . 21207
Cowen, Frederic Hymen 1852–1935
Born Hymen Frederick Cowen
Measure 7859; Romeo 13899
Cox, Albert Walter 1898–1973
As You Like It 526, 527; Cymbeline 2452;
L.L.L. 6213, 6214; Measure 7623; Merchant
8107; Merry Wives 8836; Dream 9371;

Tempest 14941; Troilus 16460; Twelfth
Night 16738; Two Gentlemen 18377;
Winter's Tale 18724
Cox, Robert
Measure 7624
Cox, W. Ralph 1884–1941
Twelfth Night 17820
Cozette, Cynthia 1953–
Sonnet 18 19354
Cozzi, Giacomo
Also known as Giacomo Corsi and as
Giacomo Conzi
Hamlet 4272
Crabtree, June
Caesar 5551; Lear 6148; Macbeth 7561;
Dream 10906; Romeo 14138; Shrew 14682;
Tempest 16214
Crabtree, Peter
Caesar 5552; Lear 6149; Macbeth 7562;
Dream 10907; Romeo 14139; Shrew 14683;
Tempest 16215
Cramer, A., arr.
Hamlet 3641
Cramer, Henri, arr.
Macbeth 7316; Merry Wives 9033; Settings
of Commemorative Pieces . . . 20964
Cramer, J., arr.
Shrew 14574
Cramer, S., arr.
Almost certainly the pseudonym of one of
the many composers who, not wishing to
sign their arrangements, published them
under the name 'Cramer'
Romeo 13666
Cramer, William Oliver, arr.
Tempest 14774
Crampton, Thomas
Henry VIII 5076
Crampton, Thomas, arr.
Cymbeline 2653
Cranmer, Damion
Antony 133
Crans, Tec
Measure 7625
Cravath, Martin
As You Like It 964
Craven, Elizabeth 1750–1828
Also known as Baroness Craven, Margravine
of Anspach
Twelfth Night 17821
Craven, John Thomas 1796–
Tempest 15531
Craven, John Thomas, arr. 1796–
Macbeth 6978; Merry Wives 8878, 8879;
Tempest 14713, 14714, 15118
Craven, Nick
Lear 5715
Crawford, G.
Coriolanus 2284

Crawford, John 1931–
As You Like It 1018, 1302; Merchant
8535; Much Ado 11425; Twelfth Night
17488, 18105; Sonnet 18 19355; Sonnet 29
19548
Crawley, Clifford
Titus 16421
Cray, Robert, arr.
Hamlet 3413
Creasey, Phyllis
Winter's Tale 18725
Crémer, H., arr.
Romeo 13667
Crerar, Louis
As You Like It 1019, 1634; Measure 7860;
Merchant 8536
Cresswell, Lyell Richard 1944–
Macbeth 7563
Cresswell, Pat
Othello 11722
Creuse, Roland
Measure 7626
Creutzburg, Werner
Dream 9372
Cribari, Donna Marie 1939–
Lear 6134
Crichton, Margaret
Cymbeline 2548; Hamlet 3702, 3754; L.L.L.
6395, 6525; Dream 10299, 10461; Much
Ado 11426; Twelfth Night 17824; Winter's
Tale 18949, 18972, 19038
Crichton, Michel
Twelfth Night 16739
Crippa, C., adapter
Tempest 15846
Cripps, A. Redgrave
Twelfth Night 17825
Crist, Bainbridge, arr. 1883–1969
Henry VIII 5178; Tempest 14775; Two
Gentlemen 18363
Crocker, Ray Dean 1949–
Hamlet 4064; Winter's Tale 18726
Croft, William 1678–1727
Titus 16426
Crofts, J.
As You Like It 1635; Cymbeline 2661;
Twelfth Night 17826
Crofut, William 1934–
Twelfth Night 16740
Croisez, A., arr.
Cymbeline 2840
Crompton, R. M., arr.
Romeo 13116
Crook, John
Merchant 8108
Crook, Stephen
Dream 9373
Crooks, John
Errors 2060

Croom, John 1941–
  Tempest 15824
Crosby, Werner
  All's Well 98
Cross, David
  Twelfth Night 16741
Cross, Lucy
  As You Like It 528
Cross, Robert 1899–
  Merchant 8537
Crosse, Gordon 1937–
  Cymbeline 2817; 1 Henry IV 4327; 2 Henry
  IV 4540; Lear 5716; Dream 10774
Crossley, T. Hastings 1846–
  Sonnet 98 20180
Croteau, Leo Francis P.
  Hamlet 4203
Crouch, Frederick William, arr. flor. 1808–1833
  Dream 10813; Othello 12060, 12061
Crouch, Rollings Edward, arr.
  Tempest 15079
Crow, Edwin John 1841–
  As You Like It 1020
Crowell, Joan
  Tempest 16198
Crowell, Mabel N.
  Dream 10596
Crowther, George W. F.
  Romeo 13900
Croy, Jamie
  Measure 7627
Cruft, Adrian Francis 1921–1987
  Dream 10597; Romeo 13901; Tempest
  16020; Settings of Commemorative
  Pieces . . . 21117
Cruickshank, William Alexander Campbell
  1854–1934
  Twelfth Night 17827
Cseh, Tamás 1943–
  As You Like It 529
Cserepes, Károly
  Twelfth Night 16742
Csire, József 1926–
  Sonnet 2 19188
Cui, Tsezar' Antonovich 1835–1918
  Othello 12287
Cuissét, Frank F. 1812–
  Merchant 8538
Culshaw, Adrian, in part arr.
  Errors 2061
Cumming, Richard 1928–
  As You Like It 530, 531, 1021, 1303;
  Hamlet 4091; 1 Henry IV 4328; Henry V
  4814; Caesar 5289; Lear 5717; L.L.L. 6215;
  Macbeth 6781; Merry Wives 8837; Dream
  9374; Romeo 13177; Shrew 14278; Tempest
  14942, 14943; Troilus 16461; Twelfth
  Night 16743, 17489, 17679, 17688, 17700,
  17828, 18106; Sonnet 29 19549

Cummings, James Joseph Aloysius 1950–
  Pericles 12552; Shrew 14279
Cummings, James Joseph Aloysius, arr.
  1950–
  Pericles 12554
Cummings, William Hayman 1831–1915
  L.L.L. 6362; Othello 12495
Cummings, William Hayman, arr. 1831–1915
  Tempest 14715
Cummings-Knight, Geoffrey
  Dream 10141
Cummins, Rick 1947–
  Dream 9375; Romeo 13178; Shrew 14280
Cunio, Angelo
  Hamlet 3919
Cunio, Angelo, arr.
  Macbeth 7317, 7318
Cunneen, Paddy
  Macbeth 6782
Cunningham, Michael G. 1937–
  Macbeth 7392; Sonnet 1 19178; Sonnet 2
  19189; Sonnet 3 19197; Sonnet 4 19201;
  Sonnet 5 19207; Sonnet 6 19215; Sonnet
  28 19534
Cunningham, Robert E., Jr.
  Sonnet 18 19356
Curran, Alvin S. 1938–
  Othello 11723; Settings of Commemorative
  Pieces . . . 21208
Cursch-Bühren, F. Th., arr.
  Lear 6059
Curschmann, Carl Friedrich 1805–1841
  Cymbeline 2662; Romeo 14140
Curtis, Irene
  Macbeth 6783
Curwin, Clifford Crawley
  Twelfth Night 18107
Cushing, Charles Cook 1905–1982
  Tempest 14944
Cusins, William George 1833–1893
  L.L.L. 6650
Custard, Reginald Goss, arr.
  Dream 9655, 9656
Cuvillier, Charles Louis Paul 1877–1955
  Merry Wives 8838
Cyr, Gordon Conrad 1925–
  Cymbeline 2549; Measure 7861; Twelfth
  Night 17829; Sonnet 66 19909
Cyriax, Horst
  Errors 2062
Czajkowski, Michael 1939–
  Lear 5718
Czerny, Carl 1791–1857
  Also known as Charles Czerny
  Settings of Commemorative Pieces . . . 21016
Czerny, Carl, arr. 1791–1857
  Also known as Charles Czerny
  Dream 10130, 10814; Othello 12062,
  12457; Twelfth Night 18069

Czubaty, Roman
As You Like It 532
Czyż, Henryk 1923–
Romeo 13179

D

da Castrovillari, Daniele
Also known as Daniele di Castrovillari
Antony 365
Da Costa, [?]
Hamlet 3920
Da Venezia, Franco 1876–1937
Tempest 16021
Dadge, Ralph
As You Like It 1022
Daffner, Hugo 1882–1936
Macbeth 7260
Dagosto, Sylvain, arr.
Romeo 13668
Dahlquist, Jack Edward 1954–
Settings of Commemorative Pieces . . .
21017
Dailly, Yvan   –1983
Antony 134; Hamlet 3012; Measure 7628;
Merchant 8109; Troilus 16462; Twelfth
Night 16744
Dakin, C.
As You Like It 533
Dal, Hans
Hamlet 3013
Dalayrac, Nicolas-Marie 1753–1809
Romeo 13633
D'Albert, Charles Louis Napoléon, arr.
1809–1886
Macbeth 7319, 7320
Dalbotten, Ted 1922–
Born Charles Eric Dalbotten
As You Like It 1949; Coriolanus 2387;
Cymbeline 2550; Hamlet 4065; 1 Henry IV
4492; 2 Henry IV 4663; Henry VIII 5077,
5227; Caesar 5535; Lear 6112; L.L.L. 6379;
Merchant 8720; Dream 10747; Richard III
13042, 13064; Romeo 14027; Tempest
16164; Troilus 16578; Winter's Tale 19130
Dalby, John
Dream 9376; Othello 11724
Dalby, Martin 1942–
L.L.L. 6651; Measure 7862; Settings of
Commemorative Pieces . . . 21118
Dale, Benjamin James 1885–1943
Tempest 16022; Twelfth Night 17490,
17830
Dale, Frederic
As You Like It 534
Dale, Jim
Winter's Tale 18727, 18728

d'Alessandro, Michele, arr.
Merry Wives 9183
dall'Argine, Costantino
Merry Wives 9245; Dream 10775; Settings
of Commemorative Pieces . . . 20919
d'Alquen, Johann Peter Cornelius
Twelfth Night 17491
Daltry, Joseph S.
As You Like It 1838; L.L.L. 6396; Merchant
8539; Twelfth Night 17831
Daltry, Joseph S., arr.
Dream 10371
Damase, Jean-Michel 1928–
As You Like It 535
Damashek, Barbara
Othello 11725; Shrew 14281, 14282
Damasse, Max
Much Ado 11058
Dambis, Pauls 1936–
Sonnet 5 19208; Sonnet 7 19220; Sonnet
26 19510; Sonnet 31 19633; Sonnet 33
19649; Sonnet 39 19683; Sonnet 40 19688;
Sonnet 102 20219; Sonnet 154 20545
Damcke, Berthold 1812–1875
Merry Wives 9216
Damrosch, Leopold 1832–1885
Merchant 8540; Romeo 13635; Settings of
Commemorative Pieces . . . 21018
Damrosch, Walter Johannes, arr. 1862–1950
Dream 9657
Dana, Arthur, arr.
Cymbeline 2724, 2725
Danblon, Paul 1931–
Coriolanus 2285; Macbeth 6784
Danby, John, arr. [circa 1757]–1798
As You Like It 410
Dancla, Jean Baptiste Charles, arr. 1817–1907
Dream 10815
d'Andréa, Oswald Antoine Marie
Macbeth 6785; Tempest 14945
D'Angelo, Nicholas V.
Merchant 8110
Dan'kevych, Konstantyn Fedorovych
1905–1984
Hamlet 3014; Much Ado 11059; Othello
11726, 12385
Dankworth, John Philip William 1927–
All's Well 99; Antony 355; As You Like It
965, 1975; Errors 2264; Coriolanus 2398;
Cymbeline 2551, 2860; Hamlet 4204;
1 Henry IV 4503; 2 Henry IV 4675; Henry V
4836; 1 Henry VI 4883; 2 Henry VI 4927;
3 Henry VI 4964; Henry VIII 5237; Caesar
5553; K. John 5652; Lear 6150; L.L.L. 6526,
6684; Macbeth 7371, 7497, 7564; Measure
8041; Merchant 8765; Merry Wives 9261;
Dream 9377, 10294, 10491, 10908; Much
Ado 11637; Othello 12496; Pericles 12610;
Richard II 12775; Richard III 13072; Romeo

Dankworth, John Philip William (*cont.*)
14141; Shrew 14684; Tempest 15826,
16216; Timon 16384; Titus 16429; Troilus
16581; Twelfth Night 16745, 17492,
17724, 17725, 17832, 18108, 18291; Two
Gentlemen 18496, 18653; Winter's Tale
19142; Sonnet 18 19357; Sonnet 23 19489;
Sonnet 24 19494; Sonnet 155 20583;
Complaint 20585; P. Pilgrim 20752; Phoenix
20768; Lucrece 20782; Venus 20810;
Settings of Commemorative Pieces . . . 20920
Dankworth, John Philip William, arr. 1927–
Henry V 4820; Caesar 5503; Sonnet 40
19689; Sonnet 147 20507
Dannreuther, Edward George 1844–1905
Also known as Eduard Dannreuther
As You Like It 1304; L.L.L. 6350, 6397,
6527; Twelfth Night 17493, 17833, 18109
Danoff, William T.
Twelfth Night 16746
Danon, Oskar 1913–
Much Ado 11060
Dansie, Redgewell
Tempest 15532, 15883
Danzi, Franz Ignaz 1763–1826
Antony 366
Darbo, Ralph
Antony 135
Darke, Robert
Tempest 16249
Darling, Maude
Timon 16385
Darnton, Philip Christian 1905–1981
Lear 5719; Merchant 8111; Romeo 13180
Darondeau, Henry 1779–1865
Othello 12021
Dart, Robert Thurston, arr. 1921–1971
As You Like It 1433
Dart, William, in part arr.
Romeo 13181
Darvas, Ferenc
L.L.L. 6324
D'Arville, G.
Tempest 15642
Dăscălescu, Camelia 1921–
Errors 2063; Merry Wives 8839
Datin, Jacques Jean Marie   –1973
Much Ado 11061
d'Auberge, Alfred, arr.
Shrew 14601
Daubney, Brian Blyth 1929–
Cymbeline 2552; L.L.L. 6528; Dream 10492;
Much Ado 11427; Tempest 15533, 15643,
15798; Twelfth Night 17494, 17689,
17834, 17835, 18292
Dauner, Wolfgang
Tempest 14946
Daus, Avraham 1902–1974
Sonnet 155 20561

Daussoigne Méhul, A., arr.
Dream 10816
Davenport, Dennis
As You Like It 1305
Davenport, Francis William 1847–1925
Twelfth Night 18212
David, Félicien César 1810–1876
All's Well 74
Dávid, Gyula 1913–1977
Antony 136; Hamlet 3015; Much Ado
11062; Othello 11727, 11728; Richard III
12815
David, Hod
Tempest 14947
David, Thomas Christian 1925–
Settings of Commemorative Pieces . . . 21209
Davidson, Harold, arr.
Tempest 14776
Davidson, Hugh Hanson 1930–
Cymbeline 2453
Davidson, Jerry F. 1942–
Sonnet 155 20562
Davidson, Malcolm Gordon 1891–1949
As You Like It 1636, 1839
Davie, Cedric Thorpe 1913–1983
As You Like It 1637; Henry VIII 4973,
5078; Lear 5720; Measure 7629; Merchant
8112, 8113; Dream 9378, 10493; Twelfth
Night 16747; Two Gentlemen 18378
Davies, D.
As You Like It 1306
Davies, Henry Walford 1869–1941
Cymbeline 2553; Henry V 4805; Henry VIII
5079; K. John 5643; Dream 10494; Richard
II 12757; Twelfth Night 17495, 17836,
18110; Winter's Tale 18973, 19072
Davies, Henry Walford, arr. 1869–1941
As You Like It 1434
Davies, Hugh Seymour 1943–
Twelfth Night 16748
Davies, Ivor Richard
As You Like It 1638; Tempest 15644
Davies, Lane
Shrew 14283
Davies, Peter Maxwell 1934–
As You Like It 536; Hamlet 3016; Lear
5721; Dream 9379; Richard II 12637;
Settings of Commemorative Pieces . . .
21119
Davies, Terry 1955–
Hamlet 3017; Richard III 12816
Davies, Vincent
Romeo 14028
Davies, Vincent, adapter
Hamlet 4205
[Davis, Meyer, arr.]
Shrew 14602
Davis, Albert O., arr.
Dream 9658

Davis, Angelita
As You Like It 1882
Davis, Carl 1936–
Antony 137; 1 Henry IV 4329; 2 Henry IV
4541; Lear 5722; L.L.L. 6216; Macbeth
6786; Measure 7630; Merchant 8114; Much
Ado 11063; Pericles 12553; Richard III
12817; Shrew 14284; Tempest 14949
Davis, Carl, in part arr. 1936–
Merchant 8115
Davis, Eleanor Maud 1889–1973
Two Gentlemen 18497
Davis, John David [1867]–1942
Dream 10495
Davis, John Freeman 1835–[circa 1916]
Cymbeline 2818
Davis, Katherine Kennicott 1892–1980
Also known under the pseudonym 'Clare
Goodhall'
Dream 10496
Davis, R. E.
As You Like It 1840
Davis, William Robert
Antony 292
Davison, James William 1813–1885
Settings of Commemorative Pieces . . . 21120
Davy, John 1763–1824
Hamlet 3720; Sonnet 61 19851; Sonnet 139
20462; Sonnet 149 20525; P. Pilgrim
20613, 20614
Davy, John, in part arr. 1763–1824
Tempest 14950
Davy, John, arr. 1763–1824
Tempest 14716, 14777, 15119, 15482,
16223
Davydov, Aleksandr Davydovich 1849–1911
Much Ado 11428
Dawes, Frank, arr.
As You Like It 411; Tempest 14778
Day, J. K.
[J. King Day?]
Twelfth Night 18066
Day, Julius Grant
As You Like It 1883
Daymond, Emily Rosa
Twelfth Night 17837
de Almeida, António Vitorino
Measure 7631
De Angelis, Arturo 1879–
Tempest 16250
de Banfield, Raffaello 1922–
Hamlet 4066; Much Ado 11064
de Bohun, Lyle 1927–
Pseudonym used by Clara Lyle Boone
Sonnet 65 19889
de Bourguignon, Francis Leon 1890–1961
Dream 9380
de Brayer, Jules, in part arr.
Dream 9381; Tempest 14951

de Brayer, Jules, arr.
Cymbeline 2454; Lear 5723
de Bréville, Pierre Eugène Onfroy
1861–1949
Tempest 14952
de Bromhead, Jerome 1945–
Much Ado 11638
de Bruce, Robert
Sonnet 18 19358; Sonnet 30 19600; Sonnet
53 19756; Sonnet 104 20234; Sonnet 105
20247
de Cairos-Rego, Rex 1886–
Much Ado 11429; Twelfth Night 17838;
Sonnet 29 19550; P. Pilgrim 20615
de Castéra, René 1873–1955
As You Like It 1023, 1307; Much Ado
11430
de Castrone, Mathilde, arr.
Othello 12063
de Clerque, Adrian
Twelfth Night 16749
de Cor-de-Lass, José
Also known as José de Cor de Lass
Lear 6070
de Crescenzo, C., arr.
Dream 9659
de Falla, Manuel 1876–1946
Also known as Manuel de Falla y Matheu
Othello 11729
de Ferranti, Zani, arr.
Othello 12064
de Filippi, Amedeo 1900–
Twelfth Night 17383, 18213; Settings of
Commemorative Pieces . . . 21183
de Fossa, François, arr.
Much Ado 11622
de Freitas, Frederico 1902–1980
Merry Wives 8840; Twelfth Night 16750
de Frumerie, Gunnar 1908–
Dream 10598
de Gamberini, Elisabett 1731–1765
Also known as Elisabetta de Gambarini
Tempest 15799
de Garaudé, Alexis Albert Gauthier, arr.
Tempest 15422
de Groot, Theo
Troilus 16463
de Haan, Willem
Macbeth 6787
de Hartog, Eduard 1829–1909
Macbeth 7426; Merchant 8691
de Joncières, Victorin 1839–1903
Pseudonym used by Félix Ludger
Rossignol
Hamlet 3018
De Jong, Conrad John 1934–
Troilus 16571
de Jong, E.
Tempest 16023

de Jong, Sarah Margaret 1952–
Measure 7632; Dream 9382; Two
Gentlemen 18379
de Koven, Henry Louis Reginald 1859–1920
As You Like It 1308; Lear 6030; L.L.L. 6373;
Merchant 8541; Tempest 15884; Twelfth
Night 17839, 18111
de Kruyf, Ton 1937–
Sonnet 5 19209; Sonnet 6 19216; Sonnet 7
19221; Sonnet 18 19359; Sonnet 73 19990
De La Borde, Jean-Benjamin-François
1734–1794
Also known as Jean-Benjamin-François de
Laborde
Merry Wives 9246
de la Cour, Anselme, arr.
Dream 10782
de Lagniel, Gordone
[Also known as Mayes Dickens de Lagniel
Donoho]
Macbeth 7261; Merchant 8482
de Lagoanère, Oscar Louis Antoine Ferdinand
1853–1918
Macbeth 6788
de Lalande, Richard
Shrew 14285
de Lano, C. S.
Dream 10599
de Lara, Isidore 1858–1935
Pseudonym used by Isidore Cohen
Lear 6181
De Lisle, Bernard Charles March Phillipps
Sonnet 98 20181
de Löetz, Paul
As You Like It 2002
de Madina, Francisco
Romeo 13182
de Maerschalk, Willy
Merry Wives 8841
De Maistre, [?]   –1875
Known as Mme. la baronne De Maistre and
as Baronne Almaury de Maistre; [possibly
Sylvie De Maistre, pseudonym used by
Suzanne Gabrielle Maitre?]
Antony 367
de Marez Oyens, Gerrit Hendrik 1922–
Merchant 8668; Romeo 13865
de Marez Oyens, Tera 1932–
Macbeth 7375; Richard II 12753
de Meester, Louis
Richard II 12638
de Mihalovich, Ödön Péter József 1842–1929
Romeo 13183; Timon 16378
de Mondonville, Jean-Joseph Cassanéa
1711–1772
Venus 20812
de Montéclair, Michel Pignolet 1667–1737
Also known as Michel Pinolet de Montéclair
Dream 10955

de Orellana, I. A.
Dream 10497
de Paris, Edouard
Winter's Tale 19103, 19104
de Pietri, Stephen
As You Like It 537
de Prosse, Angelo
Much Ado 11065
de Regt, Hendrik 1950–
Measure 7863; P. Pilgrim 20616, 20617,
20618, 20619, 20620; Phoenix 20757;
Venus 20790
de Ridder, Allard 1887–1966
Dream 10600
de Ronssecy, Madam, arr.
Cymbeline 2854
de Roo-Vierdag, Corry 1925–
Dream 9383; Winter's Tale 18729
de Roos, Robert
Merchant 8116
de Ruiter, Wim 1943–
Hamlet 3921
De Sabata, Victor 1892–1967
Merchant 8117
de Sarasate, Pablo, arr. 1844–1908
Romeo 13669
de Saussine, Henri 1859–1940
Merchant 8396
De Smet, Raoul 1936–
Hamlet 4153; Caesar 5544
De Smet, Robin, arr. 1935–
Errors 2035; Othello 12518
de Solla, Isidore
Two Gentlemen 18498
de Souza, F.
Twelfth Night 17840
de Swert, Jules, arr. 1843–1891
Tempest 14779, 14780
de Turckheim, Cyril
Twelfth Night 16751
de Vallombrosa, Amédée   –1968
Twelfth Night 16752
De Vito, Albert Kenneth 1919–
Twelfth Night 17841
Deacon, Edward King
Cymbeline 2819
Deal, Dennis
Hamlet 4092
Deale, Edgar Martin 1902–
As You Like It 1309; Cymbeline 2554;
Othello 12288; Twelfth Night 17842,
18112; Winter's Tale 19039
Dean, Donn, arr.
Dream 9660
Deane, Charles
Dream 10956
Deane, J. H.
Macbeth 7427

Dearle, Edward 1806–1891
Measure 7864; Much Ado 11431
Debussy, Achille Claude 1862–1918
As You Like It 538, 948; Hamlet 3020; Lear
5724, 6071; Dream 10601; Romeo 13670;
Tempest 16217; Settings of Commemorative
Pieces . . . 21298
Dec, Walenty 1857–1938
Twelfth Night 16753
Decourcelle, Maurice Henri, arr.
Romeo 13671, 13672, 13673, 13674
Decsényi, János 1927–
Errors 2064; Macbeth 7377; Romeo 13855;
Tempest 15987
Dedić, Arsen 1938–
Othello 11730
Defesch, Willem 1687–[1757?]
Surname also known as de Fesch, de Veg, de
Feghe, and du Feche
Tempest 14953, 15508, 15885, 15971
Deffès, Louis Pierre 1819–1900
Merchant 8397
Deiro, Pietro, Jr., arr.
Romeo 13584, 13585, 13586
Deis, Carl, arr.
Errors 2036; Hamlet 2971
Dejarnette, Monroe C.
Macbeth 6789; Othello 11731
Déjazet, Ernest, arr.
Othello 12065
Déjazet, Eugène 1819–1880
Romeo 13675
Déjazet, Jules, arr.
Othello 12066
Dejours, Olivier 1950–
Lear 5727
del Campo y Zabaleta, Conrado 1878–1953
Romeo 13636
Del Frate, Raffaele
Tempest 15403
del Maglio, F., arr.
Dream 9661
Delahaye, L. L., arr.
Macbeth 7321; Dream 9662
Delambre, Marcel
Titus 16399
Delamorinière, Guy-Frédéric
Macbeth 6790; Merry Wives 8842; Romeo
13184
Delaney, Robert Mills 1903–1956
As You Like It 1024; Tempest 15645
Delannoy, Marcel François Georges
1898–1962
Coriolanus 2286; Hamlet 3571; 1 Henry IV
4330; 2 Henry IV 4542; Merry Wives 8843;
Dream 10143
Delerue, Georges Henri Jean-Baptiste 1925–
Antony 138; Coriolanus 2287; Hamlet
3021; Caesar 5290; Macbeth 6791; Merry

Wives 8844; Romeo 13185; Tempest 14954;
Twelfth Night 16754; Sonnet 56 19792
Delibes, Clément Philibert Léo, adapter
1836–1891
L.L.L. 6675
Delibes, Clément Philibert Léo, arr.
1836–1891
Merry Wives 8990, 8991
DeLigio, Francis
Macbeth 7262
Delinger, Lawrence Ross 1937–
All's Well 11; Coriolanus 2288; Hamlet
3022, 3023; 1 Henry IV 4331; Caesar 5291;
Lear 5728; Macbeth 6792; Dream 9384,
9385; Othello 11732, 11733, 11734;
Pericles 12555; Richard II 12639; Richard
III 12818; Romeo 13186, 13187; Twelfth
Night 16755; Winter's Tale 18730; Sonnet
18 19360; Settings of Commemorative
Pieces . . . 20836
Delioux, Charles, arr. 1830–1880
Also known as Charles Delioux de Savignac
Dream 9663; Romeo 13640
Delius, Frederick Theodore Albert 1862–1934
As You Like It 1310; Romeo 14077
Dello Joio, Norman Joseph 1913–
Antony 139
Delsart, Jules, arr. 1844–1900
Also known as Jules Delsaert
Othello 12415
Demian, Vilmos 1910–
Richard III 12819
Demol, Pierre
Lear 6151
Demone, Richard
Caesar 5539
Demuth, Norman Frank 1898–1968
All's Well 12; As You Like It 1639; K. John
5586; Macbeth 6793; Dream 10321; Much
Ado 11066; Tempest 14955, 16024; Titus
16400; Twelfth Night 18113; Winter's Tale
19073
Denis, Didier 1947–
Merchant 8118
Denison, Eva
Tempest 14956
Denni, Lucien 1886–1947
Romeo 14142; Settings of Commemorative
Pieces . . . 21019
Dennis, Brian Jonathan Charles 1941–
Tempest 15502, 15534, 15646, 15863
Dennis, Paul, arr.
Two Gentlemen 18572
Dennis, Robert
1 Henry IV 4332; Merry Wives 8845;
Winter's Tale 18731
Dennison, Peter John, arr. 1942–
Tempest 15445

Denny, William Douglas 1910–1980
  Antony 140
Densinger, Charles W.
  Measure 7633
Dent, Edward Joseph 1876–1957
  Merchant 8119; Twelfth Night 17496
Dent, Edward Joseph, arr. 1876–1957
  Hamlet 3854; Dream 10199
Denys, Christopher
  Dream 9386
Denza, Luigi [1846–1922]
  Twelfth Night 18326
Depas, Ernest Lambert Joseph, arr.　–1889
  Othello 12067
Deransart, Louis Édouard　–1905
  Tempest 16025, 16026
Derbès, Jean 1937–1982
  Settings of Commemorative Pieces . . . 21210
Derfin, Josef
  Hamlet 3024; Measure 7634; Richard III
  12820; Timon 16315
Derfin, Josef, arr.
  Caesar 5370
Dermo, John
  Lear 5729
Derzhanovskii, V., arr.
  Romeo 13799
Des Marais, Paul Emile 1920–
  As You Like It 539
Desch, Otmar
  Dream 9387
Desgranges, Félix Pierre Émile Adolphe
  [1866?]–1920
  1 Henry IV 4494; 2 Henry IV 4667; Merry
  Wives 9237
Deshayes, Henri Frédéric [1838?]–1913
  Hamlet 3922
Deshevov, Vladimir Mikhailovich 1889–1955
  Lear 5730; Othello 11735
Desmarets, Henri 1661–1741
  Also known as Henry Desmarets and under
  the surnames Desmarest, Desmarestz, and
  Desmarais
  Venus 20813
Desormes, Louis César 1841–1898
  Pseudonym used by Louis César Marchionne
  Antony 368; Hamlet 3923
Desplat, Alexandre
  Romeo 14043
Desportes, Yvonne Berthe Melitta 1907–
  Caesar 5292
Despréaux, Jean-Étienne 1748–1820
  Othello 12449
Dessau, Paul 1894–1979
  Coriolanus 2388; Sonnet 8 19236; Sonnet
  32 19642; Sonnet 88 20100; Settings of
  Commemorative Pieces . . . 21265
Desslyn, Guy, arr.
  Two Gentlemen 18573

Detoni, Dubravko 1937–
  Macbeth 6794
Détrée, Roberto C.
  Dream 9388; Troilus 16464; Twelfth Night
  16756
Deutsch, Herbert A. 1932–
  Othello 11736; Richard III 12821,
  12822
Deval, Harry
  Merchant 8120; Dream 9389
Devaux, Alfred, arr.
  Merry Wives 9001; Dream 10817; Othello
  12068
Devereaux, L., arr.
  Cymbeline 2654
Devienne, François 1759–1803
  Also known as François de Vienne
  Caesar 5554
Devine, John Kevin 1953–
  Merchant 8669
Devreese, Frederik 1929–
  Merchant 8121
Devriès, Ivan Daniel Marcel Louis 1909–
  Hamlet 3025; Othello 12386; Shrew 14286
d'Evry, Edward
  Sonnet 18 19361
Dexter, Harry
  Much Ado 11432
Dexter, Harry, arr.
  Henry VIII 5195, 5196; Dream 9664, 9665;
  Much Ado 11558; Romeo 13979
Di Domenica, Robert 1927–
  Twelfth Night 17497, 17843, 18114
Diabelli, Anton, arr. 1781–1858
  Othello 12069, 12070, 12071
Diack, John Michael, adapter 1869–1946
  Twelfth Night 17844
Diack, John Michael, arr. 1869–1946
  As You Like It 412, 1435; Cymbeline 2726,
  2727; L.L.L. 6685; Tempest 14781
Diamond, David Leo 1915–
  Romeo 13188, 13902; Tempest 14957,
  15535, 15647, 15821, 15886, 15972,
  16027; Timon 16379; Sonnet 10 19278;
  Sonnet 18 19362; Sonnet 29 19551; Sonnet
  30 19601; Sonnet 36 19671; Sonnet 41
  19703; Sonnet 71 19940; Sonnet 147
  20508; Sonnet 150 20532
Dibdin, Charles 1745–1814
  Errors 2065; Hamlet 4206; Dream 9390;
  Settings of Commemorative Pieces . . . 21020,
  21021, 21024, 21025, 21026, 21121
DiBucci, Michelle
  Twelfth Night 16758
Dick, Charles George Cotsford 1846–1911
  Much Ado 11639; Two Gentlemen 18656
Dick, Charles George Cotsford, in part arr.
  1846–1911
  Merchant 8122

Dicker, Seymour, arr.
  As You Like It 1436; Twelfth Night
  17309
Dickinson, Peter, arr. 1934–
  Antony 301; Cymbeline 2728; Two
  Gentlemen 18574
Dickinson, William E.
  Romeo 13189
Dicks, Ernest Alfred 1865–
  As You Like It 1311; Dream 10322, 10393;
  Two Gentlemen 18499
Dickson, Andrew
  Merchant 8123; Dream 9391
Didam, Otto 1890–1966
  Romeo 13637
Dieckmann, Carl-Heinz 1923–
  Errors 2066
Diegel, Reinhard
  Troilus 16465
Diemer, Emma Lou 1927–
  As You Like It 1312; L.L.L. 6398; Measure
  7865; Much Ado 11433; Twelfth Night
  17845; Sonnet 18 19363
Diemer, Frederick
  Tempest 14958
Dien, Achille, arr.
  Dream 10818
Dienel, Otto, arr.
  Dream 9666
Diercks, John H. 1927–
  Dream 10498
Diesendruck, Tamar 1946–
  Sonnet 43 19723; Sonnet 76 20054
Dietmar-Richter, Kurt
  Much Ado 11067
Dietrich, Albert Hermann 1829–1908
  Cymbeline 2455, 2456
Dietrich, Karl
  As You Like It 540
Dieval, Jack 1920–
  Hamlet 4207
Dignum, Charles [circa 1765]–1827
  Hamlet 3721; Merchant 8434; Settings of
  Commemorative Pieces . . . 21027, 21277
Dilsner, Laurence
  Twelfth Night 17846
d'Indy, Paul Marie Théodore Vincent
  1851–1931
  Antony 313
d'Indy, Paul Marie Théodore Vincent, arr.
  1851–1931
  1 Henry IV 4511; 2 Henry IV 4680; Much
  Ado 11379
Dinjian, Deran Sarkis
  As You Like It 541
Dinn, Freda, arr.
  L.L.L. 6217, 6351, 6399, 6529, 6652
Dinn, Noel
  Tempest 16182

Dinnen, Rod
  1 Henry IV 4333
Dintrich, Michel Albert 1933–
  Merchant 8124
Dirks, Dieter
  Errors 2067
Dittersdorf, Karl Ditters von 1739–1799
  Merry Wives 9006; Tempest 15404
d'Ivry, Paul Xavier Desiré 1829–1903
  Also known as Marquis d'Ivry and under the
  pseudonym 'Richard Yrvid'
  Romeo 13638
Dix, J.
  As You Like It 1640; Merchant 8542
Dixon, Chris
  Richard II 12640
Dixon, Christopher
  Also known as Christopher Dixon of York
  Measure 7866
Dixon, Ed
  Merchant 8398
Dixon, Mike
  Dream 9392
Djonov, Dimiter
  Merchant 8125
Dobrokhotov, B. V., arr.
  Tempest 15381
Dobrzański, Jan
  As You Like It 542
Docker, Robert, arr.
  As You Like It 759
Dodd, J. Douglas, in part arr.
  Romeo 13190
Dodds, James
  Settings of Commemorative Pieces . . .
  20921
Dodge, Walt
  Tempest 14959
Dodgson, Stephen 1924–
  1 Henry IV 4334; 2 Henry IV 4543; 1 Henry
  VI 4850; 2 Henry VI 4892; 3 Henry VI
  4935; L.L.L. 6218; Macbeth 6795; Dream
  10603
Dods, Marcus 1918–1984
  Pericles 12556
[Dodworth, Charles R.]
  Shrew 14287
Dodworth, Charles R.
  K. John 5587; L.L.L. 6219
Dodworth, [Harvey B.]
  Richard II 12641; Twelfth Night 16759
Dodworth, Harvey B.
  Hamlet 3026; Lear 5731; Settings of
  Commemorative Pieces . . . 20837
Döhler, Théodore, arr.
  Also known as Theodor von Döhler
  Macbeth 7322
Dold, Karl Heinz
  Coriolanus 2289

Dolgorukov, Pavel Ivanovich 1787–1845
  Coriolanus 2382
Dollar, Clyde D.
  Macbeth 6796
Dollase, Jürgen
  Settings of Commemorative Pieces . . . 21211
Dolmetsch, Carl Frederick, ed. 1911–
  Anthologies 21354; 21359
Dolmetsch, Eugène Arnold, arr. 1858–1940
  Dream 10200
Domhardt, Gerd
  Merry Wives 8846
Dominique, Claude
  Pseudonym used by Claude Marie Concordel
  Merchant 8126
Dommann, Hanspeter
  Dream 9393; Tempest 14960
Donajowski, Ernest, arr.
  Dream 9667
Donat, Misha
  Lear 5732; Othello 11737
Donceanu, Felicia 1931–
  Measure 7636; Twelfth Night 16760
Donchev, Kiril
  As You Like It 543; Hamlet 3027; Lear
  5733; L.L.L. 6220; Romeo 13191; Shrew
  14288; Twelfth Night 16761
Doniger, Paul E.
  Hamlet 3028; Macbeth 6797
Doniger, Paul E., in part arr.
  Pericles 12557
Donizetti, Gaetano 1797–1848
  Romeo 14192; Settings of Commemorative
  Pieces . . . 20922
Donnell, Edith
  Winter's Tale 18732
Donner, Henrik Otto 1939–
  Richard III 12823; Sonnet 19 19463; Sonnet
  66 19910; Sonnet 135 20441; Sonnet 136
  20443
Donovan, David
  Richard III 12824
Donovan, Tom
  As You Like It 544
Dooley, Roger B.
  Settings of Commemorative Pieces . . .
  21028
Doolittle, Quenten 1925–
  Cymbeline 2457; Measure 7637; Twelfth
  Night 18115
Doppler, Árpád 1857–1927
  Much Ado 11361
Doppler, Charles, arr. 1826–
  Romeo 13676
Doppler, J. H., arr.
  Merry Wives 9034
Doran, Matt Higgins 1921–
  Sonnet 18 19364; Sonnet 71 19941; Sonnet
  128 20390

Dorati, Antal, arr. 1906–
  Romeo 14080
Doret, Gustave 1866–1943
  Caesar 5293
Dörffel, Alfred, arr. 1821–1905
  Merry Wives 9035, 9036; Othello 12072
Doria, Georges
  Hamlet 3924
Doris, Hubert
  Henry V 4712; 1 Henry VI 4851; 2 Henry VI
  4893; 3 Henry VI 4936; Richard III 12825
Dorn, Edouard 1838–1923
  Pseudonym used by Joseph Leopold Roeckel
  Merchant 8785; Tempest 16028
Dorn, Edouard, arr. 1838–1923
  Pseudonym used by Joseph Leopold Roeckel
  Merry Wives 9037; Dream 10819; Othello
  12073; Shrew 14575, 14576
Dorn, Heinrich 1804–1892
  Caesar 5294
Dorn, Theo
  Shrew 14289; Troilus 16466; Twelfth Night
  16762; Two Gentlemen 18380
Doron, Huldah
  Winter's Tale 18733
Dorren, Joep
  Cymbeline 2458
D'Orso, F.
  Hamlet 3925
Douard, Alexis, arr.   –1896
  Hamlet 3642
Doubrava, Jaroslav 1909–1960
  Dream 10144
Dougherty, Mervyn
  Caesar 5295
Douglas, Clive
  Troilus 16467
Douglas, David
  Winter's Tale 18931
Douglas, Dennis
  As You Like It 545
Douglas, Ernest, arr.
  Dream 9668
Douglas, Hugh A.
  Romeo 14044
Douglas, Johnny, arr.
  Cymbeline 2729
Douglas, Keith, arr. 1903–
  Romeo 14081
Douglas, Roy, arr.
  As You Like It 905; Henry V 4810; Othello
  11704; Tempest 16138
Douliez, Jean François
  Macbeth 6798
Doury, Pierre Charles
  Hamlet 3029
Douty, Nicholas 1870–1955
  L.L.L. 6400; Twelfth Night 17498

DoVale, Dove K. M.
  Hamlet 4208
[Dowland, John] [1562–1626]
  P. Pilgrim 20621
Doyle, Pat
  Twelfth Night 16763
Draeseke, Felix August Bernhard 1835–1913
  Caesar 5500, 5501
Draghi, Giovanni Battista
  [circa 1640]–1708
  Tempest 15405
Drake, Addie H.
  Romeo 13903
Drake, Mervyn
  Lear 5734
Drakeford, Richard Jeremy 1936–
  As You Like It 546; L.L.L. 6401; Tempest
  14961
Drakeford, Richard Jeremy, in part arr. 1936–
  Lear 5735; Macbeth 6799; Merchant 8127;
  Dream 9394; Twelfth Night 16764; Winter's
  Tale 18734
Drayton, Harry U.
  Twelfth Night 17499, 17847
Drayton, Paul
  L.L.L. 6221
Drdla, Franz
  Tempest 16029
Dremliuha, Mykola Vasyl'evych 1917–
  Sonnet 18 19365; Sonnet 30 19602; Sonnet
  31 19634; Sonnet 60 19821; Sonnet 81
  20066
Dress, Michael [1935]–1975
  Antony 141; Hamlet 3030; Richard III
  12826; Tempest 14962, 16183; Titus 16427
Dressel, Erwin
  Tempest 14963
Dressler, Friedrich August   –1919
  Macbeth 7263
Drew, Geoffrey
  Hamlet 3031
Drewniak, Horst
  Hamlet 3032; Twelfth Night 16765
Drewnick, Eberhard
  Much Ado 11068
Drexler, J., arr.
  Merry Wives 9038, 9039
Dreyer, Ernst, arr.
  Merry Wives 9040
Dreyfuss, Randolph
  Twelfth Night 16766
Driessler, Johannes 1921–
  Henry VIII 5080
Driffield, Edward Townshend 1851–
  Dream 10909; Twelfth Night 17848
Dring, Madeleine 1923–1977
  As You Like It 1025, 1313, 1641; L.L.L.
  6402; Measure 7867; Twelfth Night 17500,
  17849; P. Pilgrim 20622

Driver, Roger
  Othello 11738
Drogin, Barry J., in part arr. 1960–
  Twelfth Night 16767
Dronsfield, John
  Merry Wives 8847
Drouet, Jean-Pierre André 1935–
  Lear 5736; Othello 11739
Drouet, Louis François Philippe, arr.
  1792–1873
  Othello 12074
Druesedow, Jean
  Twelfth Night 16768
Druick, Don 1945–
  Winter's Tale 18951
Drury, Marian, in part arr.
  Shrew 14290
Du Bois, François Clément Théodore, arr.
  1837–1924
  Also known as Théodore Dubois
  Hamlet 3643
du Plessis, Hubert L.
  Twelfth Night 17501, 17850, 18116
Dubiel, Jerzy
  Twelfth Night 16769
Dubinsky, Leon
  Much Ado 11069
Dubois, Jean-Baptiste
  Macbeth 7264
Dubovský, Milan
  Lear 5737; Othello 11740
Ducat, Vivian
  Dream 9395
Ducelle, Paul
  Dream 10604
Duchemin, Charles Jean Batiste 1827–
  As You Like It 1314; Settings of
  Commemorative Pieces . . . 21029
Duclos, Pierre 1929–1973
  Macbeth 7428
Dudarenko, Aleksander
  Hamlet 3033; Dream 9396
Dudley, Grahame
  As You Like It 547
Dudley, Jack
  Macbeth 6800
Duey, Philip, arr.
  Two Gentlemen 18575
Dufaure, Albert, arr.
  Dream 9669, 9670
Duff, Arthur K.
  Two Gentlemen 18500
Duffy, John 1928–
  All's Well 13; Antony 142; As You Like It
  548; Errors 2068; Coriolanus 2290; Hamlet
  3034, 3035, 3036, 3037; 1 Henry IV 4335; 2
  Henry IV 4544, 4545; Henry V 4713; Henry
  VIII 4974; Caesar 5296; Lear 5738; Macbeth
  6801, 6802, 7513; Measure 7638; Merchant

Duffy, John (*cont.*)
8128, 8129; Merry Wives 8848; Dream
9397, 9398; Much Ado 11070; Othello
11741; Richard II 12642, 12643; Romeo
13192; Shrew 14291, 14292; Tempest
15406; Titus 16401; Twelfth Night 16770
Dufour, Denis
Sonnet 107 20270
Dufour, Louis, arr. –1908
Tempest 15494
Dugend, Enno 1915–1980
As You Like It 549; Hamlet 3038; Caesar
5297; Lear 5739, 5740, 5741; Macbeth
6803, 6804, 6805; Merchant 8130; Merry
Wives 8849; Dream 9399; Othello 11742;
Romeo 13193; Shrew 14293; Tempest
14964; Twelfth Night 16771
Duggan, Joseph Francis 1817–[1894]
Also wrote under the pseudonym 'Fred Beyer'
As You Like It 550; Dream 10378, 10394,
10468; Tempest 15503, 15822; Two
Gentlemen 18501
Duggan, Joseph Francis, arr. 1817–[1894]
Also wrote under the pseudonym 'Fred Beyer'
Tempest 14782
Dugnani, D., arr.
Hamlet 4148
Duhamel, Antoine 1925–
Sonnet 8 19237
Duit, Erke
Richard III 12827
Dukas, Paul Abraham 1865–1935
Lear 6072; Tempest 14965, 15407
Duke, John
[John Woods Duke (1899–1984)?]
Sonnet 29 19552
Duke, Lewis Byron
As You Like It 1026; Measure 7868;
Merchant 8543; Sonnet 73 19991
Dula, Henry, arr. 1920–
Also writes under the pseudonym 'Lynn
Palmer'
Cymbeline 2730; Dream 9671; Romeo
13677; Two Gentlemen 18576
Dulac, Maurice
Settings of Commemorative Pieces . . . 21030
Dulay, Arthur, in part arr.
Antony 143; As You Like It 551; Hamlet
3039; Macbeth 6806; Merchant 8131;
Richard II 12644; Shrew 14294
Dulay, Arthur, arr.
Henry VIII 4981
Dulova, V., arr.
Romeo 13800
Dumitrescu, Ion 1913–
Hamlet 3040; Lear 5742; Macbeth 6807;
Merry Wives 8850
Dumond, Arnaud Jacques Victor
Othello 11743

Dumoulin, [?]
Romeo 13904
Dunaev, S., arr.
Dream 9672
Duncan, Chester Thomas Alexander
Winchester 1913–
Coriolanus 2291; Measure 7869; Troilus
16468; Winter's Tale 18735; Settings of
Commemorative Pieces . . . 20838
Duncan, Martin
Pericles 12558; Shrew 14295; Tempest 14966
Duncan, Timothy W. 1952–
Hamlet 3041; Merchant 8132; Dream 9400,
9401; Twelfth Night 16772
Duncan, Trevor 1924–
Macbeth 7514
Duncan, William Edmondstoune 1866–1920
As You Like It 1027; Cymbeline 2663;
Hamlet 3714, 3850; L.L.L. 6530; Twelfth
Night 17851; Sonnet 29 19553; Sonnet 30
19603; Sonnet 60 19822; Sonnet 87 20085;
Sonnet 128 20391
Duncan, William Edmondstoune, arr. 1866–1920
Tempest 14717, 14783
Duncombe, William Duncombe Van Der Horst
–[before 1951]
Much Ado 11071; Twelfth Night 17502
Dunhill, Thomas Frederick 1877–1946
As You Like It 1315, 1642; Henry VIII
5081; Merchant 8544; Dream 10395,
10605, 10606, 10607, 10941; Much Ado
11434; Tempest 15536, 15648, 15649,
15887; Twelfth Night 17503, 17852,
18117; Two Gentlemen 18502
Dunhill, Thomas Frederick, arr.
1877–1946
Much Ado 11535, 11536; Othello 12251
Dunn, Anita Sutcliffe
As You Like It 1643
Dunn, James Philip 1884–1936
As You Like It 1316, 1644; Twelfth Night
17853; P. Pilgrim 20623
Dunn, John
Hamlet 3926
Dunn, Tom
L.L.L. 6326
Dünnebier, Otto
Tempest 14967
Dünnwald, Josef
Macbeth 6808; Shrew 14296
Dunstan, Ralph 1857–1933
Dream 10396
Dunstan, Ralph, arr. 1857–1933
Tempest 15812
Dunstan, Ralph, ed. 1857–1933
Anthologies 21321; 21322
Duparc, Marie Eugène Henri Fouques
1848–1933
Cymbeline 2512; Lear 5990

Dupont, Gabriel Édouard Xavier 1878–1914
 Hamlet 4209
Duprato, Jules 1827–1892
 Hamlet 4210
Dupré, Desmond John, arr. 1916–1974
 Tempest 15057
Dupré, Marcel Jean Jules –1971
 Lear 5743
Duprez, Gilbert-Louis 1806–1896
 Romeo 13642
Dupuis, Sylvain 1856–1931
 Macbeth 7429
Dupuy, Jean-Baptiste-Edouard-Louis
 [circa 1770]–1822
 Hamlet 3042
Durand, Émile 1830–1903
 Hamlet 4211
Dure, Robert George 1934–
 Lear 6034
Durek, Josef S., arr.
 Much Ado 11349
Durkee, Norman
 Merry Wives 8851; Richard III 12828
Durst, Matthias 1815–1875
 Richard III 12829
Dussek, Jan Ladislav 1760–1812
 Othello 12536
Duthoit, William James, arr.
 Errors 2210; Romeo 13587; Shrew 14603
Dutkiewicz, Andrzej
 Two Gentlemen 18381
Duval, Frank 1942–
 Twelfth Night 16773
Duvernoy, Henry, arr.
 Macbeth 7323
Duvernoy, Victor Alphonse 1842–1907
 Tempest 15408
Dvarionas, Balys Dominiko 1904–1972
 Othello 11744; Twelfth Night 16774
Dvoirin, Meer Iurmovich 1910–
 Othello 11745; Romeo 13194
Dvořák, Antonín Leopold 1841–1904
 Othello 12387; Romeo 13905; Twelfth Night
 17384
Dvořák, Josef
 Winter's Tale 18736
Dvorine, Shura
 1 Henry IV 4461; 2 Henry IV 4627; Romeo
 14088
Dvorkin, Judith
 Tempest 14968
Dyal, Myron
 Caesar 5298
Dyce-Sombre, Mary Anne
 Also known as Hon. Mary Anne Jervis and as
 Mrs. David O. Dyce-Sombre
 As You Like It 1028
Dyer, Chouteau
 Macbeth 6809

Dyer-Bennet, Richard 1913–
 Winter's Tale 18737; Settings of
 Commemorative Pieces . . . 20839, 20840
Dyson, George 1883–1964
 Henry V 4799; L.L.L. 6531; Winter's Tale
 18998
Dzerzhinskii, Ivan Ivanovich 1909–1978
 Shrew 14297
Dzierżanowski, Maciej
 Twelfth Night 16775

E

Eakin, Charles [1927–]
 Tempest 14969
Earhart, Will 1871–1960
 Henry VIII 5238
Earhart, Will, arr. 1871–1960
 Macbeth 7565; Richard III 13073
Earl, David
 Hamlet 3572
Earle, Frederick, arr.
 Much Ado 11537
Earle, William Benson
 Macbeth 7400; Merchant 8421; Dream
 10499; Twelfth Night 18077
Earnest, David
 Measure 7639
Easdale, Brian 1909–
 Hamlet 3043; Macbeth 6810; Merchant
 8133, 8134; Much Ado 11435, 11611;
 Romeo 13195
Easson, James 1895–
 Tempest 15537, 15650
East, Jack F. 1944–
 Macbeth 6811
Eastland, Basil F. R.
 Dream 9402
Eastman, Julius
 Othello 11746
Eastwood, Thomas Hugh 1922–
 Hamlet 3044; K. John 5588; Shrew 14568;
 Settings of Commemorative Pieces . . .
 20841
Eaton, John Charles 1935–
 Tempest 15409
Ebbekke, Hans
 Merchant 8135
Ebdon, Thomas 1738–1811
 Cymbeline 2861
Ebel, Otto, arr.
 Merry Wives 9041
Eben, Petr 1929–
 Hamlet 3045; Venus 20784; Settings of
 Commemorative Pieces . . . 20842
Eberlin, Johann Ernst 1702–1762
 Richard III 13082

Ebers, Walter, arr.
  Merry Wives 9042
Ebert, Hans
  Hamlet 3046; Titus 16402
Eberwein, Traugott Maximilian
  1775–1831
  Macbeth 6812, 7430
Ebner, Emil
  Twelfth Night 16776
[Eccles, John] [(circa 1668)–1735]
  Merchant 8726
Eccles, [John] [(circa 1668)–1735]
  Measure 7640
Eccles, John [circa 1668]–1735
  Hamlet 3047; Henry V 4840; Macbeth
  6813; Troilus 16469; Twelfth Night 18268
Eccleston, Colleen 1958–
  As You Like It 552; L.L.L. 6670
Ecke, Frederick W.
  Lear 5744; Shrew 14298
Ecke, Frederick W., in part arr.
  Merchant 8136; Much Ado 11072
Ecke, Frederick W., arr.
  Cymbeline 2731; Merry Wives 9043; Much
  Ado 11538
Eckerberg, Sixten 1909–
  Much Ado 11073
Eckert, Karl
  Errors 2069; Twelfth Night 16777
Eckert, Louis V.
  Settings of Commemorative Pieces . . . 21122
Eckstein, Gary
  Twelfth Night 16778
Eckstein, Maxwell 1905–1974
  Settings of Commemorative Pieces . . . 21123
Eckstein, Maxwell, arr. 1905–1974
  Dream 9673
Edander, Gunnar 1942–
  Winter's Tale 19137
Eddy, Hiram Clarence, arr. 1851–1937
  Dream 9674
Edelmann, Toni 1945–
  Lear 6022; Dream 9403; Othello 11747,
  12217, 12235, 12289; Sonnet 66 19911
Eder, Helmut
  Hamlet 3048; Lear 5745; Merchant 8137;
  Dream 9404; Much Ado 11074; Othello
  11748; Richard II 12645; Troilus 16470
Edeson, Donald John Joseph Scott
  As You Like It 1317; Merchant 8545;
  Twelfth Night 17854
Edgar, Edward
  As You Like It 1841
Edgerton, Brian
  Richard III 12830
Edis, Stephen
  Antony 144
Edmonds, Paul N. 1873–1939
  Twelfth Night 17855; P. Pilgrim 20624

Edmunds, Christopher Montague 1899–
  Sonnet 71 19942
Edmunds, John 1913–1986
  Also known as John St. Edmunds
  As You Like It 1029; Hamlet 3703, 3755;
  L.L.L. 6403; Measure 7870; Twelfth Night
  17504, 17856
Edmunds, John, adapter 1913–1986
  Also known as John St. Edmunds
  Anthologies 21362
Edmunds, John, arr. 1913–1986
  Also known as John St. Edmunds
  Hamlet 2911; Dream 10201, 10202, 10203,
  10204; Tempest 14718
Edmundson, Garth 1895–
  Measure 7871; Tempest 16030
Edwards, Allan
  Twelfth Night 16779
Edwards, Edward Bartholomew, ed.
  1873–1948
  Anthologies 21318
Edwards, Franklin Ryan
  Hamlet 3049; Tempest 14970
Edwards, Gus Simon 1879–1945
  Romeo 14089
Edwards, Leo 1886–1978
  As You Like It 1030; Measure 7872
Edwards, Paul Christison 1955–
  Measure 7873; Much Ado 11436
Edwards, Richard 1524–1566
  Also known as Richard Edwardes
  Romeo 14193
Edwards, Stephen
  As You Like It 553
Edwards, Walter Strong
  Twelfth Night 17857
Edwin, John
  Timon 16377
Effinger, Cecil S. 1914–
  L.L.L. 6222
Egan, Daniel
  Winter's Tale 18738
Egan, Paul
  Measure 7641
Egerbladh, Birgitta 1956–
  Tempest 14971
Eggen, Arne 1881–1955
  Cymbeline 2513; Winter's Tale 19141
Eggenhofer, Werner
  Lear 5746
Eggert, Moritz
  Settings of Commemorative Pieces . . . 20843
Egorov, Aleksandr Aleksanrovich, arr.
  1887–1959
  Winter's Tale 18878
Ehl, Albrecht 1939–
  As You Like It 554; Hamlet 3050; Lear
  5747; Dream 9405; Twelfth Night 16780;
  Settings of Commemorative Pieces . . . 20844

Ehlert, Louis 1825–1884
  Winter's Tale 19105
Ehret, Walter Charles, arr. 1918–
  As You Like It 1437; Shrew 14604
Ehricht, Thomas
  Shrew 14299
Ehrlich, C. F. 1807–1887
  Othello 12389
Ehrström, Jarl Otto Sigurd 1891–
  As You Like It 555
Eichhorn, Bernhard 1904–
  Antony 145; Errors 2070; Cymbeline 2459;
  Hamlet 3051, 4093; Macbeth 6815, 6816;
  Much Ado 11075; Othello 11749; Richard
  III 12831; Tempest 14972
Eichhorn, Bernhard, arr. 1904–
  Dream 10820
Eichhorn, Gregor
  Hamlet 3052; Macbeth 6817; Shrew 14300;
  Winter's Tale 18739
Eiges, Oleg Konstantinovich 1905–
  Twelfth Night 18118
Eilenberg, Robert Braun 1873–
  Hamlet 3927
Eisenstein, Linda
  Hamlet 4094
Eisler, Hanns 1898–1962
  Hamlet 3053, 3695; Measure 8032; Sonnet
  66 19912
Eisrich, Karl Traugott 1770–[1835]
  Dream 10776
Ėkhala, O.
  Romeo 13196
Ekimovskii, Viktor, arr.
  Hamlet 3414
El-Dabh', Halim Abdul Messieh 1921–
  Also known as Halim El-Dabh
  Antony 266
Eldh, Kiki
  Dream 9406; Twelfth Night 16781
Elfers, Konrad
  K. John 5589; Lear 5748; Macbeth 6818;
  Troilus 16471
Elgar, Edward William 1857–1934
  Cymbeline 2876; 1 Henry IV 4476; 2 Henry
  IV 4651; Henry V 4817; Lear 5991; Othello
  12514; Romeo 14194; Tempest 16251,
  16252; Settings of Commemorative
  Pieces . . . 20923
Eliáš, Pavel
  Dream 9407
Elias, Sheldon 1945–
  As You Like It 556; Settings of
  Commemorative Pieces . . . 20845
Elkamp, H. 1812–1862
  As You Like It 1645
Ella, [John] [1802–1888]
  L.L.L. 6363

Ellerton, John Lodge 1801–1873
  Born John Lodge
  Dream 10356
Elling, Catharinus 1858–1942
  Dream 9408; Twelfth Night 16782, 17505,
  17858, 18119; Sonnet 18 19366; Sonnet 31
  19635
Ellingford, Herbert Frederick, arr. 1876–1966
  Merry Wives 9044; Othello 11718
Ellington, Edward Kennedy 1899–1974
  Also known as Duke Ellington
  Antony 314; Hamlet 3928; Henry V 4819;
  Caesar 5502; Macbeth 7431; Dream 10608;
  Othello 12390; Romeo 13906, 14195;
  Shrew 14656; Timon 16316; Settings of
  Commemorative Pieces . . . 21124
Elliot, Charles S., arr.
  Dream 9675
Elliot, Muriel
  As You Like It 557; L.L.L. 6404
Elliott, James 1783–1856
  Measure 7874; Two Gentlemen 18503
Elliott, James William, arr. 1833–1915
  Tempest 14719
Elliott, Mark A.
  Merry Wives 8852
Elliott, Percy
  Dream 10609
Elliott, William
  Henry V 4714; Othello 11750; Winter's Tale
  18740
Ellis, Arthur
  Tempest 14973
Ellis, Cathleen
  Dream 9409
Ellis, E. Vicki
  Twelfth Night 16783
Ellis, Osian 1928–
  Twelfth Night 17859
Elliston, Marion
  As You Like It 949; Cymbeline 2514; Hamlet
  3573; Merry Wives 9007; Dream 10145;
  Tempest 15410; Winter's Tale 18932
Elmore, Robert Hall 1913–
  Caesar 5491
Elrington, S. N., Jr.
  Dream 10910
Elsea, Peter 1947–
  1 Henry IV 4336; Macbeth 6819, 6820,
  6821
Elsner, Herbert
  Shrew 14301
Elsner, Horst
  Lear 5749; Shrew 14302
Elton, Antony 1935–
  As You Like It 1318; Merchant 8546;
  Twelfth Night 17506; Sonnet 71 19943
Elwell, Herbert 1898–1974
  Dream 10447

Elwyn-Edwards, Dilys
    Née Roberts
    Twelfth Night 17507, 17860
Emanuel, Louis, arr.
    As You Like It 413; Macbeth 6979; Merry
    Wives 8880; Settings of Commemorative
    Pieces . . . 21125
Emge, Adolf
    Twelfth Night 16784
Emmerich, Robert 1836–1891
    Cymbeline 2664
Emmerson, Simon Thomas 1950–
    Hamlet 4067; Dream 10500; Tempest
    15651; Twelfth Night 17508; Sonnet 30
    19604
Emmert, Adam Josef 1765–1812
    Tempest 15411
Emmert, František
    Two Gentlemen 18459
Emrich, Jürgen
    Twelfth Night 16785
Emrick, George
    P. Pilgrim 20625
Ender, Edmund Sereno
    As You Like It 1031
Ender, Fr., arr.
    Dream 9676
Enders, Harvey, arr.
    As You Like It 1736
Endsley, Gerald, arr.
    Dream 10205
Enfield, Patrick Keen 1929–
    As You Like It 1319; Cymbeline 2665; L.L.L.
    6405, 6406; Tempest 15652, 15653; Two
    Gentlemen 18504
Engel, A. Lehman 1910–1982
    Hamlet 3054; 1 Henry IV 4337; Henry VIII
    4975; Caesar 5299; Macbeth 6822; Measure
    7642; Romeo 13197; Shrew 14303;
    Tempest 14974; Twelfth Night 16786
Engel, Paul 1920–
    Measure 8028; Dream 10610
Engelbach, Jerry, in part arr.
    Pericles 12559
Engelbogen, Eric
    Antony 146
Engelmann, H.
    As You Like It 1884
Engelmann, Hans Ulrich 1921–
    As You Like It 558; Hamlet 3055, 3056,
    3574, 4095; Macbeth 6823; Merchant
    8436; Tempest 14975, 14976, 16199;
    Twelfth Night 16787
Engerman, John 1950–
    Twelfth Night 16788
Engleberg, Niels Cary
    As You Like It 950
Engleman, Joseph, arr.
    Lear 6093

Englert, Giuseppe G. 1927–
    Macbeth 7265
Englund, Adolf
    Dream 10611
Enke, Heinrich, arr. 1881–1859
    Also known as Heinrich Encke
    Hamlet 3145; Caesar 5509; Merry Wives
    9045
Enna, August 1860–1939
    Antony 369, 370
Enos, Joseph Thomas 1911–
    Sonnet 27 19520; Sonnet 30 19605
Enright, Nick
    Hamlet 3057
Epstein, Alvin 1926–
    Merchant 8547
Epstein, David Mayer 1930–
    Caesar 5300
Epstein, Paul Arnold 1938–
    Macbeth 6824
Epsten, Chip
    Richard III 12832
Ercolano, Christiaan
    Romeo 13198
Ergmann, Auguste, arr.
    Dream 10821
Erickson, Frank, arr. 1923–
    Romeo 13588, 13980
Eriksson, Gunnar
    Hamlet 3058
Eriksson, Josef 1872–1957
    As You Like It 559, 1032, 1320, 1592,
    1821
Erkel, Gyula
    Winter's Tale 18741
Erlanger, David
    Errors 2071; Much Ado 11076; Twelfth
    Night 16789
Ermel, Alexis, arr.
    Romeo 13678
Ernemann, Moritz
    As You Like It 1321
Ernest, Gustav
    Dream 10612
Ernryd, Bengt 1943–
    Richard III 12833; Twelfth Night
    16790
Ernst, Édouard, arr.
    Othello 12075
Ernst, Heinrich Wilhelm, arr. 1814–1865
    Dream 10822; Othello 12076
Erskine, Charles
    Sonnet 18 19367
Erskine, Peter 1954–
    Dream 9410; Richard II 12646
Erskine, Robert
    As You Like It 560
Erzakovich, Boris Girshevich 1908–
    Othello 11751

Escher, Rudolf George 1912–1980
  Sonnet 43 19713
Esperon, Manuel
  Romeo 14045
Esposito, Michele 1855–1929
  Othello 12391
Estes, Charles 1946–
  As You Like It 562, 563; Errors 2072;
  Hamlet 3059; 1 Henry IV 4338; Caesar
  5301; L.L.L. 6223; Macbeth 6825; Merry
  Wives 8853; Dream 9411, 9412; Much Ado
  11077, 11078; Romeo 13199; Shrew
  14304; Tempest 14977; Twelfth Night
  16791; Two Gentlemen 18382
Estrada, Carlos, in part arr. 1909–1970
  Caesar 5302
Esty, Robert Malcolm, III
  Twelfth Night 18279
Ettinger, Max Markus Wolf 1874–1951
  Merry Wives 8854; Twelfth Night
  18214
Ettling, Émile, arr.
  Hamlet 3644; Macbeth 7324
Eubanks, Charles G. 1942–
  Othello 12392
Evans, Archibald, arr.
  Merchant 8302
Evans, C., arr.
  Othello 12519
Evans, Colin
  Macbeth 6826
Evans, D. T.
  Two Gentlemen 18505
Evans, David
  Othello 11752
Evans, David Emlyn 1843–1913
  Merchant 8437
Evans, Edward G., Jr.
  1 Henry IV 4478; 2 Henry IV 4653; Merry
  Wives 9218; Settings of Commemorative
  Pieces . . . 21126
Evans, Edwin, Sr., arr. 1844–1923
  Lear 6060; Merry Wives 9046; Dream 9677;
  Much Ado 11350; Settings of
  Commemorative Pieces . . . 20965
Evans, George, arr.
  As You Like It 1218; Much Ado 11589
Evans, Howard, arr.
  Romeo 13589
Evans, Jack
  Twelfth Night 16792
Evans, Samuel
  Merchant 8438
Evdokimov, V., arr.
  Shrew 14644
Evett, Robert, arr. 1922–1975
  Twelfth Night 18316
Evetts, Edgar Thomas, arr.
  P. Pilgrim 20709

Ewan, Murray
  Twelfth Night 16793
Ewing, M. Porteous
  Richard II 12758
Ewing, Montague
  Dream 10614
Ewing, Montague, arr.
  Romeo 13981
Eyser, Eberhard 1932–
  Macbeth 7432
Eytle, Tommy
  Measure 7643

F

Fabiani, Viktor
  Othello 11753; Twelfth Night 16794
Fabrizi, Vincenzo 1764–[after 1812]
  Tempest 16253
Faccio, Francesco Antonio 1840–1891
  Hamlet 3575
Faerber, Adolf, arr.
  Hamlet 4189
Faerber, Douglas K.
  Hamlet 3060; Macbeth 6827; Troilus 16472
Faerber, Jörg 1929–
  Hamlet 3061; Shrew 14305; Twelfth Night
  16795; Two Gentlemen 18383
Fagge, Arthur, arr. 1864–1943
  As You Like It 414, 1438
Faktorovich, Natan Grigor'evich 1909–1967
  Romeo 13200
Falchi, Stanislao 1851–1922
  Caesar 5504
Falk, Julien Isaac
  K. John 5590; Macbeth 6828
Falk, Richard 1878–1949
  Twelfth Night 17385
Fallmann, W. A., arr.
  Also known as W. A. Fallman
  Othello 12077, 12190
Fallon, Larry
  Sonnet 18 19368
Fanciulli, Francesco 1853–1915
  Othello 12393
Fane, John 1784–1859
  Also known as The Earl of Westmoreland
  and as Lord Burghersh
  Tempest 16165; P. Pilgrim 20626
Fanimokun, N. O. A.
  L.L.L. 6407
Faning, Joseph Eaton 1850–1927
  Merchant 8439
Fantapié, Henri Claude Émile 1938–
  Titus 16403
Fantel, Hans
  Much Ado 11079

Farberman, Harold 1929–
    Twelfth Night 17726
Fardig, Elsie
    Richard III 12834
Farina, Guido 1903–
    Twelfth Night 17386
Farinelli, Giuseppe 1769–1836
    Pseudonym used by Giuseppe Francesco Finco
    Romeo 14196
Faris, Alexander
    Much Ado 11080; Romeo 14090
Farkas, Ferenc 1905–
    As You Like It 564, 1033, 1322, 1646,
    1842, 1885; Hamlet 3062; Macbeth 6829;
    Romeo 13201; Shrew 14306; Timon 16317;
    Twelfth Night 16796
Farland, Alfred A., arr. 1864–1954
    Cymbeline 2732
Farley, Roland 1892–1932
    L.L.L. 6532
Farmer, Henry, arr.
    Dream 9678; Othello 12078
Farmer, Thomas   –1688
    Troilus 16473
Farnell, George H., arr.
    Dream 9679
Färnlöf, Bertil
    Romeo 13202
Farquhar, David Andross 1928–
    Lear 5750; Measure 7644; Dream 9413,
    10350, 10501; Richard III 12835; Romeo
    13203; Tempest 14978, 15654; Twelfth
    Night 18120; Winter's Tale 18974
Farquharson, James M.
    Hamlet 3063
Farr, Ian
    Tempest 14979
Farran, Ramon
    Settings of Commemorative Pieces . . .
    21031
Farrant, George
    Much Ado 11437
Farrar, Ernest Bristow 1885–1918
    As You Like It 1323; Henry V 4821; Twelfth
    Night 17861; Winter's Tale 18975
Farrar, Geraldine, arr. 1882–1967
    Romeo 13876
Farrell, Colin
    As You Like It 565
Farrell, Dennis M. 1940–
    Sonnet 1 19179
Farwell, Arthur George 1877–1952
    As You Like It 1964; Merry Wives 9248
Farwell, Arthur George, in part arr.
    1877–1952
    Tempest 15412; Settings of Commemorative
    Pieces . . . 20924
Fasanotti, F., arr.
    Othello 12079

Fátyol, Tibor
    Twelfth Night 16797
Faulkes, William 1863–1933
    As You Like It 1034, 1647; Hamlet 3756;
    Henry VIII 5082; Measure 7875; Merchant
    8548; Much Ado 11438; Othello 12290;
    Twelfth Night 17509, 17862, 18121; Two
    Gentlemen 18506
Fauré, Gabriel Urbain 1845–1924
    Caesar 5303; Merchant 8727, 8766
Fauss, M. Michael 1950–
    Dream 9414, 9415; Othello 11754, 12218,
    12236; Romeo 13204
Favarger, Réné
    Dream 10615; Tempest 16031
Favarger, Réné, arr.
    Merry Wives 9047; Dream 10823, 10824;
    Romeo 13679
Favre, Pierre
    Hamlet 3064
Fawcett, E., arr.
    Tempest 14784
Fax, Mark
    Richard III 12836
Fay, Thomas
    Romeo 13205, 13206
Fazarro, Susan
    Tempest 15413
Fearis, J. S.
    Dream 10616
Federle, Hel[muth] M.
    Titus 16428
Fehmel, Klaus 1932–1980
    Twelfth Night 17387
Feidje, Aasmund
    As You Like It 566
Feingold, Ellen Bower 1930–
    Also known as Ellen Bower
    Lear 5751; Merchant 8138; Dream 9416;
    Twelfth Night 16798
Fekete, Ivan
    Merry Wives 8855
Fekete, Zoltan, arr. 1909–
    Tempest 16129
Felciano, Richard James 1930–
    Measure 7876; Merchant 8549; Merry
    Wives 9204
Fel'dman, K. V.
    Winter's Tale 19106
Felix, Julie
    Twelfth Night 18122
Fellmer, Helmut
    As You Like It 567
Fellowes, Edmund Horace, arr. 1870–1951
    As You Like It 415, 416, 1439, 1440, 1441
Fellows, George William 1939–
    Hamlet 3578
Fén Zhōnghuá 1926–
    Merry Wives 8856

Fenby, Eric William, arr. 1906–
  Romeo 14082, 14083
Fenigstein, Claude S.
  Dream 10957; Othello 11755
Fennimore, Joseph 1940–
  As You Like It 1035; Twelfth Night 17510;
  Sonnet 19 19464; Sonnet 29 19554; Sonnet
  73 19992; Sonnet 76 20044; Sonnet 115
  20302
Fenollosa, W. S.
  As You Like It 1648
Fenton, George
  Antony 147; As You Like It 568; Hamlet
  3065; Caesar 5304; Macbeth 6830; Measure
  7645; Merchant 8139; Much Ado 11081;
  Twelfth Night 16799
Fenwick, Edward John 1932–
  1 Henry IV 4339
Fenwick, Edward John, in part arr. 1932–
  As You Like It 569
Fenwick, Edward John, arr. 1932–
  Hamlet 3596
Ferber, Richard
  Dream 10617
Ferenczy, Oto 1921–
  Sonnet 43 19714; Sonnet 128 20392;
  Sonnet 147 20509
Fergus, John 1767–1825
  Cymbeline 2862
Fergus, M. Phyllis, in part arr.
  Shrew 14307
Fergus, Malcolm C.
  Romeo 13207
Feritto, John
  Shrew 14308
Fernström, John 1897–1961
  Hamlet 3066; Merchant 8140; Dream 9417;
  Shrew 14309
Ferrante, Aurtur, arr. 1921–
  Romeo 13590
Ferrari, Gustave 1872–1948
  Hamlet 3067
Ferrata, Giuseppe 1865–1928
  L.L.L. 6408, 6533
Ferrazano, Anthony Joseph
  Sonnet 18 19369
Ferreira, Nelson
  Macbeth 6831
Ferrero, Lorenzo 1951–
  Tempest 14980
Ferrers, Herbert [1878?]–1958
  As You Like It 1036, 1649
Ferroni, Vincenzo 1858–1934
  Macbeth 7266; Romeo 13643
Ferstl, Erich
  As You Like It 570; Errors 2073; L.L.L.
  6224; Timon 16318
Fesperman, John, Jr. 1925–
  Macbeth 6832

Fetler, Paul, in part arr. 1920–
  As You Like It 571
Feyer, George, arr.
  Shrew 14605
Ffoulkes, Sydney
  As You Like It 572, 1650; L.L.L. 6409;
  Romeo 13208
Fiałkowski, Stanisław
  Much Ado 11082
Fibich, Zdeněk 1850–1900
  Also known as Zdenko Fibich
  Othello 12394; Romeo 13209; Tempest
  14981, 15414, 16032
Ficher, Jacobo 1896–1978
  Hamlet 3929
Fiebach, Otto 1851–1937
  Caesar 5305; Twelfth Night 16800
Fieber, Günter Pavel
  Macbeth 7515
Fiebig, Kurt 1908–
  Shrew 14310
Fiedler, Valentin
  Tempest 14984
Field, John
  Winter's Tale 18933
Field, Keith Ross 1929–
  Dream 10323, 10397
Field, Robin 1935–
  Dream 10502; Othello 12291; Tempest
  15888; Twelfth Night 18123
Fielden, Thomas Perceval 1883–1974
  Shrew 14311; Tempest 15800
Fietz, Erhard
  Hamlet 3068
Figg, Joe
  Much Ado 11083
Fikejz, Daniel 1954–
  Errors 2074
Filby, William Charles, arr.
  Macbeth 7325; Dream 10783
Filip, Jaroslav
  L.L.L. 6225; Romeo 13210
Finarovskii, Grigorii Abramovich 1906–
  Shrew 14312
Fincham, Peter
  Merchant 8141; Othello 11756; Romeo
  13211; Winter's Tale 18742
Finck, Herman 1872–
  Henry V 4715; Henry VIII 5233; Caesar
  5505; Twelfth Night 16801
Finck, Herman, arr. 1872–
  Cymbeline 2733; Merry Wives 9048; Dream
  9680; Romeo 13680
Finckel, Edwin Alexander 1917–
  Dream 9418; Tempest 14985
Findlay, Alec Stuart 1918–
  As You Like It 1324, 1651; L.L.L. 6410,
  6534; Merchant 8440; Othello 12292; Two
  Gentlemen 18471

Fine, Vivian 1913–
Twelfth Night 17511
Finger, Gottfried [*circa* 1660]–1730
Also known as Godfrey Finger
Macbeth 6833
Fink, Eugenie Valeska
Macbeth 6834
Fink, Michael 1939–
Hamlet 3817; Tempest 15655, 15656,
15889; Twelfth Night 17512; Winter's Tale
18999
Fink, Robert
Hamlet 3069, 3930
Finke, Fidelio, arr.
Merry Wives 9049
Finkel'shtein, Izrail' Borisovich 1910–
Antony 148
Finley, Lorraine Noel 1899–1972
Tempest 16033; Twelfth Night 18215
Finn, William
Much Ado 11084
Finney, Ross Lee 1906–
Merchant 8488
Finnissy, Michael Peter 1946–
1 Henry IV 4340; Sonnet 61 19847
Finzi, Gerald Raphael 1901–1956
Antony 293; As You Like It 1037, 1325;
Cymbeline 2555; L.L.L. 6226, 6352, 6411,
6535, 6653; Twelfth Night 17513, 17863;
Two Gentlemen 18507; Sonnet 15 19316;
Sonnet 18 19370
Fiorentino, Robert
As You Like It 573; Merchant 8142; Much
Ado 11085; Shrew 14313
Fiori, Giovanni
Hamlet 3070
Fischer, G., arr. [flor. 1865]
Romeo 13681, 13682
Fischer, Günther 1944–
Richard III 12837
Fischer, Jan Frank 1921–
Also known as J. F. Fišer
Antony 149; As You Like It 574; Errors
2075; Hamlet 3071, 3072, 3073; Macbeth
6835, 6836; Merry Wives 8857, 8858,
8859; Romeo 14093; Shrew 14314; Twelfth
Night 16802, 16803; Winter's Tale 18743
Fischer, Peter 1929–
Antony 150; As You Like It 575, 576;
Coriolanus 2292, 2293; Caesar 5306, 5307;
Lear 5752, 6121; L.L.L. 6227; Macbeth
6837, 6838, 7516; Measure 7646; Dream
9419; Much Ado 11086; Richard III 12838;
Romeo 13212; Twelfth Night 16804, 16805;
Winter's Tale 18744
Fischer, Rolf
Twelfth Night 16807
Fischer-Münster, Gerhard 1952–
Sonnet 18 19324

Fischer-Schwaner, Ludwig
Hamlet 3074
Fišer, Luboš
Lear 5753
Fisher, Aidan Hugh 1959–
Tempest 16034
Fisher, Charles R.
Dream 10618
Fisher, John Abraham 1744–1806
Macbeth 6839, 7401; Tempest 14986
Fisher, John Daniel
Sonnet 141 20472
Fisher, Katherine Danforth 1913–
Sonnet 155 20563
Fisher, Peter
L.L.L. 6228; Dream 9420
Fisher, William Arms 1861–1948
As You Like It 1038; Much Ado 11439
Fishlock, Clive
Much Ado 11087
Fishman, Martin
Merchant 8143
Fisin, James 1755–1847
Cymbeline 2863; Hamlet 3723
Fisk, Bessie
Twelfth Night 16808
Fisk, Elsie Irene
Much Ado 11088
Fiske, John
Measure 7877
Fiske, Milton
As You Like It 1039; Merchant 8550;
Tempest 15890; Twelfth Night 17864;
Winter's Tale 19131
Fiske, Roger 1910–1987
L.L.L. 6412
Fistoulari, Gregor
Hamlet 3931
Fitch, Theodore Frank 1901–
Richard III 13046
Fithian, James Hampton
Measure 7878
Fittelberg, Gregor, arr.
Romeo 13801
Fitzgerald, Augustine
P. Pilgrim 20627
Fitzwilliam, Edward Francis
1824–1857
Merry Wives 9210; Dream 10398
Fizéarfizet, C. F., arr.
Cymbeline 2734
Flagel, Claude
Othello 11757
Flaksman, Michael
Caesar 5308; Lear 5754
Flanagan, Thomas J., Jr. 1927–
Romeo 13833; Sonnet 71 19944
Fleischer, Ned B.
Dream 9421

Fleischmann, Johann Friedrich Anton
1766–1798
Tempest 15415
Fleming, Keith
Hamlet 3075
Fleming, Robert James Berkeley 1921–1976
Merchant 8551
Fletcher, Horace Grant 1913–
As You Like It 1326; Two Gentlemen 18384
Fletcher, Percy Eastman 1879–1932
Merchant 8144; Twelfth Night 18327;
Settings of Commemorative Pieces . . . 21127
Fletcher, Percy Eastman, arr. 1879–1932
Tempest 14785
Fletcher, Stanley 1910–
Cymbeline 2556; Lear 5755; L.L.L. 6413,
6536; Measure 7879; Dream 10503; Much
Ado 11440; Winter's Tale 19040
Flindt, Minna
L.L.L. 6537
Flink, A. J., arr.
Othello 12425
Flint, D. Frame
As You Like It 1327; L.L.L. 6414
Flitner, Carl 1838–1906
Winter's Tale 18745
Flood, Buster
Twelfth Night 16809
Florath, Albert
Richard III 12839
Florencie, Jacques
Pseudonym used by Jacques Georges Wilmann
As You Like It 577
Florian, Mircea
Pericles 12560; Romeo 13213
Flosman, Oldřich 1925–
Much Ado 11089; Romeo 13835; Shrew
14569
Flothuis, Marius Hendrikus 1914–
Romeo 13907
Flothuis, Marius Hendrikus, arr. 1914–
Dream 10206
Flotow, Friedrich Adolf Ferdinand von
1812–1883
Also known as Freiherr von Flotow
Hamlet 3076; Merchant 8145; Winter's Tale
18746
Fluck, Alan
Hamlet 3077
Flury, Roman
1 Henry IV 4341; 2 Henry IV 4546; Henry V
4716; Richard II 12647; Richard III 12840
Flux, Neville
Errors 2248
Foerster, Josef Bohuslav 1859–1951
Caesar 5309; L.L.L. 6229, 6654; Macbeth
7433; Merchant 8399, 8692; Shrew 14657;
Twelfth Night 16810, 18216; Winter's Tale
19107

Fogg, Charles William Eric 1903–1939
Errors 2249; Tempest 15657
Foley, Daniel Charles 1952–
Sonnet 61 19852; Sonnet 87 20086
Folprecht, Zdeněk 1900–
L.L.L. 6690
Fones, Anthony F., arr.
Romeo 13591
Fonseca, Fernando 1947–
Caesar 5310; Dream 9422; Two Gentlemen
18460
Fontana, Caetan, arr.
Macbeth 7326
Fontana, Uranio 1815–1881
Lear 6152
Fontmichel, Hippolyte-Honoré-Joseph
1799–1874
Also known as Court de Fontmichel
Hamlet 3579
Foote, Arthur William 1853–1937
As You Like It 1328; L.L.L. 6538; Much Ado
11441
Foote, Guthrie, arr.
Merry Wives 9164
Forbes, Sebastian 1941–
Merchant 8441, 8552; Othello 12219;
Tempest 15658; Sonnet 73 19993; Sonnet
129 20410
Forbes, Watson, arr. 1909–
Merry Wives 9165
Forchhammer, Th., arr.
Hamlet 3981
Ford, C. Edgar
Dream 10619
Ford, Gertrude Castellow
Settings of Commemorative Pieces . . . 20846
Ford, Gertrude Castellow, arr.
P. Pilgrim 20628
Ford, Thomas [circa 1580?–1648]
Also known as Thomas Forde
Much Ado 11442
Forest, George C.
Merry Wives 8860
Forest, Jean Kurt 1909–1975
Hamlet 3580; Romeo 14094
Forman, Edmund, adapter
Shrew 14685
Forneris, R.
Othello 12397
Forrest, George
Othello 12472
Forrest, Hamilton
As You Like It 578
Forrester, James Cliffe 1860–1941
Twelfth Night 17865
Forró, Daniel
Troilus 16474
Forsblad, Leland
As You Like It 1652

Forster, C[uthbert]
  As You Like It 1040
Forsyth, Cecil 1870–1941
  As You Like It 1653; Dream 10504
Forsyth, G. Forbes, arr.
  Othello 12252
Forte, James 1936–
  Romeo 13214
Fortia de Piles, Alphonse-Toussaint-Joseph-
    André-Marie-Marseille 1758–1826
  Also known as Conte de Fortia de Piles
  Venus 20814
Fortner, Wolfgang 1907–1987
  As You Like It 1041; Cymbeline 2557;
  Hamlet 3791; Lear 6031; L.L.L. 6415, 6539;
  Macbeth 7393; Measure 7880; Othello
  12293; Twelfth Night 17514, 17678,
  17866; Winter's Tale 18747; Sonnet 18
  19371; Sonnet 20 19476; Sonnet 22 19484;
  Sonnet 91 20118
Forval, Pierre, arr.
  Merchant 8742
Foss, Hubert James 1899–1953
  Cymbeline 2558, 2834; L.L.L. 6416, 6671;
  Tempest 15538, 15659, 16184; Twelfth
  Night 17867, 18124, 18269
Foss, Hubert James, arr. 1899–1953
  Merry Wives 9166, 9167; Settings of
  Commemorative Pieces . . . 21022
Foss, Lukas 1922–
  [Born Lukas Fuchs]
  Hamlet 3811; Caesar 5494; Measure 8042;
  Merchant 8483, 8670; Dream 10456;
  Tempest 15862, 15891; Twelfth Night
  17727
Foss, Lukas, in part arr. 1922–
  [Born Lukas Fuchs]
  Tempest 14987
Fossey, Léon, arr. 1829–1877
  Othello 12080
[Foster, John, arr.]
  Twelfth Night 17951
Foster, Arnold Wilfrid Allen, arr. 1898–1963
  Dream 10207, 10208
Foster, Donald L. 1944–
  Twelfth Night 16811
Foster, Gertrude Elaine
  Macbeth 6840
Foster, Myles Birket 1851–1922
  As You Like It 1329, 1654
Foster, R.
  Tempest 15892
Foster, Stephen Collins 1826–1864
  Hamlet 4273; Romeo 13871
Fougstedt, Nils-Eric 1910–
  Hamlet 3078
Foulds, John Herbert 1880–1939
  As You Like It 966; Cymbeline 2460; Henry

VIII 4976, 5214; Caesar 5311; Merry Wives
  8861
Foulds, John Herbert, arr. 1880–1939
  Lear 6170
Fouret, Maurice Pierre 1888–1962
  L.L.L. 6230
Fowler, Frederick, arr.
  As You Like It 1174; Tempest 15058
Fowler, Jennifer 1939–
  Hamlet 3932
Fox, A.
  [Arthur Makinson Fox?]
  Twelfth Night 17868
Fox, Arthur Makinson
  Henry VIII 5083; Measure 7881; Much Ado
  11090, 11444; Winter's Tale 18748
Fox, Aynsley
  Othello 11758
Fox, Charles 1940–
  Hamlet 4096; Dream 10146
Fox, Frederick Alfred 1931–
  1 Henry IV 4342
Fox, George E.
  Much Ado 11445; Othello 12220; P. Pilgrim
  20629
Foy, M. E.
  Lear 6182
Frackenpohl, Arthur Roland 1924–
  As You Like It 1330; Hamlet 3724; L.L.L.
  6378; Twelfth Night 18125
Fraggi, Hector Michel
  Macbeth 6841
Fragson, Harry, adapter   –1913
  Settings of Commemorative Pieces . . .
  21032
France, William Edward 1912–
  As You Like It 1331, 1655; Twelfth Night
  17869
Franceschina, John
  As You Like It 579; Hamlet 3079; Caesar
  5312; Dream 9423; Othello 11759; Tempest
  14988, 14989
Franchi, Dorothea Anne 1920–
  Twelfth Night 16812
Franchomme, Auguste, arr. 1808–1884
  Othello 12081
Francis, Theodore, arr.
  Dream 9681
Francis, William T.
  Romeo 14143
Francisci, Luciano
  Errors 2076
Francisci, Maurizio
  Errors 2077
Franck, César-Auguste-Jean-Guillaume-
    Hubert 1822–1890
  Romeo 14197
Franck, Johann Wolfgang 1644–[circa 1710]
  Timon 16319

Franck, Maurice 1897–
  Coriolanus 2390
Francker, Otto
  Macbeth 6842
Franco, Johan Henri Gustave 1908–
  Tempest 14990; Sonnet 18 19372; Sonnet
  27 19521; Sonnet 71 19945; Sonnet 123
  20364; Settings of Commemorative
  Pieces . . . 20925, 21033
Francœur, François 1698–1787
  Dream 10958
François, Jean-Charles
  Richard III 12841
Frangeš, Neven
  Hamlet 3080; Caesar 5313; Romeo 13215
Frangipane, Ronald George
  L.L.L. 6231
Frank, Alan Clifford, arr. 1910–
  Merry Wives 9168
Frank, Ernst 1847–1889
  Tempest 15416
Frank, Marcel Gustave, arr. 1909–
  Twelfth Night 17390
Frank, Reinhard
  Othello 11760
Frankel, Benjamin 1906–1973
  Caesar 5314; Macbeth 6843; Romeo 13908;
  Settings of Commemorative Pieces . . .
  21128, 21129
Frankel, Steven, arr.
  Tempest 15059
Frankenburger, Paul 1897–
  Born Paul Shaul Ben-Haim
  Troilus 16475
Franklin, Malvin M. 1889–
  Romeo 14095
Fränzl, Ignaz 1736–1811
  Caesar 5315; Macbeth 6844
Fraser, Donald
  Antony 151; Hamlet 3081; Lear 5756;
  Romeo 13216; Twelfth Night 16813
Fraser, Norman George 1904–
  Tempest 15660
Fraser, Shena Eleanor 1910–
  As You Like It 1656; Dream 10324; Tempest
  15661
Frazelle, Kenneth
  Sonnet 30 19606
Frazzi, Vito 1888–1975
  Lear 5992
Frechter, Colin, arr.
  Two Gentlemen 18577
Fredelius, Yngve Marten 1956–
  Twelfth Night 16814
Freed, Dorothy Whitson 1919–
  Née Doorly
  Hamlet 3757; Twelfth Night 17870
Freedman, Harry 1922–
  As You Like It 580, 1042, 1332, 1657;

  Much Ado 11091, 11446; Romeo 13644;
  Twelfth Night 16815, 16816, 17515,
  17871, 18126
Freeland, Michael
  K. John 5591
Freer, Eleanor 1864–1942
  Née Everest
  Twelfth Night 17872
Freivogel, David
  Romeo 13217
Fremont, Rob
  As You Like It 581
French, Joan
  Twelfth Night 16817
Fretheim, Barbara
  Pericles 12561
Freudenberg, Wilhelm 1838–1928
  Antony 371; Romeo 13218; Titus 16430
Freuhm, Hermann
  Errors 2078
Frey, E. H., arr.
  [Hugo Frey (1874–1952)?]
  Merry Wives 9050
Frey, Hugo 1874–1952
  [E. Hugo Frey?]
  Settings of Commemorative Pieces . . .
  21130
Frey, Hugo, arr. 1874–1952
  [E. Hugo Frey?]
  Romeo 13982
Freyer, Hans Dietrich
  As You Like It 582
Frezza, Christine
  Née Chester
  All's Well 14; Antony 152; As You Like It
  583, 584; Errors 2079, 2080, 2081;
  Cymbeline 2461; Hamlet 3082, 3083;
  1 Henry IV 4343; Henry V 4806; Caesar
  5316, 5317; Lear 5757; L.L.L. 6232, 6233;
  Macbeth 6845; Measure 7647, 7648;
  Merchant 8146, 8147, 8148; Merry Wives
  8862, 8863; Dream 9424, 9425, 9426;
  Much Ado 11092, 11093; Othello 11761;
  Richard III 12842, 12843, 12844; Romeo
  13219, 13220, 13221; Shrew 14315,
  14316; Tempest 14991; Twelfth Night
  16818, 16819; Two Gentlemen 18385,
  18461; Winter's Tale 18749
Frezza, Christine, in part arr.
  Née Chester
  Much Ado 11094; Othello 11762
Fribec, Krešimir 1908–
  Romeo 13645
Fricker, Herbert Austin, arr. 1868–1943
  Dream 9682
Fricker, Peter Racine 1920–
  K. John 5592; Dream 10620; Othello 12398;
  Twelfth Night 17873; Settings of
  Commemorative Pieces . . . 21131

Frid, Géza 1904–
  Twelfth Night 16820, 17516, 17874, 18127
Frid, Grigorii Samuilovich 1915–
  Sonnet 12 19284; Sonnet 27 19522; Sonnet
  29 19555; Sonnet 50 19745; Sonnet 153
  20539
Fried, Martin
  Richard III 12845
Friedel, Kurt-Joachim 1921–
  Sonnet 155 20564
Friedman, Allan Jay
  Settings of Commemorative Pieces . . . 20926
Friedman, Gary William
  Macbeth 6846; Merry Wives 8864
Friedman, Joel J.
  As You Like It 585; Much Ado 11095
Friedman, Sid
  Settings of Commemorative Pieces . . . 20927
Friedrich, Eduard Ferdinand
  Dream 10621
Friedrich, Matthias
  Twelfth Night 16821
Fries, Herbert 1926–
  Caesar 5318; Macbeth 7267; Tempest
  14992
Fristorp, Göran 1948–
  Errors 2082
Fritsch, Alfred
  Dream 9427
Fritsch, Johannes G. 1941–
  Dream 10147; Twelfth Night 16822, 16823
Fritz, Sherilyn Gail 1957–
  Hamlet 3933; Lear 5758; Dream 9428
Fritzen, Heinz Joachim
  Dream 9429
Froggatt, Raymond
  Settings of Commemorative Pieces . . . 20928
Frogworth, A. C.
  Pseudonym used by Jonathan C. Brown
  Twelfth Night 18128
Fröhlich, Christian
  Much Ado 11096; Winter's Tale 18750
Fröhlich, Friedrich Theodor 1803–1836
  Cymbeline 2559, 2666; Twelfth Night
  17517, 17690, 17875, 18129
Frohlich, Otto
  Caesar 5319
Frohman, Walter David
  Macbeth 6847
Fromm, Herbert 1905–
  Cymbeline 2560; L.L.L. 6540; Merchant
  8553; Dream 10505; Tempest 15662,
  15847
Frost, Charles Joseph, arr.
  Dream 9683
Fry, Christopher 1907–
  Winter's Tale 18751
Fry, William Henry 1813–1864
  Lear 5993; Macbeth 7434

Fryer, George Herbert 1877–1957
  Twelfth Night 17876; Sonnet 71 19946
Fù Tiān Xūn
  Othello 11763
Fuchs, Géorges Frédéric, arr.
  1752–1821
  Much Ado 11623
Fuchs, Hermann
  Errors 2083; Dream 9430; Richard II 12648;
  Two Gentlemen 18386
Fuchs, Janet
  Richard III 12846
Fuchs, Kenneth
  Twelfth Night 16824
Fuchs, Michael
  Sonnet 155 20551
Fuchs, Tilo, [in part arr.?]
  Dream 9431
Fueter-Graf, Daniel
  Lear 5759; Twelfth Night 18217
Fuleihan, Anis 1900–1970
  Also known as Anīs Fulaihān
  Hamlet 3934
Fuleihan, Anis, arr. 1900–1970
  Also known as Anīs Fulaihān
  Lear 6061; Merchant 8743; Dream 9684;
  Much Ado 11351
Fulton, Robert Norman 1909–1980
  As You Like It 1043, 1333, 1658, 1822,
  1843, 1956; Merry Wives 8865; Othello
  12294; Tempest 15893; Twelfth Night
  17518, 17877; Winter's Tale 18753
Fumagalli, Carlo, arr.
  Othello 12191
Fumagalli, Luca, arr.
  Dream 9685
Furrer, Walter 1902–1978
  Hamlet 3084; Macbeth 6848; Romeo 13222;
  Shrew 14317; Tempest 14993; Twelfth
  Night 16825
Furst, William
  Romeo 13223; Twelfth Night 16826
Furst, William, in part arr.
  Merry Wives 8866
Fusco, Giovanni 1906–
  Merchant 8149
Fuß, Hans
  Twelfth Night 16827
Fussell, Charles C. 1938–
  Cymbeline 2515
Füssl, Karl Heinz 1924–
  L.L.L. 6417, 6541
Futterer, Carl 1873–1927
  Twelfth Night 16828
Fuzzy 1939–
  Pseudonym used by Jens Wilhelm Pedersen
  As You Like It 586; Errors 2084; Hamlet
  3085; Macbeth 6849; Romeo 13224;
  Twelfth Night 16829, 16830

Fuzzy, in part arr. 1939–
Pseudonym used by Jens Wilhelm Pedersen
Dream 9432, 9686

G

Gabichvadze, I., arr.
Hamlet 3582
Gabichvadze, Revaz Konrat'evich 1913–
Hamlet 3581
Gabler, Friedrich, arr.
Dream 9687
Gabold, Ingolf 1942–
Hamlet 3827; Tempest 15860
Gabriel, Joseph D., [in part arr.]
Macbeth 6850
Gabriel, [Mary Ann or Mary Anne] Virginia
1825–1877
Also known as Mrs. George E. March
Henry VIII 5084; Tempest 16254
Gabriel, Ulrich
Shrew 14318
Gabriel, Ulrich, arr.
Shrew 14606
Gabrielski, Louis
Cymbeline 2667
Gachechiladze, E., arr.
Othello 12032
Gachechiladze, G.
Othello 11764
Gade, Niels Vilhelm 1817–1890
Hamlet 3935; Lear 5760
Gadsby, Henry Robert 1842–1907
As You Like It 1886
Gadzhiev, Rauf Soltan 1922–
Romeo 14097
Gaertner, Katarzyna
Twelfth Night 16831
Gaffe, George 1849–
Dream 10506
Gaffield, Eleanor Neidich
Much Ado 11097
Gagić, Bogdan 1931–
Hamlet 3086; Caesar 5320; Twelfth Night
16832
Gak, A.
Much Ado 11098
Gál, Hans 1890–1987
Merchant 8554; P. Pilgrim 20630
Galan, Juraj
Troilus 16476
Gale, James Randolph Courtenay
As You Like It 1044
Gale, Percival
Hamlet 4274
Galea, Manuel, [in part] arr.
Lear 5994

Gall, Jan Karol 1856–1912
As You Like It 1334, 1659; Hamlet 3792;
L.L.L. 6418; Measure 7882; Twelfth Night
17388, 17519; Winter's Tale 19041
Galli, Raffaello, arr.
Romeo 13775
Galliard, John Ernest 1687–1749
Caesar 5540; Measure 7883
Gallieri, C., arr.
Othello 12082
Galloway, Michael
Macbeth 7537
Galuppi, Baldassare 1706–1785
Coriolanus 2412
Gambaro, Vicenzo, arr.
Othello 12083
Gamble, Judith 1953–
Caesar 5321; Dream 9433; Richard II 12649
Gamblin, [?]
Lear 5761
Gambogi, Frederica Elvira   –1940
Cymbeline 2668; Measure 7884
Gann, Angela
As You Like It 587; Dream 9434; Winter's
Tale 18754
Ganz, Wilhelm, arr. 1832–1914
Macbeth 7415; Merry Wives 9051; Dream
10825
Gào Yiànshēng 1940–
Lear 5762
Garant, Serge 1929–1986
Sonnet 61 19853; Sonnet 88 20101; Sonnet
133 20436; Sonnet 136 20444; Sonnet 149
20526
Garat, Pierre-Jean
Hamlet 4275
Garbarek, Jan
Dream 9435
Garbett, Arthur Selwyn
As You Like It 1335
García, Manuel del Popolo Vicente Rodríguez
1775–1832
Romeo 14198
García Robles, José 1835–1910
Caesar 5478
G[ardiner?], W[illiam?] [1770–1853]
Measure 7885
Gardiner, Henry Balfour 1877–1950
Cymbeline 2561; L.L.L. 6542; Tempest
15663
Gardiner, Henry Balfour, arr. 1877–1950
Hamlet 3758
Gardner, A. L., in part arr.
Macbeth 7538
Gardner, Charles 1836–
Merchant 8442, 8671; P. Pilgrim 20631
Gardner, John Linton 1917–
All's Well 15; As You Like It 1045, 1336,
1337, 1660, 1661, 1662, 1663, 1950;

Gardner, John Linton (*cont.*)
Cymbeline 2562, 2563, 2669, 2670; Hamlet 3087, 3834; Henry VIII 5085; Caesar 5322; K. John 5593; Lear 5763; L.L.L. 6419; Measure 7886, 7887; Merchant 8555, 8556; Dream 10748; Much Ado 11447; Romeo 13854; Tempest 15664, 15848; Twelfth Night 16833, 17520, 17701, 17728, 17729, 17878; Two Gentlemen 18508; Sonnet 12 19285; P. Pilgrim 20632; Settings of Commemorative Pieces . . . 21034
Gardner, Kevin
Othello 11765
Gardner, Worth
Hamlet 3088
Gardo, Ryszard
Antony 153; Hamlet 3089; Lear 5764; Romeo 13225; Troilus 16477
Gariachikh, V. I.
Hamlet 3090
Gariboldi, Giuseppe, arr. 1833–1905
Macbeth 7327; Romeo 13683
Garland, Hugh 1882–1955
Pseudonym used by William Henry Anderson
Dream 10325
Garletskii, I., arr.
Othello 11812
Garlick, Antony 1927–
Measure 7888; Merchant 8557; Dream 10399
Garner, Ned
Caesar 5323
Garnett, Louise
Née Ayres
Dream 10400, 10431, 10470, 10507, 10756; Tempest 15539; Settings of Commemorative Pieces . . . 20847
Garrett, Gaynor D.
As You Like It 1338
Garrett, Jean Wilfrid
Coriolanus 2294
Garrido-Lecca, Celso 1926–
Shrew 14319
Gärtner, Alfred 1909–1970
Tempest 14994
Garvarentz, Georges
Romeo 14046
Garvin, Kevin
As You Like It 588; Merchant 8150; Dream 9436
Gaslini, Giorgio
Richard II 12650
Gasparini, Carlo Francesco 1668–1727
Hamlet 4276
Gass, I.
As You Like It 1664
Gates, John 1926–
Shrew 14320
Gatsenko, A., arr.
Othello 11813

Gattie, Mrs. John Byng
Dream 10458
Gatty, Nicholas Comyn 1874–1946
As You Like It 1046; Henry VIII 5086; Macbeth 7268; Tempest 15417
Gaujac, Edmond Germain 1895–1962
Coriolanus 2391; Romeo 13646
Gauk, Aleksandr Vasil'evich 1893–1963
Macbeth 6851
Gaul, Alfred Robert 1837–1913
As You Like It 1047, 1339, 1665; Henry VIII 5087; Dream 10401, 10508; Tempest 15830, 15864; Troilus 16572; Twelfth Night 17879, 18293; P. Pilgrim 20633; Venus 20791; Settings of Commemorative Pieces . . . 21035
Gaul, Harvey Bartlett 1881–1945
Also wrote under the pseudonyms 'Will Deems', 'Lester Jenks', and 'Monte Wellings'
Othello 12221; Richard II 12754; Romeo 13830, 13846, 14144; Tempest 15832; Sonnet 18 19373
Gautier, Léonard
Also known as Leonard Gautier
Romeo 13909
Gautier, Léonard, arr.
Also known as Leonard Gautier
Dream 9688, 10166
Gavall, John, arr.
As You Like It 417, 1442; Twelfth Night 17761
Gavazzeni, Gianandrea 1909–
Settings of Commemorative Pieces . . . 21212
Gavins, Robert
As You Like It 590
Gavrilov, A.
Romeo 13226
Gaythorne, R., arr.
Twelfth Night 17917
Gazeau, Hélène Fanny Marcelle
Macbeth 6852
Gaztambide, Joaquín Romualdo 1822–1870
Also known as Joaquín Romualdo Gastambide and as Joaquín Romualdo Gaztambide y Garbayo
Merry Wives 9249; Dream 10777; Settings of Commemorative Pieces . . . 20929
Gazzola, Giannandra
Macbeth 6853
Gebauer, Étienne-François, arr. 1777–[1822 or 1823]
Much Ado 11624
Gebhardt, Reinhard W.
Twelfth Night 18328
Gebler, Adolphe
Caesar 5324; Macbeth 6854
Gedike, Aleksandr Fedorovich 1877–1957
Macbeth 7269
Gedzhadze, Iraklii Aleksandrovich 1925–
Hamlet 3091

Geehl, Henry Ernest, arr. 1881–1961
 Cymbeline 2735, 2736; Henry VIII 5179;
 Macbeth 7440; Dream 9689, 9690; Tempest
 14720, 14786
Geibel, Adam
 Cymbeline 2671
Geißler, Fritz 1921–1984
 Hamlet 3092; Dream 10148
Geisthardt, Hans Joachim
 Dream 9437; Twelfth Night 16834
Gelber, Stanley Jay 1936–
 Twelfth Night 17389
Gellert, Johann Ludwig 1827–1913
 Dream 10959
Gémignani, Vincent Émile Arthur 1939–
 Caesar 5325; Macbeth 6855; Dream 9438
Gems, Jonathan 1952–
 Romeo 14047
Gendlin, Frances O.
 Hamlet 3759
Genée, Rudolf
 L.L.L. 6234
Generali, Pietro 1773–1832
 Pseudonym used by P. Mercandetti
 Lear 6135
Génin, Paul Agricole, arr. 1829–1903
 Settings of Commemorative Pieces . . . 20966
Gensler, Lewis
 Romeo 14145
Gentry, Bruce
 Much Ado 11099
Genzmer, Harald 1909–
 As You Like It 1049; L.L.L. 6374, 6420,
 6543; Tempest 15849
George, Charles 1893–
 Settings of Commemorative Pieces . . .
 20930
George, Graham 1912–
 Cymbeline 2564; Hamlet 3093, 3725; Lear
 5765; Dream 9439; Much Ado 11100;
 Othello 11766; Tempest 14995
Georges, Alexandre 1850–1938
 Antony 372; Venus 20815
Gerard, Mike
 Hamlet 3094
Gerber, René 1908–
 Dream 10149; Romeo 13647
Gere, Richard, in part arr.
 Dream 9440
Gergeiy, János
 Twelfth Night 16835
Gerhard, Fritz Christian 1911–
 As You Like It 591; Lear 5995; Macbeth
 6856; Measure 7649
Gerhard, Roberto 1896–1970
 Coriolanus 2295; Cymbeline 2462; Lear
 5766; Macbeth 6857; Dream 9441; Pericles
 12562, 12563; Romeo 13227; Shrew
 14321; Tempest 15418

Gericke, Wilhelm, arr. 1845–1925
 Cymbeline 2737
German, Edward 1862–1936
 Born German Edward Jones
 As You Like It 592, 1341; Hamlet 3940;
 Henry VIII 4977, 5089; Dream 10778;
 Much Ado 11101; Othello 12295, 12399;
 Richard III 12847; Romeo 13228; Tempest
 16255; Twelfth Night 16836; Two
 Gentlemen 18509; Settings of
 Commemorative Pieces . . . 21267
Germanov, Sergei Leonidovich 1899–
 Also known as Sergei Leonidovich Gorbenko-
 Germanov
 Othello 11767
Gerner, Hermann
 Twelfth Night 16837
Gernet, Rainer
 Tempest 14996
Geronimo, L.
 Hamlet 3942
Gerschefski, Edwin 1909–
 Coriolanus 2296; Lear 5767, 6073
Gerster, Ottmar
 As You Like It 594; Shrew 14322
Gerstman, Blanche Wilhelminia 1910–1973
 As You Like It 1050; Merchant 8443;
 Tempest 14997, 15540, 15665, 15801,
 15894, 15973; Twelfth Night 17881; Sonnet
 18 19374; Sonnet 29 19556
Gervasio, Raffaele 1910–
 Merchant 8151
Gerville, Léon Pascal, arr.
 Merchant 8597
Gessner, John
 Tempest 14998
Getselev, Boris Semenovich 1940–
 Sonnet 54 19767
Getty, Arthur Radcliffe
 Twelfth Night 17882
Getty, Gordon Peter 1933–
 1 Henry IV 4462; 2 Henry IV 4628; Henry V
 4800
Gevaert, François-Auguste 1828–1908
 Lear 6153
Gevaert, François-Auguste, arr.
 1828–1908
 Errors 2259; Romeo 13813
Geyer, Eberhard
 Dream 9442
Ghiglia, Benedetto
 Antony 154; As You Like It 595; Measure
 7650; Much Ado 11103; Troilus 16478
Ghisi, Federico 1901–1975
 Dream 10150
Ghislanzoni, Alberto 1897–
 Lear 5996
Giannelli, E., adapter
 Romeo 14199

Giannini, Vittorio 1903–1966
L.L.L. 6655; Merry Wives 9250; Dream
10780; Romeo 14098; Shrew 14570;
Sonnet 34 19665; Sonnet 57 19808; Sonnet
61 19861; Sonnet 91 20124; Sonnet 95
20143; Sonnet 137 20451; Sonnet 148
20524; Sonnet 150 20534; Sonnet 151
20536; Venus 20809
Giard, Charles
Dream 10622
Gibbens, John Jeffrey 1955–
Sonnet 97 20160
Gibbons, Mark
As You Like It 951
Gibbs, Alan 1932–
As You Like It 1887; 1 Henry IV 4479;
2 Henry IV 4654; Henry VIII 5090; Lear
6074; Merry Wives 9219; Dream 10623;
Much Ado 11597; Tempest 16035
Gibbs, Cecil Armstrong 1889–1960
As You Like It 1051, 1342; Cymbeline 2565;
Henry VIII 5091; L.L.L. 6544, 6545; Dream
10357, 10403, 10510, 10911; Twelfth
Night 16838, 17392, 17883, 17884, 18130
Gibbs, Michael Clement 1937–
Macbeth 7435; Sonnet 18 19452; Settings of
Commemorative Pieces . . . 21132, 21133
Gibling, Sophie Pauline
Romeo 13229
Gibson, Alexander 1926–
Hamlet 3095; Richard III 12852
Gibson, Henry
Hamlet 3096
Gibson, John
Romeo 13230
Gibson, Richard
Settings of Commemorative Pieces . . .
21195
Gibson, S. Archer
As You Like It 1343
Gide, Casimir 1804–1868
Hamlet 3943
Gideon, Miriam 1906–
Sonnet 8 19238; Sonnet 19 19465; Sonnet
33 19650; Sonnet 71 19947; Sonnet 123
20365
Giebel, Reinhard
Tempest 14999
Giejesse, Jay
Twelfth Night 16839
Gierschner, C. F. J. 1794–1860
As You Like It 1344
Gieseker, [?]
Richard III 12853
Gifford, Helen 1935–
All's Well 16; Macbeth 6858; Merchant
8152; Much Ado 11104; Othello 11768;
Pericles 12564; Winter's Tale 18755; Sonnet
121 20360

Gilbert, Alfred
Settings of Commemorative Pieces . . .
21037
Gilbert, E. Ouseley
Settings of Commemorative Pieces . . .
20931
Gilbert, Ernest Thomas Bennett 1833–1885
Henry VIII 5092; Dream 10781, 10912;
Tempest 16036; Settings of Commemorative
Pieces . . . 20932
Gilbert, Fred
Merry Wives 9008
Gilbert, Henry Franklin Belknap 1868–1928
Merchant 8558
Gilbert, James
Merchant 8153; Merry Wives 9009; Settings
of Commemorative Pieces . . . 21269
Gilbert, Norman 1912–
L.L.L. 6546; Much Ado 11448
Gilbert, Stephen
Antony 155
Gilbert, Walter
Richard III 13074
Gilchrist, William Wallace 1846–1916
Tempest 16166
Gilford, Nancy, arr.
Dream 10767
Gill, Frank
Hamlet 3097
Gill, Harry
Dream 10326
Gillar, Jaroslav 1942–
Hamlet 3098; Merchant 8154
Gillen, Theodore
Merry Wives 9011
Gilles, Constantin   –1934
Cymbeline 2864; Dream 10913; Settings of
Commemorative Pieces . . . 21213
Gillet, Ernest, arr.
Romeo 13684
Gillick, Emelyn Mildred Samuels 1948–
Macbeth 6859
Gilmore, B., arr.
Romeo 13592
Gilson, Paul 1865–1942
Henry VIII 5215; Richard III 13052
Ginot, Marc
Winter's Tale 19138
Ginsburg, Gerald M. 1932–
Winter's Tale 19000, 19074
Ginsburg, Isaac   –[before 1963]
Sonnet 18 19375
Ginton, Jules
Othello 11769
Giordanengo, Jean Pierre Henri
Dream 9443
Giordani, Giuseppe [circa 1753]–1798
Also known as 'Giordanello'
Coriolanus 2413

Giordani, Tommaso 1730–1806
  Cymbeline 2865; Measure 7889; Othello
  12296; P. Pilgrim 20635
Giorza, Paolo 1832–1914
  Hamlet 4154; Merry Wives 9251; Dream
  10785; Settings of Commemorative
  Pieces . . . 20933
Giovanni, Paul
  Twelfth Night 16841
Girard, L., arr.
  Macbeth 7328; Romeo 13685, 13686
Girnatis, W.
  Dream 9444
Gironce, A., arr.
  Hamlet 3645, 3646, 3647; Lear 6171
Girvin, Richard
  Macbeth 6860
Gisler, Anton
  Dream 9445
Gitschel, Hans Georg
  Hamlet 3099; Caesar 5326; Merchant 8155;
  Much Ado 11105; Othello 11770; Romeo
  13231
Gitter, Paul
  Macbeth 6861
Giuliani, Mauro, arr.
  Othello 12084
Giuliani, Mich., arr.
  Othello 12085
Gladkov, Gennadii Igorevich 1935–
  Shrew 14323
Gladstone, Francis Edward 1845–1928
  Twelfth Night 17885
Glandien, Lutz 1954–
  Twelfth Night 16842
Glaser, Joseph
  Hamlet 3100
Glaser, Werner Wolf 1910–
  Romeo 13232
Glass, Paul, arr. 1910–
  Dream 10209
Glass, Philip 1937–
  Dream 9446
Glasser, Stanley 1926–
  Romeo 13233
Glatz, Helen Sinclair 1908–
  Merchant 8156; Much Ado 11106; Romeo
  13234
Glatz, Helen Sinclair, in part arr. 1908–
  Merry Wives 8867
Glazunov, Aleksandr Konstantinovich
  1865–1936
  Sonnet 66 19913; Sonnet 147 20510
Glendinning, Richard Rashleigh
  Cymbeline 2672
Glière, Reinhold Moritsevich 1875–1956
  Othello 11771
Glinka, Mikhail Ivanovich 1804–1857
  Hamlet 3583

Gloger, [?]
  Richard III 12854
Glonti, Feliks Filipp Petrovich 1927–
  Antony 267; Othello 11772; Sonnet 155
  20565
Glover, Charles William 1806–1863
  As You Like It 1888, 1976; Hamlet 3944;
  Macbeth 7436; Tempest 16037
Glover, James Mackey 1861–1931
  Antony 338
Glover, John
  Merchant 8400
Glover, Marsha
  Merchant 8401
Glover, Stephen Ralph 1812–1870
  As You Like It 1889; Dream 10914; Romeo
  13910; Twelfth Night 18218; P. Pilgrim
  20636; Settings of Commemorative
  Pieces . . . 21038
Glover, Stephen Ralph, arr. 1812–1870
  Tempest 14787; Twelfth Night 16671
Glover, William Howard 1819–1875
  Romeo 14029
Glover-Kind, John A.
  Romeo 14146
Głowiński, Andrzej 1938–
  Hamlet 3101; Dream 9447; Richard II
  12651; Romeo 13235; Tempest 15000;
  Twelfth Night 16843; Settings of
  Commemorative Pieces . . . 20848
Glukh, Mikhail Aleksandrovich 1907–
  Sonnet 34 19662; Sonnet 102 20220
Gobatti, Stefano 1852–1913
  Also known as Stefano Gobati
  Lear 6183
Gobbaerts, Jean Louis, arr. 1835–1886
  Also wrote under the pseudonyms 'L.
  Streabbog', 'Ludovic', and 'Lévi'
  Dream 9691, 9692, 10826
Gobbi, Henri, arr.
  Dream 9693
Godard, Benjamin Louis Paul 1849–1895
  Much Ado 11107
Godfrey, Adolphus Frederick, arr.
  Errors 2037; Romeo 13687
Godfrey, Charles, the Elder, arr. 1790–1863
  Dream 9694
Godfrey, Charles, the Younger, arr.
  1839–1919
  All's Well 76; Macbeth 6883; Othello 12192;
  Romeo 13688
Godfrey, Charles George, arr. 1866–1935
  Cymbeline 2738
Godfrey, Daniel Eyers, arr. 1868–1939
  Also known as Dan Godfrey, Jr., although
  not to be confused with Dan Stuart Godfrey
  (1893–1935), who was also known as Dan
  Godfrey, Jr.
  As You Like It 593; Hamlet 3648; Henry

Godfrey, Daniel Eyers (*cont.*)
VIII 4982, 4983, 4984; Macbeth 7176;
Merchant 8347; Merry Wives 9052; Much
Ado 11102; Richard III 12848; Romeo
13689
Godfrey, H. Graham
Dream 10404; Twelfth Night 17521
Godfrey, Percy
Dream 10151
Godley, Elisabeth
Twelfth Night 16844
Godøy, Rolf Inge 1952–
Sonnet 79 20061
Goebbels, Heiner
Othello 11773
Goehr, Alexander 1932–
Troilus 16570; Settings of Commemorative
Pieces . . . 20937
Goepp, Philip Henry 1864–1936
As You Like It 1345, 1667
Goering, Richard
Shrew 14324; Twelfth Night 16845
Goerner, Carl
Richard III 13053
Goetsch, Georg
Tempest 15001
Goetz, Hermann Gustav 1840–1876
Shrew 14571
Goeyvaerts, Karel 1923–
Sonnet 8 19239; Sonnet 59 19811
Gofton, Richard
Shrew 14325
Goland, Arnold, arr.
Dream 10126
Gold, Ernest 1921–
Born Ernest Goldner
Sonnet 18 19376
Gold, G., arr.
Hamlet 3937
Goldani, Franco
K. John 5594
Goldberg, Isaac
As You Like It 1052, 1668; Merchant 8559;
Much Ado 11449; Twelfth Night 17522
Goldberg, Jon, arr.
Henry VIII 5014
Goldberg, Jonathan D., in part arr. 1964–
Dream 9448
Goldberg, Julius, arr.
Merry Wives 9053
Goldblatt, Maurice Henry 1883–1962
As You Like It 1890
Goldecke, Mike
Romeo 13236
Golden, John L.
Othello 12497
Goldenberg, Mark
Settings of Commemorative Pieces . . . 21134
Goldenthal, Elliot
Dream 9449; Tempest 15002

Goldman, Edwin Franko, arr. 1878–1956
As You Like It 418; Tempest 14788
Goldman, Jack
Macbeth 6862
Goldman, Maurice, arr. 1910–
Merry Wives 9184
Goldmann, Friedrich
Hamlet 3102; Measure 7651; Much Ado
11108; Romeo 13237
Goldmark, Carl 1830–1915
Tempest 16038; Twelfth Night 16846;
Winter's Tale 18934
Goldmark, Rubin 1872–1936
Dream 10624
Goldner, Wilhelm, arr.
Dream 9695
Goldsbrough, Arnold, arr.
Henry VIII 5098
Goldschmidt, Berthold 1903–
As You Like It 596; Errors 2250; Winter's
Tale 18756
Goldschmidt, G., arr.
Merry Wives 9054
Goldstaub, Paul 1947–
As You Like It 1891; Richard II 12652,
12769; Shrew 14658; Tempest 15003,
16039; Twelfth Night 17523, 17730,
17886, 18131, 18261; Two Gentlemen
18387
Goldstein, J.
Pseudonym used by Frederic Brown
Twelfth Night 18132
Goldstein, Lee
Hamlet 3103
Golinelli, Stephano, arr. 1818–1891
Settings of Commemorative Pieces . . . 20910
Golland, Abram Isaevich 1911–
Twelfth Night 16847
Golob, Jani
Hamlet 3104
Goltermann, Georg E., arr.
Dream 10827
Golub, David B. 1949–
Macbeth 6863
Golub, Peter 1952–
1 Henry IV 4344; K. John 5595; Measure
7890; Dream 9450; Richard II 12653;
Romeo 13238
Golubentsev, Aleksandr Aleksandrovich 1899–
Othello 11774; Shrew 14326
Gomer, Llywelyn 1911–
Pseudonym used by Gomer Llewellyn Jones
Tempest 16040
Gomion, L., arr.
Othello 12086
Gooch, Warren Peter 1953–
Dream 9451, 10625
Goodall, Cecil
Merchant 8560

Goodban, Henry William, arr.
  Settings of Commemorative Pieces . . .
  21039
Goode, Daniel 1936–
  Tempest 15004, 15666
Gooding, David 1935–
  Othello 11775; Tempest 15005
Goodman, David B. 1953–
  Dream 9452
Goodman, John I. 1937–
  Cymbeline 2566; L.L.L. 6421, 6547; Much
  Ado 11450; Twelfth Night 17887
Goodrich, Florence A.
  Dream 10786
Goorhuis, Rob 1948–
  Henry VIII 5093
Goossen, Jacob Frederic 1927–
  Antony 294; As You Like It 1053, 1346;
  Dream 10511; Much Ado 11451; Othello
  12222, 12237; Tempest 15667, 15895,
  16041; Twelfth Night 17524; Two
  Gentlemen 18511
Gorb, Adam
  As You Like It 597
Gorbulskis, Benjaminas Iokubo 1925–
  Shrew 14327
Gordigiani, Luigi, arr. 1806–1860
  Macbeth 7329
Gordon, Glenn Charles
  Macbeth 7270
Gordon, Hugh, arr.
  Dream 9696
Gordon, John 1915–
  Hamlet 3105; Henry V 4717
Gordon, Peter, in part arr. 1951–
  Othello 12022, 12193
Gordon, Philip 1894–1983
  Merchant 8561
Gordon, Philip, arr. 1894–1983
  Romeo 13424; Twelfth Night 17762
Gordon, Sheridan
  As You Like It 1977
Gordon, William
  Two Gentlemen 18512
Gore, Richard Taylor
  Hamlet 3818
Görgen, Martin, [arr.]
  Macbeth 7330; Merry Wives 9185; Othello
  12194
Gorham, Carl
  As You Like It 598
Goria, Alexandre Édouard
  Hamlet 3945; Tempest 16042
Goria, Alexandre Édouard, arr.
  Othello 12087
Goriachikh, Vladimir Ivanovich 1929–
  Hamlet 3106
Gorin, Katharine Douglas
  Romeo 13239

Gormack, Robert
  Hamlet 3107
Gorney, Jay
  Hamlet 4155
Goršič, Edvard
  Hamlet 3108
Gorter, A., arr.
  Merry Wives 9055
Gorton, Belle Lodema
  As You Like It 1054, 1669; Hamlet 3866;
  Henry VIII 5094; Lear 6032; L.L.L. 6548;
  Measure 7891; Dream 10327, 10405; Much
  Ado 11452; Tempest 15541, 15896; Twelfth
  Night 17888; Winter's Tale 18976, 19042;
  Sonnet 104 20235; P. Pilgrim 20637
Gossec, François-Joseph 1734–1829
  Tempest 16200
Gößling, Werner
  L.L.L. 6235; Merchant 8157
Göthel, Lothar
  As You Like It 599
Gotovac, Pero 1927–
  Macbeth 6864; Richard II 12654
Gottschalk, Louis Moreau, arr. 1829–1869
  Dream 10828; Settings of Commemorative
  Pieces . . . 20967
Göttsching, Rudolf
  Hamlet 3744
Gottshall, William 1955–
  Twelfth Night 17889
Götzloff, Friedrich
  Twelfth Night 17525
[Gouge, George] [–1730?]
  [Also known under the names 'Mr. George'
  and 'Mr. Goudge']
  Settings of Commemorative Pieces . . .
  20849
Gough, Christine
  All's Well 17; Two Gentlemen 18388
Gould, William Monk 1858–1923
  Two Gentlemen 18513
Gounod, Charles François 1818–1893
  Henry VIII 5240; Romeo 13648
Goupil, Émile Alphonse, arr.   –1937
  Othello 12088
Gout, Alan, arr.
  Romeo 14092
Gover, Gerald Maxwell 1914–
  K. John 5653; Richard II 12759; Sonnet 18
  19377; Sonnet 30 19607
Gow, David 1924–
  Twelfth Night 17526, 17702, 17746,
  17890, 18133
Gow, George Coleman 1860–1938
  As You Like It 1055, 1670
Gowers, Patrick
  Hamlet 3109
Grabert, Martin 1868–
  Dream 10626

Grabu, Louis
  Also known as Lewis Grabue, Louis Grabut, and Louis Grebus
  Timon 16320
Grace, Harvey 1874–1944
  Winter's Tale 19149
Graczol, Frank
  As You Like It 600; Dream 9453
Grädener, Carl Georg Peter 1812–1883
  Twelfth Night 17527
Graf, L., arr.
  Merry Wives 9056
Graf, Rudolf
  Hamlet 3110; Merchant 8158; Dream 9454
Graff, Alfons
  Measure 7892
Grah, Bill
  Dream 9455
Graham, Colin
  Merchant 8159
Graham, Irvin 1909–
  Pseudonym used by Irvin Abraham
  Shrew 14584
Grahn, Ulf-Åke W. 1942–
  Tempest 15006, 15007
Grainger, George Percy, arr. 1882–1961
  Adopted the name Percy Aldridge Grainger
  Othello 12253; Twelfth Night 17763
Gram, Peder 1881–1956
  Settings of Commemorative Pieces . . . 20850, 21135
Grana, Edgar D.
  Errors 2085
Granahan, G.
  Twelfth Night 18134
Granath, Mats
  Macbeth 6865
Grandauer, G.
  Caesar 5327
Grandi, Alfredo
  Hamlet 4157
Grandinger, H. F.
  P. Pilgrim 20638
Grandjean, Axel Carl William 1847–1932
  Lear 5768
Grano, Romano
  2 Henry IV 4547
Granquist, Gunnar Eric
  Twelfth Night 17891
Grant, Paul
  Dream 9456
Grant, William Parks 1910–
  L.L.L. 6549; Macbeth 7437; Twelfth Night 17731
Grant-Schaefer, George Alfred 1872–1939
  As You Like It 1892; Dream 10960
Graun, Karl Heinrich [1703?]–1759
  Antony 373; Coriolanus 2414; Hamlet 3111

Graves, Ralph, Jr.
  Two Gentlemen 18462
Graves, Richard Harding, arr. 1926–
  Dream 10277, 10278, 10279
Graves, Rupert
  1 Henry IV 4345
Graves, Rupert, arr.
  Richard II 12687
Gray, Alan 1855–1935
  Cymbeline 2567; Twelfth Night 17892
Gray, Alan, arr. 1855–1935
  Macbeth 7526; Richard II 12708
Gray, Charles
  Pericles 12565
Gray, G. Allan [1903]–1973
  L.L.L. 6236; Much Ado 11109; Twelfth Night 16848
Gray, John flor. 1985
  Othello 11776; Pericles 12566; Tempest 15008
Gray, John flor. 1850
  Tempest 16218
Grayson, Charles, arr.
  Two Gentlemen 18578
Grazia, E. N.
  Pseudonym used by Mrs. Bourne
  Measure 7893
Graziano, John M. 1938–
  Romeo 13860
Greasby, James
  Hamlet 3112
Greatorex, Edward
  Henry VIII 5095
Greaves, Ralph 1889–1966
  Twelfth Night 17528
Greaves, Ralph, arr. 1889–1966
  Henry VIII 5096; Merry Wives 9169
Greaves, Richard
  Tempest 16256
Grechuta, Marek
  Othello 11777
Green, David Llewellyn
  Sonnet 2 19190; Sonnet 12 19286; Sonnet 73 19994; Sonnet 119 20350; Sonnet 120 20356
Green, Philip –1982
  Othello 12450
Green, Ray Burns 1908–
  Macbeth 7539
Green, R[ussell?]
  Twelfth Night 18135
Green, Shannah
  Tempest 15542, 15668
Green, Sydney, arr.
  As You Like It 1443
Greenan, Owen Emmons
  Henry V 4834
Greenbaum, Hyam, arr.
  Tempest 15276

Greenbaum, Matthew Jonathan 1950–
  Merry Wives 8868; Richard III 12855;
  Shrew 14328
Greenberg, Laura 1942–
  Sonnet 29 19557; Sonnet 73 19995
Greenberg, Noah, arr. 1919–1966
  As You Like It 1444
Greene, Maurice 1695–1755
  Henry VIII 5097
Greene, R.
  As You Like It 1347; Dream 10328
Greene, W. H.
  Dream 10627
Greenhill, Harold Walter 1902–
  Twelfth Night 17893
Greenhill, James Harrison 1840–
  As You Like It 1348; Cymbeline 2568;
  Measure 7894; Winter's Tale 19001; Sonnet
  100 20207
Greenlee, Dillon
  Errors 2086
Greenstein, Michael Harvey
  Also known as Michael Harvey
  Hamlet 3946
Greenwald, Martin
  Hamlet 3947
Greenwell, Peter
  Merchant 8753
Greenwood, J. A., arr.
  Dream 9697, 10829
Greenwood, John Danforth Herman
  1889–1975
  Merchant 8160; Dream 9457, 10301, 10329
Greer, Herb
  Antony 156; As You Like It 601; Errors
  2087, 2088; 1 Henry IV 4346; 2 Henry IV
  4548; Lear 5769; Measure 7652; Dream
  9458; Twelfth Night 16849
Grégoir, Jacques Mathieu Joseph 1817–1876
  Hamlet 3948
Grégoir, Jacques Mathieu Joseph, arr.
  1817–1876
  Dream 10830; Romeo 13690
Gregory, Tom
  Settings of Commemorative Pieces . . . 20938
Grémaud, Stéphane Jean
  Coriolanus 2297; Romeo 13761; Troilus
  16479
Grenfell, Dolores
  Merchant 8676
Gress, Richard 1893–
  Twelfth Night 18136
Greß, Theo
  1 Henry IV 4347; 2 Henry IV 4549; Lear
  5770
Gresser, Hans
  Shrew 14329
Grétry, André-Ernest-Modeste 1741–1813
  Errors 2258; Othello 11778, 12298

Greville, M., arr.
  As You Like It 1946
Greville, Ursula
  Winter's Tale 19075
Grey, Gerald, arr.
  Two Gentlemen 18579
Griebling, Karen Jean 1957–
  Richard III 13032
Grieg, Edvard Hagerup 1843–1901
  Macbeth 7438; Dream 10961
Griesbach, John Henry 1798–1875
  Dream 10628
Griesbach, John Henry, in part arr.
  1798–1875
  Tempest 15009
Griesbach, John Henry, arr. 1798–1875
  Tempest 14721, 14789, 15483
Griesbach, Karl-Rudi 1916–
  Sonnet 51 19749; Sonnet 55 19778; Sonnet
  99 20199; Settings of Commemorative
  Pieces . . . 21214
[?Grieth, Walther]
  Shrew 14330
Griffith, Bobby Glenn, Jr. 1957–
  Macbeth 6866
Griffith, Bobby Glenn, Jr., in part arr. 1957–
  Merchant 8161
Griffith, William [1876?]-
  Twelfth Night 17894; P. Pilgrim 20639
Griffiths, George Richard, arr.
  Dream 9698
Griffiths, Joe
  Hamlet 3113
Griffiths, T.
  Merchant 8444
Griffiths, Thomas Vernon 1894–
  Caesar 5328
Grigoriu, Theodor 1926–
  As You Like It 602; Macbeth 6867; Tempest
  15010; Twelfth Night 16850
Grimm, Carl Hugo 1890–
  Tempest 15669
Grimpe, Alex
  Richard III 12856
Grimshaw, Arthur Edmund, arr. 1864–1913
  Hamlet 3941, 3949
Grimshaw, W.
  Settings of Commemorative Pieces . . . 21040
Grīnblats, Romualds [Samuilovych] 1930–
  Merry Wives 8869
Grobe, Charles, arr. [circa 1817]–1879
  Dream 10831
Groenevelt, Edward F.
  Much Ado 11453
Grohmann, C[arl] T[heodor], arr.
  Some imprints bear the name 'Carlo T.
  Grohmann'
  Merry Wives 9186; Othello 12195; Richard
  III 13062

Grönemeyer, Herbert
  Merchant 8162
Grooms, Calvin, arr.
  Pseudonym used by Lee Orean Smith
  Cymbeline 2739; Merry Wives 9057
Groschwitz, G., arr.
  As You Like It 914
Grosheim, Georg Christoph 1764–1841
  Dream 10152
Gross, Charles
  Lear 5771, 5772; Macbeth 6868; Richard III
  12857
Gross, Eric 1926–
  Cymbeline 2463; Merchant 8562; Winter's
  Tale 18958, 18977, 19002, 19043, 19077
Großkopf, Gerd
  Romeo 13240
Grossman, Ludwik 1835–1915
  Lear 6075
Grossman, Robert
  As You Like It 603; Dream 9459; Twelfth
  Night 16851
Großmann, Gustav
  Shrew 14331
Grosvenor, Norman de l'Aigle
  Much Ado 11454; Tempest 15670
Grote, B. Allison
  Romeo 14147
Groth, Howard
  Shrew 14585
Grove, Rick
  Much Ado 11110
Grovlez, Gabriel, arr.
  Dream 10602
Gruber, Agatha E., in part arr.
  Much Ado 11112
Gruenberg, Louis 1884–1964
  Antony 268
Gruenwald, R.
  Antony 269; As You Like It 604, 1893;
  Caesar 5506
Grünauer, Ingomar
  Hamlet 3114, 4277; Much Ado 11113,
  11114; Twelfth Night 16852, 16853
Grund, Bert
  Much Ado 11115; Twelfth Night 16854
Grundy, Enid
  Dream 10629
Grunes, David J., arr.
  Romeo 13802
Gruntz, George 1932–
  Antony 157; Hamlet 4097; K. John 5596;
  Measure 7653; Richard III 12858; Romeo
  13241; Shrew 14332; Troilus 16480;
  Twelfth Night 16855; Lucrece 20772;
  Settings of Commemorative Pieces . . .
  21041
Gruodis, Juozas Mato 1884–1948
  Hamlet 3115

Gruss, Theodor, arr.
  Merry Wives 9058
'Gryphon'
  Tempest 15011
Gubby, Roy Dawson 1911–
  Sonnet 18 19325
Gudmundsen-Holmgreen, Pelle 1932–
  Hamlet 3116; Sonnet 8 19240
Guenther, Ralph R. 1914–
  Sonnet 17 19320; Sonnet 18 19378
Guernsey, Wellington
  As You Like It 1894; Twelfth Night 18219
Guest, Douglas Albert, arr. 1916–
  Dream 10424; Tempest 15841
Guetzkow, Lauris Steere
  Twelfth Night 17895; Sonnet 55 19779
Guézec, Jean-Pierre 1934–1971
  Much Ado 11116
Gugl, Gerhard 1921–
  Settings of Commemorative Pieces . . . 21042
Guglielmi, Pietro Alessandro 1728–1804
  Antony 374
Guglielmi, Pietro Carlo [circa 1763]–1817
  Romeo 13762
Gui, Vittorio 1885–1975
  Romeo 14030
Guichard, A., arr.
  Romeo 13691, 13692, 13693
Guilbaut, E., arr.
  Hamlet 3649
Guilmartin, Kenneth Kells 1946–
  Dream 9460
Guilmartin, Kenneth Kells, arr. 1946–
  Cymbeline 2475
Gulda, Friedrich 1930–
  Measure 7803
Gülke, Peter
  All's Well 18; Hamlet 3117; Dream 9461;
  Romeo 13242; Twelfth Night 16856
Gulliver, John
  Merchant 8163
Gumbert, Ferdinand, arr. 1818–1896
  Hamlet 3650
Gundry, Inglis 1905–
  Caesar 5545; Merchant 8754; Othello
  12299
Gung'l, Joseph 1810–1889
  Dream 10630
Günther, Jens-Uwe 1937–
  All's Well 83; As You Like It 967, 1587;
  Cymbeline 2520; Hamlet 3118; 2 Henry IV
  4642, 4648, 4649; Henry VIII 5040, 5210;
  Caesar 5485; L.L.L. 6646; Macbeth 7376;
  Measure 7812; Merchant 8164; Dream
  9462, 9463, 10455; Richard II 12655;
  Romeo 13243; Shrew 14586; Timon 16321;
  Troilus 16562
Günther, Jens-Uwe, arr. 1937–
  Dream 10210

Gurgel, Gaó, arr.
Romeo 13983
Gurlitt, Cornelius 1820–1901
Dream 10631
Gurlitt, Manfred 1890–[1972]
Antony 335; 2 Henry IV 4664; Caesar 5536;
Richard II 12774; Richard III 13065; Romeo
14031; Troilus 16579
Gurney, Ivor Bertie 1890–1937
As You Like It 1056, 1671; Henry VIII
5100, 5101; L.L.L. 6422, 6550; Measure
7895; Tempest 15671; Twelfth Night
17529, 18137
Gürtler, Carl
Caesar 5329
Gustafson, Don
Romeo 14200
Gustafson, Dwight Leonard 1930–
1 Henry IV 4348; Tempest 15012
Gustafson, Stig, arr.
Winter's Tale 18807
Gustin, L. V.
Twelfth Night 18329
Gutwein, Daniel
Antony 158
Guylott, Robert 1794–1876
As You Like It 1978
Guzman, Rodolfo
Much Ado 11117
Gwanga, Jonas
Othello 11780
Gwyn, Jennifer
As You Like It 1957
Gyring, Elizabeth 1906–1970
Henry VIII 5102; Tempest 15974
Gyrowetz, Adalbert 1763–1850
Hamlet 3584; Macbeth 7566

H

H., J.
Cymbeline 2866
Haack, Friedrich Wilhelm 1760–1827
Surname known in a number of forms, e.g.,
Haacke, Haak, and Haake
Tempest 15419
Haarklou, Johannes 1847–1925
Caesar 5330
Haase, Michael
Caesar 5331
Hába, Alois, arr. 1893–1972
Tempest 15353
Haberbier, Ernst 1813–1869
Othello 12400
Habersack, Karl 1907–
Sonnet 54 19768; Sonnet 78 20057; Sonnet
84 20074

Hackbarth, Horst
Shrew 14333
Hadley, Helen
Merchant 8165
Hadley, Henry Kimball 1871–1937
As You Like It 1349; Hamlet 3740;
Merchant 8563; Othello 12401; Twelfth
Night 17896
Hadley, Patrick Arthur Sheldon 1899–1973
Twelfth Night 16857
Hadzidakis, Manos
Dream 9464
Haensch, E., arr.
As You Like It 915; Merry Wives 9059
Haentjes, Werner 1923–
Antony 159; As You Like It 605; Hamlet
3119; Lear 5773; Macbeth 6869, 6870;
Dream 9465; Sonnet 18 19453
Hafermalz, Wilhelm
L.L.L. 6238; Much Ado 11118; Romeo
13244
Hagedorn, Helmut
Much Ado 11119
Hagemann, Philip 1932–
Twelfth Night 17530, 17703, 17897,
18138; Sonnet 18 19379; Sonnet 29 19558
Hagen, Daron Aric 1961–
Tempest 15672, 15802, 15827, 15850,
15897
Hager, Johannes 1822–1898
Pseudonym used by Johann Hasslinger von
Hassingen
Tempest 16043
Hagi, Kyoko 1956–
Macbeth 7386, 7402, 7408
Hague, Albert
Lear 6136
Hahn, Reynaldo 1874–1947
Merchant 8402; Much Ado 11120
Haigh, Thomas 1769–1808
Macbeth 6871
Haigh, Thomas, in part arr. 1769–1808
Macbeth 6982
Haigh, Thomas, arr. 1769–1808
Macbeth 6980, 6981; Tempest 14722
Hailey, Gary
Merchant 8166
Haimo, Ethan Tepper 1950–
Macbeth 7387
Haines, Chauncey
Two Gentlemen 18657
Haines, Herbert Edgar 1880–1923
As You Like It 1965
Haines, Roger
Merchant 8167, 8403
Hainton, Herbert H., in part arr.
Othello 11781
Haire, Paula Loraine
Merchant 8168

Haite, John James, arr.
  Dream 9699; P. Pilgrim 20710
Hakanen, Karl
  Dream 9466
Hála, Kamil
  Dream 9467
Halaczinsky, Rudolf
  Hamlet 3120
[Halas, František] [1901–1949]
  Cymbeline 2880
Halbach, Erich
  Macbeth 6872
Haldene, Verner
  Merry Wives 8870
Hale, Alfred Matthew   –1960
  Merchant 8564; Tempest 15420; Sonnet 59
  19812; Sonnet 60 19823; Sonnet 61 19854;
  Sonnet 104 20236; Sonnet 105 20248;
  Sonnet 106 20260; Sonnet 110 20288;
  Sonnet 116 20316
Hálek, Václav 1937–
  All's Well 19, 20, 21; As You Like It 606;
  Hamlet 3121; Macbeth 6873; Measure
  7654; Merchant 8169; Dream 9468; Othello
  11782; Romeo 13245, 13246, 13247;
  Twelfth Night 16858
Hales, Hubert James 1902–1965
  Cymbeline 2569; Henry VIII 5216;
  Merchant 8565, 8693; Dream 10432;
  Twelfth Night 18220; Winter's Tale 18757,
  18959, 18978, 19003, 19044, 19078
Halévy, Jacques François Fromental Élie
  1799–1862
  Born Lévy
  Romeo 14201; Tempest 15421
Halffter, Ernesto Escriche 1905–
  Othello 11783
Halford, John
  Twelfth Night 18139
Hall, A.
  Othello 12300
Hall, Carol [1936–   ]
  L.L.L. 6239
Hall, Charles
  Errors 2089
Hall, Charles King, arr. 1845–1895
  Much Ado 11539
Hall, Frances Evelyn
  Much Ado 11121
Hall, G.
  Twelfth Night 17531
Hall, George
  As You Like It 607; Measure 7655;
  Merchant 8170; Othello 11784; Twelfth
  Night 16859
Hall, George, in part arr.
  Twelfth Night 16860
Hall, J. D.
  Romeo 13248

Hall, John Gerald 1905–
  Dream 9469, 10512
Hall, Pauline 1884–1969
  As You Like It 609; Hamlet 3122, 4212;
  Caesar 5332; Lear 5774; Merry Wives 8871;
  Dream 9470; Shrew 14334
Hall, Richard 1903–1982
  Merchant 8728; Winter's Tale 18758;
  Sonnet 38 19679; Sonnet 75 20034; Sonnet
  76 20045; Sonnet 78 20058
Hallauer, Dankwart 1936–
  Lear 5775; Macbeth 6874
Hallberg, Bengt 1932–
  P. Pilgrim 20640
Hallberg, David
  Dream 10962
Halldén, Björn 1862–1935
  L.L.L. 6240
Halldén, Björn, in part arr. 1862–1935
  Lear 5776
Halldén, Björn, arr. 1862–1935
  Merchant 8172
Halle, Richard L., arr.
  Merry Wives 9060
Halliday, G. C.
  As You Like It 610
Halliday, Jim, in part arr.
  Much Ado 11122
Hallstrom, Henry 1906–
  Dream 9471, 10406, 10448, 10469, 10513
Hallström, Ivar Christian 1826–1901
  Merchant 8171
Halm, August Otto 1869–1929
  Cymbeline 2464; Dream 9472; Much Ado
  11123; Tempest 15013; Twelfth Night
  16861, 17532, 17680, 17898, 18140;
  Winter's Tale 18759
Halmrast, Tor 1951–
  Othello 12451
Halpern, Sidney
  Macbeth 7271
Halvorsen, Johan 1864–1935
  As You Like It 611; Hamlet 3123; 1 Henry
  IV 4349; 2 Henry IV 4550; Macbeth 6875;
  Merchant 8173, 8174; Much Ado 11124
Halvorsen, Johan, in part arr. 1864–1935
  Shrew 14335
Halvorsen, Johan, arr. 1864–1935
  Richard III 12981
Halvorsen, Tom Harry
  Dream 9473
Ham, Albert 1858–1940
  Two Gentlemen 18514
Hamand, Louis Arthur
  Tempest 15673
Hambraeus, Bengt 1928–
  Othello 11785; Tempest 15014, 15898
Hamel, Eduard 1811–
  All's Well 78

Hamel, Peter Michael
As You Like It 612
Hamel, Walter E.
Much Ado 11125
Hames, Richard David 1945–
Troilus 16576
Hamilton, Marcia
As You Like It 1672
Hamilton, Richard
Errors 2090; Two Gentlemen 18389
Hamlyn, Mark
Lear 5777
Hammond, Michael
Merchant 8175; Dream 9474
Hampton, Richard 1937–
Othello 11786
Hanan, Stephen 1947–
Pseudonym used by Stephen Hanan Kaplan
Measure 8035
Hancock, Elizabeth E.
Twelfth Night 16862
Hancock, Oliver John 1965–
Caesar 5333
Hancock, Paul 1952–
Sonnet 27 19523; Sonnet 29 19559; Sonnet
97 20161
Hancock, Stephen
K. John 5597; Lear 5778; Twelfth Night
16863
Hand, Colin 1929–
L.L.L. 6551
Handel, George Frideric 1685–1759
Antony 350; Caesar 5559; Measure 8036;
Much Ado 11612; Settings of
Commemorative Pieces . . . 21136
Handleigh, Robert
Tempest 15015
Handman, Lou 1894–1956
As You Like It 1979
Hänel, Harry
1 Henry IV 4350; 2 Henry IV 4551
Hanell, Robert
Hamlet 3124
Hanke, Karl 1754–1835
Macbeth 6876
Hanmer, Ronald, arr.
Dream 9700
Hannenford, Noel, arr.
Henry VIII 5180
Hänleßz, Manfred
Dream 9475; Romeo 13249
Hansen, Burrell F.
Macbeth 7540
Hanson, Bob
Macbeth 6877
Hanson, Raymond 1913–1976
Othello 11787
Häntsch, Gottfried
Twelfth Night 16864

Hanuš, Jan 1915–
Othello 12023; Sonnet 60 19824; Sonnet
116 20317
Harada, Mark
Dream 9476
Harbage, Alfred Bennett, ed. 1901–
Anthologies 21358
Harbaugh, Carla M.
As You Like It 1673
Harbison, John Harris 1938–
Merchant 8176, 8694; Winter's Tale
18935; Sonnet 59 19813; Sonnet 102
20221
Harcourt, J. Arthur 1852–
Merchant 8566
Hardee, Noble A.
Tempest 15674
Hardin, Burton Ervin 1936–
Henry V 4718
Harding, Robert
Hamlet 3125; Macbeth 6878
Hardy, Judith
Coriolanus 2298
Hardy, Steven 1953–
As You Like It 613; Dream 9477; Much Ado
11126; Tempest 15016; Twelfth Night
16865
Hardy, T. Maskell
L.L.L. 6552; Settings of Commemorative
Pieces . . . 21043
Hardy, T. Maskell, arr.
As You Like It 419, 1445; Much Ado 11540
Hardy, T. Maskell, ed.
Anthologies 21347; 21348
Hare, Edwin C. F., arr.
Dream 9701
Hare, Nicholas, arr.
Othello 12520; Settings of Commemorative
Pieces . . . 21283
Harington, Henry 1727–1816
As You Like It 2003; Merchant 8773;
Twelfth Night 18067
Harker, Arthur Clifford
Henry VIII 5103
Harker, F. Flaxington 1876–1936
As You Like It 1350
'Harlequin'
[Pseudonym used by ?]
Two Gentlemen 18515
Harleßz, Martin
Dream 9478
Harline, Leigh 1907–1969
Lear 6122
Harman, Adrian
L.L.L. 6241
Harman, Carter 1918–
Twelfth Night 18280
Harmer, Dennis
Othello 11788

Harper, C.
Twelfth Night 17533
Harper, Edward James 1941–
Sonnet 2 19191; Sonnet 8 19241; Sonnet
102 20222
Harper, Wally 1941–
Romeo 13763, 13765
Harper, William, in part arr.
Caesar 5334
Harpham, James
Settings of Commemorative Pieces . . .
20851
Harraden, R. Ethel
Also known as Mrs. Frank Glover
Much Ado 11455
Harrell, Gordon, arr.
Tempest 14948
Harrex, Patrick 1946–
Measure 7896; Merchant 8567; Othello
12301
Harries, David 1933–
Settings of Commemorative Pieces . . .
21215
Harris, A.
Twelfth Night 17534
Harris, Cuthbert 1870–1932
As You Like It 1674; Dream 10632, 10915
Harris, Cuthbert, arr. 1870–1932
As You Like It 1446; Cymbeline 2740;
Tempest 14790
Harris, Edward
[Edward C. Harris (1899–   )?]
As You Like It 1351; L.L.L. 6553
Harris, Edward C. 1899–
Dream 10514
Harris, G. J.
Dream 9479
Harris, Herbert
Hamlet 3126
Harris, J. Thorne
Tempest 16044
Harris, James
Tempest 16257
Harris, Joseph John, arr. 1799–1869
Dream 10832, 10833
Harris, Roger W. 1940–
Tempest 16258
Harris, Russell G. 1914–
Macbeth 6879
Harris, W[illiam] H[enry] [1883–1973]
K. John 5598
Harris, William Victor, arr. 1869–1943
Henry VIII 5181
Harris-Weston, R.
Settings of Commemorative Pieces . . . 21270
Harrison, Julius Allen Greenway 1885–1963
Antony 356; As You Like It 1675; Dream
10330, 10515; Twelfth Night 17535,
17536, 17681, 17899, 18141

Harrison, Julius Allen Greenway, in part arr.
1885–1963
As You Like It 614
Harrison, Julius Allen Greenway, arr.
1885–1963
As You Like It 1048, 1340, 1666; Henry
VIII 5088; Dream 10402, 10509; Tempest
15831, 15865; Troilus 16573; Twelfth
Night 17880, 18294; P. Pilgrim 20634;
Settings of Commemorative Pieces . . .
21036
Harrison, Lou 1917–
Winter's Tale 18760
Harrison, Sidney, arr. 1903–
As You Like It 1447
Harriss, Alfred
Twelfth Night 17537
[Harroway, John, arr.] [1810–1857]
Hamlet 4213; Lear 6154; Romeo 14149
Harroway, John 1810–1857
Romeo 14150
Harroway, John, in part arr. 1810–1857
Macbeth 7567
Harroway, John, arr. 1810–1857
Merchant 8774; Othello 12498; Richard III
13076
Hart, Fritz Bennicke 1874–1949
Hamlet 3950; Henry VIII 5104; Twelfth
Night 17393
Hart, James 1647–1718
Tempest 15424
Hart, Jonathan
Tempest 15017
Hart, Joseph Binns, arr. 1794–1844
Macbeth 6983
Harthan, Hans, arr.
Cymbeline 2741
Hartley, B. W.
As You Like It 1352
Hartley, James
Caesar 5335; Shrew 14336
Hartley, Walter Sinclair 1927–
Henry VIII 5105, 5217
Hartmann, Albert, arr.
Dream 10834
Hartmann, Edmund
Macbeth 7394
Hartmann, Gerhard
Much Ado 11127
Hartmann, H., arr.
Merry Wives 9061, 9062
Hartmann, Karl Amadeus 1905–1963
Macbeth 6880, 7272
Hartung, C. F., arr.
Merry Wives 9063
Hartwig-Steller, Maxi-Charlott 1929–
Coriolanus 2373; Romeo 14151, 14152,
14153, 14154; Settings of Commemorative
Pieces . . . 21137

Harty, Herbert Hamilton, arr. 1879–1941
  Hamlet 4190
Harvey, J. flor. 1910
  Twelfth Night 18330
Harvey, Jonathan 1939–
  Dream 10749
Harvey, Rupert
  Much Ado 11128; Winter's Tale 18761
Harvey, W. T.
  Twelfth Night 16866
Hásek, Josef
  Timon 16322
Hashagen, Klaus 1924–
  Dream 9480
Hashiba, Kiyoshi
  Twelfth Night 16867
Hasquenoph, Pierre Louis Marie 1922–1982
  As You Like It 952
Hasse, Johann Adolf 1699–1783
  Also known as Johann Adolphe Hasse
  Dream 10963
Hassenstein, Paul, arr.
  Merry Wives 9064
Hassler, Simon 1832–1901
  Hamlet 3127, 3951; Merchant 8177;
  Twelfth Night 16868
Hassloch, Karl 1769–1829
  Macbeth 7498
Hastings, Ross, arr. 1915–
  Merry Wives 9187, 9188
Hately, Walter 1843–
  Dream 10964
Hathaway, Daniel
  As You Like It 615; Merry Wives 8872
Hathaway, Joseph William George 1870–1956
  Merchant 8445
Hatton, John Liptrot 1809–1886
  Also wrote under the pseudonym 'P. B. Czapek'
  As You Like It 2004; Hamlet 3129; 1 Henry
  IV 4504; Henry VIII 4993, 5106; K. John 5599;
  Lear 5779; Macbeth 6881, 6882; Merchant
  8178, 8568; Dream 10407; Much Ado 11129;
  Tempest 15018; Twelfth Night 18142; Two
  Gentlemen 18654; Winter's Tale 18762
Hatton, John Liptrot, in part arr. 1809–1886
  Also wrote under the pseudonym 'P. B. Czapek'
  Richard II 12656
Hatton, John Liptrot, arr. 1809–1886
  Also wrote under the pseudonym 'P. B. Czapek'
  Macbeth 6984; Much Ado 11541; Othello
  12089
Haubenstock-Ramati, Roman 1919–
  Sonnet 53 19757; Sonnet 54 19769
Haubiel, Charles Trowbridge 1892–1978
  Tempest 16259; Settings of Commemorative
  Pieces . . . 20852
Haug, Hans
  Caesar 5336; Much Ado 11130; Twelfth
  Night 16869

Haūgland, A. Oscar 1922–
  L.L.L. 6423; Twelfth Night 17900; Sonnet 1
  19180
Hauk, Günter
  Dream 9481; Romeo 13250
Haun, Kathryn Reece
  Romeo 14032
Hauschild, Wolf-Dieter
  Errors 2091; Much Ado 11131
Hauser, Eric, arr.
  Dream 9702
Hauser, Frank
  Hamlet 3130
Häusler, Emil
  Twelfth Night 16870
Hausser, Henri, arr.
  Dream 9703
Havelka, Svatopluk
  Romeo 13251
Havens, Mabel Fielder, in part arr.
  Winter's Tale 18763
Havergal, Henry
  Macbeth 6884
Haverkampf, Ulrich, arr.
  Twelfth Night 17224
Hawkes, William Henry, arr.
  Merry Wives 9065, 9066
Hawkins, George, arr.
  Romeo 13694
Hawkins, H. A.
  Dream 9482
Hawkins, John 1944–
  As You Like It 1994
Hawksworth, John
  Settings of Commemorative Pieces . . .
  21138
Hawley, Charles Beach 1858–1915
  As You Like It 2005
Haworth, Francis 1905–
  As You Like It 953; Macbeth 6885, 7444;
  Romeo 13911; Tempest 15019
Hawthorne, Tim
  Twelfth Night 16871
Hay, Walter Cecil 1828–1905
  Tempest 16260
Hayashi, Hikaru
  Antony 160; Merry Wives 8873
Hayden, William
  Antony 315; As You Like It 1895; Dream
  10633; Tempest 16045
Haydn, Franz Joseph 1732–1809
  Hamlet 3131; Lear 5780; Tempest 16261;
  Twelfth Night 18068; Settings of
  Commemorative Pieces . . . 21299
Haydn, Franz Joseph, arr. 1732–1809
  L.L.L. 6424
Hayes, Barry
  Dream 9483

Hayes, Fanny M.
  Cymbeline 2570; Settings of Commemorative
  Pieces . . . 21044
Hayes, H. L.
  Twelfth Night 16872
Hayes, Philip 1738–1797
  As You Like It 1844
Hayes, Truman Daniel 1918–
  Antony 295; Macbeth 7395; Much Ado
  11592; Othello 11789; Twelfth Night
  16873, 18221
Hayes, William [1706?]–1777
  Merchant 8755
Haynes, A. P.
  Macbeth 6886
Haynes, Antony
  1 Henry IV 4351; Shrew 14337
Haynes, Walter Battison, arr. 1859–1900
  Hamlet 3137
Haywood, Ernest, arr.
  Cymbeline 2742
Hazard, Jim
  Macbeth 6887
Hazel, Edward
  Lear 6076, 6077
Heacock, Richard
  Dream 9484
Head, Michael Dewar 1900–1976
  Merchant 8446
Heale, Hélène 1855–
  As You Like It 1057, 1353, 1676; Cymbeline
  2673; Tempest 15899; Two Gentlemen
  18516; Venus 20792
Heale, Hélène, arr. 1855–
  As You Like It 420, 1175, 1354; Errors
  2038; Cymbeline 2655, 2743; Macbeth
  7406; Dream 9704, 10131, 10307, 10553,
  10835, 10836; Tempest 15305, 15306,
  15307, 16224; P. Pilgrim 20728
Heap, Charles Swinnerton 1847–1900
  Two Gentlemen 18517
Hearne, Isabel
  Cymbeline 2820, 2821; Hamlet 3952, 3953;
  2 Henry VI 4922; Lear 6078; L.L.L. 6656;
  Dream 10634, 10635; Winter's Tale 19108,
  19109; Venus 20801
Hearne, John Michael 1937–
  As You Like It 616, 1058; Lear 5781; Dream
  9485; Pericles 12567; Tempest 15020;
  Twelfth Night 16874; Sonnet 60 19825;
  Sonnet 65 19890; Settings of
  Commemorative Pieces . . . 21300
Heartz, H. L., arr.
  Cymbeline 2744; Two Gentlemen 18580
Heath, John Rippiner 1887–
  Hamlet 3954; Dream 10636; Romeo
  13912
Heath, Reginald
  Tempest 16046

Heathcote, Evelyn D.
  Henry VIII 5107
Heathcote, Gilbert [1765–1829]
  Hamlet 3726
Heaton, Theodore
  Merchant 8786
Hecker, Robert Ira 1947–
  Known as Zeke Hecker
  L.L.L. 6672; Dream 9486; Othello 12452;
  Pericles 12602; Shrew 14338; Tempest
  15021; Twelfth Night 18270
Heckman, Don
  Hamlet 3132
Hector, Chastey William George, arr.
  Tempest 14791
Hedger, John R.
  As You Like It 1355, 1677; Twelfth Night
  17538, 17901
Hedwall, Lennart 1932–
  Hamlet 3133, 3704, 3760, 3867
Heenan, Ashley David Joseph 1925–
  Measure 7897
Hegedus, Gabor
  Also known under the pseudonym 'B. B.
  Gabor'
  Othello 12499
Heiden, Bernhard 1910–
  1 Henry IV 4352; Tempest 15022
Heidingsfeld, Ludwig 1854–1920
  Lear 6079
Heifetz, Jascha, arr. 1901–1987
  Cymbeline 2644; Dream 9705; Romeo
  13803; Winter's Tale 18957
Heilmann, Harald 1924–
  As You Like It 1059, 1678; Merchant 8447
Heilner, Irwin 1908–
  Sonnet 76 20046
Heim, Ernst, arr.
  Othello 12090
Heimann, Julius
  Twelfth Night 16875
Heimler, Hans
  Henry V 4719; Tempest 15023
Hein, Silvio
  Settings of Commemorative Pieces . . . 21271
Heindrichs, Heinz-Albert
  Dream 9487; Much Ado 11132; Romeo
  13252; Two Gentlemen 18390
Heinefetter, Wilhelm [circa 1833]–
  Macbeth 6888
Heininen, Paavo Johannes 1938–
  Sonnet 130 20421
Heinrich, Adel Verna 1926–
  As You Like It 954; Hamlet 3585, 3586;
  Henry VIII 5036; Caesar 5479; Macbeth
  7373, 7383, 7388; Othello 12024; Pericles
  12603; Richard II 12749; Romeo 13766;
  Shrew 14650; Timon 16370; Sonnet 8
  19229; Sonnet 102 20213; Sonnet 106

20257; Sonnet 128 20379; Sonnet 141 20471
Heinrich, Max 1853–1916
  Richard III 13047
Heinz, Albert, arr. 1822–1911
  Also known as Albert Heintz
  Caesar 5453
Heinze, Helmut
  Macbeth 6889
Heise, Peter Arnold 1830–1879
  As You Like It 1060, 1356, 1679; Hamlet 3793; Henry VIII 5108; Merchant 8569; Much Ado 11456; Othello 12302; Twelfth Night 17539, 18143
Heisig, Wolfgang
  Dream 9488
Helasvuo, Esa
  Dream 9489
Helber, Kurtz
  Caesar 5337
Helberger, Heinzpeter 1912–
  Tempest 15900; Winter's Tale 18965; Sonnet 24 19495; Sonnet 55 19780; Sonnet 65 19891
Helfer, Walter
  Sonnet 18 19380
Hellawell, Piers Rupert Henry Duncan 1956–
  Hamlet 3955
Helldén, Daniel 1917–
  As You Like It 968, 1680; Hamlet 3830
Hellem, Mark D. 1957–
  Hamlet 4158; Henry VIII 5234; Lear 6137; Sonnet 73 20028
Hellemann, Christian
  Dream 10637
Heller, Eddie
  Henry VIII 5241
Heller, M. P., arr.
  Merry Wives 9067
Heller, Stephen, arr. 1813–1888
  Cymbeline 2745; Dream 9706
Hellermann, William David 1939–
  Tempest 16235
Helliger, Richard
  Macbeth 6890; Romeo 13253; Twelfth Night 16876
Hellman, Ivar 1891–
  Hamlet 3134
Hellmundt, Gottfried
  Romeo 13254
Helm, Everett Burton 1913–
  Antony 306
Helmann, Aleksandr 1912–1954
  Sonnet 73 20029
Hely-Hutchinson, Christian Victor 1901–1947
  Antony 161; Henry VIII 5109; L.L.L. 6425, 6554; Macbeth 6891, 6892; Much Ado 11457; P. Pilgrim 20641

Hely-Hutchinson, Christian Victor, arr. 1901–1947
  Othello 12521
Helyer, Jack, arr.
  [Also known as Edmund Victor Helyer?]
  Othello 11719
Hemann, Carl, arr.
  Dream 10837
Hemenway, Edith 1926–
  Merchant 8570; Tempest 15675
Hemery, Valentine, arr.
  Dream 9707
Hemmer, Eugene Ralph 1929–1977
  Twelfth Night 17540, 17682, 17704, 17902, 18144
Hemmer, Martha Maycox 1914–1983
  Macbeth 7445; Dream 10433; Romeo 13827, 13852, 13879
Hemmerlein, J. J. A., arr.
  Dream 10838
Hempel, F. C.
  Measure 7656; Shrew 14339
Hemy, Henri Christopher
  Tempest 16047
Henault, Franz, arr.
  Dream 10839
Henderson, Alva 1940–
  Tempest 15425
Henderson, Charles E. 1907–1970
  Hamlet 4098
Hendrichs, Hans Albert
  Hamlet 3135
Hendricks, Thomas Manley 1949–
  Romeo 13824
Henley, William, arr.
  Othello 12522
Henly, Mary
  L.L.L. 6242
Hennagin, Michael 1936–
  As You Like It 1681, 1951
Henneberg, Richard 1853–1925
  Macbeth 6893
Henning, Carl Wilhelm 1784–1867
  Caesar 5338
Henning, Erwin
  [Erwing Arthur Henning (1910–   )?]
  Measure 7657
Henning, Franz, arr.
  Much Ado 11352
Henrich, Hermann 1891–
  Much Ado 11362
Henrion, Paul 1819–1901
  Othello 12500
Henry, Dean
  Othello 11790
Henschel, George 1850–1934
  Born Isidor Georg Henschel
  Hamlet 3136, 3956; Caesar 5339; Lear 6155; Twelfth Night 17541;

Henschel, George (*cont.*)
  Winter's Tale 18764; Sonnet 105 20249, 20255
Hensel, Johann Daniel 1757–1839
  Tempest 15426
Henselt, Adolphe, arr. 1814–1889
  Also known as Adolph Henselt and as Adolf von Henselt
  Dream 10840
Henshilwood, Donald
  Dream 9490, 9491
Hensley, Harold Glenn 1922–
  Settings of Commemorative Pieces . . . 21278
Henze, Hans Werner 1926–
  As You Like It 1896; Hamlet 3957; L.L.L. 6327; Macbeth 7446; Dream 10638, 10639; Richard III 13054, 13079; Romeo 13913; Tempest 16048; Twelfth Night 18222; Sonnet 129 20416
Heppener, Robert 1925–
  Tempest 15024
Héquet, Charles Joseph Gustave 1803–1865
  Lear 5997
Hera, Willi
  Othello 11791
Herbage, Julian, in part arr.
  As You Like It 617, 618, 1958; Much Ado 11133
Herbeck, Johann 1831–1877
  Also known as Ritter von Herbeck
  As You Like It 1357
Herberigs, Robert 1886–1974
  Antony 270; Hamlet 3958; Merry Wives 9220; Romeo 13914
Herbert, John Bunyan 1852–1927
  As You Like It 1358; L.L.L. 6426; Dream 10331; Tempest 15901; Twelfth Night 17542
Herbert, John Bunyan, ed. 1852–1927
  Anthologies 21325
Herbert, Seligman Walter 1902–1975
  Shrew 14340
Herbert, Theodore, arr.
  Merry Wives 9068; Dream 9708
Herbert, Victor August 1859–1924
  As You Like It 1966
Herbert, Victor August, arr. 1859–1924
  Dream 9709
Herbert-Caesari, E.
  Hamlet 3813
Herbolsheimer, Bern Hart 1948–
  As You Like It 1061, 1359; Hamlet 3705; 2 Henry IV 4637; Henry VIII 5110; Measure 7898; Merchant 8571; Much Ado 11381; Othello 12303; Twelfth Night 17705
Herder, Ronald 1930–
  As You Like It 619
Herf, Franz Richter 1920–
  Errors 2092

Herfeld, Arno
  Dream 9492
Herman, Adolphe, arr.
  Othello 12091; Romeo 13695, 13696
Herman, Jules, arr.
  Romeo 13697; Settings of Commemorative Pieces . . . 20968
Herman, Mary
  Richard III 12859
Hermann, Friedrich, arr. 1828–1907
  Merry Wives 9069, 9070; Dream 9710, 9711, 9712; Romeo 13966
Hermann, Ulrich 1937–
  Hamlet 3138; Tempest 15025
Hernandez, Larry D. 1960–
  Macbeth 6894
Hernandez-Gonzalo, Gisela [1910?]–1971
  Hamlet 3139
Hérold, Louis Joseph Ferdinand 1791–1833
  1 Henry IV 4512; 2 Henry IV 4681
Hérold, Louis Joseph Ferdinand, arr. 1791–1833
  Othello 12092
Herouet, Marc
  Tempest 15026
Herr, Robert C.
  Lear 6123
Herriman, Jack
  Tempest 15027
Herrmann, Bernard 1911–1975
  Hamlet 4099; Lear 6124; Macbeth 6895; Richard III 13068; Romeo 14048; Twelfth Night 18271
Herrmann, Ed
  Hamlet 3140
Herrmann, Theodor, arr.
  Dream 10841
Herschel, William 1738–1822
  Born Friedrich Wilhelm Herschel
  Macbeth 7403
Herschell, Richard Farrer 1878–1929
  Much Ado 11134; Two Gentlemen 18391
Hertel, Piotr
  As You Like It 620, 621; Coriolanus 2299; Hamlet 3141; 1 Henry IV 4353; Romeo 13255; Shrew 14341
Hertel, Thomas
  As You Like It 622; 1 Henry IV 4354; 2 Henry IV 4552; Dream 9493, 9494; Winter's Tale 18765
Hertz, Henryk
  As You Like It 623
Hertz, Michał 1844–1918
  As You Like It 624; Twelfth Night 16877
Herz, Henri, arr. 1803–1888
  Also known as Heinrich Herz
  Dream 10842, 10843; Othello 12093
Herzberg, Hans
  Twelfth Night 16878

Heseltine, John LeRoy, in part arr.
L.L.L. 6243; Winter's Tale 18766
Hesford, Michael Bryan 1930–
As You Like It 1360; L.L.L. 6427; Romeo
13866; Twelfth Night 17543; Settings of
Commemorative Pieces . . . 21045
Hesford, Michael Bryan, arr. 1930–
Dream 10211; Othello 12523, 12524
Hess, J. Ch[arles], arr.
Romeo 13698
Hess, Ludwig 1877–1944
Twelfth Night 17394
Hess, Nigel 1953–
Errors 2093; Hamlet 3142; Caesar 5340;
Much Ado 11135, 11382, 11458; Othello
11792; Troilus 16481; Winter's Tale 18767;
Settings of Commemorative Pieces . . . 20853
Hesselberg, Edouard, arr.
Cymbeline 2746
Hessenberg, Kurt 1908–
Tempest 15028, 16049
Hester, Jeffrey Richards
Lear 6156
Hester, Wesley Hal 1933–
Twelfth Night 17395; Settings of
Commemorative Pieces . . . 20939
Hetea, Ion
Timon 16323
Hetsch, Karl Ludwig Friedrich 1806–1872
Macbeth 6896; Much Ado 11136
Heuberger, Richard F. J. 1850–1914
Twelfth Night 17397
Heuberger, Richard F. J., arr. 1850–1914
Merry Wives 9071
Heuser, Kurt
Antony 162; Hamlet 3143; 1 Henry IV
4355; 2 Henry IV 4553; Caesar 5341;
Measure 7658; Merry Wives 8874; Much
Ado 11137, 11138; Richard III 12860,
12861; Shrew 14342; Tempest 15029;
Timon 16324; Troilus 16482; Twelfth Night
16879
Heuss, Alfred Valentin 1877–1934
Sonnet 81 20067
Heward, Leslie Hays 1897–1943
Hamlet 3587; Dream 10408, 10516
Hewitt, [?], arr.
Dream 9713
Hewitt, John Hill, in part arr. 1801–1890
Dream 10153
Hewitt, Thomas James 1880–
Dream 10640
Hewitt-Jones, David Anthony 1926–
Known professionally as Tony Hewitt-Jones
As You Like It 1682; L.L.L. 6555; Dream
10517; Richard II 12657; Tempest 15676,
15851
Hewson, Chris
Twelfth Night 16880

Hewson, Richard
Antony 163; Romeo 13256
Hey, C. E.
Twelfth Night 17903
Heyde, J. F.
Twelfth Night 17904
Heyl, Paul R.
Much Ado 11459
Heyman, Werner
Hamlet 4100; Merchant 8729
Heynen, Walter
Othello 11793
Heyral, Marc
Romeo 14155
Heyward, Berry
Henry VIII 4994
Heywood, Ian
Merchant 8404
Hicklin, Don
All's Well 22; As You Like It 625
Hickling, Wilfred, arr.
Two Gentlemen 18581
Hickson, Robert 1951–
Macbeth 6897; Measure 7659
Hickson, Robert, in part arr. 1951–
1 Henry IV 4356
Hidas, Frigyes 1928–
All's Well 23; Caesar 5342
Hieß, Karl
Shrew 14343
Higdon, Greg S.
Measure 7660; Two Gentlemen 18392;
Winter's Tale 18768
Higgins, Benjamin Pearce
Tempest 15030; Twelfth Night 16881
Higgins, Benjamin Pearce, in part arr.
Richard II 12658
Higginson, Gary Michael 1952–
L.L.L. 6428; Sonnet 8 19242; Sonnet 76
20047
Higgs, Henry Marcellus   –1929
Antony 316; As You Like It 1897; Hamlet
3959; Henry VIII 5218; Caesar 5507; L.L.L.
6244, 6657; Macbeth 7447; Merchant
8695; Merry Wives 9221; Dream 10641;
Othello 12402; Romeo 13915; Tempest
16050; Winter's Tale 19110
Higgs, Henry Marcellus, arr.   –1929
Henry VIII 5021, 5022; Twelfth Night 17186
Higgs, Jessica
Romeo 13257
Hignard, Jean Louis Aristide 1822–1898
Hamlet 3588
Hiketick, Patrick
Winter's Tale 18769
Hilb, Birdie E.
As You Like It 2006
Hilb, Emil, arr.
Romeo 13984

Hildebrand, Ernst 1918–
  Merchant 8405
Hildemann, Wolfgang 1925–
  Settings of Commemorative Pieces . . . 21140
Hiles, Henry 1826–1904
  As You Like It 1361; Dream 10642
Hiles, John, arr. 1810–1882
  Dream 9714
Hilf, Arno, arr.
  Othello 12094
Hill, [?]
  Twelfth Night 16882
Hill, Ada Marion
  Romeo 13258
Hill, Alex E.
  Romeo 13259
Hill, D. M., arr.
  Measure 7806
Hill, Harrison
  Romeo 14156
Hill, Henry
  Tempest 16262
Hill, Hoagie K.
  Dream 9495
Hill, Jackson 1941–
  Sonnet 64 19872
Hill, Mirrie Irma 1926–
  Merchant 8448; Tempest 15902
Hill, Richard, in part arr. 1942–
  Settings of Commemorative Pieces . . .
  20854
Hill, W. Hayes
  Much Ado 11139
Hiller, Ferdinand 1811–1885
  Cymbeline 2674; Twelfth Night 17905,
  18223
Hiller, Ferdinand, arr. 1811–1885
  Hamlet 3558
Hiller, Harry Croft
  Much Ado 11460
Hiller, Wilfried
  Dream 9496
Hillmar, Kurt
  Twelfth Night 16883
Hills, William, adapter
  Dream 10518
Hilpipre, Gérard 1959–
  Sonnet 44 19724; Sonnet 73 19996; Sonnet
  146 20491
Hilprecht, Uwe 1939–
  As You Like It 626; Merchant 8179
Hilprecht, Uwe, in part arr. 1939–
  Dream 9497
Hilton, John, the Younger 1599–1667
  As You Like It 1845
Hime, Edward Laurence 1823–
  Dream 10365; Twelfth Night 18072
Hime, Edward Laurence, arr. 1823–
  Two Gentlemen 18364

Himmel, Friedrich Heinrich 1765–1814
  Tempest 15427
Hind, John
  As You Like It 1362; Merchant 8572;
  Twelfth Night 17544; Winter's Tale 19079
Hind O'Malley, Pamela 1923–
  As You Like It 1683
Hindley, David
  Shrew 14344
Hink, Antje
  Twelfth Night 16884
Hinkelbein, Susanne
  Romeo 13260
Hinman, Mildred
  Henry VIII 5111
Hinrichs, A.
  Antony 164
Hinton, Arthur, arr. 1869–1941
  Dream 10212
Hirsch, Bernie, arr.
  Dream 10213
Hirsch, Fritz
  Twelfth Night 17545
Hirsch, Stephen A.
  As You Like It 1062
Hirschbach, Hermann 1812–1888
  Also wrote under the pseudonym 'Henry
  Largo'
  Hamlet 3144; Caesar 5508; Othello 12025
Hirst, George
  Richard III 12862
Hively, Wells 1902–1969
  Twelfth Night 17732
Hlávka, Zdeněk
  Dream 9498; Twelfth Night 16885
Hoag, Charles Kelso 1931–
  Cymbeline 2571; Lear 6019
Hoar, Robert
  Sonnet 18 19381
Hoard, Bruce
  Lear 5782
Hoard, Bruce, in part arr.
  Hamlet 3146
Hobart, Daniel J.
  Merchant 8756
Hobbs, Christopher
  Hamlet 3147
Hobbs, John William 1799–1877
  All's Well 100; Tempest 16167
Hobday, Rachael
  Othello 12304
Hobson, Ian
  Dream 9499
Hobson, Richard
  As You Like It 627
Hoby, John Charles James
  As You Like It 1063, 1684
Hock, Jan Nepomucen
  Macbeth 6898; Tempest 15031

Höckner, Hilmar, arr.
Dream 10214
Hodge, [Muriel Talbot?]
Measure 7899
Hodge, Muriel Talbot
Merchant 8573
Hodson, George Alexander –1863
Merry Wives 9238
Hoérée, Arthur Charles Ernest
1897–1986
Pseudonym used by Pedro Lipton
All's Well 24; Richard III 12863
Höffer, Paul 1895–1949
Coriolanus 2300
Hoffman, Theodore B. 1925–
Hamlet 3148; Macbeth 7448, 7499;
Merchant 8180; Tempest 15032; Twelfth
Night 16886
Hoffmann, Ernst Theodor Amadeus
1776–1822
Merry Wives 9012
Hoffmann, Heinz
Much Ado 11140
Hoffmann, Willi
Macbeth 6899
Hoffmeister, Franz Anton 1754–1812
Tempest 15428
Höfgen, Christian
Measure 7661
Hofmann, [?]
Merry Wives 9013
Hofmann, Hans
Richard III 12864
Hofmann, Heinrich Karl Johann 1842–1902
Hamlet 4214; Othello 12501; Romeo 14157;
Tempest 16219
Hofmann, Klaus
Hamlet 3149; Measure 7662; Shrew 14345;
Twelfth Night 16887
Hofmann, Richard, arr. 1831–1909
Also known as Richard Hoffman
Cymbeline 2747; Merry Wives 9072, 9073;
Dream 9715; Othello 12196; Shrew 14577,
14578
Hogan, John Morris
Settings of Commemorative Pieces . . . 21046
Hogarth, George, arr. 1783–1870
As You Like It 421; Cymbeline 2847;
Macbeth 6985; Tempest 14723, 14792
Högberg, Per 1957–
Hamlet 4101
Högenhaven, Knud 1928–1987
Sonnet 8 19243; Sonnet 106 20261; Sonnet
128 20393
Hogg, Philippa Stewart
Measure 7663
Hoggard, Lara, arr.
As You Like It 1448; Othello 12308;
Tempest 15966; Twelfth Night 17310

Hohensee, Wolfgang 1927–
Shrew 14346
Hohmeyer, Jim
Tempest 15033
Hoiby, Lee 1926–
As You Like It 628; Hamlet 3150; L.L.L.
6245; Merry Wives 8875; Richard III
12865; Shrew 14347; Tempest 15034,
15429; Twelfth Night 16888, 17546,
17906, 18145; Winter's Tale 18770
Hoile, Martin
Richard III 12866
Holbrooke, Josef Charles 1878–1958
Also known as Joseph Holbrooke
Romeo 13826, 13916, 14033; Tempest
16051
Hold, Trevor James 1939–
As You Like It 1064; Henry VIII 5112;
Macbeth 7389; Measure 8044; Dream
10358, 10519; Much Ado 11461; Tempest
15543, 15677, 15903; Twelfth Night
18146; Winter's Tale 19150
Holder, Christopher
Measure 7664
Holder, Joseph William 1764–1832
Much Ado 11640
Holder, Joseph William, arr. 1764–1832
Hamlet 3722
Holdridge, Lee Elwood
Henry VIII 5113; Shrew 14678
Holenia, Hanns 1890–1972
Twelfth Night 17398
Holford, Franz
Twelfth Night 17547
Holland, Caroline
Sonnet 71 19948
Holland, Dulcie Sybil 1913–
Dream 10643; Twelfth Night 17907;
P. Pilgrim 20642
Holland, Johann David 1746–1827
Hamlet 3151
Hollander, Benoit 1853–1942
Tempest 16220
Holländer, Friedrich 1896–
Caesar 5343
Hollander, John, [in part arr.]
Twelfth Night 16889
Holliday, John C.
Dream 10644
Hollingsworth, John, arr. 1916–1963
Romeo 13985
Holloway, Merle
As You Like It 1065
Holloway, Robin 1943–
Othello 12441
Holm, Mogens Winkel 1936–
Twelfth Night 16890
Holmboe, Vagn 1909–
Caesar 5344; L.L.L. 6429, 6556

Holmek, Yngve 1911–
  Hamlet 3152
Holmes, Alfred 1837–1876
  Romeo 13917; Settings of Commemorative
  Pieces . . . 21141
Holmes, Alfred, arr. 1837–1876
  Dream 9716
Holmes, Henry, arr. 1839–1905
  Dream 9717
Holmes, Richard
  Errors 2094
Holmes, Rupert
  Twelfth Night 16891
Holmes, William Henry, arr. 1812–1885
  Errors 2039; Dream 9718; Twelfth Night
  16672; Two Gentlemen 18365
Holmström, Carita 1954–
  Romeo 13261
Holst, A. Moller, arr.
  Cymbeline 2748
Holst, Gustav Theodore 1874–1934
  Born Gustavus Theodore von Holst
  As You Like It 1363; Twelfth Night 17548
Holst, Gustav Theodore, in part arr. 1874–1934
  Born Gustavus Theodore von Holst
  1 Henry IV 4463; 2 Henry IV 4629; Sonnet
  12 19294; Sonnet 19 19474
Holst, Gustav Theodore, arr. 1874–1934
  Born Gustavus Theodore von Holst
  Settings of Commemorative Pieces . . . 20940
Holst, Imogen Clare, arr. 1907–1984
  As You Like It 1449; Dream 10136, 10215;
  Tempest 15060; Twelfth Night 16708,
  17311; Winter's Tale 19026; Sonnet 43
  19712; Settings of Commemorative
  Pieces . . . 21142
Holstein, Jean Paul 1939–
  Hamlet 4068
Hölszky, Adriana 1953–
  Sonnet 64 19873
Holt, Henry
  As You Like It 629
Holten, Bo 1948–
  Sonnet 8 19244
Holterdorf, Theodor
  Lear 5783; Dream 9500; Romeo 13262;
  Winter's Tale 18771
Holý, Ondřej František 1747–1783
  Also known as Andreas Franz Holly
  Hamlet 3153; Macbeth 6900
Hölzel, G. 1813–1883
  Twelfth Night 17549
Holzmann, Rudolf, arr. 1910–
  Dream 10216
Homewood, Bill
  Twelfth Night 16892
Homs, Joaquím 1906–
  Also known as Joaquím Homs Oller
  Sonnet 147 20511

Honegger, Arthur 1892–1955
  Hamlet 3154; Tempest 15035, 15544,
  15678, 15904, 16052; Winter's Tale 18772
Honey, Albert
  L.L.L. 6430; Twelfth Night 18262
Honig, Michael
  Dream 9501
Honolka, Kurt, adapter 1913–
  Tempest 15430
Hood, Tim
  Dream 9502
Hook, James [1746?]–1827
  As You Like It 1980; Cymbeline 2881;
  Dream 9503; Othello 12305
Hooker, Paul Scott
  Tempest 15036
Hookham, George
  Twelfth Night 17908
Hooper, Elric
  Lear 5784
Hope, Claude
  Pseudonym used by Neal Hemachandra
  Measure 8037
Hopkins, Antony 1921–
  Born Antony Reynolds
  All's Well 25; Antony 165, 166, 167;
  Coriolanus 2301; Hamlet 3155; Henry V
  4720, 4721; Caesar 5345, 5346; K. John
  5600; Lear 5785, 5786; Macbeth 6901,
  6902; Othello 11794; Romeo 13263, 14049;
  Troilus 16483; Twelfth Night 16893
Hopkins, Douglas
  Cymbeline 2572
Hopkins, Franklin 1879–
  As You Like It 1066, 1685; Henry VIII
  5114; L.L.L. 6364; Twelfth Night 17910;
  Two Gentlemen 18518
Hopkins, Gerard Manley 1844–1889
  Henry VIII 5115; Much Ado 11373; Two
  Gentlemen 18519; Winter's Tale 18960
Hopp, Julius 1819–1885
  Hamlet 3589
Horder, Mervyn 1910–
  As You Like It 1067, 1364, 1686; Cymbeline
  2573; L.L.L. 6431; Twelfth Night 17911,
  18147; Two Gentlemen 18520
Horelick, Stephen C.
  Henry V 4722; Twelfth Night 16894
Horký, Karel 1909–
  Hamlet 3590
[Horn, Charles Edward] [1786–1849]
  As You Like It 1068, 1959
Horn, August, arr. 1825–1893
  Cymbeline 2749; Caesar 5524; Dream 9719,
  9720
Horn, Charles Edward 1786–1849
  As You Like It 630, 1981; Macbeth 6903;
  Merchant 8730; Merry Wives 8876; Dream
  10332, 10353, 10359, 10757, 10787;

Tempest 15037, 15038; Sonnet 18 19382;
Sonnet 40 19690, 19701; Sonnet 57 19802;
Sonnet 60 19826; P. Pilgrim 20643, 20644,
20744, 20745; Venus 20793, 20807;
Settings of Commemorative Pieces . . . 21301
Horn, Frederick
  Hamlet 4102
Horn, Hans Werner
  Macbeth 6904
Horn, Roderick
  Much Ado 11141
Horncastle, Frederick William
  Twelfth Night 17683
Horne, Elsie E., arr.
  Cymbeline 2750
Hornyak, Andrew
  Dream 9504; Twelfth Night 16895
Horovitz, Joseph 1926–
  As You Like It 631, 1069, 1365, 1687;
  Macbeth 7273; Tempest 15039; Twelfth
  Night 16896; Settings of Commemorative
  Pieces . . . 21047
Horowitz, Jeffrey
  Dream 9505
Horr, Peter, arr.
  Dream 10844
Horrocks, Amy Elise 1867–1919
  As You Like It 1070; 1 Henry IV 4513
Horrocks, Herbert
  Dream 10520
Horsley, Charles Edward 1822–1876
  Twelfth Night 17733
Horsley, William 1774–1858
  Macbeth 7568; Tempest 16263
Horsley, William, arr. 1774–1858
  As You Like It 1176; Dream 10554; Tempest
  15120; P. Pilgrim 20711
Horton, John
  Merchant 8574
Horusitzky, Zoltán 1903–
  Sonnet 71 19949; Sonnet 73 19997; Sonnet
  75 20035
Horvit, Michael M. 1932–
  Sonnet 18 19383; Sonnet 57 19803; Sonnet
  104 20237
Horwitz, Albert
  Lear 6184
Hosalla, Hans Dieter 1919–
  Shrew 14348, 14349
Hosfeld, Samuel
  Cymbeline 2822
Hösl, Hans Wilhelm
  Errors 2095
Hosmer, Elmer Samuel 1862–
  As You Like It 1366
Hosmer, Lucius, arr. 1870–1935
  Dream 9721
Hossack, Grant
  As You Like It 632

Hostié, D., arr.
  Othello 12095
[Hotchkis], John
  Hamlet 3156
Hotchkis, John
  Henry V 4723; Lear 5787; Macbeth 6905;
  Measure 7665; Merry Wives 8888; Pericles
  12568; Richard II 12659; Twelfth Night
  16897
Hotham, Charles
  As You Like It 1071, 1688
Houdy, Pierick 1929–
  Macbeth 6906
Houghton, Phillip
  Winter's Tale 18773
Houkom, Alf
  Merchant 8575
Houston, Christopher
  Twelfth Night 16898
Houston, Levin, III
  Lear 5788
Hovhaness, Alan 1911–
  [Born Alan Hovaness Chakmakjian]
  Pericles 12604; Sonnet 29 19560; Sonnet
  30 19608
Howard, Brian
  Macbeth 6907
Howard, Dean C. 1918–
  Tempest 15040
Howard, Samuel 1710–1782
  Dream 10758
Howarth, Elgar 1935–
  Romeo 13918; Settings of Commemorative
  Pieces . . . 21143
Howarth, Harry H. 1931–
  Winter's Tale 18774
Howe, Albert Percy, arr.
  Dream 10217; Twelfth Night 18305; Two
  Gentlemen 18582
Howe, Mary Alberta Carlisle 1882–1964
  Also known as Mrs. Walter Bruce
  Twelfth Night 17912; Winter's Tale
  19028
Howell, Dorothy [1898]–1982
  As You Like It 1898; Winter's Tale 18936
Howell, Peter
  Dream 9506
Howell, T., arr.
  Cymbeline 2855
Howells, Herbert Norman 1892–1983
  As You Like It 1689, 1690; Cymbeline 2574;
  Dream 10645; Tempest 15679; Twelfth
  Night 17913
Howells, William Archibald
  Two Gentlemen 18521
Howenstein, J. H.
  Cymbeline 2575
Howes, Christopher Campbell
  Twelfth Night 16899

Howorth, Wayne, arr. 1895–
  Errors 2040
Howson, Frank A.
  Hamlet 3157; Twelfth Night 16900
Howson, Frank A., arr.
  Macbeth 7177
Hoyland, Victor 1945–
  Tempest 16264
Hristić, Stevan 1885–1958
  Dream 9507; Tempest 15041
Hristić, Zoran 1938–
  Macbeth 6908; Measure 7666; Dream
  9508
Huáng Hăiyìn, arr.
  Othello 11814
Huang Ji-mao
  Merchant 8757
Huáng Píng 1945–
  Othello 12026
Hubad, Samo 1917–
  Hamlet 3158
Hubarenko, Vitalyi Sergeevych 1934–
  Twelfth Night 16901
Hubbell, Raymond 1879–1954
  Romeo 14202
Huber, F., arr.
  Merry Wives 9074
Huber, Heinrich
  Caesar 5347; Measure 7667; Dream 9509;
  Othello 11795; Twelfth Night 16902
Huber, Paul 1918–
  Tempest 15042
Huber, Rudolf
  Hamlet 3159; Merchant 8181; Troilus
  16484
Hubicki, Margaret Olive 1915–
  Née Mullins; once wrote under the pseudonym
  'Katharine Lovell' (see also Lovell)
  Tempest 15680
Hübner, Jaroslav
  Antony 168; Hamlet 3160; Measure 7668;
  Richard III 12867; Romeo 13264; Tempest
  15043
Hübner, Wilhelm
  Errors 2096; Tempest 15044
Hudson, Henry
  As You Like It 1072, 1367; Dream 10333;
  Much Ado 11462; Tempest 15681, 15905;
  Two Gentlemen 18522; P. Pilgrim 20645
Hudson, Henry, arr.
  Dream 9722, 9723
Hudson, Robert 1732–1815
  As You Like It 2007
Hudson, Will, arr. flor. 1945
  Errors 2211
Hudson, William H. flor. 1915
  Henry V 4724; Richard III 12868
Hüe, Georges Adolphe 1858–1948
  Dream 10965

Hueber, Kurt Anton 1928–
  As You Like It 633; Twelfth Night 16903,
  18224
Huebner, William Michael
  Sonnet 116 20318
Hufeld, Arno
  Measure 7669
Hüffer, Franz 1843–1889
  Also known as Francis Hueffer
  Measure 7900
Hug, Lars
  Hamlet 3161
Hughes, R.
  L.L.L. 6345; Shrew 14587; P. Pilgrim 20749
Hughes, Raymond
  As You Like It 634
Hughes, Richard Samuel 1855–1893
  Tempest 16265
Hughes, Robert J., arr. 1912–
  Two Gentlemen 18583
Hughes, Robert W. 1912–
  Antony 169; Hamlet 3162; Henry V 4841;
  Macbeth 6909, 6910; Merchant 8787;
  Richard II 12660
Hughes, Rupert 1872–1956
  L.L.L. 6346; Sonnet 71 19950
Hughes, T[homas]
  Richard III 12869; Winter's Tale 18775;
  Settings of Commemorative Pieces . . .
  21048
Hugon, Georges 1904–1980
  Hamlet 3960; Tempest 16053
Hulbert, Hugh Reginald 1884–
  Henry VIII 5116
Hull, Arthur Eaglefield 1876–1928
  Also known as Arthur Eaglefield-Hull
  As You Like It 1368
Hull, Arthur Eaglefield, arr. 1876–1928
  Also known as Arthur Eaglefield-Hull
  As You Like It 1450; Othello 12248; Twelfth
  Night 17764
Hullah, John Pyke, arr. 1812–1884
  Merchant 8635; Dream 10132; Much Ado
  11007; Tempest 14724, 14793, 15061,
  15838; Two Gentlemen 18533; Winter's
  Tale 19011
Hülphers, Bo 1934–
  Romeo 13265
Humel, Gerald 1931–
  Macbeth 6911; Much Ado 11142; Othello
  12027; Twelfth Night 16904
Humfrey, Pelham 1647–1674
  Also known as Pelham Humphrey
  Othello 12223, 12307; Tempest 15431,
  15906
Hummel, Bertold 1925–
  Lear 5789
Hummel, Ferdinand 1855–1928
  Antony 170; Coriolanus 2302

Hummel, Franz
  As You Like It 635; Much Ado 11143;
  Richard II 12661
Hummel, Karl
  Coriolanus 2303
Humperdinck, Engelbert 1854–1921
  As You Like It 636; Merchant 8182; Romeo
  13266; Tempest 15045; Twelfth Night
  16905; Winter's Tale 18776
Humphries, Frederick
  Richard III 13055
Humphries, L.
  Sonnet 37 19675; Settings of
  Commemorative Pieces . . . 21256
Hundley, Richard 1931–
  L.L.L. 6432
Hunt, Kenneth
  Lear 5790
Hunt, Wynn 1910–
  As You Like It 1691; Twelfth Night 17914
Hünten, Franz, arr. 1793–1878
  Also known as François Hünten
  Merry Wives 9075; Othello 12096, 12097
Hunter, Emily Walker
  Two Gentlemen 18658
Hunter, Frank
  Twelfth Night 16909
Huntington, E. S. S.
  Settings of Commemorative Pieces . . .
  21049
Huntley, Hal, arr.
  Cymbeline 2751
Hurd, Daniel George 1918–
  Hamlet 3591
Hurd, Michael John 1928–
  Hamlet 3163, 4278; Henry VIII 5117;
  Phoenix 20758
Hurník, Ilja 1922–
  Dream 9510; Romeo 13267
Hurt, Jim
  Merchant 8184
Huse, Carolyn Evans
  As You Like It 2008
Huss, Henry Holden 1862–1953
  As You Like It 969, 1369
Huston, Thomas Scott, Jr. 1916–
  As You Like It 1899
Hutcheson, Ernest, arr. 1871–1951
  Dream 9724
Hutchings, Dick
  Merchant 8185
Hutchings, Peter
  Dream 10789
Hutchinson, Frederick William Hutchinson
  Cymbeline 2675
Hutchinson, Joseph T. 1849–
  As You Like It 1370; Merchant 8449
Hutchinson, Lesley
  Romeo 13268

Hutchinson, Thomas
  Merchant 8450; Romeo 13841; Tempest
  15988; Winter's Tale 19004
Hutchinson, William Marshall 1854–1933
  Also wrote under the pseudonyms 'Julian
  Mount' and 'Josef Meissler'
  As You Like It 1371; Hamlet 4215; Dream
  10521; Tempest 16054; Twelfth Night
  17915
Huttenbach, Otto
  Twelfth Night 16910
Huttenbach, Trude
  Twelfth Night 16911
Hüttenstrasser, Michael
  Winter's Tale 18779
Hutter, Herman 1846–1926
  Coriolanus 2374
Huttunen, Markku
  1 Henry VI 4852; 2 Henry VI 4894; 3 Henry
  VI 4937
Huzella, Elek 1915–1971
  Sonnet 73 19998
Hvoslef, Ketil 1939–
  K. John 5601; Lear 5791; Richard II 12662;
  Richard III 12870
Hyde, Frederick S.
  Hamlet 3164; Macbeth 6912
Hyde, Thomas A.
  Sonnet 4 19202; Sonnet 65 19892
Hye-Knudsen, Johan 1896–1975
  Shrew 14350
Hye-Knudsen, Johan, in part arr. 1896–1975
  As You Like It 637
Hylton-Edwards, Stewart
  Hamlet 3165; Twelfth Night 16912
Hyman, Richard R. 1927–
  As You Like It 1073, 1372, 1692; L.L.L.
  6433, 6557; Measure 7901; Much Ado
  11463; Twelfth Night 17550, 17918,
  18148; Two Gentlemen 18523; Winter's
  Tale 19005, 19045, 19080
Hyson, Winifred Prince 1925–
  Tempest 15545
Hytti, Antti
  Macbeth 6913
Hywel, John 1941–
  As You Like It 638

I

Iarovyns'kyi, Borys 1922–
  Richard III 12871
Ibert, Jacques François Antoine 1890–1962
  Antony 171; Macbeth 6914
Ibert, Jacques François Antoine, [in part] arr.
  1890–1962
  Dream 9511

Ibeson, Joseph Edgar
 Dream 10646
Ible, W.
 Two Gentlemen 18659
Idle, Frank
 Dream 10966
Idler, Werner
 K. John 5602; Twelfth Night 16913
Ihlenfeld, Eckart
 Hamlet 3166; Measure 7670; Shrew 14351;
 Troilus 16485
Ikebe, Shinichiro
 As You Like It 639; Hamlet 3167; Caesar
 5348; Measure 7671; Dream 9512; Othello
 11796, 11797
Ikebe, Shinichiro, in part arr.
 Much Ado 11144
Iles, Edward
 L.L.L. 6558; Measure 7903
Ilgenfritz, McNair [1887?]–1953
 As You Like It 1074
Iliev, Iliya
 Sonnet 50 19746
Iliev, Konstantin Nikolov 1924–
 Lear 5792
Iliff, Geoff
 As You Like It 640
Ilinski, Janos
 Also known as Graf Janos von Ilinski, Janus
 d'Ilinski, and Johann Graf Stanislaus Ilinski
 Romeo 13919
Illenberger, Anton
 Shrew 14352
Imbrie, Andrew Welsh 1921–
 Merchant 8186, 8576
Incho, W.
 Dream 10647
Ingersoll, E. P.
 Cymbeline 2676
Ingham, Richard 1804–1841
 Dream 10916
Inglis, Gordon
 Titus 16404
Ingman, Yngve
 Othello 11798; Shrew 14353
Ingraham, George
 Two Gentlemen 18524
Ingram, Harold
 Hamlet 3168; Settings of Commemorative
 Pieces . . . 21284
Ingram, Harold, arr.
 Merchant 8331
Ingram, Ted, arr.
 Romeo 13593, 13594, 13595, 13596
Ionescu, Lucian
 Cymbeline 2465; Hamlet 3169; Richard III
 12872
Ippolitov, Pavel Afanas'evich 1889–1947
 Caesar 5349; Richard III 12873

Ippolitov-Ivanov, Mikhail Mikhailovich
 1859–1935
 Dream 10917; Sonnet 18 19384; Sonnet 33
 19651; Sonnet 71 19951; Sonnet 73 19999;
 Sonnet 92 20125; Sonnet 98 20182; Sonnet
 99 20200; Sonnet 106 20262; Sonnet 109
 20279; Sonnet 149 20527
Ireland, John Nicholson 1879–1962
 Caesar 5350; Dream 10648; Tempest
 15682; Twelfth Night 18225; Winter's Tale
 19046
Irmler, Alfred
 Dream 9513
Irvin, Nathaniel 1951–
 Dream 9514; Shrew 14354
Irving, K. Ernest 1878–1953
 As You Like It 1076; Hamlet 3170; Macbeth
 6915; Merry Wives 8889; Othello 11799,
 12310; Shrew 14355; Twelfth Night 17551,
 17920, 18226, 18227
Irving, K. Ernest, arr. 1878–1953
 Richard II 12628
Irving, Robert Augustine 1913–
 As You Like It 641; Hamlet 3171
Isaac, Merle J., arr.
 Romeo 13945, 13948
Isaacson, B.
 Hamlet 3172; Richard III 13057
Isaacson, B., in part arr.
 Henry V 4725
Isakova, Aida Petrovna 1940–
 Hamlet 3592
Isebring, Leif
 As You Like It 642
Ištván, Miloš
 Caesar 5352
Iurovskii, Vladimir Mikhailovich
 1915–1972
 Othello 12028
Ivanov, Azariia, arr.
 Hamlet 3415
Ivanova, Lidia
 Settings of Commemorative Pieces . . .
 21216
Ivers, Peter
 As You Like It 643
Ives, Charles Edward 1874–1954
 · Tempest 15683
Ivey, Herbert
 Antony 317; Dream 10649; Twelfth Night
 18228
Ivey, Jean Eichelberger 1923–
 Macbeth 7449; Tempest 16055, 16056,
 16168; Sonnet 98 20183
Iwamoto, Keiji
 Dream 9515

J

Jacchia, Agide, arr. 1875–1932
Othello 12197

Jackman, Percy
Much Ado 11464

Jackman, Percy, arr.
Dream 10845

Jackson, George Knowil [1757]–1822
Two Gentlemen 18660

Jackson, Jolyon
Twelfth Night 16914

Jackson, Lilian
Shrew 14356

Jackson, Nelson
Hamlet 4216; Romeo 14158

Jackson, Nelson, in part arr.
Two Gentlemen 18655

Jackson, Nelson, arr.
Two Gentlemen 18584

Jackson, Robert
Dream 10918

Jackson, Samuel P., arr. 1818–1885
Dream 9725; Tempest 14794

Jackson, Seymour
As You Like It 644

Jackson, W.
Tempest 15684

Jackson, W., arr.
Merchant 8744

Jackson, W. F. W.
As You Like It 1373

Jackson (of Exeter), William 1730–1805
Cymbeline 2867; L.L.L. 6365; Measure 7904

Jackson (of Exeter), William, in part arr.
1730–1805
Dream 10919; Tempest 14795, 16221

Jacob, Benjamin, arr. 1778–1829
Also known as Benjamin Jacobs
Macbeth 6986

Jacob, Gordon Percival Septimus 1895–1984
All's Well 26; Antony 172; As You Like It
645, 1694; Cymbeline 2576; Hamlet 3173,
3819; Henry V 4822; Henry VIII 4995;
L.L.L. 6559, 6560; Merchant 8187, 8696;
Dream 10650; Tempest 16057; Twelfth
Night 18229; Phoenix 20767

Jacob, Gordon Percival Septimus, arr.
1895–1984
Dream 9726, 10218

Jacobi, Georges 1840–1906
Dream 10154

Jacobowski, Richard
Two Gentlemen 18393

Jacobs, I.
Much Ado 11465

Jacobs, Kris, in part arr.
Merry Wives 8890

Jacobson, Maurice 1896–1976
Also wrote under the pseudonym 'John
Bateson'
Antony 173, 296; Caesar 5353; Macbeth
6916; Tempest 16266

Jacobson, Maurice, in part arr. 1896–1976
Also wrote under the pseudonym 'John
Bateson'
Hamlet 3174

Jacobson, Maurice, arr. 1896–1976
Also wrote under the pseudonym 'John
Bateson'
Hamlet 3706, 3761, 3835, 3868; Othello
12254; Winter's Tale 19027, 19047, 19076

Jacques, Thomas Reginald 1894–1969
Henry VIII 5118

Jacques, Thomas Reginald, in part arr.
1894–1969
Henry V 4726

Jacques, Thomas Reginald, arr. 1894–1969
Dream 10219, 10220

Jadassohn, Salomon, arr.
Merry Wives 9076; Shrew 14579

Jadin, H. [flor. 1880]
Othello 12403

Jadin, Hyacinthe, arr. 1769–1802
Much Ado 11625

Jaell, Alfred, arr. 1832–1882
Merry Wives 9077; Romeo 13699

Jaffe, Gerald
Twelfth Night 16915

Jahn, Otto 1813–1869
Twelfth Night 17552

Jahn, Thomas 1940–
1 Henry IV 4465; 2 Henry IV 4631; Merry
Wives 9014

Jakobowski, Edward
Pseudonym used by Edward Belville
Antony 174; Tempest 16058

Jakša, Lado
Twelfth Night 16916

Jalas, Armas Jussi Veikko 1908–
Measure 7672

Jalinek, Miki
Richard III 12874

Jámbor, Jenő
Macbeth 6917; Much Ado 11145

James, Christopher
Sonnet 116 20319

James, Dorothy E. 1901–1982
As You Like It 646

James, Margaret
Merry Wives 8891

James, Michael
Hamlet 3175

James, Philip 1890–1975
Sonnet 19 19466

James, Robert McElhiney, arr. 1939–
Romeo 13986

James, Robert Meredith 1919–
  Errors 2097; Caesar 5354; Macbeth 6918;
  Tempest 15048; Settings of Commemorative
  Pieces . . . 21144
Janitzkowski, Walter
  Twelfth Night 16917
Jannoch, Hans Peter
  Hamlet 3176; Romeo 13269; Troilus 16486
Jannotta, Roger, arr.
  Twelfth Night 16757
Janovický, Karel, arr. 1930–
  Tempest 15062; Settings of Commemorative
  Pieces . . . 21145
Jans, Alaric Rokko
  As You Like It 647; Dream 9516; Much Ado
  11146; Richard III 12875; Twelfth Night
  16918
Jansa, Leopold, arr. 1795–1875
  Merry Wives 9078; Othello 12098
Jansen, F. Gustav, arr.
  Hamlet 3938; Dream 9727
Jansen, Johann Friedrich Anton, arr.
  Othello 12099, 12100, 12101
Jansen, Pierre Georges Cornil 1930–
  Hamlet 4103; Macbeth 6919; Romeo 13270;
  Sonnet 147 20512
Janson, Alfred 1937–
  Othello 11800
Janssens, Peter 1934–
  All's Well 27; As You Like It 648; Errors
  2098; Hamlet 3177; Lear 5793; Richard II
  12663; Shrew 14357; Twelfth Night 16919
Janssens, Pit
  Twelfth Night 16920
Jaques-Dalcroze, Émile 1865–1950
  Settings of Commemorative Pieces . . . 21196
Jarc, Matjaž 1954–
  Coriolanus 2304
Jarmołowicz, Bohdan
  As You Like It 649
Jarnach, Philipp 1892–1982
  Twelfth Night 17921, 18149
Jarre, Maurice Alexis 1924–
  All's Well 28; Macbeth 6920; Merchant
  8188; Dream 9517; Richard II 12664;
  Tempest 15049
Jarrett, Brian C. 1925–
  Sonnet 8 19245
Jarrett, Jack M. 1934–
  As You Like It 1374, 1695; Two Gentlemen
  18525
Järvinen, Martti-Mikael
  Merchant 8189
Jastrzębski, Mirosław
  Dream 9518; Romeo 13271
Jaubert, Maurice Jacques-Joseph-Eugène
  1900–1940
  1 Henry IV 4357; 2 Henry IV 4554
Jedwabski, Erich
  Twelfth Night 16921

Jeffers, Ronald Harrison 1943–
  Hamlet 3178
Jefferson, Peter
  Merchant 8577
Jeffreys, John 1927–
  As You Like It 1375; L.L.L. 6434; Measure
  7907; Much Ado 11466; Tempest 15685,
  15907; Twelfth Night 17922, 18150
Jeger, Benedikt
  Merchant 8190
Jelde, Tassilo 1943–
  As You Like It 650; Hamlet 3179; Measure
  7673; Richard II 12665; Shrew 14358;
  Twelfth Night 16922
Jelínek, Miki
  Romeo 13272
Jénei, Zoltán
  Measure 7674; Timon 16325
Jenkins, Charles
  Twelfth Night 16923
Jenkins, Cyril 1889–1978
  Also known as D. Cyril Jenkins
  As You Like It 1077, 1376; Coriolanus 2383
Jenkins, Cyril, arr. 1889–1978
  Also known as D. Cyril Jenkins
  As You Like It 1451; Tempest 14796,
  14797; Two Gentlemen 18585
Jenkins, David 1848–1915
  Dream 10790; Tempest 15433
Jenkins, David flor. 1980
  Twelfth Night 16924
Jenkins, David 1848–1915
  P. Pilgrim 20750
Jenkins, Edmund Thornton 1894–1926
  Much Ado 11147
Jenkins, Karl
  Settings of Commemorative Pieces . . . 21146
Jenkins, Robert, in part arr.
  Twelfth Night 16925
Jenner, Harold
  As You Like It 1377; Twelfth Night 17923
Jensche, H., arr.
  Twelfth Night 18248
Jensen, Adolf 1837–1879
  Othello 12311
Jensen, Paul
  [Paul Arthur Jensen?]
  Much Ado 11148; Richard II 12666
Jensen, Paul Arthur
  Dream 10155
Jeppesen, Knud Christian 1892–1974
  As You Like It 1078, 1696; L.L.L. 6435,
  6561
Jeremiáš, Jaroslav 1889–1919
  Twelfth Night 16926, 17553
Jeremiáš, Otakar 1892–1962
  Settings of Commemorative Pieces . . . 21184
Jeremiáš, Otakar, arr. 1892–1962
  Macbeth 7479

Jeremias, Wolfgang
  Lear 5794; Macbeth 6921
Jerome, Benjamin M. 1881–1938
  Cymbeline 2882; Hamlet 4159
Jerome, Benjamin M., arr. 1881–1938
  Settings of Commemorative Pieces . . .
  21077
Jersild, Jørgen 1913–
  Hamlet 3180
Jervis, St. Vincent
  Twelfth Night 17554; Sonnet 71 19952
Jervis-Read, Harold Vincent 1883–1945
  Twelfth Night 18230
Jessett, Michael, arr.
  Hamlet 3762
Jesson, Roy
  Dream 9519; Tempest 15050
Jex, David N. 1950–
  Sonnet 55 19781
Jezovšek, Janko
  Measure 7675
Jiáng Hóng Shēng 1930–
  Lear 5795; Macbeth 6922; Tempest 15051
Jíra, Milan 1935–
  Settings of Commemorative Pieces . . . 21217
Jirák, Karel Boleslav 1891–1972
  Hamlet 3181, 4217; Twelfth Night 16927;
  Settings of Commemorative Pieces . . . 21147
Jirko, Ivan 1926–1978
  Macbeth 7450; Twelfth Night 17399
Jírovec, Vojtěch 1763–1850
  Hamlet 3593
Joachim, Joseph 1831–1907
  Hamlet 3961; 1 Henry IV 4480; 2 Henry IV
  4655
Jóhannsson, Magnús Blöndal
  Hamlet 3182
Johansen, Svend Aaquist 1948–
  Romeo 13273, 13920, 13921, 13922
Johanson, Sven-Eric 1919–
  As You Like It 1079, 1378, 1697; Cymbeline
  2577, 2677; Hamlet 3183; L.L.L. 6562;
  Merchant 8578; Twelfth Night 17924; Two
  Gentlemen 18526
Johansson, Bengt Viktor 1914–
  P. Pilgrim 20646, 20647
Johansson, Björn Emanuel 1913–1983
  Troilus 16487; Sonnet 8 19246; Sonnet 18
  19385; Sonnet 20 19477; Sonnet 26 19511;
  Sonnet 36 19672; Sonnet 46 19729; Sonnet
  56 19793; Sonnet 81 20068; Sonnet 116
  20320; Sonnet 144 20480; P. Pilgrim
  20648
Johansson, Thomas, in part arr. 1958–
  Hamlet 3184
John, Alan
  Romeo 13274; Twelfth Night 16928
John, Aloys, in part arr.
  Dream 9520; Twelfth Night 16929

John, Dominic
  Merchant 8788
John, Elton Hercules 1947–
  Born Reginald Kenneth Dwight
  Hamlet 3594
John, Hermann, arr.
  Macbeth 7470
Johns, Donald 1926–
  As You Like It 651
Johnsen, Dan
  Errors 2099
Johnson, Allen
  Macbeth 6923
Johnson, Bernard
  Twelfth Night 17925
Johnson, Craig
  Lear 5796
Johnson, George F.
  Measure 7908
Johnson, James
  Richard III 12876
Johnson, John St. Anthony
  Macbeth 6924
Johnson, Lockrem 1924–1977
  Lear 5797
Johnson, Madeleine
  Measure 7909
Johnson, Ralph
  Romeo 13275
Johnson, Reginald
  As You Like It 1379; Much Ado 11598
Johnson, Robert [circa 1583]–1633
  Cymbeline 2678; Macbeth 6925; Tempest
  15052, 15686, 15908; Winter's Tale 18780,
  18961, 19006, 19139
Johnson, Stuart
  Antony 175; Hamlet 3185; Lear 5798;
  Measure 7676; Richard II 12667; Tempest
  15070; Winter's Tale 18781
Johnson, Stuart, in part arr.
  Macbeth 6928
Johnson, William Noel 1863–1916
  2 Henry IV 4638, 4668; Shrew 14359;
  Sonnet 18 19386; Settings of
  Commemorative Pieces . . . 21218
Johnson, William Noel, in part arr. 1863–1916
  Othello 11801
Johnston, Benjamin Burwell, Jr. 1926–
  Shrew 14361; Tempest 15687; Sonnet 56
  19794; Sonnet 119 20351
Johnstone, Maurice 1900–1976
  Tempest 16059; Sonnet 75 20036
Jolas, Betsy 1926–
  [Born Elizabeth Illouz]
  Dream 10651; Tempest 15071
Jolivet, André 1905–1974
  Coriolanus 2305
Jolly, Margaret
  Othello 12312; P. Pilgrim 20649

Jommelli, Nicolò 1714–1774
Also known as Niccolò Jomelli
Coriolanus 2415
Jones, Chuck
Measure 7677
Jones, Clifford Ernest Barnett 1943–
Hamlet 3595
Jones, D. T.
Settings of Commemorative Pieces . . . 21272
Jones, Edward
Pseudonym used by Edward Stephen
Antony 176; Hamlet 3186; Othello 11802;
Winter's Tale 18782
Jones, Henry Festing 1851–1928
Twelfth Night 17926
Jones, John Owen 1876–1962
As You Like It 1080; Twelfth Night 17927
Jones, Ken
Settings of Commemorative Pieces . . .
21148
Jones, Ken, arr.
Settings of Commemorative Pieces . . .
21139
Jones, Lewis 1933–
As You Like It 1900; Lear 6113; Macbeth
7500
Jones, Marvin
Twelfth Night 16930
Jones, Quentin Robert 1951–
Lear 5799; Twelfth Night 16931
Jones, Raymond
Romeo 13276
Jones, Robert F. 1947–
1 Henry IV 4358
Jones, Robert W.
Dream 10522
Jones, Rulon
Hamlet 3844
Jones, Samuel 1935–
Hamlet 3187
Jones, V.
Twelfth Night 17928
Jonson, William, arr.
Romeo 13597
Jonsson, Josef 1887–1969
Hamlet 3188
Jopson, Anthony
Dream 9521
Jorck, Carl
Hamlet 3963
Jordahl, Robert Arnold 1926–
Measure 7910; Merchant 8579; Dream
10523; Othello 12313; Twelfth Night
17555, 17929
Jordan, Chris
Tempest 15072
Jordan, Jules 1850–1927
Two Gentlemen 18527; Settings of
Commemorative Pieces . . . 21219

Jordan, Sverre 1889–1972
Romeo 13277; Settings of Commemorative
Pieces . . . 21149
Jordan, Thomas
Twelfth Night 16932
Jordan, Wolfgang, arr.
Romeo 14084
Josefs, Hermann
[Hermann Josephs?]
Merchant 8191; Sonnet 116 20339
Joseph, Jane M.
Dream 10360, 10462
Josephs, Hermann
[Also known as Hermann Josefs?]
Errors 2100; Measure 7678; Dream 9522
Josephs, Wilfred 1927–
1 Henry IV 4359; 2 Henry IV 4555; Tempest
15073
Josif, Enrico 1924–
Hamlet 3189, 3964
Josten, Werner Erich 1885–1963
Hamlet 3965
Joubert, John 1927–
P. Pilgrim 20650; Phoenix 20759
Jowett, Albert
As You Like It 1380
Jozefović, Oskar 1890–1941
Settings of Commemorative Pieces . . . 21185
J:son Lindh, Björn 1944–
[Note that 'J:son Lindh' is his correct legal
surname]
Hamlet 3190
Judd, Percy 1892–
L.L.L. 6436, 6563; Winter's Tale 19048
Judd, Peter
Richard III 12877
Jullien, Louis 1812–1860
Born Julien. Also published under a number
of his other thirty-five given names (listed in
Grove 6, Vol. 9, p. 748, as having been
'bestowed by his 36 godfathers, members of
the Sisteron Philharmonic')
Tempest 15434
Junger, Ervin 1931–
Romeo 13278
Jungmann, Albert 1824–1892
Hamlet 4279
Just, Herbert, arr.
Dream 10221
Just, Johann August [circa 1750]–1791
Merchant 8789

K

Kaan, Jindřich 1852–1926
Also known as Jindřich Kaan z Albestu
Hamlet 3966; Caesar 5355

Kabakov, Joel
1 Henry IV 4360; Merchant 8192
Kabalevskii, Dmitrii Borisovich 1904–1987
As You Like It 652; Measure 7679; Romeo
13279, 13923; Sonnet 8 19247; Sonnet 13
19296; Sonnet 27 19524; Sonnet 30 19609;
Sonnet 71 19953; Sonnet 76 20048; Sonnet
81 20069; Sonnet 90 20111; Sonnet 102
20223; Sonnet 153 20540
Kabeláč, Miloslav 1908–1979
Hamlet 3967; Settings of Commemorative
Pieces . . . 21150
Kabisch, Ernst
Twelfth Night 17556
Kaeuffer, Ollivier
Pseudonym used by Joseph Dominique Viacava
Shrew 14362; Two Gentlemen 18394
Kaffka, Johann Christoph 175[4]–1815
Pseudonym used by Johann Christoph
Engelmann
Antony 271
Kagan, Alex
As You Like It 653; Errors 2198
Kagel, Mauricio
Lear 5800
Kagen, Sergius 1909–1964
Hamlet 3598
Kagen, Sergius, arr. 1909–1964
Dream 10222, 10223; Tempest 14725,
14726; Timon 16345; Twelfth Night 18298,
18317
Kaidan, S.
Othello 11803
Kainulainen, Timo
Hamlet 3191
Kaipainen, Jouni Ilari 1956–
Titus 16405, 16422; Sonnet 8 19248
Kaiser, Albert E., in part arr.
As You Like It 654
Kaiser-Lindemann, Wilhelm 1940–
Dream 9523
Kaizar, Peter
Othello 11804
Kalach, Jiří 1934–
Twelfth Night 16933
Kalas, Janet 1959–
Romeo 13280
Kaldor, Connie
Winter's Tale 18783
Kalender, Sabahattin
Errors 2101; Hamlet 3192
Kalkbrenner, Friedrich Wilhelm Michael, arr.
1785–1849
Twelfth Night 16673
Kalliwoda, [Johann Wenzel?] [1801–1866]
[Also known as Jan Křtitel Václav Kalivoda]
Cymbeline 2466
Kalliwoda, Wilhelm 1827–1893
Macbeth 6929

Kallosh, Shandor Ernestovich 1935–
Macbeth 6930
Kallstenius, Edvin, arr. 1881–1967
Dream 9524
Kalniņš, I.
Hamlet 3193
Kalniņš, Imants Avgustovich 1941–
Much Ado 11149; Sonnet 56 19798
Kalniņš, Jǎnis A. 1904–
Hamlet 3599
Kalomba, Tshisungu
Macbeth 6931
Kalomiris, Manolis 1883–1962
Macbeth 6932
Kamaldinov, Georgii Konstantinovich
1907–
Twelfth Night 16934
Kamenogradskii, E. P.
Hamlet 3194; Two Gentlemen 18395
Kaminsky, Laura 1956–
Sonnet 8 19249; Sonnet 14 19298; Sonnet
65 19893
Kammerer, David
Hamlet 3195
Kancheli, Giia Georgii Aleksandrovich 1935–
As You Like It 655; Hamlet 3196; Lear
5801; Richard III 12878; Settings of
Commemorative Pieces . . . 21220
Kanne, Friedrich August 1778–1833
Measure 7911; Tempest 16267
Kantardjiev, Nickola
Romeo 13281; Twelfth Night 16935
Kapp, Eugen Arturovich 1908–
Merchant 8193; Much Ado 11150
Kappey, Jacob Adam, arr.
Merchant 8414; Merry Wives 9189; Dream
9728; Romeo 13700
Kapstad, Egil 1940–
Lear 5802
Karaev, Kara Abul'faz 1918–1982
Also known as Kara Abdul'faz Karaev
Antony 177; Hamlet 3197; Othello 11805;
Winter's Tale 18784
Karavaichuk, O.
Romeo 13282
Kardaś, Grzegorz
Much Ado 11151; Romeo 13283
Karel, J. O.
Macbeth 6933; Merchant 8194; Merry
Wives 8892; Twelfth Night 16936
Karel, Rudolf 1880–1945
Shrew 14588
Karetnikov, Nikolai Nikolaevich 1930–
Lear 5803
Karg-Elert, Sigfrid, arr. 1877–1933
1 Henry IV 4477; 2 Henry IV 4652; Henry V
4818
Karger, Reinhard
Dream 9525

Kari, Erkki
1 Henry VI 4853; 2 Henry VI 4895; 3 Henry
VI 4938
Karkoff, Maurice 1927–
Caesar 5356
Karnecki, Zbigniew
As You Like It 656; Richard III 12879;
Romeo 13284; Twelfth Night 16937, 17400
Karosas, Juozas 1890–1981
Sonnet 155 20566
Karr, Henry, arr. 1784–1842
Much Ado 11626
Kashperov, Vladimir Nikitich 1827–1894
Tempest 15435
Kas'ianov, Aleksandr Aleksandrovich 1891–
Twelfth Night 16938
Kasics, Tibor   –1986
1 Henry IV 4361; 2 Henry IV 4556;
Macbeth 6934; Measure 7680; Twelfth
Night 16939
Kasilag, Lucrecia R.
As You Like It 657; Hamlet 3198; Merchant
8195; Dream 9526; Romeo 13285; Twelfth
Night 16940
Kašlík, Ivan
Merchant 8196
Kasper, Virgilius
Merry Wives 8893
Kaspersen, Jan
All's Well 29; As You Like It 658; Hamlet
4104; Macbeth 6935
Kass, J., arr.
Romeo 13565, 13987
Kassel, Marsha
Sonnet 73 20000
Kastal'skii, Aleksandr Dmitrievich 1856–1926
Lear 5804
Kaszycki, Jerzy
All's Well 30; Hamlet 3199; Romeo 13286
Kaszycki, Lucjan M.
As You Like It 659; Hamlet 3200; Macbeth
6936; Merry Wives 8894; Dream 9527
Katin, Peter Roy 1930–
Hamlet 3201; Othello 11806
Katsman, Klara Abramovna 1916–
Antony 178
Katzenstein, Emil
Tempest 16268
Katzer, Georg 1935–
Dream 10156; Settings of Commemorative
Pieces . . . 21221
Kauffman, Gary Neil
Much Ado 11152
Kauffmann, Emil 1836–1909
Antony 297; Twelfth Night 17557
Kaufman, I., arr.
Hamlet 3416, 3417; Othello 11815
Kaufmann, Dieter 1941–
Othello 11807

Kaufmann, Nico
1 Henry IV 4362; 2 Henry IV 4557
Kaufmann, Serge Léon Henri 1930–
Measure 7681; Merry Wives 8895
Kaun, Hugo 1863–1932
1 Henry IV 4482; 2 Henry IV 4657; Merry
Wives 9222
Kay, Andrew
Twelfth Night 16941
Kay, Don 1933–
L.L.L. 6564; Twelfth Night 16942; Winter's
Tale 19049
Kay, Hershy, arr. 1919–1981
Twelfth Night 17374
Kay, Paul, arr.
Romeo 13950
Kay, Robert
Tempest 15074
Kay, Ulysses Simpson 1917–
Hamlet 4218; Twelfth Night 17558; Settings
of Commemorative Pieces . . . 21285
Kaye, Deena
Merry Wives 8896
Kaye, Ernest
Twelfth Night 17559
Kayser, Leif 1919–
Hamlet 4105; Settings of Commemorative
Pieces . . . 20855
Kayser-Schlömer, Wilhelm
Hamlet 3202; Twelfth Night 16943
Kazanli, Nikolai Ivanovich 1869–1919
Tempest 15436
Kazasoglou, George 1910–
Also known as George Kazasoglu
As You Like It 660; Winter's Tale 18785
Kean, Edmund 1789–1833
Hamlet 3727
Keane, David Roger 1943–
As You Like It 661; Macbeth 6937; Tempest
15075
Keane, Robert John 1948–
Hamlet 3203; Twelfth Night 16944; Sonnet
87 20087
Kearns, William Henry 1794–1846
Macbeth 7541
Kearton, Joseph Harper 1848–
Two Gentlemen 18528
Keats, Horace
Lear 6157
Keck, Michael
Henry V 4727; Lear 5805; Macbeth 6938;
Pericles 12569; Shrew 14363
Keefe, H. F.
Romeo 14203
Keel, James Frederick 1871–1954
Cymbeline 2578; Henry VIII 5119; L.L.L.
6437, 6565; Dream 10524; Much Ado
11467; Tempest 15546, 15688; Winter's
Tale 19007, 19050; Sonnet 18 19387

Keel, James Frederick, arr. 1871–1954
  As You Like It 1452; Othello 12255
Keighley, Thomas 1869–1935
  L.L.L. 6566; Merry Wives 9223
Keighley, Thomas, arr. 1869–1935
  As You Like It 1453; Merry Wives 9079
Keil, Harry
  Dream 9528
Keiper, William
  All's Well 31
Keiser, Reinhard 1674–1739
  Caesar 5560
Keith, Lester W.
  Dream 10921
Kelemen, László
  Lear 5806
Kellam, Ian
  Coriolanus 2306; Hamlet 3204; Macbeth
  6939; Othello 11808; Romeo 13287;
  Tempest 15076, 15077; Twelfth Night
  16945
Kellan, I.
  [Ian Kellam?]
  Sonnet 18 19388
Keller, Albert
  As You Like It 1982
Keller, F. J.
  Cymbeline 2823
Keller, Robert, arr.
  Twelfth Night 17459; Winter's Tale 18929
Keller, Wilhelm
  Hamlet 3205
Kelley, Edgar Stillman 1857–1944
  Also known as Edgar Stillman-Kelley
  Macbeth 6940, 7451
Kelley, Edgar Stillman, adapter 1857–1944
  Also known as Edgar Stillman-Kelley
  Winter's Tale 18786
Kelly, Bryan 1934–
  Henry V 4728; Lear 5807; Dream 9529;
  Richard II 12668; Tempest 16060, 16061
Kelly, Frederick Septimus 1881–1916
  Sonnet 18 19389
Kelly, Michael 1762–1826
  Hamlet 3728; Richard II 12669; Tempest
  15078
Kelly, Michael, arr. 1762–1826
  Macbeth 6987
Kelly, Ruth Sterne
  Sonnet 18 19390
Kelly, T.
  L.L.L. 6438
Kelly, Thomas J.
  As You Like It 1698
Kelsh, Peter 1940–
  L.L.L. 6439, 6567
Kelterborn, Louis 1891–1933
  Hamlet 3206; Settings of Commemorative
  Pieces . . . 20856

Kelterborn, Rudolf 1931–
  Hamlet 3600; Sonnet 43 19715
Kember, Gordon
  Settings of Commemorative Pieces . . . 20857
Kemble, Eleanor
  P. Pilgrim 20651
Kemble, Vivian
  Caesar 5357
Kemmer, Nicolas
  Pericles 12570; Troilus 16488
Kemner, Gerald
  Macbeth 6942
Kemp, Ian, arr.
  Romeo 13988
Kemp, Joseph 1778–1824
  Errors 2246; Hamlet 3729; L.L.L. 6338;
  Othello 12314; Romeo 13847
Kemp-Potter, Joan
  Tempest 15081
Kempff, Wilhelm 1895–
  Hamlet 3601
Kenel', Aleksandr Aleksandrovich 1898–1970
  Much Ado 11153; Othello 11809; Twelfth
  Night 16946
Kenin, Eliot
  Settings of Commemorative Pieces . . . 21050
Kennan, Kent Wheeler 1913–
  Twelfth Night 16947
Kennedy, Gilbert
  Antony 179; As You Like It 662, 663;
  Hamlet 3207; 1 Henry IV 4363; Lear 5808;
  L.L.L. 6246; Merchant 8197, 8198; Much
  Ado 11154, 11155; Richard II 12670;
  Tempest 15082, 15083; Twelfth Night
  16948, 16949; Winter's Tale 18787
Kennedy, Jack
  Much Ado 11156
Kennedy, John Brodbin 1934–
  Hamlet 4219
Kennedy, Spruhan
  As You Like It 1699
Kenny, James C.
  As You Like It 664
Kenny, John Francis 1957–
  Tempest 15437
Kent, Edward
  Othello 12502
Kent, Richard Layton 1916–
  L.L.L. 6568; Merchant 8451
Kent, Steven
  Tempest 16185
Kerckhoff, Bernard
  Macbeth 7569
Kerényi, Gábor
  Dream 9530
Kereselidze, Archil Pavlovich 1912–1971
  Antony 180; Romeo 13288
Kern, Carl Wilhelm
  Tempest 16062

Kerner, Jenő
Merchant 8199
Kerr, Mark Ralph George 1817–1900
Cymbeline 2679
Kershaw, Ernest, arr.
Cymbeline 2752; Two Gentlemen 18586
Kerzanet, Jean André Léon Louis
Also known under the pseudonym 'Michel Valmer'
K. John 5603
Kessel'man, A.
Othello 11810; Romeo 13289; Shrew 14364
Kessinger, Jim
Errors 2102
Kessler, John
Measure 7912
Kesti, Jouni
As You Like It 665
Ketèlbey, Albert William 1875–1959
Also wrote under the pseudonyms
'A. William Aston', 'Raoul Clifford',
'Geoffrey Kaye', and 'Anton Vodorinsky'
As You Like It 1081
Ketelle, S. W., arr.
Also known as S. W. Ketell
Dream 10846
Ketterer, Eugène, arr. 1831–1870
All's Well 77; Hamlet 3651, 3652; Macbeth 7331, 7332; Othello 12102; Romeo 13701
Ketting, Piet 1904–
Winter's Tale 19143; Sonnet 8 19250; Sonnet 113 20296; Sonnet 154 20546
Keurvels, Edoardo 1853–1916
Hamlet 3208
Keyper, Frantz, arr. 1792–1859
Settings of Commemorative Pieces . . . 20861
Keys, Ivor 1919–
Cymbeline 2579
Keyser, Harry Assur
Othello 12404
Keyser, Irene Lamb
Dream 10652
Khachaturian, Aram Il'ich 1903–1978
Lear 5809; Macbeth 6943, 6944; Othello 11811; Romeo 13290; Winter's Tale 18788; Settings of Commemorative Pieces . . . 20858
Khachaturian, Emin Levonovich, arr. 1930–
Othello 11816
Khachaturian, Karen Surenovich 1920–
Merry Wives 8897; Two Gentlemen 18396
Khan, George 1938–
Macbeth 6945
Khan, Steve
Macbeth 6946
Khapava, L.
Othello 11817
Khrennikov, Tikhon Nikolaevich 1913–
Much Ado 11157, 11363, 11364, 11599

Kiallmark, George, arr. 1781–1835
Two Gentlemen 18366
Kieffer, Detlef 1944–
Sonnet 155 20567
Kienzl, Wilhelm, arr.
Dream 9729
Kieserling, Richard
As You Like It 1082
Kiesewetter, Peter 1945–
Dream 10750; Tempest 15547, 15689, 15909; Sonnet 60 19827; Sonnet 87 20088; Sonnet 146 20492
Kiesewetter, Tomasz Marian 1911–
Twelfth Night 16950; Two Gentlemen 18397
Kießig, Georg 1885–
Hamlet 3209; Caesar 5358; Lear 5810; Macbeth 6947; Romeo 13291; Shrew 14365; Twelfth Night 16951
Kikkawa, Kazuo 1954–
L.L.L. 6440, 6569
Kilar, Wojciech
Antony 181; Errors 2103; Hamlet 3210; 1 Henry IV 4364; 2 Henry IV 4558; K. John 5604
Kilburn, Nicholas 1843–1923
As You Like It 1083
Killmayer, Wilhelm 1927–
As You Like It 1084; Cymbeline 2680; 1 Henry IV 4365; 2 Henry IV 4559; Measure 7913; Tempest 15690, 15910; Twelfth Night 17560, 18151; Winter's Tale 18789, 19081
Killorin, Joseph
Merry Wives 8898
Kilpinen, Yrjö 1892–1959
Cymbeline 2681; Othello 12315
Kim, Yong Man
Hamlet 4106
Kimball, Eugene
Macbeth 6948
Kimmins, Grace Thyrza Hannam, ed.
Anthologies 21320
Kincaid, Don
As You Like It 666; Errors 2104; Cymbeline 2467
Kines, Tom, ed. 1922–
Anthologies 21355
King, Alfred
Measure 7914
King, Betty Lou Jackson
Settings of Commemorative Pieces . . . 21222
King, Bob Brown
Merchant 8406
King, David 1949–
Errors 2105; Dream 9531
King, David [UK]
Errors 2106, 2107; Hamlet 3211; Titus 16406

King, Matthew Peter [*circa* 1773]–1823
Hamlet 3884; Lear 6037; L.L.L. 6342, 6380;
Macbeth 7370, 7381, 7384, 7404, 7409;
Merchant 8452, 8580; Romeo 13857;
Troilus 16568; Twelfth Night 17426;
Sonnet 109 20280; P. Pilgrim 20652;
Settings of Commemorative Pieces . . .
21223
King, Robert D., arr.
Dream 10224
King, Stanford, arr. 1912–
Romeo 13702
Kingsford, Winifred, arr.
Twelfth Night 17909
Kingsley, Ben 1943–
As You Like It 667; Tempest 15084
Kingsley, Gershon 1925–
Twelfth Night 16952
Kingsley, Herbert
Shrew 14366
Kinkee, F. R.
As You Like It 668
Kinkel, Charles [1832–   ]
Dream 10967
Kinross, John, arr.
As You Like It 1454; Much Ado 11542
Kipper, Hermann
Othello 12474
Kiran, Hartvig 1911–1978
Hamlet 4220
Kirby, Paul 1903–1971
As You Like It 1901
Kirby, Percival Robson 1887–
Henry VIII 5120; Tempest 15085; Twelfth
Night 16953, 17930
Kirchin, Basil
Richard III 12880
Kirchner, Georg, arr.
Measure 7807
Kirchner, Hermann 1861–1928
Twelfth Night 17401
Kirchner, Volker David
Tempest 15086, 15087
Kirk, Theron Wilford 1919–
As You Like It 1085, 1381; L.L.L. 6441,
6570; Dream 10409; Much Ado 11383;
Tempest 15803; Twelfth Night 17931
Kirk-Burnnand, T. J.
Caesar 5359
Kirkpatrick, John 1947–
Twelfth Night 16954
Kirkpatrick, John, in part arr. 1947–
Twelfth Night 16955
Kistetenyi, Melinda 1928–
Sonnet 155 20568
Kisza, Stanisław, arr.
Dream 9730
Kitcat, Cecil
Antony 182; L.L.L. 6247

Kjær, Torben 1946–
Hamlet 3968; Tempest 16063; Sonnet 8
19251; Sonnet 18 19391; Sonnet 65 19894
Kjelland, Olav
Coriolanus 2307
Klami, Uuno Kalervo 1900–1961
Lear 5811, 6080
Klatovsky, Richard
Caesar 5360
Klatzow, Peter
Tempest 15088; Winter's Tale 18790
Klauser, Karl, arr. 1823–1905
Dream 9731
Klauß, Karl
Pericles 12571
Klauwell, Otto Adolf 1851–1917
Macbeth 7452
Klauwell, Otto Adolf, arr. 1851–1917
Cymbeline 2753
Klebe, Giselher 1925–
Caesar 5480
Kleefeld, Wilhelm Joseph, arr. 1868–
Much Ado 11353
Kleiberg, Ståle 1958–
Sonnet 30 19610; Sonnet 33 19652; Sonnet
60 19828
Klein, Joseph 1801–1862
As You Like It 1700; Cymbeline 2682;
Hamlet 3707, 3794; Merchant 8581;
Twelfth Night 17561; Winter's Tale 19132
Klein, Lothar 1932–
Errors 2108; 1 Henry IV 4366; Measure
7915; Merchant 8582; Richard III 12881;
Tempest 15911
Kleiner, Arthur
Hamlet 3212
Kleinheinz, Franz Xaver 1765–1832
Hamlet 4107
Kleinmichel, Richard, arr. 1846–1901
Dream 9732; Othello 12103; Romeo 13566
Kleinsinger, George 1914–1982
Settings of Commemorative Pieces . . . 20859
Klemetti, Heikki Valentin 1876–1953
Much Ado 11600
Klemetti, Heikki Valentin, in part arr.
1876–1953
As You Like It 669
Klempíř, Jaromír 1944–
As You Like It 670
Klempner, V.
Othello 11818
Klenovskii, Nikolai Semionovich 1853–1915
Antony 183
Klepka, Paul
Othello 12316
Kliebert, Karl 1849–1907
Romeo 13924
Kliem, Franz
Merchant 8200; Romeo 13292

Klindworth, Karl, arr. 1830–1916
　Romeo 13989
Kling, H., arr.
　Romeo 13567, 13568, 13569
Klobe, Eberhard
　Shrew 14367
Klose, Francis Joseph, arr. 1784–1830
　Dream 10847
Klose, Friedrich 1862–1942
　Macbeth 6949
Klosé, Hyacinthe Éléonore, arr.
　Dream 10848
Kloss, Wilhelm
　Dream 10653
Kloth, Timothy Tom 1954–
　Shrew 14368
Klotz, Jeffrey
　Two Gentlemen 18398
Klug, Ernst 1905–1985
　Macbeth 6950
Klughardt, August
　Lear 5812
Klusák, Jan 1934–
　Hamlet 3213; Macbeth 6951; Romeo 13293;
　Timon 16326; Twelfth Night 17402; Two
　Gentlemen 18399
Knabl, Rudolf G.
　Hamlet 3214; Twelfth Night 16956
Knape, Walter 1906–
　Dream 10654, 10655; Twelfth Night
　18231
Knauer, Hans-Jürgen
　Coriolanus 2308; Shrew 14369; Troilus
　16489
Knaup, Karl Heinz
　Dream 9532
Knecht, Justin Heinrich 1752–1817
　Tempest 16201
Knieper, Jürgen
　Hamlet 4108; Measure 7682; Twelfth Night
　16957
Knight, Gwen
　Henry VIII 4996
Knight, Henry
　As You Like It 1382; Henry VIII 5121
Knight, Joseph Philip 1812–1887
　Also wrote under the pseudonym 'Philip
　Mortimer'
　Dream 10922; Romeo 14204
Knight, Richard
　Merchant 8583
Knittl, Karel 1853–1907
　Winter's Tale 19111
Knobel, Theo
　Dream 9533
Knopfler, Mark
　Romeo 14159
Knotzinger, Günther
　Coriolanus 2309

Knowles, Arthur R.
　Romeo 14160
Knussen, Oliver 1952–
　Hamlet 3969, 3970, 4222
Knyvett, William 1779–1856
　P. Pilgrim 20653
Kober, Dieter, arr.
　Dream 10225
Koblenz, Babette 1956–
　Macbeth 7274
Kocáb, Michael
　Othello 11819
Koch, Caspar Petrus, arr. 1872–1970
　Dream 9733
Koch, Frederick 1928–
　Errors 2199; Hamlet 3215; Richard III
　12882
Koch, Hansgeorg
　Measure 7683, 7684; Dream 9534; Much
　Ado 11159; Tempest 15089; Winter's Tale
　18791
Koch, Johannes Hermann Ernst 1918–
　Henry VIII 5122
Koch, John G. 1928–
　As You Like It 1383; Hamlet 3763; Twelfth
　Night 17562
Kochan, Günter 1930–
　2 Henry VI 4921; Caesar 5493; Sonnet 94
　20136
Kochbeck, Jürgen-Georg, in part arr. 1955–
　Also known as George Kochbeck
　Hamlet 3216
Kochurov, Iurii Vladimirovich 1907–1952
　Macbeth 6952, 7453
Kocsis, Zoltán, arr.
　Romeo 13570
Kocyba, Tadeusz
　Twelfth Night 16958
Kodály, Zoltán 1882–1967
　Henry VIII 5123; Merchant 8584
Ködderitzsch, Uwe
　Cymbeline 2468
Koder, Urban
　As You Like It 671; Dream 9535
Kœckert, Gustave Adolphe Jean　–1948
　Hamlet 3217
Koehler-Wümbach, Wilhelm, arr.
　Merry Wives 9080
Koehne, Graeme
　Twelfth Night 16959
Koennecke, Fritz 1876–
　Tempest 15438
Koering, René 1940–
　Hamlet 4161; Macbeth 7542; Sonnet 24
　19496
Koff, Charles, arr.
　Cymbeline 2754
Koffman, Adolph
　Tempest 16269

Kogel, Gustav Friedrich, arr. 1849–
Merry Wives 9081
Kogtev, V.
Errors 2109; Two Gentlemen 18400
Köhler, Henning
Twelfth Night 16960
Köhler, Louis, arr. 1820–1886
Dream 9734
Köhler, Lutz
Merchant 8201
Köhler, Wolfgang 1923–
Caesar 5510
Kohs, Ellis Bonoff 1916–
Caesar 5361; Macbeth 6953
Kojetinsky, Maximilian
Hamlet 3218
Kolditz, Hans, arr. 1923–
Romeo 13598
Kolman, Peter 1937–
Romeo 13925
Kolmanovskii, Eduard Savel'evich 1923–
Twelfth Night 16961
Kol'tsov, Petr Fedorovich 1904–
Othello 11820
Kölz, Ernst 1929–
Romeo 13294
Komives, Janos 1932–
Othello 11821
Komorowski, Ryszard
Merry Wives 8899
Kon, Boleslaw
Romeo 13295
Kondek, Charles
Tempest 15090
Kondorossy, Leslie 1915–
Sonnet 25 19504; Sonnet 60 19829; Sonnet 71 19954; Sonnet 104 20238; Sonnet 116 20321; Sonnet 126 20372; Sonnet 128 20394; Sonnet 145 20484; Sonnet 149 20528
Kondracki, Michał 1902–1984
Hamlet 3219
Kondrat'ev, Sergei Aleksandrovich 1896–1970
Shrew 14370
Konieczny, Zygmunt
Hamlet 3220; Macbeth 7517; Dream 9536; Much Ado 11160
Konietzny, Heinrich 1910–1983
Romeo 13296
Konietzny, Stefan
Timon 16327
König, Christa
Pericles 12572
Konjović, Petar 1883–1970
Dream 9537, 10656
Kont, Paul 1920–
Tempest 15091; Twelfth Night 16963, 17563, 17706, 17932, 18152

Kool, Jaap
Coriolanus 2310
Kopelent, Marek 1932–
Richard III 12883
Koplow, Philip
Othello 11822
Kopp, Ladislaus
Hamlet 3221
Koppel, Herman David 1908–
K. John 5605; Macbeth 7275; Richard III 12884; Romeo 13297
Koppel, Thomas 1944–
Dream 9538; Troilus 16490
Koppitz, C.
Henry VIII 4997
Koráb, J., arr.
Othello 12396
Koreniak, P.
Othello 11823; Romeo 13298
Koreshchenko, Arsenii Nikolaevich 1870–1921
Twelfth Night 16964
Korn, Harold
Sonnet 18 19392
Korn, Peter Jona 1922–
Much Ado 11468
Korngold, Erich Wolfgang 1897–1957
As You Like It 672, 1086, 1384, 1701, 1995; Much Ado 11161, 11469, 11601; Othello 11824, 12317; Romeo 14050; Tempest 16270; Twelfth Night 16965, 17564, 17684, 17707, 17933, 18153; Winter's Tale 19151; Sonnet 130 20422
Korngold, Erich Wolfgang, arr. 1897–1957
Dream 9735
Korostelev, A. V.
Errors 2110
Kortes, Sergei Al'bertovich 1935–
L.L.L. 6442, 6571; Much Ado 11470; Sonnet 25 19505; Sonnet 147 20513
Kos-Anatol'skyi, Anatolyi Iosyfovych 1909–1983
Sonnet 155 20569
Koschinsky, Fritz 1903–1969
1 Henry IV 4367; Twelfth Night 16966, 18232
Kosina, Jiří
Merchant 8202; Shrew 14371; Twelfth Night 16967
Kosiol, Peter
Merry Wives 8900
Kosma, Joseph 1905–1969
Macbeth 7518; Romeo 14051
Kossmaly, Karl 1812–1893
Twelfth Night 17565
Košťál, Arnošt 1920–
Measure 7685; Merry Wives 8901
Kostal, Irwin James, arr. 1911–
Romeo 13599

Kosteck, Gregory W. 1937–
  Tempest 15691
Kostelanetz, André, arr. 1901–1980
  Shrew 14607
Kostić, Vojislav 1931–
  As You Like It 673; Lear 5813; Richard II
  12671; Winter's Tale 18792
Kostřiba, Josef
  Macbeth 6954
Koswell, Gordon David
  Cymbeline 2580
Kosztolnyik, Penelope
  Twelfth Night 16968
Kotoński, Włodzimierz
  Dream 9539
Kouba, Stefan
  1 Henry IV 4368; 2 Henry IV 4560; Caesar
  5362; Merchant 8203; Dream 9540; Much
  Ado 11163; Richard II 12672
Kovač, Ivan 1937–
  Antony 272
Kovařovic, Karel 1862–1920
  Winter's Tale 18793
Kowalowski, Zenon
  L.L.L. 6248; Merchant 8204
Kowarski, Erik
  Dream 9541
Kox, Hans 1930–
  Coriolanus 2311; Caesar 5363; Macbeth
  7454; Merchant 8407; Richard II 12673;
  Romeo 14099; Sonnet 53 19764; Sonnet
  116 20343
Kozakevich, Anna Abramovna 1914–
  Othello 11825
Kraehenbuehl, David
  Tempest 15092
Kral', K. I.
  Othello 12318
Kralik von Meyrswalden, Mathilde
  Also known as Mathilde von Kralik
  Cymbeline 2683; Othello 12319
Kramer, Alan H.
  Tempest 15439
Kramer, Arthur Walter, arr. 1890–1969
  Henry VIII 4985
Krasnogliadova, Vera Vladimirovna 1902–
  Sonnet 7 19222; Sonnet 155 20570
Kratochvíl, Martin
  Hamlet 3222
Kraus, E., arr.
  Dream 9736
Kraus, George 1912–
  Twelfth Night 16969
Kraus, John
  Macbeth 6955
Kraus, Karlo 1940–
  Hamlet 3223
Krause, Joachim
  Twelfth Night 16970

Krause, Richard
  Tempest 16271
Krause, Robert James 1943–
  Winter's Tale 18794
Krauss, Michael
  Merchant 8731
Krausse, Theodor, arr.
  Dream 10849
Krawinkel, Paul
  Errors 2111; Dream 9542
Kreglow, Margaret
  Winter's Tale 18795
Krein, Aleksandr Abramovich 1883–1951
  Othello 12029; Romeo 13299
Krein, Michael   –1966
  Dream 10657
Krejčí, Iša Frantisek 1904–1968
  As You Like It 674; Errors 2200; Twelfth
  Night 16971
Křenek, Ernst 1900–
  Dream 9543, 10525
Krenz, Jan 1926–
  Antony 184
Kresky, Jeffrey Jay 1948–
  1 Henry IV 4471; Tempest 16169
Kretschmar, F. W., arr.
  Macbeth 7252
Kretschmer, William F., arr.
  Merry Wives 9082; Dream 9737
Kreuder, Peter [1906]–1981
  Winter's Tale 18796
Kreussel, Lutz-Peter
  Shrew 14372
Kreutz, Arthur 1906–
  As You Like It 1385; Hamlet 3224; Much
  Ado 11471; Twelfth Night 17934
Kreutzer, Conradin 1780–1849
  Also known as Conrad Kreuzer
  Lear 6185
Kreutzer, Léon Charles François 1817–1868
  Tempest 16064
Kreutzer, Rodolphe 1766–1831
  Antony 375; Cymbeline 2837
Křička, Jaroslav 1882–1969
  Winter's Tale 18797
Krieger, Edino
  Dream 9544
Krigar, Hermann
  Cymbeline 2684
Krigbaum, Charles Russell 1929–
  Lear 5814
Krijn, Onno Maarten 1957–
  Hamlet 3730
Kristinus, Carl Raimund, arr.
  Cymbeline 2755
Kriukov, Vladimir Nikolaevich 1902–1960
  Merchant 8205; Romeo 13300
Krivitskii, D.
  Twelfth Night 16972

Kroeger, Ernest Richard 1862–1934
  Dream 10658
Krogseth, Gisle 1952–
  Tempest 15093
Krogulski, Władysław 1840–1926
  Merchant 8206
Krohn, Max 1886–
  Lear 5815; Much Ado 11164; Richard II
  12674; Twelfth Night 16973, 17403;
  Winter's Tale 18798
Krönin, J., arr.
  Dream 10794
Kropatschek, Hermann   –[before 1987]
  As You Like It 675; Hamlet 3225; 1 Henry
  IV 4369; 2 Henry IV 4561; K. John 5606;
  Macbeth 6956; Measure 7686; Merchant
  8207; Dream 9545; Much Ado 11165;
  Richard II 12675; Richard III 12885;
  Romeo 13301; Shrew 14373; Tempest
  15094; Twelfth Night 16974; Winter's Tale
  18799
Krstić, Milivoje 1917–1988
  Twelfth Night 16975
Krtschil, Henry
  As You Like It 676
Kruchinin, K., arr.
  Othello 12033
Krueger, Paul H.
  Caesar 5546
Krug, Arnold 1849–1904
  Othello 12405
Krug, Reinhold
  Shrew 14374
Krüger, Carl
  Much Ado 11166; Winter's Tale 18800
Krüger, Wilhelm, arr. 1820–1883
  Hamlet 3653; Macbeth 7333
Kruse, Karl
  Measure 7687
Kruse, Werner
  Hamlet 3226; Measure 7688; Much Ado
  11167; Shrew 14375; Twelfth Night 16976
Krütsch, Franz
  Dream 9546; Richard III 12886
Kryzhanovskyi, B.
  Othello 11826
Krzemieński, Witold 1909–
  As You Like It 677; L.L.L. 6249; Twelfth
  Night 16977
Krzemieński, Witold, arr. 1909–
  Dream 9738
Kubik, Gail Thompson 1914–1984
  Coriolanus 2400; Tempest 16236
Kubizck, Karl Maria 1925–
  Twelfth Night 17734
Kučera, Antonín
  Twelfth Night 16978
Kučera, Václav 1929–
  Hamlet 3971; Sonnet 12 19287

Küchenmeister, A., arr.
  Merry Wives 9083
Kücken, Friedrich Wilhelm 1810–1882
  Cymbeline 2685; L.L.L. 6443; Much Ado
  11609
Kudriavtsev, [?]
  Hamlet 3227
Kuehmann, Karen 1954–
  Errors 2112; Shrew 14376; Twelfth Night
  16979
Kufferath, Hubert Ferdinand, arr. 1818–1896
  Dream 9739
Küffner, Joseph, arr. 1776–1856
  Also known as Josef Küffner
  Othello 12104, 12105, 12106
Kuhe, Wilhelm, arr.
  Cymbeline 2756; Macbeth 7334, 7335;
  Merry Wives 9084; Dream 10850; Othello
  12198; Romeo 13703; Tempest 14798; Two
  Gentlemen 18587
Kuhl, Rolf
  1 Henry IV 4370; 2 Henry IV 4562
Kuhlau, Friedrich Daniel Rudolph 1786–1832
  Settings of Commemorative Pieces . . . 20860
Kuhlau, Friedrich Daniel Rudolph, arr.
  1786–1832
  Othello 12107
Kühm, Otto Julius, arr.
  Dream 9740
Kuhn, Hans-Peter
  Macbeth 6957
Kuhn, Max 1896–
  As You Like It 1386; Othello 12320; Twelfth
  Night 17566
Kühn, Rudi
  Shrew 14377
Kühne, Rolf
  Errors 2113
Kuhni, Chris
  As You Like It 678; Cymbeline 2469; Lear
  5816; Merchant 8208; Richard III 12887
Kula, Ryszard
  1 Henry IV 4371; 2 Henry IV 4563; Henry V
  4729; Merchant 8209; Merry Wives 8902
Kulesha, Gary Alan 1954–
  All's Well 32; Henry VIII 4998, 5219;
  Measure 7689; Merchant 8210; Dream
  9547
Kulesha, Gary Alan, in part arr. 1954–
  L.L.L. 6250
Kuliev, Tofik Alekper 1917–
  Twelfth Night 16980
Kulins, Hedwig, arr.
  Twelfth Night 16806
Kulish, Marlowe Francis 1952–
  Tempest 15692; Twelfth Night 17567
Kuljerić, Igor 1938–
  Hamlet 3228; Dream 9548; Richard III
  13033

Kummer, Clare
    Tempest 16272
Kún, László
    Henry VIII 5124
Kunad, Rainer 1936–
    Errors 2114; Cymbeline 2470; Lear 5817;
    Much Ado 11168, 11169; Richard III
    12888; Shrew 14378; Tempest 15095;
    Troilus 16491, 16492
Kunad, Rainer, in part arr. 1936–
    As You Like It 679; Dream 9549; Othello
    11827
Kunkel, [George?]
    Settings of Commemorative Pieces . . . 21151
Kunkel, George, arr.
    Merry Wives 9085
Kunz, Alfred Leopold 1929–
    As You Like It 1087; Sonnet 18 19393
Kunz, Ernst 1891–
    Richard II 12770
Kunzen, Friedrich Ludwig Aemilius
    1761–1817
    Also known as Friedrich Ludwig Aemilius
    Kuntzen
    Tempest 16273; Anthologies 21343
Kupka, Karel 1927–
    Twelfth Night 16981
Kuriia, A.
    Hamlet 3229
Kurka, Robert Frank 1921–1957
    Caesar 5511
Kurtág, György 1926–
    Hamlet 3230
Kurtz, James L. 1936–
    As You Like It 1088, 1387; Dream 10157;
    Tempest 15693, 16202; Twelfth Night
    17568
Kurylewicz, Andrzej 1932–
    Dream 9550; Romeo 13302; Tempest
    16065; Twelfth Night 16982
Kurz, Siegfried 1930–
    As You Like It 680; Errors 2115; Hamlet
    3231; K. John 5607; Macbeth 6958;
    Measure 7690; Dream 9551; Much Ado
    11170; Shrew 14379; Twelfth Night 16983
Kurzbach, Paul 1902–
    Romeo 14100
Kusche, Ludwig
    Troilus 16493
Küster, Hermann 1817–1878
    Also known as 'Lehmann'
    Othello 12321; Tempest 15912; Twelfth
    Night 18154
Kusterer, Arthur 1898–1967
    Macbeth 6959; Twelfth Night 17404
Kuttner, Alfred J.
    Hamlet 3232
Kuzmich, Natalie 1932–
    L.L.L. 6572

Kuzmin, Mikhail Alekseevich 1875–1936
    Twelfth Night 16984
Kvapil, Radoslav, arr.
    Macbeth 7480
Kvernadze, Aleksandr Bidzina Aleksandrovich
    1928–
    Dream 9552
Kymlicka, Milan 1936–
    L.L.L. 6251

L

La Cerva, Patricia Ann, ed.
    Anthologies 21360
La Forge, Frank 1879–1953
    K. John 5642; Measure 7916; Tempest
    15548
La Forge, Frank, arr. 1879–1953
    Errors 2041
La Montaine, John 1920–
    Hamlet 3820; Sonnet 14 19299, 19302;
    Sonnet 18 19394, 19454; Sonnet 40 19691,
    19699; Sonnet 71 19955, 19975; Sonnet 98
    20184, 20196; Sonnet 105 20250, 20254
La-Rosa-Parodi, Armando 1904–1977
    Twelfth Night 16985
La Violette, Wesley 1894–1978
    Merchant 8408
Labis, Raoul Charles, arr.   –1973
    Much Ado 11354
Laborit, Henri Philippe Georges
    Shrew 14380
Labroca, Mario 1896–1973
    Romeo 13303; Winter's Tale 18801
Lacey, Frederic William, Jr.
    Othello 12503
Lachman, Hans 1906–
    Settings of Commemorative Pieces . . .
    21224
Lachner, Franz 1803–1890
    Winter's Tale 18802
Lachner, Ignaz 1807–1895
    Merchant 8211
Lachner, Theodor, arr. 1788–1877
    Macbeth 7253
Lackey, Lionel
    Lear 5998
Lacombe, Louis 1818–1884
    Also known as Louis Trouillon-Lacombe and
    as Louis Brouillon Lacombe
    Tempest 15694
Lacombe, Louis, arr. 1818–1884
    Also known as Louis Trouillon-Lacombe and
    as Louis Brouillon Lacombe
    Dream 10851
Lacy, Frederick St. John 1862–
    Merchant 8585

Lacy, Michael Rophino 1795–1867
All's Well 79; L.L.L. 6676; Dream 10791;
Othello 12475; Richard III 13071; Romeo
14101; Twelfth Night 18281; Two
Gentlemen 18652; Sonnet 39 19686;
P. Pilgrim 20751

Lacy, Michael Rophino, arr. 1795–1867
Othello 12108

Laffont, Noël –1937
Hamlet 4162

Lafforgue, René-Louis 1917–1967
Lear 5818; Measure 7691; Shrew 14381

Lafite, Karl 1872–1945
Hamlet 3795

Laflamme, Linda
As You Like It 681; 1 Henry IV 4493;
2 Henry IV 4665; Macbeth 6960; Dream
9553; Othello 11828; Pericles 12573;
Richard III 13066; Romeo 13304

Lahmeyer, Carl
As You Like It 1388

Lahusen, Christian 1886–
L.L.L. 6252

Laidlaw, Alexander H., Jr.
Romeo 14102

Laidlaw, Paul
As You Like It 682

Laidlow, Elizabeth
Lear 5819

Laine, Reino
Dream 9554

Laing, Alan
Errors 2116; Hamlet 3233, 3234; Caesar
5364; Lear 5820; L.L.L. 6253; Macbeth
6961; Dream 9555; Tempest 15096;
Troilus 16494; Twelfth Night 18272;
Settings of Commemorative Pieces . . .
20863

Laing, Alan, in part arr.
Dream 9556

Lair, Robert
Henry V 4730; Macbeth 6962; Merchant
8212; Othello 11829; Richard III 12889;
Shrew 14382

Laisné, Jean Charles Louis 1932–
Macbeth 6963

Laitinen, Pekka 1946–
Lear 5821

Laitman, Lori 1955–
Also known as Lori Laitman Rosenblum
Shrew 14383

Lake, H[arold?] C.
Tempest 15695

Lake, Richard D.
Sonnet 116 20322

Lally, Jimmy, arr.
Errors 2212, 2213; Shrew 14608

Lam, Baid, in part arr.
Winter's Tale 18803

Lama, Serge 1943–
Pseudonym used by Serge Chauvier
Othello 12504

Lamb, John David 1935–
As You Like It 1089; Hamlet 3764; 2 Henry
IV 4639; Measure 7917; Twelfth Night
17935

Lambard, Benjamin
As You Like It 1702

Lambert, John Arthur Neill 1926–
Henry V 4731; Caesar 5365; Merry Wives
8903; Much Ado 11171

Lambert, John Arthur Neill, in part arr. 1926–
Merchant 8213; Richard III 12890

Lambert, John Arthur Neill, arr. 1926–
Tempest 15318

Lambert, Leonard Constant 1905–1951
Cymbeline 2581; Hamlet 3235; Romeo
13767

Lambert, Leonard Constant, arr. 1905–1951
Dream 10226, 10227, 10228; Tempest
14727

Lambertson, Chester Lee
Dream 9557; Richard III 12891; Twelfth
Night 16986

Lambrechts, Jean 1936–
As You Like It 970; Hamlet 3715; Henry V
4807; Macbeth 7379; Merry Wives 8904,
9224; Tempest 15861; Twelfth Night
16987, 17735

Lamming, Frank M.
Twelfth Night 16988

Lamming, Frank M., arr.
Dream 9741

Lamothe, Georges Marie Émile, arr. –1894
Macbeth 7336; Romeo 13704

Lamotte, Nicolas-Antony, arr. 1819–1912
Merry Wives 8992, 8993, 8994; Dream
10852

Lampe, J. Bodewalt, arr. 1869–1929
Romeo 14096

Lampe, John Frederick [circa 1703]–1751
K. John 5608; Dream 10158; Romeo 13305;
Winter's Tale 18804, 18950, 18979

Lampersberg, Gerhard 1928–
Sonnet 26 19509; Sonnet 27 19514; Sonnet
28 19533; Sonnet 73 20001; Sonnet 97
20162

Lampl, Hans, in part arr.
Henry V 4732; Much Ado 11172; Tempest
15097

Lamy, François
Hamlet 3236; Othello 11830

Lance, J. F., arr.
Othello 12109

Lancelott, F.
Measure 7918

Lander, Cyril Bertram
Tempest 15696

Landowski, Marcel François Paul Evenos Marc
1915–
Macbeth 7570
Landowsky, Paul
Dream 9558
Landy, Robert J.
Tempest 15440
Lane, David, in part arr.
Othello 11831
Lane, Edgar A.
K. John 5644
Lane, Gerald M., arr.
Two Gentlemen 18588
Lang, Edith
As You Like It 1389
Láng, István 1933–
Measure 7692; Romeo 13926; Twelfth Night
18322
Lang, Max 1917–1987
All's Well 33; Antony 185; Hamlet 3237;
Lear 5822; Macbeth 6964; Measure 7693;
Merchant 8214; Much Ado 11173
Lang, Philip J., arr.
Othello 12473
Langdon, Christopher S., ed.
Anthologies 21350
Langdon, Richard, arr.
[circa 1729]–1803
Merchant 8061
Lange, Arthur 1888–1956
Romeo 14052
Lange, Richard, arr.
Dream 9742
Langer, Eduard, arr. 1835–1905
Hamlet 3467, 3472, 3473; Tempest 16130,
16131
Langer, F. 1815–1895
Hamlet 3972
Langer, Jan Kazimierz
Two Gentlemen 18401
Langerstädt, E., arr.
Merry Wives 9086
Langey, Otto
1 Henry IV 4514; 2 Henry IV 4682
Langgaard, Rued 1893–1952
Hamlet 3973
Langley, Bernard Peter Francis 1929–
Sonnet 106 20263
Langlois, Dominique Michel Jacques
K. John 5609
Langnese, Rolf 1904–1968
As You Like It 683; Hamlet 3238; Henry V
4733; Caesar 5366; Lear 5823; Macbeth
6965; Measure 7694; Much Ado 11174;
Richard III 12892; Romeo 13306; Shrew
14384; Twelfth Night 16989, 16990;
Winter's Tale 18805
Lanier, Hal
Tempest 15098

Lankester, Michael
Measure 7695; Romeo 13307; Shrew 14385;
Twelfth Night 16991; Two Gentlemen 18402
Lansky, Paul 1944–
Sonnet 73 20002
Lantz, David, III
L.L.L. 6573
Lanza, Gesualdo
Dream 10659
Lanzon, Simon
Richard III 12893
Laptenko, Iu.
Two Gentlemen 18403
Laquai, Reinhold 1894–1957
Timon 16380; Winter's Tale 19112
Laquidara, Charles
Richard III 12894
Largent, Daniel
As You Like It 684
Larmanjat, Jacques 1878–1952
Hamlet 3239
Larsen, Elizabeth Brown 1950–
[Née Reece]; also known as Libby Larsen
Tempest 15549, 15697, 15913, 15975
Larsen, Jeff
Twelfth Night 16992
Larson, Nils 1902–
Twelfth Night 16993, 18233
Larsson, Lars-Erik Vilner 1908–
Tempest 16066; Winter's Tale 18806
Larsson, Lucas
Lear 5824
Laru, Tony 1949–
Pseudonym used by Antonio Gonzalez
Settings of Commemorative Pieces . . . 21051
L[asker], V[ally]
Othello 12322
Lasker, Vally, arr.
1 Henry IV 4464; 2 Henry IV 4630; Sonnet
12 19295; Sonnet 19 19475
Lasry, Jacques Isaac 1918–
Dream 9559
Lassen, Eduard 1830–1904
Hamlet 3708, 3741, 3746, 3765, 3836,
3869, 3882; Henry V 4734; 1 Henry VI
4854; 2 Henry VI 4896; 3 Henry VI 4939;
Henry VIII 5125; Richard II 12676
Lassowsky, Jaropolk
Hamlet 3240
Last, Joan
Dream 10942
Lastovetskyi, M.
Merry Wives 8905
Laszlo, Alexander 1895–[before 1982]
Dream 9560; Settings of Commemorative
Pieces . . . 21152
Lathrop, Child, arr.
Hamlet 4112; Settings of Commemorative
Pieces . . . 20869

Lathrop, Marion Nugent, arr.
  Hamlet 4113; Settings of Commemorative
  Pieces . . . 20870
Lathrop, Roy, arr.
  As You Like It 1455
Lattuada, Felice 1882–1962
  Tempest 15441
Laub, Mark, arr.
  Romeo 13600, 13601
Lauer, Wolfgang   –1984
  Dream 9561
Laufer, Beatrice 1923–
  Merchant 8790
Lauglane, Georges Jean Louis   –1918
  Hamlet 4223
Laurence, G. F. Handel
  Settings of Commemorative Pieces . . .
  21153
Laurendeau, Louis-Philippe, arr. 1861–1916
  Merry Wives 9087
Laurie, Alison Margaret, arr.
  Twelfth Night 18299, 18306, 18318
Lauska, Franz Seraphinus, arr. 1764–1825
  Tempest 15466
Lavagnino, Angelo Francesco 1909–
  Othello 11832
Lavenu, Louis Henry, arr. 1818–1859
  Dream 10372
Lavigna, Vincenzo 1776–1836
  Coriolanus 2416
Lavignac, Albert, arr.
  Dream 9743
Lavignino, Alberto
  1 Henry IV 4372; 2 Henry IV 4564
Law, Alice
  Cymbeline 2582
Law, Hamilton
  As You Like It 1390
Law, Mary
  1 Henry VI 4855; 2 Henry VI 4897; 3 Henry
  VI 4940; Richard III 12895
Lawes, Henry 1596–1662
  Sonnet 116 20323
Lawes, Hubert, arr. 1939–
  Romeo 13990
Lawrence, Alan
  As You Like It 685; Merchant 8215
Lawrence, Thomas Montagu 1909–
  Cymbeline 2686; Henry VIII 5126
Lawson, Gary
  Shrew 14686
Lawson, Malcolm Leonard 1849–
  Much Ado 11472; Twelfth Night 18331
Lawson, Mark
  Tempest 15099
Lawson, Robert
  Macbeth 6966
Laycock, Arthur, arr.
  Merchant 8303

Layer, Friedemann
  Hamlet 3241
Layland, W.
  L.L.L. 6444
Layland, William, arr.
  Tempest 14799
Lazarev, Eduard Leonidovich 1935–
  Antony 273
Lazarus, Frank
  Lear 5825
Lazarus, Henry, arr. 1815–1895
  As You Like It 422
Lazell, Leonard, arr.
  Dream 10229, 10230
Lazzari, Sylvio 1857–1944
  Hamlet 3974
Le Borne, Fernand 1862–1929
  Antony 376
Le Boucher, Maurice Georges Eugène
  1882–1964
  Hamlet 3242
Le Breton, Mahoni, arr.
  Merry Wives 9247
Le Brum, George, arr.
  Richard III 13075
Le Brunn, George
  As You Like It 1983; Merchant 8791
Le Corbeiller, Charles   –1894
  Hamlet 3975; Dream 10968
Le Corbeiller, Charles, arr.   –1894
  Dream 10853
Le Duc, [?]
  Caesar 5367
Le Flem, Paul 1881–1984
  Macbeth 7276, 7519
le Fleming, Christopher Kaye 1908–1985
  As You Like It 1391
Le Gallienne, G.
  Sonnet 71 19956; Sonnet 87 20089; Sonnet
  128 20395
Le Grand, Robert Louis Iwan   –1964
  Macbeth 7455
Le Lacheur, Rex Arthur 1920–1984
  Merchant 8672; Romeo 13839; Sonnet 116
  20324
Le Rey, Frédéric Albert 1858–1942
  Shrew 14589
Le Roux, Maurice Anne Fernand 1923–
  Caesar 5368
Le Thière, Charles
  Two Gentlemen 18661
Le Thière, Charles, arr.
  Errors 2042
Lea, A[nthony]
  Dream 9562
Leach, John 1931–
  Measure 7696; Tempest 15100
Leach, S. W.
  Twelfth Night 17736

Leadbetter, Martin John 1945–
  Henry V 4823
Leahy, Frank
  Twelfth Night 18282
Leandre, Joëlle Jeanne Lucienne 1951–
  Coriolanus 2312; Romeo 13768; Troilus
  16495
Lear, Arthur
  Tempest 15698
Lear, Thomas
  Merchant 8697
Leavitt, Jonathan Gilbert
  Hamlet 4224
Lebeau, Alfred, arr.
  Romeo 13705
Lebherz, Harald
  Tempest 15101
Lebič, Lojze 1934–
  Twelfth Night 16994
Leblanc, Daniel
  Dream 9563
Lebrun, Paul 1863–1920
  Lear 6114
Lecarpentier, Adolphe Clair, arr. 1809–1869
  Also known as Adolphe-Clair Le Carpentier
  Dream 10854; Othello 12110; Romeo
  13706; Settings of Commemorative
  Pieces . . . 20969
Lecocq, Alexandre-Charles 1832–1918
  Cymbeline 2838
Lecocq, Alexandre-Charles, in part arr.
  1832–1918
  Othello 12111
LeCompte, Calvin
  Errors 2118
Ledent, Robert
  Hamlet 3243; Shrew 14386; Twelfth Night
  16995
Lederer, W.
  Dream 9564
Ledger, Philip Stevens, arr. 1937–
  Dream 10231
Leduc, Alphonse, arr. 1804–1868
  Also known as Alphonse Leduc père
  Dream 10855; Tempest 14800
Lee, Chris H.
  L.L.L. 6254
Lee, Ernest Markham 1874–1956
  As You Like It 1703; Dream 10660, 10661;
  Tempest 15550, 15699
Lee, Ernest Markham, arr. 1874–1956
  Cymbeline 2757; Dream 9744; Two
  Gentlemen 18589
Lee, George Alexander 1802–1852
  Twelfth Night 18332; Settings of
  Commemorative Pieces . . . 21052
Lee, George Alexander, in part arr. 1802–1852
  As You Like It 1902; L.L.L. 6658; Macbeth
  7456; Dream 10856; Tempest 16067

Lee, James Turle, arr.
  Tempest 14801
Lee, John
  Hamlet 3976
Lee, M[aurice?], arr.
  Shrew 14580
Lee, Maurice, arr.
  Dream 9745, 10857; Tempest 14728
Lee, Noël 1924–
  Hamlet 3244, 3766, 3796, 3837, 3870;
  Henry VIII 5127, 5128; Measure 7697,
  7919, 7920; Two Gentlemen 18529; Sonnet
  18 19395; Sonnet 19 19467; Sonnet 29
  19561; Sonnet 73 20003; Sonnet 147
  20514
Lee, Ronald Gregg, in part arr. 1960–
  Twelfth Night 16996
Lee, Ronald Gregg, arr. 1960–
  Twelfth Night 17612
Lee, Rupert E.
  Dream 9565
Lee, Sebastian, arr. 1805–1887
  Macbeth 7337; Dream 10858
Lees, Benjamin 1924–
  Lear 5826, 6081
Lees, Carol
  As You Like It 686; Othello 11833
Lees, Heath
  Othello 11834
Lees, P. J., arr.
  Settings of Commemorative Pieces . . . 21023
Lefébure-Wély, Louis James Alfred 1817–1869
  Born Lefébre
  Dream 10662
Lefébure-Wély, Louis James Alfred, arr.
  1817–1869
  Born Lefébre
  Hamlet 3654
Lefebvre, Channing 1895–
  Henry VIII 5129
Lefebvre, François Charlemagne, fils
  1775–1839
  Venus 20816
Lefèvre, Victor-Gustave 1831–1910
  Romeo 13308, 13927
Legg, James, Jr. 1962–
  Caesar 5487; Dream 10311, 10379;
  Tempest 16068
Legouix, Isidore Édouard 1834–1916
  Othello 12476
Legov, Max
  Much Ado 11365
Legrand, [Jean-Pierre] [1734–1898]
  Merry Wives 9239
Leguerney, Jacques Alfred Georges Émile
  1906–
  Twelfth Night 17569
Lehane, Maureen, arr.
  Tempest 15220

Lehár, Franz 1870–1948
Merry Wives 9265
L[ehmann], A[melia] [circa 1835]–
Née Chambers; also known as Mrs. Rudolf Lehmann
As You Like It 2009; Measure 7921
Lehmann, [?]
Romeo 13769
Lehmann, Günther
Shrew 14387
Lehmann, Liza 1862–1918
Née Elizabeth Nina Mary Frederika Lehmann; also known as Mrs. Herbert Bedford
As You Like It 1392, 1704, 1705, 1967; L.L.L. 6574; Merchant 8453, 8586, 8587; Dream 10334, 10336, 10352; Much Ado 11473; Twelfth Night 17737, 17936; Two Gentlemen 18530; Sonnet 105 20251
Lehmann, Markus Hugo 1919–
As You Like It 687; Dream 9566; Twelfth Night 16997
Lehn, Erwin
Errors 2119
Lehrman, Leonard J. 1949–
Sonnet 18 19396
Lehto, Frederick E.
As You Like It 688
Leibrock, Joseph Adolph, arr. 1808–1886
Lear 6062
Leich, Roland Jacobi 1911–
Lear 5827; Richard III 12896
Leicht, Arno
Much Ado 11175
Leichtling, Alan Robert 1947–
Tempest 16274; Sonnet 29 19562
Leidgebel, Amandus Leopold 1816–
Lear 6082
Leidzén, Erik William Gustav, arr. 1894–1962
Errors 2214; Lear 6172; Merchant 8745
Leigh, Henry S., arr.
Caesar 5561
Leigh, Mitch 1928–
Born Irwin Mitchnick
Sonnet 130 20423
Leigh, Walter 1905–1942
Henry V 4842; Henry VIII 4999; Dream 9567
Leighton, Kenneth 1929–
As You Like It 1706; 1 Henry IV 4373; 2 Henry IV 4565; Merry Wives 8906
Leighty, Stephen
Tempest 15102
Leistner, Siegfried
Twelfth Night 16998
Leistner-Mayer, Roland 1945–
Sonnet 15 19307; Sonnet 116 20325; Sonnet 146 20493
Leitch, Donovan 1946–
Also known as 'Donovan'
As You Like It 1707

Leitner, Max
Coriolanus 2313; Caesar 5369; K. John 5610; Much Ado 11176; Shrew 14388
Leitner, Max, arr.
Measure 7635
Lejet, Edith Jacqueline Marie 1941–
Hamlet 4069
Lekeu, Jean Joseph Nicolas Guillaume 1870–1894
Hamlet 3977, 3978
Lemaire, Cor
Dream 9568, 9569
Lemare, Edwin Henry, arr. 1865–1934
Henry VIII 4986, 4987, 4988, 4989, 4990; Merry Wives 9088; Dream 9746; Othello 12525; Romeo 13991
Lemêtre, Jean-Jacques
1 Henry IV 4374; Richard II 12677; Twelfth Night 16999
Lemke, Jürgen
Winter's Tale 18808
Lemke, Jürgen, in part arr.
Hamlet 3245
Lemmon, Jeremy
Settings of Commemorative Pieces . . . 21186
Lemmon, Jeremy, in part arr.
Antony 186; Henry V 4735; Dream 9570
Lemmons, Jaak-Nicholaas 1823–1881
Also known as Nicolas Jacques Lemmens
Lear 6158
Lemoine, Antoine Marcel, arr. 1763–1817
Much Ado 11627; Romeo 13634
Lemoine, Léon, arr. 1855–1916
Dream 9747
Lendvay, Kamilló 1928–
Sonnet 75 20037
Lennox, Eva U.
Much Ado 11474
Lenormand, René, arr. 1846–1932
Merry Wives 9217
Lenschow, Charles, arr.
Dream 9748
Lenton, John [1656?–1718?]
Othello 11835
Lenz, Klaus 1940–
Measure 7698; Pericles 12574
Lenz, Leopold 1803–1862
Macbeth 7571
Léon, Laurent
Othello 11836, 12323
Leonard, Beldon, arr.
Two Gentlemen 18590
Léonard, Hubert, arr.
Dream 10859
Leonard, Mamie Grace 1909–
Sonnet 1 19181; Sonnet 78 20059
Leonard, Matthew
Macbeth 6967

Leonard, Ruth
Winter's Tale 18809
Leonard, Stanley Sprenger 1931–
Sonnet 116 20307
Leonard, Stuart B.
Dream 10526
Leonardi, Lino
As You Like It 689
Leoncavallo, Ruggero 1857–1919
Also known, incorrectly, as Ruggiero
Leoncavallo
Dream 10160
Leoni, Alberto
Tempest 16275
Leoni, Pasquale
Hamlet 3979
Leonov, Apollon Mikhailovich 1894–
Othello 11837; Shrew 14389
Leonte, Chrestos
Shrew 14390
Leopold, Bohuslav, arr.
Richard III 13056
Leopold I 1640–1705
Holy Roman Emperor
Timon 16388
Leppard, Raymond John 1927–
Cymbeline 2471; L.L.L. 6255; Dream 9571;
Romeo 13309; Tempest 15103, 15104;
Twelfth Night 17000; Two Gentlemen
18404
Leroux, Félix, arr. –1894
Othello 12112; Romeo 13707, 13708
Leroux, Xavier Henry Napoléon 1863–1919
Venus 20817
Leroux, Xavier Henry Napoléon, arr.
1863–1919
Macbeth 7462
Lerstad, Terje Bjørn 1955–
Sonnet 27 19531; Sonnet 28 19539; Sonnet
66 19914; Sonnet 128 20405; Sonnet 147
20515; P. Pilgrim 20654
Lesjak, Borut 1931–
Twelfth Night 17001
Leslee, Ray 1953–
Errors 2201; Hamlet 4163; 1 Henry IV
4375; Lear 5828; L.L.L. 6328; Macbeth
6968; Measure 7699; Merchant 8216;
Merry Wives 8907; Dream 10161; Pericles
12605; Richard II 12678; Romeo 13310;
Shrew 14591; Tempest 15105; Twelfth
Night 17002, 17003; Winter's Tale 18810;
Sonnet 41 19705; Sonnet 91 20123; Sonnet
116 20340; Settings of Commemorative
Pieces . . . 20941, 20942
Leslie, D.
[Desmond Leslie?]
Tempest 16069
Leslie, Desmond
Antony 187; Hamlet 3246; Henry V 4736;

Caesar 5371; Lear 5829; Macbeth 6969;
Measure 7700; Dream 9572; Othello 11838;
Richard III 12897; Tempest 15106
Leslie, Henry David 1822–1896
2 Henry IV 4646; Merchant 8454, 8486;
Settings of Commemorative Pieces . . .
21053
Leslie, Henry David, arr. 1822–1896
Cymbeline 2656; Dream 10373
Leslie, Kevin 1960–
As You Like It 690; Hamlet 3247; Dream
9573; Twelfth Night 17004
Lessard, John Ayres 1920–
Henry VIII 5130; Dream 10434; Tempest
15700, 15914
Lessem, Alan
Lear 5830
Lester, Thomas William 1889–1956
As You Like It 1393, 1708; L.L.L. 6353;
Much Ado 11475; Tempest 15551; Twelfth
Night 17570, 17937; Two Gentlemen 18531
Lester, William, in part arr.
Shrew 14391
Lesur, Daniel [1908–]
Shrew 14392
Leszczyńska, Franciszka
Twelfth Night 17005
Letelier, Miguel
Merchant 8217; Othello 11839
Lethbridge, Lionel
Merchant 8218, 8588
Lethbridge, Lionel, arr.
Much Ado 11559
Letorey, Omer Claude 1873–1938
Macbeth 6970; Romeo 14053
Letts, Egerton
Measure 7922
Leukauf, Robert
All's Well 34; Lear 5831; Othello 11840;
Troilus 16496; Twelfth Night 17006
Leuschner, [?]
Macbeth 7457
Levandowski, Thomas
Romeo 13311
Leveaux, David
Hamlet 3248
Levenson, Michael
Tempest 15107
Lévêque, Émile, arr.
Also known as Émile Lévèque
Hamlet 3655
Leveridge, Richard [1670?]–1758
1 Henry IV 4376; L.L.L. 6445, 6575;
Macbeth 6971; Dream 10162, 10751; Two
Gentlemen 18532
Levey, Andrew James
As You Like It 691; Romeo 13312, 13928;
Twelfth Night 17007, 17938, 18155;
Winter's Tale 18811

Levey, Harold
Caesar 5372
Levey, Richard Michael 1811–1899
Antony 188
Levey, Sivori
As You Like It 692, 1394; Merchant 8219;
Tempest 15552
Levey, Sivori, arr.
As You Like It 1456; Cymbeline 2868;
Merchant 8589; Romeo 14161; Tempest
15701; Twelfth Night 17765, 18295
Levey, William Charles 1837–1894
Antony 189; Romeo 14054
Lèvi, Edgardo, arr.
Tempest 15121
Levi, Paul Alan 1941–
As You Like It 693; Macbeth 7007; Much
Ado 11177; Tempest 15108
Levin, Barbara
As You Like It 1709; Hamlet 3767
Levin, Gregory 1943–
Dream 9574; Twelfth Night 17008, 17571,
17939
Levine, Henry, arr. 1892–
Dream 9749
Levitan, Alan
Much Ado 11178
Levitan, Dan
Dream 9575
Levy, Harold 1894–
Hamlet 3249
Levy, Ronald M. 1951–
Sonnet 29 19563
Lewin, Frank 1925–
As You Like It 694; Dream 9576; Shrew
14393; Tempest 15109, 15110; Twelfth
Night 17009
Lewis, Anthony Carey, arr. 1915–1983
Macbeth 6988; Tempest 15063
Lewis, C. A.
Merchant 8590
Lewis, Gene 1940–
As You Like It 695; Hamlet 3250; Twelfth
Night 17010
Lewis, John Richard
Twelfth Night 17011
Lewis, Leon 1890–1961
Merchant 8792
Lewis, Malcolm Wallace, Jr. 1925–
Troilus 16561
Lewis, Maurice Anthony 1915–
As You Like It 1090, 1710; Tempest 15702
Lewis, Michael J.
Caesar 5373; Settings of Commemorative
Pieces . . . 20864
Lewis, Paul
Hamlet 3251
Lewis, William Rees 1910–
As You Like It 2010

Ley, Henry George 1887–1962
Merchant 8455
Ley, Henry George, arr. 1887–1962
Henry V 4780
Leybach, Ignace Xavier Joseph, arr.
1817–1891
Hamlet 3656; Macbeth 7338; Dream 10860,
10861; Othello 12113; Romeo 13709,
13710
Leyton, Steve
Dream 9577
Liáng Jíngmíng 1939–
All's Well 35
Liatoshyns'kyi, Borys Mykolaiovych
1895–1969
Romeo 13313, 13929
Liberace, George J. 1911–1983
Settings of Commemorative Pieces . . .
20943
Liberovici, Sergio 1930–
As You Like It 696; Errors 2120; Henry V
4737; Lear 5832; Merchant 8220; Richard II
12679; Tempest 15111; Titus 16407
Liberto, Joseph C.
Tempest 16276
Libkin, Maida 1952–
As You Like It 697
Lichtenberg, Andrew
Macbeth 7008
Lichter, Robert
Othello 11841
Liddell, Claire E.
Merchant 8221, 8591; Twelfth Night
17012, 17572, 17747, 18156
Lidgey, Charles Albert –1924
As You Like It 1395
Liebeck, Pamela
Antony 190; Hamlet 3252
Liebermann, Rolf 1910–
As You Like It 698; Measure 7701; Dream
9578; Tempest 15112; Twelfth Night
17013; Winter's Tale 18812
Liebl, Siegfried
Merry Wives 8908
Liebling, Estelle 1880–1970
Dream 10435
Liebling, Estelle, arr. 1880–1970
Hamlet 3657; Dream 9364; Two Gentlemen
18367
Liebrecht, Marc
L.L.L. 6256
Lieckfeldt, Eberhard
Antony 191; Richard III 12898
Lieven, Nils
L.L.L. 6257
Lievens, Eugeen
Macbeth 7009
Liftl, Franz J., arr.
Merry Wives 9089, 9090

Ligeti, György Sándor 1923–
    Tempest 15443
Lilburn, Douglas Gordon 1915–
    Cymbeline 2583; Hamlet 3253, 3254;
    2 Henry IV 4566; Henry V 4738; Macbeth
    7010; Merchant 8222; Dream 9579; Much
    Ado 11384; Othello 11842, 12324; Tempest
    15113
Lilburn, Douglas Gordon, in part arr. 1915–
    1 Henry IV 4377
Lillo, Giuseppe 1814–1863
    Merry Wives 9252; Dream 10792;
    Settings of Commemorative Pieces . . .
    20944
Limb, Roger
    Macbeth 7011
Lincoln, Charles
    As You Like It 1091, 1396; Cymbeline 2584,
    2687; Henry VIII 5131; L.L.L. 6576; Dream
    10527; Much Ado 11476; Tempest 15915;
    Twelfth Night 17940; Two Gentlemen
    18534; Winter's Tale 19008
Lincoln, Thomas, arr.
    As You Like It 1177; Much Ado 11543
Lindberg, Robert, in part arr.
    Dream 9580
Lindblad, Otto 1809–1864
    Henry VIII 5132
Lindemann, Otto, arr. 1879–
    Romeo 14085
Linder, G., arr.
    Romeo 13711
Lindgren, Bo
    Lear 5833
Lindquist, Frank, in part arr.
    Shrew 14394
Lindsay, Sylvia
    Antony 192
Lindsey, Edwin S.
    Hamlet 3602
Lindsey, Mort 1923–
    As You Like It 955
Lindup, David
    Merry Wives 9205; Settings of
    Commemorative Pieces . . . 21154
Linjama, Jouko 1934–
    As You Like It 699
Link, Joachim-Dietrich 1925–
    Errors 2121; Cymbeline 2688; Hamlet 3255,
    3797; 1 Henry IV 4378; L.L.L. 6446, 6577;
    Measure 7702; Much Ado 11179, 11477;
    Shrew 14395; Twelfth Night 17014, 18157;
    Winter's Tale 19009
Link, Peter
    Errors 2122; Much Ado 11180
Linke, Hans-Michael
    Twelfth Night 17015
Linley, George 1798–1865
    Othello 12505

Linley, Thomas, Sr. 1732–1795
    Henry VIII 5000; Macbeth 7012; Romeo
    13315; Tempest 15114; Settings of
    Commemorative Pieces . . . 21054
Linley, Thomas, Sr., arr. 1732–1795
    Macbeth 6989; Tempest 15080
Linley, Thomas, Jr. 1756–1778
    Tempest 15115; Settings of Commemorative
    Pieces . . . 21055
Linley, William 1771–1835
    All's Well 84; Antony 298; As You Like It
    1092, 1397, 1823, 1866; Cymbeline 2585;
    Hamlet 3256, 3838; 2 Henry IV 4640;
    Henry VIII 5133, 5220; Lear 6026; Macbeth
    7572; Measure 7923; Merchant 8592;
    Dream 10361, 10969; Much Ado 11385,
    11478; Othello 12224, 12325; Tempest
    15804, 16226; Twelfth Night 17573,
    17941; Two Gentlemen 18535; Winter's
    Tale 19010; Venus 20794; Settings of
    Commemorative Pieces . . . 20865
Linley, William, in part arr. 1771–1835
    As You Like It 423; Cymbeline 2594
Linley, William, arr. 1771–1835
    As You Like It 1857; Cymbeline 2657;
    Dream 10308, 10555; Tempest 14729,
    14802, 15122, 15484; Twelfth Night 17312
Linley, William, ed. 1771–1835
    Anthologies 21309
Linsel, Eckhard, arr.
    Settings of Commemorative Pieces . . .
    21266
Linstaedt, Axel
    Two Gentlemen 18463
Linstead, George Frederick 1908–1974
    Merchant 8593
Linter, Ricardo, arr.   –1886
    Dream 10795
Linton, Arthur Henry
    As You Like It 1398, 1711; Twelfth Night
    17942; Two Gentlemen 18536
Liotta, A.
    Romeo 13770
Lipkis, Larry 1951–
    Lear 6115; Tempest 16170
Lippol'd, Max, arr.
    Tempest 16132
Lisk, Edward Lee
    As You Like It 1399
Lisle, Vernon 1906–
    Sonnet 18 19459
Lissmann, Kurt 1902–1983
    Sonnet 65 19895
List, Franz, arr.
    Dream 9908
List, Karl
    Dream 9581; Much Ado 11181; Shrew
    14396; Troilus 16497; Twelfth Night
    17016; Winter's Tale 18813, 18814

Lister, Craig
Twelfth Night 17017
Lister, John Rodney 1951–
Measure 7924; Merchant 8594; Dream
10449; Settings of Commemorative Pieces . . .
21225
Listov, Konstantin Iakovlevich 1900–
Othello 11843
Liszt, Franz 1811–1886
Born Ferenc Liszt
Hamlet 3980; Tempest 16070
Liszt, Franz, arr. 1811–1886
Born Ferenc Liszt
Cymbeline 2758; Hamlet 3559; 1 Henry IV
4515; 2 Henry IV 4683; Lear 6063, 6173,
6174; Dream 9750, 10862; Othello 12114;
Romeo 13712
Litaize, Gaston Gilbert 1909–
Richard II 12680
Litolff, Henry Charles 1818–1891
Lear 5999
Litolff, Henry Charles, arr. 1818–1891
Othello 12115
Litta, Paolo
Antony 274
Little, James Hyatt, arr.
Macbeth 6990
Littlejohn, Joan Anne 1937–
As You Like It 1093, 1400, 1712, 1848;
L.L.L. 6578; Measure 7925; Merchant 8595;
Dream 10528; Tempest 15553, 15703;
Twelfth Night 17574, 17943, 17944,
18158; Sonnet 18 19397; Sonnet 57 19804;
Sonnet 71 19957; Sonnet 73 20004; Sonnet
98 20185; Sonnet 104 20239; Sonnet 116
20326; P. Pilgrim 20655
Littlewood, Christopher 1946–
As You Like It 700, 2011; Merchant 8223,
8224; Much Ado 11182
Littoff, Maxim
Pseudonym used by Maxwell Eckstein
As You Like It 1903
Liú Rùzhēng
Much Ado 11183
Livens, Leo
Two Gentlemen 18662
Liverman, Hubert
Caesar 5374
Lizaso, Nydia Pereyra
Also known as Nydia Pereira Lizaso
Merchant 8225; Twelfth Night 17018
Llorca, Hervé Michel André 1951–
Hamlet 3257; 1 Henry IV 4495; 2 Henry IV
4669
Lloret, José
Dream 10163
Lloyd, Charles Harford 1849–1919
Dream 10410

Lloyd, Richard
As You Like It 701; Merchant 8226; Dream
9582; Much Ado 11184; Othello 11844;
Romeo 13316; Tempest 15130; Twelfth
Night 17019
Lloyd, Richard G.
Dream 9583
Lloyd, S. O., arr.
Cymbeline 2848
Lloyd-Howells, David 1942–
Phoenix 20760
Lobanov, P. M.
Othello 12326
Löbbert, Wolfgang
Richard III 12899
Lobdell, Edith
Merchant 8227
Lochy, Claude
Troilus 16498; Twelfth Night 17020
Locke, Matthew [1621?]–1677
Also known as Matthew Lock
Hamlet 3851; Henry VIII 5001, 5135;
Macbeth 7013; Tempest 15444
Lockett, David
Tempest 15131
Locknane, Clement
Cymbeline 2689; Macbeth 7014
Lockwood, Anne
Twelfth Night 17021
Lockwood, Normand 1906–
Macbeth 7015; Dream 9584
Loder, Edward James 1813–1865
As You Like It 1401; Measure 7926; Dream
9585, 10366, 10411, 10793; Sonnet 18
19398; Sonnet 71 19958
Loder, Edward James, arr. 1813–1865
As You Like It 424; Cymbeline 2759;
Macbeth 6991; Tempest 14730, 14803,
15485; Twelfth Night 16674, 18018
Loeb, David 1939–
Sonnet 5 19210; Sonnet 71 19959; Sonnet
128 20396
Loepelmann, Jens, in part arr.
Hamlet 3258
Loeschhorn, Carl Albert, arr. 1819–1905
Merry Wives 9091
Loevendie, Theo 1930–
Venus 20785
Loew, Ossip
Hamlet 3987
Loewe, Johann Carl Gottfried 1796–1869
Hamlet 3798; Othello 12327; Twelfth Night
17575
Löffler, Hellmuth
Errors 2123, 2124; Coriolanus 2314; Hamlet
3259, 3260; 1 Henry IV 4379; 2 Henry IV
4567; 1 Henry VI 4856; 2 Henry VI 4898;
3 Henry VI 4941; Macbeth 7520; Measure
7703; Merchant 8228; Richard II 12681;

Löffler, Hellmuth (*cont.*)
   Richard III 12900; Romeo 13317; Troilus
   16499; Twelfth Night 17022
Löffler, Wolfgang　–1984
   Measure 7704; Richard III 12901; Romeo
   13318, 13319; Tempest 15132
Loftus, Mrs. George
   Dream 10923
Logan, Frederic Knight 1871–1928
   Two Gentlemen 18663
Logar, Mihovil 1902–
   Antony 275; Lear 6000; Merchant 8409;
   Dream 10664
Logeart, Gustave Léopold, arr.　–1903
   Lear 6064
Lohberg, Hans
   As You Like It 702; Tempest 15133
Löhr, Hermann Frederic 1872–1943
   Settings of Commemorative Pieces . . . 21056
Löhr, Richard Harvey 1856–
   Antony 318, 319; Hamlet 3988; L.L.L.
   6659; Dream 10665; Much Ado 11602;
   Richard II 12771; Shrew 14659; Tempest
   15448, 15449, 16071; Twelfth Night 18234;
   Winter's Tale 19113; Sonnet 97 20174
Lohse, Uwe
   Macbeth 7016
Lokshin, Aleksandr Lazarevich 1920–
   Hamlet 4225; Sonnet 66 19915; Sonnet 73
   20005
Lombardi, Luca
   Hamlet 4226
Lombardo, Carmen
   Romeo 14162
Lombardo, Robert M. 1932–
   Tempest 15134; Twelfth Night 17023
Lonati, Edmond
   Dream 10863
London, Edwin 1929–
   Errors 2125; Hamlet 4070; Dream 9586;
   Twelfth Night 17024
Long, John P.
   Romeo 14163
Long, Robert
   Henry V 4739; Twelfth Night 17025;
   Winter's Tale 18815
Longden, Robert
   Twelfth Night 17026
Longley, Thomas
   Lear 6186
Longmire, John Basil Hugh 1902–
   As You Like It 1402; L.L.L. 6447, 6579;
   Twelfth Night 17027; Two Gentlemen 18537
Longstaff, Brian
   Tempest 15135
Longuich, Heinz-Martin
   Twelfth Night 17028
Loomis, Clarence 1889–1965
   Lear 5834; Macbeth 7458

Loomis, Harvey Worthington 1865–1930
   Also wrote under the pseudonym 'Walter F.
   Scollard'
   Cymbeline 2472, 2473, 2690; Merchant
   8424; Othello 12225; Tempest 16277;
   P. Pilgrim 20656
Lopas, Algimantas
   Settings of Commemorative Pieces . . .
   21226
Lopez, Francis 1916–
   Romeo 14164
Lopez Buchardo, Carlos 1881–1948
   Romeo 13320
López-Morillas, Julian 1947–
   1 Henry VI 4857; 2 Henry VI 4899; Lear
   5835; Merchant 8229; Dream 9587; Pericles
   12575; Two Gentlemen 18405
Lorenz, Carl Adolf 1837–1923
   Also known as Adolph Lorenz
   As You Like It 1996; Errors 2202
Loreto, Vittore
   Pseudonym used by Ernest Barnard
   Hamlet 3989
Loschelder, Franz
   Much Ado 11185
Loth, Louis Leslie 1888–
   Romeo 14165
Lothar, Friedrich Wilhelm, arr. 1885–
   Dream 10232
Lothar, Mark [1903]–1985
   All's Well 36; As You Like It 703; Hamlet
   3261, 3262; Caesar 5375; Lear 5836, 5837,
   5838; L.L.L. 6258; Measure 7705; Merry
   Wives 8909; Much Ado 11186; Othello
   11845, 11846; Richard II 12682; Richard III
   12902; Romeo 13321; Shrew 14397,
   14398; Tempest 15136; Twelfth Night
   17029; Two Gentlemen 18406, 18644
Lothar, Mark, in part arr. [1903]–1985
   Romeo 13322
Lotichius, Erik 1929–
   Much Ado 11479; Twelfth Night 17576,
   17945, 18159; Sonnet 60 19830
Lott, Edwin Matthew, arr.
   Dream 9751
Lotter, Adolf, arr.
   Merry Wives 9260
Lotz, Marie
   Romeo 13323
Loucheur, Raymond 1899–
   Coriolanus 2392
Loudová, Ivana 1941–
   Romeo 13930
Louhensalo, Tapio
   Merry Wives 8910
Louis, Émile O.
   Much Ado 11480
Louis, Émile O., arr.
   Othello 12116

Louis, Nicolas, arr. –1857
Macbeth 7339; Othello 12117
Louvier, Alain Maurice Jean Marie 1945–
Hamlet 4071
Lovatt, Samuel Ernest
As You Like It 1094; Merchant 8456; Much
Ado 11481; Winter's Tale 19133, 19152;
Sonnet 29 19564
Love, Ron
Hamlet 3263
Lovell, Katharine 1915–
Pseudonym once used by Margaret Olive
Hubicki (see also Hubicki, Margaret Olive)
Hamlet 3990; Henry V 4824; L.L.L. 6660;
Merry Wives 9225; Dream 10666; Tempest
16072
Lovelock, William 1899–
As You Like It 1713; Winter's Tale 19051;
Sonnet 73 20006
Low, James
Much Ado 11187
Löw, Josef, arr. 1834–1886
Shrew 14581
Low, Reg
Settings of Commemorative Pieces . . . 21057
Lowe, Claude Egerton 1860–
As You Like It 1849
Lowe, Claude Egerton, arr. 1860–
Tempest 15294
Lowell, Oscar
Romeo 13931
Lowens, Irving 1916–1983
Twelfth Night 17577
Lowery, Ray
Hamlet 3264
Lowrey, Norman Eugene 1944–
Twelfth Night 17030; Sonnet 8 19252;
Sonnet 60 19831; Sonnet 146 20494;
Settings of Commemorative Pieces . . . 21058
Lowry, Todd, in part arr.
Tempest 15137
Lowther, Toupie
Antony 377
Lowthian, Caroline [circa 1860]–
Also known as Mrs. Cyril A. Prescott
Dream 10164, 10165
Luard-Selby, Bertram 1853–[1918]
As You Like It 1095, 1403; L.L.L. 6580;
Measure 7927
Lubahn, P.
Othello 12477
Lubalin, Paul
Othello 12453
Lubetsky, Ronald Stuart 1959–
Sonnet 60 19832
Luboff, Norman 1917–
Much Ado 11641
Lucardo, L.
Romeo 13932

Lucas, Clarence Reynolds 1866–1947
As You Like It 1904; Macbeth 7459; Othello
12406; Tempest 16073; Settings of
Commemorative Pieces . . . 20945
Lucas, Leighton 1903–1982
Twelfth Night 17578
Lucke, K. E.
As You Like It 1404; Tempest 15916
Luckenbach, Lorine B.
Caesar 5512
Lucraft, H.
As You Like It 1096, 1405, 1714; Much Ado
11482; Tempest 15917; Twelfth Night
17946; Two Gentlemen 18538
Ludt, Finn 1918–
Macbeth 7017; Twelfth Night 17031
Ludwig, Carl Joachim 1938–
1 Henry IV 4380; 2 Henry IV 4568;
Macbeth 7521; Sonnet 1 19182; Sonnet 15
19308; Sonnet 29 19565; Sonnet 91 20119;
Sonnet 100 20208
Ludwig, Otto 1813–1865
Romeo 13771
Ludwig, Peter
Othello 11847; Richard II 12683; Richard III
12903
Luening, Otto Clarence 1900–
Lear 5839
Luff, Enid Meirion 1935–
Née Roberts
Dream 9588, 10667; Sonnet 18 19399;
Sonnet 31 19636; Sonnet 98 20186
Luigini, Alexandre, arr.
Romeo 13713
Luís, Cláudio
Tempest 15138
Lukáš, Zdeněk
As You Like It 704
Łukaszewski, Wojciech
All's Well 37
Lumby, Herbert Horace
As You Like It 1406, 1715; Measure 7928;
Twelfth Night 17947
Lumsdaine, David 1931–
Tempest 16074
Lund Christiansen, Charlotte
Shrew 14399
Lund Christiansen, Toke
Shrew 14400
Lundquist, Torbjörn 1920–
Coriolanus 2315
Lundsten, Ralph 1936–
Dream 9599; Troilus 16500
Lunssens, Martin 1871–1944
Caesar 5513; Romeo 13933; Timon 16381
Lupovici, Patrice
Twelfth Night 17032
Luscomb, Fred
Caesar 5514

Lust, Louis César Marie   –1919
    Merry Wives 9253
Lütgen, Bernard
    Merchant 8596; Dream 10529
Luther, Carola
    Romeo 13324
Lutosławski, Witold 1913–
    Macbeth 7018; Merry Wives 8911; Twelfth
    Night 17033
Lutyens, Agnes Elisabeth 1906–1983
    Antony 193; As You Like It 705; Hamlet
    3265, 4109; Henry VIII 5002; Caesar 5376;
    Twelfth Night 18160
Lutyens, Sally Speare 1927–
    Dream 9589
Lutz, Wilhelm Meyer [1822?]–1903
    Tempest 16186
Lützow-Holm, Ole 1954–
    Settings of Commemorative Pieces . . . 20866
Lux, Friedrich 1820–1895
    Coriolanus 2417
Lygon, Frederick
    Also known as Earl of Beauchamp
    Sonnet 54 19770
Lynas, F.
    [Frank Lynes (1858–1913)?]
    Caesar 5377
Lynes, Frank, arr. 1858–1913
    As You Like It 1150
Lynn, Gary
    Tempest 15139
Lynner, Brian
    Hamlet 3266; L.L.L. 6259; Much Ado
    11188; Titus 16408
Lyon, James 1872–1949
    Dream 10463
Lyon, Nicholas 1948–
    Also known as Nicolas Lyon
    Hamlet 3267; 1 Henry IV 4381; 2 Henry IV
    4569; Romeo 13325
Lyon, Thomas   –1837
    L.L.L. 6366
Lysberg, Ch[arles] B., arr.
    Hamlet 3658; Romeo 13714
Lysenko, Mykola Vitaliiovych 1842–1912
    Hamlet 3268
Lyster, Fred
    Much Ado 11189

M

M., H. B.
    As You Like It 1407
Maasz, Gerhard 1906–
    Dream 9590; Romeo 13326; Tempest 15140
Macarig, Hector
    Othello 12478
MacCarthy, Hector 1888–
    Romeo 14205
MacCunn, Hamish 1868–1916
    As You Like It 2012; 2 Henry IV 4684;
    Macbeth 7019; Romeo 13858; Twelfth Night
    17948
MacDermot, Galt Arthur Terence [1928]–
    Cymbeline 2474; Hamlet 4110, 4164;
    Troilus 16559; Twelfth Night 17034,
    18283; Two Gentlemen 18464; Sonnet 29
    19566
MacDonald, Catherine 1940–
    Tempest 15141; Twelfth Night 17035
MacDonald, Fraser Pringle 1912–
    Settings of Commemorative Pieces . . . 21187
MacDonald, Ian 1937–
    Coriolanus 2316
MacDonald, Katie
    Twelfth Night 17036
MacDonald, Robert David
    Coriolanus 2317
MacDougall, Robert Bruce 1931–
    Lear 6138; Dream 9591; Tempest 15142;
    Timon 16328
MacDowell, Edward Alexander 1860–1908
    Also wrote under the pseudonyms 'Edgar
    Thorn' and 'Edgar Thorne'
    Hamlet 3991; Much Ado 11603; Twelfth
    Night 17949
MacDowell, Edward Alexander, arr.
    1860–1908
    Also wrote under the pseudonyms 'Edgar
    Thorn' and 'Edgar Thorne'
    Macbeth 7472; Romeo 13953
MacEnulty, Rosalind
    As You Like It 706
MacEnulty, Rosalind, ed.
    Anthologies 21361
Macfarren, George Alexander 1813–1887
    As You Like It 1097, 1408, 1716; Cymbeline
    2586, 2691; Hamlet 3992; Henry VIII 5136;
    L.L.L. 6367, 6448, 6581; Measure 7929;
    Merchant 8598, 8698; Dream 10412,
    10530, 10668; Much Ado 11483; Romeo
    13934; Twelfth Night 17579, 17950; Two
    Gentlemen 18539; P. Pilgrim 20657;
    Settings of Commemorative Pieces . . . 21059
Macfarren, George Alexander, arr.
    1813–1887
    As You Like It 1457; Twelfth Night 18070;
    Settings of Commemorative Pieces . . . 21155
Macfarren, Walter Cecil 1826–1905
    Henry V 4825; Dream 10669; Othello
    12407; Shrew 14660; Two Gentlemen
    18540, 18645; Winter's Tale 19114;
    P. Pilgrim 20658
MacGregor, Joanna 1959–
    Hamlet 3269; Romeo 13327; Twelfth Night
    17037

Mácha, Otmar 1922–
Dream 9592
Machavariani, Aleksei Davidovich
1913–
Hamlet 3603; Lear 5840; Othello 12030,
12408, 12409, 12410; Richard III 12904
Machell, David
Tempest 15704
Machl, Tadeusz, arr.
Dream 9752
Machts, Carl
Othello 12411
Maciejewski, Roman 1910–
Macbeth 7020
MacInnes, Donald
Settings of Commemorative Pieces . . . 20867
MacIntyre, David 1952–
Hamlet 3270; Romeo 13328
Macirone, Clara Angela 1821–1914
Henry V 4837; Measure 7930; Two
Gentlemen 18541; Winter's Tale 18980,
19052, 19082
Mack, Adrian
Macbeth 7021
Mack, Andrew
Othello 12506
Mack, David
Settings of Commemorative Pieces . . . 21156
MacKaye, Percy Wallace 1875–1956
Hamlet 4111; Settings of Commemorative
Pieces . . . 20868
Mackenroth, Steven
Settings of Commemorative Pieces . . . 21060
Mackenzie, Alexander Campbell 1847–1935
Coriolanus 2318, 2384; Merchant 8599;
Othello 12328; Richard II 12684; Twelfth
Night 18235; Sonnet 18 19400; Sonnet 29
19567; Sonnet 61 19855; Sonnet 99 20201;
P. Pilgrim 20659; Settings of
Commemorative Pieces . . . 21061
Mackerras, Alan Charles MacLaurin 1925–
Lear 5841
Maclean, Alexander Morarven 1872–1936
Also known as Alick Maclean
Shrew 14680
MacMillan, Ernest Alexander Campbell
1893–1973
Twelfth Night 17952
MacMurrough, D[ermot?] [1872–1943]
Pseudonym used by H. R. White
Shrew 14661; Winter's Tale 19115
MacNeil, Alan
Macbeth 7277
Maconchy, Elizabeth 1907–
Hamlet 3768; Measure 7931; Dream 10970;
Othello 12238; Twelfth Night 17580, 18161
Maconie, Robin John 1942–
Sonnet 155 20571; Settings of
Commemorative Pieces . . . 21258

Madarász, Iván 1949–
Errors 2203
Madden, William James
Settings of Commemorative Pieces . . . 21062
Maddison, George W.
Hamlet 3731
Mader, Richard 1930–
Hamlet 3271; Romeo 13329; Twelfth Night
17038
Maderna, Bruno 1920–1973
As You Like It 971; Coriolanus 2319;
Hamlet 4280; Caesar 5378
Madetoja, Leevi Antti 1887–1947
Antony 194
Madsen, Gunnar
Caesar 5379
Maganini, Quinto E., arr. 1897–1974
Macbeth 7552, 7553
Magazzari, Gaetano, arr. [circa 1808]–1872
Othello 12118
Magee, John Thomas
Merchant 8410
Magee, Rusty
Twelfth Night 17039
Magg, Kyril, arr. 1945–
Dream 9753
Maggiore, Francesco [circa 1720]–1782
Coriolanus 2418
Magner, Charles, arr.
Dream 9754
Magnus, D. 1828–1883
Also known as Désiré Magnus; pseudonyms
used by Magnus Deutz
1 Henry IV 4483; 2 Henry IV 4658; Merry
Wives 9226
Magwili, Dom
Twelfth Night 17040
Maher, Amy Grace
Hamlet 3272
Mahler, Gustav, arr. 1860–1911
Dream 10864
Mahon, Herbert
Romeo 13836, 13859
Mahon, Patricia
Lear 5842
Maiboroda, Heorhii Ilarionovych 1913–
Lear 5843, 6083
Mailley, Frank
As You Like It 1717
Maillot, Jean 1911–
Othello 11848
Mailman, Martin 1932–
Cymbeline 2692; Henry V 4804; Henry VIII
5037, 5038; Measure 7932; Twelfth Night
17953
Maiman, Z., arr.
Hamlet 3474
Maingueneau, Louis-Gustave-Jacques   –1950
Romeo 13330

Mainzer, J.
    Henry VIII 5138
Mais, Chester L. 1936–
    Romeo 13856
Maister, Nigel
    Hamlet 3273
Maixner, Vincenc
    Coriolanus 2320
Majer, Milan 1895–1967
    Settings of Commemorative Pieces . . . 21188
Majewski, Hans-Martin 1911–
    Hamlet 3274; Twelfth Night 17041
Major, Bradshaw
    All's Well 38
Major, John Stenson
    L.L.L. 6347
Major, Josh[ua], arr.
    Twelfth Night 17823
Makachinas, T.
    Antony 195
Makhlin, V.
    Othello 11849
Maklakiewicz, Jan Adam 1899–1954
    Caesar 5380; Much Ado 11190; Othello
    11850; Romeo 13331
Maklakiewicz, Zdzisław
    Shrew 14401
Malamet, Marsha
    Tempest 15450
Malásek, Jiří
    Shrew 14592
Malát, Jan, arr. 1843–1915
    Twelfth Night 17411
Malawski, Artur 1904–1957
    Dream 9593; Tempest 15143
Maldonati, G.
    Romeo 13772
Malec, Ivo 1925–
    Lear 5845; Macbeth 7022
Małecki, Maciej 1940–
    As You Like It 707; Macbeth 7023; Measure
    7706; Shrew 14402
Malhocký, Pavel
    Two Gentlemen 18407
Malin, Donald Franklin, ed. 1896–
    Anthologies 21356
Malipiero, Gian Francesco 1882–1973
    Antony 276; Caesar 5481; Macbeth 7501;
    Romeo 13773
Mallandaine, John E., arr.
    Twelfth Night 16675
Malling, Otto Valdemar, arr. 1848–1915
    Settings of Commemorative Pieces . . . 20862
Mallinson, James Albert 1870–1946
    Much Ado 11651; Sonnet 109 20281
Mallis, Constantine Alexander Hagi
    Also wrote under the pseudonyms 'Alex Los
    Angeles', 'Guy Puck', and 'Rex Oberon'
    Dream 10167

Malmgren, Jens Ole 1946–
    Hamlet 3604
Mal'ter, L., arr.
    Othello 12034
Mamangakis, Nicos
    Also known as Nikos Mamangakis
    Othello 11851
Manaev, Evgenii Vasil'evich 1910–
    Twelfth Night 17042
Manassen, Alex 1950–
    Troilus 16564
Mancinelli, Luigi 1848–1921
    Dream 10168
Mancini, Henry, arr. 1924–
    Romeo 13425
Mandée, Rudolf Maria
    Merchant 8230
Mandel, Petr 1938–
    All's Well 88; As You Like It 708; Errors
    2126; Dream 9594; Much Ado 11191;
    Shrew 14403; Twelfth Night 17043
Mandelbaum, Mayer Joel 1932–
    Merchant 8457
Mander, Henry
    As You Like It 1905; Merchant 8699;
    Tempest 16075
Mander, Henry, arr.
    Tempest 14804
Mandozzi, Graziano
    Macbeth 7024; Shrew 14404
Manevich, Aleksandr Mendelevich 1908–
    As You Like It 709, 1906
Manfroce, Nicola Antonio 1791–1813
    Also known as Niccolò Manfroce and Nicolò
    Manfroce
    Dream 10971
Mangelsdorff, Arthur
    Tempest 15705
Mangin, Eugène Édouard, arr. 1837–1907
    Macbeth 7340; Tempest 15495
Mangoianu, Ştefan 1922–1979
    Errors 2127; Lear 5846; L.L.L. 6260; Othello
    11852; Pericles 12576
Mangold, Johann Wilhelm 1796–1875
    Hamlet 3275; Macbeth 7025; Merchant
    8231
Mann, A., arr.
    Twelfth Night 16676
Mann, John David 1954–
    Tempest 15706
Mann, Leslie Douglas 1923–1977
    As You Like It 1409, 1718; P. Pilgrim
    20660
Manne, Sheldon 1920–1984
    1 Henry IV 4382
Manners, Richard
    Errors 2128
Mannes, Leopold Damrosch 1899–1964
    Tempest 15144

Manney, Charles Fonteyn 1872–1951
  Henry VIII 5139; Othello 12226
Mannfred, Heinrich, arr.
  Merry Wives 9092
Manning, Edward Betts 1874–1948
  As You Like It 1098, 1410, 1719; Twelfth
  Night 17954
Manning, Jack
  Macbeth 7026
Manns, August Friedrich, arr. 1825–1907
  Merry Wives 9093, 9094
Mansfield, Johnathan
  Winter's Tale 18816
Mansfield, Orlando Augustine 1863–1936
  2 Henry VI 4920; Richard II 12772
Mansfield, Orlando Augustine, arr. 1863–1936
  Henry VIII 5182; Much Ado 11544
Mansfield, Purcell James 1889–1968
  As You Like It 1099, 1720; Much Ado
  11484; Tempest 15554, 15707
Mansfield, Purcell James, arr. 1889–1968
  Hamlet 4007; Henry VIII 5183
Mantalto, Richard
  Dream 9595
Manusardi, Giuseppe Lodi
  Dream 10798
Manykin-Nestruev, Nikolai Aleksandrovich
  1869–
  Caesar 5381
Mar, Kathy
  Romeo 13332
Mar-Haim, Yossi
  Also known as Joseph Marchaim
  Dream 9596; Romeo 13333, 13334
Marais, [Josef] [1905–   ]
  Twelfth Night 18162
Marbe, Myriam 1931–
  Also known as Myriam Marbé
  As You Like It 710; Tempest 15145
Marcel, Luc-André 1919–
  Also known as André Lucien Marcel and as
  Marcel Luc-André
  Macbeth 7027
Marchant, Arthur William 1850–1921
  L.L.L. 6582
Marchetti, Filippo 1831–1902
  Romeo 13774
Marchisio, Giovanni
  Merry Wives 9190
Marco, Tomás [circa 1942]–
  Macbeth 7028
Marcucci, Stefano
  Shrew 14405
Marcus, Ada Belle Gross 1929–
  As You Like It 972; Sonnet 29 19568
Marcus, Bernard
  Hamlet 4072
Marden, Robert, arr.
  Dream 9755

Mareček, Maximilián 1821–1892
  Hamlet 3605
Maréchal, Charles Henri 1842–1924
  As You Like It 1907; Othello 12412
Mareo, Eric, arr.
  Cymbeline 2760
Marescalchi, Luigi
  Romeo 13782
Margetson, Edward 1891–1962
  Twelfth Night 17955
Margoni, Alain André Armand 1934–
  Merry Wives 8912
Margoshes, Steven
  Dream 10170
Mariani, Giuseppe, arr.
  Hamlet 3577; Dream 9756
Marie, William Constant Frédéric
  –1933
  Hamlet 3993
Marillier, Glyn
  Tempest 15146
Marinelli, Gaetano 1754–1820
  Antony 378
Mariolozzo, Gratiano
  Shrew 14406
Marklund, Ola
  Macbeth 7029
Markopoulos, Jannis
  Tempest 15147
Markowski, Andrzej 1924–
  Much Ado 11192; Shrew 14407
Marks, G. W., arr.
  Also known as Marcks. Not to be confused
  with Johannes Brahms' pseudonym, 'G. W.
  Marks'. [Possibly a pseudonym commonly
  used by a variety of arrangers associated
  with the publisher Aug. Cranz.]
  Hamlet 3659; Macbeth 7341; Othello
  12119; Romeo 13715
Marks, James Christopher, Jr. 1863–
  Twelfth Night 18333
Marks, Michael 1963–
  Also known as Michael Zliwokram
  As You Like It 711
Marks, Thomas Osborne 1845–
  Two Gentlemen 18542
Marland, Albert, arr.
  Romeo 13992
Maronde, Mark E. 1957–
  Sonnet 27 19525; Sonnet 138 20454
Marr, Johnny
  Settings of Commemorative Pieces . . .
  21279
Marriott, Bryant
  Coriolanus 2321
Marriott, Charles Handel Rand 1831–1889
  Merchant 8700; Dream 10670; Tempest
  16076; Twelfth Night 18236; Settings of
  Commemorative Pieces . . . 21157

Marsden, Evan
  Pseudonym used by Eric Marco
  1 Henry IV 4484; 2 Henry IV 4659
Marsden, J. H.
  As You Like It 1100
Marsh, Alphonso, Sr. 162[7]–1681
  Measure 8034; Much Ado 11613
Marsh, J.
  As You Like It 1101
Marshall, Derrick
  Dream 9597
Marshall, Frederick
  Cymbeline 2476; Henry V 4740; 1 Henry VI
  4858; 2 Henry VI 4900; 3 Henry VI 4942;
  Henry VIII 5003; Caesar 5382; Othello
  11853; Timon 16329; Troilus 16501
Marshall, Jim
  Shrew 14408
Marshall, Nicholas 1942–
  L.L.L. 6449, 6583
Marshall-Hall, George William Louis
  1862–1915
  Also known as George W. L. Marshall Hall
  Romeo 13783
Martaine, G., arr.
  Merry Wives 9095
Martell, E.
  Much Ado 11193
Martelli, Henri 1895–1980
  Settings of Commemorative Pieces . . . 20871
Mártha, István
  Macbeth 7030
Marthaler, Christoph
  Hamlet 3276; Merchant 8232
Martin, Charles André Gabriel 1929–
  Tempest 15148
Martin, Christopher
  Titus 16409
Martin, Deborah
  1 Henry VI 4859; 2 Henry VI 4901; 3 Henry
  VI 4943; Merchant 8233; Othello 11854;
  Richard III 12905; Twelfth Night 17044;
  Kinsmen 19161
Martin, Easthope [1847]–1925
  As You Like It 1102
Martin, Frank 1890–1974
  Romeo 13335; Tempest 15451, 15509,
  15555, 15708, 15918, 15986, 16077,
  16078, 16079
Martin, George Dudley
  Winter's Tale 19116
Martin, George William, arr. 1828–1881
  Macbeth 6992
Martin, Gilbert M. 1941–
  Twelfth Night 17956
Martin, Henry, arr.
  Macbeth 7342
Martin, Hugh, arr. 1914–
  Errors 2215

Martin, J. McKay, arr.
  Dream 10865
Martin, James
  1 Henry IV 4383; Caesar 5383
Martin, Judith Reher
  Dream 10171
Martin, Philip
  As You Like It 1721; Hamlet 3821; L.L.L.
  6584; Tempest 16171; Twelfth Night 17957
Martin, Robert
  Merchant 8234
Martín y Soler, Atanasio Martín Ignacio
  Vicente Tadeo Francisco Pellegrin
  1754–1806
  Shrew 14593
Martinez, Isidora
  Two Gentlemen 18543
Martinez, Sabu
  Tempest 15149
Martini, Ettore 1865–
  Hamlet 4165; Settings of Commemorative
  Pieces . . . 20946
Martini, Johann Paul Aegidius 1741–1816
  Born Johann Paul Aegidius Schwarzendorf;
  also known as Martin, as Martini il Tedesco,
  and as Jean Paul Egide Martini
  1 Henry IV 4516; 2 Henry IV 4685
Martirano, Salvatore 1927–
  As You Like It 1103; Lear 6159; L.L.L. 6450,
  6585; Dream 10531; Tempest 15976
Marton, Rumiana
  All's Well 39; Antony 196; As You Like It
  712; Errors 2129, 2130, 2131; Merchant
  8235; Merry Wives 8913; Dream 9598;
  Othello 11855; Romeo 13336; Twelfth Night
  17045; Two Gentlemen 18408; Winter's
  Tale 18817
Marty, Georges 1860–1908
  Hamlet 4281
Marvin, Mel 1941–
  As You Like It 713; Cymbeline 2477;
  Tempest 15150; Twelfth Night 17046;
  Winter's Tale 18818
Marx, Adolf Bernhard 1795–1866
  Twelfth Night 17581
Marx, Henry, arr.   –1888
  Errors 2260; Romeo 13716, 13717, 13718
Marx, Karl Julius 1897–
  Merchant 8491; Romeo 13867
Marzials, Théophile Jules Henri 1850–1920
  As You Like It 1104, 1411, 1722; Cymbeline
  2587, 2693; L.L.L. 6586; Twelfth Night
  18334; Two Gentlemen 18544
Mascagni, Pietro 1863–1945
  Lear 6001
Mason, Daniel Gregory 1873–1953
  Measure 7933; Tempest 15709
Mason, Jack, arr. 1906–1965
  Romeo 13602; Shrew 14609

Mason, William, arr.
  Also known as William Mason of Lincoln
  Dream 9757
Massara, Pino 1931–
  Pseudonym used by Giuseppe Previde Massara
  As You Like It 714
Massarani, R.
  Macbeth 7031
Massenet, Jules Émile Frédéric
  1842–1912
  Macbeth 7460; Othello 12417; Romeo
  13935; Tempest 16080
Massey, Andrew
  Lear 5847
Massis, Amable Pierre Eugène 1893–1980
  Antony 197; Lear 5848
Másson, Áskell 1953–
  Macbeth 7032
Masson, D[iego Luc]
  Lear 5849
Masters, William J. Chalmers 1818–1893
  Dream 10671, 10672
Maters, Theodore
  Hamlet 3277
Mathews, Glenn
  Hamlet 3278; L.L.L. 6261; Macbeth 7033;
  Merchant 8236
Mathews, Henry, arr.
  Settings of Commemorative Pieces . . . 20905
Mathey, Paul 1909–
  Twelfth Night 17582, 17708, 17958, 18163
Mathias, Georges Amédée Saint-Clair
  1826–1910
  Hamlet 3994
Mathias, William 1934–
  As You Like It 715, 1102, 1105, 1412, 1723;
  Cymbeline 2588; Much Ado 11485; Tempest
  15710; Winter's Tale 19013; P. Pilgrim
  20661; Settings of Commemorative
  Pieces . . . 21227
Mathieson, Muir 1911–1975
  Othello 12454
Mathieson, Muir, arr. 1911–1975
  Hamlet 3514, 3515; Henry V 4781; Richard
  III 13015, 13016; Settings of
  Commemorative Pieces . . . 20897, 20898
Mathisen, Leo 1906–1969
  Hamlet 4227; Romeo 14166
Matsumura, Teizo 1929–
  Merchant 8237
Matt, E.
  Pericles 12577
Matter, René Jean 1921–
  Macbeth 7034
Matthes, Wilhelm 1889–
  As You Like It 716
Mattheson, Johann 1681–1764
  Antony 277; 1 Henry IV 4517; 2 Henry IV
  4686

Matthews, Colin
  Macbeth 7035
Matthews, David
  Errors 2132
Matthews, Jennie
  Dream 9600
Matthews, Louise
  Hamlet 3769
Matthews, Peter J.
  Macbeth 7543
Matthey, Alphonso
  Twelfth Night 17738
Matthey, Jul. H., arr.
  Hamlet 3939
Matthus, Siegfried 1934–
  Lear 5850, 5851; L.L.L. 6691; Macbeth
  7036; Dream 9601; Tempest 15151
Matuszczak, Bernadetta 1937–
  Romeo 13784
Matveev, Iu.
  Romeo 13337
Matz, Peter
  Twelfth Night 17405; Settings of
  Commemorative Pieces . . . 20947
Maucksch, Hans-Jörg
  Richard III 12906
Maurice, Alphonse 1862–1906
  Twelfth Night 17583
Maurice, Louis
  Also known as Louie Maurice
  Romeo 13338, 13936
Maurick, Ludwig 1898–
  Dream 9602; Much Ado 11194
Maury, Henry Lowndes 1911–1975
  L.L.L. 6451
Mausz, Erwin
  As You Like It 717; Othello 11856; Winter's
  Tale 18819
Maw, Nicholas 1935–
  Lear 6084
Maxwell, Charles [1892–1962]
  Caesar 5384
Maxwell, Isobel
  Dream 10532
Maxwell, J. Geddes
  As You Like It 1413
Maxwell, Michael Somerset Cullen 1921–
  Dream 9603
May, Arletta
  Measure 8045
May, D. M. H., arr.
  Romeo 13719
May, Frederick M., in part arr.
  1911–1985
  Coriolanus 2322
May, Hans 1891–
  Dream 9604
Mayer, Eckehard
  Tempest 15152

Mayer, Henry 1925–
  Romeo 14167
Mayer, Josef A.
  Twelfth Night 17047
Mayer, Michael A.
  Dream 9605
Mayer, William Robert 1925–
  Tempest 16227
Mayer-Cosacchi, Joachim
  Dream 9606
Mayes, Rodney, arr.
  Dream 9758
Mayeur, L., arr.
  Hamlet 3660
Maynard, Walter
  Pseudonym used by Willert Beale
  Macbeth 7573
Maynard, Walter, arr.
  Pseudonym used by Willert Beale
  Dream 9759
Mayne, Leslie
  Caesar 5385; Merry Wives 8914
Mayor, Charles 1876–1950
  Hamlet 4228
Mayr, Fr., arr.
  Dream 10275
Mayr, Johannes Simon 1763–1845
  Also known as Giovanni Simone Mayer
  Tempest 16278
Mazurek, Bohdan
  Macbeth 7037
Mazzocchetti, Germano
  Dream 9607
McAfee, Donald L. 1935–
  Sonnet 18 19401
McAllester, David Park 1916–
  Twelfth Night 17048
McAuliffe, Jason
  As You Like It 1414; Merchant 8484, 8600;
  Dream 10436; Sonnet 8 19253; Sonnet 29
  19569; Sonnet 49 19738; Sonnet 87 20090
McAven, Peter
  Twelfth Night 17049
McBain, Kenneth
  Dream 9608
McCabe, James C., arr.
  Tempest 15046; Winter's Tale 18777
McCabe, John 1939–
  Settings of Commemorative Pieces . . . 21228
McCabe, Richard
  Romeo 13339
McCarty, Randy
  Errors 2133
McCaskey, John Piersol, arr.
  Merry Wives 8881
McCauley, William Alexander 1917–
  Settings of Commemorative Pieces . . . 20872
McClenahan, Andrew
  Errors 2204

McClung, Samuel W.
  All's Well 40
McClung, Samuel W., in part arr.
  Dream 9609
McColley, Tom
  1 Henry VI 4860; 2 Henry VI 4902; 3 Henry
  VI 4944; Richard III 12907
McCollin, Frances
  As You Like It 1415
McCombs, Ralph L. F.
  Twelfth Night 17959
McConathy, Osbourne, arr. 1875–1947
  Two Gentlemen 18591
McConathy, Osbourne, ed. 1875–1947
  Anthologies 21324
McConnehea, Ron
  Antony 198
McCrary, Margaret
  Merchant 8238
McCubbin, David
  Much Ado 11195
McCulloch, William Campbell, Jr.
  As You Like It 1106
McCurrach, Hector
  1 Henry IV 4384; K. John 5611; Macbeth
  7038
McCurrach, Hector, in part arr.
  Hamlet 3279; Dream 9610; Twelfth Night
  17050
McDonald, Ian Donald 1937–
  Dream 9611; Richard III 12908
McDonald, Molly
  As You Like It 718
McElyea, Hugh M.
  Romeo 13340
McEwen, John Blackwood 1868–1948
  Othello 12227, 12239
McFadden, E. A., in part arr.
  Twelfth Night 17051
McFarland, Ron
  Lear 5852
McGilvra, Douglas 1945–
  Also known under the pseudonym 'Brian
  Oaks'
  Tempest 16172; Winter's Tale 19134
McGlinchey, Liz
  As You Like It 719; Pericles 12578
McGovern, Barry
  Merchant 8239
Mcgrah, N.
  As You Like It 1416; Twelfth Night 17584
McGrath, Joseph John 1889–1968
  Merchant 8601
McGregor, Nigel
  As You Like It 720
McGuire, Edward 1948–
  Macbeth 7039
McGuire, Gaywood
  Settings of Commemorative Pieces . . . 21063

McKay, George Frederick, arr. 1899–1970
  Lear 6175
McKee, Malcolm
  Dream 9612; Tempest 15153
McKelvey, Lori
  Much Ado 11196
McKennitt, Loreena
  Two Gentlemen 18409
McKenzie, Sandra
  As You Like It 721; Macbeth 7040;
  Merchant 8240; Much Ado 11197; Richard
  II 12685; Richard III 12909; Twelfth Night
  17052
McKillen, Arch Alfred 1914–
  Sonnet 29 19570
[McKinney, Howard D.]
  Romeo 14168
McKinney, John
  As You Like It 722; Tempest 15154
McKinney, Mac
  Twelfth Night 17053
McLaughlin, James M., arr.
  Two Gentlemen 18592
McLean, Wallace Donald, II 1944–
  Dream 9613; Tempest 15790
McLeod, Jennifer Helen 1941–
  Hamlet 3280; Troilus 16502; Twelfth Night
  17054
McLin, Edward, arr.
  Dream 9760
McLin, Lena
  Lear 6044
McLoughlin, Peter Paul
  Errors 2134; Tempest 15155; Twelfth Night
  17055
McMahon, Eugene
  Hamlet 3281; Macbeth 7041
McMurdie, Joseph 1792–1878
  Settings of Commemorative Pieces . . . 21280
McNabb, Lenore
  Merchant 8241
[McNaught, William Gray], arr. [1849–1918]
  Dream 10556, 10557; Much Ado 11545;
  Tempest 14731
McNaught, William Gray, arr. 1849–1918
  As You Like It 1178
McNeff, Steve
  Dream 9614
McNeil, James Charles 1902–
  Hamlet 4229
McNiven, David
  Errors 2135
McPartland, [Margaret] Marian, arr.
  [1920]–
  Née Turner; previously used the stage name
  'Marian Page'
  Romeo 13603
McPeek, Benjamin Dewey, arr. 1934–1981
  Hamlet 3597

McPhail, P. Morghean
  Macbeth 7042
McQuaid, John 1909–
  Macbeth 7372; Tempest 16081
McTee, Cindy Karen 1953–
  Lear 6020, 6036, 6046
Meacham, F. W., arr.
  Hamlet 4160
Meade, David
  Dream 9615
Meale, Richard Graham 1932–
  Lear 5853
Mechem, Kirke Lewis 1925–
  Much Ado 11486; Sonnet 98 20187
Medek, Tilo 1940–
  Errors 2136; Hamlet 3282, 3995, 3996;
  K. John 5646; Macbeth 7043; Shrew
  14409, 14662
Mederitsch, Johann Georg Anton
  1752–1835
  Also known as Johann Mederitsch-Gallus
  and as Johann Gallus
  Hamlet 3283; Macbeth 7044; Tempest
  15156; Twelfth Night 18164
Medtner, Nikolai Karlovich 1880–1951
  Hamlet 3997; Lear 6085
Meek, Kenneth 1908–1976
  Hamlet 3998
Meerovich, I.
  [Il'ia Mikhailovich Meerovich (1906–   )?]
  Measure 7707
Meerovich, I. M.
  [Il'ia Mikhailovich Meerovich (1906–   )?]
  Two Gentlemen 18410
Meerovich, Il'ia Mikhailovich 1906–
  Hamlet 3284
Mees, Arthur 1850–1923
  Merchant 8242
Mees, Siegbert
  Dream 9616
Megvinetukhutsesi, Konstantin Vasil'evich
  1891–1972
  Lear 5854; Othello 11857; Richard III
  12910; Shrew 14410
Méhul, Étienne-Nicolas 1763–1817
  Othello 12479
Meier-Waelde, Ingeborg
  Twelfth Night 17056
Meik, Siegfried
  Merchant 8243
Meima, Herman 1905–
  As You Like It 1107; Cymbeline 2589;
  Henry VIII 5140
Meiners, Giovanni Battista 1826–1897
  Richard III 13083
Meinhart, Günter
  Romeo 13341
Meinung, Carl Johan, in part arr.
  Merchant 8244

Meisel, Edmund
    Hamlet 3285
Meissner, Hjalmar 1865–
    Merry Wives 8915
Meissner, Werner 1926–
    Hamlet 3286; Henry VIII 5004; Lear 5855;
    Measure 7708; Merry Wives 8916; Dream
    9617; Twelfth Night 17057; Two Gentlemen
    18411
Meister, Arnold
    Twelfth Night 17058
Meister, Georges, arr.   –1902
    Romeo 13571
Meixner, Rudi 1924–1984
    Hamlet 4230
Mekeel, Joyce H. 1931–
    Macbeth 7045; Othello 11858; Richard III
    12911
Mélat, Maurice 1910–
    Romeo 13342
Melchers, Klaus
    As You Like It 723; Lear 5856
Melfi, Maurizio
    1 Henry IV 4385; 2 Henry IV 4570; Henry V
    4741; Merry Wives 8917
Melis, László
    Twelfth Night 17059
Mellers, Wilfrid Howard 1914–
    As You Like It 1108, 1417, 1724; Hamlet
    3770, 4073; Measure 7934; Dream 10364,
    10533; Tempest 15556, 15711; Twelfth
    Night 17060; Winter's Tale 19053
Mellinger, Michael 1920–
    As You Like It 724; Errors 2137; Merchant
    8245; Much Ado 11198; Tempest 15157;
    Twelfth Night 17061
Mellnäs, Arne
    Measure 7709
Mellon, Alfred 1821–1867
    Measure 7935; Settings of Commemorative
    Pieces . . . 21064, 21065
Mellon, Alfred, arr. 1821–1867
    Settings of Commemorative Pieces . . .
    21098
Melnick, Peter R.
    Winter's Tale 18937
Melnotte, Claude
    Dream 10673
Melnotte, Claude, arr.
    Merry Wives 9096
Melo, Richard F.
    Antony 199
Mendelsohn, J. Arko
    As You Like It 1109
Mendelssohn, Arnold Ludwig 1855–1933
    As You Like It 1110, 1725; Cymbeline 2590;
    Measure 7936; Much Ado 11487; Twelfth
    Night 17585, 18165; Settings of
    Commemorative Pieces . . . 21229

Mendelssohn, Jakob Ludwig Felix 1809–1847
    Also known as Felix Mendelssohn-Bartholdy
    Hamlet 3606; Dream 9618, 9619, 10674;
    Tempest 15452
Menges, Herbert 1902–1972
    Antony 200, 201; Coriolanus 2323; Hamlet
    3287, 3288; 1 Henry IV 4386; 2 Henry IV
    4571, 4572; Henry V 4742; Lear 5857,
    5858; Macbeth 7046; Measure 7710, 7711,
    7712; Merchant 8246, 8247; Othello 11859,
    11860; Richard II 12686; Richard III 12912,
    12913; Shrew 14411; Tempest 15158;
    Twelfth Night 17062, 18273; Two
    Gentlemen 18651; Winter's Tale 18820;
    Settings of Commemorative Pieces . . .
    20873, 20874, 20875, 20876, 20877
Menges, Herbert, in part arr. 1902–1972
    Henry VIII 5005; L.L.L. 6262; Winter's Tale
    18821
Mennie, Ian 1934–
    1 Henry IV 4387; Henry VIII 5006;
    Macbeth 7047; Othello 11861; Twelfth
    Night 17063
Menotti, Gian Carlo 1911–
    Romeo 13343
Menozzi, Giovanni, arr.
    Romeo 13776, 13777, 13778
Mentel, Janusz
    As You Like It 725
Menzies, Roderick B. 1951–
    As You Like It 726; L.L.L. 6263
Menzies, Roderick B., in part arr. 1951–
    Dream 9862
Mercadal y Pons, Antonio 1850–1873
    Romeo 13785
Mercadante, Giuseppe Saverio Raffaele
    1795–1870
    Also known under the pseudonym
    'Francesco Saverio Mercadante'
    Hamlet 4166; 1 Henry IV 4466; 2 Henry IV
    4632; Henry V 4801; Merchant 8793; Titus
    16431
Mercadante, Giuseppe Saverio Raffaele, arr.
    1795–1870
    Also known under the pseudonym
    'Francesco Saverio Mercadante'
    Othello 12120
Mereu, Jean
    Lear 5859
Merikanto, Frans Oskar 1868–1924
    Winter's Tale 19083
Merkel, Gustav Adolph, arr. 1827–1885
    Dream 9761
Merkù, Pavle 1927–
    Hamlet 3289
Merlet, Michel Marie Joseph Antoine 1939–
    Hamlet 4074
Mermoud, Robert 1912–
    Shrew 14412

Meroz, Guy
  Much Ado 11199
Merritt, George
  Much Ado 11488
Merryman, Marjorie 1951–
  Tempest 15504, 15984
Merson, Billy
  Othello 12537
Mersson, Boris E. 1921–
  Othello 11862; Twelfth Night 17064
Mersson, Boris E., arr. 1921–
  Tempest 14904
Merta, Vladimír
  Twelfth Night 17065
Mertel, G.
  Romeo 13786
Mertoni, Carlo
  Two Gentlemen 18664
Merwin, Royal Andrews
  As You Like It 1111
Messiaen, Olivier 1908–
  Romeo 14188
Messimer, Donn Gene 1957–
  Sonnet 130 20424; Sonnet 138 20455;
  Sonnet 146 20495
Messinger, Dominick
  Hamlet 3290
Mestral, Patrice 1945–
  Romeo 13344
Mestrozi, Paul 1851–1921
  Merchant 8775
Metcalf, Jo Anne 1958–
  Hamlet 3291; Measure 7713
Metcalf, Jo Anne, in part arr. 1958–
  As You Like It 727
Metis, Frank W., arr. 1925–
  As You Like It 1693; Measure 7902; Twelfth
  Night 17919
Métral, Pierre 1936–
  Merry Wives 8918
Metzdorff, Richard 1844–1919
  Lear 6086
Metzler, Friedrich 1910–1979
  All's Well 41; Hamlet 3292
Meugé, Georges
  All's Well 104
Meves, Augustus, arr.
  Othello 12121
Mewes, Erich
  As You Like It 728; Hamlet 3293; K. John
  5612; Dream 9863, 9864; Twelfth Night
  17066
Mey, August, arr.
  Hamlet 3661
Meyder, Karl, in part arr.
  Winter's Tale 18822
Meyer, Cornell
  As You Like It 729

Meyer, Ernst Hermann 1905–
  Tempest 15805
Meyer, Georg
  Shrew 14413; Winter's Tale 18823
Meyer, George W.
  Hamlet 4282
Meyer, Guy
  As You Like It 956
Meyer, Hans Bruno
  Macbeth 7048; Twelfth Night 17067
Meyer, J., arr.
  Dream 9762
Meyer, Louis H.
  Caesar 5515, 5516; Dream 10172,
  10675
Meyerhold, Kazimierz 1886–1956
  Caesar 5386; Merchant 8248
Meynell, H. A.
  2 Henry IV 4573
Michael, Friedrich, arr.
  Merry Wives 9097
Michael, Nick
  Merchant 8249
Michaelides, Peter 1930–
  K. John 5613
Michalski, C.
  Two Gentlemen 18412
Michalski, Stanisław
  Romeo 13345
Michel, Virgil
  Coriolanus 2419
Micheuz, Georges 1805–1882
  Also known as Georg Micheuz. Pseudonym
  used by Jurij Mihevec
  Romeo 13937
Micheuz, Georges, arr. 1805–1882
  Also known as Georg Micheuz. Pseudonym
  used by Jurij Mihevec
  Settings of Commemorative Pieces . . . 20970
Michniewski, Wojciech 1947–
  Tempest 15159
Micu, Eugeniu 1910–1982
  Merchant 8411
Middenway, Ralph 1932–
  As You Like It 730, 1908; Tempest 15453;
  Twelfth Night 17068
Middleton, Elwyn, arr.
  Tempest 14805
Middleton, Hubert Stanley
  As You Like It 1726, 1824; Hamlet 3839,
  3871; Henry VIII 5141; L.L.L. 6452, 6587;
  Measure 7937; Merchant 8602; Dream
  10534; Much Ado 11386, 11489; Othello
  12240, 12329; Romeo 13825; Tempest
  15852, 15977; Troilus 16565; Twelfth
  Night 17960, 18166; Two Gentlemen
  18545; Winter's Tale 18981, 19084
Mieg, Peter 1906–
  As You Like It 731

Mielck, Ernst Leopold Christian
   1877–1899
   Macbeth 7463
Miessner, William Otto 1880–1967
   As You Like It 732; Tempest 15160
Migne, Joël
   Lear 5860
Mignone, Francisco 1897–1980
   Romeo 13346
Mihály, András 1917–
   Merry Wives 8919
Mikhailovich, M.
   Errors 2138; Shrew 14414
Mikorey, Franz, arr.
   Measure 7808
Mikuła, Marzena
   Richard III 12914
Mikuszewski, Stefan
   As You Like It 733
Milburn, Rob
   Othello 12455
Miles, Russell Hancock 1895–
   L.L.L. 6453
Milford, Robin Humphrey 1903–1959
   As You Like It 1418, 1727, 2013; Hamlet
   3822, 3999, 4167; Measure 7938; Dream
   10676; Tempest 16082; Settings of
   Commemorative Pieces . . . 21230
Milhaud, Darius 1892–1974
   Hamlet 4114; Caesar 5387; Macbeth 7049;
   Romeo 13347; Winter's Tale 18824
Milhaud, Darius, arr. 1892–1974
   Dream 9976
Milićević, Aleksandar
   Hamlet 3294
Millar, Michael
   Othello 12480
Millars, Francis Joseph Haydn, arr.
   Merry Wives 9098
Miller, Annie Z., arr.
   As You Like It 1458
Miller, Ashley, arr.
   Errors 2216
Miller, Brian
   Dream 9865; Romeo 13348; Winter's Tale
   18825
Miller, Carl, arr.
   Othello 12256
Miller, Charles Allen 1937–
   Cymbeline 2694; Twelfth Night 18167;
   Winter's Tale 18826
Miller, Claudine
   Richard II 12688
Miller, E.
   Hamlet 3732
Miller, Frederick, arr.
   Romeo 13426
Miller, George John, arr.
   Richard III 12849; Tempest 16123

Miller, Glenn
   Macbeth 7278
Miller, Lewis Martin 1933–
   Henry V 4826
Miller, Malloy M. 191[8]–1981
   Richard III 12915
Miller, Marjorie Freeland
   Much Ado 11200
Miller, Michael Richard 1932–
   As You Like It 1909
Miller, Philip Lieson, ed. 1906–
   Anthologies 21351; 21352
Miller, Ralph Dale 1909–
   Venus 20802
Miller, Tony
   Tempest 15161
Milligan, Harold Vincent 1888–1951
   Much Ado 11652
Milligan, Harold Vincent, arr.
   1888–1951
   Othello 12281; Tempest 15197
Mills, Terry
   Romeo 13349
Mills-Cockell, John 1943–
   Hamlet 3295; Dream 9866, 9867, 9868;
   Romeo 13350, 13351; Tempest 15162,
   15163; Twelfth Night 17069
Millward, W., arr.
   Dream 9763
Milner, A.
   [Anthony Francis Dominic Milner (1925–   )
   or Arthur Frederick Milner ([1894]–1972)?]
   Merchant 8701; Tempest 16083
Milner, Anthony Francis Dominic 1925–
   Macbeth 7385
Milner, Arthur Frederick [1894]–1972
   Henry VIII 5142
Milorava, Shota Ermolaevich 1925–
   Othello 11863
Milton, Carl, arr.
   Romeo 13720, 13721
Milton, James
   Dream 9869; Tempest 15164
Milveden, Ingmar 1920–
   Antony 202
Mine, Ann
   Macbeth 7050
Minervini, Serge
   Much Ado 11201
Minetti, Carlo
   As You Like It 1419
Mingardo, Raffaele
   Tempest 15165
Minns, Paul
   Macbeth 7051
Minster, [?]
   Errors 2139
Miranda, Carlos 1945–
   Tempest 15166

Miranda, Carlos, in part arr. 1945–
Dream 10174; Romeo 14103
Miranda, Carlos, arr. 1945–
Dream 9764
Miroglio, Francis Édouard 1924–
1 Henry VI 4861; 2 Henry VI 4903; 3 Henry VI 4945
Mirsch-Riccius, Erich, arr.
As You Like It 962
Mirt, Alessandro 1925–
Hamlet 3709; Merchant 8603, 8684; Tempest 15712
Mirzoian, A.
Richard III 12916
Mishkin, Henry G.
Macbeth 7052
Mishkin, Henry G., in part arr.
Tempest 15167
Missa, Edmond Jean Louis 1861–1910
Cymbeline 2516; Lear 5861
Misterly, Eugene William 1926–
Henry V 4802
Mitchell, Alastair
Richard II 12760
Mitchell, John Robert Glyn 1946–
As You Like It 1112
Mitchell, Ken 1940–
Othello 12481
Mitchell-Davidson, Paul
Caesar 5388
Mitchell-Davidson, Paul, in part arr.
Settings of Commemorative Pieces . . . 21158
Mitrup, C.
Hamlet 4000
Mitschke, Herbert
Romeo 13352
Miyoshi, Ko
Twelfth Night 17070
Mizerit, Klaro M.
Hamlet 3296
Mizuno, Situko 1934–
Romeo 13353
Mkrtychian, Nikita Grigor'evich 1901–
Twelfth Night 17071
M'Leod, R.
As You Like It 1728
Młodziejowski, Jerzy 1909–1985
Measure 7714; Twelfth Night 17072, 17073
Mobbs, Kenneth William 1925–
Dream 9870
Möckel, Hans
Errors 2140
Mockridge, Cyril John 1896–1979
Hamlet 4115
Mockwitz, Friedrich, arr. 1785–1849
Lear 6176; Macbeth 7166; Dream 9765
Model', V., arr.
Romeo 13390

Modestini, Mario
Merchant 8250
Modoi, Evalyn, in part arr.
Twelfth Night 17074
Moeckel, Charles 1926–
Romeo 13787
Moeckels, Hans
Shrew 14415
Moehlmann, R. L. 1907–1972
K. John 5647
Moeran, Ernest John 1894–1950
As You Like It 1420, 1729; Hamlet 3297; L.L.L. 6454, 6588; Much Ado 11490; Othello 12330; Tempest 15919; Twelfth Night 17586; Winter's Tale 19054
Moevs, Robert Walter 1920–
Sonnet 64 19874
Moffat, Alfred Edward, arr. 1866–1950
Dream 10233, 10234; Othello 12122; Tempest 14732, 14733, 14806
Mohaupt, Richard 1904–1957
Macbeth 7586; Much Ado 11604
Mohler, Philipp Heinrich, arr. 1908–1982
Dream 9871
Mohr, Adolf
Hamlet 3298
Möhrens, Theo
Merchant 8251; Shrew 14416
Möhring, Ferdinand 1816–1887
Cymbeline 2695
Moir, F[rank Lewis?] [1852–1902]
Merchant 8458
Mokranjać, Vasilije 1923–
Hamlet 3299; Macbeth 7053
Molchanov, Kirill Vladimirovich 1922–
Macbeth 7279; Romeo 14104
Mollenhauer, Edward 1827–1914
Also known as Eduard Mollenhauer
Hamlet 3300, 4001; Henry VIII 5007, 5143; Caesar 5389; Much Ado 11202; Othello 11864; Romeo 13354; Winter's Tale 18827
Möller, Håkan
Hamlet 3301
Mollicone, Henry 1946–
Antony 307; 1 Henry IV 4388; Merry Wives 8920
Monaco, James V. 1885–1945
Settings of Commemorative Pieces . . . 21259
Mönch, F. K.
As You Like It 1113
Monck, G. S.
Merchant 8252
Monckton, Lionel 1861–1924
Merchant 8253, 8604
Monday, Mark
As You Like It 734
Moniuszko, Stanisław 1819–1872
Hamlet 3302, 3771, 4002; Merchant 8254; Merry Wives 9099; Dream 9872

Monk, Peter Anthony 1946–
    Tempest 15510, 15557, 15713, 15920,
    15978
Monks, Christopher
    Cymbeline 2478; Hamlet 3303; Measure
    7715
Monn-Iversen, Egil, arr.
    Dream 10235
Monroe, Michael
    Tempest 16188
Montague, G., arr.
    Hamlet 4056
Montague, Lily, arr.
    Two Gentlemen 18593
Montanari, Angelo, arr.
    Lear 6054
Monteux-Brisac, [?]   –1928
    Othello 11865
Montgomery, Robert Bruce 1921–1978
    As You Like It 1731; L.L.L. 6589; Measure
    7939; Merchant 8605; Romeo 14055;
    Tempest 15714; Twelfth Night 17587,
    17961; Two Gentlemen 18546
Montgomery, William Henry
    [circa 1811]–1886
    As You Like It 1910; Errors 2251; Hamlet
    3304, 4003; Henry V 4743; Macbeth 7464;
    Dream 9873; Pericles 12579; Tempest
    16084; Settings of Commemorative
    Pieces . . . 21159
Montgomery, William Henry, in part arr.
    [circa 1811]–1886
    Winter's Tale 19140
Montgomery, William Henry, arr.
    [circa 1811]–1886
    Macbeth 6993, 6994; Merry Wives 9002,
    9100, 9101; Dream 9766, 10866
Monti, [Victor-Emmanuel-Marie-François?]
    Romeo 14105
Montijn, Aleida
    Merchant 8255; Dream 9874; Troilus
    16503; Twelfth Night 17075; Two
    Gentlemen 18413
Monza, Carlo
    Coriolanus 2420
Moody, Marie
    Hamlet 4004; Lear 6087; Othello 12418
Moolman, Philip
    Hamlet 3305
Moór, Emanuel 1863–1931
    As You Like It 1422; Cymbeline 2591;
    Twelfth Night 17588
Moor, Karel 1920–
    Errors 2141; Merry Wives 8921
Moorat, Joseph Samuel Edward 1864–1938
    Also wrote under the pseudonym 'Joseph S.
    Ward'
    As You Like It 1114; Cymbeline 2696; L.L.L.
    6590; Othello 12331; Tempest 15168

Moore, Carman Leroy 1936–
    Timon 16330
Moore, Christopher, arr.
    Dream 10142
Moore, David A. 1948–
    Sonnet 29 19571
Moore, Donald I., arr.
    Othello 12199
Moore, Douglas Stuart 1893–1969
    As You Like It 1732; Much Ado 11203,
    11491; Twelfth Night 17076, 17589
Moore, Dudley 1935–
    Coriolanus 2324; Settings of
    Commemorative Pieces . . . 21273
Moore, Edward C.
    Measure 7940; P. Pilgrim 20662
Moore, Frank L[edlie]
    Hamlet 3306; Twelfth Night 17077
Moore, J. Charles
    Othello 12538
Moore, Jeremy
    Romeo 13355
Moore, Margery
    Cymbeline 2592
Moore, Michael
    Romeo 13356; Twelfth Night 17078
Moore, Paul
    Measure 7716
Moore, Sandy
    Hamlet 3307; Tempest 15169
Moore, Winifred
    L.L.L. 6591
Moorhead, John, arr.   –1804
    Othello 12297
Morales, Meliseo 1838–1908
    Antony 379; Romeo 14206
Moralt, Louis
    Tempest 16279
Morcillo, Fernando Garcia
    Romeo 14056
Moreau, Jacky
    Winter's Tale 18828
Morel, Jean-Marie
    Romeo 13938
Morel, Joseph Raoul François d'Assise 1926–
    Settings of Commemorative Pieces . . . 21302
[?Morelli, Cesare]
    Hamlet 3852
Morera, Enrique 1865–1942
    [Also known as Enrique Morera y Viura]
    Shrew 14417
Moret, Norbert 1921–
    Coriolanus 2393
Moret, Victor, arr.
    Dream 10867
Morgan, Pamela
    Tempest 16189
Morgan, Robert flor. 1970
    Winter's Tale 18829

Morgan, Robert Orlando 1865–
Dream 10413, 10677
Morgan, Vincent
Macbeth 7054
Morgan, William Perry
Winter's Tale 18830
Morgenstern, Sam
Merchant 8256
Morgenstern, Sam, arr.
Dream 9767
Morgeson, Eric
Hamlet 3607
Mori, Frank 1820–1873
Measure 7941
Mori, Kurato
Romeo 13357
Mori, Nicolas, arr. 1797–1839
Othello 12123
Morison, Jessie
Two Gentlemen 18665
Moritz, Franz
Tempest 16280
Morlacchi, Francesco Giuseppe Baldassare
1784–1841
Merchant 8794
Morley, Glenn 1952–
Macbeth 7055; Tempest 15170
Morley, Thomas [circa 1557]–1602
As You Like It 1423, 1825; Twelfth Night
17962; P. Pilgrim 20663
Morley, Thomas, arr. [circa 1557]–1602
Twelfth Night 17766
Moroni, Luigi
Hamlet 4168
Morris, Haydn 1891–1965
As You Like It 1115, 1476
Morris, Hayward, arr.
Twelfth Night 17396
Morris, John [Leonard] 1926–
Antony 203; As You Like It 735, 1116;
Errors 2142; Hamlet 3308, 3309, 4116;
1 Henry IV 4389, 4505; 2 Henry IV 4574;
Caesar 5390; Lear 5862; L.L.L. 6264;
Macbeth 7056; Measure 7717; Merchant
8732; Richard III 12917; Romeo 13358,
13359; Tempest 15171, 15921; Titus
16410; Twelfth Night 17079
Morris, Leonard, arr.
As You Like It 608
Morris, Roger
Romeo 14169
Morrison, Michael
Measure 7718; Othello 11866; Twelfth
Night 17080
Morrissey, John J. 1906–
Caesar 5391
Morrow, Macklin, in part arr.
Twelfth Night 17081

Mors, Rudolf 1920–
As You Like It 736; Errors 2143, 2144;
Hamlet 3310; Measure 7719; Merchant
8257, 8258; Merry Wives 8922; Dream
9875; Much Ado 11204, 11205; Twelfth
Night 17082, 17083; Two Gentlemen
18414; Winter's Tale 18831
Morse, Theodore F., arr. [1873–1924]
Dream 9768
Mortellari, C. Michele, arr.
Also known as 'M. C. Mortellari' and
as 'Michele C. Mortellari, the
Younger'
Othello 12124, 12125, 12126
Mortellari, Michele [1750?]–1807
Venus 20818
Mortelmans, Lodewijk 1868–1952
Macbeth 7502
Mortensen, Otto 1907–
Othello 11867
Mortensen, Otto, arr. 1907–
Measure 8033
Mortimer, Terry
Merchant 8259
Morton, David
Tempest 16203
Morton, Louise
Twelfth Night 17084
Mosca, Luca 1957–
Dream 10175
Moscheles, Ignaz, arr. 1794–1870
Merry Wives 9003; Dream 10868
Moselli, Egisto, arr.
Othello 12127
Moser, Andreas, arr. 1859–1925
Othello 12128
Moss, Katie 1881–
Twelfth Night 18335
Moss, Lawrence Kenneth 1927–
Tempest 16281
Moss, M. Hugh
Sonnet 18 19402
Moss, Matthew, arr.
Macbeth 7343
Moss, Piotr
Hamlet 3311; Tempest 15172; Twelfth Night
17085
Moss, R. Britton
Richard III 13044
Moss, William A., Jr.
Dream 9876
Mottl, Felix, arr. 1856–1911
Much Ado 11355
Mottram, Charles H. G.
Twelfth Night 17963
Motzan, Otto 1880–1937
Romeo 14106
Mouen, Grafton
L.L.L. 6265

Moulaert, Pierre 1907–1967
  Hamlet 3312; Henry V 4744; Caesar 5392;
  Richard II 12689; Romeo 13360
Moulaert, Raymond 1875–1962
  Othello 12332
Moule, Kenneth, arr.
  Shrew 14610
Moule-Evans, David 1905–
  L.L.L. 6592; Twelfth Night 17964
Mount, George, arr.
  Twelfth Night 16677
Mouton, Hubert Henri François   –1954
  Hamlet 3662; Lear 5725; Romeo 13722;
  Twelfth Night 17344, 17345; Settings of
  Commemorative Pieces . . . 20971
Moylan, William David 1956–
  Sonnet 12 19288; Sonnet 15 19309
Moyzes, Alexander 1906–
  Hamlet 3313; Winter's Tale 18832
Mozart, Wolfgang Amadeus 1756–1791
  Baptised Joannes Chrysostomus Wolfgangus
  Theophilus Mozart
  Hamlet 4283; L.L.L. 6677; Tempest 15454
Mozin, [?], arr.
  Known as 'Mozin le jeune'
  Merry Wives 9244
Mudie, Thomas Molleson, arr. 1809–1876
  Also known as Thomas Mollison Mudie
  Merry Wives 9102
Mueller, Marcia Ann
  Sonnet 18 19403
Mueller, Mark
  As You Like It 737
Mueller, Otto-Werner, arr. 1926–
  Dream 10236
Mugnié, Jean
  1 Henry IV 4518; 2 Henry IV 4687
Mühldorfer, Wilhelm Carl 1836–1919
  Cymbeline 2479; Merchant 8260; Richard
  III 12918, 13058
Mühlenfeldt, Carl
  Dream 10678
Mukhamedzhanov, Sydykh 1924–
  Tempest 16282
Mukle, A. V.
  As You Like It 738
Mulcahy, Lance
  Much Ado 11206; Settings of
  Commemorative Pieces . . . 20948, 20949
Muldowney, Dominic 1952–
  Antony 204; Macbeth 7057, 7280; Much
  Ado 11207; Othello 11868; Richard III
  12919; Shrew 14418
Mulford, Don
  Errors 2261
Mulhare, Mirta T.
  Othello 12482
Muling, Vladimir
  Caesar 5393

Mullen, A[lfred Frederick?], arr. [–1881]
  Tempest 14807
Mullen, Alfred Frederick, arr.   –1881
  Merry Wives 8882
Mullen, Frederic
  Also wrote under the pseudonym 'Gustave
  Lind'
  Hamlet 4005; Twelfth Night 18238
Mullen, Michael Livingston
  Tempest 15173
Müller, Adolf, Sr. 1801–1886
  Born Adolf Schmid; also known as Adolph
  Müller
  Antony 339; Hamlet 3314; 1 Henry IV
  4519; 2 Henry IV 4688; Macbeth 7058,
  7522; Merchant 8261; Othello 12456;
  Richard III 12920; Romeo 14057
Müller, August Eberhard 1767–1817
  Romeo 13361
Müller, Carl, arr.
  Settings of Commemorative Pieces . . . 20906
Muller, Ed., arr.
  Othello 12129
Müller, Edmund
  Twelfth Night 17086
Müller, Fritz
  As You Like It 739; Hamlet 3315; Caesar
  5394; Much Ado 11208
Müller, Gerhild
  Errors 2145; Hamlet 3316; Measure 7720;
  Much Ado 11209
Müller, Gottfried
  Hamlet 3826
Müller, Heiner
  Merchant 8262; Twelfth Night 17087
Müller, Heinz
  Shrew 14419
Müller, Hermann
  Twelfth Night 17088
Müller, Hermann, arr.
  Dream 10237
Müller, J.
  L.L.L. 6455
Müller, J. Frederick, arr.
  Romeo 13604, 13993
Müller, Julius E., arr.
  Dream 10869
Müller, Karl 1818–1894
  Othello 12419
Muller, Stephen
  Hamlet 4117
Müller, Wenzel 1767–1835
  Tempest 15455
Müller-Adolphi, H.
  Romeo 13362
Müller-Blattau, Gabriele
  Dream 9877
Müller-Kopp, Bert
  As You Like It 740

Müller-Sybel, Franz Peter
Hamlet 3317; Macbeth 7059
Mullinar, Michael, arr. [1896?]–1973
Merry Wives 9170; Dream 10238; Tempest
15432
Mullins, [?]
Romeo 13788
Mullins, Hugh Englis 1922–198[3]
L.L.L. 6329; Sonnet 155 20572
Mullot, Émile, arr. –1906
Macbeth 7344; Romeo 13723
Mulvihill, Jerome Jacques
Also known as Jerry Mulvihill
As You Like It 1733
Mumby, Frank
Pericles 12580
Munakata, Kuniyoshi
Hamlet 3608
Münch, Gerhard 1907–
Dream 9878
Munck, G. J.
Romeo 13872
Mund, Jakub
Coriolanus 2325
Mundella, Emma 1858–1896
Dream 10535, 10972
Müntz-Berger, Joseph, arr. 1769–1844
Othello 12130
Münzer, Fritz
Richard III 12921
Munzer, Markus
Macbeth 7523
Murby, Thomas
Hamlet 4170; Henry V 4835; Macbeth
7544; Merchant 8758; Dream 10799,
10924; Shrew 14681; Tempest 16204;
Settings of Commemorative Pieces . . .
20950
Murphy, Robert 1948–
L.L.L. 6266; Dream 9879; Troilus 16504
Murphy, Robert [US]
Merchant 8263
Murphy, Val
As You Like It 741
Murphy, Walter, arr.
Romeo 13994
Murphy, William
Dream 10925
Murray, Alan Robert 1890–
Twelfth Night 17965
Murray, Dom Gregory, arr.
Also known as Anthony Gregory Murray
Dream 10239; Settings of Commemorative
Pieces . . . 21286
Murrill, Herbert Henry John 1909–1952
Richard III 12922; Twelfth Night 17590,
17966
Murzin, V., arr.
Romeo 13089

Muscarelli, G., arr.
Dream 10870
Musch, Dietrich
As You Like It 742
Musgrave, Frank –1888
Much Ado 11210
Musgrave, Frank, arr. –1888
Othello 12507
Musgrave, George W., arr.
Macbeth 7345
Musgrave, Thea 1928–
Dream 9880; Phoenix 20761
Mussi, A., arr.
Settings of Commemorative Pieces . . . 20934
Mussorgsky, Modest Petrovich, arr.
1839–1882
Lear 5669
Mustacchi, Joseph
As You Like It 957
Muth, Lucille
Settings of Commemorative Pieces . . . 21066
Muthspiel, Christian
Romeo 13363
Muurikoski, Antero
Merry Wives 8923
Muzio, Emanuele, arr. 1825–1890
Macbeth 7346
Myers, Elizabeth
Dream 9881
Myers, Jack
Dream 10536
Myers, James E.
Also known under the pseudonym 'Jimmy
DeKnight'
Twelfth Night 18336
Myrow, Fredric 1939–
1 Henry IV 4390

N

Nabokov, Nicolas 1903–1978
L.L.L. 6330
Nadelmann, Leo 1913–
Measure 7721
Naderman, François Joseph, arr. 1773–1835
Othello 12131
Naftel, Frederick Paul 1956–
Twelfth Night 17591; Sonnet 73 20007;
Sonnet 81 20070; Sonnet 87 20091; Sonnet
129 20411
Nagler, F., arr.
[Franciscus Johannes Nagler (1873–1957)?]
Merry Wives 9103
Nahay, Paul Lawrence 1958–
Much Ado 11642; Sonnet 8 19254
Naicimbene, Mario
Romeo 14058

Nakapkin, V., arr.
Romeo 13883
Nałęcz, Wojciech
1 Henry IV 4391; 2 Henry IV 4575
Nangle, Philip
Hamlet 3318
N[apier], W[illiam] [1740–1812]
Measure 7942
Napoli, Jacopo 1911–
L.L.L. 6661
Nápravník, Eduard Francevič 1839–1916
Tempest 15456
Nardin, Anthony Attilio
Measure 7943
Nardo, Don
Richard III 13034
Nares, James 1715–1783
Cymbeline 2593, 2869
Narici, Louis, arr.
Merchant 8746; Dream 10871
Nash, Doris Louise
Merchant 8264
Nash, Paul 1948–
Macbeth 7060; Dream 9882
Nash, Stewart
Sonnet 104 20240
Nash, Winifred M.
Hamlet 4231
Nasidze, Sulkhan Ivanovich 1927–
Much Ado 11211
Nasolini, Sebastiano [circa 1768–1806 or
1816]
Antony 380
Nass, Hermann
Twelfth Night 17089
Nassau, Paul 1930–
Caesar 5547; Macbeth 7545
Natanek, Adam
Richard II 12690
Natschinski, Thomas
Dream 9883
Natusch, Kurt
Errors 2146; Much Ado 11212
Nava, Franz, arr.
[Pseudonym used by ?]
Macbeth 7347
Naylor, Bernard James 1907–1986
Lear 5863; Macbeth 7061; Twelfth Night
17592, 18168; Sonnet 97 20163; Sonnet 98
20188; Sonnet 99 20202
Naylor, Bernard James, arr. 1907–1986
Hamlet 3710, 3772
Naylor, E. flor. 1845
Also known as Miss Naylor
Merchant 8459
Naylor, Edward Woodall, ed. 1867–1934
Anthologies 21323
Naylor, John 1838–1897
Twelfth Night 17090, 17593

Naylor, Peter Russell 1933–
Tempest 15174; Twelfth Night 17967
Nebelsiek, Paul Oskar
Dream 9884, 9885
Nebeský, Pravoš
As You Like It 743; Macbeth 7062;
Merry Wives 8924; Shrew 14420; Troilus
16505
Nechiporenko, A., arr.
Lear 5844
Necke, Hermann, arr. 1850–1912
Merry Wives 9104, 9105
Nedbal, Oskar 1874–1930
Romeo 14107
Neden, Harold
Merchant 8606; Tempest 15715
Needham, Alicia Adélaïde 1875–
As You Like It 1477; Twelfth Night 17968
Neef, Wilhelm 1916–
Romeo 13364; Winter's Tale 18833;
Settings of Commemorative Pieces . . . 20951
Neefe, Christoph Gottlob 1748–1798
Macbeth 7063
Neff, Jerome
Measure 7944
Neff, Wilhelm
Much Ado 11213
Negri, Gino 1919–
Dream 9886; Pericles 12581; Shrew 14421
Negri, Luigi, arr.
Merry Wives 9004
Neidlinger, Günter
Hamlet 3319
Neidlinger, William Harold 1863–1924
Romeo 14170
Neighbarger, Randy
Richard II 12691
Nelsen, Duane
Errors 2147
Nelson, Paul 1929–
Twelfth Night 17091, 17594, 17969, 18169
Nelson, Ralph Conrad
Twelfth Night 17092
Nelson, Robert 1941–
All's Well 42; Errors 2148; Hamlet 3320;
Lear 5864; L.L.L. 6267; Measure 7722;
Merchant 8265; Dream 9887; Othello
11869; Richard III 12923; Tempest 15175;
Two Gentlemen 18415; Winter's Tale 18834
Nelson, Robin
Othello 11870, 11871; Tempest 15176;
Twelfth Night 17093
Nelson, Sidney, arr. 1800–1862
As You Like It 425, 426; Tempest 14734,
14735, 14808, 14937, 14938, 15123
Nemerowsky, A., arr.
Othello 12132
Nessler, Robert [1919–   ]
Macbeth 7064

Nestor, Carl
  Winter's Tale 19014
Nešvera, Josef 1842–1914
  Winter's Tale 18938
Nett, Dieter
  Tempest 15177
Nettlefold, F. J.
  Merchant 8460; Sonnet 65 19896; Sonnet
  104 20241
Nettles, Joyce
  Twelfth Night 17094
Neubert, Günter 1936–
  Othello 11872
Neufeld, Kenneth
  Twelfth Night 17595, 17709, 17970
Neumane, [?], arr.
  1 Henry IV 4467; 2 Henry IV 4633
Neumann, Richard
  Twelfth Night 17095
Neumann, Ulrik
  As You Like It 744
Neuner, Carl Borromäus 1778–1830
  Venus 20819
Neustedt, Charles, arr.
  Hamlet 3663; Othello 12133; Settings of
  Commemorative Pieces . . . 20972
Neuwirth, H.
  Hamlet 4118
Nevi, Pio, arr.
  Merry Wives 9191
Nevin, Ethelbert Woodbridge 1862–1901
  Occasionally wrote under the name Ethelbert
  Woodbridge
  As You Like It 1911; Hamlet 4006; L.L.L.
  6354
Nevin, George Balch 1859–1933
  As You Like It 1478; L.L.L. 6456; Merchant
  8776; Much Ado 11492; Twelfth Night
  17971
Newcomb, Wilburn W., ed.
  Settings of Commemorative Pieces . . . 21287
Newell, Joseph Edward 1843–
  Also wrote under the pseudonyms 'Carlo
  Murretti' and 'Nicola Podesta'
  Dream 10414, 10437; Settings of
  Commemorative Pieces . . . 21303
Newell, Joseph Edward, arr. 1843–
  Also wrote under the pseudonyms 'Carlo
  Murretti' and 'Nicola Podesta'
  Macbeth 7441; Tempest 15295
Newhall, J. Lincoln
  As You Like It 1117
Newman, Eldridge
  Dream 10800
Newman, Joel, arr.
  Settings of Commemorative Pieces . . .
  21288
Newman, Lillian, arr.
  Dream 9769

Newman, Sidney 1906–1971
  Much Ado 11214, 11493
Newman, Taze W.
  Dream 10679
Newson, George 1932–
  Othello 12420; Tempest 16205; Winter's
  Tale 18939, 19117, 19118; Sonnet 116
  20338
[Newton, Ernest Richard, ed.] [–1929]
  Anthologies 21313; 21326; 21327; 21328;
  21329; 21330; 21331; 21332; 21333;
  21334; 21335; 21336; 21337; 21338;
  21339; 21340; 21341; 21342; 21344
Newton, Dan
  Much Ado 11215
Newton, Ernest, arr.
  Cymbeline 2761
Newton, Ernest Richard   –1929
  As You Like It 1479, 1997; Henry VIII
  5144; Dream 9888, 10176, 10337, 10537,
  10680; Tempest 15457; Two Gentlemen
  18547; Winter's Tale 18940; Settings of
  Commemorative Pieces . . . 21160
Newton, Ernest Richard, arr.   –1929
  As You Like It 427, 1459, 1460; Much Ado
  11546; Tempest 14809; Twelfth Night
  17313
Newton, Larry
  Henry VIII 5242
Newton, Richard
  As You Like It 1912
Newton, Rodney Stephen 1945–
  Lear 6088; Macbeth 7584; Sonnet 30
  19611; Sonnet 31 19637; Sonnet 53 19758;
  Sonnet 57 19805; Sonnet 87 20092; Sonnet
  97 20164
Newton, Rolfe
  All's Well 43
Neyer, Ernest
  Hamlet 3321
Nichol, Henry Ernest
  Othello 12333; Troilus 16577
Nicholl, Horace Wadham 1848–1922
  Hamlet 4008
Nicholl, Horace Wadham, arr. 1848–1922
  As You Like It 1536
Nicholls, Frederick C. 1871–
  Tempest 15558, 15716
Nicholls, Paul Charles Alexander 1954–
  Tempest 15559, 15717, 15922
Nicholls, William Heller, arr.
  Dream 9770; Two Gentlemen 18594
Nichols, Kelly Dawn 1957–
  As You Like It 958; Macbeth 7281; Dream
  10177
Nick, Edmund Joseph 1891–1974
  Dream 9889, 9890
Nicks, George
  Twelfth Night 18073, 18078

Nicks, George, arr.
  Hamlet 3322, 3711, 3742, 3745, 3773,
  3840, 3872, 3883
Nickson, John A.
  Measure 7945
Nicolai, Carl Otto Ehrenfried 1810–1849
  As You Like It 1118, 1480; 2 Henry IV
  4672; Merry Wives 9015; Dream 10801;
  Twelfth Night 18284; Settings of
  Commemorative Pieces . . . 21231
Nicolini, Giuseppe 1762–1842
  Also known as Giuseppe Niccolini
  Coriolanus 2421
Nicolosi, Roberto 1914–
  Errors 2149
Nidi, Alessandro
  1 Henry IV 4392; 2 Henry IV 4576
Niebergall, Johannes
  Dream 9891
Niehaus, Manfred
  Romeo 13365
Nielsen, Carl August 1865–1931
  Tempest 16228; Settings of Commemorative
  Pieces . . . 21067
Nielsen, Svend 1937–
  Sonnet 30 19612; Sonnet 64 19875; Sonnet
  73 20008
Nielsen, Tage 1929–
  As You Like It 1586; Macbeth 7410;
  Merchant 8423
Nieman, Alfred 1913–
  Also writes under the pseudonym 'Robert
  Legray'
  Dream 10681; Twelfth Night 17972
Niemen, Czesław
  Hamlet 3323; Dream 9892
Niemeyer, Wolfgang H. 1951–
  Sonnet 24 19492; Sonnet 60 19815; Sonnet
  116 20308
Niessner, Wolfgang
  Twelfth Night 17096
Nieto, Manuel 1844–1915
  Othello 12483
Niles, John Edward, arr.
  L.L.L. 6337
Niles, Marion A.
  Much Ado 11216
Nilson, Einar 1881–
  As You Like It 745; Errors 2150; 2 Henry IV
  4577; Much Ado 11217; Romeo 13366
Nimtz, Roderick E.
  Dream 9893
Nin-Culmell, Joaquín María 1908–
  Cymbeline 2480
Ninat, Claude
  Richard II 12692; Twelfth Night 17097
Nishida, Glenn
  Macbeth 7065

Nissim, Mico Jacques
  Tempest 15178
Nixon, Henry Cotter 1842–1907
  Dream 10682
Niziurski, Mirosław
  L.L.L. 6268; Macbeth 7066; Twelfth Night
  17098
Noble, F. C., arr.
  Macbeth 6995
Noble, Harold 1903–
  As You Like It 1734
Noble, Harold, arr. 1903–
  Tempest 14810
Noble, Jules, arr. 1862–1902
  Merry Wives 9192
Noble, Thomas Tertius 1867–1953
  As You Like It 1119
Nocella, Joseph Anthony
  Sonnet 97 20165
Noel, Joscelyn
  As You Like It 1913
Noeltner, Robert H., arr.
  Shrew 14611; Two Gentlemen 18465
Nogaideli, G.
  Twelfth Night 17099
Nölck, August
  Hamlet 4009
Noll, Albert W.
  As You Like It 1914
Noll, Diether
  Winter's Tale 18835
Noll, Dietrich J.
  Dream 9894
Nona, M. W., arr.
  Merry Wives 9106
Nono, Liugi 1924–
  Twelfth Night 17100
Norby, Erik 1936–
  Sonnet 8 19255; Sonnet 112 20293; Sonnet
  128 20397; Sonnet 130 20425; Sonnet 137
  20446; Sonnet 154 20547
Nordgren, Pehr Henrik 1944–
  Lear 5865
Nordheim, Arne 1931–
  Hamlet 3324; Lear 5866; Macbeth 7067;
  Othello 11873; Tempest 15505
Nordheim, Arne, in part arr. 1931–
  Tempest 15458
Nordman, Chester, arr.
  Romeo 13995
Nordmann, Rudolf, arr. 1796–1867
  Also known as Rudolph Nordmann.
  Pseudonyms used by George Frederick Harris
  As You Like It 428, 429; Errors 2043;
  Merry Wives 8883, 9107; Settings
  of Commemorative Pieces . . . 20907,
  21161
Nordoff, Paul 1909–1977
  Antony 205; Othello 12334; Romeo 13367

Nørgård, Per 1932–
Romeo 14108
Norman, Frederik Vilhelm Ludvig 1831–1885
Antony 320
Norman, Philip Thomas 1953–
Measure 7723; Romeo 13368
Normile, Joseph P.
Twelfth Night 17101
Normino, O. H. arr.
As You Like It 1915
Norris, Harry B.
As You Like It 1984
Norris, Thomas 1741–1790
Cymbeline 2870; Tempest 15179
North, Alex 1910–
Antony 340; Coriolanus 2326; Richard III 12924
North, R. D., in part arr.
Merchant 8266; Winter's Tale 18836
Northcote, Sydney, arr.
As You Like It 430, 431; Henry VIII 5184
Northrop, Suzane 1948–
Lear 6002
Northway, William Rufus, Jr.
Dream 10538
Norton, William George 1913–
Tempest 15180; Twelfth Night 17102, 17103
Noskowski, Zygmunt 1846–1909
Coriolanus 2375
Nosov, Ivan Alekseevich 1900–
Shrew 14422
Nottingham, Charles Henry
Dream 10683
Nova Sondag, Jacqueline [1935]–1975
Caesar 5395; Macbeth 7068
Novák, Jan 1921–
Caesar 5396
Novák, Milan 1927–
1 Henry IV 4393; 2 Henry IV 4578; Richard II 12693
Novák, Vítězslav 1870–1949
Tempest 15459
Novello, Ivor 1893–1951
Hamlet 4171; Henry V 4745; Lear 6125
Novello, Vincent, arr. 1781–1861
Macbeth 6996; Dream 10558
Novick, David
Merchant 8267
Novotný, Jaroslav
Shrew 14423
Novozhilov, N.
Othello 11874; Romeo 13369
Nowacki, Alfons
As You Like It 746, 747; Errors 2151;
Cymbeline 2481; Hamlet 3325; Measure
7724; Merry Wives 8925; Dream 9895,
9896; Richard II 12694; Shrew 14424;
Tempest 15181; Troilus 16506; Twelfth
Night 17104; Winter's Tale 18837

Nowotny, Karl, arr.
Merry Wives 9108; Twelfth Night 18179
Nugent, Claud
Caesar 5541; K. John 5614
Nun, Stephanie
Tempest 15182
Nunn, Edward Cuthbert [1868]–1914
Winter's Tale 19085
Nunzio, Charles, arr.
Shrew 14612
Nur, Shabda 1937–
Also known as Thomas Kemper Wirtel
Hamlet 4261
Nürnberg, Karlheinz 1918–
Antony 278; Merchant 8412; Timon 16371;
Winter's Tale 18941
Nurock, Kirk 1948–
Caesar 5397
Nussio, Otmar 1902–
1 Henry IV 4485; 2 Henry IV 4660; Merry
Wives 9227
Nyberg, Åke
Winter's Tale 18838
Nyiregyházi, Ervin, arr. 1903–
Hamlet 3982
Nystroem, Gösta 1890–1966
Merchant 8268, 8702; Dream 10973;
Tempest 15183, 15560, 15806, 15923;
Settings of Commemorative Pieces . . . 21162

O

Ó Gallchobhair, Eamonn   –[circa 1973]
Antony 206
Ó Murnaghan, Art
Richard III 12925
Oak, Kilsung
Sonnet 73 20009
Oakes, Isaire Hesse
As You Like It 1120; Cymbeline 2697;
Tempest 15561, 15718, 15924
Oakey, George, arr. 1841–
As You Like It 432, 1179, 1858; Errors
2044; Cymbeline 2658, 2762; Dream 10133,
10309, 10374, 10559, 10920; Tempest
14811, 16225; P. Pilgrim 20612, 20729
Oakley, Samuel Harold
Two Gentlemen 18548
Oberbrunner, Carl
As You Like It 1735
Oberhoffer, Robert Werner
Merchant 8607
Oberholzer, Otto 1858–1901
Merry Wives 9228; Shrew 14425; Winter's
Tale 19119
Oberndorfer, Marx E. 1876–
Sonnet 29 19572

Oberthür, Charles [Karl] 1819–1895
  Macbeth 7465; Tempest 16085; Settings of
  Commemorative Pieces . . . 21163
Oberthür, Charles [Karl], arr. 1819–1895
  Othello 12134
Oboussier, Robert 1900–1957
  Sonnet 31 19638
O'Brien, J. Vick
  Merchant 8269
O'Brien, Peter
  Dream 9897
O'Byrne, Joan
  Much Ado 11218
Occioni, P.
  All's Well 89
Ochalski, Tomasz
  Dream 9898; Othello 11875
O'Connor, Eustace
  Sonnet 36 19673
Octavian, Mircea
  As You Like It 748
Oczko, Michael
  All's Well 44
O'Day, Robert
  Hamlet 4232
Odegard, Peter Sigurd
  Coriolanus 2327; Othello 11876
O'Dell, Gwyl
  Twelfth Night 17105
Odenz, Leon
  Dream 10802
Odland, Bruce 1952–
  Errors 2152; Macbeth 7069; Dream 9899;
  Romeo 13370; Tempest 15184; Twelfth
  Night 17106
Odoevskii, Vladimir Fedorovich, arr.
  1804–1869
  Othello 12135
Odom, John
  Much Ado 11219
O'Donoghue, Rory 1949–
  Hamlet 4119
Oehlenschläger, Adam Gottlob 1779–1850
  Dream 10539; Twelfth Night 17596
Oelschlegel, Alfred, arr. 1847–1915
  Caesar 5525; Merry Wives 9109, 9110;
  Dream 9771; Othello 12136, 12137
Oerton, Trevor, arr.
  Errors 2244
Oesten, Théodore, arr. 1813–1870
  Also known as Theodore Oesten and as
  Theodor Oesten
  Macbeth 7348; Othello 12138; Romeo
  13724; Settings of Commemorative
  Pieces . . . 20973
Oettel, Fritz
  Macbeth 7070; Twelfth Night 17107
Ogden, John
  Twelfth Night 17108

Ogilvy, Alfred Walter
  As You Like It 1481, 1737
O'Gorman, George Joseph 1917–
  Cymbeline 2595; Twelfth Night 17973,
  18170
Ohana, Maurice Michael 1914–
  Lear 6139; Dream 9900
O'Hare, Christopher, arr.
  Henry VIII 5053
O'Horgan, Thomas flor. 1950
  Tempest 15185
O'Horgan, Tom flor. 1975
  Tempest 15186
Oia, E.
  Lear 5867
Øian, Johan, arr.
  Hamlet 4221
Ojanen, Eero 1943–
  Richard III 12926; Tempest 15187
Okada, Kazuo
  Twelfth Night 17109
O'Kelly, Joseph
  Tempest 16283
O'Kelly, Joseph, arr.
  Merry Wives 8995; Dream 10872
Oldfield, Derek
  All's Well 45; Caesar 5398, 5399; L.L.L.
  6269; Twelfth Night 17110
Olds, William Benjamin 1874–
  As You Like It 1121
O'Leary, Arthur, arr. 1834–1919
  Tempest 14812
Olenev, Iu., arr.
  Hamlet 3468; Romeo 13996
Oliphant, Thomas, arr. [1799?]–1873
  Much Ado 11547; Othello 12257
Oliver, Colin George Henry
  As You Like It 1482; Tempest 15719
Oliver, Grant
  Tempest 15853
Oliver, Harold 1942–
  Tempest 15720
Oliver, Herbert 1883–
  Twelfth Night 17974; Sonnet 18 19404
Oliver, Stephen 1950–
  Antony 207; As You Like It 749; Coriolanus
  2328; Cymbeline 2482, 2833; L.L.L. 6270;
  Measure 7725; Dream 9901, 9902; Much
  Ado 11220; Othello 11877, 11878; Pericles
  12582, 12583; Richard II 12695; Romeo
  13371; Shrew 14426, 14427, 14428;
  Tempest 15188; Troilus 16507, 16508;
  Winter's Tale 18839; Settings of
  Commemorative Pieces . . . 20878
Olivier, Laurence Kerr 1907–
  Romeo 13372
Olon-Scrymgeour, John
  Hamlet 3326; Merchant 8270; Two
  Gentlemen 18416

Olsen, Karsten
  Dream 9903
Olsen, Otto Norman
  Dream 10178
Olsson, Margery, arr.
  Dream 10240
'Omega'
  Twelfth Night 17111
O'Neal, Danny
  Lear 6003
O'Neill, Norman Houstoun 1875–1934
  As You Like It 1483, 1960; Hamlet 3327;
  Henry V 4746; Caesar 5400; Macbeth 7071;
  Measure 7726; Merchant 8271, 8608, 8703;
  Merry Wives 8926; Twelfth Night 17598,
  17975, 18274; Lucrece 20773, 20777;
  Settings of Commemorative Pieces . . . 20879
O'Neill, Norman Houstoun, in part arr.
  1875–1934
  Lear 5868
Onnertz, Michael
  Lear 5869
Operti, G.
  Caesar 5401, 5517; Lear 5870
Operti, G., arr.
  Hamlet 3664; Romeo 13725
Opieński, Henryk 1870–1942
  Caesar 5402; Tempest 15189
Oram, Daphne Blake 1925–
  Hamlet 3328
Oranskii, Iu.
  Twelfth Night 17112
Oranskii, Viktor Aleksandrovich 1899–1953
  Also known as Viktor Aleksandrovich
  Oranskii Gershov
  Errors 2153; Lear 5871; Merry Wives 9152
Orchard, William Arundel 1867–1961
  Dream 10541
Orff, Carl 1895–1982
  Dream 9904, 9905, 9906, 9909, 9910,
  9911
Orff, Carl, arr. 1895–1982
  As You Like It 939
Orland, Ferdinando 1774–1848
  Lear 6140
Orlov, Vasilii Mikhailovich 1858–1901
  Shrew 14429
Ornadel, Cyril 1924–
  Also writes under the pseudonym 'Simon
  Anderson'
  All's Well 47; Errors 2154; 1 Henry IV
  4394; 2 Henry IV 4579; L.L.L. 6271;
  Richard II 12696; Romeo 13373; Shrew
  14430; Troilus 16509; Winter's Tale 18840
Orost, W. G., arr.
  Tempest 14813
Orpin, [?]
  'Mr. Orpin of Bath'; [also known as Orpen]
  Measure 7946

Orr, Donald
  Dream 9912
Orr, Robin Kemsley 1909–
  Born Robert Kemsley Orr
  Winter's Tale 18841
Ortega, Sergio
  Romeo 13374
Ortmann, Otto Rudolph 1889–1979
  Dream 10684
Ory, Jean-Marie
  Henry VIII 5008
Osborn, Donald N. 1926–
  Caesar 5403
Osborn, H.
  Othello 12335
Osborne, George Alexander 1806–1893
  Lear 6187
Osborne, George Alexander, arr.
  1806–1893
  Romeo 13726
Osborne, Mabel C.
  As You Like It 1122, 1484, 1738
Osborne, Willson -[before 1982]
  Twelfth Night 17976
Osgood, Heinrich, in part arr.
  As You Like It 750
O'Shea, John A., arr.
  Two Gentlemen 18595
Osmond, Clara
  Dream 10685
Osmond, Cuthbert
  P. Pilgrim 20664
Osolnik, Peter
  As You Like It 751; Macbeth 7072
Ostendorf, Jens Peter
  K. John 5615; Much Ado 11221; Richard III
  12927; Titus 16411
Ostrander, Allen, arr.
  Tempest 14736
Ostrčil, Otakar 1879–1935
  Cymbeline 2517
O'Sullivan, Michael George
  Tempest 15190
Oswald, James 1711–1769
  Macbeth 7073
Oţeanu, Smaranda 1941–
  Henry V 4812
Othon, [?], adapter
  Macbeth 7282
Ots, Kh.
  Antony 208
Ottman, Clara S.
  Shrew 14431
Oughton, Ruth
  Dream 9913
Oury, Anna Caroline, arr. 1808–1880
  Née de Belleville; also known as Emilie
  Anna-Caroline Oury
  Merry Wives 9111; Dream 10873

Ouseley, Frederick Arthur Gore 1825–1889
  Hamlet 4284
Ouseley, Frederick Arthur Gore, arr.
  1825–1889
  Timon 16333, 16346
Ovanin, Nikola Leonard 1911–
  Tempest 15925
Overbeck, Christian Adolf 1755–1821
  As You Like It 1123
Overton, Hall 1920–1972
  Caesar 5404
Overton, William Ted
  Errors 2205
Ovitt, Jack W.
  K. John 5616; Othello 11879; Richard II
  12697
Owen, Alexander, arr. 1851–1920
  Richard III 12850
Owen, J., arr.
  Tempest 14814
Owen, John Jones
  [John Owen Jones (1876–1962)?]
  Dream 10438; Settings of Commemorative
  Pieces . . . 21304
Owens, Christopher
  Twelfth Night 17599

P

Paatashvili, Guram Rubenovich
  Settings of Commemorative Pieces . . .
  21164
Paccione, Paul 1952–
  Winter's Tale 19055
Pacey, Denis
  Hamlet 3329
Pacheco, Carmen S.
  Hamlet 4233
Pacher, J. Adalbert, arr.
  Dream 10874
Pächter, Hans
  As You Like It 1916
Pachulski, Heinrich, arr. 1857–1921
  Hamlet 3469
Pacini, Giovanni 1796–1867
  Merchant 8795; Othello 12484
Paciorkiewicz, Tadeusz 1916–
  Much Ado 11222
Packer, Albert William
  As You Like It 1739
Packer, Randall 1953–
  Tempest 16284
Padilla, Mario
  Richard III 12928
Paer, Ferdinando 1771–1839
  Also known as Ferdinando Paër
  Antony 381

Pagan, José
  Romeo 13375
Pagani, Mauro 1946–
  Dream 10179
Page, Nathaniel Clifford, arr.
  As You Like It 1461; Cymbeline 2763, 2764,
  2765
Paine, John Knowles 1839–1906
  As You Like It 1917; Tempest 16086
Paisible, James [circa 1650–circa 1721]
  Also known as Paisable, Peasable, and
  Peasible
  1 Henry IV 4496; Timon 16332
Pakker, Hendrikus L. 1952–
  Sonnet 8 19230; Settings of Commemorative
  Pieces . . . 20880
Pala, Johan, arr.
  Othello 12139
Paledes, Stephen P.
  As You Like It 752; Twelfth Night 17113
Palester, Roman 1907–
  Lear 5872
Palester, Roman, arr. 1907–
  Dream 9772
Pałłasz, Edward 1936–
  Hamlet 3330; 1 Henry VI 4862
[Palm, Mati], arr. [1942–   ]
  Dream 10241
Palm, Guje
  Othello 11880
Palmer, Cedric King
  Romeo 13997
Palmer, Geoffrey Molyneux 1882–
  Twelfth Night 17600, 17977
Palmer, Robert Henry Charles 1916–
  Henry VIII 5145
Palmieri, Benedetto, arr.
  Othello 12200
Paltsits, Florence
  Tempest 15191
Palumbo, Costantino 1843–1928
  Macbeth 7466
Palumbo, Rodolphe Onofrio 1926–
  Macbeth 7074; Tempest 15192, 16173
Panella, John V.
  Macbeth 7283
Pannain, Guido 1891–1977
  Hamlet 4010
Pannell, Raymond 1935–
  As You Like It 753; Measure 7727; Merry
  Wives 8927
Panni, Marcello, arr. 1940–
  Dream 10242
Panting, Dave
  Tempest 16190
Panula, Jorma 1930–
  As You Like It 754
Panula, Sami
  Timon 16335

Papale, Henry 1937–
Tempest 15721; Twelfth Night 17685
Papavoine, Louis Auguste 1729–1790
Merry Wives 9153
Pape, Johnathon 1955–
As You Like It 755
Pape, Louis
Winter's Tale 18842
Papini, Guido 1847–1912
Dream 10686
Papini, Guido, arr. 1847–1912
Dream 10613
Papp, Zoltán
As You Like It 756
Parès, Gabriel Philippe Charles, arr. –1934
Hamlet 3665; Lear 6177
Park, James M. 1942–
Titus 16423; Settings of Commemorative
Pieces . . . 21165
Park, John 1804–1865
As You Like It 1740; Cymbeline 2596;
Hamlet 3799; Henry VIII 5146; L.L.L. 6457;
Much Ado 11494; Twelfth Night 17601
Park, John, adapter 1804–1865
As You Like It 1124
Park, Maria Hester 1775–1822
Also known as Maria Hester Parke and as
Mrs. John Beardmore
As You Like It 1741; Cymbeline 2871;
Twelfth Night 17602
Parke, Bob
As You Like It 757
Parker, Clifton 1905–
As You Like It 758, 1485, 1742; L.L.L.
6272; Merry Wives 8928; Much Ado 11223;
Othello 11881, 11882; Romeo 13376;
Tempest 15193, 15194
Parker, Francine
Twelfth Night 17114
Parker, Henry T. 1845–1917
As You Like It 1125, 1486, 1918; Cymbeline
2698; Henry VIII 5147; Lear 6089; Dream
10338; Much Ado 11495; Othello 12336;
Romeo 13939; Tempest 15722; Twelfth
Night 17603, 17978
Parker, Henry T., arr. 1845–1917
As You Like It 433; Tempest 14815
Parker, Henry Taylor 1867–1934
Much Ado 11496
Parker, Horatio William 1863–1919
As You Like It 1126; Twelfth Night 18337
Parker, J. Harleston
Hamlet 4172
Parker, James
Lear 5873
Parker, James Mavin 1934–
Twelfth Night 17115; Sonnet 3 19198;
Sonnet 15 19310; Sonnet 18 19405; Sonnet
24 19497; Sonnet 29 19573; Sonnet 50

19747; Sonnet 53 19759; Sonnet 55
19782; Sonnet 113 20297; Sonnet 130
20426; Sonnet 144 20481; Sonnet 146
20496
Parker, Jim
Hamlet 4120
Parker, K.
Othello 11883
Parkman, Hakan 1955–
Hamlet 3331
Parks, Van Dyke
1 Henry IV 4395
Parmelee, Mabel Lainhart
Winter's Tale 18843
Parnell, Claude W.
As You Like It 1743; Tempest 15723;
Sonnet 30 19613
Parnes, Randy
Dream 9914
Parodi, Renato 1900–
Twelfth Night 18239
Parrillo, John J.
Antony 209; Shrew 14594; Twelfth Night
17116
Parrott, Horace Ian 1916–
Macbeth 7467; Romeo 13940, 13941;
Shrew 14663; Twelfth Night 18240
Parry, Charles Hubert Hastings 1848–1918
As You Like It 1127, 1487, 1744; Cymbeline
2597; L.L.L. 6368, 6593; Measure 7947,
7948, 7949; Merchant 8609; Othello 12337;
Richard II 12761; Tempest 15724; Twelfth
Night 17979; Sonnet 18 19406; Sonnet 29
19574; Sonnet 30 19614; Sonnet 32 19643;
Sonnet 71 19960; Sonnet 87 20093; Sonnet
109 20282; P. Pilgrim 20665; Settings of
Commemorative Pieces . . . 21305
Parry, John 1776–1851
Hamlet 3733; L.L.L. 6339, 6673; Merry
Wives 8929; P. Pilgrim 20666
Parry, Joseph Haydn 1864–1894
L.L.L. 6686, Sonnet 18 19407; Sonnet 19
19468
Partch, Harry 1901–1974
Romeo 13377
Partlan, Bill
Shrew 14432
Parton, Jeff
Hamlet 3332; 1 Henry IV 4396; 2 Henry IV
4580; Henry V 4747; Macbeth 7075; Dream
9915; Much Ado 11224; Othello 11884;
Romeo 13378; Twelfth Night 17117
Parwez, Akmal 1948–
As You Like It 1128; Measure 7950;
Merchant 8610; Twelfth Night 17980
Pasatieri, Thomas John 1945–
Lear 6160; Richard II 12751; Romeo 13379,
13837; Tempest 16285; Sonnet 73 20010

P[ascal], F[lorian], arr. [1847–1923]
[Pseudonym used by Joseph Benjamin
Williams]
Cymbeline 2849; Dream 10375

Pascal, Florian 1847–1923
Pseudonym used by Joseph Benjamin Williams
As You Like It 1129, 1488; Errors 2247;
Henry VIII 5148; L.L.L. 6375; Measure
7951; Merchant 8777; Dream 10339,
10415; Much Ado 11497; Twelfth Night
17981; P. Pilgrim 20667; Venus 20795

Pascal, Prosper, adapter [circa 1825]–1880
L.L.L. 6678

Pascoe-Williams, Leonard
Also known as Leonard Pascoe Williams
Henry VIII 5149; L.L.L. 6458, 6594

Pascuttini, Kreso
Hamlet 3333

Pasfield, William Reginald 1909–
Dream 10687

Pasfield, William Reginald, arr. 1909–
Othello 12360; Twelfth Night 18031

Pasmore, Henry Bickford 1857–1944
Settings of Commemorative Pieces . . . 21068

Pasquali, Nicolò [circa 1718]–1757
Also known as Niccolo Pasquali
Romeo 13380; Tempest 15926

Pasquet, E.
Also known as Mme. Pasquet
Hamlet 4011, 4234

Passani, Émile Barthélemy 1905–1974
Sonnet 128 20398

Pasta, Giuditta, arr.
Othello 12140

Pasternack, Josef Alexander 1881–1940
Measure 7952

Patacchi, Val
Much Ado 11225

Paterson, Charles
Twelfth Night 17604, 17982

Patriquin, Donald Charles Harvey 1938–
As You Like It 1489, 1745; Measure 7953

Pattenhausen, Hellmuth 1896–1979
Cymbeline 2699, 2872; Two Gentlemen
18549

Patterson, Andy J. 1929–
Hamlet 3734; Romeo 13849; Sonnet 65
19897

Patterson, Dixi
Lear 5874

Pattison, [Thomas Mee?] [1845–   ]
As You Like It 1746

Patton, Chris
Two Gentlemen 18417

Pattrick, Laughton
Hamlet 3334

Pauels, Heinz 1908–
All's Well 48; As You Like It 760; Hamlet
3335; Measure 7728; Much Ado 11226;
Richard II 12698; Richard III 12929; Shrew
14433; Twelfth Night 17118

Pauer, Ernst, arr. 1826–1905
Merry Wives 9112; Dream 9773, 9774,
9775, 10243, 10875; Shrew 14582

Paul, Arth[ur]
As You Like It 761

Paul, Walter, arr.
Shrew 14613

Paull, James 1957–
Twelfth Night 17119

Paull, Steven J.
Kinsmen 19162

Pauls, Raimonds 1936–
Sonnet 56 19799; Sonnet 61 19860; Sonnet
92 20129

Paulus, Stephen Harrison 1949–
Hamlet 3823

Paumgartner, Bernhard 1887–1971
Lear 5875; Dream 9916, 9917; Twelfth
Night 17120, 17121

Paumgartner, Bernhard, in part arr. 1887–1971
Twelfth Night 17122

Pavchinskii, S., arr.
Hamlet 3983

Pawlak, Stanisław
Romeo 13381

Pawlicki, Norbert
Twelfth Night 17123

Pawlicki, Zbigniew
Macbeth 7076

Pawłowski, Bogdan
Henry V 4748; Lear 5876; Richard III
12930; Romeo 13382; Shrew 14434

Pawłowski, Walerian 1920–
1 Henry IV 4397; 2 Henry IV 4581; Othello
11885

Pawluśkiewicz, Jan Kanty
Troilus 16510

Paxton, William 1737–1781
Tempest 15833

Paychère, Albert 1889–1970
Coriolanus 2329

Payer, Friedrich, arr.
Hamlet 3666; Merry Wives 9113; Romeo
13727

Payne, Maggi 1945–
Winter's Tale 18844

Payne, Richard 1843–1884
Henry VIII 5150

Paynter, John 1931–
Henry V 4803, 4815

Pears, Peter, arr. 1910–1986
Dream 10244; Twelfth Night 18307, 18319

Pearsall, Robert Lucas 1795–1856
Often ennobled his name to 'de Pearsall'.
Also wrote under the pseudonym
'G. Berthold' (see also Berthold, G., adapter)
Macbeth 7077, 7468; Measure 7954

Pearson, Arthur
  As You Like It 1130
Peartree, Clifford
  Merry Wives 8930
Peaslee, Richard Cutts 1930–
  Antony 210; 1 Henry IV 4398; Macbeth
  7078; Merchant 8272; Dream 9918, 10295,
  10302, 10377, 10441, 10444, 10542;
  Richard III 12931; Troilus 16511; Settings of
  Commemorative Pieces . . . 20881
Peck, Dennis 1914–
  As You Like It 1131, 1490, 1747; Cymbeline
  2700; Much Ado 11498; Pericles 12609;
  Tempest 15927; Twelfth Night 17983; Two
  Gentlemen 18550
Pedersen, Gunner Møller 1943–
  Hamlet 3336
Pedrell, Felipe 1841–1922
  Lear 5877
[Peed, Thomas Thorpe]
  Settings of Commemorative Pieces . . . 21069
Peele, Dudley
  As You Like It 1132
Peers, Jennie, arr.
  Hamlet 3337
Peeters, Emil 1893–1974
  Antony 211; Errors 2155; Coriolanus 2330;
  1 Henry IV 4399; 2 Henry IV 4582; Henry V
  4749; 1 Henry VI 4863; 2 Henry VI 4904;
  Henry VIII 5009; Caesar 5405; K. John
  5617; L.L.L. 6273; Macbeth 7079, 7080;
  Merchant 8273, 8274; Richard II 12699;
  Richard III 12932, 12933; Romeo 13383,
  13384; Shrew 14435; Tempest 15195; Titus
  16412; Winter's Tale 18845
Peile, [?], arr.
  Tempest 14816
Peile, F. O. Kinsey
  Twelfth Night 18338
Peiniger, Otto
  As You Like It 1491
Peixinho, Jorge 1940–
  Macbeth 7081
Peleg, Frank
  As You Like It 762; Romeo 13385; Shrew
  14436
Pelissier, Victor [circa 1740/1750–circa 1820]
  Surname also known as Pelesier, Pelliser,
  and Pellisier
  Tempest 16229, 16230
Pelissier, Victor, in part arr.
  [circa 1740/1750–circa 1820]
  Surname also known as Pelesier, Pelliser,
  and Pellisier
  Tempest 15196
Pelletier, Jean Claude
  Dream 9919
Pelzer, Anne W.
  Tempest 16087

Pembaur, Karl Maria 1876–1939
  As You Like It 1492; Hamlet 3338; Othello
  12338; Richard III 12934; Twelfth Night
  17124
Pembaur, Karl Maria, in part arr. 1876–1939
  Hamlet 3339
Pen, Ronald
  As You Like It 763
Pender, Tom
  Cymbeline 2598; Sonnet 18 19408
Penderecki, Krzysztof 1933–
  Troilus 16512, 16513
Pengov, Tomaž
  Measure 7729
Penn, William Albert 1943–
  All's Well 49; As You Like It 764, 765;
  Errors 2156; Hamlet 3340; Henry V 4750;
  Caesar 5406; Lear 5878, 5879; L.L.L. 6274;
  Macbeth 7082, 7083; Measure 7730, 7731;
  Merry Wives 8931; Dream 9920, 9921,
  9922, 9923; Much Ado 11227; Pericles
  12584, 12606; Richard II 12700, 12701;
  Richard III 12935; Romeo 13386; Tempest
  15198; Titus 16413; Twelfth Night 17125;
  Two Gentlemen 18418, 18419; Settings of
  Commemorative Pieces . . . 21189
Penn, William H.
  As You Like It 1919
Penny, Ethel M.
  As You Like It 1748
Penny, M[artin?]
  Cymbeline 2599
Penny, Martin, arr.
  Dream 10137
Pépin, Jean Josephat Clermont 1926–
  Merchant 8275; Twelfth Night 17126
Pepperdine, Warren
  Othello 11886
[Pepusch, Johann Christoph] [1667–1752]
  1 Henry IV 4400
Pepusch, Johann Christoph 1667–1752
  Tempest 16286; Timon 16336; Venus 20820
Perabo, Johann Ernst 1845–1920
  Hamlet 3855
Perak, Rudolf 1891–
  Romeo 13387
Percival, Frank, arr.
  Dream 9776
Percy, [?]
  Merry Wives 9229
Percy, John 1749–1797
  As You Like It 1749; L.L.L. 6595; Merchant
  8461; Dream 9924, 10340, 10464; Much
  Ado 11643; Othello 12339; Romeo 14171;
  Twelfth Night 17605
Peress, Maurice 1930–
  All's Well 50
Peress, Maurice, arr. 1930–
  Romeo 13605

Perez, David 1711–1778
Also known as Davide Perez
Caesar 5562
Perkins, Charles Callahan
Dream 10688
Perkins, Horace 1901–[circa 1983]
Merchant 8276
Perkins, Roger
Richard III 12936; Twelfth Night 17127
Perkinson, Coleridge-Taylor 1932–
Othello 11887
Permann, J., arr.
Hamlet 3667
Pernice, A. Nicholas 1957–
Tempest 15199
Perosi, Dom Lorenzo 1872–1956
Romeo 13789
Perrenoud, Jean-Frédéric 1912–
Sonnet 29 19575; Sonnet 60 19833; Sonnet
73 20011
Perrier, E., arr.
Hamlet 3668
Perrin, Mac, arr.
Merry Wives 9114
Perring, James
Settings of Commemorative Pieces . . .
21070
Perrucci, Mario 1934–
L.L.L. 6275
Perry, Floyd
As You Like It 766
Perry, Harold, arr.
Romeo 14086
Persichetti, Vincent 1915–1987
Lear 6004; Tempest 15501
Persico, Mario 1892–1977
Shrew 14595
Pert, Morris 1947–
Macbeth 7084
Perti, Giacomo Antonio 1661–1751
Coriolanus 2422
Peška, Vlastimil
Shrew 14437
Peskanov, Alexander
Romeo 13388
Peterkin, George Norman 1886–1982
As You Like It 1750; Lear 6161
Petersén, Gösta 1949–
Dream 9925
Petersen, Marian
Henry V 4751
Petersen, Wilhelm 1890–1957
Hamlet 3800; Macbeth 7085; Othello
12340; Twelfth Night 17606; Settings of
Commemorative Pieces . . . 21232
Peterson, Oscar Emmanuel, arr. 1925–
Romeo 13606
Pethel, Stanley 1950–
Twelfth Night 17128

Pether, Henry E.
Settings of Commemorative Pieces . . . 21071
Petin, Nikola 1920–
Hamlet 4012
Petit, Jean-Claude
Othello 12508
Petit, Raymond 1893–
Settings of Commemorative Pieces . . .
21233
Petosa, James
Tempest 15461
Petr, Zdeněk 1919–
As You Like It 767; Much Ado 11228
Petrella, Errico 1813–1877
Merchant 8796
Petrič, Ivo 1931–
Macbeth 7086
Petrocelli, Gabriel, arr.
Romeo 13427
Petrov, A., arr. flor. 1900
Macbeth 7422
Petrov, Andrei Pavlovich 1930–
Romeo 13389
Petrov, Vadim
Shrew 14438
Petrovič, Boško 1935–
Othello 11888
Petrovics, Emil 1930–
Antony 212
Petsch, Hans 1891–[before 1987]
Hamlet 3341; Caesar 5407; Much Ado
11229; Othello 11889; Richard III 12937
Pett, Eustace
Merchant 8704
Pettengill, Richard
Dream 9926
Pettigrew, Robert
Twelfth Night 17129
Petyrek, Felix 1892–1951
Othello 11890
Petzold, Winfried
As You Like It 768
Peyton, Malcolm C. 1932–
As You Like It 1133; Henry VIII 5151;
Sonnet 7 19223; Sonnet 8 19256
Pezzi, Vincenzo, arr.
Romeo 13998
Pfautsch, Lloyd 1921–
As You Like It 1134; Henry VIII 5152
Pfeiffer, Georges Jean, arr. 1835–1908
Hamlet 4191
Pfister, Hugo 1914–1969
Othello 11891
Pflanz, Ludwig
Dream 9927
Pflüger, Andreas 1941–
Dream 9928
Pfriemer, Ernst
Macbeth 7087

Philidor, François-André Danican 1726–1795
1 Henry IV 4520; 2 Henry IV 4689; Merry
Wives 9254
Philipp, Isidor, arr. 1863–1958
Also known as Isador Edmond Philipp; also
wrote under the pseudonym 'Sam. Phitt'
Hamlet 4192; Dream 9777
Philipp, Jobst
Errors 2157; Shrew 14439; Twelfth Night
17130
Phillips, B.
As You Like It 1135
Phillips, Bryony 1948–
Sonnet 116 20327
Phillips, Burrill 1907–
Merchant 8611
Phillips, Dan, arr.
Henry V 4782
Phillips, Henry 1801–1876
Lear 6162; Dream 10367
Phillips, James Carlisle, III 1951–
Twelfth Night 17607
Phillips, Kim
Hamlet 3342
Phillips, Linda 1924–
Also known as Mrs. L. Kauffmann
Twelfth Night 17984
Phillips, Montague Fawcett 1885–1969
As You Like It 1493, 1751; Dream 10689;
Much Ado 11499
Phillips, Paul Schuyler 1956–
Pericles 12585
Phillips, Wilfred Hudson, arr.
Cymbeline 2766
Philpot, Michael Peter 1954–
L.L.L. 6596; Much Ado 11500; Tempest
15725
Phipps, [Thomas Blomer?], arr. [1796–1849?]
Macbeth 6997
Phipps, Thomas Blomer, arr. 1796–1849
Settings of Commemorative Pieces . . . 21166
Phipps, William H.
Dream 10690
Piantanida, Gaetano, arr.
Lear 6141
Piatti, Carlo Alfredo 1822–1901
Also known as Alfred Piatti
Sonnet 139 20463
Piazzolla, Astor
Dream 9929
Piccinni, Louis Alexandre 1779–1850
Also known as Luigi Alessandro Piccinni, as
Lodovico Alessandro Piccini, and as Louis-
Alexandre Piccini
Macbeth 7524
Piccinni, Vito Niccolò Marcello Antonio
Giacomo 1728–1800
Also known as Nicola Piccini
Coriolanus 2423

Piccioli, Giuseppe 1905–1961
Hamlet 3343
Picek, Josef
Othello 11892
Picka, František
Hamlet 3344; Macbeth 7088; Merchant
8277; Much Ado 11230; Othello 11893;
Richard III 12938; Shrew 14440; Twelfth
Night 17131; Winter's Tale 18846
Pickerill, E. C.
Errors 2158
Pickerill, W.
Caesar 5408; Macbeth 7089; Sonnet 18
19409
Piechler, Arthur 1896–1974
Hamlet 3345; Sonnet 76 20049; P. Pilgrim
20668, 20669
Pierné, Henri Constant Gabriel 1863–1937
Coriolanus 2331; Hamlet 3346
Pierson, Henry Hugo 1815–1873
Born Henry Hugh Pearson; also wrote under
the pseudonym 'Edgar Mannsfeldt'. On some
scores is printed 'Henri Hugo Pierson'.
As You Like It 1752, 1920; Cymbeline 2600;
Hamlet 4013; Caesar 5409; Macbeth 7469;
Measure 7955; Merchant 8612; Romeo
13942; Twelfth Night 18241; Two
Gentlemen 18551; Settings of
Commemorative Pieces . . . 21072
Pietrapertosa, Jean, arr.
Romeo 13728
Pietsch, Wolfgang
Merry Wives 8932; Othello 11894; Romeo
13391; Troilus 16514; Twelfth Night 17132
Piggott, Harry Edward [1878?]–1966
Two Gentlemen 18552
Pijper, Willem Frederik Johannes 1894–1947
Hamlet 4262; Tempest 15200
Pilati, Mario, arr. 1903–1938
Shrew 14596
Pilhofer, Herbert
Hamlet 3347; Henry V 4752; Caesar 5410;
Much Ado 11231; Richard III 12939
Pilkington, Michael, arr.
As You Like It 434; Henry VIII 5099
Pillaut, Léon 1833–1903
Winter's Tale 18942
Pillinger, Wolfgang
Twelfth Night 17133
Pimsleur, Solomon 1900–1962
Sonnet 8 19257; Sonnet 18 19410; Sonnet
29 19576; Sonnet 30 19615; Sonnet 33
19653; Sonnet 66 19916; Sonnet 73 20012;
Sonnet 97 20166; Sonnet 106 20264;
Sonnet 116 20328
Pinchard, Lester
As You Like It 769; Merchant 8278
Pine, Tyrrell
Settings of Commemorative Pieces . . . 20882

Pinedo, Cesar Hector
  Merchant 8613
Pinkard, Maceo 1897–1962
  Othello 12539
Pinkham, Daniel Rogers, Jr. 1923–
  Troilus 16515; Sonnet 97 20167
Pinkham, Daniel Rogers, Jr., arr. 1923–
  Twelfth Night 18300
Pinkston, Joan
  As You Like It 770; 1 Henry IV 4401;
  2 Henry IV 4583; Henry V 4753; 3 Henry VI
  4946; Henry VIII 5010; Lear 5880, 5881;
  Richard II 12702; Richard III 12940;
  Twelfth Night 17134
Pinkstone, Donna, in part arr.
  Macbeth 7090
Pinsuti, Ciro Ercole 1829–1888
  Also known as Il Cavaliere Pinsuti
  As You Like It 1985; Hamlet 4235;
  Merchant 8279, 8413, 8487, 8614; Dream
  10974; Much Ado 11501
Piotrowski, Zbigniew
  Hamlet 3348
Piovani, Nicola
  Timon 16337
Piper, Martin
  Othello 11895
Pirchner, Werner
  Tempest 15202
Pirkis, Bessie L'Evesque
  Sonnet 128 20399
Pirotta, Manoel 1962–
  Antony 213
Pirumov, Aleksandr Ivanovich 1930–
  Sonnet 25 19506; Sonnet 71 19961
Pischinger, Alajos, arr.
  Hamlet 3669
Pisk, Paul Amadeus 1893–
  Much Ado 11232; Sonnet 8 19258; Sonnet
  55 19783
Pisk, Paul Amadeus, in part arr. 1893–
  Macbeth 7091; Dream 9930
Pistor, Judith
  Tempest 15203; Winter's Tale 18847
Pitcher, Richard James
  Cymbeline 2701; Tempest 15928
Pitcher, Richard James, arr.
  As You Like It 1462
Pitcher, Stephen
  As You Like It 771; Errors 2159; Hamlet
  3349; 1 Henry IV 4402; Measure 7732;
  Much Ado 11233; Pericles 12586, 12587;
  Richard III 12941; Romeo 13392; Twelfth
  Night 17135
Pitfield, Thomas Baron 1903–
  Merchant 8615; Othello 11896, 12341,
  12342; Tempest 15204, 15807
Pitot, Genevieve 1901–1980
  Hamlet 4173

Pitot, Genevieve, arr. 1901–1980
  Shrew 14614
Pitt, A.
  Pseudonym used by Eric Spear
  As You Like It 1921; Hamlet 4014;
  Merchant 8705; Merry Wives 9230; Dream
  10691; Romeo 13943; Tempest 16088;
  Twelfth Night 18242, 18243; Winter's Tale
  18982, 19056
Pitt, Percy 1870–1932
  Richard II 12703, 12773; Shrew 14664
Pittas, Christos
  Merchant 8280; Troilus 16516
Pittrich, Georg 1870–1934
  Twelfth Night 17136
Pizer, Elizabeth Faw Hayden 1954–
  Sonnet 30 19616
Pizzardi, Flaviano
  1 Henry IV 4403; 2 Henry IV 4584; Henry V
  4754; Merry Wives 8933
Pizzetti, Ildebrando 1880–1968
  As You Like It 772; Romeo 13790
Plaetner, Jørgen 1930–
  Hamlet 4174
Platen, Horst 1884–
  Macbeth 7092
[?Platt, Martin L.]
  As You Like It 959
Platt, Martin L.
  Lear 5882; Measure 7733; Richard II 12704
Platt, William 1867–
  Twelfth Night 17608
Platzman, Eugene, arr.
  Macbeth 7294
Pless, Hans 1884–1966
  [Pseudonym used by Hans Pischinger?]
  Macbeth 7284
Pleyel, Camille 1788–1855
  Tempest 16287
Pleyel, Camille, arr. 1788–1855
  Othello 12141
Płoszaj, Anny
  Hamlet 3350
Plum, Abram
  Much Ado 11234
Plummer, Roy
  Romeo 14207
Plumstead, Mary 1905–1980
  Née Frost
  Measure 7956; Much Ado 11502; Tempest
  15726
Plumstead, W. H., arr.
  As You Like It 435; Measure 7906
Poćwierz, Antoni
  L.L.L. 6276
Podaševský, Alexandr
  1 Henry IV 4404; 2 Henry IV 4585; Caesar
  5411; Lear 5883; Romeo 13393; Shrew
  14441; Twelfth Night 17137

Podel'skii, Gennadii Viacheslavovich 1927–
As You Like It 773
Podestà, Carlo 1847–1921
Much Ado 11366
Podrazil, Johann, arr.
Dream 9778
Pogodin, G.
Romeo 13394
Pogodin, Sergei Aleksandrovich 1896–
Lear 6005
Pohl, Richard, arr. 1826–1896
Romeo 13572
Pohlman, Ray
Othello 12037
Pointer, John   –1934
Merchant 8616
Pointer, John, arr.   –1934
Two Gentlemen 18510
Pointon, Malcolm
Hamlet 3351; Romeo 13395
Poldini, Ede 1869–1957
Twelfth Night 18244
Polferov, Iakov Iakovlevich 1891–1966
Antony 214
Polianich, Aleksandr Aleksandrovich
1895–1968
Also known as Polianichenko
Lear 5884; Othello 11897; Twelfth Night
17138
Poliart, Jean-Louis
Twelfth Night 17139
Polifrone, Jon J. 1937–
Tempest 15205
Politser, E.
Twelfth Night 17140
Pollack, Christian
Hamlet 3352; Measure 7734; Much Ado
11235
Pollarolo, Carlo Francesco [circa 1653]–1723
Coriolanus 2424
Pololáník, Zdeněk 1935–
Lear 5885; Macbeth 7093; Merchant 8281;
Othello 11898; Romeo 13396
Polonskii, Artur Moritsevich 1900–
Much Ado 11236
Polonskii, V.
Much Ado 11237
Polovinkin, Leonid Alekseevich 1894–1949
Tempest 16089
Polsterer, Rudolf
Sonnet 98 20189
Polycarpou, Peter
Antony 215
Pommer, W. H.
Much Ado 11503
Ponc, Miroslav 1902–1976
As You Like It 774; Errors 2160; Henry V
4755; Lear 5886; Macbeth 7094; Measure
7735; Merchant 8282; Merry Wives 8934;

Much Ado 11238; Othello 11899; Shrew
14442, 14443; Tempest 15206; Twelfth
Night 17141; Winter's Tale 18848
Poniridis, Georgios 1892–
Settings of Commemorative Pieces . . .
21190
Pontet, Henry
Pseudonym used by Théodore Auguste Marie
Joseph Piccolomini
L.L.L. 6687
Ponti, Hugh
Dream 10692
Poole, Henry James
Lear 6163
Poole, Jeffrey J., arr.
Tempest 14817
Poole, Roderick
Dream 9931
Pope, David
Dream 9932; Romeo 13397; Winter's Tale
18849
Pope, Logan
Twelfth Night 17142
Popławski, Marceli 1882–1948
Twelfth Night 17143
Popov, Gavriil Nikolaevich 1904–1972
Lear 6006
Popp, Wilhelm, arr. 1828–1902
Merry Wives 9115; Twelfth Night 17346
Port, Frederick
Antony 216; Hamlet 3353; 1 Henry IV
4405; Henry V 4756; Macbeth 7095
Porta, Bernardo 1758–1829
Romeo 14208
Portch, Margaret
Dream 10693
Porteous, Norman
Much Ado 11504
Porter, Bella C.
Twelfth Night 17985
Porter, Cole Albert 1891–1964
Romeo 14059; Shrew 14597; Sonnet 155
20582
Porter, William Quincy 1897–1966
Antony 217; L.L.L. 6459, 6679; Merry
Wives 8935; Dream 9933; Much Ado
11631
Portman, Rachel
Twelfth Night 17144
Portnoff, Misha 1901–
Also known as Mischa Portnoff
Merry Wives 8936
Portnoff, Westley 1910–
Merry Wives 8937
Portoalegre, Válter Schultz
Hamlet 3354
Poser, Hans 1917–1970
Hamlet 3355

Pospíšil, Miloš 1934–
  As You Like It 775; Romeo 13398; Tempest
  15207; Twelfth Night 17145, 17146
Post, Douglas
  As You Like It 776; Caesar 5412; Dream
  9934; Richard III 12942; Tempest 15208,
  15462; Twelfth Night 17147
Post, Joseph
  1 Henry IV 4406
Poston, Elizabeth 1905–1987
  As You Like It 1494; Tempest 15209;
  Twelfth Night 17148
Poston, Elizabeth, in part arr.
  1905–1987
  Twelfth Night 17149
Poston, Elizabeth, arr. 1905–1987
  Tempest 15064
Pottebaum, William G. 1930–
  Dream 9935
Potter, D. E., arr.
  Romeo 13999
Potter, Philip Cipriani Hambly 1792–1871
  Also known as Philip Cipriani Hambley Potter
  Antony 322; Cymbeline 2824; Tempest
  16090
Potter, Philip Cipriani Hambly, arr.
  1792–1871
  Also known as Philip Cipriani Hambley Potter
  Othello 12142
Pottle, Samuel 1934–1978
  Tempest 15210
Pötzsch, J. Wilh[elm], arr.
  Macbeth 7254
Poulenc, Francis Jean Marcel 1899–1963
  Merchant 8617; Romeo 13399
Pounds, Charles Courtice 1862–1927
  Twelfth Night 17150, 17986
Powell, Dean, in part arr.
  Tempest 15211
Powell, Mel 1923–
  Born Melvin Epstein
  As You Like It 1495
Powell, Thomas 1776–[after 1860]
  Hamlet 4015
Pownall, Mary Ann 1751–1796
  Also known as Mrs. Pownall and, in the UK,
  as Mrs. Wrighten
  Cymbeline 2702; Measure 7957
Powroźniak, Józef, arr. 1902–
  Dream 9779
Pozdneev, Aleksei Alekseevich 1904–
  Othello 11900; Romeo 13400; Shrew
  14444; Twelfth Night 17151
Praeger, Ferdinand, arr. 1815–1891
  Dream 10784
Prahl, Victor, arr.
  Twelfth Night 17487
Pratt, Alfred
  Dream 10694; Winter's Tale 19057

Pratt, Silas Gamaliel 1846–1916
  Hamlet 4016, 4017; Settings of
  Commemorative Pieces . . . 21167
Pratt, Sophie
  Tempest 15212
Pratten, Catherina Josepha, arr. 1821–1895
  Née Pelzer; also known as Madame Sidney
  Pratten
  As You Like It 1986
Pratten, William Sidney
  P. Pilgrim 20670
Prehn, Holger, in part arr.
  As You Like It 777
Preis, Karl
  L.L.L. 6460; Measure 7958; Dream 10416;
  Romeo 13873; Twelfth Night 17987; Two
  Gentlemen 18553; P. Pilgrim 20671
Preizner, M.
  All's Well 51
Prejzner, Tadeusz
  Dream 9936
Prendergast, Arthur Hugh Dalrymple
  Measure 7959; Twelfth Night 17988
Prendiville, H., arr.
  Merry Wives 9116
Presser, Gábor 1948–
  Dream 9937
Preston, Herbert M., arr.
  Dream 9780
Preston, Robert Williamson
  Merchant 8415
Presuhn, Alexander
  As You Like It 778; Errors 2161; Hamlet
  3356; Measure 7736; Merchant 8283
Preuss, Rainer
  Lear 5887
Previn, Charles 1888–
  Richard III 12943
Price, Beryl 1912–
  Much Ado 11505
Price, Richard Maldwyn 1890–1952
  Henry V 4827
Pride, John
  Tempest 15727
Prideaux, George
  Hamlet 3357; Tempest 15213
Pridham, John 1818–1896
  Tempest 16091
Priestley-Smith, Hugh
  Twelfth Night 17609, 17989
Priestman, Brian 1927–
  Lear 5888
Priestman, Brian, in part arr. 1927–
  Othello 11901
Prigmore, James 1943–
  Macbeth 7096
Prigozhin, Liutsian Abramovich 1926–
  Twelfth Night 17152, 17990; Settings of
  Commemorative Pieces . . . 21234

Přikryl, M.
Much Ado 11239
Prin, Yves Léon Francis 1933–
As You Like It 779
Prince, Robert 1929–
Macbeth 7097; Much Ado 11240
Prince, Rosalie M.
Dream 10975
Pring, J.
[Jacob Cubitt Pring (1771–1799)?]
Merchant 8618
Pring, Jacob Cubitt 1771–1799
Much Ado 11387
Pringle, Robert Wallace
Tempest 16092
Pringsheim, Klaus 1883–1972
Caesar 5413; Lear 5889; Othello 11902;
Richard II 12705; Shrew 14445
Prioleau, Judith
Tempest 15728
Prior, Claude Henri
Much Ado 11241; Romeo 13401
Pritchett, John
Hamlet 3358
Pritsker, David Abramovich 1900–1978
Sonnet 61 19856; Sonnet 70 19930; Sonnet
96 20144; Sonnet 97 20168; Sonnet 99
20203
Probst, Dominique-Henri 1954–
Lear 5890; Macbeth 7098; Richard III
12944
Proch, Heinrich 1808–1878
Merry Wives 9154
Procner, Jerzy
Tempest 15214
Procter, Robert
Hamlet 4121
Proctor, Charles 1906–
Henry VIII 5153
Proctor, David
1 Henry IV 4407
Prohaska, Carl 1869–1927
Cymbeline 2601; Twelfth Night 17610
Prokof'ev, Sergei Sergeevich 1891–1953
Antony 341, 357; Hamlet 3359, 3609;
Romeo 13791, 13944, 13946, 13949,
13951
Promnitz, Wilfried
Merchant 8284
Prosser, Ruth
As You Like It 1136
Prószyński, Stanisław 1926–
Dream 9938
Protheroe, Brian
As You Like It 780; Caesar 5414; Measure
7737; Dream 9939; Winter's Tale 18850
Protheroe, Daniel 1866–1934
Henry VIII 5154; Twelfth Night 17991,
17992

Protheroe, Daniel, arr. 1866–1934
Cymbeline 2767
Prout, Ebenezer 1835–1909
Twelfth Night 18245
Pruden, Larry Carrol 1925–
Hamlet 3361; Tempest 16093
Prudent, Émile B.
Tempest 16094
Prulière, Jules Joseph Marius, arr.
–1945
Cymbeline 2841
Pruslin, Naum 1877–1944
Dream 9940
Pruszak, Jan
Much Ado 11242
Prutsman, Harriet Theo
Tempest 15215
Przybylski, Bronisław Z.
Tempest 15216
Pscherer, Adolf
Richard III 12945; Romeo 13402
Puccini, Giacomo 1858–1924
Lear 6007
Puerner, Charles
As You Like It 781; Macbeth 7099
Puget, Paul Charles Marie 1848–1917
Much Ado 11367; Tempest 15217
Pugni, Cesare 1805–1870
Macbeth 7547
Pujol, Emilio
Romeo 14060
Pulli, Pietro
Coriolanus 2425
Pul'ver, Lev Mikhailovich 1883–1970
Lear 5891
Purcell, Arthur, arr.
Romeo 13729
Purcell, Daniel 1660–1717
Hamlet 4285; Macbeth 7100; Shrew 14679
Purcell, Henry 1659–1695
Macbeth 7101, 7525; Measure 8046; Dream
10180; Richard II 12706; Tempest 15218;
Timon 16338; Twelfth Night 18296, 18302,
18311
Purcell, Thomas
Winter's Tale 18851
Purday, Charles Henry 1799–1885
Dream 10926
Purdy, William
Macbeth 7548
Purefoy, Juliene
As You Like It 782
Purgol'd, Nadezhda, arr.
Romeo 14000
Purser, John Whitley 1942–
Caesar 5415; Dream 9941; Tempest 15222;
Twelfth Night 17153
Putnam, George David
Sonnet 18 19411

Pütz, Eduard 1911–
    Merchant 8706
Pütz, Johannes
    Caesar 5416
Pye, Kellow John 1812–1901
    Cymbeline 2703; P. Pilgrim 20672
Pyle, Gerry
    Hamlet 3610

Q

Qu Yong-ji
    Merchant 8759
Quesnel, Steven R.
    L.L.L. 6332
Quilter, Roger Cuthbert 1877–1953
    As You Like It 783, 1137, 1496, 1753,
    1850, 1922; Cymbeline 2602, 2704; Hamlet
    3774; Henry VIII 5155; L.L.L. 6597;
    Measure 7960; Merchant 8619; Dream
    10269; Much Ado 11506; Tempest 15562,
    15729, 15929; Twelfth Night 17611,
    17993, 18171; Two Gentlemen 18554;
    Winter's Tale 19058
Quincy, George 1944–
    Richard III 12946
Quine, Hector, arr.
    Cymbeline 2768; Merry Wives 9171
Quinn, J. Mark 1936–
    Pseudonym used by James J. Quinn
    Settings of Commemorative Pieces . . .
    21073

R

R., J. A., arr.
    Dream 9781
Raaj, Prayag
    Antony 343; Othello 12458
Rabaud, Henri 1873–1949
    Antony 218
Rabaud, Henri, arr. 1873–1949
    Merchant 8285
Rabaud, Hippolyte, arr.
    Hamlet 3670
Rabe, Folke 1935–
    1 Henry IV 4408; 2 Henry IV 4586
Raben, Peer 1940–
    Caesar 5417; Merchant 8286; Much Ado
    11243; Romeo 13804; Shrew 14446;
    Twelfth Night 17154
Rabenalt, Peter
    All's Well 52; Winter's Tale 18852
Rabenstein, Hans-Martin
    Romeo 13403

Race, Steve 1921–
    K. John 5618; Richard III 12947; Twelfth
    Night 17155
Rachinskii, Ivan Ivanovich 1861–1921
    Cymbeline 2705; Tempest 15855
Račiūnas, Antanas 1905–
    Sonnet 155 20573
Radchenko, Oleksandr 1894–1975
    Hamlet 3362; Lear 5892; Othello 11903
Radcliffe, J.
    Tempest 15730
Radecke, Albert Martin Robert 1830–1911
    K. John 5619, 5648; Timon 16386
Radford, Robert H.
    Sonnet 18 19412
Radić, Dušan 1929–
    Dream 9942
Radicati, Felice Alessandro 1778–1823
    Coriolanus 2426
Radin, Oscar
    Lear 5893; Macbeth 7102; Othello 11904;
    Richard III 12948
Radó, Aladár 1882–1914
    Merchant 8416
Radwan, Stanisław
    All's Well 53; Hamlet 3363; Lear 5894;
    Troilus 16517, 16518
Radzievskyi, N.
    Othello 11905
Rae, Allan
    Much Ado 11244; Tempest 15223; Troilus
    16519
Raff, Joseph Joachim 1822–1882
    Macbeth 7471; Dream 10943; Othello
    12421; Romeo 13952; Tempest 16095
Raff, Joseph Joachim, arr. 1822–1882
    Romeo 13730
Raffman, Relly 1921–
    Merry Wives 9206; Sonnet 18 19413;
    Sonnet 30 19617; Sonnet 87 20094;
    P. Pilgrim 20673
Raffone, Nicola
    Macbeth 7103
Ragland, Jim
    Winter's Tale 18853
Raguin, Daniel
    Tempest 15224
Rahe, Anne
    Richard III 12949
Rahikainen, Esko
    L.L.L. 6598
Rahner, Hans, arr.
    Othello 12201
Rainone, John
    Much Ado 11245
Rajičić, Stanojlo 1910–
    Dream 9943; Romeo 13404
Raka Cameng, Anak Agung
    Tempest 15225

Rakhmaninov, Sergei Vasil'evich
  1873–1943
  Richard II 12750
Rakhmaninov, Sergei Vasil'evich, arr.
  1873–1943
  Dream 9782
Rakhmanov, Nikolai Nikolaevich 1892–1964
  Also known as Nikolai Nikolaevich
  Rakhmanov-Sokolov
  Hamlet 3364; Twelfth Night 17156
Rakhmanov, P.
  Twelfth Night 17157
Rakov, N[ikolai Petrovich], arr. [1908–   ]
  Hamlet 3418
Raleigh, Stuart W. 1940–
  Hamlet 3365
Ralke, Donald Edward
  Hamlet 3366; Henry V 4757; Romeo 13405
Ralph, Robert
  Twelfth Night 18172
Ralston, Alfred
  1 Henry IV 4409; 2 Henry IV 4587
Ralston, Frances Marion 1875–1952
  Dream 10695
Ramans, Çederts 1927–
  Twelfth Night 17158
Ramella, Giuseppe, arr.
  Tempest 15442
Ramin, Günter 1898–1956
  As You Like It 785; Twelfth Night 17159
Ramin, Sid, arr. 1924–
  Romeo 13607
Ramsay, Charlotte Fanning   –1904
  Also known as Lady Ramsay of Banff
  Sonnet 18 19414
Ramsdell, E. C.
  Romeo 13954
Ramsey, Basil, arr. 1929–
  As You Like It 1421, 1730
Ramsey, Carol
  Twelfth Night 17160
Ran, Shulamit 1949–
  Othello 12245
Randall, Ronald Francis
  Hamlet 4018
Randegger, Alberto 1832–1911
  Sonnet 109 20283
Randel, Andreas, in part arr. 1806–1864
  Macbeth 7104
Randel, Andreas, arr. 1806–1864
  Macbeth 6715
Randon, Camille
  Caesar 5563
Rangström, Ture 1884–1947
  Coriolanus 2332; Hamlet 3367; 1 Henry IV
  4410; 2 Henry IV 4588; Lear 5895; Macbeth
  7105; Tempest 16096
Rani, Bulo C.
  Romeo 13406

Ranieri, Silvio, arr.
  Merry Wives 9117
Ránki, György
  All's Well 54; Dream 9944
Ranta, Sulho Veikko Juhani 1901–1960
  Merchant 8287, 8707; Othello 11906
Raphael, Juliet
  Sonnet 29 19577
Raphael, Mark
  Sonnet 18 19415
Raphling, Sam 1910–
  As You Like It 973, 1952; Hamlet 3611;
  2 Henry VI 4925; Macbeth 7503; Merchant
  8721; Dream 10752; Othello 12442; Romeo
  14034; Tempest 16174; Twelfth Night 18263
Rapley, Edmond Felton, arr. 1907–
  Errors 2217; Romeo 13608; Shrew 14615
Raposo, Joseph
  As You Like It 786; Hamlet 3368
Rapp, Thomas D.
  Sonnet 65 19898
Rasely, Charles W. 1921–
  Sonnet 18 19416
Raskin, David
  Othello 12459
Rasmus, Tyra
  Merchant 8288
Rasmussen, Geraldine Dorothy 1925–
  As You Like It 1138; Hamlet 3612, 3856;
  Caesar 5482, 5495; Lear 6021; Merchant
  8677
Rastrelli, Joseph 1799–1842
  Also known as Goseffo Rastrelli and as
  Giuseppe Rastrelli
  Macbeth 7106
Ratcliffe, Desmond, arr. 1917–
  As You Like It 436; Twelfth Night 17314
Rathaus, Karol 1895–1954
  Henry VIII 5156; Merchant 8289
Rathbone, Christopher Bruce 1947–
  As You Like It 1826; Coriolanus 2333; Lear
  5896; L.L.L. 6277; Dream 9945; Sonnet 18
  19417
Rathbone, George 1874–
  Henry VIII 5157; Merchant 8462; Two
  Gentlemen 18555
Rathbone, George, arr. 1874–
  As You Like It 1463
Rathjens, Klaus-Joachim
  All's Well 55
Rathrobert, F.
  Tempest 16097
Ratiu, Adrian 1928–
  Measure 7961; Merchant 8620; P. Pilgrim
  20674
Ratti, Leopoldo, arr.
  Othello 12143, 12144, 12145
Rauber, François
  Dream 9946

Rauch, J. N., arr.
Dream 9783, 9784
Rauh, Adam
Dream 9947
Raukhverger, Mikhail Rafailovich 1901–
Merry Wives 8938
Rautavaara, Einojuhani 1928–
Sonnet 12 19289; Sonnet 18 19418; Sonnet
73 20013
Rauzzini, Venanzio 1746–1810
Dream 10976
Rauzzini, Venanzio, arr. 1746–1810
Cymbeline 2856
Raven, Richard, arr.
Errors 2218
[Ravenscroft, Thomas] [circa 1582–circa
1635]
Twelfth Night 17691
Ravnkilde, Niels 1823–1890
Romeo 14172
Rawlings, Thomas A., arr. 1775–[circa 1850]
Cymbeline 2659; Dream 10376
Rawls, Adelaide Miller
Much Ado 11246
Rawsthorne, Alan 1905–1971
Also wrote under the pseudonym 'Pandora'
As You Like It 1139; Hamlet 3369, 3841;
Lear 5897; L.L.L. 6461; Dream 10696;
Othello 12343; Tempest 15563; Sonnet 18
19419; P. Pilgrim 20675
Ray, Helen Davis
Much Ado 11247
Ray, Satyajit 1922–
Antony 344; Othello 12460
Raymond, Eduard 1812–
Tempest 15463
Raymond, Emma Marcy
As You Like It 787
Raymond, Louisa
As You Like It 1754
Raynaud, Armand 1848–1900
Also known as Armand Reynaud
Lear 6008
Raynor, John 1909–1970
As You Like It 1498, 1755; Cymbeline 2603,
2706; Measure 7962; Much Ado 11507;
Twelfth Night 17613, 17994
Razlag, Filip
Antony 219; As You Like It 788; Lear 5898;
Othello 11907; Shrew 14447; Tempest
15226; Troilus 16520; Twelfth Night
17161, 17162; Winter's Tale 18854
Rea, Alan 1933–
Merry Wives 9155
Read, Gardner 1913–
Dream 10697
Reaks, Brian Harold James 1920–
Tempest 15227, 15564, 15930; Twelfth
Night 17163, 17614

Reale, Paul Vincent 1943–
Hamlet 4075
Reay, Samuel 1822–1905
As You Like It 1499; Measure 7963;
P. Pilgrim 20676
Reay, Samuel, arr. 1822–1905
Dream 9785
Rebel, François 1701–1775
Dream 10977
Rechberger, Herman 1947–
Dream 9948
Rechid Rey, Djemal 1904–
Hamlet 3370
Rechnitzer-Möller, Hennig 1889–
Sonnet 18 19420; Sonnet 71 19962
Rechter, Yoni
Twelfth Night 17164
Reckers, Dieter
Coriolanus 2389
Redding, Joseph D.
Romeo 14173
Redeghieri, Fulvio
Macbeth 7107
Redern, Friedrich Wilhelm 1802–1883
Also known as Graf von Redern
Tempest 16098
Redfield, Liza
Errors 2162
Redford, J. A. C. 1953–
Macbeth 7108; Dream 9949
Redhead, Alfred Edward [1857?]–1937
Twelfth Night 18339
Redhead, Alfred Edward, arr.
[1857?]–1937
As You Like It 437
Redlich, Hans Ferdinand, ed. 1903–1968
Twelfth Night 18323; Settings of
Commemorative Pieces . . . 21289
Redman, Douglas
Winter's Tale 19059
Redstone, William
Macbeth 7109
Reece, Helen
Merchant 8290
Reed, Alfred 1921–
Hamlet 4019; Dream 10698; Othello 12344,
12422; Tempest 15228, 15731
Reed, Franklin
Othello 11908
Reed, Marion Guendolen
Romeo 13407
Reed, Michael
Merchant 8291
Reed, Thomas German 1817–1888
Romeo 13408
Reed, Thomas German, arr. 1817–1888
Macbeth 6998
Reed, William
Merchant 8463

Reed, William Henry 1876–1942
Tempest 16099
Reed, William Henry, arr. 1876–1942
Dream 10245
Reed, William Leonard, arr. 1910–
Dream 10246
Reekes, J[ohn?]
L.L.L. 6666; Romeo 14035; Twelfth Night
17995; Sonnet 18 19421; Sonnet 33 19654;
Sonnet 87 20095; Sonnet 97 20169; Sonnet
98 20190; Venus 20796
Rees-Davies, Ieuan
Twelfth Night 17996
Reesen, Emil 1887–1964
As You Like It 789; Hamlet 3371; Shrew
14448; Twelfth Night 17165
Reesen, Emil, in part arr. 1887–1964
As You Like It 790; Merchant 8292; Othello
11909
Reesen, Morten, arr. 1928–1961
As You Like It 791, 792
Reeve, George W.
Settings of Commemorative Pieces . . .
20883
Reeve, William 1757–1815
As You Like It 1987; Hamlet 4236; 1 Henry
IV 4506; Romeo 14174
Reeves, Ernest
Tempest 16100
Reeves, Ernest, arr.
Dream 10247
Reeves, Geoffrey
Caesar 5418
Reeves, Ike
Sonnet 18 19422; Settings of
Commemorative Pieces . . . 21306
Regan, Andy
Much Ado 11248; Tempest 15229
Regan, Michael James 1947–
As You Like It 1756; L.L.L. 6462; Dream
10543; Much Ado 11508; Twelfth Night
17615
Reggio, Pietro Francesco [1632?]–1685
Tempest 15464
Regi, A.
Merry Wives 8939
Regondi, Guilo, arr. 1822–1872
Othello 12146, 12147
Rehman, Carl
Romeo 14175
Reibold, Bruno, arr.
Dream 9786
Reich, Johannes
Twelfth Night 17166
Reicha, Antoine-Joseph 1770–1836
Also known as Antonín Rejcha and as
Anton Rejcha
Hamlet 3857

Reichardt, Johann Friedrich 1752–1814
Also wrote under the pseudonym 'Trahcier'
As You Like It 1757; Cymbeline 2707;
Macbeth 7110; Measure 7964; Dream
10978; Tempest 15465
Reichardt, Luise
[Louise Reichardt (1779–1826)?]
Henry VIII 5158
Reichel, Adolph 1820–1896
Also known as Adolf Reichel
L.L.L. 6463, 6599; Twelfth Night 17997
Reichenbach, Horst
Much Ado 11249
Reichlin, Gerald
Caesar 5419
Reif, Paul 1910–1978
Hamlet 3613; Sonnet 73 20014
Reiff, Antony
Also known as Anthony Reiff
Tempest 15230
Reiff, Lily
Dream 10979
Reiff, Wilhelm 1833–1870
Caesar 5420; Merchant 8293; Winter's Tale
18855
Reijnders, Nard 1951–
Lear 5899; Dream 9950
Reimann, Aribert 1936–
Lear 6009; Sonnet 43 19716; Sonnet 65
19899; Sonnet 137 20447
Reimann, Ralf Rainer
Twelfth Night 17167
Reinecker, Gunther
Othello 11911
Reinthaler, Karl Martin 1822–1896
As You Like It 1758; Othello 12423
Reisacher, John
As You Like It 793; Errors 2163; Hamlet
3372; Merchant 8294; Merry Wives 8940;
Much Ado 11250; Romeo 13409; Shrew
14449; Twelfth Night 17168
Reisch, Friedrich
Tempest 15231
Reise, Jay 1950–
Antony 308
Reise, Karl
Hamlet 3373
Reißiger, Carl 1798–1859
Macbeth 7111
Reizenstein, Franz Theodor 1911–1968
Measure 7738
Reizman, Shosh
Also known as Shosh Reisman
Macbeth 7112; Romeo 14061
Rektorys, Artuš 1935–
Hamlet 3374; Othello 11912; Romeo
13410
Rémusat, Jean, arr. 1815–1880
Othello 12148

Remy, Francis
    Cymbeline 2873
Renaud de Vilbac, Alphonse Zoé Charles
    1829–1884
    Also known as Alphonse-Zoé-Charles
    Renaud de Vilback and as Alfonse Charles
    Renaud de Vilback
    Hamlet 4020
Renaud de Vilbac, Alphonse Zoé Charles, arr.
    1829–1884
    Also known as Alphonse-Zoé-Charles
    Renaud de Vilback and as Alfonse Charles
    Renaud de Vilback
    Dream 9787, 9788; Romeo 13731, 13732
Renault, C., arr.
    Hamlet 3671
Rennert, Wolfgang
    Timon 16353
Renosto, Paolo 1935–
    Macbeth 7285
Renton, Victor
    Tempest 16101
Renzi, Armando 1915–
    Much Ado 11251
Repossy, Charles, arr. 1847–1902
    Merry Wives 9193; Othello 12202
Reppond, Gene
    Twelfth Night 17169
Respighi, Elsa, arr. 1895–
    Née Olivieri-Sangiacomo
    Lucrece 20770
Respighi, Ottorino 1879–1936
    Hamlet 3614; Lucrece 20769
Restrepo, Juan Luis
    Macbeth 7113
Retford, M., arr.
    Henry VIII 5023; Othello 12526, 12527;
    Shrew 14360
Rettich, Wilhelm 1892–
    Sonnet 8 19259; Sonnet 18 19423; Sonnet
    128 20400
Reutter, Hermann 1900–1985
    Hamlet 3615, 3775, 3809, 3842, 3858,
    3873
Revallo, Jozef
    Tempest 15232
Révillon, Ferdinand
    Tempest 16102
Revuts'kyi, Lev Mykolaiovych 1889–1977
    Errors 2164; Lear 5900
Rex, Gary
    Sonnet 18 19424; Sonnet 19 19469; Sonnet
    40 19692; Sonnet 55 19784; Sonnet 60
    19834; Sonnet 62 19862; Sonnet 66 19917;
    Sonnet 121 20358; Sonnet 138 20456;
    Sonnet 145 20485; Sonnet 147 20516;
    Sonnet 148 20521
Rexhäuser, Ferdinand 1924–
    Shrew 14450

Rexhäuser, Ferdinand, arr. 1924–
    As You Like It 940
Rey, Cemal Reşit 1904–
    Lear 5901; Macbeth 7114; Much Ado
    11252; Tempest 15233
Rey, Horst
    Merchant 8295
Rey, Jean-Baptiste 1734–1810
    Lear 5902; Macbeth 7115
Reyes, James E.
    Othello 11913
Reynardson, Herbert Frederick Birch
    Twelfth Night 18173
Reynolds, Alfred 1884–1969
    Merchant 8296; Much Ado 11253, 11605;
    Shrew 14451, 14665
Reynolds, B.
    [Barbara Reynolds?]
    As You Like It 1140
Reynolds, Barbara
    As You Like It 1500
Reynolds, Charles Tom 1865–
    As You Like It 1501
Reynolds, Roger Lee 1934–
    Tempest 15234
Reznick, David
    Hamlet 4076; Measure 8030; Twelfth Night
    18264; Settings of Commemorative
    Pieces . . . 21235
Reznikov, N.
    Lear 5903
Rheinberger, Josef Gabriel 1839–1901
    Also known as Joseph Gabriel Rheinberger,
    as Josef Gabriel von Rheinberger, and as
    Gabriel Josef Rheinberger
    Errors 2252; Shrew 14666
Rhodes, Harold William 1889–1956
    Henry VIII 5159
Rhys, Stephen 1926–
    Sonnet 155 20574
Riario Sforza, Giovanni 1769–1836
    Dream 10980
Ribári, Antal 1924–
    Sonnet 113 20298; Sonnet 119 20352
Ricci, Clara Ross
    As You Like It 1502; Henry VIII 5160;
    Tempest 15931
Ricci, Luigi, arr.
    Lucrece 20771
Rice, Eric
    Tempest 15235
Rice, P.
    Romeo 13955
Rice, Paul Francis 1949–
    As You Like It 1827
Rich, Marie
    Tempest 15732
Richards, Arthur
    As You Like It 1759

Richards, Henry Brinley 1817–1885
Dream 10699; Tempest 16103
Richards, Henry Brinley, arr. 1817–1885
Merry Wives 8884; Dream 10876; Romeo
13733, 13734; Twelfth Night 16678, 18071
Richards, John Eric 1921–
Tempest 15733; Sonnet 73 20015
Richards, Richard
Tempest 16104
Richardson, Alfred Madeley 1868–1949
As You Like It 1503, 1760; Much Ado
11509; Shrew 14687; Tempest 15734,
15932; Twelfth Night 17998; Venus
20797
Richardson, Norman, arr.
Richard III 13017
Richardson, Thomas
P. Pilgrim 20677
Richmond, Eero 1938–
Measure 7965; Merchant 8621; Tempest
15933
Richmond, Jeff
Tempest 15236
Richmond, Legh 1772–1827
Merchant 8622
Richter, Carl, arr.
Pseudonym used by Henry Dellafield. [Carl
Arthur Richter (1883–1957)?]
Cymbeline 2769; Merry Wives 9118; Two
Gentlemen 18596
Richter, Kurt Dietmar, arr. 1931–
L.L.L. 6325
Rickard, Gene Paul
Much Ado 11254; Settings of
Commemorative Pieces . . . 21197
Rickards, Ernest H.
L.L.L. 6464, 6600
Rickett, Edmond W.
As You Like It 794; Errors 2165; Hamlet
4122; Macbeth 7116; Dream 10759
Riddle, Ron
[Ronald William Riddle (1934–   )?]
As You Like It 795
Riding, Henry
Cymbeline 2604
Ridley, Helen
Dream 9951
Ridley, Sebastian Claude
Dream 10700; Tempest 16105
Ridout, Alan John 1934–
L.L.L. 6601; Dream 10544; Tempest 15808,
16106; Troilus 16569; P. Pilgrim 20678
Riedl, Josef Anton 1927–
Antony 220; Tempest 15237
Riedlbauch, Václav 1947–
Lear 6116; Macbeth 7286, 7504; Sonnet 75
20038
Riege, Ernest 1885–1976
Much Ado 11606

Riegger, Wallingford Constantin 1885–1961
Also wrote under the pseudonyms 'Z.G.' and
'Gerald Wilfring Gore'
Sonnet 138 20457
Riegger, Wallingford Constantin, arr.
1885–1961
Also wrote under the pseudonyms 'Z.G.' and
'Gerald Wilfring Gore'
Cymbeline 2770; Two Gentlemen 18597
Riem, Wilhelm Friedrich 1779–1857
Twelfth Night 17616
Ries, Ferdinand 1784–1838
Macbeth 7407
Ries, Ferdinand, arr. 1784–1838
Errors 2045, 2046; Two Gentlemen 18368
Riesenfeld, Hugo 1879–1939
Tempest 16288
Rieti, Vittorio 1898–
As You Like It 1504
Rietz, August Wilhelm Julius 1812–1877
As You Like It 796; Hamlet 3375; Macbeth
7117; Tempest 15467, 16107; Twelfth
Night 17170; Settings of Commemorative
Pieces . . . 20884
Rigby, H.
Tempest 15565
Rihm, Alexander, arr.
Lear 6065
Rihm, Wolfgang 1952–
Hamlet 4175, 4286
Riley, Alice C. D., adapter
Settings of Commemorative Pieces . . . 20952
Riley, Dennis 1943–
Antony 309; Richard II 12755
Riley, John, arr.
Errors 2245
Riley, Tim 1966–
As You Like It 797
[Rimbault, Edward Francis, ed.]
[1816–1876]
Anthologies 21316
Rimbault, Edward Francis, arr. 1816–1876
Macbeth 6814, 6926, 6999, 7349; Dream
9789, 9790, 9791; Othello 12309; Tempest
14818, 14819
Rimmer, Drake
Othello 12424
Rimmer, Drake, arr.
Henry VIII 5024
Rimmer, John Francis 1939–
Dream 9952
Rimmer, W[illiam] [1862–1936]
As You Like It 1923; Hamlet 4021; Measure
8029; Twelfth Night 18246; Two Gentlemen
18646; Winter's Tale 19120
Rimskaia-Korsakova, Nadezhda Nikolaevna,
arr. 1848–1919
Née Purgol'd
Romeo 14001

Ringuet, Leon
    Romeo 13956
Rintel, Wilhelm 1818–
    [Also wrote under the pseudonym 'W. Litner']
    Twelfth Night 17406
Riotte, Philipp Jakob 1776–1856
    Tempest 15468
Ripley, Frederic H., arr.
    Cymbeline 2771; Two Gentlemen 18598
Risher, Anna Priscilla
    As You Like It 1141; L.L.L. 6602; Tempest
    15934; Twelfth Night 17999
Ritchie, Anthony Damian 1960–
    L.L.L. 6662
Ritchie, John Anthony 1921–
    As You Like It 798, 1761; Henry VIII
    5011; Caesar 5421, 5422; Tempest 15238,
    15735
Ritchie, Roy 1954–[before 1985]
    Hamlet 3376
Ritchie, Tom Vernon 1922–
    Merchant 8464
Ritsher, Louise
    Merchant 8297
Ritter, Ernst Wilhelm, arr.
    Dream 10877; Shrew 14583
Ritter, Frédéric Louis [1824]–1891
    Othello 12426
Ritter, H.
    Tempest 15469
Ritter, Peter 1763–1846
    Merry Wives 9156; Tempest 15470
Ritter, Théodore 1841–1886
    Pseudonym used by Théodore Bennet
    Dream 10701
Ritter, Théodore, arr. 1841–1886
    Pseudonym used by Théodore Bennet
    Merry Wives 9119; Dream 9792; Romeo
    13573, 13574, 13735
Rittman, Trude, arr.
    Shrew 14616
Rivalet, Andrei
    Shrew 14452
Rivers, Gertrude Eloise
    Macbeth 7382
Rivers, Patrick C., arr.
    Tempest 14820
Rivier, Jean 1896–
    1 Henry IV 4411; 2 Henry IV 4589
Rivière, Jules 1819–1900
    Antony 323
Rivière, Jules, arr. 1819–1900
    Romeo 13898
Rix, Carol May
    Macbeth 7118
Rix, Frank Reader, arr. 1853–
    Two Gentlemen 18599
Roach, Maxwell 1924–
    Dream 9953

Robb, Graham 1950–
    Tempest 15239
Robbins, John
    As You Like It 1988
Roberton, Hugh Stevenson 1874–1952
    Cymbeline 2605; Merchant 8465; Tempest
    15736
Roberton, Hugh Stevenson, arr.
    1874–1952
    As You Like It 438; Tempest 15839
Roberts, Charles J., arr. 1868–1957
    Merry Wives 9120; Dream 9793, 10878
Roberts, Clifford 1889–
    Tempest 15240
Roberts, Gertrud Hermine Kuenzel 1906–
    Tempest 15241
Roberts, Henry Stephen
    As You Like It 2014
Roberts, Jane A. 1933–
    Twelfth Night 17171
Roberts, Rick
    Tempest 15242; Twelfth Night 17172
Roberts, Stefan
    Dream 10760
Roberts, Timothy, arr.
    Timon 16347
Roberts, Virginia Anne
    Merchant 8623
Robinson, Andrew
    Much Ado 11255
Robinson, Charles Wyndham
    As You Like It 799, 1762; Twelfth Night
    17173, 17617, 18174
Robinson, James
    As You Like It 1142
Robinson, Lavan
    Dream 9954
Robinson, Stanford F. H. 1904–1984
    Merchant 8298
Robinson, Stanford F. H., arr. 1904–1984
    As You Like It 439; Merchant 8747; Dream
    10248
Robinson, Stuart K.
    Shrew 14453
Robison, Steve
    Macbeth 7119
Robuschi, Ferdinando 1765–1850
    Caesar 5564
Rocco, Davor 1948–
    Hamlet 3377; Romeo 14062
Rochard, Jules
    As You Like It 2015
Rochard, Jules, arr.
    Macbeth 7000; Merry Wives 8885; Dream
    9794, 9795, 10879; Tempest 14737,
    14821, 15124; Twelfth Night 16679; Two
    Gentlemen 18369
Rochberg, George 1918–
    Lear 6090

Roche, Alexander D.
Tempest 16289
Rock, Michael   −1809
Macbeth 7368
Rock, William
As You Like It 1505
Rockstro, William Smith, arr. 1823−1895
Dream 10880
Roderick Jones, Richard Trevor 1947−
As You Like It 1961; Errors 2257; Cymbeline
2835; Macbeth 7120; Measure 7739;
Merchant 8733; Dream 9955, 10761; Much
Ado 11256; Othello 12461; Tempest 15243,
16191; Twelfth Night 18275; Settings of
Commemorative Pieces . . . 20885
Rodgers, John Arthur
As You Like It 1506
Rodgers, Mary 1931−
Also known as Mary Rodgers Guettel
As You Like It 1507; Dream 10417; Tempest
15566, 15737; Twelfth Night 18000
Rodgers, Richard Charles 1902−1979
Errors 2206; Much Ado 11368
Rodmann, Harry
Twelfth Night 17174
Rodrigo, Joaquin 1902−
Two Gentlemen 18420
Rodriguez, Andre
Troilus 16521
Rodriguez, Robert Xavier 1946−
Macbeth 7121
Roeckel, A., arr.
Macbeth 7255
Roeckel, Jane
Also wrote under the pseudonym 'Jules de
Sivrai'
Tempest 16108
Roemheld, Heinz 1901−
Settings of Commemorative Pieces . . . 21261
Roff, Joseph 1910−
Merchant 8678; Othello 12345; Tempest
15738
Roffe, Alfred Thomas, arr. 1808−1871
Dream 10159
Roffman, Frederick S.
Twelfth Night 17175
Roger, Kurt George 1895−1966
As You Like It 1143; Tempest 15739, 15935
Roger-Ducasse, Jean Jules, arr. 1873−1954
Lear 5726
Rogers, Bernard 1893−1968
Hamlet 4022
Rogers, Clara Kathleen 1844−1931
Née Barnett; also known as Clara Doria
Twelfth Night 18074
Rogers, E. W.
Merry Wives 9157
Rogers, Eric   −1981
Antony 345; Caesar 5542

Rogers, James Hotchkiss 1857−1940
Much Ado 11510
Rogers, Leonard L.
1 Henry IV 4472
Rogers, Paul [I]
Macbeth 7122
Rogers, Paul [II]
Macbeth 7123
Rögner, Heinz 1929−
Macbeth 7124; Romeo 13411
Rogowski, Ludomir Michał 1881−1954
As You Like It 800; 1 Henry IV 4412;
2 Henry IV 4590; Othello 11914; Winter's
Tale 18856
Rohde, Rolf
Measure 7740
Rohe, Robert Kenneth 1920−
Dream 9956
Rohe, Robert Kenneth, in part arr. 1920−
Twelfth Night 17176
Röhl, Uwe
Measure 7741
Röhlig, Eginhard
Tempest 15244
Rohrkamp, Michael
Dream 9957
Rokhlina, E.
Two Gentlemen 18421
Roland, G. F.
Dream 10702
Roldan, Francisco
Two Gentlemen 18422
Rolfe, Walter, arr.
Dream 9796
Rolle, Johann Heinrich 1718−1785
Tempest 15471
Romani, G., arr. 1917−
Romeo 13736
Romano, Giuseppe, arr.
Settings of Commemorative Pieces . . .
20911
Romberg, Sigmund 1887−1951
Romeo 14109
Rome, Harold Jacob 1908−
Romeo 14063; Twelfth Night 18285
Romeo, James Joseph 1955−
Othello 12427
Róna, Frigyes
Romeo 13412
Ronger, Florimond 1825−1892
Wrote under the pseudonym 'Hervé'
Romeo 14110
Ronsheim, John Richard 1927−
Also known as John-Richard Ronsheim
Sonnet 100 20209
Röntgen, Johannes 1898−1969
Sonnet 8 19260
Ronzi, Gaspare
Romeo 13805

Roos, André
    L.L.L. 6278; Macbeth 7125; Measure 7742;
    Dream 9958
Root, George Frederick 1820–1895
    Cymbeline 2883
Rootham, Cyril Bradley 1875–1938
    Much Ado 11511; Tempest 15740; Sonnet
    18 19425
Rootham, Cyril Bradley, arr. 1875–1938
    Dream 10249, 10250
Roper, Edgar Stanley, arr. [1879?]–1953
    Merry Wives 9172
Roques, Jean Léon, arr. 1839–
    Cymbeline 2842; Richard III 13036
Rorem, Ned 1923–
    All's Well 101; Henry V 4828; Lear 6091;
    Merchant 8708; Dream 10703; Othello
    12428; Romeo 13957; Tempest 16109,
    16290; Sonnet 8 19273; Sonnet 30 19630;
    Sonnet 33 19655; Sonnet 60 19844; Sonnet
    129 20412; P. Pilgrim 20679
Rose, Barbara
    Hamlet 3378
Rose, Cyrille, arr. 1830–[circa 1902]
    Hamlet 3672
Rose, David [1919–   ]
    Romeo 13413
Rose, Ina Wolf
    Sonnet 18 19426
Rose, John Luke 1933–
    As You Like It 1508; Macbeth 7473; P.
    Pilgrim 20680
Roseberry, Eric Norman 1930–
    Coriolanus 2334
Rosebrook, Leon
    Macbeth 7549
Roseingrave, Thomas 1688–1766
    Also known as Thomas Rosengrave
    Timon 16354
Rösel, Arthur
    Lear 5904; Richard III 12950, 12951;
    Romeo 13414
Roselius, Ludwig Wilhelm 1902–1977
    As You Like It 1509, 1763
Rosellen, Henri 1811–1876
    Winter's Tale 19121
Rosellen, Henri, arr. 1811–1876
    Othello 12149, 12150; Romeo 13737;
    Tempest 15423; Settings of Commemorative
    Pieces . . . 20974
Rosellin, Léon
    Romeo 14111
Rosen, Albert
    Errors 2166
Rosen, Jerome William 1921–
    Othello 11915
Rosen, Lewis Maxwell
    L.L.L. 6680

Rosen, Zvi
    Errors 2167
Rosenberg, Hilding 1892–1985
    Merchant 8299; Richard III 12952; Twelfth
    Night 17177
Rosenberg, Hilding, arr. 1892–1985
    Romeo 13481
Rosenberg, Kai 1898–1977
    Macbeth 7126, 7127; Measure 7743
Rosenberg, Philip
    All's Well 56; Hamlet 3379; 1 Henry IV
    4413; Lear 5905; L.L.L. 6279; Macbeth
    7128; Much Ado 11257; Othello 11916;
    Romeo 13415; Shrew 14454; Tempest
    15245
Rosenberg, Philip, arr.
    Dream 9797; Twelfth Night 16612
Rosenberg, Rick
    Lear 6011
Rosenberg, Vilhelm 1862–1944
    Othello 11917; Shrew 14455
Rosenboom, David 1947–
    Tempest 16237
Rosenfeld, Gerhard 1931–
    Richard II 12709
Rosenfeld, Isidor
    Richard III 13059
Rosengart, Lucien
    Winter's Tale 18857
Rosenmüller, Henri, arr.
    Tempest 14738, 14822, 15125
Rosewig, Albert Henry 1846–1929
    Settings of Commemorative Pieces . . . 21168
Rosner, Bernice 1912–
    Dream 10704
Rosolak, Stephen, arr.
    As You Like It 589
Ross, Edith Irene
    Also known as Irene Varley Ross
    As You Like It 1510; Twelfth Night 18001
Ross, Hugh, arr.
    [Hugh Cuthbert Melville Ross (1898–   )?]
    Sonnet 66 19921
Ross, Robert A. M.
    Sonnet 130 20427
Ross, Theodor
    Pericles 12588
Rosse, Frederick 1867–1940
    Merchant 8300, 8624
Rosse, Frederick, arr. 1867–1940
    Much Ado 11548
Rossellini, Renzo 1908–1982
    Winter's Tale 19153
Rossetter, G.
    Merchant 8625
Rossi, Giuseppe 1761–
    Dream 10981
Rossi, Lauro 1810–1885
    Antony 382; Macbeth 7550

Rossi, Nick, adapter 1924–
As You Like It 1851
Rossini, Gioachino Antonio 1792–1868
MSS signed 'Gioachino'; commonly known
as Gioacchino Rossini
Othello 12038; Romeo 14176
Rößler, Klaus
Twelfth Night 17178
Rößler, Wolfgang
Dream 9959
Rota, Giuseppe, arr.
Othello 12151
Rota, Nino 1911–1979
Also known as Nino Rinaldi
Much Ado 11258; Romeo 13416, 13417,
13418; Shrew 14456; Twelfth Night 17179
Roters, Ernst 1892–1961
Hamlet 3616; Dream 9960; Twelfth Night
17180
Roth, Alfred, arr.
Dream 9798
Roth, David A.
Sonnet 116 20329
Roth, Michael S. 1954–
As You Like It 801; Cymbeline 2483; Romeo
13429; Shrew 14457
Roth, Michael S., in part arr. 1954–
As You Like It 802
Rothenborg, Niels
Lear 5906
Rothenhagen, Franz
Merchant 8305
Rother, Werner
As You Like It 803; Macbeth 7129; Measure
7744; Much Ado 11259; Richard II 12710;
Romeo 13430; Twelfth Night 17181
Rothmüller, Aron Marko 1908–
Sonnet 30 19631
Roti, Ugo
Dream 10270
Rötsch, Heinrich
Henry V 4758; 1 Henry VI 4864; 2 Henry VI
4905; 3 Henry VI 4947; Richard II 12711
Rousseau, Jean Jacques 1712–1778
Othello 12346
Roussey, Maria
Twelfth Night 17182
Routh, Francis 1927–
As You Like It 1144; Hamlet 3776; Henry
VIII 5161; Much Ado 11512
Routier, Léon, arr.   –1895
Romeo 13738
Rövenstrunck, Bernhard 1920–
As You Like It 1145, 1764; Henry VIII
5162; L.L.L. 6465, 6603; Merchant 8466;
Dream 10465, 10545; Richard II 12756;
Sonnet 66 19918
Rovics, Howard, in part arr. 1936–
Winter's Tale 18858

Rowland, Alexander Campbell 1826–1896
Twelfth Night 18075
Rowland, David
Antony 221
Rowley, Alec 1892–1958
As You Like It 1511, 1765; L.L.L. 6604;
Dream 10705; Much Ado 11513; Twelfth
Night 18175; Winter's Tale 18983, 19015,
19086
Rowley, Alec, arr. 1892–1958
As You Like It 440, 441; Cymbeline 2619;
Merchant 8099; Two Gentlemen 18493
Roy, Klaus George 1924–
As You Like It 804; Othello 11918
Roy, Klaus George, in part arr. 1924–
Twelfth Night 17183
Rôze, J. H. Raymond 1875–1920
Also known as Raymond Roze and as
Raymond Rôze-Perkins
Antony 222; 1 Henry IV 4414; Henry V
4759; Caesar 5423; K. John 5620; Dream
10418; Much Ado 11260; Shrew 14458;
Tempest 15246; Sonnet 40 19693, 19702;
P. Pilgrim 20746
Rôze, J. H. Raymond, [in part] arr.
1875–1920
Also known as Raymond Roze and as
Raymond Rôze-Perkins
Merry Wives 8941
Rôze, J. H. Raymond, in part arr. 1875–1920
Also known as Raymond Roze and as
Raymond Rôze-Perkins
Dream 9961
Rôze, J. H. Raymond, arr. 1875–1920
Also known as Raymond Roze and as
Raymond Rôze-Perkins
Dream 9799
Rózsa, Miklós Nicholas 1907–
Hamlet 4123; Caesar 5424; Merchant 8734;
Othello 12462
Różycki, Ludomir 1884–1953
Merchant 8306
Rubbra, Charles Edmund 1901–1986
Also known as Edmund Duncan-Rubbra
As You Like It 1512; Henry VIII 5163;
Macbeth 7130; Measure 7966; Two
Gentlemen 18556
Ruben, Paul
L.L.L. 6681
Rubens, Hugo 1905–[before 1983]
L.L.L. 6663
Rubens, Paul Alfred 1875–1917
Caesar 5549; Measure 8038; Much Ado
11261; Shrew 14459; Twelfth Night 17184,
17185; Kinsmen 19170, 19174
Rubenson, Albert 1826–1901
Caesar 5518
Rubenstein, Eli
Hamlet 4176

Rubenstein, Marc
Richard III 12953
Rubenstein, Mical D. 1959–
Tempest 15247
Rüber, Ottmar
Winter's Tale 18859
Rubin, Amy
Cymbeline 2484; Romeo 13431
Rubin, Marcel 1905–
Merry Wives 8942; Shrew 14460
Rubinstein, Anton Grigor'evich 1829–1894
Antony 324
Rubinstein, Arthur
Caesar 5425; Macbeth 7131; Othello
11919
Rubinstein, Beryl 1898–1952
Dream 10706
Rubinstein, John Arthur, arr. 1946–
Twelfth Night 17391
Rubio, Robert
Dream 9962
Ruch, Hannes
Twelfth Night 18340
Ruddell, Bruce
Errors 2168; Macbeth 7132
Rüdenauer, Meinhard 1941–
Sonnet 40 19694
Rudnicki, Marian Teofil 1888–1944
Antony 223
Ruffin, L., arr.
Merry Wives 9121
Rüggeberg, Michael 1941–
As You Like It 805, 806; Macbeth 7133,
7134, 7527; Dream 9963; Much Ado 11262
Ruhm, Franz Karl
Dream 9964
Rummel, Ch., arr.
Merry Wives 9234
Rummel, Joseph, arr. 1818–1880
Macbeth 7350; Merchant 8348; Dream
10663, 10881; Othello 12152; Settings of
Commemorative Pieces . . . 20975, 20976
Rung, Frederik, in part arr. 1854–1914
Twelfth Night 17187
Rung, Henrik 1807–1871
As You Like It 807, 1766, 1852; Cymbeline
2485, 2708, 2825; Tempest 15472; Twelfth
Night 17188
Runge, John, arr.
Twelfth Night 18308
Runnström, William 1951–
Caesar 5426
Rushton, Liza
As You Like It 1767
Rushton, William Lowes
As You Like It 1989; Coriolanus 2399;
Cymbeline 2874; Hamlet 4237; Lear 6164;
Macbeth 7574; Dream 10927; Much Ado
11644; Othello 12509; Romeo 14177;

Tempest 16231; Twelfth Night 18320;
Winter's Tale 19144; Sonnet 146 20497
Russell, Anna, adapter 1911–
Stage name used by Claudia Anna Russell-
Brown
Hamlet 4177
Russell, George Allen 1923–
Othello 12172
Russell, Henry, [adapter] 1812–1900
Merry Wives 9005
Russell, Olive Nelson 1905–
Née Nelson; also known as Mrs. Clarence H.
Russell
Merchant 8467
Russell, Richard
Romeo 13432; Twelfth Night 17189
Russell, Welford Hamilton 1900–
As You Like It 1146, 1513, 1768; Measure
7967; Twelfth Night 17618, 18002
Russell, [William Henry?] [1777–1813]
Henry VIII 5012
Russell, William Henry 1777–1813
Hamlet 3735
Russo, Louis
Shrew 14461
Russo, William A. 1928–
Othello 12173; Twelfth Night 18003
Russotto, Chaim Nesvizhsky 1869–1925
Lear 6126
Rust, Friedrich Wilhelm 1739–1796
Lear 6092
Rust, W., arr.
Romeo 13561
Rustichelli, Carlo
Dream 9965
Ruth, Anita
As You Like It 808
Ruthardt, Adolf, arr.
Cymbeline 2772
Rutherford, R[obert?]
As You Like It 1514
Rutter, John 1945–
As You Like It 1147, 1515; L.L.L. 6605;
Merchant 8626
Ruyneman, Daniel 1886–1963
Sonnet 76 20050; Sonnet 98 20191;
P. Pilgrim 20681
Ruzicka, Jiri
Lear 5907
Růžička, Petr
Richard III 12954; Twelfth Night 17190
Ryall, David
As You Like It 809
Ryan, Anthony Wayne 1951–
Antony 346; 1 Henry IV 4473; Dream 9966
Rybář, Jaroslav 1942–
Dream 9967
Rydberg, Steven Maurice
Dream 9968; Romeo 13433

Ryder, A. H., arr.
  Two Gentlemen 18600, 18601
Rydman, Kari 1936–
  Troilus 16522
Ryelandt, Joseph 1870–1965
  Dream 10707
Ryley, Geoffrey Charles Edward
  P. Pilgrim 20682
Ryvkin, G.
  Romeo 13434

S

Saar, Louis Victor Franz, arr. 1868–1937
  Dream 9800; Two Gentlemen 18602
Saar, R. W., arr.
  Cymbeline 2773; Dream 9801, 9802
Sabo, William J.
  As You Like It 810; Twelfth Night 17619
Sabon, E., arr.
  Romeo 13739
Sacchi, Vincenzo
  Antony 279
Sachau, Jean H.
  Hamlet 4238
Sack, Richard F.
  Twelfth Night 17710
Sackville, Arthur
  As You Like It 1516
Sadero, Geni 1866–1961
  Pseudonym used by Eugenia Scarpa
  Othello 11920
Sadler, Michael
  Tempest 15248
Saenger, Gustav 1865–1935
  Also wrote under the pseudonym 'W. F.
  Ambrosio'
  As You Like It 811; Merchant 8307; Shrew
  14462; Twelfth Night 17191
Saenger, Gustav, arr. 1865–1935
  Also wrote under the pseudonym 'W. F.
  Ambrosio'
  Cymbeline 2774; Dream 9803
Sæverud, Harald Sigurd Johan 1897–
  Lucrece 20778, 20783
Safford, Charles L.
  Caesar 5427
Safonov, K.
  Shrew 14463
Safouan, Ismaïl
  Tempest 15249
Sager, Sidney
  Richard II 12712; Romeo 13435
Saguer, Louis 1907–
  Hamlet 4077
Sahl, Michael 1934–
  Hamlet 4023; Othello 11921

Sailer, H.
  Twelfth Night 17192
Saint Quentin, Edward
  One of the twenty-eight pseudonyms used by
  Alfred William Rawlings
  Tempest 16291
Saint-Saëns, Charles Camille 1835–1921
  Hamlet 4239; Henry VIII 5243; Macbeth
  7287; Romeo 13806
Saint-Saëns, Charles Camille, arr. 1835–1921
  Hamlet 3560; Dream 9804, 10882, 10883
Sakač, Branimir 1918–1979
  Tempest 15250
Sala Rafel, C., arr.
  Hamlet 3673
Salabert, Francis, arr. 1884–1946
  Merchant 8771; Romeo 14002
Saladino, Michele, arr. 1835–1912
  Othello 12203
Salaman, Charles 1814–1901
  Assumed the name Charles Kensington
  Salaman
  Winter's Tale 19145; Sonnet 44 19725;
  Settings of Commemorative Pieces . . . 21074
Salbert, Dieter
  As You Like It 812
Sale, John Bernard 1779–1856
  As You Like It 1148
Saleh, Karl-Heinz
  Hamlet 3380, 4124
Salieri, Antonio 1750–1825
  Hamlet 4287; Merry Wives 9158
Salisbury, John, arr.
  Dream 10560
Salkeld, Robert, arr. 1920–
  Dream 10251, 10252, 10768
Sallinen, Aulis 1935–
  Henry V 4843
Salmhofer, Franz 1900–1975
  As You Like It 813; Errors 2169; 1 Henry VI
  4865; Lear 5908; Measure 7745; Merchant
  8308; Merry Wives 8943; Dream 9969;
  Othello 11922; Pericles 12589; Richard III
  12955; Romeo 13436; Tempest 15251;
  Timon 16383; Twelfth Night 17193;
  Winter's Tale 18860
Salminen, Matti
  Dream 9970
Salmon, Lucretia
  Merchant 8309
Salomé, Théodore César, arr. 1834–1896
  Dream 9805
Salomon, Hector, arr. 1838–1906
  Romeo 13740, 13741
Salomon, Johann Peter 1745–1815
  Dream 10368
Salomon, K.
  [Karel Salomon, also known as Karel Salmon
  (1897–   )?]
  Tempest 15809

Salsbury, Janet Mary 1881–
    Hamlet 4240; L.L.L. 6688; Dream 10928
Salter, Lionel 1914–
    Othello 12347
Salter, Mary Elizabeth 1856–1938
    Née Turner
    Romeo 14209
Salter, Timothy John 1942–
    Sonnet 30 19618
Salvayre, Gaston 1847–1916
    Pseudonym used by Gervais Bernard Salvayre
    Richard III 13035
Salz, Simon 1955–
    Dream 9971
Salzedo, Leonard Lopés 1921–
    Hamlet 3874; Settings of Commemorative
    Pieces . . . 21169
Salzman, Tim, arr.
    Henry V 4783
Samaras, Spyridon Filiskos [1863?]–1917
    Also known as Spiros Samaras
    Shrew 14641
Samazeuilh, Gustave Marie Victor Fernand,
    arr. 1877–1967
    Merchant 8772
Samet, E., arr.
    Merry Wives 9122
Saminsky, Lazare 1882–1959
    Tempest 16292
Sammons, Albert, arr. 1886–1957
    Merchant 8304
Sampson, George 1861–1949
    L.L.L. 6376
Sampson, Godfrey
    As You Like It 1517, 1769
Sams, Jeremy
    Measure 7746; Merry Wives 8944; Dream
    9972; Tempest 15252
Sams, Jeremy, in part arr.
    As You Like It 814
Samuel, Harold 1879–1937
    As You Like It 815; L.L.L. 6466, 6606, 6674
Samuel, Harry Cecil 1927–
    Lear 6094
Samuel, Rhian 1944–
    P. Pilgrim 20683
Samuelson, Arvid, arr.
    Much Ado 11549; Tempest 15486
Sánchez-Gabanyach, Francisco di Paolo 1845–
    Also known as Francisco de Paolo Sanchez-
    Gabanach
    Othello 12463
Sand, Paul
    Tempest 15253
Sandberger, Adolf 1864–1942
    Twelfth Night 18247
Sanders, Greg 1957–
    Measure 7968; Tempest 15741; Twelfth
    Night 18004

Sanders, Marvin
    Merchant 8310
Sanders, Richard
    [Richard Charles Sanders (1949–   )?]
    Tempest 15473
Sanderson, Wilfrid Ernest 1878–1935
    Dream 10450
Sandler, Mitchell
    Macbeth 7135; Shrew 14464; Troilus
    16523
Sandow, Gregory 1943–
    Hamlet 3381; Macbeth 7528
Sandresky, Margaret Vardell 1921–
    Dream 10982
Sandroff, Howard F. 1949–
    Tempest 15474
Sandström, Sven-David 1942–
    Romeo 13840
Sanz, Rocio 1934–
    Also known as Carmen Rocío Sanz Quiros
    Macbeth 7136; Tempest 15254
Sapienza, Antonio S. 1794–1855
    Merry Wives 8945
Sapp, Gary J. 1944–
    Errors 2235
Saracino, Doriano
    Caesar 5428
Sargent, Harold Malcolm Watts, arr.
    1895–1967
    As You Like It 442; Hamlet 3516; Henry V
    4784
Sarjeant, James
    As You Like It 1149; 2 Henry IV 4644; Two
    Gentlemen 18557
Sárossy, Endre
    As You Like It 816
Sarson, Hilda May [1901?]–1958
    Cymbeline 2606; L.L.L. 6607
Sáry, László 1940–
    Coriolanus 2335
Sassaroli, Vincenzo 1820–1904
    Richard III 13084
Satanowski, Jerzy
    Errors 2170; Hamlet 3382, 3383; Dream
    9973, 9974; Richard III 12956; Timon
    16355; Two Gentlemen 18423
Satie, Erik Alfred Leslie 1866–1925
    Dream 9975, 10708
Sato, Hiroshi
    Romeo 13437
Sato, Masaru
    Hamlet 4125; Macbeth 7529
Sats, Il'ia Aleksandrovich 1875–1912
    Hamlet 3384
Satter, Gustav 1832–1879
    Caesar 5519; Tempest 16110
Saudek, Vojtěch 1951–
    As You Like It 974; Hamlet 3859; Macbeth
    7396; Dream 10451; Romeo 13861; Twelfth

Night 18176; Sonnet 11 19281; Sonnet 12
19290; Sonnet 15 19311; Sonnet 16 19317
Sauer, Emil, arr. 1882–1942
Dream 9806
Sauer, Ludwig, arr.
Romeo 13575
Sauguet, Henri 1901–
Pseudonym used by Henri-Pierre Poupard
As You Like It 817; Cymbeline 2486; Lear
6188; Measure 7969; Othello 11923;
Tempest 15255; Twelfth Night 17194;
Sonnet 43 19717; Sonnet 155 20575
Saumell, Manuel, arr. 1817–1870
Also known as Manuel Saumell Robredo
Macbeth 7351
Saunders, Herbert Max   –1983
Dream 10929
Saunders, Neil Nathaniel, arr. 1918–
Othello 12348
Sauvage, Emil
Lear 6012
Sauvageau, Jean
Othello 11924
Savage, Jim
As You Like It 818
Savagnone, Giuseppe, arr. 1902–
Twelfth Night 16906
Savard, Augustin Marie Emmanuel
1861–1942
Also known [incorrectly] as Marie-
Emmanuel-Augustin Savard
Lear 6095
Savel'ev, Boris Vladimirovich 1896–
Romeo 13438
Savery, Finn 1933–
Richard II 12713
Savin, Dragutin 1915–
As You Like It 819; Lear 5909; Shrew
14465; Twelfth Night 17195
Savin, Igor 1946–
Dream 9977
Sawtell, Paul 1906–[before 1980]
Lear 6127
Sawyer, Frank E.
Two Gentlemen 18558
Saxe, Serge
Tempest 16111
Saya, Mark 1954–
Twelfth Night 18005
Saylor, Richard 1926–
Macbeth 7137
Sbragia, Giancarlo
Othello 11925
Scaife, Frederick Ellis 1880–
Romeo 14178
Scanzello, Charles J. 1935–
Antony 299; As You Like It 820, 1152,
1225, 1518, 1593, 1770, 1828, 1853;
Hamlet 3718, 3777, 3801, 3875; Measure

7970; Merchant 8627; Dream 9978, 10452,
10546; Much Ado 11388, 11514; Othello
12228, 12241, 12349; Romeo 13439;
Tempest 15567, 15742, 15823, 15856,
15936, 15979; Troilus 16566; Twelfth
Night 17620, 17711, 18006, 18177; Two
Gentlemen 18559; Winter's Tale 18963,
18964, 18984, 19016, 19060, 19087
Scaramuzza, Vicente
Hamlet 3617
Scarchiapone, Cosmos
Winter's Tale 18861
Scarlatti, Alessandro 1660–1725
Coriolanus 2427
Scarlatti, Domenico 1685–1757
Hamlet 4288
Scarlatti, Giuseppe 1723–1777
Coriolanus 2428
Scarsbrook, Frederick, arr.
Tempest 14739, 14823, 15487
Schaad, Roar 1941–
Sonnet 71 19963
Schaaf, Daniel E.
Lear 6013; Macbeth 7288
Schaaf, Edward Oswald
As You Like It 1924; Cymbeline 2826
Schachner, Joseph Rudolf 1821–1896
As You Like It 1153; Settings of
Commemorative Pieces . . . 21075
Schad, Joseph, arr.
Romeo 13742
Schaefer, Albert   –1942
Also known as Albert Schäfer
Cymbeline 2827
Schaefer, Albert, arr.   –1942
Also known as Albert Schäfer
Merry Wives 9123
Schaefer, David Alan
All's Well 94; Much Ado 11632
Schäfer, [?]
Twelfth Night 18341
Schäfer, Alexander Nikolajewitsch 1866–
Hamlet 4024
Schäfer, Hans-Georg
Two Gentlemen 18424
Schäfer, Karl, arr.
Romeo 14003
Schäffer, Bogusław 1929–
Troilus 16524; Settings of Commemorative
Pieces . . . 21236
Schäffer, Karl Friedrich Ludwig 1746–1817
Macbeth 7138; Tempest 15475
Schafmeister, Heinrich
Tempest 15256
Schall, Claus Nielsen 1757–1835
All's Well 80; Macbeth 7289; Romeo 13807
Schartau, Herbert William [1859?]–1915
Dream 10930; Tempest 15937

Scharwenka, Ludwig Philipp, arr. 1847–1917
  Hamlet 3561; Romeo 14127
Schatte, [?]
  Macbeth 7139, 7474
Schaum, Sylvia, arr.
  Two Gentlemen 18603
Schaumburg, Ronald G.
  Romeo 13440; Tempest 15257
Scheinpflug, Paul 1875–1937
  Settings of Commemorative Pieces . . . 21170
Scheit, Karl, arr. 1909–
  Settings of Commemorative Pieces . . .
  21290, 21291
Schenck, Elliott
  Tempest 15258
Schenck, Elliott, arr.
  Cymbeline 2775; Two Gentlemen 18604
Schibler, Armin 1920–
  Tempest 15259
Schick, Otto, arr.
  Merry Wives 9124; Dream 9807
Schick, Philippine 1893–1970
  Settings of Commemorative Pieces . . . 21237
Schick, Philippine, arr. 1893–1970
  Winter's Tale 18925
Schierhorn, Paul
  As You Like It 821
Schieve, Catherine
  Much Ado 11263
Schiffel, E., arr.
  Merry Wives 9125
Schifrin, Lalo Boris 1932–
  Hamlet 3385
Schildknecht, Björn 1905–1946
  Antony 224; Caesar 5429; Much Ado 11264
Schildknecht, Björn, arr. 1905–1946
  As You Like It 854
Schill, Rolf
  Hamlet 3386; 1 Henry IV 4415; Dream
  9979, 9980; Othello 11926; Romeo 13441
Schiller, Leon 1887–1954
  [Also known as Leon Schiller de Schildenfeld]
  Coriolanus 2336; Much Ado 11265
Schiller, Leon, in part arr. 1887–1954
  [Also known as Leon Schiller de Schildenfeld]
  Twelfth Night 17196
Schiltz, [H.], arr.
  Romeo 13743, 13744, 13745
Schimm, Günter
  Measure 7747; Dream 9981; Troilus 16525,
  16526; Winter's Tale 18862
Schimon, Adolf, arr. 1820–1887
  Romeo 13746
Schindler, Kurt 1882–1935
  L.L.L. 6467
Schiøtz, Henrik, arr.
  Much Ado 11550
Schipper, Walter
  Hamlet 3387; Richard III 12957

Schirmer, Tim
  Errors 2171, 2172; Hamlet 3388; L.L.L.
  6280; Merchant 8311; Merry Wives 8946;
  Dream 9982; Romeo 13442, 13443; Shrew
  14466; Titus 16414; Two Gentlemen 18425
Schirmer, William Louis 1941–
  Othello 11927; Twelfth Night 17197,
  17739; P. Pilgrim 20684
Schirren, Ferdinand
  Antony 225
Schiwa, [?]
  Lear 6014
Schjelderup, Gerhard Rosenkrone 1859–1933
  Macbeth 7290
Schlawing, Helmuth
  Errors 2173; 1 Henry IV 4416; 2 Henry IV
  4591; Shrew 14467
Schleiffelder, Felix
  1 Henry IV 4417; 2 Henry IV 4592; Caesar
  5430; Winter's Tale 18863
Schlemm, Gustav Adolf 1902–
  Measure 7971; Dream 10382
Schlemüller, Hugo 1872–1918
  All's Well 102
Schlepegrell, F.
  Othello 12429
Schlesinger, Hans
  All's Well 57
Schloesser, Carl Wilhelm Adolphe
  1830–1931
  Dream 10709
Schlösser, Louis 1800–1886
  Macbeth 7140; Richard III 12958
Schlotel, Brian
  Henry VIII 5164; Much Ado 11515
Schlottmann, Louis 1826–1905
  Romeo 13958
Schmalstich, Clemens 1880–1960
  Errors 2253
Schmalstich, Clemens, arr. 1880–1960
  Tempest 15047; Winter's Tale 18778
Schmid, Adolf, in part arr. 1878–1958
  Merchant 8312; Richard II 12714; Tempest
  15260; Winter's Tale 18864
Schmid, Adolf, arr. 1878–1958
  Othello 12528
Schmid-Kayser, Hans, arr.
  Cymbeline 2776
Schmidt, Christfried
  Richard III 12959
Schmidt, Joye Zelda 1930–
  Winter's Tale 19061
Schmidt, Peter
  Hamlet 3389
Schmidt, Wilfried
  Hamlet 3390
Schmidt-Isserstedt, Hans 1900–1973
  As You Like It 822; Much Ado 11266;
  Romeo 13444

Schmitt, Florent 1870–1958
Antony 226; Macbeth 7390
Schmitt, Florent, arr. 1870–1958
Romeo 14087
Schmitz, Alan W. 1950–
Caesar 5483
Schmoll, Joseph
Hamlet 3391; Richard II 12715
Schmorl, Wolfgang
Macbeth 7141
Schnabel, Gottfried
1 Henry IV 4418; 2 Henry IV 4593; Caesar
5431; Much Ado 11267; Richard III 12960;
Winter's Tale 18865
Schnebel, Dieter 1930–
Macbeth 7142, 7291
Schnecker, Peter August 1850–1903
As You Like It 1925
Schneidenbach, Mario
Twelfth Night 17198
Schneider, Elisabeth
Merchant 8313
Schneider, F.
Hamlet 3392
Schneider, F. H., arr.
Merry Wives 9126
Schneider, Friedrich
Lear 5910
Schneider, Gary Michael 1922–
Merchant 8314
Schneider, Georg Abraham 1770–1839
K. John 5621; Richard III 12961; Romeo
13445
Schneider, Horst
Romeo 13446
Schneitzhoeffer, Jean-Madeleine
Tempest 15476
Schnoor, Heinr[ich] Christ[ian]
As You Like It 1519
Schobeß, Rainer
Richard III 12962
Schoeck, Othmar Gottfried 1886–1957
Timon 16372
Schoenfeldt, Alice Watson
Sonnet 137 20448
Schofer, Marvin
Romeo 13447
Schöll, Klaus
As You Like It 823
Scholter, Hugo 1932–
As You Like It 824; Measure 7748; Romeo
13448; Twelfth Night 17199
Scholter, Hugo, in part arr. 1932–
Merry Wives 8947; Much Ado 11268;
Sonnet 8 19274; Sonnet 21 19482; Sonnet
23 19491; Sonnet 38 19682; Sonnet 116
20341
Scholz, Bernhard E. 1835–1916
Twelfth Night 17621

Schön, Eduard 1825–1879
Wrote under the pseudonym 'E[duard]
S[chön] Engelsberg'
As You Like It 1520; Twelfth Night 17622
Schönbach, Dieter 1931–
All's Well 58; As You Like It 825; Hamlet
3393, 3394; 1 Henry IV 4419; 2 Henry IV
4594; Henry V 4760; 1 Henry VI 4866;
2 Henry VI 4906; 3 Henry VI 4948; Caesar
5432; K. John 5622, 5623; Lear 5911,
5912, 6128; Macbeth 7143, 7144, 7145;
Merry Wives 8948; Dream 9983, 9984,
9985; Much Ado 11269, 11270; Othello
11928; Pericles 12590; Richard II 12716,
12717; Richard III 12963, 12964, 12965;
Romeo 13449, 13450, 13451; Shrew
14468, 14469, 14470, 14471; Tempest
15261, 15262; Timon 16356; Troilus
16527; Twelfth Night 17200, 17201
Schönbach, Dieter, in part arr. 1931–
Dream 9986
Schönberg, Stig Gustav 1933–
Sonnet 1 19183; Sonnet 29 19578; Sonnet
64 19876; Sonnet 75 20039; Sonnet 92
20126; Sonnet 93 20131; Sonnet 130
20428; Sonnet 143 20476; Sonnet 146
20498; Sonnet 147 20517
Schöne, R.
Sonnet 37 19677; Settings of
Commemorative Pieces . . . 21262
Schöner, Eberhard
Dream 9987
Schönfeld, Georg
Merry Wives 9255
Schortemeier, Dirk
Hamlet 3395
Schottmiller, Steve, in part arr.
Romeo 13452
Schreiber, Hans 1912–1969
Hamlet 3396; Macbeth 7146
Schreiber, Michael
Two Gentlemen 18426
Schreiber, Thomas
Much Ado 11516
Schreibman, Phillip
Shrew 14472
Schreiner, Adolf, arr.
Merry Wives 9127; Dream 9808
Schreiner, Adolf D. 1841–1894
Hamlet 4025
Schreiter, Ryszard
Romeo 13453; Twelfth Night 17202
Schröder, Anna Christina
Hamlet 3397
Schroeter, [?]
Measure 7972
Schröpfer, Wilfried
Lear 5913; Richard III 12966; Two
Gentlemen 18427

Schubert, Artur
Much Ado 11271
Schubert, F. L., arr.
Dream 9809, 9810
Schubert, Franz Peter 1797–1828
Antony 300; Cymbeline 2709; Tempest
15477; Two Gentlemen 18560
Schulkowsky, Robyn
As You Like It 826
Schuller, Gunther Alexander 1925–
As You Like It 1154; L.L.L. 6341; Twelfth
Night 17623, 17712, 18007; Sonnet 87
20096
Schult, Ernest
Romeo 13454; Twelfth Night 17203
Schultz, Andrew
Richard III 12967
Schultz, Chester Verco 1945–
As You Like It 1155; Cymbeline 2607;
Tempest 15743
Schultz, Donna Gartman
As You Like It 1771; Hamlet 3778; Much
Ado 11517
Schultz, Greg, in part arr.
L.L.L. 6281
Schultz, Richard
Othello 12350
Schultz, Svend Simon 1913–
Hamlet 3398; Macbeth 7147; Much Ado
11272; Romeo 13455; Twelfth Night 17204
Schultz, Svend Simon, in part arr. 1913–
Othello 11910, 11929
Schultze, Max, arr.
Caesar 5526; Merry Wives 9128
Schultze, Norbert 1911–
Merchant 8315; Twelfth Night 17205
Schulz, Johann Abraham Peter 1747–1800
As You Like It 1522
Schulz, Karl-Heinz
Dream 9988
Schulz, P., arr.
Dream 9811
Schulz-Beuthen, Heinrich 1838–1915
Lear 6096
Schulzová, Anežka, arr. 1870–1905
Tempest 14983
Schuman, Max, arr.
Merry Wives 9129
Schuman, William Howard 1910–
Henry VIII 5013, 5165, 5221, 5222
Schumann, Robert Alexander 1810–1856
Hamlet 3618, 4026, 4241; Caesar 5520;
Macbeth 7475; Twelfth Night 18178
Schunke, Charles, arr. 1801–1839
Dream 10884
Schupman, Edwin
Measure 7749
Schurmann, Gerard 1928–
Lear 5914

Schuster, Ignaz 1779–1835
Hamlet 4126; Othello 12464; Romeo
14064
Schütz, Hans Georg 1912–
Othello 12510
Schuurman, Max 1889–1955
Much Ado 11273; Tempest 15263
Schwabe, Michael K.
Romeo 13456
Schwalm, Robert, arr. 1845–
Dream 9812
Schwanbeyer, Ferdinand
Romeo 13848
Schwanenberger, Johann Gottfried
[1740]–1804
Surname also known as Schwanenberg,
Schwanberger, Schwanberg, and Schwanburg
Romeo 13808
Schwartz, Francis 1940–
Tempest 16238
Schwartz, Jean 1878–1956
Hamlet 4242, 4243; Macbeth 7575; Romeo
14112; Settings of Commemorative
Pieces . . . 21076
Schwartz, Kenneth
Dream 10271
Schwartz, Paul 1907–
Shrew 14473, 14667
Schwartzman, Evan J. 1955–
Tempest 15568, 15744; Sonnet 35 19668
Schwarz, Ira Paul 1922–
As You Like It 827; Dream 9989; Winter's
Tale 18866
Schwarz, Reinhard
Richard II 12718
Schwarz, Ulrich 1952–
As You Like It 828
Schwedeler, Raimund 1925–
Macbeth 7576; Sonnet 54 19771; Sonnet 55
19785; Sonnet 56 19795; Settings of
Commemorative Pieces . . . 21191
Schweitzer, Anton 1735–1787
Richard III 13085
Schweppe, Michael
Caesar 5433
Schwertfeger, Eva
Dream 9990
Schwimm, Ulrich
Shrew 14474
Schwittmann, W., arr.
Dream 9813
Sciammarella, Valdo 1924–
Twelfth Night 17206
Sciarrino, Salvatore 1947–
Macbeth 7292
Scognamiglio, Gaetano
Othello 12174
Scolari, Giuseppe
Coriolanus 2429

Scotland, John
Dream 10983
Scott, Austin
Much Ado 11274
Scott, Bennett
Merchant 8797
Scott, Charles Kennedy 1876–1965
Tempest 15745
Scott, Cyril Meir 1879–1970
As You Like It 1772; Cymbeline 2787; Much
Ado 11518; Othello 11930; Tempest 16112;
Lucrece 20774
Scott, Derek Brian 1950–
Sonnet 27 19526; Sonnet 49 19739; Sonnet
113 20299
Scott, John
Antony 227; Settings of Commemorative
Pieces . . . 20953
Scott, John Prindle 1877–1932
Romeo 14179
Scott, Nathan George 1915–
Errors 2262; Sonnet 18 19427
Scott, Phillip
Tempest 15264
Scrimger, John
Dream 9991, 9992; Othello 11931; Romeo
13457; Shrew 14475
Scull, G. C.
As You Like It 1524
Scull, Harold Thomas
Othello 12351
Sculthorpe, Peter Joshua 1929–
Lear 5915; Much Ado 11275; Twelfth Night
17207
Seaman, Barry 1946–
As You Like It 1773; Dream 10547; Sonnet
43 19718; Sonnet 66 19919; P. Pilgrim
20685
Seaman, Gerald Roberts 1934–
Tempest 15265
Searle, Humphrey 1915–1982
Antony 228, 280, 347; Hamlet 3399, 3619,
4244; Troilus 16528
Searle, Willis
Dream 9993
Secchi, Adrian
L.L.L. 6282; Macbeth 7148; Othello 11932;
Shrew 14476; Twelfth Night 17208
Secker, John Charles 1961–
P. Pilgrim 20686
Secluna, Clive
Merchant 8316; Twelfth Night 17209
Sedlář, Josef
Hamlet 3400; Merchant 8317; Romeo
13458
Sedmidubský, Miloš 1924–
Merchant 8318
Seeger, Peter R. 1919–
Tempest 15746

Seeholt, Robert, in part arr.
Twelfth Night 17210
Seiber, Mátyás György 1905–1960
Sonnet 18 19428
Seiber, Mátyás György, arr. 1905–1960
As You Like It 443; L.L.L. 6498
Seidel, Friedrich Ludwig 1765–1831
Coriolanus 2337; Macbeth 7149; Romeo
13459
Seidl, Stefan, arr.
As You Like It 941
Seidmann, Bernhard
Shrew 14477
Seifriz, Max
Tempest 15266; Winter's Tale 18867
Seigner, Michel
Dream 9994
Seiler, Hans
Tempest 16113
Sekacz, Ilona 1948–
As You Like It 829; Cymbeline 2487, 2488,
2489; Hamlet 3401; Henry VIII 5016; Lear
5916, 6129; Macbeth 7150; Measure 7750;
Merchant 8319, 8320; Dream 9995; Much
Ado 11276; Romeo 13460, 13461; Troilus
16529; Twelfth Night 17211
Seki, Tadaakira
Merchant 8321; Dream 9996; Much Ado
11277; Romeo 13462
Selby, Philip 1948–
As You Like It 1156; Cymbeline 2788
Sell, Colin
K. John 5624
Sell, David
Twelfth Night 17212
Sellé, William Christian
Dream 10710; Twelfth Night 17740
Sellenick, [Adolphe Valentin], arr.
[circa 1816]–1893
Romeo 13747
Selnes, Johan
Sonnet 116 20330
Seltzer, Dov 1932–
Tempest 15267
Selwyn, David Morton 1951–
Romeo 13463
Séméladis, Victor
Lear 6015
Semenoff, Ivan 1917–1972
Also known as Ivan Kogan-Semenoff
Hamlet 3402; Othello 11933
Semini, Carlo Florindo 1914–
Tempest 16232
Semmelbeck, Gustav
Hamlet 3403; Caesar 5434; Much Ado
11278; Timon 16357
Semmler, Rudolf H. Mathias 1904–
Twelfth Night 17213; Two Gentlemen
18428

Senator, Ronald 1926–
    Sonnet 8 19231; Sonnet 55 19776; Sonnet
    65 19885; Sonnet 97 20150
Seng, John, arr.
    Romeo 13609
Sénia, Jean-Marie Pierre N.
    1 Henry IV 4497; 2 Henry IV 4670; Merry
    Wives 9240; Romeo 13464; Tempest 15268
Serebrier, José 1938–
    Coriolanus 2338; Lear 5917; Romeo 13465
Serocki, Kazimierz 1922–1981
    As You Like It 830; Coriolanus 2339; Lear
    5918
Serov, Aleksandr Nikolaevich 1820–1871
    Merry Wives 9160
Serpette, Henri Charles Antoine Gaston
    1846–1904
    Dream 10984; Settings of Commemorative
    Pieces . . . 21274
Serry, John
    Tempest 15269
Sersam, Rolf 1946–
    As You Like It 831; Twelfth Night 17214
Seserko, Joseph
    Dream 9997
Settle, Ronald
    Merchant 8322; Twelfth Night 18008
Settle, Ronald, in part arr.
    Hamlet 3404; Caesar 5435; Twelfth Night
    17215
Severn, Edmund 1862–1942
    Dream 10711
Severn, Thomas Henry 1801–1881
    Romeo 13874
Severns, J. G.
    Tempest 15270
Severns, W. F.
    Henry V 4838
Sexton, Peter M.
    Two Gentlemen 18429
Seydelmann, Franz 1748–1806
    Shrew 14690
Seyfried, Ignaz Xaver 1766–1841
    Also known as Ritter von Seyfried
    Caesar 5436; Dream 10803
Seyler, Joseph A.
    Hamlet 4027
Seymour, John Laurence 1893–
    Measure 7804; Two Gentlemen 18466
Sfetsas, Kyriacos 1945–
    Hamlet 4028
Sgarini, Raffaele, arr.
    Othello 12153
Shackleton, J. Howard, arr.
    Dream 9814
Shakespeare, Laura
    Lear 5919
Shakespeare, William 1849–1931
    Hamlet 4029

Shakhbagian, G.
    Othello 11934
Shalit, Daniel
    1 Henry IV 4420; 2 Henry IV 4595;
    Merchant 8323
Shanidze, Sh., arr.
    Othello 12035
Shapey, Ralph 1921–
    Hamlet 3405
Shapiro, Alexandra 1962–
    As You Like It 1157, 1774
Shapiro, Gerald Mark, in part arr. 1942–
    Lear 5920
Shapiro, Michael Jeffrey 1951–
    As You Like It 1775; Tempest 15747;
    Winter's Tale 19088
Shaporin, Iurii Georgii Aleksandrovich
    1887–1966
    Errors 2174; 1 Henry IV 4421; 2 Henry IV
    4596; Lear 5921; Merry Wives 8949; Much
    Ado 11279; Twelfth Night 17216
Shaposhnikov, Adrian Grigor'evich
    [1887?]–1967
    Lear 5922; Othello 11935
Sharman, Cecil 1894–
    Henry VIII 5166; L.L.L. 6468, 6608;
    Merchant 8628; Dream 10341
Sharp, Cecil James 1859–1924
    Kinsmen 19171, 19175
Sharp, Cecil James, in part arr. 1859–1924
    Dream 9998
Sharpe, Cedric, arr. 1891–
    As You Like It 444; Othello 12258
Sharpe, Evelyn A., arr.
    Also known as Evelyn Sharpe Saville
    As You Like It 445; Tempest 14824
Sharpe, Herbert Francis 1861–1925
    Hamlet 3716; Dream 10931
Sharpe, R.
    Tempest 16114
Shatirian, Sergei Aleksandrovich 1907–
    Hamlet 3406; Lear 5923; Othello 11936
Shavers, Bruce Jeffrey 1958–
    Measure 7973; Merchant 8629
Shaw, C., arr.
    As You Like It 1568
Shaw, Christopher 1924–
    Cymbeline 2490
Shaw, Diccon
    As You Like It 832; Henry VIII 5017; Romeo
    13466; Tempest 15271, 15272; Troilus
    16530; Two Gentlemen 18430; Winter's
    Tale 18868
Shaw, Geoffrey Turton 1879–1943
    As You Like It 833, 1854; Cymbeline 2608;
    L.L.L. 6283, 6609; Merchant 8630; Dream
    9999, 10419, 10466, 10548; Much Ado
    11519; Richard II 12763; Tempest 15810;
    Twelfth Night 17217, 17686, 18180

Shaw, Geoffrey Turton, arr. 1879–1943
  Tempest 14825; Twelfth Night 16622
Shaw, James 1842–
  As You Like It 1776
Shaw, Martin Edward Fallas 1875–1958
  As You Like It 1158, 1777; L.L.L. 6469;
  Dream 10000, 10342, 10420, 10457,
  10549; Much Ado 11520; Richard II 12764;
  Tempest 15748; Twelfth Night 17624,
  17625, 18181; Winter's Tale 18869, 18985
Shaw, Martin Edward Fallas, arr.
  1875–1958
  Dream 10253; Tempest 14740; Twelfth
  Night 18309
Shaw, Martin Edward Fallas, ed.
  1875–1958
  Sonnet 146 20499
Shaw, Phillip
  L.L.L. 6284; Winter's Tale 18870
Shaw, R., arr.
  Much Ado 11551
Shaw, Roland, arr.
  Shrew 14617; Two Gentlemen 18605
Shaw, Thomas [circa 1760–circa 1830]
  Merchant 8324
Shawn, Allen
  Hamlet 3407; Henry V 4761; Measure 7751;
  Dream 10001
Shazman, Poldi
  Merry Wives 8950; Dream 10002; Romeo
  14065; Twelfth Night 17218; Settings of
  Commemorative Pieces . . . 20886
Shearer, Clarence Maynard 1940–
  Cymbeline 2789; Measure 7974
Shearing, George Albert 1919–
  As You Like It 1159; Much Ado 11521;
  Sonnet 8 19261
Shearwood, James
  Hamlet 3408
Shebalin, Vissarion Iakovlevich 1902–1963
  Hamlet 3409; Shrew 14642
Shedlock, John South, arr. 1843–1919
  Dream 10254; Tempest 14741
Sheehan, Robert
  As You Like It 1525
Sheehan, Robert, adapter
  L.L.L. 6610
Sheffield, Yorke
  Cymbeline 2491; Much Ado 11610; Othello
  11937; Richard III 12968; Winter's Tale
  18871, 18872
Shefter, Bert Abram 1904–
  Lear 6130
Shefter, Bert Abram, adapter 1904–
  As You Like It 1990
Sheibler, Truvor Karlovich 1900–1960
  Shrew 14478
Shelley, Harry Rowe 1858–1947
  Romeo 13809

Shelley, Harry Rowe, arr. 1858–1947
  As You Like It 446; Tempest 14742;
  Winter's Tale 19012
Shen, Hsueh-Yung
  L.L.L. 6470
Shèn Lì Qún
  Twelfth Night 17407
Shenshin, Aleksandr Alekseevich 1890–1944
  Twelfth Night 17408
Shephard, Richard 1949–
  As You Like It 834; Dream 10003
Shepherd, David Allan
  Dream 10351
Shepherd, Stuart Paul
  Settings of Commemorative Pieces . . . 21198
Shepperd, J. O., arr.
  Macbeth 7001
Sheridan, Louisa H.
  Othello 12512
Sherman, Abe
  Troilus 16531
Sherman, Sylvia
  Much Ado 11280
Sherman, Terrence
  Macbeth 7151; Dream 10004; Richard III
  12969, 12970
Sherwin, Manning 1902–1973
  Settings of Commemorative Pieces . . . 20954
Sherwood, William Hall, arr. 1854–1911
  Macbeth 6941
Shǐ Jǐ Huá
  Twelfth Night 17409
Shield, William 1748–1829
  Hamlet 4127; 2 Henry IV 4643; Henry VIII
  5018; Dream 10369; Othello 12244;
  Tempest 15811; P. Pilgrim 20687, 20688;
  Settings of Commemorative Pieces . . . 21078
Shierhorn, Paul
  1 Henry IV 4422; 2 Henry IV 4597
Shiffer, Kate U.
  As You Like It 1991
Shiffler, Harrold C. 1918–
  As You Like It 835; Twelfth Night 17219
Shifrin, Seymour J. 1926–1979
  All's Well 87; Lear 6117; Sonnet 60 19835;
  Sonnet 106 20265
Shigeto, Yoichi
  1 Henry VI 4867; 2 Henry VI 4907; 3 Henry
  VI 4949
Shipley, R., arr.
  Othello 12259
Shire, David
  As You Like It 836
Shires, Norman
  Twelfth Night 17220
Shkurovich, L., arr.
  Othello 12036
Shliuzberg, M.
  Romeo 13467

Shokhin, L., arr.
Cymbeline 2777
Shore, Susan
Dream 10005
Short, Michael 1937–
As You Like It 1160; Hamlet 3736;
Merchant 8631; Tempest 15749; Sonnet 8
19262; Sonnet 18 19429; Sonnet 33 19656;
Sonnet 60 19836; Sonnet 96 20145
Shostakovich, Dmitrii Dmitrievich 1906–1975
Hamlet 3410, 3421, 3423, 4030, 4245,
4246; Lear 5924, 5925; Macbeth 7551;
Sonnet 66 19920
Showard, Charles
Richard III 12971
Shropshire, Noble
1 Henry IV 4423; 2 Henry IV 4598; Lear
5926; Merchant 8325; Dream 10006; Much
Ado 11281; Richard II 12719
Shtaiher, Volodymyr 1900–
Merry Wives 8951; Twelfth Night 17221
Shudson, Hodd
Tempest 15273
Shuler, Craig, in part arr.
L.L.L. 6285
Shumilov, G.
Dream 10007
Shute, Edwin
Tempest 16115
Sibelius, Jean Julias Christian 1865–1957
Romeo 14210; Tempest 15274, 16116;
Twelfth Night 17222, 17626, 18182
Siboni, Erik A. V. 1828–1892
Othello 11938, 12430
Sicard, Jeff
Othello 11939
Sidebotham, M. A.
L.L.L. 6355
Sidonia
[Pseudonym?]
Measure 7975
Sieber, H.
Richard III 12972
Siebert, Ludwig
Shrew 14479; Sonnet 18 19457
Siegel, Louis
Hamlet 3425
Siegel, Wayne 1953–
Hamlet 4031
Siegemund, Klaus
Dream 10008
Siegler, Osmar
Othello 11940
Siegmeister, Elie 1909–
Dream 10272; Othello 12485
Sigel, Steve 1952–
Winter's Tale 18873
Sigurbjörnsson, Þorkell 1938–
Merchant 8326

Šikola, Zdeněk
Coriolanus 2340; Measure 7752; Merchant
8327; Richard II 12720
Silberberg, Sol
Hamlet 3620
Silberflug, Elster
As You Like It 837
Silcher, Friedrich 1789–1860
As You Like It 1526
Silner, Carlo
Romeo 14211
Silva, Reynold
Much Ado 11282
Silveira, Miroel
As You Like It 838
Silver, Alfred Jethro, arr.
Henry VIII 5185
Silver, Charles 1868–1949
Shrew 14645
Silver, Frederick 1936–
Also known as Fred Silverberg
Sonnet 18 19430; Sonnet 61 19857
Silver, Sheila Jane 1946–
L.L.L. 6471
Silverman, Stanley Joel 1938–
Errors 2175; Coriolanus 2341; Caesar 5437;
Lear 5927; L.L.L. 6286; Merchant 8328;
Dream 10009, 10273; Much Ado 11283;
Othello 11941; Richard III 12973; Shrew
14480; Tempest 15277, 15278
Silversher, Michael
Twelfth Night 17225
Silverthorne, Hugh, arr.
Merry Wives 8886; Dream 9365, 10173
Silvestri, Martin
Hamlet 3426
Simeone, Harry 1911–
As You Like It 975
Simiele, Robert
As You Like It 839
Simmonds, Thomas F.
As You Like It 1161
Simms, Henry, arr. 1804–1872
Twelfth Night 16680; Two Gentlemen 18370
Simon, Anton Iul'evich 1850–1916
Henry VIII 5019; Merchant 8329
Simon, John [UK]
Richard II 12721
Simon, John [US]
Lear 5928, 6165; Settings of
Commemorative Pieces . . . 20955
Simon, Ladislav 1929–
As You Like It 840; Coriolanus 2342;
1 Henry IV 4424; 2 Henry IV 4599; Caesar
5438; K. John 5625; Othello 11942; Shrew
14481, 14482; Troilus 16532; Winter's Tale
18874
Simon, Zoltán
Winter's Tale 18875

Simoni, Wolfgang
  Lear 5929
Simpson, Claude Mitchell, arr. 1910–
  Dream 10255; Settings of Commemorative
  Pieces . . . 21292
Simpson, Dudley George 1922–
  Hamlet 3427; 1 Henry VI 4868; 2 Henry VI
  4908; 3 Henry VI 4950; Richard III 12974;
  Winter's Tale 18876
Simpson, Frederick James 1856–
  L.L.L. 6611
Simpson, Richard   –1876
  Antony 302; As You Like It 1162, 1163,
  1221, 1778, 1779, 1780, 1781, 1782,
  1783, 1829; Cymbeline 2609, 2610, 2790,
  2791; Henry VIII 5167; L.L.L. 6348, 6472,
  6612; Measure 7976, 7977, 7978, 7979;
  Merchant 8632, 8633; Dream 10362,
  10421, 10550; Much Ado 11374, 11522;
  Othello 12352; Romeo 13868; Tempest
  15569, 15570, 15750, 15751, 15813,
  15938, 15980; Twelfth Night 17627,
  17628, 17741, 18009, 18183; Two
  Gentlemen 18616, 18617; Winter's Tale
  19017, 19062, 19089; Sonnet 1 19184;
  Sonnet 2 19192; Sonnet 3 19199; Sonnet 4
  19203; Sonnet 5 19211; Sonnet 6 19217;
  Sonnet 7 19224; Sonnet 8 19263; Sonnet 9
  19276; Sonnet 10 19279; Sonnet 11 19282;
  Sonnet 12 19291; Sonnet 13 19297; Sonnet
  14 19300; Sonnet 15 19312; Sonnet 16
  19318; Sonnet 17 19321; Sonnet 18 19431;
  Sonnet 19 19470; Sonnet 20 19478; Sonnet
  21 19480; Sonnet 22 19485; Sonnet 23
  19490; Sonnet 24 19498; Sonnet 25 19507;
  Sonnet 26 19512; Sonnet 27 19527; Sonnet
  28 19535; Sonnet 29 19579; Sonnet 30
  19619; Sonnet 31 19639; Sonnet 32 19644;
  Sonnet 33 19657; Sonnet 34 19663; Sonnet
  35 19669; Sonnet 36 19674; Sonnet 37
  19678; Sonnet 38 19680; Sonnet 39 19684;
  Sonnet 40 19695; Sonnet 41 19704; Sonnet
  42 19706; Sonnet 43 19719; Sonnet 44
  19726; Sonnet 45 19728; Sonnet 46 19730;
  Sonnet 47 19733; Sonnet 48 19736; Sonnet
  49 19740; Sonnet 50 19748; Sonnet 51
  19750; Sonnet 52 19752; Sonnet 53 19760;
  Sonnet 54 19772; Sonnet 55 19786; Sonnet
  56 19796; Sonnet 57 19806; Sonnet 58
  19810; Sonnet 59 19814; Sonnet 60 19837;
  Sonnet 61 19858; Sonnet 62 19863, 19864;
  Sonnet 63 19867; Sonnet 64 19877; Sonnet
  65 19900; Sonnet 66 19922; Sonnet 67
  19927; Sonnet 68 19928; Sonnet 69 19929;
  Sonnet 70 19931; Sonnet 71 19964; Sonnet
  72 19976; Sonnet 73 20016; Sonnet 74
  20031; Sonnet 75 20040; Sonnet 76 20051;
  Sonnet 77 20056; Sonnet 78 20060; Sonnet
  79 20062; Sonnet 80 20064; Sonnet 81
  20071; Sonnet 82 20072; Sonnet 83 20073;
  Sonnet 84 20075, 20076; Sonnet 85 20077;
  Sonnet 86 20078; Sonnet 87 20097; Sonnet
  88 20102; Sonnet 89 20103, 20104; Sonnet
  90 20112; Sonnet 91 20120, 20121; Sonnet
  92 20127; Sonnet 93 20132; Sonnet 94
  20137; Sonnet 95 20140; Sonnet 96 20146;
  Sonnet 97 20170; Sonnet 98 20192; Sonnet
  99 20204; Sonnet 100 20210; Sonnet 101
  20212; Sonnet 102 20224; Sonnet 103
  20228; Sonnet 104 20242; Sonnet 105
  20252; Sonnet 106 20266; Sonnet 107
  20271; Sonnet 108 20275; Sonnet 109
  20284; Sonnet 110 20289, 20290; Sonnet
  111 20291; Sonnet 112 20294; Sonnet 113
  20300; Sonnet 114 20301; Sonnet 115
  20303; Sonnet 116 20331; Sonnet 117
  20345; Sonnet 118 20349; Sonnet 119
  20353; Sonnet 120 20357; Sonnet 121
  20359; Sonnet 122 20361; Sonnet 123
  20366; Sonnet 124 20369, 20370; Sonnet
  125 20371; Sonnet 126 20373; Sonnet 127
  20376; Sonnet 128 20401; Sonnet 129
  20413; Sonnet 130 20429; Sonnet 131
  20432; Sonnet 132 20434; Sonnet 133
  20437; Sonnet 134 20438; Sonnet 135
  20442; Sonnet 136 20445; Sonnet 137
  20449; Sonnet 138 20458; Sonnet 139
  20464, 20465; Sonnet 140 20469; Sonnet
  141 20473; Sonnet 142 20475; Sonnet 143
  20477; Sonnet 144 20482; Sonnet 145
  20486; Sonnet 146 20500; Sonnet 147
  20518; Sonnet 148 20522; Sonnet 149
  20529; Sonnet 150 20533; Sonnet 151
  20535; Sonnet 152 20538; Sonnet 153
  20541; Sonnet 154 20548, 20549; P.
  Pilgrim 20689, 20690, 20691, 20692,
  20693, 20694, 20695, 20696, 20697,
  20698, 20699, 20700, 20701, 20702,
  20703, 20704, 20705, 20706; Phoenix
  20762; Lucrece 20775; Venus 20798
Simpson, S. B.
  Much Ado 11284
Simpson, William W. 1945–
  Measure 8039
Sims, Thos. H., arr.
  Romeo 14148
Simun, Francis
  Macbeth 7152
Sinagra, Antonio
  Tempest 15279
Sinclair, Dane, arr.
  As You Like It 561
Sinclair, G. R., arr.
  Othello 12529
Singelée, Jean Baptiste, arr. 1812–1875
  Hamlet 3674; Dream 10885; Othello
  12154

Singer, André 1907–
  Also known under the pseudonym
  'Alexander Ross'
  Twelfth Night 17226
Singer, Joseph
  Twelfth Night 17227
Singer, Louis C. 1912–1966
  Errors 2219; Romeo 13610, 13611; Shrew
  14618, 14619
Singer, Malcolm John 1953–
  Macbeth 7153; Measure 7753
Singer, Otto, arr. 1833–1894
  Lear 6178; Romeo 13576, 13577
Singer, Otto, Jr., arr.
  As You Like It 916; Cymbeline 2877;
  Macbeth 7484; Measure 7809
Singer, Otto [Jr.], arr.
  Lear 6108
Sired, W. G.
  Dream 10274
Sirli, Vasile
  Richard III 12975
Sirmay, Albert, arr. 1880–1967
  Errors 2220, 2221; Shrew 14620, 14621
Sirota, Robert Benson 1949–
  Settings of Commemorative Pieces . . .
  21238
Sisson, Marion Grace
  Shrew 14483
Sisson, Richard 1957–
  As You Like It 841; Othello 11943
Sitsky, Larry 1934–
  L.L.L. 6473
Sitt, Hans 1850–1922
  Macbeth 7476
Sitt, Hans, arr. 1850–1922
  Tempest 15332
Siuda, Wolfgang 1952–
  Measure 7754
Siwe, Thomas V. 1935–
  Othello 11944
Siwek, Zbyhněv
  Macbeth 7154
Sixt, Paul
  1 Henry IV 4425; 2 Henry IV 4600
Skalkottas, Nikolaos 1904–1949
  Also known as Nikos Scalcotas and as Nicos
  Scalcotas
  Henry V 4762
Skeaping, Roddy
  Twelfth Night 17228
Skeoch, Fraser
  1 Henry IV 4426
Škerjanc, Lucijan Marija 1900–1973
  Much Ado 11285
Skiles, Marlin Henderson 1906–
  Hamlet 3812
Skinner, Frank C., arr. 1897–1968
  Two Gentlemen 18606

Skinner, William
  Hamlet 3428
Sklenička, Karel
  Macbeth 7155; Much Ado 11286
Skolnik, William 1950–
  Romeo 13468; Twelfth Night 17229
Skoumal, Petr 1938–
  Hamlet 3429; Dream 10010; Romeo 13469;
  Tempest 15280; Twelfth Night 17230
Skrzek, Józef
  Othello 11945
Slade, Julian Penkivil 1930–
  Antony 229, 351; As You Like It 842; Errors
  2236; Merchant 8330; Dream 10011,
  10012, 10013; Much Ado 11287, 11614;
  Shrew 14484; Two Gentlemen 18431
Slater, David Dick 1869–1942
  Much Ado 11523
Slater, Gordon Archbold 1896–1979
  Winter's Tale 19018
Slater, Jack
  Kinsmen 19163
Slater, Neil
  Sonnet 29 19580
Slaughter, A. Walter 1860–1908
  Settings of Commemorative Pieces . . .
  20887
Slaughter, A. Walter, in part arr. 1860–1908
  As You Like It 843
Slavický, Milan 1947–
  Hamlet 4032
Slim, Harry Colin 1929–
  1 Henry IV 4427
Šlitr, Jiří 1924–1969
  Sonnet 51 19751
Slonov, Iurii Mikhailovich 1906–
  Much Ado 11288
Sloper, Edmund Hugh Lindsay 1826–1887
  Tempest 16117
Smale, Percy W. de Courcy
  As You Like It 1527
Smallwood, William 1831–1897
  As You Like It 1926; Cymbeline 2828;
  Hamlet 4033; Romeo 13959
Smallwood, William, arr. 1831–1897
  As You Like It 1947; Dream 9815; Twelfth
  Night 18237
Smart, Gary L. 1943–
  Tempest 15478
Smetana, Bedřich 1824–1884
  Macbeth 7477; Richard III 12976, 13060;
  Twelfth Night 17410; Settings of
  Commemorative Pieces . . . 21171
Smiley, Pril 1943–
  Lear 5930; Macbeth 7156, 7157; Dream
  10014; Richard III 12977, 12978; Twelfth
  Night 17231
Smit, Leo, arr. 1921–
  Romeo 13612

Smit Sibinga, Theo H. 1899–1958
  Merchant 8332
Smith, A., arr.
  Romeo 13613
Smith, Alexander
  Much Ado 11289
Smith, Barron, arr.
  Romeo 13614
Smith, Boyton 1837–
  As You Like It 1927
Smith, Carl
  K. John 5626; L.L.L. 6287; Merchant 8333;
  Much Ado 11290; Richard III 12979; Two
  Gentlemen 18432; Kinsmen 19164
Smith, Clive
  Lear 5931
Smith, David Stanley 1877–1949
  1 Henry IV 4486; 2 Henry IV 4661; Henry V
  4839; Troilus 16533
Smith, Edward Sydney 1839–1889
  Dream 10713
Smith, Edward Sydney, arr. 1839–1889
  Dream 9816, 9817
Smith, Edwin
  [Edwin Smith, one of several pseudonyms
  used by Franz Behr (1837–1898)?]
  Tempest 15752
Smith, Frank H.
  Coriolanus 2343
Smith, George Stuart
  Much Ado 11645
Smith, Hale 1925–
  L.L.L. 6474
Smith, Ian
  Hamlet 3430; Shrew 14485
Smith, James G.
  As You Like It 1528
Smith, Jim
  Merchant 8417; Dream 10015
Smith, John Christopher 1712–1795
  Henry VIII 5168, 5235; L.L.L. 6343, 6682;
  Dream 10276; Much Ado 11524, 11633;
  Tempest 15479, 15939, 16206
Smith, John Gregory
  As You Like It 1529
Smith, John Stafford 1750–1836
  As You Like It 1784, 1855; L.L.L. 6475;
  Measure 7980
Smith, Joseph Leopold 1881–1952
  Also known as Leo Smith
  Henry VIII 5244
Smith, Joseph Leopold, arr. 1881–1952
  Also known as Leo Smith
  Tempest 14860
Smith, L.
  Winter's Tale 19019
Smith, Malcolm Wallace 1944–
  Hamlet 3431; Tempest 15281; Sonnet 18
  19432; Sonnet 60 19838; Sonnet 71 19965

Smith, Raymond Allyn, arr.
  Cymbeline 2778
Smith, Robert 1922–
  Twelfth Night 18010
Smith, Roger, arr.
  Macbeth 7352
Smith, Stephen
  Macbeth 7158
Smith, Walter Ernest
  Merchant 8468
Smith, William Marion
  Macbeth 7159
Smith, William Russell 1927–
  Lear 6016; Tempest 15488; Twelfth Night
  17629
Smith, William Seymour [1836?]–1905
  As You Like It 1928; Macbeth 7577; Merry
  Wives 9231; Dream 10712; Much Ado
  11607; Romeo 13960; Tempest 16118,
  16119; Twelfth Night 18249, 18250, 18251
Smith, Wilson George 1855–1929
  Merchant 8709
Smith Brindle, Reginald 1917–
  2 Henry IV 4647; Macbeth 7397; Merchant
  8469; Much Ado 11525; Othello 12229
Smithers, Don LeRoy 1933–
  As You Like It 844
Smolanoff, Michael Louis 1942–
  Much Ado 11526
Smolover, Raymond 1921–
  Merchant 8679
Smyth, Ethel Mary 1858–1944
  Antony 325
Smyth, Ethel Mary, arr. 1858–1944
  Hamlet 4034
Sneath, Elias Hershey, arr.
  Macbeth 7578; Richard III 13077
Snel, Joseph François, arr. 1793–1861
  Dream 10886
Snook, Michael
  Settings of Commemorative Pieces . . . 21263
Snyder, Jack
  Macbeth 7293
Snyder, Stephen
  L.L.L. 6333
Sobieski, Andrzej 1937–
  Tempest 15282
Sobolewski, Fryderyk Edward [1808]–1872
  Also known as Johann Friedrich Eduard de
  Sobolewski
  Cymbeline 2518
Söderlundh, Lille Bror 1912–1957
  As You Like It 845; Merchant 8334; Romeo
  13470; Twelfth Night 17232, 17233,
  17630, 18011, 18184
Söderman, Johan August 1832–1876
  Coriolanus 2344; Richard III 12980; Timon
  16358; Settings of Commemorative
  Pieces . . . 21172

Sofsky, Max
  Sonnet 29 19581; Sonnet 116 20332
Sojka, František 1933–1984
  Shrew 14486
Sokolov, Nikolai Aleksandrovich 1859–1922
  Othello 12353; Winter's Tale 18877
Sokolov, V., arr.
  Cymbeline 2779
Sokolov, Vladimir Aleksandrovich
  Dream 10016
Sokolov, Vladimir Timofeevich 1830–1890
  Othello 12354
Sola, Carlo [Michelangelo], arr. 1786–[after
  1829]
  Othello 12155
Sola, Jose
  Romeo 14066
Solazzi, Ugo, arr.
  Romeo 14120
Soldan, Kurt, arr.
  Macbeth 7353; Merry Wives 9130
Soleil, Didier
  Pseudonym used by Paulette Ghestem
  Lear 6097
Soler, Josep 1935–
  Sonnet 155 20576; Settings of
  Commemorative Pieces ... 21239, 21240
Solie, John
  Lear 5932
Solin, Lev L'vovich 1923–
  Antony 230, 326
Solin, Lev L'vovich, arr. 1923–
  Hamlet 3419, 3422
Soliva, Carlo Evasio, arr. 1792–1851
  Othello 12156
Solov'ev, Nikolai Feopemptovich 1846–1916
  Lear 6189
Soltanoff, Philip
  Dream 10017
Somary, Johannes 1935–
  Settings of Commemorative Pieces ... 21241
Somer, Louis Henri 1901–1966
  Twelfth Night 18252
Somers, Harry Stewart 1925–
  Macbeth 7160; Dream 10018, 10019,
  10471; Tempest 15828
Somers, Paul M.
  Macbeth 7161
Somerset, Mary Hurd
  Also wrote under the pseudonym 'Maud
  Somerset'
  P. Pilgrim 20707
Somervell, Arthur 1863–1937
  As You Like It 1164, 1785, 1859; Henry
  VIII 5169; Measure 7981; Tempest 16120;
  Twelfth Night 18012, 18253; Winter's Tale
  19020, 19090; Sonnet 71 19966
Somervell, Arthur, arr. 1863–1937
  As You Like It 1464; Twelfth Night 18310

Somerville, Reginald 1867–
  Settings of Commemorative Pieces ... 21275
Sommerfeld, Willy 1904–
  As You Like It 846, 847; Measure 7755;
  Much Ado 11291; Romeo 13471; Shrew
  14487, 14488; Tempest 15283; Twelfth
  Night 17234, 17235; Winter's Tale 18879
Sommerlatte, Ulrich 1914–
  Twelfth Night 17631
Sommerlatte, Ulrich, arr. 1914–
  Othello 12511
Sommerro, Henning 1952–
  Hamlet 3432
Sommi-Picenardi, Guido 1894–
  Macbeth 7162
Son, Yung Wha 1954–
  Macbeth 7481
Sonder-Mahnken, Roland
  Coriolanus 2345; 1 Henry IV 4428; 2 Henry
  IV 4601; Henry V 4763; Shrew 14489
Sonneborn, Daniel
  Tempest 16192
Sonnenburg, Klaus 1927–
  As You Like It 848; Macbeth 7163; Othello
  11946; Richard II 12722; Richard III 12982;
  Romeo 13472; Twelfth Night 17236, 17237
Sonnenburg, Klaus, in part arr. 1927–
  Hamlet 3433
Sønstevold, Gunnar 1912–
  Much Ado 11292; Tempest 15284
Sorbon, Kurt
  Winter's Tale 19154
Sosārs, Burhards 1890–1953
  Settings of Commemorative Pieces ...
  20888
Soteriou, Mia
  Romeo 13473
Soukup, Vladimír 1930–
  Antony 281
Soulé, Anne, in part arr.
  Romeo 13474
Sousa, John Philip, arr. 1854–1932
  Hamlet 3128; Merry Wives 9131; Othello
  12204
Souster, Timothy Andrew James 1943–
  Tempest 15506
Southam, T. Wallace 1900–
  Much Ado 11527
Southgate, William David 1941–
  As You Like It 849; Hamlet 3434; L.L.L.
  6288; Macbeth 7164; Merry Wives 8952;
  Othello 11947; Twelfth Night 17238
Southworth, W.
  As You Like It 1929
Sowerbutts, John Albert   –1970
  Much Ado 11528
Sowinski, Albert [1803?]–1880
  Born Wojciech Sowiński
  Dream 10714; Othello 12431

Soyer, Adolphe-François, arr. 1865–1919
Cymbeline 2843; Merry Wives 9194; Othello
12205
Spacks, Barry
Tempest 15489
Spada, Pietro, arr.
Dream 9818
Spadaccino, Silvano
Othello 11948
Spalder, Frithjof, arr.
Merry Wives 9173, 9174, 9175
Spalding, Albert, arr. 1888–1953
Cymbeline 2780
Spangler, David
Troilus 16534
Spark, William, in part arr. 1823–1897
Settings of Commemorative Pieces . . .
21173
Spark, William, arr. 1823–1897
Dream 9819; Tempest 14743, 14826,
15065
Speaight, Joseph 1868–1953
Dream 10715; Romeo 13961; Tempest
16121; Winter's Tale 19122
Spearing, Robert Michael 1950–
L.L.L. 6476, 6613; Romeo 14036
Spedding, Frank Donald 1929–
Titus 16424
Speer, William Henry 1863–1937
As You Like It 2016
Speidel, Wilhelm 1826–1899
Twelfth Night 17632
Speidel, Wilhelm, arr. 1826–1899
Dream 9820
Spelman, Peter
As You Like It 1968
Spencer, Marguerita 1892–
Née MacQuarrie
As You Like It 1786; Cymbeline 2792; L.L.L.
6477; Dream 10343; Tempest 15940;
Twelfth Night 18013; Two Gentlemen
18618; Settings of Commemorative
Pieces . . . 21307
Spencer, Robert
Merchant 8335
Spencer, Williametta 1931–
As You Like It 1530; Tempest 15571,
15753, 15941; Twelfth Night 17633, 18014
Spendiarov, Aleksandr Afanas'evich
1871–1928
Merchant 8336; Othello 11949, 12230
Spevak, Harver
Lear 5933
Speyer, W.
Two Gentlemen 18619
Spialek, Hans, arr. 1894–1983
Errors 2222
Spicker, Max, arr. 1858–1912
Othello 12206; Tempest 14827

Spies, Claudio 1925–
Sonnet 5 19212; Sonnet 18 19433; Sonnet
27 19528; Sonnet 28 19536; Sonnet 43
19720; Sonnet 60 19839; Sonnet 71 19967;
Sonnet 104 20243; Sonnet 115 20304;
Sonnet 116 20333; Sonnet 119 20354;
Sonnet 137 20450
Spies, F., arr.
Merry Wives 9132
Spies, Leo 1899–1965
As You Like It 850, 1165, 1531, 1787,
1860; Hamlet 3435; 1 Henry IV 4429; 2
Henry IV 4602; L.L.L. 6344; Dream 10020,
10716; Romeo 13810, 13962; Twelfth Night
17239, 17634; Settings of Commemorative
Pieces . . . 21079
Spies, Leo, in part arr. 1899–1965
Errors 2176
Spiller, Isaac
Macbeth 7579; Othello 12513; Richard III
13078; Romeo 14180
Spindler, Franz Stanislaus 1759–1819
Dream 10985
Spink, Ian Walter Alfred, arr. 1932–
Cymbeline 2631; Macbeth 6927; Measure
8017; Tempest 15066; Winter's Tale 18962
Spira, Rudolf, arr.
Winter's Tale 18752
Spitzer, Jan
Richard III 12983; Romeo 13475
Spizizen, Louise Myers 1928–
Sonnet 27 19529
Spohr, Louis 1784–1859
Macbeth 7165
Spratlan, Lewis 1940–
Hamlet 3436; Measure 7756
Spray, Philip M. 1954–
Hamlet 3437; Measure 7757; Merry Wives
8953; Dream 10021; Romeo 13476; Twelfth
Night 17240
Sprayberry, Robert Jones 1952–
Hamlet 3860; Romeo 13477
Springer, Erma D.
As You Like It 851
Springer, Melvyn
1 Henry IV 4430; 2 Henry IV 4603
Spyrka, Edward
Shrew 14490
Squire, William Henry, arr. 1871–1963
Twelfth Night 16619
Srebotnjak, Alojz 1931–
Twelfth Night 17241
Srebotnjak, Alojz, in part arr. 1931–
Tempest 15285
Srnka, Jiří 1907–1982
Hamlet 3438; Macbeth 7167; Merry Wives
8954, 8955, 8956, 8957; Dream 10022,
10023, 10024; Romeo 14067; Twelfth Night
17242

Šrubař, Jan
    Othello 11950
St. Amand, A.
    Macbeth 7580
St. Clair, Floyd J., arr. 1871–1942
    Richard III 12851
St. John, Kathleen Louise 1942–
    Sonnet 29 19582; Settings of
    Commemorative Pieces . . . 21242
St. Leger, Frank
    Othello 11951
Stack, Bernadette
    Winter's Tale 18880
Stade, Friedrich, arr. 1844–1928
    Romeo 13578
Stadtfeld, Christian Josef Anton Franz
    Alexander 1826–1853
    Hamlet 3621
Staeps, Hans Ulrich, arr. 1909–
    Dream 10256
Staffelli, Attilio 1894–1957
    Lear 6099
Stafford, C. Lloyd
    Cymbeline 2611
Stahl, Frederic, arr.
    Macbeth 7256
Stalling, Christian
    Twelfth Night 17243
Stallybrass, James S., arr.
    Macbeth 7002
Stamper, David 1883–1963
    Romeo 14181; Settings of Commemorative
    Pieces . . . 21080
Stamper, R.
    Macbeth 7168
Stanchevaia, R.
    Merry Wives 8958
Standke, O., arr.
    Dream 9821
Staněk, Josef
    Much Ado 11293
Stanford, Charles Villiers 1852–1924
    Much Ado 11369; Twelfth Night 17635,
    18015, 18185; Winter's Tale 19155
Stanislaus, Frederick 1844–1891
    As You Like It 1166, 1532; Henry VIII
    5170; L.L.L. 6478; Measure 7982; Much
    Ado 11529; Twelfth Night 18016
Stanislaus, Henri
    Pseudonym used by J. Herbert Marshall
    Lear 6100; Much Ado 11608; Tempest
    16122
Stanislaw, C. Francis J.
    Hamlet 3622; Sonnet 57 19809; Sonnet 62
    19866
Stanley, Charles John 1713–1786
    L.L.L. 6369
Stanley, Gerald
    Cymbeline 2829

Stanley, Helen Gatlin 1930–
    Tempest 15843
Stanley, Michael 1956–
    Winter's Tale 18881
Stanley, Mildred Couture
    As You Like It 1588
Stansbury, George Frederick 1800–1845
    Dream 10762
Stansbury, George Frederick, in part arr.
    1800–1845
    Settings of Commemorative Pieces . . . 20889
Starer, Robert 1924–
    Henry VIII 5041; Tempest 16293
Stark, Fleurette 1932–
    Twelfth Night 17636
Stärk, Wilhelm
    Merchant 8337, 8338; Romeo 13478;
    Shrew 14491
Starke, H., arr.
    Merry Wives 9133
Starke, Peter
    Henry V 4764
Staskowiak, Dietmar
    Hamlet 3439, 4128; Twelfth Night 17244
Stattersfield, Peter 1926–
    Settings of Commemorative Pieces . . .
    20957
Stauffer, Aubrey, arr.
    Dream 9822
Stavenhagen, Bernhard 1862–1914
    Twelfth Night 17637
Steadman, Robert
    Winter's Tale 18882
Stearns, Carolyn
    Twelfth Night 17245
Stearns, Peter Pindar 1931–
    Tempest 15942
Štědroň, Miloš 1942–
    Merry Wives 8959
Steel, Alfred G.
    As You Like It 1788
Steel, Christopher 1939–
    1 Henry IV 4474; L.L.L. 6340; Richard II
    12752; Tempest 15859, 15985
Steele, James Aloysius
    Dream 10717
Steele, Porter, arr.
    1 Henry IV 4470; 2 Henry IV 4636; Merry
    Wives 9197
Steenberg, Julius 1830–1911
    As You Like It 1533; Hamlet 3802; Much
    Ado 11530; Twelfth Night 17638
Steer, Michael 1946–
    Coriolanus 2346; Caesar 5439
Stefanović, Ivana
    Macbeth 7169
Steggall, Reginald 1867–1938
    Cymbeline 2793; Henry VIII 5171; Measure
    7983; Two Gentlemen 18620

Stegmann, Karl David 1751–1826
Also known as Carl David Stegmann
Lear 5934; Macbeth 7170
Stegmann, W. G.
[G. W. Stegmann?]
Lear 5935
Stegmayer, Ferdinand 1803–1863
[Also known as Ferdinand Stegmeyer]
Cymbeline 2794
Stegmayer, Matthäus 1771–1820
Merry Wives 9241
Steibelt, Daniel Gottlieb 1765–1823
Romeo 13811
Stein, Alan 1949–
Twelfth Night 17246
Stein, Gottfried 1932–
1 Henry IV 4431; 2 Henry IV 4604
Stein, Jürgen
Merchant 8339
Stein, Ronald 1930–
Othello 11952
Stein, Stacy
Two Gentlemen 18433
Steinbach, Emil 1849–1919
Hamlet 4035
Steinberg, Paul 1946–
Macbeth 7171
Steinbrecher, Alexander
All's Well 59; Othello 12465; Shrew 14492
Steinbrook, David Herman 1941–
Sonnet 73 20017
Steiner, Emma R.
As You Like It 852
Steiner, Eric, arr.
Macbeth 7354
Steinert, Alexander Lang, in part arr.
1900–1982
Romeo 13479
Steinke, Greg A. 1942–
Dream 10025; Shrew 14493; Tempest
15286; Twelfth Night 17247; Sonnet 18
19434; Sonnet 53 19761; Sonnet 98 20193;
Settings of Commemorative Pieces . . .
20890
Steinkopf, Hanns
Measure 7758
Steinkühler, Emil 1824–1872
Twelfth Night 17412
Steinmayer, Otto, in part arr.
Tempest 15287
Stenhammar, Karl Vilhelm Eugen 1871–1927
Also known as Wilhelm Stenhammar
As You Like It 853, 1167, 1969; Hamlet
3440; Henry VIII 5172; Lear 5936; Romeo
13480; Twelfth Night 17413
Ştephănescu, George 1843–1925
Hamlet 3441; Caesar 5440; Shrew 14494
Stephano, Ch., arr.
Tempest 15126

Stephen, David 1869–1946
As You Like It 1168; Twelfth Night 17639
Stephen, R.
Dream 10551
Stephen-Samuels, Patrick 1940–
As You Like It 1169, 1789; Measure 7984;
Tempest 15288
Stephens, [John] [circa 1720–1780]
Tempest 15834
Stephenson, Morton 1884–
Settings of Commemorative Pieces . . . 20891
Stephenson, Pat
L.L.L. 6289
Stephenson, Robin
L.L.L. 6614; Winter's Tale 19135
Stepp, Joachim
As You Like It 855
Steptoe, Roger Guy 1953–
As You Like It 1224; L.L.L. 6615
Stern, Gunter
Sonnet 18 19435
Sternberg, Erich-Walter 1891–1974
Sonnet 146 20501
Sternberg, Friwi
Romeo 13482; Shrew 14495
Sterne, Colin Chase 1921–
Henry VIII 5173; Caesar 5441; Measure
7759; Tempest 15572, 15754
Sterne, Richard L.
Antony 231; Hamlet 3442
Sternefeld, Daniel 1905–
Settings of Commemorative Pieces . . . 21192
Sternfeld, Frederick William, ed. 1914–
Anthologies 21357
Sternfels, Karl
Shrew 14496
Stevens, [?]
Cymbeline 2492
Stevens, Clive
Kinsmen 19165
Stevens, Denis William, arr. 1922–
As You Like It 856, 1465, 1847
Stevens, Evelyn Sutton
Much Ado 11294
Stevens, Halsey 1908–
L.L.L. 6616; Settings of Commemorative
Pieces . . . 21243
Stevens, Joan Frances 1921–
Née Wollerman
Tempest 15289, 15573, 15755
Stevens, Paul James 1930–
Also writes under the pseudonym 'Paul James'
Sonnet 155 20577
Stevens, Richard John Samuel 1757–1837
As You Like It 1170, 1534, 1861, 1992;
Cymbeline 2612; Hamlet 3737; Henry VIII
5174; Merchant 8634; Dream 10363,
10552, 10986; Much Ado 11531, 11646;
Tempest 15835; Twelfth Night 17640,

Stevens, Richard John Samuel (*cont.*)
    17742, 18017; Two Gentlemen 18434,
    18470, 18621; P. Pilgrim 20708; Settings of
    Commemorative Pieces . . . 21081
Stevens, Richard John Samuel, arr.
    1757–1837
    Cymbeline 2857
Stevens, William P.
    L.L.L. 6370
Stevens, William Seaman 1778–
    Romeo 14037
Stevenson, Alexander
    Dream 10932
Stevenson, Frederick
    Tempest 15943
Stevenson, Holly
    Richard III 12984
Stevenson, John Andrew 1761–1833
    Hamlet 3712, 3738, 3779; Measure 7985;
    Merchant 8636; Dream 10933; Shrew
    14646; Tempest 15574; Twelfth Night
    18079, 18186, 18286; P. Pilgrim 20712
Stewart, Humphrey John [1854]–1932
    Born Humphrey John Stark
    Tempest 16124
Stewart, John
    Hamlet 3443
Stewart, Louis
    Dream 10026
Stewart, Robert
    Shrew 14497
Stewart, Robert Prescott 1825–1894
    Settings of Commemorative Pieces . . . 21082
Steymans, Herwig
    Richard III 12985
Stich, Joseph, arr.
    Measure 7810
Stichini, Placido 1860–1897
    Othello 12207
Stickles, William C., arr. 1883–1971
    Errors 2223, 2224, 2225, 2226, 2227,
    2228, 2229, 2230; Romeo 13615, 13616,
    13617, 13618, 13619, 13620, 13621,
    13622, 13623, 13624; Shrew 14622,
    14623, 14624, 14625, 14626, 14627,
    14628, 14629, 14630, 14631, 14632
Stieber, Hans 1886–1969
    Twelfth Night 17248
Stieber, Hans, arr. 1886–1969
    Dream 10257
Stierlin-Vallon, Henri 1887–1952
    Tempest 15290
Stiles, George 1961–
    Hamlet 3444; L.L.L. 6290; Othello 11953;
    Sonnet 18 19458
Stillinger, Gertrude Metcalf
    Henry VIII 5175
Stillman, Richard
    Hamlet 3445

Stivín, Jiří
    Hamlet 3446; L.L.L. 6291
Stocco, Clemente, arr.
    Romeo 13779
Stock, David Frederick 1939–
    Hamlet 3447; Macbeth 7172; Othello
    11954; Romeo 13483
Stockmeier, Wolfgang, arr. 1931–
    Hamlet 3984
Stocks, Harold Carpenter Lamb
    [1885?]–1956
    Dream 10561
Stoecklin-Prietto, Carmen
    As You Like It 1790
Stoepel, Robert August 1821–1887
    As You Like It 857; Macbeth 7173, 7482;
    Merchant 8340; Othello 11955; Richard III
    12986
Stoepel, Robert August, in part arr.
    1821–1887
    Hamlet 3448; Twelfth Night 17249
Stoessel, Albert Frederic 1894–1943
    As You Like It 1537
Stogorskii, Aleksandr Pavlovich, arr. 1910–
    Much Ado 11158
Stoianovskaia, G.
    Romeo 13484
Stoker, Richard 1938–
    Henry VIII 5176; Tempest 15490; Troilus
    16535; Twelfth Night 17748
Stokes, Charles, arr. 1784–1839
    Macbeth 7003, 7213
Stokes, George
    As You Like It 1181, 1538, 1791; Cymbeline
    2795; Measure 7986; Dream 10344, 10422,
    10562; Much Ado 11552; Tempest 15944;
    Twelfth Night 18019; Two Gentlemen
    18622
Stoklasa, Zdeněk
    Romeo 13485; Timon 16359
Stokłosa, Janusz 1954–
    Measure 7760; Titus 16415
Stoll, D.
    [David Stoll? Dennis Stoll?]
    Antony 327
Stolz, L.
    Merchant 8341
Stolz, Robert 1880–1975
    Hamlet 4247; Romeo 14068
Stone, David, arr. [1922–   ]
    Merry Wives 9176; Dream 9823, 9824
Stone, J. T., arr.
    As You Like It 447; Macbeth 7355; Tempest
    14744, 14828, 15127
Stone, Jeremy
    Hamlet 3449
Stone, Norman Murray 1890–
    As You Like It 1182; Cymbeline 2613; L.L.L.
    6617; Twelfth Night 17641

Stone, Norman Murray, arr. 1890–
As You Like It 448; Cymbeline 2781; Hamlet
3780; L.L.L. 6499; Measure 8018; Othello
12260; Tempest 14829; Twelfth Night
17315; Two Gentlemen 18607

Stör, Carl
Henry V 4765; 1 Henry VI 4869; 2 Henry VI
4909; 3 Henry VI 4951; Macbeth 7174;
Richard II 12723; Twelfth Night 17250

Stora, Jean-Pierre-Salomon
Othello 11956

Storace, Stephen John Seymour 1762–1796
Errors 2238; Venus 20821

Storch, Anton Maria 1813–1887
Romeo 14113

Storch, Howard V.
Richard III 12987

Storm, Wayne
As You Like It 1970

Stothart, Herbert 1885–1949
Romeo 13486

Stout, Alan Burrage 1932–
Tempest 15578, 15945; Two Gentlemen
18623

Stoye, Karl
Twelfth Night 17251

Stradal, August, arr. 1860–
Hamlet 3985

Strait, David
Settings of Commemorative Pieces . . . 20892

Stramm, Gottfried
As You Like It 858; Dream 10027; Othello
11957; Richard II 12724; Romeo 13487,
13488; Shrew 14498; Titus 16416

Strand, Ragnvald Edvard 1910–
Sonnet 8 19264

Strandberg, Newton D. 1921–
Dream 10718

Stranders, Percy
Dream 10719

Strange, Mary A.
Shrew 14499

Strano, Alfredo
Twelfth Night 17252

Stransky, Josef, arr. 1872–1936
Much Ado 11356

Strasser, Jani 1901–1978
Merchant 8342

Straube, Klaus
Hamlet 3450

Straus, Ludwig, arr. 1835–1899
Merry Wives 9134

Strauss, Heinrich
Hamlet 3451

Strauss, Isaac, arr. 1806–1888
Hamlet 3675, 3676, 3677

Strauss, Johann Baptist 1825–1899
Known as Johann Strauss, Sohn
Twelfth Night 17414

Strauss, Joseph 1793–1866
Richard III 12988

Strauss, [Jules], arr.
Romeo 13748

Strauss, Richard Georg 1864–1949
Hamlet 3781, 3843, 3876; Macbeth 7483;
Romeo 13489

Strauss, Ronald Hugh
Sonnet 140 20470

Stravinsky, Igor Fedorovich 1882–1971
Antony 232; L.L.L. 6334, 6479; Tempest
15756; Sonnet 8 19265

Stravinsky, Soulima, arr. 1910–
Dream 9825

Strayhorn, William 1915–1967
Antony 328; Hamlet 4036; Henry V 4829;
Caesar 5528; Macbeth 7485; Dream 10720;
Othello 12432; Romeo 13963; Shrew
14668; Settings of Commemorative
Pieces . . . 21174

Streatfield, Valma Jane 1932–
Née Paterson
Sonnet 18 19436

Streck, Jürgen 1948–
Troilus 16536

Street, Joseph
Two Gentlemen 18647

Street, Wolcott Davenport
Sonnet 30 19620

Strehlow, John
Tempest 15291

Streulens, Herman
Measure 7761; Dream 10028; Much Ado
11295

Strick, Susan
Merchant 8343

Strickland, William 1914–
1 Henry IV 4432; Caesar 5442

Stricklen, Edward Griffith 1880–
Twelfth Night 17253

Strilko, Anthony 1931–
Hamlet 4248

Strindberg, Carl Axel 1845–1927
Shrew 14500

Strobach, Franz
Othello 11958, 12355

Strobl, Heinrich
As You Like It 1930

Strodel, Otto
Hamlet 3452

Strohbach, Siegfried 1929–
Much Ado 11296; Othello 11959; Troilus
16537; Twelfth Night 17254; Settings of
Commemorative Pieces . . . 21244

Stroiński, Marian 1907–1957
Dream 10029

Strom, K.
[Kurt Richard Strom (1903–   )?]
Romeo 13490

Strombergs, Alfred 1922–
As You Like It 1183; Twelfth Night 17642
Stromenger, Karol 1885–1975
L.L.L. 6292; Othello 11960; Shrew 14501
Strong, George Templeton 1856–1948
Also known as George Templeton-Strong
Hamlet 4037; Dream 10721; Othello 12433;
Sonnet 49 19741
Strube, Gustav 1867–1953
Dream 10722
Strunk, Steven Gerhardt 1943–
Tempest 15579, 15757, 15946
Stueber, Carl, arr.
Othello 12157
Stultz, Marie Irene 1945–
As You Like It 1184, 1792; Hamlet 3824;
L.L.L. 6618; Sonnet 73 20018; Venus 20799
Stümer, Marie W.
Dream 10934
Stuntz, Joseph Hartmann 1793–1859
Winter's Tale 18883; Settings of
Commemorative Pieces . . . 21245
Sturiale, Grant 1957–
Twelfth Night 17255
Stürmer, Bruno 1892–1958
Henry V 4766; Much Ado 11553
Stuten, Jan 1890–1948
Cymbeline 2493; L.L.L. 6293; Merchant
8344; Dream 10030; Tempest 15292;
Twelfth Night 17256; Winter's Tale 18884
Stutz, Philippe, arr.
Hamlet 3678
Styne, Jule Kerwin 1905–
Also known as Jules Stein and as Julius Stein
Romeo 14115
Sū Jin Zùo
Twelfth Night 17415
Suben, Joel Eric 1946–
As You Like It 859
Subotnik, Morton 1933–
Lear 5937
Suchoff, Benjamin, arr. 1918–
Hamlet 3420
Suckling, Norman Charles, arr. 1904–
Measure 8019
Sudds, William F. 1843–1920
Dream 10935
Suett, Richard 1755–1805
Twelfth Night 17257
Suffern, Carlos 1905–
Lear 6101
Sugarman, Louis, arr.
Romeo 14004
Suk, Josef 1874–1935
Winter's Tale 19123
Suk, Josef, arr. 1874–1935
Othello 12388
Suk, Váša 1861–1933
Winter's Tale 19125

Šulek, Stjepan 1914–1986
Coriolanus 2376; Tempest 15491
Sullivan, Arthur Seymour 1842–1900
As You Like It 1222, 1539; Henry VIII
5020, 5177; Macbeth 7175; Merchant
8345, 8470, 8485, 8760; Merry Wives
8960; Much Ado 11554; Othello 12356,
12486; Tempest 15293; Timon 16382;
Twelfth Night 18020
Sullivan, Thomas D.
P. Pilgrim 20713
Sulyok, Tamás
Lear 5938; Richard III 12989
Sulzer, Julius 1834–1891
Antony 233; Hamlet 3453; 1 Henry IV
4433; 2 Henry IV 4605; Henry V 4767;
Richard II 12725
Summerly, Alan
Romeo 13964
Sumner, Louise
Romeo 13491
Sumsion, Herbert Whitton, arr. 1899–
Merchant 8748
Sundell, Steven L. 1946–
Romeo 13850
Sundstrøm, Andy 1940–
Othello 11961; Troilus 16538
Surdin, Morris 1914–1979
Merchant 8349; Twelfth Night 17258
Susa, Conrad 1935–
All's Well 60, 61; Antony 234, 235, 236,
237; As You Like It 860, 861, 862, 863, 864;
Errors 2177; Coriolanus 2347, 2348;
Cymbeline 2494; Hamlet 3454, 3455;
1 Henry IV 4434, 4435; 2 Henry IV 4606;
Henry V 4768; Henry VIII 5026; Caesar
5443, 5444; K. John 5627; Lear 5939, 5940,
5941, 5942; L.L.L. 6294, 6295; Macbeth
7178, 7179; Measure 7762, 7763, 7764;
Merchant 8350; Merry Wives 8961, 8962;
Dream 10031, 10032, 10033; Much Ado
11297, 11298, 11299, 11300; Othello
11962, 11963, 11964, 11965; Richard II
12726, 12727, 12728; Richard III 12990,
12991, 12992, 12993, 12994; Romeo
13492, 13493, 13494, 13495, 13496; Shrew
14502, 14503, 14504; Tempest 15298;
Timon 16360; Troilus 16539; Twelfth Night
17259, 17260, 17261, 17262, 17263,
17264, 17265, 17266, 17267, 17268; Two
Gentlemen 18435, 18436; Winter's Tale
18885, 18886; Sonnet 18 19326; Sonnet 27
19532; Sonnet 29 19541; Sonnet 30 19590,
19591; Sonnet 60 19816; Sonnet 73 19979;
Sonnet 116 20309; Sonnet 130 20430;
Settings of Commemorative Pieces . . . 20893
Susa, Conrad, in part arr. 1935–
Hamlet 3456, 3457; 2 Henry IV 4607; L.L.L.
6296; Tempest 15299

Sushkova, L.
Lear 5943
Suter, Hans
Lear 5944
Suter, Robert 1919–
As You Like It 1931
Sutermeister, Heinrich 1910–
Romeo 13815; Tempest 15492
Sutherland, Margaret Ada 1897–
Dream 10034, 10563; Twelfth Night 18021;
Settings of Commemorative Pieces . . .
21246, 21264
Sutkowski, Stefan
Twelfth Night 17269
Sutor, Wilhelm 1774–1828
Macbeth 7180
Sutro, Ottilie, arr.
Dream 9826
Suttle, Raymond
Hamlet 3458
Suycott, Forest
Caesar 5445
Sveinbjörnsson, Sveinbjörn 1847–1926
Tempest 16294
Svendsen, Johan Severin 1840–1911
Romeo 13965
Svensson, Sven Erik Emanuel 1899–1960
Twelfth Night 18254
Sveshnikov, Aleksandr Vasil'evich 1890–
Twelfth Night 17270
Svetel, H.
Twelfth Night 17271
Sviridov, Georgii Iurii Vasil'evich 1915–
As You Like It 1185; Hamlet 3803; L.L.L.
6619; Othello 11966, 12231, 12242,
12357; Twelfth Night 18187
Svoboda, Milan
Hamlet 3459
Swackhamer, John M.
Hamlet 3460
Swados, Elizabeth 1951–
As You Like It 865
Swaffield, Ronald
Two Gentlemen 18624
Swain, Freda Mary 1902–1985
As You Like It 1793; Sonnet 18 19437;
Sonnet 30 19621; Sonnet 40 19696; Sonnet
53 19762; Sonnet 65 19901; Sonnet 102
20225
Swan, Billy
As You Like It 866
Swann, Donald Ibrahim 1923–
As You Like It 1186, 1540; Romeo 14182
Swanson, Howard 1907–1978
Hamlet 4249
Swanson, Walter Donald 1903–
As You Like It 867; Measure 7987;
Merchant 8351, 8639; Twelfth Night
17643, 18022

Swart, Glenn
Hamlet 3461
Swatton, H. T., arr.
Dream 9827
Swayne, Giles Oliver Cairns 1946–
Cymbeline 2796; Tempest 15758, 15947
Swedberg, Torbjörn 1959–
Also known as Torbjörn Svedberg
Macbeth 7181
Sweeney, Elsie Irwin
Winter's Tale 18887
Sweeney, Eric John 1948–
Twelfth Night 18023
Sweeney, Glen
Macbeth 7182
Sweeting, Edward Thomas, arr. 1863–1930
As You Like It 1466; Tempest 14830
Swenson, Warren Arthur 1947–
Macbeth 7183; Romeo 13842; Tempest
15580, 15759
Swettenham, Neal
Richard III 12995
Święcicki, Mateusz
As You Like It 868; Twelfth Night 17272
Swier, Charles F. 1918–
As You Like It 869; Coriolanus 2349; Henry
VIII 5027; L.L.L. 6335; Merchant 8352;
Merry Wives 9161; Tempest 15300; Twelfth
Night 17416
Świezy, [Władysław?]
Hamlet 3462
Swift, Gertrude H.
Cymbeline 2797
Swift, Richard G. 1927–
As You Like It 870; Lear 5945; Macbeth
7184
Swinburne, William H.
Dream 10345
Swingle, Ward Lemar 1927–
As You Like It 1541
Swinstead, Felix Gerald 1880–1959
Merchant 8710
Swisher, Gloria Agnes Wilson 1935–
Also known as Mrs. Donald Prevost Swisher
Twelfth Night 18024; Sonnet 2 19193;
Sonnet 18 19438; Sonnet 38 19681; Sonnet
116 20334
Sykes, Charles T., arr.
Twelfth Night 16681
Sykes, Harold Hinchcliffe
As You Like It 1794
Symon, Jon
Macbeth 7295
Symonds, Norman 1920–
Othello 11967; Shrew 14505
Symons, Dom Thomas 1887–1975
Twelfth Night 17644
Synková, Katarína
Tempest 15301

Szabados, Béla Antal 1867–1936
  Othello 12175
Szabo, Csaba 1936–
  Romeo 13497; P. Pilgrim 20714; Lucrece
  20776
Szántó, Tivadar 1877–1934
  Romeo 14116
Szczepanek, Włodzimierz
  Cymbeline 2495; Othello 11968
Szczerbakanik, Jolanta
  Romeo 13498
Székely, Emeric, arr.
  Hamlet 3679
Szeligowski, Tadeusz 1896–1963
  Dream 10035; Much Ado 11301; Twelfth
  Night 17273
Szenkar, Mischa
  Much Ado 11302
Szervánszky, Endre 1911–1977
  Macbeth 7185
Szigeti, István
  Richard II 12729
Szokolay, Sándor 1931–
  Hamlet 3623
Sztojanovits, Jenő
  Othello 12176
Szymanowska, Maria Agata
  1789–1831
  Née Wołowska
  Othello 12358

T

T., C., arr.
  Merchant 8638
Tabrar, Joseph
  Romeo 14183
Tachihara, Yo
  Merry Wives 8963
Taggart, Mark
  Hamlet 3463
Tagliapietra, G., arr.
  [Gino Tagliapietra (1887–1954)?]
  Dream 9828
Takács, Jenő 1902–
  Cymbeline 2614
Takemitsu, Toru 1930–
  Lear 6131
Taktakishvili, Otar Vasil'evich 1924–
  Lear 5946; Winter's Tale 18888
Talexy, Adrien, arr. 1820–1881
  Dream 10887; Romeo 13641, 13749
Tallman, Randolph
  Dream 10280, 10380, 10472, 10564
Talma, Louise Juliette 1906–
  Hamlet 3861; Sonnet 29 19583; Sonnet 98
  20194; Sonnet 104 20244

Tamás, János 1936–
  Winter's Tale 18889
Tamblyn, William 1941–
  L.L.L. 6297; Measure 7765
Tamchina, Jürgen
  Measure 7766; Dream 10036; Richard II
  12730; Romeo 13499; Twelfth Night
  17274
Tamplin, Augustus Lechmore 1837–1889
  K. John 5649
Taneev, Aleksandr Sergeevich 1850–1918
  Hamlet 4038
Taneev, Sergei Ivanovich, arr.
  1856–1915
  Romeo 13877
'Tangerine Dream'
  Macbeth 7186
Tanner, John
  1 Henry IV 4436
Tanner, Mary Creusa
  Romeo 13500
Tants, Robert
  As You Like It 871, 1542; Errors 2178;
  1 Henry IV 4437; Lear 5947; Measure 7767;
  Merry Wives 8964; Dream 10037; Much
  Ado 11303; Othello 11969; Richard II
  12731; Richard III 12996; Romeo 13501;
  Shrew 14506; Tempest 15302
Tants, Robert, arr.
  Twelfth Night 16907
Tapp, Frank, arr.
  Henry VIII 5197
Tapp, Frank Harold
  Tempest 16125
Taranu, Cornel 1934–
  Hamlet 3464; Othello 11970
Taraszjewicz, Alina
  Romeo 13816
Tarenskeen, Boudewijn
  Troilus 16540
Tariot, Alexandre
  Hamlet 4039
Tariverdiev, Mikael Leonovich 1931–
  Sonnet 102 20214, 20226; Sonnet 117
  20344, 20346
Tarn, Colin
  Merry Wives 8965
Tarpey, W. Kingsley
  Twelfth Night 18025
Tarr, Edward Hankins, arr. 1936–
  Timon 16348
Tass, Erik
  All's Well 62; Errors 2179; Cymbeline 2496;
  Hamlet 3465; Measure 7768; Merchant
  8353; Romeo 13502, 13503; Tempest
  15303; Twelfth Night 17275; Two
  Gentlemen 18437; Winter's Tale 18890
Tate, Clarke, arr.
  As You Like It 1003

Tate, Phyllis 1911–1987
Pseudonym used by Margaret Duncan
As You Like It 976, Phoenix 20763

Tatton, Jack Meredith 1901–1970
As You Like It 1187

Taube, Evert 1889–1976
Sonnet 30 19622; Sonnet 60 19840; Sonnet 64 19878; Sonnet 65 19902

Taubert, Karl Gottfried Wilhelm 1811–1891
As You Like It 1543; Henry VIII 5187; L.L.L. 6480, 6620; Macbeth 7296; Merchant 8640; Dream 10565, 10723; Othello 11971; Tempest 15304; Twelfth Night 17417, 17645, 18026

Taubmann, Otto 1859–1929
Merchant 8418

Taubmann, Otto, arr. 1859–1929
Lear 6066

Taurman, Mikanna, arr.
Henry VIII 5015

Tauro, Erna 1916–
As You Like It 872

Tausch, Julius 1827–1895
As You Like It 873; Twelfth Night 17276

Tausig, Carl 1841–1871
Also known as Karol Tausig
Hamlet 3986

Tavan, Émile, arr.
Hamlet 3680; Romeo 13750

Tayler, E. Douglas
Merchant 8471

Taylor, Billee
Romeo 14184

Taylor, C.
Phoenix 20764

Taylor, Clifford Oliver 1923–1987
As You Like It 1594; Lear 6045; Merchant 8490; Dream 10442; Othello 12372; Settings of Commemorative Pieces . . . 21083

Taylor, Colin [1881?]–1973
Hamlet 4250; Dream 10724; Winter's Tale 18986

Taylor, Dorothy Janet
Twelfth Night 17277

Taylor, Franklin, arr. 1843–1919
Merchant 8761; Tempest 15296

Taylor, Horace
L.L.L. 6621

Taylor, J. A.
Measure 7988

Taylor, Jane, arr.
Tempest 14745

Taylor, Jeffrey
[Jeffrey Ayres Taylor (1945–   )?]
As You Like It 874

Taylor, Jeremy James
As You Like It 875

Taylor, Joseph Deems 1885–1966
Settings of Commemorative Pieces . . . 20894

Taylor, Laura Wilson 1819–1905
Née Barker; also known as Mrs. Tom Taylor
As You Like It 876; Measure 7989

Taylor, Madeleine Peck
Sonnet 18 19439

Taylor, Michael
Othello 12487

Taylor, Philip
[Philip Hilton Taylor (1951–   )?]
Two Gentlemen 18467

Taylor, Stainton de B., arr.
Henry V 4811

Taylor, Stanley
Merchant 8354

Taylor, Stephen
Merry Wives 8966

Taylor, William Frederick 1835–1887
Tempest 16126

Taylor, William Frederick, arr. 1835–1887
Tempest 14831

Tchaikovsky, Peter Ilich 1840–1893
Hamlet 3466, 3470, 4040, 4251; Othello 12177; Romeo 13817, 13875, 13967, 14185; Tempest 16127

Tchaikowsky, André 1935–1982
Merchant 8419; Tempest 15581, 15760, 15948; Sonnet 49 19742; Sonnet 61 19859; Sonnet 75 20041; Sonnet 89 20105; Sonnet 90 20113; Sonnet 104 20245; Sonnet 146 20502

Teicher, Louis, arr. 1924–
Romeo 13625

Teitel'baum, I.
Othello 11972

Telfer, John
As You Like It 877; L.L.L. 6298; Dream 10038; Shrew 14507; Winter's Tale 18891

Telma, Maurice
One of the sixty-two pseudonyms used by Charles Arthur Rawlings; see also Bonheur, Theodore
Dream 10725; Romeo 14009

Temmingh, H.
Errors 2180

Tempest, Leslie
As You Like It 1932; Tempest 16133

Tepper, Albert 1921–
As You Like It 878, 879, 1188, 1544, 1795; Errors 2254; Hamlet 3476, 3477; Henry VIII 5188; Caesar 5446; Lear 5948; L.L.L. 6299, 6300, 6481, 6622, 6664; Macbeth 7187; Merchant 8711; Merry Wives 8967, 9232; Dream 10039, 10040, 10041, 10042; Much Ado 11304, 11560; Othello 11973, 11974; Romeo 13504, 13505, 13506, 14010; Shrew 14508, 14509, 14669; Tempest 15308, 15309; Twelfth Night 17278, 17279, 17646, 18027; Two Gentlemen 18438; Winter's Tale 18892

ter Jung, Willi
  Twelfth Night 17280
Terashima, Rikuya 1964–
  Hamlet 4078
Terni, Paolo
  All's Well 63
Terral, Claude François René 1935–
  Hamlet 3478
Terry, George N., arr.
  Errors 2231; Romeo 13525; Shrew 14633;
  Settings of Commemorative Pieces . . . 21260
Terry, John S.
  Tempest 16295
Terschak, Adolf 1832–1901
  Romeo 14011
Terterian, Avet Rubenovich 1929–
  Richard III 13037
Terzian, Alicia 1936–
  Romeo 14038
Tessarin, Angelo, arr.
  Romeo 13780, 13781
Testi, Flavio 1923–
  Richard III 13038; Sonnet 19 19471; Sonnet
  71 19968
Thalberg, Sigismond Fortuné François, arr.
  1812–1871
  Dream 9829; Othello 12158
Thatcher, Reginald Sparshatt 1888–1957
  Tempest 15949
Thau, Wilhelm
  Hamlet 3624
[Theil, G.], arr.
  Dream 9830
Theil, Fritz 1886–
  Lear 6102
Thelen, Adolf, arr.
  Dream 10258
Thelen, Albert
  Tempest 15310
Theobald, James Chester 1950–
  Hamlet 4060
Theobald, James Chester, arr. 1950–
  As You Like It 1467; Settings of
  Commemorative Pieces . . . 21175
Thesing, James J.
  1 Henry IV 4438; 2 Henry IV 4608; 1 Henry
  VI 4870; Lear 5949; Macbeth 7188; Troilus
  16541
Theusner, Christoph, in part arr.
  Twelfth Night 17281
Thewlis, Stephen H.
  Lear 5950; Merry Wives 8968; Dream
  10043; Shrew 14510; Tempest 15311
Thiele, Eduard 1812–1895
  As You Like It 880
Thiele, Manfred
  Hamlet 3479
Thiele, Manfred, arr.
  Hamlet 3562

Thieme, Hermann Ernst Maria 1924–
  Also known as Ernst Maria Hermann Thieme
  Errors 2181; Measure 7769, 7770; Romeo
  13507; Shrew 14511
Thiman, Eric Harding 1900–1975
  As You Like It 1545; Cymbeline 2615;
  Henry VIII 5189; L.L.L. 6623; Macbeth
  7486; Dream 10566, 10726; Much Ado
  11561, 11562; Tempest 16134; Twelfth
  Night 18028; Two Gentlemen 18625
Thiman, Eric Harding, arr. 1900–1975
  Twelfth Night 17316
Thingnæs, Frode 1940–
  P. Pilgrim 20715
Thiriet, Maurice Charles 1906–1972
  Othello 12178
Thode, Scott
  Merry Wives 8969
Thom, Paul 1941–
  Coriolanus 2350
Thomas, Andrew William 1939–
  Cymbeline 2830; Sonnet 129 20414;
  Settings of Commemorative Pieces . . .
  21247
Thomas, Benjamin
  Henry VIII 5190; Measure 7990
Thomas, Bill 1952–
  Twelfth Night 17282
Thomas, Charles Louis Ambroise 1811–1896
  Hamlet 3625; Merry Wives 9256; Dream
  10804, 10805; Tempest 15493; Settings of
  Commemorative Pieces . . . 20958
Thomas, Janet
  Dream 10044
Thomas, John 1826–1913
  Also known as 'Pencerdd Gwalia'
  Twelfth Night 18343
Thomas, Peter
  Richard III 12997
Thomas, Robert Harold 1834–1885
  As You Like It 1933; Macbeth 7357; Twelfth
  Night 18342
Thomas, Robert Harold, arr. 1834–1885
  Macbeth 7356; Merry Wives 9135
Thomas, Rudolph, arr.
  Dream 10259
Thomas, Timothy J.
  Dream 10045
Thomass, Eugen 1927–
  Othello 11975
Thomé, Francis 1850–1909
  Born François Luc Joseph Thomé
  Romeo 13508
Thommessen, Olav Anton 1946–
  Lear 5951; Macbeth 7189; Romeo 13509;
  Shrew 14512; Tempest 15312
Thompson, Clyde Douglas 1947–
  K. John 5628; Dream 10046; Titus 16417;
  Two Gentlemen 18439

Thompson, John
[John Sylvanus Thompson (1889–   )?]
Dream 10727
Thompson, Leslie
As You Like It 1796; Tempest 15761;
Winter's Tale 19063
Thompson, Lewis S.
Hamlet 4178
Thompson, Orlando Montrose 1879–[after
1944]
Sonnet 27 19530
Thompson, Randall, arr. 1899–1984
Much Ado 11587; Tempest 15784, 15961;
Twelfth Night 18056
Thompson, Roy
Winter's Tale 19021
Thompson, Van Denman 1890–1969
Tempest 16135
Thomsen, Geraldine 1917–
Also known as Geraldine Muchová-
Thomsenová
Macbeth 7297; Sonnet 155 20552
Thomsen, Martin
Hamlet 3480
Thomsen, Ole
Dream 10047
Thomsen, Reinhard
Much Ado 11305
Thomson, Bothwell, arr.
Tempest 14746
Thomson, George, adapter 1757–1851
L.L.L. 6482
Thomson, Lionel
As You Like It 881
Thomson, Millard Sponsel 1918–
As You Like It 1546; Merchant 8420
Thomson, Virgil Garnett 1896–
All's Well 85, 90; Antony 238; Hamlet
3481; K. John 5629; Lear 5952; Macbeth
7190; Measure 7771, 7991; Merchant 8355,
8489, 8641; Much Ado 11306, 11389,
11563; Othello 11976
Þórarinsson, Leifur 1934–
Twelfth Night 17283
Thorby, Philip
As You Like It 882; Dream 10048; Richard
II 12732
Thoresen, Jan
Merchant 8356
Thorley, Walter Handel
Macbeth 7487
Thorndike, Russell
Shrew 14513
Thorne, [Edward Henry] [1834–1916]
Romeo 13510
Thorne, Edward Henry 1834–1916
Cymbeline 2798; Merchant 8680
Thorne, Ken
Hamlet 4129

Thornhill, Claude, arr. 1909–1965
As You Like It 1468
Thornley, Arthur, arr.
Macbeth 7358
Thorpe, Raymond, arr.
Tempest 14747
Thurm, Joachim 1927–
Richard III 12998; Tempest 15313; Winter's
Tale 18893
Thurow, Matthias
Tempest 15314
Thybo, Leif 1922–
Sonnet 8 19266; Sonnet 18 19440
Thÿsse, Wim H. 1916–
P. Pilgrim 20716
Tiainen, Martti
Twelfth Night 17284
Tiefensee, Siegfried
Errors 2182; Macbeth 7191; Much Ado
11307; Othello 11977; Richard III 12999;
Shrew 14514; Tempest 15315; Timon
16361; Twelfth Night 17285, 17286,
17287; Two Gentlemen 18440
Tiegert, Günter
Hamlet 3482
Tierney, Harry Austin 1890–1965
Measure 8043
Tiersot, Jean-Baptiste Elisée Julien, arr.
1857–1936
Othello 11779
Tiessen, Heinz 1887–1971
Cymbeline 2497; Hamlet 3483; Measure
7772; Tempest 15316; Settings of
Commemorative Pieces . . . 20895
Tietjens, Paul 1877–1945
Merchant 8357
Tillett, Michael, arr.
All's Well 96; Tempest 16208
Tilliard, Georges Louis, fils   –1913
Caesar 5565
Tilliard, Georges Louis, fils, arr.   –1913
Macbeth 7359; Dream 9831, 10888; Othello
12159, 12160; Pericles 12611
Timmerman, John Paul, Jr.
Sonnet 18 19441
Timms, Colin
Henry V 4769
Timson, David
Winter's Tale 18894
Tindal, William
Hamlet 3739; Measure 7992
Tinney, Charles Ernest
Cymbeline 2884
Tippett, Michael Kemp 1905–
All's Well 95; Macbeth 7488; Dream 10806;
Tempest 15317, 15582, 15583, 15762,
15950, 16207
Tippett, Michael Kemp, arr. 1905–
Dream 10260; Twelfth Night 18301

Tipping, Simon
Henry V 4770; Lear 5953
Tischhauser, Franz 1927–
Two Gentlemen 18441
Tissington, H., in part arr.
Romeo 13511; Tempest 15319
Titcomb, Caldwell 1926–
Henry V 4771; Lear 5954
Titl, Anton Emil 1809–1882
Antony 239; Coriolanus 2351; Cymbeline
2498; 1 Henry IV 4439; 2 Henry IV 4609;
Caesar 5447; Macbeth 7192, 7193;
Merchant 8358; Merry Wives 9233; Much
Ado 11308; Othello 11978; Richard III
13000
Tittle, Stephen
Settings of Commemorative Pieces . . . 21199
Titus, Hiram
Hamlet 3484, 3485; Measure 7773; Dream
10049; Romeo 13512; Shrew 14515;
Twelfth Night 17288, 17289; Winter's Tale
18895
Tjeknavorian, Loris
Othello 12179
Tobani, Theodore Moses 1855–1933
Also known as Theodore Moses-Tobani
Dream 10728
Tobani, Theodore Moses, arr. 1855–1933
Also known as Theodore Moses-Tobani
As You Like It 1934; Macbeth 7360; Merry
Wives 9195; Dream 9832, 10889; Romeo
13751, 13752
Tobias, Rudol'f 1873–1918
Caesar 5529
Tobin, John, adapter 1891–
Winter's Tale 19022
Tobin, John, arr. 1891–
Cymbeline 2782; Tempest 14832
Tocchi, Gian Luca, in part arr. 1901–
Merry Wives 8970
Tocchi, Gian Luca, arr. 1901–
Merry Wives 9136
Toch, Ernst 1887–1964
As You Like It 883; Twelfth Night 17290
Todd, Paul 1952–
Errors 2183; Coriolanus 2352, 2353; Hamlet
3486; L.L.L. 6301; Merchant 8359, 8360,
8361; Merry Wives 8971; Dream 10050;
Richard III 13001; Romeo 13513, 13514;
Shrew 14516, 14517; Tempest 15320,
15321; Twelfth Night 17291, 17292
Toja, G., arr.
Settings of Commemorative Pieces . . . 20935
Tolk, Dieter
L.L.L. 6302; Shrew 14518
Tolkien, Frederick
Antony 383
Tollett, Patricia
Hamlet 3487

Tolmachev, B.
Shrew 14519
Tolman, Grace
Much Ado 11309
Tomasi, Henri 1901–1971
Coriolanus 2394; Hamlet 4041
Tomlins, Greta 1912–1972
Antony 329; Dream 10729; Othello 12434;
Shrew 14670
Tomlinson, E[rnest] [1924–]
As You Like It 1547
Tommasini, Vincenzo 1878–1950
Tempest 16296
Tompkins, George
Much Ado 11564
Tonini, Lionel Antoine
Henry VIII 5028
Tonini, Serge
Henry VIII 5029
Tonnellier, Goldsmith
As You Like It 1548
Topel, Harry, arr.
Sonnet 37 19676; Settings of
Commemorative Pieces . . . 21257
Toplis, Margot, arr.
Twelfth Night 18344
Tormis, Vel'o Rikhovich 1930–
Hamlet 4079
Tornyos, György
As You Like It 1549
Torrence, Ernest
Sonnet 18 19442
Torriana, [?]
Much Ado 11565
Torriani, E.
Romeo 14212
Torry, Jane Sloman
Dream 10936
Toska, [?], arr.
Othello 12530
Totels, Robert Edward
Twelfth Night 17647
Totzauer, Hans
Hamlet 3488; 1 Henry IV 4440; 2 Henry IV
4610; Henry V 4772; 1 Henry VI 4871;
2 Henry VI 4910; 3 Henry VI 4952; Caesar
5448; Lear 5955; Macbeth 7194; Measure
7774; Merchant 8362; Othello 11979;
Richard II 12733, 12734; Richard III 13002
Tourbié, Richard, arr.
Merry Wives 9137, 9138
Tournier, Franz André 1923–
Hamlet 3489
Tours, Berthold 1838–1897
As You Like It 884, 1830; Cymbeline 2499;
Hamlet 3490, 4042; Merchant 8363; Dream
10937
Tours, Berthold, arr. 1838–1897
Henry VIII 5025; Dream 9833, 9834, 9835

Tours, Frank E. 1877–1963
  Measure 8040
Tours, Frank E., in part arr. 1877–1963
  Shrew 14520
Toutant, William 1948–
  Richard III 13003
Tovatt, Patrick
  Much Ado 11310
Tovey, Donald Francis 1875–1940
  As You Like It 885; Measure 7993;
  Merchant 8642; Tempest 15763; P. Pilgrim
  20717
Toye, E.
  As You Like It 1189
Toye, John, in part arr.
  Shrew 14521
Toye, John Francis 1883–1964
  Merchant 8643; Much Ado 11566; Twelfth
  Night 17648, 18029
Tracey, Stan
  Hamlet 4252; Dream 10730; Settings of
  Commemorative Pieces . . . 21084
Tracy, Charles
  Settings of Commemorative Pieces . . . 21085
Trafford, Edmund 1948–
  Dream 10051
Trailin, Sergei Aleksandrovich 1872–1951
  Twelfth Night 17293; Sonnet 30 19623
Tranchell, Peter Andrew 1922–
  Macbeth 7195, 7398; Merchant 8364;
  Merry Wives 9162; Settings of
  Commemorative Pieces . . . 20979
Trapp, Herrman Emil Alfred Max 1887–1971
  Timon 16362
Traunfellner, Peter Carl 1930–
  Hamlet 3491; Romeo 13515; Tempest
  15322
Trautman, [?]
  Twelfth Night 17294
Travers, Alison
  Pseudonym used by Toni Farrell
  Twelfth Night 17743
Travis, Roy Elihu 1922–
  Tempest 15584, 15764, 15817, 15857,
  15981
Trefousse, Roger 1951–
  Hamlet 3810, 4179
Trego, H. Stafford, arr.
  Dream 9836
Treharne, Bryceson 1879–1948
  Also wrote under the pseudonym 'Chester
  Wallis'
  As You Like It 886, 1190, 1935; L.L.L.
  6624; Measure 7994; Much Ado 11567;
  Twelfth Night 17649; Sonnet 18 19443
Treharne, Bryceson, in part arr. 1879–1948
  Also wrote under the pseudonym 'Chester
  Wallis'
  Settings of Commemorative Pieces . . . 20980

Treharne, Bryceson, arr. 1879–1948
  Also wrote under the pseudonym 'Chester
  Wallis'
  As You Like It 1180; Romeo 14005
Treibmann, Karl Ottomar
  Othello 11980
Trekell, Joseph Theodore, arr.
  Dream 10890; Othello 12161
Tremain, Albert Ronald 1923–
  As You Like It 1797; L.L.L. 6483, 6625;
  Measure 7995; Much Ado 11568; Tempest
  15765; Twelfth Night 17650
Tremain, Thomas
  Measure 7996
Trémisot, Édouard 1874–1952
  Dream 10987
Trémois, Marcel Édouard   –1974
  Hamlet 3687
Trento, Vittorio 1761–1833
  Macbeth 7554
Treu, Daniel Gottlob 1695–1749
  Also known as Daniel Gottlob Trew and as
  Daniele Teofilo Fedele
  Coriolanus 2430
Trevalsa, Joan
  L.L.L. 6626
Trevor, Claude
  Much Ado 11569
Tricon, Louis-Jules   –1921
  Dream 10731
Trienes, Hermann 1872–
  Othello 12435
Trillat, Ennemond 1890–1980
  Dream 10052; Romeo 13516
Trimble, Lester Albert 1923–
  Merchant 8644
Trinder, Walter
  Dream 10346
Triphook, J. Crampton
  P. Pilgrim 20718
Trituz, Mikhail L'vovich
  Othello 11981
Trojan, Václav 1907–1983
  Dream 10053, 10054, 10055, 10281
Trombley, Richard
  Lear 5956; Dream 10056; Tempest 15323;
  Twelfth Night 17295; Sonnet 2 19195;
  Sonnet 73 20027; Sonnet 95 20142; Sonnet
  96 20149; Sonnet 138 20461
Troob, Danny
  Dream 10057
Troostwyk, Arthur, [arr.]
  Dream 10732
Troskie, Albert J. J.
  Tempest 15324
Troup, Emily Josephine   –1912
  As You Like It 1550; Cymbeline 2799
Trousselle, Josef
  Dream 10733

Trouw, Karel 1929–
    Hamlet 3492
Trowbridge, Ernest
    Tempest 16136
Trozner, József 1904–1984
    As You Like It 1551, 1798; Sonnet 73
    20019; Sonnet 75 20042; Sonnet 97 20171
Truc, Vladimír
    All's Well 64
Truhn, Friedrich Hieronymus 1811–1886
    Antony 384; Hamlet 3804; Measure 7997
Truzzi, Luigi, arr.
    Hamlet 4149, 4169
Truzzi, Paolo, arr. 1840–
    Settings of Commemorative Pieces . . . 20936
Trybuła, Andrzej
    Othello 11982
Trzaskowski, Andrzej
    Richard III 13004; Tempest 15325; Twelfth
    Night 17296
Tsabel', Fedor Ernestovich 1878–
    Othello 11983; Twelfth Night 17297
Tsangaris, Manos
    Twelfth Night 17298
Tsankov, Petur
    Shrew 14522
Tschirch, W., arr.
    Dream 9837
Tschudin, Michael
    Coriolanus 2354; Othello 11984; Romeo
    14117
Tsintsadze, Sulkhan Fedorovich 1925–
    Merchant 8365, 8712
Tsugawa, Shuichi
    Shrew 14523
Tubbs, Michael
    Lear 5957
Tubbs, Michael, in part arr.
    Twelfth Night 17299
Tubbs, Michael, arr.
    Troilus 16553
Tuček, Vincenc Tomáš Václav 1773–[circa
    1821]
    Also known as Franz Vinzenz Ferrerius Tuczek
    Hamlet 4130, 4180
Tucker, Dan
    [Daniel E. Tucker?]
    1 Henry IV 4441; Twelfth Night 17300
Tucker, Daniel E.
    Henry VIII 5191
Tuffin, Michael
    Hamlet 3493; Henry V 4773; Merchant
    8366
Tully, James Howard, arr. 1814–1868
    Tempest 14748, 14833, 15128
Tunick, Jonathan 1938–
    Timon 16373
Tunnard, T. N.
    Two Gentlemen 18442

Turkevych, Lev 1901–1961
    Hamlet 3494
Turnbull, Percy Purvis 1902–1976
    Dream 10567; Winter's Tale 19064
Turnbull, Walter
    P. Pilgrim 20719
Turner, Eustace
    Sonnet 105 20253
Turner, James, arr.
    Errors 2237
Turner, John Bradbury
    P. Pilgrim 20720
Turner, Myra Brooks 1936–
    Dream 10282
Turner, Robert Comrie 1920–
    Phoenix 20765; Settings of Commemorative
    Pieces . . . 21086
Turner, Stewart W.
    Lear 5958; Dream 10058
Turner, William, in part arr.
    As You Like It 887
Turok, Paul Harris 1929–
    Merchant 8472; Richard III 13039
Turski, Zbigniew 1908–1979
    As You Like It 888; Cymbeline 2500;
    Macbeth 7196; Dream 10283; Much Ado
    11311; Tempest 15326
Tusiacki, Tadeusz
    Hamlet 3495
Tuskiia, Iona Iraklievich 1901–1963
    Caesar 5449; Othello 11985
Tuthill, Marguerite
    Romeo 13517
Tutin, Christopher, arr.
    Dream 10261; Tempest 14749
Tutsch, G., arr.
    Macbeth 7361
Tuttle, Ron
    Twelfth Night 17301
Tvorun, Stefan Nikonovych, arr.
    Romeo 13314
Twardowski, Romuald 1930–
    Dream 10059
Twigg, Douglas J.
    Much Ado 11570
Twinn, Sydney, arr.
    As You Like It 1469
Tyler, Abram Ray, arr.
    Dream 9838
Tyler, James Henry 1940–
    Hamlet 3496
Tyler, James Henry, in part arr. 1940–
    Henry VIII 5030; Measure 7775; Romeo
    13518
Tyler, Jim, arr.
    Errors 2240
Tyrrell, John
    L.L.L. 6627

U

Ublich, Oskar
  Twelfth Night 17302
Udow, Michael 1949–
  Othello 11986
Ueno, Michiko
  Lear 6132
Ugalde, Delphine 1829–1910
  Hamlet 4253
Uglow, Richard
  Hamlet 4131
Uherek, Milan 1925–
  Antony 240; Dream 10060; Twelfth Night
  17303
Uhlmann, Otto 1891–
  Henry VIII 5192
Ulehla, Ludmila 1923–
  Also known as Ludmila Ulehla Sokoloff
  Sonnet 18 19444; Sonnet 97 20172; Sonnet
  109 20285
Ulrich, Hans, arr.
  Merry Wives 9139
Ulrich, Homer 1906–
  As You Like It 889
Ulrik, Sven 1911–1980
  Pseudonym used by Harry Jensen
  Hamlet 4254
Ultan, Lloyd 1929–
  As You Like It 1191
Underwood, Samuel William
  As You Like It 1192
Unger, Harald
  Hamlet 3497
Unger, Hermann Gustav 1886–1958
  As You Like It 1936; Hamlet 4043; Merry
  Wives 9235; Othello 12436; Tempest 15327;
  Twelfth Night 18255; Two Gentlemen 18648
Unia, Giuseppe, arr.
  Othello 12162, 12163
Unkel, Rolf 1912–
  Hamlet 3498; Measure 7776
Uno, Seiichiro
  Hamlet 3499
Untermüller, Jiří
  Othello 11987
Urai, Vilmos
  Also known under the pseudonym 'Sylvio
  Flory'
  Hamlet 4263
Urban, Max, arr.
  Macbeth 7442, 7443
Urbont, Jack
  Tempest 15766
Urich, Jean 1849–1939
  Tempest 16297
Urmuzescu, Paul 1928–
  Hamlet 3500; 1 Henry IV 4442; 2 Henry IV

4611; Lear 5959; Dream 10061; Shrew
  14524; Tempest 15328
Urner, Catherine Murphy 1891–1942
  Twelfth Night 17651
Urrows, David Francis 1957–
  Dream 10284; Tempest 15767; Winter's
  Tale 18896
Urspruch, Anton 1850–1907
  Tempest 15496
Uschmann, Hans
  Lear 5960
Usher, Julia 1945–
  Merchant 8645
Ussachevsky, Vladimir Alexis 1911–
  Lear 5961
Uttley, William 1955–
  Measure 7777; Dream 10062
Uvril, Hanns
  Shrew 14525

V

Vaccaj, Nicola 1790–1848
  Also known as Nicolò Vaccai
  Romeo 14213
Vacek, Miloš 1928–
  Shrew 14526
Vačkář, Dalibor Cyril 1906–1984
  Dream 10285
Vaculík, Pavel
  As You Like It 890
Vaille, Agnes
  Macbeth 7197
Vainberg, Moisei Samuilovich 1919–
  Sonnet 155 20578
Vakhvakhishvili, Tamara Nikolaevna
  1894–
  Othello 11988
Val'dgardt, Pavel Petrovich 1904–
  Errors 2184; Shrew 14527; Twelfth Night
  17304
Vale, Charles
  As You Like It 1552; P. Pilgrim 20721
Vale, Walter Sidney 1875–1939
  Cymbeline 2616; Settings of Commemorative
  Pieces . . . 21087
Válek, Jiří 1923–
  Antony 330, 331; Hamlet 3688, 4044,
  4045, 4046; 2 Henry VI 4923, 4924; Henry
  VIII 5223, 5224; Caesar 5530, 5531; Lear
  6103, 6104; Macbeth 7380; Romeo 14012;
  Shrew 14671, 14672; Winter's Tale 19126,
  19127, 19128; Sonnet 66 19923; Sonnet 94
  20138; Sonnet 128 20402
Valenti, Michael
  Errors 2239; Othello 11989

Valenti, Tomas
  Tempest 15329
Valentin, Patrice, arr.
  Romeo 13753
Valentini, Raffaele, arr.
  Othello 12164
Valiquet, H., arr.
  Hamlet 3681, 3682, 3683
Valls, Manuel 1920–
  Also known as Manuel Valls Gorina
  Settings of Commemorative Pieces . . .
  21248
Valverde Sanjuán, Joaquín 1875–1918
  Known as Quinito; also known as Joaquín
  Valverde y San Juan
  Dream 10286
Van, Jeffrey Wylie 1941–
  Twelfth Night 17652; Winter's Tale 18987,
  19065
van Appledorn, Mary Jeanne 1927–
  As You Like It 1193, 1799
van Arenbergh, René
  Henry V 4774
van As, Cees 1946–
  Twelfth Night 17305
van Baarens, Kees, arr. 1906–1970
  Tempest 15201
van Bruyck, Carl Debrois 1828–1902
  Lear 6105
Van Cleemput, Werner
  Sonnet 56 19797
van Crombruggen, Paul 1905–
  Pseudonym used by Vincent Christoff
  Macbeth 7198; Dream 10063
van de Velde, Wannes
  Measure 7778
van Delden, Lex 1919–
  Macbeth 7199; Sonnet 43 19721; Sonnet 44
  19727; Sonnet 47 19734
van den Abeelen, Henri
  Tempest 15814
van der Horst, Anthon 1899–1965
  Macbeth 7200
van der Pals, Leopold 1884–1966
  Dream 10064; Tempest 15330
van der Steen, Gerrit Christiaan 1907–
  Tempest 15585, 15768, 15951
Van der Stucken, Frank Valentine 1858–1929
  Tempest 15331
Van der Stucken, Frank Valentine, arr.
  1858–1929
  Merchant 8749
van der Wurff, Eric
  Dream 10065
van Dieren, Bernard Hélène Joseph 1887–1936
  Measure 7998; Sonnet 28 19537; Sonnet 30
  19624; Sonnet 43 19722
Van Dieval, Rita
  Dream 10763

van Dijck, Raymond
  Hamlet 3501
Van Dooren, Eduardo 1879–1948
  Hamlet 4047
Van Durme, Jef 1907–1965
  Antony 282; Hamlet 4048; Lear 6017;
  Richard III 13040
Van Dyke, H.
  Winter's Tale 18943
Van Etten, Jane
  Also known as Mrs. Alfred Buritt Andrews
  As You Like It 1553
Van Hecke, Mark Joseph 1949–
  Caesar 5450; Richard III 13005; Romeo
  13519
van Hemel, Oscar 1892–1981
  Sonnet 8 19267; Sonnet 71 19969; Sonnet
  138 20459; Sonnet 154 20550
Van Heusen, James 1913–
  Pseudonym used by Edward Chester Babcock
  Dream 10287
van Hulst, Gerard 1909–
  Sonnet 22 19486; Sonnet 24 19499; Sonnet
  71 19970
van Lijnschooten, Henk, arr.
  Othello 12531
van Noord, Adriaan
  As You Like It 891
van Oosterom, Richard
  Merchant 8367
van Prooijen, Cornelius Anton 1939–
  Sonnet 62 19865; Sonnet 76 20052
van Someren-Godfery, Masters   –1947
  Cymbeline 2617
van Steeden, Peter, Jr. 1904–
  Shrew 14528
van Thienen, Marcel 1922–
  Romeo 14013
Van Wart, Irving
  Hamlet 4049
van Westerhout, Nicola 1857–1898
  Also known as Niccolò van Westerhout
  Cymbeline 2519; Caesar 5532
Van Wormer, Gordon
  As You Like It 1554; Measure 7999; Twelfth
  Night 18188
van Wyk, Carl Albert 1942–
  Dream 10066; Romeo 13520
van Zutphen, Wim
  Errors 2185; Twelfth Night 17306
Vardell, Richard
  Romeo 13521
Varlamov, Aleksandr Egorovich
  1801–1848
  Hamlet 3502
Varney, Alice M.
  Much Ado 11312
Vartanian, Richard
  Shrew 14529

Vartkes, Baronijan
L.L.L. 6303
Varviso, Silvio
Romeo 13522
Vaschetti, Cesare
Hamlet 4255
Vasconcelos, Nana
Tempest 15333
Vasilenko, Sergei Nikiforovich 1872–1956
Dream 10067; Shrew 14530
Vaszy, Viktor
Sonnet 8 19268; Sonnet 66 19924; Sonnet
73 20020; Sonnet 117 20347
Vatsadze, Nugzar Mikhailovich 1937–
Caesar 5451
Vaubourgoin, Marc Jean Joseph 1907–
Coriolanus 2395
Vaughan Thomas, David 1873–1934
Henry VIII 5193; Merchant 8473; Two
Gentlemen 18626; Settings of
Commemorative Pieces . . . 21308
Vaughan Williams, Ralph 1872–1958
As You Like It 1555; Cymbeline 2618; Henry
V 4775, 4809, 4830; Henry VIII 5194, 5198;
L.L.L. 6484, 6628; Measure 8000; Merchant
8474; Merry Wives 8972, 9262; Dream
10423; Much Ado 11571; Othello 12359;
Richard II 12735; Richard III 13006; Tempest
15769, 15840, 16137; Twelfth Night 17653,
18030; Winter's Tale 19156; Sonnet 71 19971
Vaughan Williams, Ralph, in part arr.
1872–1958
As You Like It 1962; 2 Henry IV 4612,
4673; L.L.L. 6683; Merry Wives 9163; Much
Ado 11634; Richard II 12736; Twelfth Night
18276; Settings of Commemorative
Pieces . . . 20896, 20981
Vaughan Williams, Ralph, arr. 1872–1958
As You Like It 1470
Vaughan Williams, Ralph, ed. 1872–1958
Sonnet 146 20503
Vauthrot, François Eugène, arr. 1825–1871
Hamlet 3684; Settings of Commemorative
Pieces . . . 20977
Vavolo, Marco 1939–
Hamlet 3689
Vavrinecz, Mór
Macbeth 7489
Vazzana, Anthony Eugene 1922–
Antony 241
Veale, John 1922–
L.L.L. 6304; Richard III 13007
Vedernikov, A., arr.
Hamlet 3360
Veenendaal, Karel, arr.
Othello 11720
Vehar, Persis Anne 1937–
As You Like It 1589; Merchant 8681;
Twelfth Night 18076

Vella, Joseph
L.L.L. 6629
Vellucci, Paul, arr.
As You Like It 1151
Vené, Ruggero 1897–1961
Antony 303; Cymbeline 2800; Hamlet 3782;
2 Henry IV 4641; L.L.L. 6356; Measure
8001; Merchant 8646; Merry Wives 9207;
Dream 10568; Much Ado 11390, 11572;
Romeo 13862; Tempest 15770; Twelfth
Night 17654; Two Gentlemen 18627
Ventura, Livio, in part arr.
As You Like It 892
Venzago, Mario 1948–
Troilus 16542
Veracini, Francesco Maria [?1690–1750]
As You Like It 960
Verbesselt, August-Frans 1919–
Two Gentlemen 18443
Verchuren, André, arr.
Lear 6098
Vercoe, Elizabeth 1941–
1 Henry VI 4880
Verdalle, Gabriel, arr.
Romeo 13754
Verdi, Giuseppe Fortunino Francesco
1813–1901
Hamlet 3690; 1 Henry IV 4468; 2 Henry IV
4634; Lear 6018; Macbeth 7298; Merry
Wives 9177; Othello 12180; Romeo 13818;
Settings of Commemorative Pieces . . . 20982
Veremans, Renaat 1894–1969
Macbeth 7201
Verger, Christiane   –1974
Merry Wives 8973
Vernon, Joseph 1739–1782
Twelfth Night 17307, 18189; Two
Gentlemen 18444, 18628
Verroust, Stanislas, arr.
Merry Wives 8996
Versavel, Luc 1952–
Richard III 13008
Versel, Louis
Tempest 15952
Veselý, Roman, arr.
Tempest 15460
Veshchitskii, Pavel' Oskarovich, arr.
Twelfth Night 16962
Vessella, Alessandro, arr. 1860–1929
Dream 9839; Othello 12165; Romeo 14121
Veteška, Lubomír 1934–
Settings of Commemorative Pieces . . .
20983
Viard, Jean Robert
Measure 7779
Viardot-Garcia, Michelle Ferdinande Pauline,
arr. 1821–1910
Née Garcia
Romeo 13814

Vibbard, Harry L.
    Winter's Tale 19091
Vibbard, Harry L., arr.
    Dream 10335
Vicars, George Rayleigh
    Tempest 15771; Twelfth Night 18032
Viccini, Juan
    Romeo 13523
Vick, Lloyd
    Merchant 8475; Sonnet 18 19445
Vickers, Michael
    Settings of Commemorative Pieces . . . 21176
Victory, Gerard 1921–
    As You Like It 1800; Cymbeline 2620;
    Macbeth 7202; Merchant 8647; P. Pilgrim
    20722
Vidal, Paul 1863–1931
    Also known as Paul-Antoine Vidal
    As You Like It 893, 1194, 1556, 1801,
    1862; Cymbeline 2801; L.L.L. 6305, 6485,
    6630; Merchant 8368, 8476, 8648; Troilus
    16543
Vidanović, Tugomir 1937–
    Twelfth Night 17418; Sonnet 1 19185;
    Sonnet 19 19472; Sonnet 28 19538; Sonnet
    40 19697; Sonnet 46 19731; Sonnet 53
    19763; Sonnet 79 20063; Sonnet 112
    20295
Vidovszky, László 1944–
    Measure 7780
Vié, Louis, arr.
    Settings of Commemorative Pieces . . . 20978
Vierling, Georg 1820–1901
    Tempest 16139
Vigil, Federico García
    Othello 11990
Vignati, Giuseppe
    Hamlet 4289
Vila, Cirilo
    Merry Wives 8974
Vil'danov, Rumil' Dzhiangirovich 1939–
    Twelfth Night 17419
Vincent, Charles John, arr. 1852–1934
    As You Like It 1471; Othello 12261
Vincent, Charles John, ed. 1852–1934
    Anthologies 21319
Vincent, Frank
    Twelfth Night 17318
Vincent, George Frederick, arr. 1855–
    As You Like It 1472
Vine, Carl Edward 1954–
    Tempest 15334
Vine, W. Vivian W.
    L.L.L. 6486
Viner, William Letton, arr. 1790–1867
    Also known as William Litton Viner
    Errors 2047
Vinning, William S.
    Measure 7781

Vinter, Gilbert 1909–1969
    As You Like It 1937; Merchant 8713; Much
    Ado 11573
Virley, Nigel
    Much Ado 11313
Viru, Val'deko Augustovich 1925–
    Measure 7782
Visetti, Albert Anthony, arr. 1846–1928
    Tempest 14750
Vishkarev, Leonid Vasil'evich 1907–
    Othello 11991
Vishnick, Martin Lawrence 1952–
    Henry V 4831
Visser, Peter 1939–
    As You Like It 1195; Romeo 13831, 13853,
    13863, 13878
Vitkind, Zinaida, arr.
    Hamlet 3424
Vizentini, Albert, arr.
    Macbeth 7362
Vlad, Roman 1919–
    Hamlet 3503, 3504, 4132; Macbeth 7203;
    Merchant 8369; Merry Wives 8975; Dream
    10068; Othello 12466; Romeo 13524,
    14014; Tempest 15335; Twelfth Night
    17319
Vladigerov, Pančo 1899–1978
    Merchant 8370; Much Ado 11314; Twelfth
    Night 17320
Vladimirov, M. V., arr.
    Hamlet 3475
Voarino, Napoleone, arr.
    Romeo 13755
Vodopivec, Marjan
    Henry V 4776; Measure 7783; Merry Wives
    8976; Othello 11992; Romeo 13526; Shrew
    14531; Tempest 15336; Twelfth Night
    17321
Voegeli, Tom
    Measure 7784
Vogel, Hermann
    Othello 12361
Vogel, Jaroslav, arr. 1894–1970
    Winter's Tale 19124
Vogel, Max, arr.
    Merry Wives 9140
Vogel, Moritz Wilhelm, arr. 1846–1922
    Dream 10891
Vogels, Wilfried Leonard 1954–
    Coriolanus 2355
Vogl, Johann Michael 1768–1840
    Othello 11993, 12362
Vogler, Georg Joseph 1749–1814
    Also known as Abbé Vogler or Abt Vogler
    Hamlet 3505
Vogrich, Max Wilhelm Karl 1852–1916
    Measure 8002
Vogt, Heinz
    Lear 5962; Othello 11994; Tempest 15337

Vogt, Heinz, in part arr.
  Dream 10069
Voigt, Friedrich Wilhelm 1833–1894
  Othello 12437
Vol'berg, Matias Samuilovich 1899–
  Romeo 13527
Vol'berg, V.
  Lear 5963
Volckmar, A. Valentin Wilhelm, arr. 1812–1887
  Dream 9840, 10892; Othello 12166
Volkmann, Friedrich Robert 1815–1883
  Richard III 13009, 13061
Volkmann, Otto 1888–
  As You Like It 1557
von Beckerath, Alfred Wilhelm 1901–
  Two Gentlemen 18445
von Blumenthal, Josef 1782–1850
  Lear 5964
von Boguslawski, H. G. W.
  Cymbeline 2802
von Bose, Hans-Jürgen 1953–
  Sonnet 42 19707
von Boyneburgk, Friedrich 1790–1849
  As You Like It 1196, 1802; Cymbeline 2803;
  Hamlet 3805; Dream 10569; Much Ado
  11574; Othello 12232, 12363; Tempest
  15772, 15953; Twelfth Night 18033;
  Winter's Tale 19023
von Bülow, Gert
  Tempest 15338
von Bülow, Hans Guido Freiherr 1830–1894
  Caesar 5452, 5533; Romeo 14015
von Bülow, Hans Guido Freiherr, arr.
  1830–1894
  Lear 6055
von Bunding, Sigism.
  Romeo 13819
von der Meden, Edmund
  Tempest 15339; Winter's Tale 18897
von der Weeth, Michael
  Shrew 14532
von Deringer, Mikko
  Hamlet 3506; Richard III 13010
von Destouches, Franz Seraph 1772–1844
  Macbeth 7204
von Einem, Gottfried 1918–
  As You Like It 894; Macbeth 7205; Romeo
  13820
von Erlanger, Ludwig
  Cymbeline 2804
von Eybler, Josef Leopold Edler [1864]–1847
  Coriolanus 2377
von Feilitzsch, Karl 1901–
  All's Well 65; As You Like It 895; Hamlet
  3507; Macbeth 7206; Much Ado 11315;
  Othello 11995; Shrew 14533
von Gallenberg, Wenzel Robert 1783–1839
  Also known as Graf von Gallenberg
  Hamlet 4181; Macbeth 7366; Othello 12210

von Gerstenberg, Heinrich Wilhelm, adapter
  1727–1823
  Hamlet 3862
von Holst, Matthias
  Hamlet 4050; Tempest 16140
von Horn, Friedrich A.
  Winter's Tale 18898
von Hornstein, Robert 1833–1890
  As You Like It 896, 1197, 1558, 1803
von Klein, Karl August 1794–
  Othello 12438
von Koch, Erland 1910–
  Sonnet 60 19841
von Lichtenstein, Karl August 1767–1845
  All's Well 81
von Lindpaintner, Peter Josef 1791–1856
  Caesar 5454
von Miltitz, Karl Borromäus Stephan
  [1781]–1845
  Also known as Carl Borromeo Stephan von
  Miltitz
  Hamlet 3508; 1 Henry IV 4443
von Mojsisovics, Roderich Edler 1877–1953
  Also known as Roderich Edler von
  Mojsisovics-Mojsvár
  Much Ado 11370
von Noé, Günther
  Lear 5965
von Perfall, Karl 1824–1907
  Coriolanus 2356; Hamlet 3509; Caesar
  5455; Lear 5966; Macbeth 7207; Merchant
  8371; Pericles 12591; Winter's Tale 18899
von Pidoll, Carl
  Shrew 14534
von Rožycki, Ludomir [1884–1953]
  Pericles 12592
von Rumling, Sigismund 1739–1825
  Romeo 13821
von Seckendorff, Karl Siegmund 1744–1785
  Cymbeline 2805; Measure 8003; Twelfth
  Night 17655
von Skeletti, G.
  Macbeth 7490
von Suppé, Franz 1819–1895
  Also known as Franz Suppè and as
  Francesco Ezechiele Ermenegildo Cavaliere
  Suppé Demelli
  Dream 10288, 10988
von Tugginer, P.
  Hamlet 4051
von Waldburg, Hans 1804–1872
  Othello 11996
von Waldstein, Wilhelm 1897–1974
  Hamlet 4052
von Winter, Peter 1754–1825
  Dream 10289; Romeo 13822, 14016;
  Tempest 15497
von Woyrsch, Felix 1860–1944
  Hamlet 4053; Twelfth Night 17656

Vormèse, C., arr.
Othello 12416
Voronovich, I.
Shrew 14535
Vorsmann, Josef
Much Ado 11316
Vos, Wim 1958–
Coriolanus 2357
Voss, Carl
Tempest 16141
Voss, Charles, arr.
Merry Wives 9141
Voss, F. M., arr.
Cymbeline 2783
Voss, Friedrich 1930–
Hamlet 4054
Vostřák, Zbyněk 1920–1985
Sonnet 55 19787; Sonnet 127 20377;
Sonnet 129 20415; Settings of
Commemorative Pieces . . . 21088
Vowles, William
As You Like It 1198
Voynich, Ethel Lilian 1864–
Also known as Ethel Lillian Boole
Lear 6033
Vranešević, Mladen 1947–
As You Like It 897; Dream 10070; Tempest
15340
Vranešević, Predrag 1946–
As You Like It 898; Dream 10071; Tempest
15341
Vreuls, Victor-Jean-Léonard 1876–1944
Dream 10290
Vukdrogović, Mihajlo 1900–
Merchant 8372
Vulchev, Dimitur
Twelfth Night 17420; Two Gentlemen 18446
VunKannon, Raymond
Twelfth Night 17322
Vyshnegradskii, Ivan Aleksandrovich
1893–1979
Also known as Wyschnegradsky
Macbeth 7208
Vyšohlíd, Jiří 1943–
Errors 2186; Dream 10072

W

Wachs, F., arr.
Hamlet 3685
Waddington, Martin
As You Like It 899; L.L.L. 6306; Macbeth
7209; Twelfth Night 17323
Waddington, Sidney Peirce 1869–1953
Twelfth Night 18034
Wade, James Augustus, arr.
Merry Wives 8887; Tempest 14834

Wade, Simon
Dream 10073
Wadely, Frederick William 1882–1970
Dream 10938; Twelfth Night 18035
Wagenaar, Johan 1862–1941
Coriolanus 2385; K. John 5650; Shrew
14673; Twelfth Night 18256
Waglechner, Erich
As You Like It 900
Wagner, Albert
Hamlet 4055
Wagner, Carl, arr.
Tempest 14835
Wagner, Ernst David, arr. 1806–1883
Merry Wives 9142; Dream 10893
Wagner, Ferdinand
Caesar 5534; Romeo 14017
Wagner, Karl Jacob 1772–1822
Also known as Jacob Karl Wagner
As You Like It 1938; Twelfth Night 18257
Wagner, Paul, arr.
Othello 12167, 12168
Wagner, Robert 1915–
Dream 10074
Wagner, Viktor
Much Ado 11317
Wagner, Wilhelm Richard 1813–1883
Measure 7805; Romeo 14018
Wagner-Régeny, Rudolf 1903–1969
Antony 242; Coriolanus 2358; Lear 5967;
Dream 10075, 10734; Twelfth Night 17324
Wainwright, M.
Dream 10347
Waithman, R. H.
Two Gentlemen 18629
Wakasugi, Hiroshi
Caesar 5456
Walaciński, Adam
As You Like It 901, 902; Coriolanus 2359;
Hamlet 3510; Measure 7785; Tempest
15342; Twelfth Night 17325; Winter's Tale
18900, 18901
Walbaum, Glenn
Antony 243; 1 Henry IV 4444; 2 Henry IV
4613; Lear 5968; Othello 11997; Romeo
13528
Walden, Stanley
Hamlet 3511; Merchant 8735
Walker, Chris 1948–
·Antony 244; Dream 10076; Richard III
13011
Walker, Don, arr.
[Donald John Walker (1907–   )?]
Hamlet 4156
Walker, Ernest 1870–1949
As You Like It 1559, 1804; Cymbeline 2806;
Henry VIII 5199, 5200; L.L.L. 6631;
Tempest 15586, 15773, 15774; Venus
20800

Walker, George Theophilus 1922–
As You Like It 1199; Measure 8004
Walker, Henry, in part arr.
Merchant 8762
Walker, James 1929–
As You Like It 1200, 1560, 1805, 1806,
1863; Cymbeline 2501; Hamlet 3512;
Caesar 5457; K. John 5630; L.L.L. 6307,
6487, 6632; Measure 7786; Merchant 8373,
8650, 8651; Much Ado 11318, 11575,
11576; Richard III 13012; Tempest 15587,
15775, 15954; Twelfth Night 17657,
17658; Two Gentlemen 18630; Settings of
Commemorative Pieces . . . 21089, 21090
Walker, James, in part arr. 1929–
Richard II 12737
Walker, John Granville
Measure 8005; Merchant 8649
Walker, Millard C.
Hamlet 3783
Wallace, William 1860–1940
Romeo 13529
Wallace, William Vincent 1814–1865
Twelfth Night 18345
Wallace, William Vincent, arr.
1814–1865
Macbeth 7363; Othello 12169
Wallbach, Louis   –1914
As You Like It 1561
Wallbank, Newell S. 1914–
As You Like It 1562
Wallenstein, René 1947–
Timon 16374
Waller, Kenneth
Henry V 4777; L.L.L. 6308; Dream 10077;
Much Ado 11319
Wallerstein, Ferdinand
As You Like It 1939, 1998; Hamlet 4057;
L.L.L. 6689; Dream 10735; Romeo 14069;
Tempest 16142
Wallerstein, Ferdinand, arr.
Tempest 15297
Wallgren, Jan 1935–
1 Henry VI 4872; 2 Henry VI 4911; 3 Henry
VI 4953; Dream 10078; Richard III 13013
Wallin, Bengt-Årne 1926–
Macbeth 7210; Twelfth Night 17326
Wallis, Arnold J.
Twelfth Night 18036
Wallnöfer, Adolf 1854–1946
Sonnet 21 19481; Sonnet 75 20043; Sonnet
76 20053; Sonnet 94 20139; P. Pilgrim
20723
Walmisley, Thomas Forbes 1783–1866
Cymbeline 2875
Walsh, Gary
Othello 12488
Walsworth, Ivor 1909–
Henry VIII 5225

Walsworth, Ivor, arr. 1909–
Twelfth Night 16623, 17317, 17750
Walter, Heinz
As You Like It 903
Walter, Otto
Tempest 15343, 15344
Walters, Gareth 1928–
Tempest 15345
Walters, Leslie 1902–
Twelfth Night 18321
Walters, Walter Edmund 1920–
As You Like It 1201, 1807; Merchant 8652;
Twelfth Night 17659, 18037
Walthew, Richard Henry 1872–1951
As You Like It 1563; Twelfth Night 17660,
18038, 18190; Sonnet 29 19584
Walton, William Turner 1902–1983
As You Like It 904, 1808; Hamlet 3513;
3 Henry VI 4963; Macbeth 7211; Merchant
8653, 8654, 8736; Richard III 13014;
Tempest 15955; Troilus 16584
Walton, William Turner, in part arr.
1902–1983
Henry V 4778
Wambach, Emile 1854–1924
Macbeth 7581
Warbeck, Stephen 1953–
Errors 2187; Dream 10079
Ward, Edward, arr. [1896–   ]
Romeo 14006
Ward, Francis Marshall 1830–
As You Like It 1564
Ward, Frank Edwin 1872–1953
Settings of Commemorative Pieces . . .
21177
Ward, Henry
Hamlet 3517; Dream 10080; Troilus 16544;
Twelfth Night 17327, 17328; Winter's Tale
18902
Ward, Howard, arr.
Dream 9841
Ward, Kate Lucy 1833–
Tempest 16175
Ward, Michael
Dream 10081
Ward, Trisha [1964]-
Macbeth 7367
Ward-Casey, Samuel
Also known as S. Ward
As You Like It 1202; Twelfth Night 18039
Ward-Steinman, David 1936–
Twelfth Night 17329
Ware, George
Twelfth Night 17330
Ware, H. J.
Tempest 16143
Ware, William Henry
Antony 245; Coriolanus 2360; Cymbeline
2502; Hamlet 3518; Caesar 5458; K. John

Ware, William Henry (*cont.*)
5631; Lear 5969; Macbeth 7212; Two
Gentlemen 18447

Wareing, Herbert Walter 1857–1918
As You Like It 1203, 1565, 1809; L.L.L.
6633; Much Ado 11577; Twelfth Night
18040, 18191; Two Gentlemen 18631;
Winter's Tale 19066

Warlock, Peter 1894–1930
Pseudonym used by Philip Arnold Heseltine
As You Like It 1566; L.L.L. 6488; Measure
8006, 8007, 8008; Merchant 8655; Much
Ado 11578; Twelfth Night 18041; Winter's
Tale 19067

Warlock, Peter, arr. 1894–1930
Pseudonym used by Philip Arnold Heseltine
Othello 12262

Warnick, Clay, arr.
Shrew 14634

Warrell, Arthur Sydney [1882?]–1939
As You Like It 1569

Warrell, Terry
Romeo 13530

Warren, Arthur M.
Tempest 15866

Warren, Charles, arr.
L.L.L. 6237

Warren, David Alvin 1957–
Othello 11998

Warren, Joseph, arr. 1804–1881
Dream 9842

Warren, Raymond Henry Charles 1928–
Tempest 16176; Twelfth Night 17331

Warren, Samuel Prowse, arr. 1841–1915
Dream 9843, 9844, 9845

Warrington, John, arr.
[John T. Warrington (1911–1978)?]
Errors 2232, 2233; Romeo 13428; Shrew
14635, 14636, 14637

Washburn, Robert 1928–
Much Ado 11579; Twelfth Night 17661,
18042

Wassall, Grace
Also known as Grace Chadbourne
As You Like It 1204, 1570, 1810; L.L.L.
6371; Merchant 8656; Sonnet 18 19446;
Sonnet 29 19585; Sonnet 30 19625; Sonnet
65 19903; Sonnet 90 20114; Sonnet 91
20122; P. Pilgrim 20724

Waters, Charles Frederick 1895–1975
Dream 10439

Waters, J. Baguley
As You Like It 1571

Waters, Joseph Martin 1952–
Sonnet 73 20021

Waterson, James 1834–1893
Tempest 16144

Watkins, Michael Blake 1948–
Antony 332; Hamlet 3717; 1 Henry IV
4487; Much Ado 11375; Romeo 14039;

Sonnet 35 19670; Settings of
Commemorative Pieces . . . 21178

Watson, Eric 1946–
Antony 246; Macbeth 7214; Tempest 15346

Watson, Geoffrey, arr.
Othello 12263

Watson, Henry 1846–1911
Antony 247; Twelfth Night 18043; Two
Gentlemen 18632; Settings of
Commemorative Pieces . . . 20984

Watson, Mabel Madison
Winter's Tale 18988

Watson, Rosabel
Coriolanus 2361; Henry V 4785; K. John
5632; L.L.L. 6309; Timon 16363

Watson, Rosabel, in part arr.
Two Gentlemen 18448

Watson, Rosabel, arr.
Two Gentlemen 18608

Watson, Tom
Shrew 14536

Watson, W.
Settings of Commemorative Pieces . . . 21091

Watson, William Michael 1840–1889
Also wrote under the pseudonym 'Jules Favre'
As You Like It 1572, 1940; Othello 12364;
Romeo 14214; Tempest 15956

Watson, William Michael, arr. 1840–1889
Also wrote under the pseudonym 'Jules Favre'
Dream 10134, 10894; Tempest 14836

Watt, Harmon H.
Tempest 16145

Watters, Mark E.
Hamlet 3519

Watts, Ardean 1928–
Tempest 15347

Wawerski, Klemens
Errors 2188

Webb, Bruce
Twelfth Night 17332

Webb, Michael 1963–
Tempest 15348

Webb, Simon
Hamlet 3520; Merchant 8374; Dream
10082; Much Ado 11320; Twelfth Night
17333

Webbe, Samuel, the Elder 1740–1816
Macbeth 7505

Webbe, Samuel, the Elder, arr. 1740–1816
As You Like It 449; Cymbeline 2660;
Merchant 8435; Tempest 14751, 14837;
Settings of Commemorative Pieces . . .
20908

Webbe, Samuel, Jr. 1770–1843
As You Like It 1205; Merchant 8477; Merry
Wives 8977; Twelfth Night 17662; Two
Gentlemen 18633

Webbe, Samuel, Jr., arr. 1770–1843
Tempest 15577

Webber, James Plaisted
1 Henry IV 4469; 2 Henry IV 4635; Merry
Wives 9196
Webber, John
[John C. Webber (1949–   )?]
Tempest 15349
Weber, Bernhard Anselm 1764–1821
Coriolanus 2386; Merchant 8657; Othello
12365
Weber, Carl Maria Friedrich Ernst von
1786–1826
Antony 348; Cymbeline 2885; Caesar 5550;
Merchant 8375, 8658; Dream 10807; Much
Ado 11615; Romeo 13531
Weber, Christoph
Tempest 15350
Weber, Gustav 1845–1887
Lear 6106
Weber, Wolfgang, arr.
Merry Wives 9143
Weber-Harnisch, Rolf
Macbeth 7215
Webster, Peter
Caesar 5459
Weckerlin, Jean-Baptiste Théodore
1821–1910
All's Well 105
Wedemeier, Ulrich
Macbeth 7530
Weelkes, Thomas [circa 1575]–1623
P. Pilgrim 20725
Wefing, Dieter 1935–
Hamlet 3521; K. John 5633
Wehli, James M., arr.
Dream 9846
Wehr, Wesley Conrad
Twelfth Night 18192
Weidenaar, Reynold Henry 1945–
Dream 10440
Weidt, Karl 1857–1936
As You Like It 1573
Weigl, Joseph 1766–1846
Antony 385; Coriolanus 2431; Hamlet
4182; Lear 5970
Weigl, Vally 1894–1982
Also known as Valerie Weigl
Cymbeline 2621
Weihe, Heinz
As You Like It 906
Weikert, Ralf
Tempest 15351
Weil, Oscar
As You Like It 1574; Dream 10898; Much
Ado 11580; Twelfth Night 17663, 18044
Weinberger, Jaromír 1896–1967
Romeo 13532; Sonnet 155 20580
Weiner, Lawrence 1932–
Sonnet 18 19447; Sonnet 29 19586; Sonnet
73 20022

Weingartner, Paul Felix 1863–1942
Also known as Edler von Münzberg
Hamlet 3522; Lear 6107; Romeo 13823;
Tempest 15352
Weinhöppel, Kurt
Twelfth Night 17334
Weinsoff, Charles
Hamlet 3523
Weinstock, Richard
All's Well 66; Shrew 14537
Weinstock, Stephen
All's Well 67; Antony 248
Weippert, John, arr.
Twelfth Night 16682
Weis, Karel 1862–1944
Twelfth Night 17421
Weisenborn, Joseph
Tempest 16146
Weiser, Adolph
As You Like It 1575
Weisgall, Hugo David 1912–
Venus 20786
Weisgarber, Elliot 1919–
Sonnet 8 19269; Sonnet 15 19313; Sonnet
18 19448; Sonnet 30 19626
Weishappel, Rudolf 1921–
Hamlet 3524; Othello 11999
Weismann, Julius 1879–1950
Dream 10083
Weisnewski, Joseph
Errors 2189; Dream 10084; Pericles
12593
Weiss, Adolph 1891–1971
As You Like It 1576
Weiss, Anton, arr.
Two Gentlemen 18609
Weiss, Dik
Measure 7787
Weiss, Harald 1949–
As You Like It 907; Dream 10085; Much
Ado 11321; Romeo 13533
Weiß, Helmuth
Henry VIII 5201; Merchant 8492; Romeo
13869; Two Gentlemen 18640
Weiss, Julius, arr.
Merry Wives 9144
Weiss, Willoughby Hunter 1820–1867
Antony 304
Weld, Margaret
Tempest 16147
Weldon, John 1676–1736
Also known as John Welldon
Measure 7788, 8009; Tempest 15354;
Twelfth Night 18277
Welffens, Peter 1924–
Coriolanus 2362; Dream 10086; Tempest
15355
Welin, Karl-Erik 1934–
Hamlet 3694; Sonnet 60 19842

Wellesley, Garrett Colley 1738–1781
    Also known as Earl of Mornington
    Henry VIII 5202; P. Pilgrim 20726
Wellesz, Egon 1885–1974
    Tempest 16148
Wells, Thomas
    K. John 5634
Wells, Thomas H.
    Lear 5971
Welser, Irving
    Sonnet 18 19461
Welsh, Harry E.
    Much Ado 11647
Welsh, Thomas [circa 1780]–1848
    Merry Wives 8978; Sonnet 97 20176;
    Sonnet 98 20197; Sonnet 99 20206
Welstead, Jon
    As You Like It 908; Hamlet 3525; Richard
    III 13018
Wemheuer, Werner
    As You Like It 909; Hamlet 3526
Wendlandt, William
    Romeo 13534
Wenham, John
    Henry V 4786
Weninger, L., arr.
    [Leopold Weninger (1879–1940)?]
    Merry Wives 9145
Wenk, J. A. [1761?]–1786
    Hamlet 3806
Werba, Erik, arr. 1918–
    Merry Wives 9146
Werle, Lars Johan 1926–
    Dream 10291
Werner, F., arr.
    As You Like It 450
Werner, Henry 1817–1892
    Pseudonym used by Charles Balmer
    Cymbeline 2831
Werner, Kurt
    Much Ado 11322, 11323, 11324; Winter's
    Tale 18903
Werner, Kurt, in part arr.
    Errors 2190
Werner, Lothar
    Measure 7789; Much Ado 11325
Werner, Vladimír
    Romeo 13535
Wernick, Adam 1963–
    As You Like It 910, 911; Hamlet 3527; 2
    Henry IV 4614; Measure 7790; Merry Wives
    8979, 9208; Dream 10087; Much Ado
    11326; Tempest 15356; Troilus 16545;
    Twelfth Night 17335
Wernick, Adam, in part arr. 1963–
    Henry V 4787
Wernick, Dick
    [Richard F. Wernick (1934–   )?]
    Dream 10088

Wernick, Richard F. 1934–
    Tempest 15776
Wertheim, Ruth White
    Hamlet 3528
Werthemann, Carl Andreas 1878–1959
    Macbeth 7491
Werzlau, Joachim 1913–
    As You Like It 1227
Wesché, Walter 1857–
    Merchant 8478
Wesley, Samuel 1766–1837
    Measure 8010; Kinsmen 19172
Wesley, Samuel, arr. 1766–1837
    Macbeth 7004; Tempest 15129
Wesley-Smith, Martin 1945–
    Othello 12366; Tempest 15588
Wesseler, Karl
    Macbeth 7531
Wessely, Carl Bernhard 1768–1826
    Tempest 15357
Wessenberg, H. W.
    Macbeth 7492
West, Edward Roberts
    Dream 10089, 10736
West, George Frederick
    Tempest 16149
West, George Frederick, arr.
    Dream 9847, 9848; Tempest 14838
West, John
    Winter's Tale 18904
West, John Ebenezer 1863–1929
    Two Gentlemen 18634
West, John Ebenezer, arr. 1863–1929
    Henry VIII 4991, 5186; Tempest 14752;
    Twelfth Night 17767; Two Gentlemen
    18610
West, Louise Ashley
    Merchant 8376
West, William, arr. 1830–
    As You Like It 451
Westbrook, Michael 1936–
    Settings of Commemorative Pieces . . . 20985
Westbrook, William Joseph, arr. 1831–1894
    Dream 9849, 9850
Westcott, Frederic
    As You Like It 2017
Westcott, Frederic, arr.
    Dream 10262
Westergaard, Peter Talbot 1931–
    Tempest 15498, 16150
Westling, Kjell 1942–
    1 Henry IV 4445; 2 Henry IV 4615; Henry V
    4788; 1 Henry VI 4873; 2 Henry VI 4912;
    3 Henry VI 4954; Richard II 12738;
    Richard III 13019
Weston, Nick
    Troilus 16546
Weston, Pamela, arr.
    Merchant 8750

Westrich, Willi
  As You Like It 912; Hamlet 3529; Macbeth
  7216
Westrop, East John, arr. 1804–1856
  Macbeth 7005, 7006
Westrop, Thomas, arr.
  Hamlet 3530, 4080
Westrup, Jack Allan 1904–1975
  Henry VIII 5203; Measure 8011; Twelfth
  Night 17664
Westrup, Jack Allan, arr. 1904–1975
  Timon 16334, 16349
Wetzel, Justus Hermann, arr. 1879–1973
  Othello 12208
Wetzel, Le Roy 1884–
  P. Pilgrim 20730
Wetzger, Paul, arr.
  Merry Wives 9147
Wetzker, Ingo
  Hamlet 3531; Romeo 13536
Wetzler, Hermann Hans 1870–1943
  As You Like It 913
Wetzler, Johannes
  As You Like It 917; Hamlet 4133; K. John
  5635; Much Ado 11327; Romeo 13537;
  Twelfth Night 17336
Weybright, June, arr.
  Dream 9851
Weyermann, Moritz Rudolf
  As You Like It 1206; Twelfth Night 17665,
  18045, 18193
Weyse, Christoph Ernst Friedrich 1774–1842
  Macbeth 7217
Whear, Paul William 1925–
  Sonnet 8 19270; Sonnet 87 20098; Sonnet
  106 20267; P. Pilgrim 20731; Settings of
  Commemorative Pieces . . . 21179
Wheeler, Alfred
  Dream 10570; P. Pilgrim 20732
Wheeler, George D. Chetwynd
  Cymbeline 2807
Wheeler, Kenneth 1930–
  Settings of Commemorative Pieces . . . 21180
Wheeler, William Scott 1952–
  As You Like It 1811; Tempest 15982
Whelen, Christopher 1927–
  Antony 249; Coriolanus 2363; 1 Henry IV
  4446; 2 Henry IV 4616; Henry VIII 5031;
  Caesar 5460, 5461, 5462; K. John 5636;
  Lear 5972; Macbeth 7218, 7219; Merchant
  8377; Much Ado 11328; Richard II 12739;
  Richard III 13020; Tempest 15358; Timon
  16364; Twelfth Night 17337; Winter's Tale
  18905; Settings of Commemorative
  Pieces . . . 21193
Whettam, Graham 1927–
  1 Henry IV 4488; Lear 6109
Whinfield, [Walter Grenville]
  Twelfth Night 17338

Whinfield, Walter Grenville
  Cymbeline 2808; L.L.L. 6634; Measure
  8012; Twelfth Night 17666
Whitaker, George
  Twelfth Night 18046
Whitaker, John 1776–1847
  Macbeth 7532
Whitbeck, Dick
  Lear 5973; Macbeth 7220; Romeo 13538
Whitcomb, Robert Butler 1921–
  Sonnet 15 19314; Sonnet 18 19449; Sonnet
  19 19473; Sonnet 33 19658
White, A. Duane 1939–
  Caesar 5463; Romeo 13539; Shrew 14538;
  Winter's Tale 18906
White, Bruce Howard
  Twelfth Night 17339
White, Claude
  1 Henry IV 4447; L.L.L. 6310
White, Douglas Howard
  Hamlet 3532
White, Felix Harold 1884–1945
  Merchant 8714; Tempest 15858, 15957,
  16151; Sonnet 18 19455; Settings of
  Commemorative Pieces . . . 21092
White, Gary Charles 1937–
  Twelfth Night 17425
White, John [UK]
  Antony 250; Measure 7791
White, John [US]
  Tempest 15359
White, L. J.
  As You Like It 1812; Twelfth Night 18194
White, Maude Valérie 1855–1937
  Hamlet 3713, 3784; P. Pilgrim 20733
White, Michael 1931–
  As You Like It 1577; Hamlet 4081; Measure
  8013; Merchant 8659
White, Tony Joe 1943–
  Othello 12211
Whitehead, Jonathan
  Winter's Tale 18907
Whiting, Arthur Battelle 1861–1936
  As You Like It 1207
Whittaker, Mary G., arr.
  Tempest 15446
Whittaker, William Gillies, arr. 1876–1944
  Hamlet 3785; Dream 10263, 10264, 10265,
  10266, 10267; Tempest 15067, 15447;
  Timon 16350
Whittingham, Alfred, arr.
  Tempest 14839
Whittle, Chris 1927–
  Tempest 16152
Whyte, Ernest 1858–1922
  Tempest 15777, 15958; Twelfth Night
  18047
Whyte, Ian 1901–1960
  Merchant 8660

Wicenciak, Andrzej
Shrew 14539
Wichmann, Hermann 1824–1905
Othello 12367
Wichmann, Karl Horst
As You Like It 918; Hamlet 3533; 1 Henry
IV 4448; 2 Henry IV 4617; Henry V 4789;
1 Henry VI 4874; 2 Henry VI 4913; 3 Henry
VI 4955; L.L.L. 6311; Measure 7792; Much
Ado 11329; Richard III 13021; Tempest
15360; Two Gentlemen 18449
Wicht, [?]
Othello 12467
Wick, Otto, arr.
As You Like It 1075
Wickens, Dennis 1926–
Cymbeline 2622
Wickham, Florence Pauline 1882–1962
Also known as Mrs. Florence Pauline
Wickham Lueder
As You Like It 961
Widmer, Fritz
Timon 16365
Widmer, Henry 1845–1895
L.L.L. 6312; Merry Wives 8980; Dream
10090
Widmer, Henry, in part arr. 1845–1895
As You Like It 919; Shrew 14540; Twelfth
Night 17340
Widmer, Henry, arr. 1845–1895
Two Gentlemen 18371, 18611
Widor, Charles Marie Jean Albert
1844–1937
Twelfth Night 17341
Wiechowicz, Stanisław 1893–1963
Winter's Tale 18908
Wiedecke, A.
Tempest 16153
Wiegand, George, arr.
Merry Wives 9148
Wiemann, Beth
Hamlet 3534; Dream 10091
Wiener, Jean Albert Henri 1896–1982
Dream 10092
Wieselman, Douglas
Errors 2191
Wieslander, Ingvar 1917–1963
Much Ado 11330; Twelfth Night 17347;
Winter's Tale 18909
Wiesler, David G. 1961–
Winter's Tale 18910
Wiflin, Paul
Dream 10093
Wigglesworth, Frank 1918–
Hamlet 3535
Wight, A. N.
Shrew 14541
Wilcke, Wolfgang
Merry Wives 8981

Wilcock, F[rank S.?]
As You Like It 1578
Wilcox, Alexander Gordon 1909–
Romeo 13843; Tempest 15778
Wilcox, Larry, arr.
Errors 2234; Caesar 5548; Macbeth 7546
Wilczek, Ludwig August
Settings of Commemorative Pieces . . . 21249
Wilczyński, Marek
Henry VIII 5032; Tempest 15361
Wildberger, Jacques 1922–
Caesar 5464
Wilder, Alec 1907–1980
Born Alexander Lafayette Chew Wilder
Twelfth Night 17348
Wilder, Throop M., III
As You Like It 920; Caesar 5465; Othello
12000; Romeo 13540; Shrew 14542
Wildermere, H.
As You Like It 1941
Wildgans, Friedrich 1913–1965
Antony 251; Othello 12001
Wilding-White, Raymond 1922–
Macbeth 7221
Wilhelm, Hein[rich], arr.
Dream 10796, 10797
Wilhelm, Rolf Alexander 1927–
Caesar 5466; Romeo 13541
Wilhelmj, August Emil Daniel Friedrich Victor,
arr. 1845–1908
Othello 12170
Wilimek, Eduard 1904–
Dream 10737
Wilke, Werner
K. John 5637; Macbeth 7222
Wilkins, Ken
Merchant 8378
Wilkinson, Keith, arr.
Much Ado 11357
Wilkinson, Marc 1929–
As You Like It 921; Cymbeline 2503; Hamlet
3536, 3537, 4134; Henry V 4790; Caesar
5467; L.L.L. 6313; Macbeth 7223, 7224;
Merchant 8661; Pericles 12594; Richard II
12740; Richard III 13022; Romeo 13542;
Tempest 15589; Twelfth Night 17349
Wilkinson, Martha
Also known as Martha Groom
Twelfth Night 18346
Wilkinson, Philip George 1929–
Errors 2255; Henry V 4832; Dream 10425,
10738; Romeo 14019; Twelfth Night 17667,
18258; Winter's Tale 18989, 19024, 19129
Wilkinson, Stephen, arr.
Hamlet 2972
Willan, James Healey 1880–1968
Occasionally wrote under the pseudonyms
'Raymond Clare' and 'H. E. Leigh'
As You Like It 922, 1864; Cymbeline 2504;

Much Ado 11581; Twelfth Night 18048,
18195; Winter's Tale 18911
Willan, James Healey, in part arr. 1880–1968
Occasionally wrote under the pseudonyms
'Raymond Clare' and 'H. E. Leigh'
L.L.L. 6314; Tempest 15362
Willan, James Healey, arr. 1880–1968
Occasionally wrote under the pseudonyms
'Raymond Clare' and 'H. E. Leigh'
As You Like It 452, 1473; Hamlet 3786;
L.L.L. 6500; Othello 12264; Tempest 14840
Willcocks, Jonathan Peter 1953–
Hamlet 3879; Macbeth 7506; Measure
7811; Othello 12373
Williams, Arnold
As You Like It 1208; Twelfth Night 18049
Williams, Bryan
L.L.L. 6336; Shrew 14543
Williams, Charles A.
Merchant 8778
Williams, Charles Lee 1852–1935
Winter's Tale 19092, 19157
Williams, Christopher à Becket [1890?]–1956
L.L.L. 6635
Williams, Claude, arr.
Shrew 14638
Williams, Clifton 1923–
Cymbeline 2505
Williams, David Christmas 1871–1926
As You Like It 1579
Williams, David Henry 1919–
Hamlet 3825
Williams, Edgar Warren, Jr. 1949–
Merry Wives 8982
Williams, Edward
Troilus 16547
Williams, Francis –1978
As You Like It 1813; Merchant 8662
Williams, Frederich Henry
Henry VIII 5228
Williams, Frederick A.
[Frederic Arthur Williams (1869–1942)?]
Dream 10739
Williams, Grace Mary 1906–1977
As You Like It 1209; Cymbeline 2623;
1 Henry IV 4489; Henry VIII 5204; L.L.L.
6636; Dream 10348; Much Ado 11582;
P. Pilgrim 20735
Williams, Iwan
Measure 7793, 7794; Othello 12002
Williams, John Gerrard 1888–1947
Twelfth Night 18050, 18196; P. Pilgrim
20734
Williams, John M., arr. [1884–]
Cymbeline 2784
Williams, K. A.
Tempest 15779
Williams, Mark
As You Like It 923

Williams, Patrick
L.L.L. 6637
Williams, Richard Henry
Merchant 8663
Williams, Ronald Ray 1929–
Antony 252; As You Like It 924; Coriolanus
2364; Hamlet 3538; 1 Henry IV 4449;
2 Henry IV 4618; Henry V 4791; 1 Henry
VI 4875; 2 Henry VI 4914; 3 Henry VI
4956; Henry VIII 5033; Caesar 5468;
K. John 5638; Lear 5974; Macbeth 7225;
Othello 12003; Richard II 12741; Richard
III 13023; Romeo 13543; Timon 16366;
Titus 16418; Twelfth Night 17350
Williams, Tony
Romeo 13544
Williams, W. Albert 1909–1946
Measure 8014; Two Gentlemen 18635
Williams, Warwick, arr. –1915
Romeo 13756
Williams, William Langton [circa 1832]–1896
Cymbeline 2832; Settings of Commemorative
Pieces . . . 21093
Williams, William Langton, arr.
[circa 1832]–1896
Tempest 14842
Williams, William Sidney Gwynn 1896–1978
L.L.L. 6489, 6638
Williams, William Sidney Gwynn, arr.
1896–1978
As You Like It 1474; Tempest 14841
Williamson, Malcolm Benjamin Graham
Christopher 1931–
Cymbeline 2624; Caesar 5566; Merry Wives
8983; Tempest 15780; Twelfth Night
17668; Settings of Commemorative
Pieces . . . 20986
Williamson, Waldo
1 Henry IV 4450
Willing, Christopher Edwin, arr. 1830–1904
Dream 9852
Willink, A. H.
P. Pilgrim 20736
Willis, Constance
Tempest 15363
Willis, Thomas C.
Twelfth Night 17351
Willmott, Rod
Shrew 14544
Willner, Arthur 1881–1959
Settings of Commemorative Pieces . . . 21250
Wills, Arthur 1926–
Cymbeline 2625
[Wilson, John] [1595–1674]
Winter's Tale 19025
Wilson, Christopher 1874–1919
Antony 253; As You Like It 925, 1580; Lear
5975; Measure 7795, 8015; Merchant 8379;
Dream 10094, 10381; Much Ado 11331;

Wilson, Christopher (*cont.*)
  Othello 12004; Pericles 12595; Richard II
  12742; Twelfth Night 17669
Wilson, Florence
  Twelfth Night 18051
Wilson, Frank
  Tempest 16154
Wilson, Harry Robert 1901–1968
  Henry VIII 5205; L.L.L. 6639; Merchant
  8479; Twelfth Night 18052
Wilson, Henry James Lane 1871–1915
  Also wrote under the pseudonym 'Robert
  Batten'
  Othello 12368
Wilson, Hilda Matilda Ellen 1860–1918
  Also wrote under the pseudonym 'Douglas
  Hope'
  As You Like It 1581
Wilson, Ira B., arr. 1880–1950
  Dream 9853
Wilson, James 1922–
  L.L.L. 6640; Twelfth Night 17422; Sonnet
  55 19788
Wilson, James Steuart, arr. 1889–1966
  Dream 10268; Tempest 14844
Wilson, James Steuart, ed. 1889–1966
  Anthologies 21345; 21346; 21349
Wilson, Jeffery J. 1957–
  Dream 10095; Sonnet 8 19271
Wilson, John 1595–1674
  Measure 8016; Much Ado 11583; Tempest
  15959; P. Pilgrim 20737
Wilson, John, arr. 1595–1674
  Tempest 15068
Wilson, Mary Lee
  Errors 2192
Wilson, Mick 1943–
  Macbeth 7555, 7582; Tempest 15364
Wilson, Mortimer 1876–1932
  Twelfth Night 18053
Wilson, Mortimer, arr. 1876–1932
  Hamlet 4058
Wilson, Myra Emily
  Hamlet 4082
Wilson, Peter [I]
  Twelfth Night 17423
Wilson, Peter [II]
  Caesar 5469
Wilson, Philip, arr.
  Othello 12265
Wilson, Randal K.
  As You Like It 926
Wilson, Robert Ashley
  Merry Wives 9198
Wilson, Robert J. Barclay, arr.
  As You Like It 453; Tempest 14843
Wilson, Stanley
  Richard II 12765
Wilson, Stanley, arr.
  As You Like It 1475

Wilson, Thomas 1927–
  As You Like It 1942; Merchant 8480
Wilson, William
  Dream 10426
Wilson, William, arr.
  As You Like It 454; Dream 10895, 10896;
  Tempest 14845, 14846
Wilson-Adams, Carrie B.
  As You Like It 1210, 1582, 1814
Wilson-Dickson, Andrew G. 1946–
  Errors 2241
Wimbeck, Heinz
  Othello 12005
Wimberger, Gerhard 1923–
  As You Like It 927; Merchant 8380; Shrew
  14545; Twelfth Night 17352
Windsperger, L., arr.
  Caesar 5527; Merry Wives 9149; Dream
  9854
Windt, W. Bernard
  All's Well 68; Antony 254; As You Like It
  928; Errors 2193; Coriolanus 2365;
  Cymbeline 2506; 1 Henry IV 4451; 2 Henry
  IV 4619; Henry V 4792; 1 Henry VI 4876;
  2 Henry VI 4915; 3 Henry VI 4957; Henry
  VIII 5034; Caesar 5470; K. John 5639; Lear
  5976, 5977; L.L.L. 6315, 6316; Macbeth
  7226, 7227; Measure 7796; Merchant 8381;
  Merry Wives 8984; Dream 10096, 10097;
  Much Ado 11332; Othello 12006; Pericles
  12596; Richard II 12743; Richard III 13024;
  Romeo 13545, 13546; Shrew 14546; Timon
  16367; Titus 16419; Troilus 16548; Twelfth
  Night 17353; Two Gentlemen 18450;
  Winter's Tale 18912
Windt, W. Bernard, in part arr.
  Hamlet 3539; Merchant 8382; Tempest
  15365
Wingham, Thomas 1846–1893
  Merchant 8715
Winham, Godfrey 1936–1975
  Sonnet 26 19513; Sonnet 116 20335;
  Sonnet 117 20348
Winheld, Dan
  Twelfth Night 17354
Winkelhaus, Johannes, arr.
  Dream 10897
Winkelmann, R., arr.
  As You Like It 1521
Winkler, Georg
  Antony 255
Winkler, Otto
  Winter's Tale 18913
Winkler, Steven David 1948–
  All's Well 82, Sonnet 1 19186; Sonnet 2
  19194; Sonnet 3 19200; Sonnet 4 19204;
  Sonnet 5 19213, 19214; Sonnet 6 19218;
  Sonnet 7 19225; Sonnet 8 19272; Sonnet 9
  19277; Sonnet 10 19280; Sonnet 12 19292;

Sonnet 14 19301; Sonnet 15 19315; Sonnet
22 19487; Sonnet 30 19627, 19628; Sonnet
31 19640; Sonnet 34 19664; Sonnet 60
19843; Sonnet 64 19879, 19880; Sonnet 65
19904; Sonnet 73 20023; Sonnet 98 20195;
Sonnet 99 20205; Sonnet 107 20272,
20273; Sonnet 123 20367
Winnbust, Johan
 Hamlet 4083
Winter, Aubrey, arr. 1870–
 Hamlet 3686
Winterberger, Alexander 1834–1914
 Twelfth Night 17670
Winterbottom, Frank, arr.
 Cymbeline 2785; Dream 9855; Othello
 11721
Winterbottom, William, arr.
 Errors 2048
Winters, Geoffrey Walter Horace 1928–
 Henry VIII 5226
Winters, Kenneth Lyle 1929–
 Settings of Commemorative Pieces . . . 21251
Winters, Ralph Edrian
 As You Like It 963
Winton, S.
 Macbeth 7493
Wirén, Dag Ivar 1905–
 Hamlet 3540; K. John 5640; Merchant
 8383, 8384, 8716; Dream 10098, 10989;
 Romeo 13547
Wise, Michael E.
 Hamlet 3691
Wise, Ruth Baxter
 As You Like It 1211
Wiseman, William, arr.
 Twelfth Night 16840
Wishart, Peter Charles Arthur 1921–1984
 As You Like It 929; Errors 2194; Cymbeline
 2626; Twelfth Night 18197
Wishart, Peter Charles Arthur, arr.
 1921–1984
 Tempest 15221
Wissmann, Friedbert
 Tempest 15366
Wissmer, Pierre Alexandre 1915–
 Antony 333
Wister, Owen 1860–1938
 As You Like It 1212; L.L.L. 6641; Much Ado
 11584; Tempest 15590, 15781
Wiszniewski, Zbigniew 1922–
 Hamlet 3541
Withers, Herbert, arr. 1880–
 Dream 10578
Withrow, Miriam Fox, arr.
 Henry VIII 4992
Witmann, Gustave-Xavier, fils, arr. –1920
 Hamlet 3019
Witney, Terry
 Tempest 15367

Wittenbecher, Otto, arr. 1875–
 Merchant 8183; Twelfth Night 16908
Wittenberg, Charles
 Lear 5978
Wittenbrink, Franz
 Troilus 16549
Wittgenstein, Friedrich Ernst 1837–1915
 Also known as Graf zu Sayn-Wittgenstein-
 Berleburg
 Antony 283
Wittmann, G., arr.
 Romeo 13757
Wittmann, Hugo
 Settings of Commemorative Pieces . . . 21094
Wittmann, Maximilián 1941–
 Settings of Commemorative Pieces . . . 20987
Woberin, W., arr.
 Merry Wives 9150
Wodellon, G.
 Antony 305; Henry VIII 5206; Measure
 8020; Much Ado 11585; Twelfth Night
 17671
Wödl, Franz 1899–
 Errors 2242
Woitschach, Paul
 Pericles 12597
Wolf, Ernst Wilhelm 1735–1792
 Dream 10292
Wolf, Hugo Filipp Jakob 1860–1903
 Antony 349; Hamlet 4059; Dream 10293,
 10453, 10571; Tempest 15499, 16155
Wolf, Jaroslav 1932–
 Coriolanus 2366
Wolf, Michael J.
 Shrew 14647
Wolf, Richard
 Tempest 15368
Wolf-Ferrari, Ermanno 1876–1948
 Shrew 14648
Wolfe, Esther C.
 Twelfth Night 17355
Wölfer, Wolfgang
 L.L.L. 6317; Shrew 14547; Troilus 16550
Wolff, Bernhard, arr. [1835–1906]
 Romeo 13579
Wolff, Eduard, arr. 1816–1880
 [Also known as Édouard Wolff]
 Macbeth 7364; Othello 12171
Wolff, Julia
 Winter's Tale 18914
Woll, Erna 1917–
 Cymbeline 2810; Merchant 8664; Othello
 12369; Twelfth Night 17672; P. Pilgrim
 20738
Wollenhaupt, Hermann Adolf 1827–1863
 Lear 6110
Wolpe, Stefan 1902–1972
 Hamlet 3542; Dream 10099; Tempest
 15369; Troilus 16582

Wolpert, Franz Alfons 1917–1978
    As You Like It 1943; Dream 10100; Sonnet
    1 19187; Sonnet 66 19925; Sonnet 71
    19972; Sonnet 73 20024; Sonnet 87 20099;
    Sonnet 107 20274; Sonnet 116 20336;
    Sonnet 128 20403; Sonnet 132 20435;
    Sonnet 134 20439; Sonnet 138 20460;
    Sonnet 144 20483; Sonnet 146 20504;
    Sonnet 149 20530; Sonnet 153 20542
Wolstenholme, William, arr. 1865–1931
    Dream 9856
Wood, C.
    Richard II 12766
Wood, Charles 1866–1926
    As You Like It 1213, 1583, 1815; Henry
    VIII 5207; Measure 8021; Merchant 8481;
    Tempest 15782; Twelfth Night 18054,
    18347; Two Gentlemen 18472, 18636
Wood, Erskine
    Much Ado 11586; Tempest 15783, 15960;
    Twelfth Night 18055
Wood, Frank
    Romeo 14186
Wood, Frederic Herbert 1880–1963
    As You Like It 1831, 1865; L.L.L. 6490,
    6642; Merchant 8665; Dream 10349,
    10572; Tempest 15591, 15785, 15815,
    15983; Twelfth Night 17713, 18198;
    Settings of Commemorative Pieces . . . 21095
Wood, Frederic Herbert, arr. 1880–1963
    Tempest 14847
Wood, Henry Joseph, arr. 1869–1944
    Timon 16351
Wood, Jeffrey
    [Jeffrey Neal Wood (1954–   )?]
    Dream 10101
Wood, Joseph R., Jr. 1915–
    Twelfth Night 17356, 18259
Wood, Ralph Walter 1902–
    As You Like It 1584; Cymbeline 2627;
    Henry VIII 5208; L.L.L. 6643; Measure
    8022; Tempest 15370, 15786, 15962;
    Sonnet 64 19881; Sonnet 97 20173;
    Settings of Commemorative Pieces . . . 21252
Wood, Ruth Anne
    Macbeth 7228
Wood, Samuel Balmforth, arr.
    Cymbeline 2786; Two Gentlemen 18612
Wood, Thomas 1892–1950
    Settings of Commemorative Pieces . . . 20899
Wood, Victoria
    [Victoria Pauline Wood (1908–   )?]
    All's Well 69
Woodard, James Philips 1929–
    Sonnet 12 19293; Sonnet 18 19450; Sonnet
    30 19629; Sonnet 95 20141; Sonnet 96
    20147
Woodcock, Alan John 1947–
    Merchant 8717

Woodgate, Hubert Leslie 1902–1961
    Hamlet 3787; Dream 10740; Othello 12007;
    Twelfth Night 18199
Woodgate, Hubert Leslie, in part arr.
    1902–1961
    Tempest 15371
Woodham, Ronald Ernest 1912–
    Kinsmen 19166
Woodham, Ronald Ernest, in part arr.
    1912–
    Two Gentlemen 18451
Woodham, Ronald Ernest, arr. 1912–
    Tempest 15069
Woodhouse, Charles, arr. [1879–1939]
    Othello 12532; Two Gentlemen 18613
Woodhouse, Frederick Erwin, arr.
    Timon 16352
Woods, Frances Cunningham 1862–1929
    Tempest 15372; Two Gentlemen 18452
Woods, J. A.
    As You Like It 1944
Woodward, Kirk
    As You Like It 930
Wooldridge, John
    Tempest 15373, 15592, 15787, 15963
Woolf, Benjamin Edward 1836–1901
    Cymbeline 2809
Woolf, E.
    Winter's Tale 18915
Woolfenden, Guy Anthony 1937–
    All's Well 70; Antony 256; As You Like It
    931, 932, 933, 1214; Errors 2243;
    Coriolanus 2367, 2368; Cymbeline 2507;
    Hamlet 3543; 1 Henry IV 4452, 4453,
    4454, 4490; 2 Henry IV 4620, 4621, 4622,
    4662; Henry V 4793, 4794, 4795, 4833;
    1 Henry VI 4877, 4878, 4879; 2 Henry VI
    4916, 4917, 4918; 3 Henry VI 4958, 4959,
    4960; Henry VIII 5035; Caesar 5471, 5472,
    5473; K. John 5641; Lear 5979, 5980; L.L.L.
    6318, 6319; Macbeth 7229, 7230, 7231;
    Measure 7797; Merchant 8385, 8386, 8387;
    Merry Wives 8985, 8986, 9263; Dream
    10102, 10103, 10573, 10741; Much Ado
    11333; Othello 12008; Pericles 12598,
    12599; Richard II 12744, 12745, 12746;
    Richard III 13025, 13026, 13027, 13028,
    13029; Romeo 13548, 14020; Shrew
    14548, 14549; Tempest 15374, 15593,
    16156; Timon 16368; Titus 16420; Troilus
    16551, 16552, 16554; Twelfth Night
    17357, 17358, 17359, 18260; Winter's Tale
    18916, 18917, 18918, 19146; Kinsmen
    19167; Settings of Commemorative
    Pieces . . . 21096, 21181
Woolfenden, Guy Anthony, in part arr. 1937–
    Measure 7798
Woolgar, Alan, arr.
    Romeo 14007

Woollen, Charles Russell 1923–
  Twelfth Night 17360
Woolley, Charles
  Two Gentlemen 18637
Wordsworth, William Brocklesby 1908–
  As You Like It 1215, 1816; Cymbeline 2628;
  L.L.L. 6644; Measure 8023; Tempest 15594,
  15788, 15964; Twelfth Night 17673,
  18057, 18200; Sonnet 33 19659
[Worgan, James] [1715–1753]
  Hamlet 4290
[Worgan, John] [1724–1790]
  Tempest 16298
Worgan, John 1724–1790
  Lear 6190
Wormser, André Alphonse Toussaint, arr.
  1851–1926
  Dream 9857; Romeo 13758
Wormus, Jay
  As You Like It 934
Wornson, Douglas
  Dream 10104
Worrell, Lola Carrier
  Twelfth Night 18058
Wörsching, Fritz 1901–1976
  Twelfth Night 17361; Two Gentlemen 18453
Worsley, Frank Wallis
  Sonnet 100 20211
Woźniak, Franciszek
  Richard II 12747; Twelfth Night 17362;
  Two Gentlemen 18454
Woźniak, Tadeusz
  Dream 10105
Woźny, Michał, arr.
  Dream 9858; Romeo 13759
Wragg, Eric
  Dream 10106
Wranitzky, Paul 1756–1808
  Also known as Pavel Vranický, Wraniczky,
  and Wranizky
  Macbeth 7232; Dream 10899
Wray, John, arr.
  Two Gentlemen 18614
Wright, Adam 1810–
  As You Like It 1945; Dream 10742; Tempest
  16157
Wright, Denis Sidney Stewart [Stuart], arr.
  1895–1967
  Dream 9859; Much Ado 11055; Richard II
  12762; Romeo 13626; Twelfth Night 17816;
  Two Gentlemen 18615
Wright, Edmund
  Winter's Tale 18919
Wright, Frank, arr.
  Othello 12376
Wright, Geoffrey John Bradford 1912–
  Macbeth 7495; Dream 10764; Tempest
  16193; Troilus 16555, 16556; Two
  Gentlemen 18638; Winter's Tale 18920

Wright, Julian
  Two Gentlemen 18666
Wright, Kenneth
  Twelfth Night 17363
Wright, Margot
  Dream 10743
Wright, Maurice Willis 1949–
  As You Like It 1216
Wright, Stuart 1948–
  Macbeth 7233
Wuchner, Jürgen
  Richard III 13030
Wulff, Christian Nicolaj 1810–1856
  Tempest 15375, 16158
Wüllner, Franz 1832–1902
  Twelfth Night 17674
Wunderlich, Hans-Joachim 1918–
  Hamlet 3544
Wurm, Marie J. A. 1860–1938
  In 1893 adopted the name of 'Verne'
  As You Like It 1817
Wüsthoff, Klaus, in part arr. 1922–
  Dream 10107
Wuytack, Jos 1935–
  Hamlet 4256
Wyatt, Scott A. 1951–
  Hamlet 3545; Tempest 15376
Wyse, Barrie
  Winter's Tale 18921
Wyton, Alec 1921–
  Shrew 14550

X

Xiè Guó Huá 1940–
  Much Ado 11371
Xiè Míng 1948–
  Shrew 14551

Y

Yamashta, Stomu
  Tempest 16194
Yannatos, James D. 1929–
  L.L.L. 6320; Macbeth 7374, 7378, 7391;
  Measure 7799
Yano, Makoto
  Twelfth Night 17364
Yáo Muò
  Romeo 13549
Yates, Edmund
  Twelfth Night 18059

Yates, Roy Riley 1930–
L.L.L. 6665
Ydstie, Arlene
Hamlet 4257
Yeh, Huai-deh
Twelfth Night 17675
Yershon, Gary
Dream 10108, 10109, 10110; Tempest
15377
Yeung, Matthew
Settings of Commemorative Pieces . . .
21253
Yoder, Paul Van Buskirk, arr. 1908–
Also writes under the pseudonyms James A.
Scott and Max Thomas
Shrew 14639
York, Francis L., arr.
[Francis Lodowick York (1861–1955)?]
Romeo 14008
Yorysh, Volodymyr 1899–1945
Othello 12009
Yoshimoto, Randall
Macbeth 7234
Young, Arthur
As You Like It 1217, 1226, 1585, 1818;
Measure 8024; Dream 10574; Much Ado
11588; Twelfth Night 18060
Young, Brian
Macbeth 7235
Young, Douglas 1947–
1 Henry IV 4455; 2 Henry IV 4623; Henry V
4796; Tempest 15789
Young, Kate, in part arr.
Much Ado 11334
Young, Percy Marshall, arr. 1912–
As You Like It 455; Cymbeline 2850; L.L.L.
6501; Much Ado 11008; Tempest 14848;
Twelfth Night 16620
Young, William James 1835–
Tempest 16159; Twelfth Night 18061; Two
Gentlemen 18639
Young, William James, arr. 1835–
Tempest 14849
Young, Willie Fong
Lear 6142
Youngren, William
Hamlet 3546
Youtz, Greg
Macbeth 7236
Yrjä, Tapio
Much Ado 11335; Othello 12010
Yú Dàchéng
Twelfth Night 17365
Yú Xiao Qiū
Tempest 15378
Yuferov, Sergei Vladimirovich 1865–
Antony 284
Yzelen, D.
Hamlet 4258

Z

Zabalza y Olaso, Don Dámaso, arr.
1833–1894
Romeo 13760
Zadlo, Leszek
Dream 10111
Zafred, Mario 1922–
Hamlet 3692
Zaimont, Judith Lang 1945–
1 Henry IV 4491; Merchant 8666; Much
Ado 11590; Twelfth Night 17676, 18062;
Sonnet 71 19973
Zajc, Ivan 1832–1914
Also known as Giovanni von Zaytz
Lear 5981
Zák, Frans
Othello 12011; Shrew 14552
Zák, Frans, in part arr.
Coriolanus 2369
Zallman, Arlene Proctor 1934–
Sonnet 18 19451; Sonnet 33 19660; Sonnet
40 19698; Sonnet 128 20404
Zalva, G. L., arr. 1895–
Shrew 14640
Zamazal, Václav
Antony 257; Hamlet 3547; Romeo 13550
Zamecnik, J. S., arr. 1872–1953
Dream 9860
Zanardini, Angelo 1820–1893
Hamlet 3693
Zandonai, Riccardo 1883–1944
Romeo 14118
Zanella, Amilcare 1873–1949
Macbeth 7494
Zanetti, Leone M.
Othello 12012
Zarchen, Lee
Sonnet 116 20337
Zariņš, Margeris Ottovich 1910–
Much Ado 11336; Romeo 13551; Twelfth
Night 17366
Zarycki, Andrzej
Romeo 13552
Zavadsky, Vassily 1899–
Sonnet 55 19789; Sonnet 57 19807; Sonnet
66 19926; Sonnet 73 20025; Sonnet 96
20148
Zavalishyna, Mariia Semenivna 1903–
Sonnet 139 20466
Zbar, Michel 1942–
Hamlet 4084
Žebre, Demetrij
Romeo 13553, 13554
Zechlin, Ruth 1926–
Sonnet 155 20579
Zehms, Craig
1 Henry IV 4456; 2 Henry IV 4624

Zeidman, Boris Isaakovich 1908–
  Twelfth Night 17424
Zeitlberger, Leop[old], arr.
  Dream 9861
Zelenka, Ivan 1941–
  As You Like It 935
Železný, Lubomír 1925–1979
  Othello 12013
Zelibor, Gustav
  As You Like It 936; Cymbeline 2508; Much
  Ado 11337; Twelfth Night 17367
Zelinka, Jan Evangelista 1893–1969
  Settings of Commemorative Pieces . . . 21200
Zeller, Wolfgang
  Hamlet 4135; Measure 7800; Dream 10112;
  Troilus 16557; Winter's Tale 18922
Zelter, Karl Friedrich 1758–1832
  Lear 5982, 6027, 6038; Othello 12014,
  12233, 12243, 12370
Zemachson, Arnold 1892–1956
  Sonnet 71 19974
Zemlinsky, Alexander 1871–1942
  Also known as Alexandre von Zemlinsky
  Cymbeline 2509
Zender, Michael
  Two Gentlemen 18455
Zenk, Ludwig
  As You Like It 937
Zeppilli, Pierre Paul   –1967
  Also known as Pierre Paul Zepili
  Hamlet 3548
Zerco, T.
  Antony 258; Hamlet 4291
Zetterberg, Mark
  Much Ado 11338
Zhāng Bǎoyun 1939–
  Othello 12212
Zhāng Dìnghé 1917–
  Timon 16369
Zhāng Zhǐliáng
  Winter's Tale 18944
Zhào Hóngshēng 1925–
  Merchant 8388; Twelfth Night 17368
Zhaò Shi Jūn 1926–
  Dream 10113
Zhelobinskii, Valerii Viktorovich
  1913–1946
  Richard III 13031; Twelfth Night 17369
Zhivotov, Aleksei Semenovich 1904–1964
  Twelfth Night 17370
Zhu Zhiqi 1965–
  Much Ado 11339
Ziedner, Edvin
  Merry Wives 8987; Much Ado 11340;
  Shrew 14553; Twelfth Night 17371
Ziegler, David
  L.L.L. 6321; Winter's Tale 18923
Ziegler, Frédéric, arr.
  Much Ado 11628

Žigon, Marko 1929–
  1 Henry IV 4457; Much Ado 11341
Zilcher, Eva
  Two Gentlemen 18456
Zilcher, Hermann Karl Josef 1881–1948
  All's Well 91; As You Like It 938; Errors
  2195, 2256; Dream 10114; Shrew 14554,
  14674; Winter's Tale 18924
Zilcher, Paul, arr.
  Othello 12209
Zillig, Winfried Petrus Ignatius 1905–1963
  Errors 2196; Hamlet 3549; Caesar 5474;
  Dream 10115; Much Ado 11342; Troilus
  16560; Twelfth Night 17372
Zimmermann, Agnes Marie Jacobina
  1845–1925
  Also known as Agnes Zimmerman
  As You Like It 1219; Dream 10939
Zimmermann, Balduin
  Winter's Tale 18945
Zimmermann, Bernd Alois 1918–1970
  Antony 259; Dream 10744
Zimmermann, Johannes
  Errors 2197; Merchant 8389
Zimmermann, Johannes, in part arr.
  As You Like It 942
Zimmermann, Rolf 1925–
  Dream 10745
Zingarelli, Niccolò Antonio 1752–1837
  Caesar 5567; Romeo 14215
Zinger, G., arr.
  [Grigorii Solomonovich Zinger (1913–   )?]
  Antony 342
Zito, Tony
  Tempest 15379
Zitterbart, Fidelis
  Richard III 13063
Zoeller, Carli, arr. 1840–1889
  Also known as Karl Zoeller
  Merry Wives 9151
Zoghby, Emile Dean
  Othello 12213
Zopf, Hermann 1826–1883
  L.L.L. 6491
Zorlig, Kurt 1893–
  Dream 10900
Zorman, Moshe
  Merry Wives 8988; Othello 12015
Zorzor, Ştefan 1932–
  Coriolanus 2370; Hamlet 3550; Measure
  7801
zu Putlitz, Gustav Heinrich Gans, arr.
  1821–1890
  Also known as Edler Herr von Putlitz
  Much Ado 11358
Żuk, Edward
  Dream 10116
Zukofsky, Celia Thaew
  Pericles 12600, 12607

Żuliński, Antoni
  Shrew 14555
Żuliński, Tadeusz
  Shrew 14556
Zulueta, Jorge
  Hamlet 4183
Zumpe, Herman 1850–1903
  All's Well 46; Timon 16331; Settings of
  Commemorative Pieces . . . 21254
Zumsteeg, Johann Rudolf 1760–1802
  Also known as Johann Rudolph Zumsteeg

Hamlet 3551, 3788; Macbeth 7237;
  Othello 12016, 12234, 12371; Tempest
  15500
Zwetkoff, Peter
  Cymbeline 2510; Two Gentlemen 18457
Zwissler, Karl Maria 1900–
  Hamlet 3552; Measure 7802
Zykan, Otto J. M. 1935–
  Hamlet 3553
Zytowski, Carl Byrd, arr. 1921–
  Macbeth 7365

INDEX TO LIBRETTISTS AND OTHER WRITERS

Abbott, George Francis 1887–
Errors 2206; Much Ado 11368; Twelfth
Night 17373
Achilles, Peter
Othello 12450
Adenis, Édouard
Shrew 14645
Adenis, Eugène 1854–
Born Eugène Félix Adenis de Colombeau
Lear 5999
Adenis, Jules 1823–1900
Born Jules Adenis de Colombeau
Lear 5999; Merchant 8397
Adler, Allen
Tempest 16177
Adler, Friedrich 1857–1938
Twelfth Night 17421
Aitmatov, Chingiz 1928–
Romeo 14070
Alder, Annie 1948–
Pseudonym used by Zora Margolis Alderfer
As You Like It 1968
Aldrich, Thomas Bailey 1836–1907
Romeo 14165, 14170, 14173
Allen, Margaret
Settings of Commemorative Pieces . . . 21019
Alvey, Southwell
Romeo 14128
Amcotts, Vincent Amcotts Cracroft 1845–1881
[Born Cracroft]
Tempest 16254
Anouilh, Jean 1910–1987
Macbeth 7518; Merchant 8081; Twelfth
Night 16695, 16744, 17194
Antokol'skii, P. G.
Much Ado 11157
Anton, Eduardo
Othello 12448
Apolinar, Danny
Twelfth Night 17395; Settings of
Commemorative Pieces . . . 20939
Appel, Libby
Settings of Commemorative Pieces . . .
20824
Appleby, Kenneth
Settings of Commemorative Pieces . . .
20957
Appleyard, Fred J., Jr.
Much Ado 11629

Arkell, Reginald
Hamlet 4143; Settings of Commemorative
Pieces . . . 20915
Arnold, Matthew 1822–1888
Settings of Commemorative Pieces . . . 21017
Artmann, Hans Carl [1932]–
Two Gentlemen 18463
Ashman, Howard Elliott 1950–
Tempest 15450
Atienza, Edward Vincent 1924–
Twelfth Night 18272; Settings of
Commemorative Pieces . . . 20863
Atteridge, Harold Richard 1886–1938
Romeo 14109
Atwood, Margaret Eleanor 1939–
Settings of Commemorative Pieces . . . 21002
Auden, Wystan Hugh 1907–1973
L.L.L. 6330, 6334; Tempest 16183
Augias, Corrado
Othello 12443
Augier, Émile 1820–1889
Merchant 8691
Auzanet, Jean
Hamlet 3687
Axelrod, Dana
Winter's Tale 18931

B

B—
Settings of Commemorative Pieces . . . 20999
Bacchelli, Riccardo
Hamlet 4280
Bachmann, Ingeborg 1926–
L.L.L. 6327
Bachrach, Jacques
Romeo 14050
Bachtík, Josef
Errors 2200
Bagley, Albert
Othello 12538
Bailey, Beverly A.
Tempest 15386
Baldanza, Giovanni 1708–1789
Coriolanus 2407
Baldridge, Dale 1924–
Measure 8039

Banks, George Linnæus
Settings of Commemorative Pieces . . .
21059
Bannelier, Charles
Much Ado 11343
Bantock, Helen Francesca Maude 1868–1961
Née Helena Franceska von Schweitzer
Romeo 13652, 13970
Barber, H. W.
Macbeth 7538
Barbier, Paul Jules 1825–1901
Hamlet 3625; L.L.L. 6675; Dream 10805;
Othello 12111; Tempest 15493
Barnes, Fred J.
Romeo 14137
Barnfield, Richard 1574–1627
P. Pilgrim 20593, 20608, 20609, 20611,
20614, 20627, 20631, 20633, 20642,
20645, 20648, 20653, 20654, 20657,
20663, 20666, 20669, 20676, 20682,
20692, 20702, 20706, 20707, 20712,
20722, 20723, 20726, 20730, 20731,
20732, 20739, 20741, 20747, 20750
Barré, Pierre-Yon 1749–1832
Othello 12444
Barrie, James Matthew 1860–1937
As You Like It 904
Bartholomew, W[illiam]
Dream 10902
Batchelder, Samuel Francis 1830–1888
Hamlet 4140
Beaumont, Alexandre 1827–1909
Pseudonym used by Alexandre Beaume
Macbeth 7298; Othello 12476
Bedford, Kate
Measure 7988
Beeching, Henry Charles 1859–1919
Hamlet 3571; Henry V 4805; K. John 5643;
Richard II 12757
Beggi, Annibale   –1920
Romeo 13790
Bellamy, W. H.
Twelfth Night 18332
Beltrame, Pietro
Antony 364
Bengough, J. W.
Hamlet 4144
Bennett, Enoch Arnold 1867–1931
Antony 260
Bennett, J. M.
Settings of Commemorative Pieces . . . 21048
Bentley, Paul
Merchant 8167
Beretti, Filippo
Romeo 13782
Bergman, Boris
Settings of Commemorative Pieces... 21030
Beringer, Oscar
Twelfth Night 17384

Berio, Francesco Maria
Also known as Marchese di Salza
Othello 12017, 12038
Berman, Ken
Dream 10802
Bernardi, Carlo
Tempest 15397
Bernède, Arthur
Antony 376
Bernhard, Jim
1 Henry IV 4459; 2 Henry IV 4626
Berton, Pierre François Samuel 1842–1912
Tempest 15408
Bertossi, [?]
Othello 12478
Besant, Walter 1836–1901
Dream 10904; Tempest 16245
Betterton, Thomas [1635?]–1710
1 Henry IV 4326, 4496; Dream 10180
Bicât, Tony
All's Well 72
Bickerstaffe, Isaac [1735–1812?]
Settings of Commemorative Pieces . . . 21020
Bill, Mary Fournier
Errors 2199
Biller, Hal
Romeo 14046
Billon, Pierre
Merchant 8149
Bingham, Graham Clifton 1859–1913
Also wrote under the pseudonym 'Cockiolly
Bird'
Romeo 14194; Twelfth Night 18339
Binnie, Jean 1949–
Macbeth 7507
Birch, [?]
Much Ado 11646
Biturgiense, Fabio Dorseno Aborigene
Pseudonym used by [?]
Hamlet 4150
Black, Kitty
Settings of Commemorative Pieces . . . 20851
Blackman, J.
Hamlet 4255
Blair, Hal
Settings of Commemorative Pieces . . . 21278
Blake, G. B.
Hamlet 4140
Blanchard, Edward Litt Laman 1820–1889
Romeo 14054
Blau, Édouard 1836–1906
Much Ado 11367; Tempest 15399
Blavet, Émile Raymond 1838–1924
Richard III 13035
Block, Irving
Tempest 16177
Block, Stephanie
Macbeth 7243
Blok, Aleksandr Aleksandrovich 1880–1921
Hamlet 4245

Blom, Michael
  Hamlet 4278
Blumenthal, Julius 1892–
  Dream 10900
Bluth, Frederick L.
  Also known under the pseudonym 'Toby'
  As You Like It 951
Bogros, [?]
  Antony 367
Böhm, Jindřich 1836–1916
  Twelfth Night 17376
Boisseaux, Henri   –1863
  Merchant 8397
Boito, Arrigo 1842–1918
  Born Enrico Boito. Also known as Arrigo
  Boïto and under the pseudonym 'Tobia Gorrio'
  Hamlet 3575; 1 Henry IV 4468; 2 Henry IV
  4634; Merry Wives 9177; Othello 12180;
  Romeo 13818
Bokkadoro, Vera
  Much Ado 11364
Boll, André 1896–
  Dream 10143; Much Ado 11344; Othello
  12178
Bolton, Guy [circa 1885]–1979
  Sonnet 155 20582
Bond, Edward 1934–
  Lear 6121, 6128, 6129
Borri, Pasquale 1820–1884
  Tempest 15388
Borwicke, Lionel H.
  Hamlet 4199
Bottarelli, Giovanni Gualberto
  Antony 373
Bottòmley, Gordon 1874–1948
  Lear 6125, 6155, 6157, 6161
Bouchor, Maurice
  Cymbeline 2454
Bouilly, Jean Nicolas 1763–1842
  Cymbeline 2878
Boulton, Harold Edwin 1859–1935
  Twelfth Night 18334
Bourget, Paul Charles Joseph 1852–1935
  Tempest 16217
Bowes-Lyon, Lilian Helen 1895–
  Also known as Lillian Bowes-Lyon
  Winter's Tale 19150
Bowles, William Lisle 1762–1850
  Tempest 16226
Boye, Caspar Johannes 1791–1853
  Settings of Commemorative Pieces . . . 20860
Boyer, Lucien Jean   –1942
  Romeo 14105
Boyle, Roger [1621] 1679
  Also known as Lord Orrery (first Earl of
  Orrery)
  Henry V 4840
Bradley, David
  Caesar 5259

Bradtke, Hans
  Romeo 14167
Brahms, Caryl
  Settings of Commemorative Pieces . . .
  20938, 20986
Braun, Kazimierz
  Twelfth Night 17400
Brecht, Bertolt 1898–1956
  Coriolanus 2388, 2389; Measure 8032
Breschan, Ivo
  Hamlet 4133
Bret, Antoine 1717–1792
  Merry Wives 9153
Brieger, Nicolas
  Two Gentlemen 18463
Briggs, Rita A.
  Hamlet 3607; Settings of Commemorative
  Pieces . . . 20926
Brill, Marty
  Lear 6136
Brine, Mary D.
  Dream 10936
Brix, Bettina
  Henry VIII 5080
Bronnikov, P. K.
  Lear 6189
Brough, William
  Winter's Tale 19140
Brougham, John 1810–1880
  Settings of Commemorative Pieces . . . 21064
Bruckner, Ferdinand 1891–1958
  Pseudonym used by Theodor Tagger
  Timon 16383; Sonnet 56 19799
Bruestle, Beaumont
  L.L.L. 6335; Merry Wives 9161; Twelfth
  Night 17416
Brusati, Franco
  Romeo 13418
Bruun, Niels Thoroup 1778–1823
  Also known as Niels Thorup Bruun
  Romeo 13807
Bryan, Al
  Hamlet 4282
Buchman, Sidney 1902–1975
  Antony 340
Buck, Gene
  Romeo 14181; Settings of Commemorative
  Pieces . . . 21080
Bulla, Clyde R.
  Henry V 4802
Buonaiuti, S.
  Romeo 13762
Burch, Fred B.
  Lear 6142
Burgersdijk, L. A. J.
  Coriolanus 2371
Burke, Johnny
  Settings of Commemorative Pieces . . .
  21259

Burke, Mike
 Settings of Commemorative Pieces . . .
 20957
Burnaby, William [1673]–1706
 Twelfth Night 18267, 18268, 18277
Burnand, Francis Cowley 1836–1917
 Tempest 16186
Burnett, Jim
 Macbeth 7533
Burnside, R. H.
 Romeo 14202
Busenello, Giovanni Francesco 1598–1659
 Also known as Gian Francesco Businello
 Caesar 5558
Bussani, Giacomo Francesco [circa 1640–after
 1680]
 Caesar 5559
Butor, Michel Marie François 1926–
 Hamlet 4161; Macbeth 7542
Butti, Enrico Annibale 1868–1912
 Shrew 14641
Buzzella, Leonard
 Hamlet 4229
Byron, Henry J.
 Othello 12507
Byron, May Clarissa   –1936
 Née Gillington
 1 Henry IV 4513; Settings of
 Commemorative Pieces . . . 20931

C

Caesar, Irving 1896–
 Also known as Isador Caesar
 Romeo 14145
Cain, Henri
 Shrew 14645
Calabrese, Anthony 1938–
 Dream 10802
Calvino, Italo
 Tempest 15391
Cammarano, Salvatore 1801–1852
 Lear 6018
Capetanos, Leon
 Tempest 16194
Carcano, Giulio 1812–1884
 Hamlet 3690; Macbeth 7287
Carey, H.
 Settings of Commemorative Pieces . . . 20993
Caritas, [?]
 All's Well 104
Carpenter, Joseph Edwards 1813–1885
 Settings of Commemorative Pieces . . .
 21038, 21070
Carré, Michel Florentin 1819–1872
 All's Well 74; Cymbeline 2516; Hamlet
 3625; L.L.L. 6675; Dream 10805

Casati, Giovanni 1811–1895
 Merry Wives 9251; Dream 10785; Settings
 of Commemorative Pieces . . . 20933
Castellani, Renato 1913–
 Romeo 13524
Casting, Harry
 Merchant 8797
Caulfield, John
 [John Caulfield, the Younger (circa 1775–   )?]
 Macbeth 7567; Romeo 14150
Cayatte, Andrei
 Romeo 14051
Čech, Svatopluk 1846–1908
 Tempest 15459
Chabrol, Claude
 Hamlet 4103
Chabukiani, Vakhtang
 Hamlet 3581; Othello 12030
Chadoff, Anne
 Settings of Commemorative Pieces . . . 20917
Chambers, David L., III
 Settings of Commemorative Pieces . . . 20955
Chandler, Steve
 Measure 8037
Charell, Erik
 Dream 10287
Chivot, Henri Charles 1830–1897
 All's Well 103
Chorley, Henry Fothergill 1808–1872
 Merchant 8760; Tempest 15293
Chorpenning, Ruth
 Romeo 14041
Christiansen, Einar
 Antony 369
Christopher, Don 1938–
 Twelfth Night 17389
Cibber, Colley 1671–1757
 Hamlet 4285; Richard III 12869, 12889,
 12948, 12980; Venus 20820
Cimino, Giorgio Tommaso 1823–1905
 Merchant 8413
Clark, R. M.
 Two Gentlemen 18666
Clause, [?]
 Dream 10952
Clork, Harry
 Settings of Commemorative Pieces . . . 21261
Clothier, R. C.
 Hamlet 4184
Cmíral, Paval
 Settings of Commemorative Pieces . . . 20987
Codebò, Andrea
 Richard III 13083
Coe, E. O.
 Tempest 16209
Coghlan, E. H.
 Twelfth Night 18333
Collard, W. F.
 Merchant 8764

Collé, Charles 1709–1783
  1 Henry IV 4508, 4510; 2 Henry IV 4677,
  4679
Collet de Messine, Jean Baptiste   –1787
  Venus 20812
Collins, John 1742–1808
  As You Like It 1987; Hamlet 4236; 1 Henry
  IV 4506; Romeo 14174
Collins, William 1721–1759
  Cymbeline 2844, 2845, 2852, 2853, 2858,
  2859, 2861, 2862, 2865, 2867, 2869,
  2870, 2871, 2873, 2875
Collis, Alan
  Settings of Commemorative Pieces . . .
  20957
Collot d'Herbois, Jean-Marie [circa 1750]–1796
  Merry Wives 9239
Colman, George, the Elder 1732–1794
  Dream 9282, 9286, 10127, 10765
Colman, George, the Younger 1762–1836
  Also wrote under the pseudonym 'Arthur
  Griffinhoof of Turnham Green'
  Antony 122; 1 Henry VI 4881; 2 Henry VI
  4926; 3 Henry VI 4962
Coltellini, Marco 1719–1777
  Dream 10963
Coma, Abelardo
  Othello 12463
Comden, Betty
  Romeo 14115
Conti, Jean
  Hamlet 4162
Cooke, John, Jr.
  Shrew 14685
Cooksey, Curtis
  As You Like It 961
Cookson, Geoffrey
  Tempest 16266
Corcoran, Robert
  Hamlet 3613
Corelli, Juan 1934–
  Othello 12178
Corneau, André 1857–
  Dream 10965
Cossa, Pietro
  Antony 363
Courtneidge, Robert
  Measure 8038
Covin, Edward F.
  Two Gentlemen 18462
Cowan, David
  Winter's Tale 18930
Cowen, Isaac
  Settings of Commemorative Pieces . . .
  21074
Cowling, Charles
  Dream 10141
Cox, A. Neville
  Macbeth 7538

Crandall, Hazel Dell
  Romeo 14131; Settings of Commemorative
  Pieces . . . 21012
Crane, Harold Hart 1899–1932
  Settings of Commemorative Pieces . . . 20893
Cressonnois, L.
  Hamlet 4281
Cross, Alan Beverley 1931–
  Othello 12468
Cross, John Cartwright   –1809
  Macbeth 7244
Crouse, Russel
  Sonnet 155 20582
Crowther, John
  Settings of Commemorative Pieces . . . 20955
Cullen, R. J.
  As You Like It 904
Cumberland, Gerald 1879–1926
  Antony 353, 354, 356
Currie, Mordaunt 1894–
  Dream 10911; Twelfth Night 16838, 17392
Cuvelier de Trye, Jean Guillaume Antoine
  1766–1824
  Also known as Jean Guillaume Antoine
  Cuvelier de Trie
  Macbeth 7282; Othello 12021

D

Da Ponte, Lorenzo 1749–1838
  Born Emmanuele Conegliano
  Errors 2238; Hamlet 4283; Shrew 14593
Dabbs, G. H. R.
  Tempest 16220
dall'Angelo, Giacomo
  Antony 365
D'Amico, Masolino
  Romeo 13418
Dance, Charles 1794–1863
  Dream 10856
Dane, Clemence 1888–1965
  Settings of Commemorative Pieces . . .
  20838, 20882, 20894, 20899
d'Arien, Bernhard Christoph 1754–1793
  Antony 271
d'Arienzo, Marco
  Antony 382; Merchant 8796
Davenant, William 1606–1668
  Also known as William D'Avenant
  Henry VIII 5001; Macbeth 6705, 6826,
  6971, 7013, 7100; Measure 8034; Much
  Ado 11613; Tempest 14702, 14757, 14859,
  14885, 15037, 15038, 15078, 15196,
  15387, 15405, 15424, 15444, 15464,
  15479, 16200
Daves, Delmar
  Othello 12459

David, Worton
  Settings of Commemorative Pieces . . .
  21032
Dawkins, Dennis
  As You Like It 1963
Day Lewis, Cecil 1904–1972
  Settings of Commemorative Pieces . . . 21005
de Choudens, Paul 1850–1925
  Antony 376; Cymbeline 2516
de Cubières-Palmézeaux, Michel 1752–1820
  Pseudonym used by Michel de Cubières (who
  also wrote under a variety of other
  pseudonyms, e.g., 'P. Ignace de Castel-Vadra'
  and 'M. de Maribarou')
  Romeo 14208
de Fourcard, L.
  Romeo 14197
de Garal, Pierre
  Hamlet 3588
de Gramont, L.
  Venus 20817
de Heredia, José María 1842–1905
  Also known as José Maria de Heredia and as
  José Maria de Hérédia
  Antony 377
de Iracheta, Francisco
  Romeo 13636
de Jallais, Amédée-Jean-Baptiste Font-Réaux
  1826–1909
  Also known as Jean de Réaux
  Romeo 13675
de Jarnatt, Steven
  Hamlet 4096
de la Escosura, Patricio 1807–1878
  Merry Wives 9249; Dream 10777; Settings
  of Commemorative Pieces . . . 20929
de La Serre, Jean-Louis-Ignace 1662–1756
  Dream 10977
De Lange, Edward 1904–1949
  Dream 10287
de Melo, Thomaz
  Othello 12207
de Monvel, Jacques-Marie Boutet 1749–1812
  Also known as 'Monvel'
  Romeo 13633
de Nancourt, Jules
  Hamlet 4162
de Nîmes, Reboul
  Caesar 5563
De Noia, Nick
  Dream 10802
de Ribbing, Adolphe 1800–1884
  Also known as Comte de Ribbing and under
  the pseudonym 'de Leuven'
  All's Well 74; Merry Wives 8989, 9242,
  9249, 9251, 9252, 9256; Dream 10772,
  10777, 10785, 10792, 10804; Settings of
  Commemorative Pieces . . . 20912, 20929,
  20933, 20944, 20958

de Saint-Georges, Jules Henri Vernoy
  1799–1875
  Merry Wives 8989
de Sainte-Croix, Camille
  As You Like It 1194; Cymbeline 2801; L.L.L.
  6485; Merchant 8476
de Téramond, Guy
  Coriolanus 2390, 2391, 2392, 2394, 2395
DeCimber, Joseph V.
  Settings of Commemorative Pieces . . .
  20943
Defranceschi, Carlo Prospero
  Merry Wives 9158
Dehmel, Willy
  Othello 12510
Deicke, Günther 1922–
  Twelfth Night 17387
Dejaure, Jean-Élie Bédéno 1761–1799
  Cymbeline 2837; Much Ado 11617
Delange, Ch. M.
  Othello 12500
DeLynn, Jane
  Hamlet 4179
Denni, Gwynne
  Romeo 14142
Dent, Alan Holmes 1905–1978
  Richard III 13014
Deperis, [?]
  Othello 12478
Deschamps, Émil 1791–1871
  Lear 6015; Romeo 13562
Deshays, Émile Léon 1856–
  Shrew 14589
Détroyat, Léonce 1829–1898
  Henry VIII 5240, 5243
Devlin, John H.
  Romeo 14135
Dézamy, Adrien   –1891
  Hamlet 4253
di Villati, Leopoldo 1701–1752
  Coriolanus 2414
Dibdin, Charles, the Younger 1768–1833
  Born Charles Isaac Mungo Pitt Dibdin
  Macbeth 7532; Settings of Commemorative
  Pieces . . . 20883
Dick, Charles George Cotsford 1846–1911
  Othello 12535
Dickin, E. P.
  Twelfth Night 18289
Didelot, Roger Francis Gabriel M. 1902–
  As You Like It 952
Dorey, M.
  Settings of Commemorative Pieces . . . 20980
Döring, Johann Wilhelm 1760–
  Tempest 15426, 15469
d'Ormeville, Carlo 1842–
  Lear 6183
Douin, [?]
  Merry Wives 9254

Drake, [?]
Known as 'Dr. Drake'.
Tempest 16263
Driver, Donald
Errors 2239; Twelfth Night 17395; Settings
of Commemorative Pieces . . . 20939
Dryden, John 1631–1700
Antony 122; Dream 10180; Tempest 14702,
14757, 14859, 14885, 15037, 15038,
15078, 15196, 15387, 15405, 15424,
15444, 15464, 15479, 16200; Troilus
16469, 16473
Du Camp, Alphonse 1840–1901
Also known as Ferdinand Van Den Camp
Hamlet 4194; 1 Henry VI 4882; Henry VIII
5236; Caesar 5557; Lear 6146; Macbeth
7558; Merchant 8763; Othello 12493
Ducis, Jean François 1733–1816
Hamlet 4138, 4146, 4150, 4151, 4154,
4166, 4168, 4181; Lear 6133, 6135, 6140;
Macbeth 7264, 7547; Othello 11778,
12038, 12449
Ducreux, Louis
Merchant 8149
DuKore, Lawrence
Hamlet 3591
Dumas, Alexandre, père 1802–1870
Hamlet 4132; Othello 12466, 12472
Duncan, Ronald Frederick Henry 1914–1982
Shrew 14568; Lucrece 20779
Dunn, Geoffrey Thomas 1903–
Caesar 5566
D'Urfey, Thomas 1653–1723
Tempest 14702; Settings of Commemorative
Pieces . . . 21297
Duroc, [?]
Merry Wives 9253
Dürrenmatt, Friedrich 1921–
K. John 5573, 5589, 5596, 5602, 5605,
5606, 5612, 5615, 5623, 5625, 5635,
5637; Titus 16427
Duru, Alfred 1829–1890
All's Well 103
Dykema, Peter W.
Dream 9786

E

Edgar, Percy
Merry Wives 9260
Edwards, Richard 1524–1566
Also known as Richard Edwardes
Cymbeline 2868; Romeo 14161; Twelfth
Night 18295
Edwards, T. C.
Tempest 16265
Eggers, Hartwig Carl Friedrich 1819–1872
Macbeth 7296; Tempest 15304

Eglin, E. H.
Hamlet 4222
'Elfin'
Dream 10787
Elkin, Saul
Pericles 12605
Ellis, Harold
Caesar 5549
Engel, Samuel G.
Hamlet 4115
Es'man, V.
Romeo 14097
Estevez, Victor A.
Macbeth 7543
Evans, J. Young
L.L.L. 6686
Evans, Sebastian
Settings of Commemorative Pieces . . . 20901

F

Fabre, Émile 1869–1955
Timon 16387
Fabri, Gottfried Lebrecht, [the Younger]
Also known as Gottlieb Lebrecht Fabri, den
Jüngern
Dream 10985
Falconer, W.
Tempest 16294
Farjeon, Harry 1878–1948
Macbeth 7495
Farmer, Marjorie
Much Ado 11423
Fee, Dorothy
Merry Wives 9250; Dream 10780; Romeo
14098; Shrew 14570; Sonnet 34 19665;
Venus 20809
Feind, Barthold 1678–1721
Caesar 5560
Felner, Peter Paul
Merchant 8731
Ferrand, Humbert   –1868
Also wrote under the pseudonym 'Georges
Arandas'
Dream 10124
Ferraz Revenga, Emilio
Dream 10163
Feustking, Friedrich Christian
[circa 1678]–1739
Antony 277
Fields, James T.
Tempest 16241
Fischer, Paul
Hamlet 4247
Flachmann, Michael
Settings of Commemorative Pieces . . . 20824
Flanders, Michael 1922–1975
Romeo 14182

Flaster, Karl
Settings of Commemorative Pieces . . . 21062
Fleg, Edmond 1874–1963
Lear 5984; Macbeth 7242
Fleming, Berry
Settings of Commemorative Pieces . . . 21272
Fleres, Ugo
Tempest 15403
Flers, Pierre-Louis 1867–
Pseudonym used by Pierre-Louis Puyol
Settings of Commemorative Pieces . . . 21274
Fletcher, John 1579–1625
Measure 7696, 7795, 7820, 7840, 7841,
7858, 7866, 7883, 7889, 7926, 7940,
7942, 7945, 7955, 7963, 7980, 7996, 8016
Fogazzaro, Antonio 1842–1911
Tempest 16239
Foix, J. V.
Tempest 15418
Foppa, Giuseppe Maria 1760–1845
Hamlet 4138, 4150; Romeo 14191, 14213,
14215
Forst, J.
Romeo 14113
Fort, Paul
Dream 10950
Forzano, Giovacchino [1883]–1970
Shrew 14648
Fothergill, F.
Lear 6186
Fouques, François-Georges 1733–1825
Known under the pseudonym 'Desfontaines'
Othello 12444
Fox, Martin
Hamlet 4203
Foxwell, A. J.
Dream 10845
Fradgley, C. J.
Macbeth 7577
Francis, [?]
Dream 10769; Tempest 16196
Freda, Riccardo
Romeo 13097
Fried, Barbara
1 Henry IV 4505
Fried, Erich 1921–
Settings of Commemorative Pieces . . .
20937
Friedman, Kim
Dream 10146
Friedman, Mort
Romeo 14046
Friswell, Hain
Settings of Commemorative Pieces . . .
21091
Fritzsche, Dietmar
Shrew 14586
Fröding, Gustaf
Dream 10962, 10989

Frypés, Karel
Also known under the pseudonym
'V. Novohradský'
Twelfth Night 17421
Fulgonio, Fulvio 1832–1904
Richard III 13081
Furnival, Robert
Caesar 5373

G

Gabory, Georges 1889–
Hamlet 4193
Gaglini, Louis V.
Merchant 8756
Gallagher, F. O'Neill
Dream 10966
Gallet, Louis Marie Alexandre 1835–1898
Dream 10965; Winter's Tale 18942
Ganthony, Robert
Hamlet 4170; Henry V 4835; Macbeth
7544; Merchant 8758; Dream 10799; Shrew
14681; Tempest 16204; Settings of
Commemorative Pieces . . . 20950
Garcia, Pilar
Dream 10175
Gardel, Pierre
Venus 20816
Gargano, Aristide
Hamlet 4157
Garland, Patrick
As You Like It 2011
Garnett, Richard 1835–1906
Tempest 16251
Garrick, David 1717–1779
Macbeth 6705; Dream 9282, 9286, 10127,
10905, 10909, 10914, 10915, 10918,
10924, 10926, 10929, 10930, 10931,
10932, 10933, 10935, 10939; Romeo
13155, 13315, 13408, 13562, 14122,
14123; Shrew 14263, 14287, 14336,
14458, 14567, 14655; Tempest 14753,
14894, 15479; Winter's Tale 18675, 18678,
18699; Settings of Commemorative
Pieces . . . 20829, 20830, 20883, 20902,
20989, 20990, 20996, 21021, 21048,
21052, 21277
Garson, Barbara
Macbeth 7513, 7520
Gassman, Vittorio 1922–
Hamlet 4132; Othello 12466
Gatty, Reginald
Tempest 15417
Gavault, Paul 1867–1951
Settings of Commemorative Pieces . . . 21274
Gaythorne, R.
Cymbeline 2884

Geda, Sigitas
Romeo 14070
Geerts, Leo
Hamlet 4153; Caesar 5544
Geiger, Milton
Romeo 14042
Gelovani, Mikhail
Othello 12030
Genée, Richard
Twelfth Night 17377
Ghislanzoni, Antonio 1824–1893
Antony 379; Lear 5987
Giannini, Giuseppe Sesto
Merry Wives 9252; Dream 10792; Settings
of Commemorative Pieces . . . 20944
Gibson, William 1914–
Settings of Commemorative Pieces . . . 20881
Gieseke, Karl Ludwig 1770–1833
[Pseudonym used by Johann Georg Metzler.]
Also known as Giesecke
Hamlet 4130
Gilbert, William Schwenck 1836–1911
Hamlet 4122; Macbeth 7246; Othello
12486
Gildon, Charles [1665?]–1724
Measure 8046
Gimbel, Norman
Dream 10146
Goddard, Julia
Hamlet 3814
Goethe, Johann Wolfgang von 1749–1832
Romeo 13361
Gold, Barry
1 Henry IV 4461; 2 Henry IV 4627; Romeo
14088
Goldschmidt, Miriam
Hamlet 3574
Goldsmith, Oliver 1728–1774
Twelfth Night 18331
Golisciani, Enrico 1848–1918
Antony 362; Cymbeline 2519
Gollmick, Karl A. 1796–1866
Twelfth Night 17412
Gooch, Steve 1945–
Romeo 14047
Good, Jack
Othello 12211
Gordin, Jacob
Lear 6126
Gordon, Barbara
Settings of Commemorative Pieces . . . 20954
Gordon, James B.
Richard III 12780
Gordon, Leo V.
Richard III 12780
Gordon, Ruth
Othello 12462
Gore-Davids, Ethel
Hamlet 4240; L.L.L. 6688; Dream 10928

Gorton, Ron
Romeo 14046
Gotter, Friedrich Wilhelm 1746–1797
Romeo 13560; Tempest 15404, 15415,
15419, 15426, 15427, 15454, 15465,
15500
Gozenpud, Abram Akimovich 1908–
Shrew 14642
Graczyk, Ed
Hamlet 3610
Graham, Ronny
Hamlet 4116; Merchant 8732
Granville, George [1667?]–1735
Also known as Viscount Lansdowne
Merchant 8726, 8751, 8755
Graves, Robert Ranke 1895–1985
Also wrote under the pseudonym 'John Doyle'
Settings of Commemorative Pieces . . . 21031
Gray, Nora
Romeo 13787
Gray, Stanhope
Tempest 16291
Grayson, Charles 1905–1973
Errors 2206; Hamlet 4098
Green, Adolph
Romeo 14115
Green, Bernard 1927–
Also known as Benny Green
Shrew 14610
Green, Dennis
Tempest 15450
Greenwood, John Ormerod
As You Like It 1950; Hamlet 3834;
Merchant 8556; Dream 10748; Much Ado
11447; Romeo 13854; Tempest 15848;
Sonnet 12 19285; Settings of
Commemorative Pieces . . . 21034
Greenwood, Thomas Longden
Romeo 14054
Greville-Bell, Anthony
Settings of Commemorative Pieces . . . 20864
Griffin, Bartholomew
P. Pilgrim 20620, 20737
Griffiths, E. M.
As You Like It 1971
Grillparzer, Franz 1791–1872
Romeo 13558
Gross, Carl
Winter's Tale 18926
Grossmith, George, Jr. 1874–1935
Caesar 5549
Gryphius, Andreas 1616–1664
Dream 10753
Gsovsky, Tatjana 1901–
Hamlet 3566; Romeo 13810
Guare, John 1928–
Two Gentlemen 18464
Guastalla, Claudio 1880–
Lucrece 20769

Guénée, A.
Antony 368
Guenther, John 1911–
Hamlet 4092
Guérin de Litteau, Hippolyte Louis
[1797]–1861
Hamlet 4211
Gugg, Roland
Errors 2242
Guillaume, Jules
Hamlet 3621
Guille, N.
Caesar 5478

H

H., W.
Twelfth Night 18346
Haavikko, Paavo
Henry V 4843
Hadot, Térence
All's Well 74
Hammerstein, Oscar, II 1895–1960
Romeo 14050
Haraucourt, Edmond 1856–1942
Merchant 8727, 8766
Harlacher, A.
Much Ado 11361
Harny de Guerville, [?]
Tempest 16195
Harrington, J. P.
As You Like It 1983
Harris, Augustus
Settings of Commemorative Pieces . . . 20887
Harris, Lionel
Errors 2236
Harrowing, Sydney
Settings of Commemorative Pieces . . . 21043
Hart, Lorenz Milton 1895–1943
Also known as Larry Hart
Errors 2206; Much Ado 11368
Hart, Moss 1904–1961
Hamlet 4099; Lear 6124; Richard III 13068;
Romeo 14048; Twelfth Night 18271
Hashimoto, Shinobu
Hamlet 4125; Macbeth 7529
Hassall, Christopher 1912–1963
Hamlet 4171; Troilus 16584
Hauptmann, Gerhart 1862–1946
Hamlet 3339, 4135
Havard, William
Settings of Commemorative Pieces . . .
21010
Hawkins, Hettie M.
Twelfth Night 18327
Haym, Nicola Francesco 1678–1729
Coriolanus 2402; Caesar 5559

Hebbel, Friedrich 1813–1863
L.L.L. 6691
Hellberg, Martin
Much Ado 11213
Henneberg, Claus H. 1936–
Lear 6009
Henry, Louis 1784–1836
Pseudonym used by Louis-Henri Bonnachon
Hamlet 4181; Macbeth 7547; Othello
12210
Henschel, Helen Henriette
Dream 10220
Hensel, Karl Friedrich
Tempest 15455
Henze, Hans Werner 1926–
Macbeth 7272
Herder, Johann Gottfried 1744–1830
Caesar 5537
Hermann, Ralph
Settings of Commemorative Pieces . . . 20943
Herrick, Robert 1591–1674
Settings of Commemorative Pieces . . . 21306
Hesse, Archie
Hamlet 4238
Heveningham, Henry
Twelfth Night 18290, 18296, 18302, 18311
Higgins, F. R.
Dream 10970
Hilliam, Bertram C.
Hamlet 4137
Hisaita, Eljiro 1898–
Hamlet 4125
Hobart, George Vere 1867–1926
As You Like It 1966; Othello 12497; Settings
of Commemorative Pieces . . . 21271
Hoblová, Alena
Dream 10281
Hoffmann, François Benoit 1768–1828
Othello 12479
Hogg, James 1770–1835
Also known as 'The Ettrick Shepherd'
Settings of Commemorative Pieces . . . 21015
Holt, Will 1929–
Twelfth Night 17373
Hood, Basil 1864–1917
Dream 10778; Settings of Commemorative
Pieces . . . 21267
Hood, Thomas 1799–1845
Also published under various pseudonyms,
e.g., 'Incog.'
Settings of Commemorative Pieces . . . 21308
Hooker, Brian
1 Henry IV 4469; 2 Henry IV 4635; Merry
Wives 9196
Hopffer, Karl Emil Heinr[ich] 1838–1877
Winter's Tale 18928
Houghton, Charlotte
As You Like It 1968
Housman, Laurence 1865–1959
As You Like It 1967

Huber, [?]
  All's Well 81
Huckell, John [1729–1771]
  Settings of Commemorative Pieces . . . 21035
Hudis, Norman 1922–
  Romeo 14055
Hueffer, Francis 1843–1889
  Romeo 13136
Hughes, Russell S.
  Othello 12459
Hull, Thomas 1728–1808
  Errors 2023, 2065; Dream 10771
Hume, Cyril
  Tempest 16177
Hume, Tobias [circa 1569]–1645
  Settings of Commemorative Pieces . . . 21296
Hunter, Anne
  Settings of Commemorative Pieces . . . 21299

I

Ide, Masato 1920–
  Lear 6131
Immerman, Karl Leberecht 1796–1840
  Tempest 15452, 16107
Impink, Craig
  Pericles 12606
Inglis, Bob
  Settings of Commemorative Pieces . . . 20918
Ionesco, Eugène 1912–
  Macbeth 7516, 7517, 7527, 7528
Ireland, William Henry 1775–1835
  Settings of Commemorative Pieces . . . 20865
Ivanovich, Christoforo 1628–1688
  Also known as Don Cristofor Ivanovich
  Coriolanus 2409
Ivory, James
  Antony 344; Othello 12460

J

Jackson, Nelson
  Macbeth 7559; Othello 12494; Romeo
  14129
Jacquemont, Maurice 1910–
  Cymbeline 2511
Jaddanbai, [?]
  Romeo 13406
Jæger, Frank
  Hamlet 4174
James, Kelli
  Winter's Tale 18931
James, Peter
  Errors 2198
Jankowski, Czesław
  Coriolanus 2375

Jaxone, H. L. D'Arcy
  Dream 10974
Jennings, Talbot
  Romeo 13486; Settings of Commemorative
  Pieces . . . 20879
Jerome, William 1865–1932
  Hamlet 4242, 4243; Macbeth 7575; Romeo
  14112; Settings of Commemorative
  Pieces . . . 21008, 21076
Jhabvala, Ruth Prawer
  Antony 344; Othello 12460
Jīn Zhì
  Much Ado 11359
Johnson, Charles
  As You Like It 1955
Jonson, Benjamin 1572–1637
  Merchant 8363; Dream 10986; Settings of
  Commemorative Pieces . . . 20981, 21053,
  21081
Joseph, Robert J.
  Tempest 16240
Josephson, Ludvig J.
  Settings of Commemorative Pieces . . . 21006

K

Kallman, Chester Simon 1921–1975
  L.L.L. 6330, 6334
Kanin, Garson
  Othello 12462
Kaplan, Stephen
  Romeo 14076
Kästner, Erich 1899–1974
  Hamlet 4212
Käutner, Helmut
  Hamlet 4093
Kearney, Ian
  Richard III 13069
Kelsey, Edward
  Dream 10789
Kemble, John
  Dream 10921
Kemble, John Philip 1757–1823
  Antony 122; Coriolanus 2360; Caesar 5458;
  Romeo 13315; Tempest 14950, 15078,
  15196; Two Gentlemen 18434; Winter's
  Tale 18690
Kennedy, Jimmy
  Romeo 14068
Kenyon, Charles
  Dream 9735
Khandamirova, A. G.
  Hamlet 3569, 3581
Kikushima, Ryuzo
  Hamlet 4125; Macbeth 7529
Kikuta, Kazuo 1908–1973
  Twelfth Night 18285

Kim, John
  Antony 346
King, Nel
  Othello 12450
Kingsley, Dorothy
  Shrew 14597
Kinkel, Gottfried
  Settings of Commemorative Pieces . . . 21094
Kishon, Ephraim 1924–
  Romeo 14065; Settings of Commemorative
  Pieces . . . 20886
Knull, Charles H. 1947–
  Lear 6134
Köllinger, Bernd
  Dream 10156
Kondos, Michael J.
  Settings of Commemorative Pieces . . . 20943
Koppel, Anders
  Macbeth 7275
Kops, Bernard 1926–
  Hamlet 4102, 4121
Korndorfer, [?]
  Tempest 15428
Körner, Thomas
  Settings of Commemorative Pieces . . . 21265
Kortunova, I.
  Merry Wives 9152
Kosta, P.
  Settings of Commemorative Pieces . . . 21200
Kozintsev, Grigorii Mikhailovich 1905–1973
  Hamlet 3423; Lear 5925
Kraft, Hy
  Lear 6136
Krásnohorská, Eliška 1847–1925
  Née Pech
  Twelfth Night 17410, 17421
Kringsteiner, Josef Ferdinand 1775–1810
  Also known as Joseph Ferdinand Kringsteiner
  Othello 12456, 12464, 12465; Romeo
  14064
[Krones, Therese] [1801–1830]
  Antony 339
Kuncová, Ludmila
  Shrew 14588
Kurosawa, Akira 1910–
  Hamlet 4125; Lear 6131; Macbeth 7529
Kvapil, Jaroslav
  Winter's Tale 18938
Kyd, Thomas 1558–1594
  Settings of Commemorative Pieces . . . 20833,
  20853, 20857, 20937

L

Lablache, Fanny Wyndham   –1877
  Née Wilton
  Hamlet 4235

Lacey, John
  Shrew 14679
Lacy, Fanny Eliza
  As You Like It 1976; Settings of
  Commemorative Pieces . . . 21039
Laforgue, Jules 1860–1887
  Hamlet 4114
Landriani, [?]
  1 Henry IV 4512; 2 Henry IV 4681
Langley, Steve
  Antony 346
Lannes, Dominique
  Romeo 14043
Lapierre, Henri
  Lear 6008
Laufs, Josef 1855–1933
  Also known as Josef Lauff and as Josef von
  Lauff
  Coriolanus 2417; Titus 16430
Laurence, French 1757–1809
  Settings of Commemorative Pieces . . . 21055
Laurents, Arthur 1918–
  Romeo 13581
Lavrovskii, Leonid
  Romeo 13791
Lawreen, J. B.
  Hamlet 4205
Lee, Bert
  Settings of Commemorative Pieces . . .
  21270
Lee, Nathaniel [1653?]–1692
  Macbeth 7525
Lee, Robert N.
  Richard III 12943
Leftley, Charles
  Dream 10969
Lega, Antonio
  Caesar 5477
Legouvé, Ernest 1807–1903
  Hamlet 4186, 4239
Leigh, Rowland 1902–1963
  Hamlet 4201; 1 Henry IV 4499
Lengyel, Melchior
  Hamlet 4100; Merchant 8729
Léon, Viktor
  Merry Wives 9265
Lester, J.
  Tempest 16260
Leterrier, Eugène [1852]–1884
  Cymbeline 2838
Letser, Torsten
  Hamlet 4101, 4128
Lewis, Joseph
  Settings of Commemorative Pieces . . .
  20917
Lifar, Serge 1905–1986
  Othello 12178
Lindsay, Howard
  Sonnet 155 20582

Linley, George 1798–1865
  As You Like It 2004
Lipton, Dan
  Romeo 14146
Lisle, Vivien
  Lear 5701
Locke, William J.
  Dream 10957
Lockman, [?]
  Lear 6190
Lodge, Thomas [1558?]–1625
  As You Like It 1956, 1958, 2009, 2016
Logan, Virginia K.
  Two Gentlemen 18663
Lollos, John 1937–
  Twelfth Night 17389
Lothar, Rudolf Spitzer 1865–
  Dream 10979
Loveman, Robert
  Romeo 14209
Lowe, [?]
  Known as Miss Lowe
  Romeo 14204
Lubitch, Ernst
  Hamlet 4100; Merchant 8729
Lucas, M. B.
  Romeo 14044
Luzzi, Eusebio
  Romeo 13555
Lyttleton, George Lyttleton 1709–1773
  Also known as 1st Baron Lyttleton
  Tempest 15943

M

M., J.
  All's Well 105
Mabley, Edward
  Dream 10272
Macchi, Gustavo 1862–1935
  Shrew 14641
MacCunn, James
  2 Henry IV 4684
Macdonald, Brian
  Romeo 13644
Macdonald, G.
  Dream 10964
MacDougall, Ranald 1915–1973
  Antony 340
Mack, Robert
  Othello 12506
MacKaye, Percy Wallace 1875–1956
  Tempest 15412; Settings of Commemorative
  Pieces . . . 20924
Mackenroth, Steven
  Dream 10280
Macnally, Leonard 1752–1820
  Twelfth Night 18265

Maeterlinck, Maurice-Polydore-Marie-Bernard
  1862–1949
  Macbeth 7519
Maffei, Andrea 1798–1885
  Macbeth 7298
Maggioni, S. M.
  Also known as S. Maggione
  Merry Wives 8998
Maguire, Patrick
  Macbeth 7563
Maillot, Jean-Christophe
  Romeo 13627
Mallio, M.
  Tempest 16253
Manas, Alfredo
  Romeo 14060
Mangione, G.
  Merchant 8149
Mankiewicz, Joseph Leo 1909–
  Antony 340; Caesar 5424
Manlove, John Gay 1931–
  Lear 5988; Shrew 14557
Mann, Seymour
  As You Like It 1990; Sonnet 18 19461
Marash, Harvey
  Pseudonym used by Harvey A. Harvey
  Measure 8037
Marcello, Marco 1820–1865
  Also known as Marcelliano Marcello
  Romeo 13774
Maren, Roger
  Macbeth 7586
Marlowe, Christopher 1564–1593
  Merry Wives 8876; P. Pilgrim 20587,
  20588, 20615, 20625, 20628, 20629,
  20637, 20638, 20640, 20641, 20647,
  20648, 20663, 20678, 20684, 20686,
  20689, 20715, 20719, 20720, 20739
Marnay, Eddy
  Romeo 14155
Marowitz, Charles 1934–
  Hamlet 4131
Marshall, Francis Albert 1840–1889
  Macbeth 7550
Martinsson, Harry
  Dream 10973
Martone, Mario
  Othello 12022
Mason, David Yates
  Dream 10764
Mastrocinque, Camillo
  Othello 12448
Matthews, E. C.
  As You Like It 1977
Mayer, Edwin Justus 1897–
  Hamlet 4100; Merchant 8729; Romeo
  14050
Maynard, Mary
  Dream 10781; Settings of Commemorative
  Pieces . . . 20932

Mazursky, Paul 1930–
    Tempest 16194
Mazzonelli, Joan Marie 1950–
    Dream 10157; Tempest 16202
McCall, Mary, Jr.
    Dream 9735
McCarthy, Jos.
    Measure 8043
McClure, Michael Thomas 1932–
    Lear 6138
McCormick, Thomas H.
    Settings of Commemorative Pieces . . . 20984
McGrath, Joseph 1930–
    Hamlet 4129
McMahon, John
    Twelfth Night 17423
McNab, Robert
    Errors 2236
Mecchi, Irene
    As You Like It 1968
Medoff, Mark Howard
    Hamlet 3578
Meehan, Thomas
    Hamlet 4116; Merchant 8732
Mehring, Walter 1896–1981
    Troilus 16582
Meier, Herbert 1928–
    Hamlet 3600; Settings of Commemorative
    Pieces . . . 20844
Meilhac, Henri 1831–1897
    Cymbeline 2879; Merry Wives 9265
Meisl, Karl 1775–1853
    Othello 12456
Melis, Hubert
    Also known as Hubert Mélis
    Merchant 8390
Menotti, Gian Carlo 1911–
    Antony 262
Meredith, Owen 1831–1891
    Pseudonym used by Edward Robert Bulwer
    Lytton (1st Earl of Lytton)
    Lear 6181
Merton, Frederic
    As You Like It 1978
Meszel, Max
    Hamlet 4176
Mészöly, Dezső
    L.L.L. 6324
Middleton, C. P.
    Settings of Commemorative Pieces . . . 21040
Middleton, Thomas [1570?]–1627
    Macbeth 6925
Millar, Michael
    Othello 12481
Miller, James
    Much Ado 11612
Miller, Ned
    Romeo 14136
Miller, Winston
    Hamlet 4115

Millevoye, Charles-Hubert 1782–1816
    Hamlet 4275
Milligan, J. L.
    Twelfth Night 18335
Mills, A. J.
    Dream 10956
Milne, J. T.
    Settings of Commemorative Pieces . . . 21093
Milton, John 1608–1674
    Dream 10227
Mitchell, Adrian 1932–
    Settings of Commemorative Pieces . . . 20985
Moine, Claude
    Hamlet 4195
Moline, Pierre Louis 1730–1820
    Romeo 14208
Moniglia, Giovanni Andrea 1624–1700
    Coriolanus 2408
Monnier, Philippe 1864–1911
    Settings of Commemorative Pieces . . . 21196
Monson, William
    Merry Wives 9155
Montgomery, James 1771–1854
    Also wrote under the pseudonyms 'Paul
    Positive' and 'Gabriel Silvertongue'
    Dream 9696
Moorcroft, C. M.
    Venus 20791
Moore, Herman
    Shrew 14561
Moore, John 1729–1802
    Hamlet 3721, 3723
Moore, Thomas 1779–1852
    Winter's Tale 19147, 19149, 19152, 19155,
    19157
Moranis, Rick
    Hamlet 4096
More, Julian
    Merry Wives 9009; Settings of
    Commemorative Pieces . . . 21269
Morell, Thomas 1703–1784
    Antony 350; Measure 8036
Morgan, MacNamara   –1762
    Winter's Tale 18679, 18680
Morland, Alfred
    Macbeth 7005
Morris, Alfred J.
    Merchant 8791
Morrisey, [Paul] [1939–   ]
    Settings of Commemorative Pieces . . .
    21279
Mortimer, John Clifford 1923–
    Twelfth Night 18272; Settings of
    Commemorative Pieces . . . 20854, 20863
Mosenthal, Hermann Salomon 1821–1877
    Cited in some sources as 'Salomon Hermann
    Mosenthal'. Also known as Ritter von
    Mosenthal
    Antony 283; Merry Wives 9015

Moss, Beatrice R.
Dream 9876
Motteux, Pierre Anthony 1660–1718
Timon 16319, 16338
Moulton, Herbert
Twelfth Night 17422
Munn, Margaret Crosby   –1946
Settings of Commemorative Pieces . . . 20852
Murger, Henry 1822–1861
Hamlet 4210, 4223
Murphy, Richard
Lear 6122
Murray, D. Christie
Merchant 8777

N

Nash, Nathaniel Richard 1913–
Born Nathaniel Richard Nusbaum
Settings of Commemorative Pieces . . . 20839
Navarro, Calisto 1847–1900
Also known as Calixto Navarro y Gonzalvo
and as Navarro Gonzalvo
Othello 12483
Neale, John Mason 1818–1866
Dream 9682
Neumann, [?]
Antony 366
Neumeier, John 1942–
Othello 12027
Nevin, Shirley Dean
Merchant 8776
Newcombe, Georgeanne Hubi 1843–1936
Also known as Georgeanne Hubi-Newcombe
Twelfth Night 18326
Nicholls, Harry
Settings of Commemorative Pieces . . .
20887
Nicholson, Hubert 1908–
Twelfth Night 18321
Nijhoff, Martinus 1894–1953
Winter's Tale 19143
Noël, Édouard Marie Émile   –1934
Dream 10984
Noris, Matteo   –1714
Coriolanus 2424, 2430
Norris, James
Romeo 14041
Norton, George A.
Merchant 8782
Nourrit, Adolphe 1802–1839
Tempest 15476
Noverre, Jean-Georges 1727–1810
Venus 20821
Noyes, Alfred 1880–1958
Settings of Commemorative Pieces . . .
20923

Nuitter, Charles-Louis-Étienne 1828–1899
Pseudonym used by Charles-Louis-Étienne
Truinet
Macbeth 7298; Othello 12476
Nunn, Trevor 1940–
Errors 2243

O

Obey, André 1892–1975
1 Henry IV 4330; 2 Henry IV 4542; Lucrece
20778, 20779
O'Brien, John
Merchant 8419
O'Donoghue, Rory
Macbeth 7533
Œris, Arsène
Hamlet 4258
Ogden, John
Troilus 16561
Oguni, Hideo 1906–
Hamlet 4125; Lear 6131; Macbeth 7529
O'Horgan, Tom
Troilus 16559
Olesen, Thøger
Hamlet 4254
Oliphant, Thomas 1799–1873
Twelfth Night 18341
Olivier, Laurence Kerr 1907–
Richard III 13014
Olmi, A. Mario
Dream 10270
Olon-Scrymgeour, John
Venus 20786
Orbán, Desző
Othello 12176
O'Reilly, P. J.
Romeo 14189
Orsini, Luigi 1875–1954
Shrew 14562
Ortego, Philip Darraugh
Hamlet 3578
Osiecka, Agnieszka
Dream 10283
Osterwald, Wilhelm
Hamlet 4214; Othello 12501; Romeo 14157;
Tempest 16219
Otčenášek, Jan
Romeo 14067, 14071, 14093, 14094, 14104
Owen, Orville W.
Settings of Commemorative Pieces . . . 21033
Owens, Rochelle
Twelfth Night 18283
Oxenford, Edward [1847?]–1929
As You Like It 1985
Oxenford, John 1812–1877
Settings of Commemorative Pieces . . . 21069

P

Pabst, Julius 1817–1881
    Settings of Commemorative Pieces . . . 20884
Pacini, Émilien Alexandre Joseph 1810–1898
    Lear 6015; Romeo 14176
Page, Edwin V.
    Romeo 14028
Pakker-Worembrand, Barbara Shelley 1952–
    Née Worembrand
    Sonnet 8 19230; Settings of Commemorative
    Pieces . . . 20880
Pankiewicz, Krzysztof
    Dream 10117
Panzieri, Lorenzo
    Macbeth 7554
Papini, Giovanni 1881–1956
    Lear 5992
Papp, Joseph 1921–
    Hamlet 4097, 4108, 4118, 4163; Much Ado
    11616; Troilus 16559; Twelfth Night 17375
Pariati, Pietro Giovanni 1665–1733
    Coriolanus 2406, 2411, 2418; Hamlet 4264,
    4268, 4276, 4288
Parker, Erik
    Hamlet 4227; Romeo 14166
Parker, Gudrun
    Settings of Commemorative Pieces . . . 20823
Parker, John
    Dream 10305
Pasqué, Ernst
    Antony 371
Patrat, Joseph 1732–1801
    Errors 2258
Patzke, Johann Samuel 1727–1787
    Tempest 15471
Pears, Peter 1910–1986
    Dream 10135, 10191
Pearson, Walter Francis
    Macbeth 7270
Pepoli, Alessandro
    Dream 10981
Pepoli, Carlo 1796–1881
    Romeo 14133
Percox, Eliza
    Settings of Commemorative Pieces . . . 21046
Perinet, Joachim 1763–1816
    Hamlet 4107, 4126
Perkins, Eleanor Ellis
    Settings of Commemorative Pieces . . . 20952
Perry, Felton
    Macbeth 7536
Peruzzini, Giovanni 1815–1869
    Hamlet 4146, 4168
Petito, Davide
    Othello 12174
Pherns, Noel
    As You Like It 1957

Phillips, Louis
    Lear 6160; Tempest 16285
Piave, Francesco Marie 1810–1876
    Macbeth 7298; Settings of Commemorative
    Pieces . . . 20909
Pietsch, Rainer
    Twelfth Night 16773
Pindar, Peter 1738–1819
    Pseudonym used by John Wolcot
    Tempest 16261
Piotrovskii, A.
    Romeo 13791
Pirandello, Luigi 1867–1936
    1 Henry IV 4507; 2 Henry IV 4676
Pirazzi, Emil 1832–1898
    Tempest 15496
Planché, James Robinson 1796–1880
    Dream 10807
Plath, Sylvia 1932–1963
    Tempest 16247, 16264, 16281, 16284,
    16290
Plessis, Pierre
    Macbeth 7276
Pokrovskii, B.
    Much Ado 11364
Polanski, Roman 1933–
    Macbeth 6755
Pope, Alexander 1688–1744
    Caesar 5538
Porter, A. M.
    Dream 10949
Porter, Andrew 1928–
    Tempest 15409
Possenti, Eligio 1886–1966
    Twelfth Night 17386
Powell, Amos
    Richard III 12780
Powell, Dawn 1900–
    Shrew 14584
Pownall, David
    Richard III 13067
Prasch, Aloys 1858–1907
    Winter's Tale 18927
Preis, Alexander
    Macbeth 7551
Presland, Eric
    Dream 10760
Pressburger, Giorgio
    As You Like It 971
Preston, Rob
    Settings of Commemorative Pieces . . . 20926
Prévert, Jacques
    Romeo 14051
Proctor, Adelaide Anne 1825–1864
    Tempest 16246
Pudalov, A.
    Antony 273
Pujol, Auguste
    Lear 6143, 6144, 6147, 6151, 6153, 6158

Q

Quantrill, D. W.
    Tempest 15396

R

Rabitti, Pietro
    Antony 279
Radet, Jean-Baptiste 1751–1830
    Othello 12444
Radlov, Sergei
    Romeo 13791
Rado, James
    Hamlet 4164
Ragni, Gerome
    Hamlet 4164
Rákosi, [?]
    Othello 12175
Raleigh, Walter [1552?]–1618
    P. Pilgrim 20592, 20625, 20637, 20638,
    20640, 20641, 20647, 20648, 20684,
    20686, 20689
Ramos Martín, José 1892–
    Dream 10163
Ravenscroft, Edward
    Titus 16425
Ray, Don
    Romeo 13632
Reichert, Heinz 1877–1940
    Cymbeline 2723
Reisch, Walter
    Othello 12454
Reisel, Zvi
    Hamlet 4176
Rejnuš, Milan
    Hamlet 3590
Renč, Václav
    Hamlet 3590; Twelfth Night 17379
Reynolds, Dorothy
    Antony 351
Reynolds, Frederick 1764–1841
    All's Well 79; Errors 2032; L.L.L. 6676;
    Dream 10127, 10791; Othello 12475;
    Richard III 13071; Romeo 14101; Shrew
    14567, 14687; Tempest 14950; Twelfth
    Night 16666, 18281; Two Gentlemen 18361,
    18652; Sonnet 39 19686; P. Pilgrim 20751
Richepin, Jacques William Théodo[re]
    1880–1946
    1 Henry IV 4494; 2 Henry IV 4667; Merry
    Wives 9237
Riehl, Wilhelm Heinrich 1823–1897
    Dream 10959
Rimbaud, Jean Nicolas Arthur 1854–1891
    Hamlet 4197, 4202, 4209, 4244

Ritterman, H.
    Hamlet 4176
Rivgauche, Michel
    Hamlet 4207
Rivoire, André
    Romeo 14053
Robb, W. Cuthbert
    Settings of Commemorative Pieces . . . 20914
Roberton, Hugh Stevenson 1874–1952
    Antony 173
Robertson, Peter
    Dream 10898
Robertson, Thomas William 1829–1871
    Settings of Commemorative Pieces . . . 21275
Robinsohn, Terese
    Hamlet 3616
Roccaforte, Gaetano
    Coriolanus 2401, 2404, 2405, 2410, 2412,
    2413, 2415, 2420, 2423, 2428, 2429
Rochon de Chabannes, Marc-Antoine-Jacques
    1730–1800
    Tempest 16200
Rode, Helge 1870–1937
    Tempest 16228; Settings of Commemorative
    Pieces . . . 21067
Roe, J. W.
    All's Well 100
Roethke, Gabriela
    Tempest 16274
Rogov, V.
    Merry Wives 8897
Rohmer, Sax 1883–1959
    Pseudonym used by Arthur Sarsfield Ward
    Settings of Commemorative Pieces . . . 21071
Rolli, Paolo Antonio 1687–1765
    As You Like It 960
Romanelli, Luigi
    Antony 385; Coriolanus 2416, 2421, 2426
Romani, Felice 1788–1865
    Hamlet 4166; 1 Henry IV 4466; 2 Henry IV
    4632; Lear 6133, 6135, 6140; Romeo
    14191, 14206, 14212, 14213; Settings of
    Commemorative Pieces . . . 20922
Römer, Georg Christian 1766–
    Merry Wives 9006, 9156
Rose, [John] [1754–1821]
    Dream 10770
Rosemon, Ethel
    Macbeth 7549
Rosi, Francesco 1922–
    Hamlet 4132; Othello 12466
Rosier, Joseph Bernard 1804–1880
    Merry Wives 9242, 9249, 9251, 9252,
    9256; Dream 10772, 10777, 10785, 10792,
    10804; Settings of Commemorative
    Pieces . . . 20912, 20929, 20933, 20944,
    20958
Ross, Adrian 1859–1933
    Cymbeline 2723

Ross, Sheridan
  Pseudonym used by Miss Maclean
  Shrew 14680
Rossato, Arturo 1882–
  Romeo 14118; Shrew 14595; Tempest
  15441
Rossetti, Dante Gabriel 1828–1888
  Born Gabriel Charles Dante Rossetti
  Hamlet 4200
Rossi, Gaetano 1772–1855
  Antony 378; Romeo 14196
Rota, Giuseppe 1822–1865
  Hamlet 4154
Rothery, W. G.
  Henry VIII 4977
Rothwell, Talbot
  Antony 345; Caesar 5542
Rouček, Rudolf
  Antony 281
Rouget de Lisle, Claude-Joseph 1760–1836
  Also known as Claude-Joseph Rouget de
  l'Isle
  Macbeth 7250; Othello 12018
Rousseau, Jean Baptiste 1670–1741
  Venus 20813
Rovira-Beleta, [?]
  Romeo 14060
Ruby, Herman
  Settings of Commemorative Pieces . . . 21080
Ruffières, [?]
  Merry Wives 9253
Ruggles, Eleanor
  Hamlet 4099; Lear 6124; Richard III 13068;
  Romeo 14048; Twelfth Night 18271
Rummo, P. E.
  Hamlet 4079
Runze, Ottokar
  Twelfth Night 16773
Ruškuc, Bogdan
  Antony 272
Russell, Harcourt
  Macbeth 7006
Russell, Helen
  Settings of Commemorative Pieces . . . 21019
Russell, Ray
  Macbeth 7548
Russillo, Joseph 1941–
  Romeo 13761

S

Sacchero, Giacomo
  Tempest 16275
Salvador, Jamie
  Romeo 14045
Salvatori, Fausto
  Dream 10168

Samson, Ch.
  Hamlet 4281
Sander, Levin Christian 1756–1819
  Tempest 16273
Sanseverino, Carlo
  Romeo 13808
Sapte, Walter, Jr.
  Antony 338
Sartre, Jean-Paul 1905–1980
  Othello 12472
Schiff, Lawrence L.
  Lear 6134
Schiller, Johann Christoph Friedrich von
  1759–1805
  Macbeth 6714, 6754, 6896, 6929, 6949,
  6958, 7024, 7111, 7117, 7149, 7165,
  7180, 7192, 7204, 7217, 7438, 7560,
  7566, 7571, 7576; Othello 12014
Schilling, Tom
  Dream 10148
Schirmer, Adolf
  Shrew 14689
Schlesinger, E. G.
  Macbeth 7538
Schmidt, Giovanni
  Dream 10944
Scholes, Percy Alfred 1877–1958
  Dream 10000; Winter's Tale 18869
Schönfeld, Alfred
  Merry Wives 9255
Schubert, Richard
  Twelfth Night 17421
Scott, William
  Settings of Commemorative Pieces . . .
  20957
Scribe, Augustin-Eugène 1791–1861
  Romeo 14201; Tempest 15421, 15452
Seay, James
  Merchant 8400
Sedaine, Michel-Jean 1719–1797
  Merry Wives 9243, 9246
Sedley, Charles [1639?]–1701
  Antony 337
Seele-Roztocki, Carolus 1930–
  Coriolanus 2373; Romeo 14151, 14152,
  14153, 14154
Ségur, Alexandre Joseph Pierre 1756–1805
  Also known as Vicomte de Ségur
  Romeo 13811
Seidl, Johann Gabriel 1804–1875
  Tempest 15468
Seitz, Dran
  As You Like It 945
Seitz, Tani
  As You Like It 945
Seldes, Gilbert
  Dream 10287
Sellers, Peter 1925–1980
  Hamlet 4129

Seriman, Zaccaria 1708–1784
Coriolanus 2425
Sertor, Gaetano   –1805
Caesar 5555, 5556, 5564, 5567; Dream 10947
Settle, Elkanah 1648–1724
Dream 10180
Seyler, Friederike Sophie 1738–1789
Née Sparmann
Dream 10899
Shadwell, Thomas [1641?]–1692
Tempest 14702, 14757, 15387, 15464;
Timon 16313, 16319, 16320, 16332, 16338
Shane, Lester
As You Like It 963
Shapiro, Mel
Two Gentlemen 18464
Shaw, Carlos Fernández
Romeo 13636; Shrew 14565
Sheffield, John 1648–1721
Also known as Duke of Buckingham
Caesar 5538, 5540
Shenshin, Afanaskii Afanas'evich 1820–1892
Also wrote under the pseudonym 'A. A. Fet'
Hamlet 4251
Sherdeman, Ted
Lear 6127
Sheridan, Richard Brinsley 1751–1816
Tempest 15115; Settings of Commemorative
Pieces . . . 21054
Sherrin, Ned
Settings of Commemorative Pieces . . .
20938, 20986
Shershenevich, Vadim Gabrielevich
1893–1942
Twelfth Night 17408
Shulgasser, Mark
Tempest 15429
Sigma, Julius
Hamlet 3624
Silva, José López
Shrew 14565
Silvani, Francesco
Coriolanus 2422
Silver, Richard L. 1955–
Also writes under the pseudonym 'Earl Revlis'
Settings of Commemorative Pieces . . . 21051
Silvestre, Paul Armand 1837–1901
Henry VIII 5243; Tempest 15408, 16297
Skinner, Ralph M.
All's Well 98
Slade, Herbert
Tempest 16249
Sløk, Johannes
Hamlet 3604
Smith, Edgar
Romeo 14143, 14175
Smith, Robert Bache 1875–1951
Romeo 14089, 14095

Snell, Gordon
Merchant 8753
Soane, George
As You Like It 1981
Söderström, Leif
Dream 10291
Sodini, Angelo
Tempest 16250
Sografi, Antonio Simone 1759–1818
Antony 374, 378, 380
Sokolovskii, A. L.
Romeo 13875
Somerset, Charles A.
Settings of Commemorative Pieces . . .
20825, 20889
Somma, Antonio 1809–1865
Lear 6018
Sondheim, Stephen Joshua 1930–
Romeo 13581
Souchay, Theodor
Richard III 13080
Southern, Terry 1924–
Hamlet 4129
Spaak, Paul 1871–
Merchant 8392; Dream 10290
Spasov, Pavel
Twelfth Night 17420
Spewack, Bella
Shrew 14597
Spewack, Samuel
Shrew 14597
Spigelgass, Leonard 1908–
Errors 2206
Spiritini, Massimo
Shrew 14563
Starling, Lynn
Romeo 14050
Stasov, Vladimir Vasil'evich 1824–1906
Othello 12177
Staton, Joseph
Shrew 14561
Stebbings, Paul
Tempest 15437
Stedman, Edmund Clarence
1 Henry IV 4502
Stein, Leo
Merry Wives 9265; Romeo 14107
Steinweg, Emil
Coriolanus 2374
Stephenson, B. C.
Dream 10951
Steppes, Adolf 1796–
All's Well 78
Stern, C. B.
Othello 12454
Stevens, Dudley
1 Henry IV 4500; 2 Henry IV 4671
Stevens, Wallace 1879–1955
Dream 10903

Stilborn, Myra Smith
  Settings of Commemorative Pieces . . .
  21307
Stone, Peter
  Othello 12472
Stonier, G. W.
  Hamlet 4109
Stoppard, Tom 1937–
  Born Thomas Straussler
  Hamlet 3080, 4134
Strachan, Alan 1946–
  Shrew 14610
Straube, Emanuel
  Dream 10288
Strutt, [?]
  Known as Mrs. Strutt
  Othello 12495
Sturgis, Julian Russell 1848–1904
  Much Ado 11369
Suarès, André 1866–1948
  Troilus 16583
Suggs, Keith
  Macbeth 7537
Sunde, Karen 1942–
  Settings of Commemorative Pieces . . .
  20826, 20836
Sutermeister, Peter
  Romeo 13815
Swaczynna, Wolfgang
  Tempest 16199
Swift, Carolyn
  Hamlet 4139
Swinburne, Algernon Charles 1837–1909
  Merry Wives 8960
Sylvester, F. O.
  As You Like It 2006
Szilágyi, L.
  Romeo 14116
Sztevanovity, Dusán
  Errors 2203

T

Tabukashvili, Revaz
  Antony 267
Tagliafico, [?]
  Hamlet 3631
Tailhade, Laurent
  Hamlet 4228
Tallman, Randolph
  Settings of Commemorative Pieces . . . 21060
Tamayo y Baus, Manuel 1829–1898
  Settings of Commemorative Pieces . . . 20837
Tanner, Tony
  Merchant 8417
Tate, Nahum 1652–1715
  Lear 5666, 5790; Richard II 12706

Taubert, Emil 1844–1895
  Twelfth Night 17417
Tavaststjerna, K. A.
  Romeo 14210
Taylor, Charles H. [1861?]–1907
  As You Like It 1965
Taylor, Michael
  Othello 12481
Tchaikovsky, Modest Ilich 1850–1916
  Richard II 12750
Teasdale, Sara 1884–1933
  Much Ado 11652
Téboul, Jacques
  Hamlet 4183
Testori, Giovanni
  Hamlet 4088
Thébaudeau, Henri
  Romeo 14043
Theobald, Lewis 1688–1744
  Settings of Commemorative Pieces . . . 20849
Thomas, Basil
  Settings of Commemorative Pieces . . . 20954
Thomas, Dave [1949?]-
  Hamlet 4096
Thomas, Jane
  Also known as Mrs. Edward Thomas
  Settings of Commemorative Pieces . . . 21037
Thomas, M. Lilly
  Hamlet 4231
Thompson, Alexander M.
  Measure 8038
Tillotson, Edith Sanford
  Dream 9853
Tindario, Dalmiro
  Also known as Dalmiro Tindaro; pseudonym
  used by G. Creglianovich
  Titus 16431
Tommasucci, Nina
  Also known as Nino Tommasucci
  Antony 360
Toole, Henry
  Settings of Commemorative Pieces . . .
  21082
Tottola, Andrea Leone   –1831
  Romeo 14192
Toulet, Paul-Jean
  As You Like It 948
Tournier, Jacques
  Cymbeline 2511
Townsend, Judith Ann
  As You Like It 1963
Townsend, Paul
  Henry V 4803
Toye, E. C.
  Twelfth Night 18325
Tožička, Bohumil 1871–
  Hamlet 4217
Tracy, Henry Chester 1876–
  Two Gentlemen 18466

Travers, Ben 1886–1980
  Romeo 14059
Treumann, Karl 1823–1877
  Romeo 14114
Trianon, Henry 1810–1896
  Lear 6152
Tsvetaeva, Marina Ivanovna Éfron 1892–1941
  Hamlet 4246
Tucker, Norman
  Tempest 15490
Tudor, Antony 1908–
  Pseudonym used by William Cook
  Romeo 14080
Turk, Roy 1892–1934
  As You Like It 1979
Turkalj, Nenad
  Richard III 13033
Turner, John Hastings
  Hamlet 4143 ; Settings of Commemorative
  Pieces . . . 20915
Turner, Montague
  Merchant 8739
Turner, Walter James Redfern 1889–1946
  Sonnet 18 19459
Tynan, Kenneth 1927–1980
  Macbeth 6755

U

Ullrich, Titus 1813–1891
  Hamlet 4241
Updike, John Hoyer 1932–
  Dream 9767
Ustinov, Peter Alexander 1921–
  Romeo 14049, 14058, 14063, 14090

V

Vaccaro, John
  Dream 10170
Vamp, Hugo
  Pseudonym used by John Robert O'Neill
  Hamlet 4213 ; Lear 6154 ; Macbeth 7580 ;
  Merchant 8774 ; Othello 12498 ; Richard III
  13076 ; Romeo 14149
Van Every, L. C.
  Settings of Commemorative Pieces . . . 21049
Vando, David
  L.L.L. 6336
Vanloo, Albert 1846–1920
  Cymbeline 2838
Varney, F. G.
  Cymbeline 2883
Vasil'ev, Vladimir
  Macbeth 7279

Vawm, Welford
  Merchant 8786
Verazi, Mattia   –1794
  Antony 358
Vestris, Armando
  Macbeth 7366
Vieillard, Pierre-Ange 1778–1862
  Also known as Pierre Ange Vieillard-
  Boismartin
  Romeo 14126
Vincy, Raymond
  Pseudonym used by Raymond Henri
  Ovanessian
  Romeo 14164
Virsaladze, S.
  Othello 12030
Volkov, N. D.
  Hamlet 3569
Voltaire 1694–1778
  Pseudonym used by François-Marie Arouet
  Caesar 5554
von Berge, Rudolf 1775–1821
  Dream 10776
von Bernbrunn, Karl 1787–1854
  Also wrote under the pseudonym 'Carl Carl'
  Macbeth 7522
von Caspar, Franz Xaver 1772–1833
  Tempest 15497
von Chézy, Wilhelmine Christiane 1783–1856
  Née von Klencke ; known as Helmine von
  Chézy
  Cymbeline 2885
von Collin, Heinrich Joseph 1772–1811
  Coriolanus 2403 ; Macbeth 7240
von Einsiedel, Friedrich Hildebrand 1750–1828
  Dream 10292 ; Tempest 15404, 15415,
  15419, 15426, 15427, 15454, 15465, 15500
von Weber, Oberst
  Dream 10152
Vonásek, Rudolf
  Dream 10144 ; Twelfth Night 17402
Vrchlický, Jaroslav 1853–1912
  Pseudonym used by Emil Bohuslav Frida
  Merchant 8399 ; Tempest 15414
Vymětal, Josef
  Twelfth Night 17421
Vyskočil, Ivan
  Hamlet 3688

W

Wagener, Terri
  Hamlet 3610
Waldron, Francis Godolphin 1744–1818
  Kinsmen 19168
Waller, John Francis 1810–1894
  Lear 6187

Walls, Donald Norman
Twelfth Night 18279
Walsh, Gary
Othello 12481
Wanamaker, Sam 1919–
Settings of Commemorative Pieces . . . 20920
Warren, Roger
Errors 2241
Wasserman, Dale 1917–
Settings of Commemorative Pieces . . . 20926
Watkins, Joseph Patrick
As You Like It 963
Watts, Frances B.
Shrew 14647
Waugh, Arthur 1866–1943
Caesar 5541
Weatherly, Frederick Edward 1848–1929
Lear 6163; Merchant 8785; Dream 10922
Webb, Mary Gladys 1881–1927
Much Ado 11611
Weiss, Jiří
Romeo 14067
Weisse, Christian Felix 1726–1804
Richard III 13085
Welles, Orson 1915–1985
1 Henry IV 4372; 2 Henry IV 4564;
Macbeth 6914
Wellmann, Paul I.
Othello 12459
Wensley, Shapcott
Dream 10937
Weslyn, Louis
Macbeth 7549
West, Paul
Hamlet 4196
Weston, R. P.
Settings of Commemorative Pieces . . . 21270
Whitehead, Douglass
Dream 10960
Whitelock, William Wallace
As You Like It 2005
Widmann, Josef Viktor 1842–1911
Also known as Joseph Viktor Widmann
Shrew 14571; Tempest 15416
Widowitz, Oskar
Twelfth Night 17398
Wilce, J.
1 Henry IV 4504
Wilde, Richard 1872–
Merchant 8418
Wilder, James A.
Hamlet 4140
Wilhelm, Julius
Romeo 14107
Wilkins, Mary E.
As You Like It 2012
Williams, Charles Walter Stansby 1886–1945
Cymbeline 2834; L.L.L. 6671; Dream 10263;
Tempest 16184; Twelfth Night 18269

Williams, Emlyn
1 Henry IV 4499; Twelfth Night 18273
Williams, Misha
Settings of Commemorative Pieces . . .
20851
Williams, Robert Folkestone [circa 1805]–1872
Dream 10923
Willner, Alfred Maria [1858?]–1929
Cymbeline 2723; Winter's Tale 18934
Wilson, Ann
Settings of Commemorative Pieces . . .
21197
Wimperis, Arthur
Measure 8038
Winther, Rasmus Villads Christian Ferdinand
1796–1876
Romeo 14172
Wodehouse, Pelham Greville 1881–1975
Sonnet 155 20582
Wolff, Pius Alexander 1782–1828
Much Ado 11615
Wood, Cyril
Tempest 16193
Woodward, Henry 1717–1777
Also known as Harry Woodward
Dream 10755; Settings of Commemorative
Pieces . . . 21255
Wright, Robert
Othello 12472
Wylie, Elinor Hoyt 1885–1928
Hamlet 4248

Y

Yates, M. E. Ashton
Cymbeline 2762
Yellen, Jack
Settings of Commemorative Pieces . . . 20991
Yordan, Philip [1913?]–
Also known as Phillip Yordan
Lear 6118; Macbeth 7514
Young, Frank B.
1 Henry IV 4459; 2 Henry IV 4626

Z

Zafred, Liliana
Also known as Lilyan Zafred
Hamlet 3692
Zahoruk, Dennis
Settings of Commemorative Pieces . . . 21263
Zakrzweski, Paul
Romeo 13763, 13765
Zamacoïs, Miguel 1866–1939
Merchant 8402

Zardi, Federico
  Merchant 8149
Zaret, Hy
  Sonnet 18 19461
Zavin, Benjamin Bernard [1920?]–1981
  Caesar 5547; Macbeth 7545
Zeffirelli, Franco 1923–
  Born Gian Franco Corsi
  Antony 262

Zeno, Apostolo 1668–1750
  Hamlet 4264, 4268, 4276, 4288
Zhōng Shǔi Hé
  Twelfth Night 17407
Zīverts, Mārtiņš 1903–
  Settings of Commemorative Pieces . . .
  20888
Zotov, Vladimir
  Merry Wives 9160